THE ISRAEL BOND OMNIBUS

by

SOL WEINSTEIN

Combustoica
a prose project of About Comics - Camarillo, California

THE CHARACTERS, PLACES AND EVENTS IN THIS MASTERWORK ARE WHOLLY FICTIONAL. ANY RESEMBLANCE, BY NAME OR OTHERWISE, TO PERSONS LIVING OR DEAD, ABOUT TO BE CONCEIVED, ABOUT TO BE BORN OR ABOUT TO DIE IS PURELY COINCIDENTAL.

Since the author has been informed that his sensitive masterworks of the real, the true espionage are popular with American servicemen, he would be grateful if his devoted readers would, upon completing them, send them to USO clubs, military bases, and hospitals, etc., instead of placing them in vaults next to precious jewels, furs and documents, or in time capsules, as so many have done. (Flattering, but unnecessary. Your sickening hero worship is ample reward.)

LOXFINGER © Sol Weinstein 1965, 2011. All rights reserved.
This novel originally appeared in abridged form in the October, 1965 issue of *Playboy*. This edition reprints the 1965 expanded novel, with new revisions made 2011 by the author.

MATZOHBALL © Sol Weinstein 1965, 1966, 2011. All rights reserved.
This novel originally appeared in abridged form in the December, 1965 issue of *Playboy*. This edition reprints the 1966 expanded novel, with new revisions made 2011 by the author.

ON THE SERVICE OF HIS MAJESTY, THE QUEEN
© Sol Weinstein 1966, 2011. All rights reserved.
An abridged version of *On the Secret Service of His Majesty, the Queen* was serialized in the July and August 1966 issues of *Playboy Magazine*.

YOU ONLY LIVE UNTIL YOU DIE
© Sol Weinstein 1968, 2011. All rights reserved.
This edition has been reedited by the original author from his 1968 novel.

Marble image from "Marbles of Hard Use" by Chefranden, used under the Creative Commons Atttribution 2.5 Generic license, readable at http://creativecommons.org/licenses/by/2.5/
Gun image from "Guns & Ammo 1" by kcdsTM (Ken), used under the Creative Commons Attribution 2.0 Generic (CC BY 2.0) license, readable at http://creativecommons.org/licenses/by/2.0/deed.en

Published by Combustoica, a prose project of About Comics.
WWW.COMBUSTOICA.COM

Rights inquiries? rights@AboutComics.com

LOXFINGER
page 5

MATZOHBALL
page 117

On the Secret Service of His Majesty, the Queen
page 239

You Only Live Until You Die
page 403

LOXFINGER

DEDICATIONS

JOE E. LEWIS
"The Aristotle of the Bottle," beloved King of the Nightclubs.

SAM AND CHAI SOORA WEINSTEIN,
the author's beloved parents.

NOMI FRIEDMAN,
the author's beloved sister.

HARRY AND BESS EISNER,
the author's beloved, hostile in-laws.

NANCY BROWN
of Plainfield, New Jersey.

GODFREY CAMBRIDGE,
who alone looks like the entire March on Washington.

NEIL LEVINSON, BERNIE GOLDBERG, IRWIN SPIEGEL, YUDEL KAPLAN, AND MIKE KEARNS,
who, with the author, comprised Trenton High School's unforgettable "The Crummy Six," who did to 11th grade French what De Gaulle is doing to us now.

STAN AND RHODA EISNER

MARK LITOWITZ, JOHNNY COATES, JR., HOWIE TEDDER, KIRK NUROCK, BEN MELZER, JAN WALLMAN, LAURA LANE, CLYDE LEIB, AUSTIN MACK, GEORGE R. BOLGE, RABBI BEN SINCOFF, BOB PINCUS, LENNIE FELDMAN

ELLIE, DAVID (008), AND JUDY WEINSTEIN,
the author's beloved wife and issue, the last named the courageous 5-year-old who, when enemies of Judaism rear their ugly heads, dons her mask and black cape and leaps from the sofa with that fearful cry: "Bat Baby Strikes Again!"

AND TO POCKET BOOKS, INC....
may we both make a little Bond bread.

Table of Contents

1 Room 1818	11
2 The Man from "Mother"	18
3 The Hebrew Himalayas	23
4 Her Nibs Digs Mibs	32
5 The Terror from the Top of the World	45
6 "Oasis Calling, Mr. Jew"	50
7 "This Can't Be the Regular Group!"	53
8 The Brave Bullring	58
9 M.	69
10 "You'll Like Mara, Mr. Bond"	79
11 "Eat, Eat, Mine Kindeleh"	89
12 Oh Hell, the Gang's All Here	92
13 The Answer	94
14 "I Am Agent D."	95
15 Parting Is Sweet	104
16 Top-Drawer Secret	113

T

1
Room 1818

Bella ciao! Bella ciao!

Two silencer-muffled shots slammed into the headboard of the bed upon which Israel Bond was making love to the impassive Oriental girl whose body, insouciantly straddled, lay beneath his eager thighs.

Even as he hurtled his body into a protective dive off the rumpled sheets into the corner of the room, upsetting a lamp, Bond's trained ears instinctively identified the weapon bent upon destroying him; the characteristic sound indicated, of course, an Italian-make gun, probably an Olivetti favored by the partisans. Wielded by a very inept assassin, Thank God!

Or so he thought until—*bella ciao!*—a third shot seared his right shoulder. He lay helpless in the corner of Room 1818 of Miami Beach's prestigious Palmetto Roach Hotel, panting, a hot streamlet of blood coursing from his grazed shoulder into the dank, matted hairs of his chest, reddening the golden chain of his mezuzah, the cylindrical symbol of his faith. The lampshade, jarred loose by his dive, had landed atop his head. I must be a ludicrous sight, he thought bitterly, a look of resignation framing his dark, cruelly handsome visage as he awaited the fourth bullet, the one that would end his life. Nay, his double life, for he had been sharing two existences—one the carefree, dashing public relations man-about-town ("Israel Bond? Oh, yes, that Hebrew chap. Loads of fun at any party ... he knows where the broads and the action are...."), and Israel Bond, prized member of a clandestine coterie, the Secret Service of the tiny democracy of Israel.

In that service he was known as Oy Oy Seven, a status which gave him license to kill. Not only was an Oy Oy holder licensed to kill, but he was also empowered to hold a memorial service over the victim. Bond thought of M., the head of the Secret Service, the only person to whom he had ever given his total love and trust, M., who had bestowed the Oy Oy rank upon him. But now, Bond reflected as he gazed into the menacing O of the Olivetti, the sallowly complexioned, wiry Levantine-type who held it had that license to kill. And he would use it.

Where would Shot No. 4 find its resting place? In his pounding heart which sounded like either the ocean's roar or the beat-beat-beat of the tom-tom as the jungle shadows fall? Between his grey eyes? Either would be mercifully quick. Or would the grinning, swarthy little man in the bellhop's uniform finish him off slowly, sadistically? Two or three in the gut? And as Bond lay moaning, would the little man grind his heel into Bond's long, tapering fingers? Splintering the bones, relishing every cracking sound? Inflicting the ultimate indignity, the ruination of a $7.50 manicure?

From a corner of a glazed eye, Bond caught the girl's face. No longer was it the sweetly obedient face of the lissome Oriental Bond had picked up a few hours ago. Its lips now were curled into a contemptuous sneer.

Of course! She was part of the cabal. He'd been had. As if she'd overheard his rueful thought, she responded with an insolent, "How big swinger rike his rittle Oriental praymate now?" And she spat into his face.

How different she had been earlier that evening at the Miami Beach Auditorium where Bond had gone with a fellow bon vivant, Seymour Feig, press agent for the Miss World Wow-Eee-Wow contest.

"Bond," Feig had winked. "One of the contestants has kind of a thing for you. She spotted you at the Boom Boom Room the other night and wants to meet you. I think you got a little action there." And Seymour had winked again, making the three-ring sign of the true ale man.

So they had met. "My name is Nu Kee," she had shyly said with Far Eastern submissiveness. Bond's eyes had twinkled. "A lovely name, my dear. Fraught with promise."

The sight of her willowy body and a curvaceous leg peeking out of a slit in her tailored cheong-sam, a Klein's original, had brought a catch to his throat.

They had cabbed it to the Eden Roc to catch the monumental Joe E. Lewis-Frank Sinatra show, Bond roaring at the puckish Joe E.'s sallies: "Show me a man who builds castles in the air and I'll show you a very stupid architect." Finally they headed to Wolfie's at 23rd and Collins where the hip, show-wise crowd went. Bond had ordered for both of them, knowingly, crisply: "Morris, we'd like two egg creams, Seventh Avenue and 28th Street style. Made properly, there should be no ice shavings in the eight-ounce Corning Ware glasses. The seltzer should be cold enough to stand on its own with a 3.5 ratio of pinpoint carbonation, roughly 1,118 bubbles to the ounce. Before the seltzer is poured, a fourth of the glass should be filled with Walker Gordon non-pasteurized milk from selected tuberculin-free Holsteins at the immaculate farm in Princeton Junction, New Jersey. Only Fox's U-Bet chocolate syrup should be used to complement the milk, both milk and syrup mixed delicately with an 1847 Rogers Brothers spoon, dairy silver, of course, in the tasteful Mrs. Aaron Burr scroll pattern, as the seltzer is added slowly, ricocheting rhythmically off the spoon."

"Boychickl, you've been around," said Morris the waiter, with new respect in his tired, I've-seen-it-all eyes.

At that point Bond had lit a filter-tipped Raleigh with his Nippo, a genuine Japanese copy of a Zippo, and had quizzed the girl.

"Whom do you represent in the Miss World Wow-Eee-Wow contest, my dear?"

She had bowed her head demurely. "Nu Kee not popurar with other girls. I am Miss Viet Cong."

Even now as he crouched like a trapped animal, Bond remembered those words. Miss Viet Cong! How did I let that one go by me? She was practically telling me she was with the opposition and like the lazy vegetable I've become I missed it. M. was right. I've let myself get soft.

And the bellhop pointing the gun? What branch of the "oppo" did he represent? Heaven knows, there were many special organizations sworn to wreak havoc upon the secret agents of Eretz Israel. The Soviet Warriors for Immolating Secretive Hebrews? Or, as it was known to the Israelis, SWISH? No, this one didn't shoot like a SWISH operative. A SWISH man would have made his first shot the last one. Perhaps, the Fraternal Egyptian Committee for Extirpating Sabras? FECES!

"No doubt, Mr. Bond," casually interjected the gun wielder, "you are curious as to who it is that will destroy you."

My God! thought Bond. They're all mind readers. His nose was assailed by the scent of the cheap oil which plastered down the Levantine's coal-black hair. Some cut-rate store junk, no doubt. Bond himself was partial to Code Ten, the hair preparation for all spies of consummate taste.

"I am a devoted member of a new terrorist group unknown to you, Mr. Bond. The Syrian Corps of Heroes for Murdering Unmercifully Craven Kikes. And now, dog of a Jew, say your infidel prayers!"

There was no time to figure out those initials, thought Bond. I've got to play my last card. And to do that I must wheedle, whine, beg.

"Please, please, let me say the final prayer. True we are mortal enemies, sir, but is it not also true that we share a common Semitic heritage? Do you not accept Moses as the spiritual predecessor of your own great Mohammed? Please, let me pray for my salvation, sir. Please ..." and he let his voice crack with emotion.

"Be quick about it!" snapped the Syrian, his finger tightening on the trigger. The girl snickered.

Bond reverentially lowered his head, muttering something in Hebrew. It was a list of all the titles of the Theodore Bikel albums he could remember, but the Syrian would not know that. Slowly, oh so slowly, his fingers slid imperceptibly down the bloodied chain ... his eyes began to close ... please, dear Lord, another precious second before the slug leaves its hot chamber ... another second....

His fingers found the mezuzah, pointed it at an angle, then squeezed the Star of David. Clearly elated at the sight of a quaking Jew, the Syrian broke into a raucous laugh.

Z-z-z-z-z-z-z-z!

No longer was the Syrian laughing. A look of amazement had come over his features. He looked dumbly at the needle which had whizzed out of the mezuzah into his hand, which was now turning numb. He pitched forward, his fingers clawing at Bond's chest. Bond sidestepped quickly. The Syrian fell face down. It had taken Molochamovis-B, the nerve poison on the needle tip, just two seconds.

He turned to the girl. Her snickering also had stilled at the startling turnabout in the situation. Bond's cold gaze made her blanch.

"Now, my 'rittle Oriental praymate'," Bond sneered, mimicking her speech, "we've a little unfinished business, haven't we? This ache in my torn shoulder isn't the only one on my Jewish body, you adorable hellcat!"

He crushed her mouth with his own, viciously drinking of her bruised lotus-petal lips. She began to scratch like a maddened jaguar, then sighed and yielded to the unstoppable bulk above her.

Occidental thighs met Oriental thighs, the latter learning the meaning of sweet surrender to a more compelling way of life. Now her scratches were loving strokings on Bond's back and the room began to swirl, spin, exploding in a 100-megaton flash of divine intensity.

Nestling in the crook of his bronzed arm and watching Raleigh smoke floating from his flared nostrils, she told him of her involvement in the affair, a contact man from the Syrian clique with the curious initials telling her Bond was an enemy of the "people's liberation" movement in Southeast Asia, the "come-on" at the beauty pageant, a Cuban refugee bellhop at the Palmetto Roach drugged and substituted for by the man whose face now met the Dupont 501 Nova Scotia pink nylon rug.

She knew too much, he realized. And had to be gotten rid of. And yet, she was so young, so lovely, and such a great piece. Perhaps, an attempt at reclamation would be worthwhile. Speaking to her softly and passionately for about ninety seconds, Bond pointed out the fallacies in her child-like devotion to the Viet Cong, gave her a reasonably detailed analysis of the true meaning of the political undercurrents in her part of the world and then, convinced she had seen the error of her ways, sent her out of his room with a friendly pat on her well-formed buttocks.

"Goodbye, Nu Kee. Now go out and win that contest. Only this time," he said huskily, "for freedom and democracy."

Her eyes misted as she stood in the doorway. "Will Nu Kee see her brave secret agent again?"

"Yes," he assured her with complete sincerity. "There must be more contacts between East and West such as we have experienced this night. Only through them can we look into each other's hearts and find the universality of purpose and basic goodness that exists deep down." Another pat on the derriere ...

and she was gone, darting like some frightened jungle bird down the corridor.

It wasn't until a moment or two after her departure that Bond realized her tidy little pile of garments—cheong-sam, bra, panties and A. S. Beck opera pumps—was still on the chair by his bed.

She seemed to be a resourceful type, he reasoned. She'll find some way to explain her condition to the hotel people.

The hotel people! By thunder, he'd forgotten the poor, drugged bellhop. Bond opened his closet and found him there, bound and gagged between two Sy Devore alpaca suits, his brown, moist eyes laden with fear.

Freeing him, Bond explained he'd been drugged by a pro-Castro provocateur (he pointed to the dead man) whom Bond had intercepted and dispatched. The man's eyes flashed fire: "Bueno, Senor Bond, bueno! Then the insult I, Juan Valdez, have endured at the hands of this Red *gusano* has been avenged by you. But, Senor Bond, your shoulder..."

"A mere scratch, Juan. But, Good Lord, it's nearly one A.M. and I'm due downstairs for an important engagement. Juan, a cup of coffee quickly. I must dress."

Glancing with satisfaction at the body, the bellhop hastened off, returning with a cup of coffee and a fresh pack of Raleighs to find Bond already dapper in a burgundy silk shantung suit with matching cummerbund, bowtie clipped onto an Arrow Gordon Dover Taper Glenn shirt, Florsheim black loafers with Roman points and a rakish tassel. He had chosen the burgundy suit for expediency. No time to dress the wound, he knew, but at least the blood flowing into the jacket would go unnoticed.

"Drink the coffee, Señor Bond. It is the very best in the world. You should know, señor, that before coming to Cuba to work in the sugar mills I lived in Colombia. The coffee of my native land is guarded by friendly shade trees on Andes mountains and only the most worthy aged beans and the finest green beans are ..."

"Yes, Juan," said Bond impatiently. "But we've a bit of a problem. The body."

"I take care of him, Señor Bond. I, too, am a patriot! I cut him up piece by piece and put him in the garbage disposal unit. Then maybe this dog float back to his Communist master. That would be the great joke, no?"

This little bellhop is a gem, Bond thought. "Burn the clothes, and throw the gun into the sea."

"Si."

Hands unsteady, Bond nevertheless managed to light a Raleigh and strode toward the elevator. His shoulder throbbed incessantly. Nerve, man, nerve! Mustn't act strange or ill at ease!

Glancing back at his room door, he became transfixed for a second. 1818. How ironic, he thought. Eighteen in Hebrew was expressed symbolically by the letters "chess-yood." Which in turn symbolized "chai," the word for "life." But there were *two* 18s. Life-life.

Of course! A double life, such as I lead. And both lives saved for me and Israel by my mezuzah, cylindrical symbol of my faith.

Perhaps, it was no mere chance that Room 1818 was assigned to me. Perhaps ...

But there was no more time to think. Bond was due downstairs in ten minutes to perform his "cover" role, the second of his lives. He must now slip into this external character, play it charmingly and well. For M. and Eretz Israel!

2
The Man from "Mother"

"... and so, charming ladies of the Upper Middle Lower Township, Pennsylvania, Chapter of Hadassah," said Bond, "your purchases of Mother Margolies' Activated Old World Chicken Soup and, indeed all of Mother's fine products, not only put the glorious culinary traditions of our ancient heritage upon your tables, nourishing your loved ones, but also assist your brethren in Eretz Israel, the Promised Land, the Land of Milk and Magnesia, to protect and defend its hallowed borders!"

Two hundred women, who had been nodding their teased hairdos approvingly all through his speech, burst into wild applause. Vivacious Mrs. Charlene Krosnick, president of the chapter which had booked the Palmetto Roach's fabulously decorated Pina Colada Room for its post-midnight brunch, beamed at Bond from her dais seat. "Tell them how, Mr. Bond! Tell them how!" And she gave his thigh a sudden squeeze.

Bond permitted a quick smile to force itself through the teeth he had been gritting for the last twenty-five minutes. Mrs. Krosnick, he noted, was quite a dish, tawny, full-breasted, possessed of two glowing schav-green eyes that held promise.

"How, you may ask, can purchasing this superior chicken soup aid Israel's gallant freedom fighters, your cousins across the sea, in their never-ending struggle? I shall now tell you a heart-warming thing: Mother Emma Margolies, the sweet, saintly old woman who has lent her skill and name to these splendid foods, has stipulated that fully twenty-five per cent—I'll repeat that—twenty-five per cent of the gross proceeds—or the Schwartz proceeds, if that happens to be your name (Explosive laughter greeted his quickly conceived witticism.)—will be donated to the Israeli Ministry of Defense, thus enabling it to acquire the cream of the world's obsolete weaponry."

An even bigger round of applause followed his revelation of Mother's charity.

"Such a brilliant speaker and so handsome, too!" said Cheer & Sorrow Secretary Mrs. Carol Bernstein, nudging Mrs. Marcia Freeman, Isometrics & Diet Cola Chairman. "Wonder if he's married."

"Nah ... those dark, cruelly handsome types with scars on their cheeks never are," responded Mrs. Freeman sagely. "So forget about him for your Merry Robin. Better she should marry that dental technician from Allentown." Thus cavalierly discarding Merry Robin's chances at the devastatingly debonair Israeli, Mrs. Freeman began to scheme: How can I get him to meet my Tara Lynne? And what's his name anyway? Her bejeweled fingers skimmed the program past "We shall all stand reverently as Mrs. Nettie Berk sings 'The Star Spangled Banner,' 'Hatikvah' and 'Hello, Dolly!'"... past "welcoming remarks by Mrs. Charlene Krosnick, president" ... lingering on "Our Guest of Honor, Mr. Israel Bond, public relations representative of Mother Margolies, Tel-Aviv, New York and Miami Beach."

Israel Bond! A wonderful name, indeed, for a man from the Holy Land. And just look at Charlene Krosnick eating him up with those greedy eyes. Not that she blamed Charlene. Charlene's husband, Max, was a fine provider and all that, but, well, dull... in the way a man can't afford to be. Mrs. Freeman, who had spent one mad impetuous night with Max at a Harrisburg motel, knew this all too well.

No, she couldn't blame Charlene. This Bond was quite a hunk of man. Though surely he needed a better tailor. His right shoulder was easily two shades darker than the rest of the suit.

At the lectern, Bond, feeling the blood soaking through, thought: Time to wind up this ghastly charade. Refreshing his parched throat with a quick, careless toss of Mother Margolies' Old World Parsley Tonic ("It Bubbles from You the Troubles"), he dragged deeply on a Raleigh and concluded: "It's been my pleasure to greet you dear Hadassah ladies, all of you truly 'N'Shay Chayil,' Women of Valor. Like so many other Israelis, I have marveled at your indefatigable good works which have culminated in the magnificent Hadassah Medical Center at Ein Kerem on the outskirts of Jerusalem. This hospital, I am informed, is adding a new wing which will house exclusively the husbands of Hadassah members who have contracted stomach disorders from their wives' cooking.

"And now other commitments dictate my regretful departure. But please do not leave. You will soon see a highly entertaining color film featuring Mother Margolies herself, who takes you on a tour of her factory. As for me, let me say 'shalom,' hoping that we shall all meet again on the slopes of Mount Tabor in Israel for the High Holy Days. In the meantime, remember our motto to be found on every can: 'Like Mother Used to Make It, Mother Makes It.' And so, shalom, shalom, I'll say shalom; it's the nicest greeting I know ... it means goodbye, salud, bon jour ... and twice as much as hello."

He sat down heavily, then rose reluctantly, painfully to acknowledge their standing ovation. As the women regained their seats, they looked at him, squeezing their support hose-covered thighs in longing, sibilant sounds escaping their lips. Mrs. Krosnick again pressed against his thigh, then blushed.

It's coming, Bond thought. He'd seen the lovely matron's eyes X-raying his body all through the speech.

The room was darkened now and on the screen Mother Margolies was dicing carrots and turnips, sprinkling her commentary with old country aphorisms for which she had become justly famous: "The fool pours tapioca down an empty coal mine, but the wise man ..."

Another squeeze on the thigh, this time more demanding.

It happened before in dozens of other places: Bronx, Teaneck, Denver, LA, Sausalito. Wherever Bond, in his cover role as Mother's spokesman, appeared there was invariably a hot-eyed, well-proportioned matron. She might be an ORT president, a JWV Auxiliary commander, a Worthy Keeper of the Seal of the Link of the Golden Chain ... and inevitably with a weary, inattentive husband named Max, Lou, Sheldon, etc., who had not been doing his homework. Ach! Stupid men they had to be to leave these treasures unattended!

Now Charlene was walking arm in arm with him, trying to make conversation as they passed through the lobby. Bond knew it would be hard for her, yet her compulsion was overpowering her. It'll be hard for me too ... with this shoulder.

In the background he could hear the Hadassah "girls," as she termed them, singing a jolly pep song-parody to the tune of Belafonte's famed Calypso song, "Matilda."

Ha-dass-ah!
Ha-dass-ah!
Ha-dass-ah! Helps poor sick Jews escape Venezuela!
All together now!
Ha-dass-ah...

"I'm glad your girls asked me down, Mrs. Krosnick. You certainly know how to handle a lovely affair."

"Oh, you'd be surprised at the way I handle an affair, Mr. Bond. And please call me Charlene."

Smiling at her clever double-entendre, Bond awaited the next incriminating sentence. "And you must call me Israel."

"I'd love to ... Israel," she gushed. Then, at a loss for more meaningful conversation, she stammered, "Did ... uh ... did you enjoy Nettie Berk's singing? She sings in our temple choir, you know. And also in our township's inter-faith Quaker chorale. Quakers are lovely people, don't you think?"

"Why, yes," he said pleasantly. "I've met many Quakers in the Middle East. Some of my best friends are Friends. Does Mr. Krosnick approve of your organizational activities, my dear?"

"Oh," she said with some petulance. "Max doesn't pay much mind to anything I do. Too busy with the country club, golf and all that. He's probably dreaming about winning the Masters right now—in our cosy master bed back home in Pennsylvania. Thirteen hundred and ninety-four miles away."

Well, Bond mused, that's that. She's made the pitch. Anyway, it's for Mother, he thought. A little consideration from me and the ladies of Middle ... Lower Upper ... or whatever the hell that township is ... will buy 150 cases of chicken soup a week. It's for Mother.

Thirty minutes later, in 1818, Bond had won Mother a convert for life.

She had become a raging, uncontrollable flood of passion, the sandbags of frustration swept away by love's sweet torrent. "Israel! Israel! My *schoenkeit*, my love! You're a continental man of the world. I'm yours to use ... yours! Make love to me ... daring love ... make French love to me! Yes, make it French!"

So he had put one of his international recordings on the phonograph and taken her violently as it spun, furnishing a uniquely Parisienne backdrop to their lovemaking. Unfortunately, he had chosen "The Recorded Speeches of Charles DeGaulle," but somehow it seemed to drive her even more insane.

Nestled in the crook of his bronzed arm, she made the horrifying discovery of his shoulder wound. "Oh, darling! And I made you love me ... with this? What pain you must have been in!"

And she hugged him with a joyous squeal when he'd gallantly responded, "Charlene, there was a far greater, sweeter pain—if you know what I mean."

"How did you get that terrible slash on your shoulder?"

Bond said airily, "Oh, I'm an Israeli secret agent and a Syrian fanatic tried to kill me."

"Be serious!" she said with mock solemnity. And he made up a story of falling in a shower.

Br-r-r-ri-i-i-ng!

The phone. Who could be calling at this hour?

An emotionless voice: "Mr. Bond? The tire of Meyer the buyer is on fire."

Click!

Bond's grey eyes narrowed. A tire-Meyer-buyer-fire message was big stuff. Something was popping. Time to send Charlene Krosnick back to her mundane suburban world. M. wanted him —fast!

3
The Hebrew Himalayas

His rented Rambler purring easily and effortlessly at thirty-eight miles an hour, Bond gunned it north on the smooth-riding, bump-free super-highway, his destination Upper New York State's famed resort center, the Catskill Mountains, known to the average man as the "Borscht Belt." But to the very "in" group Bond ran, drank, and loved with (people who were by taste, temperament, and sophistication justly entitled to include themselves in the Pepsi Generation) it was incisively termed "The Hebrew Himalayas."

M.'s urgent message, relayed through 11 1/2 (a midget whose cover roles took various forms—sometimes a Little League shortstop, other times a fireplug) had made him drop everything, which resulted in a painful buttock bruise for the ebullient Charlene Krosnick, and impelled him eagerly, tensely toward his next assignment. Trained traveler that he was, Bond had cut his packing time to a bare minimum by giving away most of his clothing to the friendly bellhop, grabbing a cab ("Driver, get me to the Miami Airport in twenty minutes and there's a box of Luden's Medicated Cough Drops in it for you!"), and churning with a powerful sprinter's closing kick into a Delta Airlines jet just as the boarding stairway was being pulled away. Three hours later in the Yucatan, his ardor cooled somewhat by his blunder, he boarded an Eastern Whisperjet for New York's Kennedy Airport. Only the urgency of the moment led him to take the Whisperjet. It was one plane he had always entertained suspicions about. True, the whispering was far superior to noisier jets, but somehow he felt the plane was plotting against him.

The flight had been uneventful, even boring, Bond thumbing listlessly through such *Reader's Digest* articles as "The Courageous Comeback of Venereal Disease," "Sex and the Single Wing," an excerpt from a best seller by a University of Pennsylvania football coach, and "Is TV Violence Affecting Our Youngsters?" an expose the *Digest* admitted in a black-bordered box preceding the story that it was forced to print posthumously, the author having been shot to death by his seven-year-old nephew during a commercial break on "Bonanza."

Of course, there had been the interlude with the stunning, vixenish stewardess, who had practically forced Bond into the lavatory while a dozen passengers, squirming with nature's call, grumbled vociferously at the sight of the OCCUPIED sign glowing for thirty-five minutes. The events in the tiny cubicle had not done Bond's aching shoulder one bit of good, Miss Bonnie Jane Abney (a former beauty pageant winner herself, incidentally: "Miss White Citizens Council" in a Selma, Alabama, summer bombing festival) practically serrating the edges of the wound with her industriously passionate teeth.

I'll have to knock off this crap, Bond told himself, shoving a Raleigh into the corner of his firm, sensual mouth. The Raleigh reminded him of the packages that had been awaiting him in his suite at the Ansonia Hotel, his plush Manhattan base of operations. Bundles and bundles ... each containing several cartons of Raleighs and heart-rending notes from the women he had known sweetly, intimately on his public relations swing throughout the United States. "When will I see you again, darling?" read the notes from Tami in Fort Wayne, Hilda in Santa Monica, Ida from Shreveport, even a special delivery from Charlene from whose lips he had recently torn his own.

All of them had noted his constant Raleigh smoking and he had hinted that a carton or two would be a nice little gift to keep his memories of them glowing like cigarette ends. The cartons, of course, had four extra coupons. In reality, Bond loathed Raleighs, but due to M.'s urging he smoked them solely to acquire the coupons.

"Ours is a penurious little Secret Service," M. had pointed out. "We need those coupons. How do you think I got your silencer and plastique bomb kit? For 1,500 coupons—that's how. You'll smoke Raleighs, Oy Oy Seven, and like it."

After a good night's sleep at the Ansonia (interrupted only by a suicidal dowager who had jumped from the ledge outside his room to the street twelve floors below, an action which elicited cheers from a good-natured throng, especially when the firemen neatly pulled the net away), Bond moseyed over to West End Avenue to make his contact and get further instructions from an agent at the Cafe Aw-Go-Go-Already who made fellafel and acted as a "mailbox" for messages.

Ah, fellafel! Israel's answer to the pizza and hotdog! Chickpeas ("hayseh arbis," as they were known to the old-line, Yiddish-speaking Jews of Eastern Europe) ground up and fried into inedible balls, covered with techina, an exquisitely uninspired sauce, then housed in an envelope of pita, the thoroughly tasteless Arab bread. Fellafel! He grew nostalgically sick to his stomach with each sniff at the counter.

Zvi Gates, the fellafel maker with the piercing eyes, had greeted him with a grin: "Back from Miami Beach, Mr. Bond? Here's a special fellafel for you."

And Bond's trembling fingers had reached into the bottom of the pita, extracting the message from M., written in invisible ink, made doubly hard to decipher since it was inscribed on invisible paper.

He had sprayed on the powders which restored visibility to the paper and its message and read:

> TO ISRAEL BOND, PUBLIC RELATIONS REPRESENTATIVE FOR MOTHER MARGOLIES: SUBJECT— 21-CASE SHIPMENT TO CATSKILLS: POSSIBILITY OF NEW TERRITORY FOR SALES OPENING UP AT THE KAHN-TIKI, LARGE HOTEL IN LOCH SHELDRAKE, N.Y. BE ON YOUR GUARD TO PREPARE SPEECH FOR DELIVERY BEFORE GREATER NEW YORK LEAGUE AGAINST ANTI-SEMITISM BY JEWS. WHILE THERE GREET RENOWNED PHILANTHROPIST LAZARUS LOXFINGER. SHALOM—M.

A seemingly innocuous message. Should it fall into alien hands the reader would deduce it had something to do with Bond's P.R. duties for the firm.

He knew, however, that the 21-case designation meant that the 21st word of each following sentence was the key word.

He counted the words deliberately, his heartstrings going zing! zing! zing!

The 21st word of the first sentence: "Guard."

Word No. 21 of the second tortuous sentence: "Loxfinger."

With blinding clarity, it was clear. Frighteningly, blindingly clear.

"Guard Loxfinger!"

Lazarus Loxfinger, septuagenarian, multimillionaire, philanthropist, whose personal story had assumed epic proportions. He had come from Argentina several years before with seemingly unlimited funds, determined to use them to make Eretz Israel a better place in which to live. His charitable works were legendary by now, the Lazarus Loxfinger League Against Constipation, the Lazarus Loxfinger Mothers March On Ringworm and Halitosis, the Loxfinger Center for Retarded Jewish Children, the Loxfinger Center for Non-Retarded Jewish Children, the Loxfinger League for Positivism in Everyday Thinking (Its members, imbued with the league's philosophy, favored pro-biotics and pro-histamines among other things.) et al. His endless generosity had caused a grateful citizenry to term him "tzaddik"—saint! And he had gone beyond mere charity. He had written a series of articles for the highly respected *Boot & Shoe Recorder* which had been given wide coverage by the press and TV the world over, becoming famous as "The Plowshare Papers," since he continually stressed the "beat swords into plowshares" theme vis-a-vis Israel and the hostile Arab diehards. His articles had noted the spiritual kinship between the Jewish state and its neighbors, pointing out the undue strain on their respective economies engendered by the arms race, offering (in his words) "... a final solution based on equitable negotiations, cultural exchange, trade and other unifying factors. To see this final solution in my lifetime is my goal, my *raison d'etre*."

And now this magnificent old man was in peril. From whom? Why? How? When?

Ergo, the hell-for-leather trip in the rented Rambler, now leaving the Harriman Exit 16 and roaring up the Quickway to the mountains. Ignoring its limitations, Bond pushed it up to forty-five. The hell with what it can stand! This baby'll have to take it.

It had been acquired from a famous car rental agency in Manhattan with an intriguing sign:

"AVIS-RENT-A-HERTZ. SURE, WE'RE NERVY, USING ANOTHER AGENCY'S CARS. BUT WE'VE GOT TO DO THINGS LIKE THIS. WE'RE ONLY NO. 2!"

Such chutzpah deserves my business, he had decided.
He jammed a Raleigh in his lips, contemptuously flicking its ashes onto the cover of a thick pamphlet on the seat next to him:

"REPORT OF THE SURGEON-GENERAL OF THE UNITED STATES ON SMOKING."

Screw it!
Hungry for the sound of a human voice as he sped down the deserted roadway, Bond flicked on the radio.
"... yessiree and yessirooney, teen timers, that was Peter Pant and the Pantyraiders rockin' and sockin' ol' Number 98 on the chart on Three-H time, the Hot Hit Hotline, on the Rockin' Robby Robbins Show on Station ROBBY and ROBBY-FM, your mad, mad mountain greenery teenery station where your Bob-Bob-Bobbin' Red Red Robin Rockin' Robby Robbins grins and spins the wacky shellacky, the chatter platters, like that last big, big one, 'Go Frug Yourself.'

"That one was for the Gangbang Gang, all of you in Miss Hepzibah Trevelyan's biology class at Novak High, all of you ... Sheri, Augie, Rocco, Dodie, Duty and Gidget ... and remember, kids, Rockin' Robby Robbins' travelin' teen bandstand, featuring such top, top recording artists as the Swine; the Scum; the Carbuncles, who made that big, big one, 'Squeeze Me'; Sneering Sammy Snot and the Sinuses; Lamount Cranston and the Shadows (Remember their big one, "Where Are You?"); Little Laura Little, your Goosey Watusi Girl; Morrie and the Morons (You all bought their golden record, "Duh, Duh, Duh."); Pregnant Peggy Prendergast ... just anybody who's anybody on the teen scene ... they'll all be there at your school next Tuesday at 4:30 P.M. to lip-synch their big, big hits and mark their X's in your autograph book. Now, that sensational group from England, Tarry Stool and the Bedpans, to sing:

Saturday night at the senior prom,
I went and blew the gym up with a homemade atom bomb,
'Cause I'm a teenage bomber! Yea, yea, yea!
I'm a—

Still hungry for the sound of a human voice, Bond changed stations. "Once again, it's time for 'Your Tum-Tum-Tummy and You,' with yours truly, Dr. Charlton Carter, your nutritionist of the airwaves, with today's topic, 'Can a Severe Heart Attack Be Beneficial in Easing Tension?'—but first a word from my sponsor, Otto's Organic Foods, a combination of nature's own whole grain okra flour with genuine crushed Indiana limestone."

Still hungry, etc., his tapering fingers dialed again.

"... with the snarlup caused by the accident at the FDR Drive near the Tri-Boro Bridge exit, motorists are advised to avoid that area. In general, if you're coming into New York, I'd say use a canoe. This is Mark Russell, your flying traffic reporter in the WDULL helicopter, speaking to you from FDR Drive where we caused the snarlup when our chopper crash-landed ..."

And another try.

"The signal you heard was a Civil Defense test. I repeat—a test. If this had been an actual alert, right now I'd be hysterical. Stay tuned ..."

A final flick of the dial.

"... the elderly Israeli philanthropist, seemingly unnerved by his brush with death at the Kahn-Tiki Hotel (Bond froze; his hands were clammy against the wheel.), vowed he would continue his attempts on behalf of Israel, his adopted homeland. Said Loxfinger: 'This cowardly attempt at assassination will only spur anew my efforts to seek a final solution for Israel in her relationships with her Arab neighbors.'

"The philanthropist then shrugged off his frightening experience and plunged into a full round of speeches and appearances at the Catskill area hotel. Meanwhile, the suspect in the shooting, who Police Chief Ed Chelland said was driving a 1963 blue Cadillac convertible, was possibly headed toward New York City. State troopers were patrolling the Quickway, hoping for an early arrest. And that's the latest on the attempt to murder Lazarus Loxfinger, Israel's old man with a heart as big as his fortune. CBS will interrupt its regular programming should further developments warrant it. Remember, when the big news breaks, CBS cracks up! This is John Cameron Facenda returning you to the program now in progress, 'Sue Stark, Girl Junkie,' which asks the question: Can a beautiful heiress from Philadelphia's Mainline find happiness as a mainliner? Yesterday, if you'll recall, Sue and her bohemian lover, Paul

Gray, an itinerant kumquat salesman, had just copped three bags of heroin from Harry (The Horse) Botoff and ..."

Two streams of Raleigh smoke jetted through his nostrils. Bond switched off the radio.

At least, Loxfinger was alive. Alive!

And if it hadn't been for my damned conceit I might have been in Loch Sheldrake thirty minutes ago. A Rocket Olds 98 would have gotten me there in time to stop this hideous thing. But I had to rent this Rambler. You know why, Bond. Because it has a bed in the back. You'd hoped for a little hanky-panky on the road, hadn't you? The whole fantasy had run through your mind a hundred times ... a car broken down, some high-breasted young thing with chopped liver-brown eyes imploring you to help her: "It got overheated, sir. You'll take me to Grossinger's in your car? Oh, bless you, sir! I could just kiss you." ... which she would, their tongues tangoing sensually against each other's gold fillings, sharing deep swigs from Bond's flask of heady, potent, aphrodisiacal Gallo Wine ... then thighs thrashing thighs ...

(Bond had always had the deepest respect for Gallo Wine, especially since he had seen their commercials on television. First of all, it came from the Wine Countree, and, secondly, each bottle bore the signatures of the Gallo Brothers on the label. Which was a proud admission that the Gallo Brothers could write their names. That kind of integrity moved a man like Bond.)

Bond, Bond told Bond, you'd better stop letting your damn, blessedly endowed genitalia rule your head. A lecher can't operate effectively as a Double Oy. Mother Margolies would have a proverb applicable to this, he thought. What had she once said? Yes ... "I cursed because I had no eyes; until I saw a cheerful man who had no head."

Wait! What had the radio bulletin said? The blue Caddy convertible was New York bound!

He pulled the Rambler over sharply, parked and lit a Raleigh. His face was icy now, lips in a tightly set vise. It was a look his enemies had learned to fear, an Israel Bond turned into a murderous machine.

He double-timed it across the north-bound section, flattening his body on the grassy medial strip. It was luxuriantly rich against his cheek—Burpee Seed, no doubt. His fingers felt the road, drawing some comfort from its texture. Portland Cement. Tops in any league!

And his right hand fondly stroked the slim, deadly item resting in his Neiman-Marcus shoulder holster.

A black speck at first ... high-tailing it south. It grew bigger. The blue Caddy! And behind it a patrol car, siren screaming, red rooftop light revolving madly.

He estimated the Caddy was hitting 150 kilos, at the very least 137.8 knots. There would be time for one shot, with luck, two.

Now he could see the face of the driver, a swarthy Levantine type, features flattened by the force of the wind. A fanatical face, maniacal eyes, teeth bared into the snarl of a rabid mongrel ...

Wang! Wang!

Bond squeezed the hair trigger on the Shar Shue Dung-55, the special that was crafted exclusively for him by Kok Eee Moon, the Hong Kong gunsmith whose clientele included other slim, well-tailored adventurers like Bond, men who casually threw down fat packets of money demanding weapons of the most exacting specifications.

The bullets had found the front tire, as Bond had intended, of the patrol car, now careening out of control. The assassin, however, startled at the reports, had taken his eyes off the road for a second, a fatal second. His own tires caught the cement ridge of the road, spinning the car into a horrible vortex.

Bond watched the Caddy leave the road, rip over some underbrush, then rip under some overbrush. It smashed into a billboard, went through it with a sickening sound of agonized metal. A flash! And the Caddy went up in a white-hot ball of flame.

Now two towering troopers were chugging from the patrol car several hundred yards up the road. They found a grim-visaged Bond staring blankly at the billboard which seconds ago had read:

> CREST TOOTHPASTE — SHOWN TO BE HIGHLY EFFECTIVE WHEN USED WITH A CONSCIENTIOUSLY APPLIED PROGRAM OF ORAL HYGIENE.

Where a curly-headed moppet had stood before her adoring mother clutching a dental report in her hand there was a gaping hole, behind which smouldered what remained of the convertible.

Bond dragged on a Raleigh. The troopers saw a hint of a smile as he said, "Crest or no Crest. Our friend sure made a hell of a cavity, didn't he?"

4
Her Nibs Digs Mibs

"WELCOME, WELCOME TO THE FABULOUS KAHN-TIKI HOTEL!"

His Rambler idled in front of the huge neon sign at the entrance to the winding lane that would take him to the hotel. He read on:

"YOU'LL ENJOY EVERY MOMENT AT THE KAHN-TIKI! POLYNESIAN DELICACIES—KOSHER STYLE! MODIFIED DIETARY LAWS (NO SMOKING DURING THE SERVING OF THE HAM SALAD)! LEARN THE LATEST JEWISH DANCES FROM THE TROPICS TAUGHT BY LITHE, OVERSEXED LATINOS!

"LEARN THE MERENGUE! THE CHA-CHA! THE PACHONGA! THE BOSSA NOVA! THE CHE GUEVARA!

"TWO HEATED SWIMMING POOLS FILLED WITH MOTHER MARGOLIES' ACTIVATED OLD WORLD CHICKEN SOUP! NOSH WHILE YOU SPLASH!

"THE ONLY HOTEL IN THE CATSKILLS WITH AN INDOOR SKI LIFT! SCHUSS ON A SIX-INCH BASE OF MATZOH MEAL!

"DON'T HIT YOUR ROTTEN, WHINING KIDS! LET OUR COLLEGE-TRAINED COUNSELLORS DO IT FOR YOU!

"MASSEUR FOR MONSIEUR! MASSEUSE FOR MRS. MONSIEUR!

"COMBINATION LOBBY-PUTTING GREEN! GOLF PRO IN RESIDENCE! OTHER PROS IN THE BAR!

"RESERVE NOW FOR PASSOVER HOLIDAYS! THRILL TO THE FERVENT CHASSIDIC CHANTING OF SEXTUPLET CANTORS—MOISHEH, MISCHEH, PISCHEH, PAYSCHEH, GRISCHEH, AND GRUSCHEH NABUTOVSKY! ACCOMPANIED BY METROPOLITAN OPERA STAR SERGIO CABRINI AND AN ALL-MORMON CHOIR!" (A distinct novelty, Bond thought. This year the cantors are Jewish.)

"ESTRELLITA AND SCHUYLER KAHN, YOUR HOSTS AT MIAMI BEACH'S GLAMOROUS PALMETTO ROACH HOTEL, HOPE YOU ENJOY THEIR MOUNTAIN RESORT AS WELL! LET'S ALL MEET AT TONIGHT'S GET-ACQUAINTED SOIREE IN THE LITVAK LUAU ROOM! FEATURING THE WEST COAST COMEDY SENSATION — HENNY BENNY LENNY! DANCE TEAM OF ROSITA AND YONKEL, 'STUPIDITY IN MOTION'! SONGS BY PERKY SONGSTRESS PATTI PERKY! HERMIE HOUSE AND HIS HOUSE HOUSE BAND FOR DANCING!"

One would need at least a two-week reservation to fully enjoy this place, Bond opined. It would take one week just to read the damn sign.
His smart Bakelite luggage stowed away, Bond warmed the tip-hungry palm of the bell captain with a shiny new Lyndon Johnson seventy-five-cent piece, frankly relishing the awed reaction. "Yes sir, Mr. Bond! Anything else, sir? Well, hope you enjoy your stay!"
He showered for three minutes under the bracing needles of Mountain Valley water, changed his suit (it was thoroughly soaked from the shower), slipping into the high-priced casual garb required in this class milieu ... skin-tight Ship N' Shore levis, burnt cantaloupe shaded crew shirt with the prize Korvette's label showing (perhaps a bit ostentatiously; it was on the breast pocket), and Mafia Raffia cord shoes.
He picked up the mauve Princess phone. "Operator, this is a Princess phone, isn't it? Good! Well, I'd like to speak to Princess Margaret." The hotel operator, Miss Studnia, unused to Bond's

dazzling spur-of-the-moment bon mots (he was as famed for his wit as Mother was for her proverbs), said, "Huh?" And Bond, sorry he'd wasted a goody on an unappreciative clod, was all business now: "Dr. Loxfinger's suite, please."

Her voice was guarded. "I'm sorry, sir, but no one is permitted to disturb the doctor ..."

"Look, honey," said Bond. "This is Israel Bond. The doctor will respond, I assure you."

"Just a minute, please, Mr. Bond."

He inhaled deeply. The Raleigh tasted strangely arid. And the Arid in his armpits felt strangely Raleigh. This is going to be one of those days, he sighed.

"Dr. Loxfinger's public relations representative will talk to you, Mr. Bond." New respect in the metallic tones. "Go ahead, Mr. Saxon."

"Mr. Bond?" A composed voice with a trace of hauteur. "Angelo Saxon here, the doctor's P.R. man. Dreadfully sorry, but he can't be disturbed now. The dreadful incident and all that. Perhaps tomorrow or—"

"Knock it off, Saxon!" Bond's rasp slashed through the room. "This is Israel Bond, security, M 33 and 1/3 section. Stop 'dreadfulling' my ass to death and tell me what's happened, how the old boy is and mach'is schnell!" In his ire he had slipped into Yiddish. Temper, temper. Can't offend the old man's flunky too much.

"Uh, perhaps first we'd best meet for a chat, Mr. Bond. See you in the Leni Lenape Lounge in ten minutes? Checko."

Well, some of the spray starch had been taken out of Mr. Saxon. Now, a friendly drink or two and he'd put the man straight.

Bond lit a Raleigh, stretched his lithe frame on the bed. His nostrils caught the scent of the cordite on his hand from the shots he had fired on the Quickway. His lips formed a moue of distaste. Not even the fine Rokeach soap had been able to dispel it.

The two burly troopers had sniffed it, too, but had held off their queries until they examined the molten mess behind the billboard. A frightened tramp who had been squatting behind the billboard had emerged screaming: "Geez, ol' Lukey can't even take a dump without them there crazy drivers a-tryin' ter run me down!" They handed him several sheets of Kleenex and booked him as a material witness.

"Okay," said one of them curtly to Bond. "I'm Trooper Crawford; this here's Trooper Broderick. Now what the hell was all this shootin' about? You damn near kilt us both."

I'd jolly well better make this good, Bond thought. He smiled: "It's all right, trooper. We're sort of in the same line of work." And he produced his gold-edged top-priority security card from his wallet. On the other side was a photo of Fay Wray.

"This don't mean a damn thing to me," snapped Crawford. "We're takin' you in."

"Call this number first," Bond said indifferently. Taken aback by his coolness in an awkward spot, the two exchanged glances and led him to their car from which they radioed their dispatcher. The latter, putting his phone up to the microphone so they could hear, dialed.

"CIA—one moment, please."

"Uh, this is Sgt. Gurski, radio dispatcher for the New York Quickway State Police. We got some guy here named Israel Bond. Says he knows you."

Bond lit a Raleigh. "Have one, lads?"

They grunted eagerly, reaching their meaty hands for the pack. "You smoke 'em, too, huh?" said Broderick, the slightly smaller one. "Us too. That's how we got the patrol car ... 15,000 coupons."

I daresay constabularies all over the world are feeling the pinch, Bond reflected. And though it stabbed his heart to do it, he reasoned it was time for a magnanimous gesture. He ripped the coupon from the pack. "Here, officer. Keep it."

"Geez," said the trooper. "You're all right, pal."

A voice crackled through the static: "Troopers, this is Monroe Goshen, head of the Mid-East section of CIA. Release Mr. Bond. I'll be responsible. This is not—I repeat—not a matter for local jurisdiction. Put him on, please."

Broderick, somewhat subdued, handed Bond his car mike. "Just talk into that, sir."

"Iz, you old Hebe sex maniac, you!" Goshen's voice was jovial, but held a note of concern. "What the hell have you mucked up now?"

"Nothing, Monroe, you old goyischeh New England lobster pot!" He heard Goshen's appreciative chuckle. They'd crossed paths before and had a warm regard for one another. In fact, it was Bond who had brought a breath of spring to Goshen's reticent, dour life, fixing up the CIA operative with his first sexual encounter at the age of 43. "Beats fishin' for stripers," the staid New Englander had admitted in a rare moment of self-revelation.

Bond swiftly explained the attempt on Loxfinger's life (which Goshen had learned anyway from one of his key sources—the Huntley-Brinkley Report), his interception of the bungler-assassin's car, the shots, the fiery climax behind the billboard. "Nothing much left of him, Monroe, but I did find a charred amulet with some symbols I'm quite familiar with. He's from the Lebanese Order for Unified Sabotage and Espionage."

"So, you got the LOUSE? Good! Listen, Iz, I'll have to do a coverup job, fast! We'll have to doctor up the story. 'Course we can't afford to have your renowned Old Man Moneybags killed on our real estate, but we do have relations with Lebanon, too. I'll have the local boys enter it as death by natural causes—vehicular accident. Tell them to forget they ever met you ... and get the hell out of there. Oh, and put the tramp in the pokey for a couple o' nights; see that he gets a big jug o' Sneaky Pete every two hours. Two nights in stir and he'll forget he ever saw anything, just chalk it up to the D.T.'s."

Goshen was on the ball, Bond thought. To the bewildered troopers: "You heard him, fellas."

"Sure thing, Mr. Bond. Say, uh ..." Crawford paused. He had something on his mind. "You mean to say that you shot out our front rubber on spite? You planned it that way?"

"Of course," Bond smiled. It sounded lame even to his own ears. (Gottenu! I've got to get back to the range and do some serious practicing!) "You see, lads, if you had been forced to shoot him it would have been embarrassing for three countries. His, Lebanon, would have denied any knowledge of his murder mission, accused yours of collusion with 'Zionist imperialists,' etc. When I deliberately forced you out of the picture I simplified matters for everybody. Now our story is that during the chase he swerved off the road and bang-o! We'll just say he was a kook with a personal grudge against Loxfinger."

They seemed highly satisfied with the explanation. "Hey, that's a fancy heater you got there, Mr. Bond. Can we look at it?"

Bond let them examine the Shar Shue Dung-55, noting with annoyance that there was a bit of dandruff on its hair trigger. Have to pay more attention to my equipment, he admitted.

He had shaken hands with them, given each man another Raleigh, and Ramblered north, with a farewell wave.

I guess the flashback killed the ten minutes, Bond reckoned. He started for the lounge and his meeting with Saxon. On the elevator he bumped into a girl. "Beg your pardon."

She said nothing, content to flash a look of utter disgust.

She's a smasher! Bond thought. Sullen savage loveliness ... full, pouting lips, eyes of Brillo black and bluish highlights, a heart-stopping shape, hugged affectionately by leotards of sheerest net lace. Her proud defiant breasts were completely uncovered. If this damn elevator doesn't stop in three seconds I'm going to crush those maddening rosebud nipples in my aching teeth, he swore vehemently.

Rosebud! He smiled a secretive smile. Odd to think of that word now. As a child he'd had a sled by that name. Wonder what ever happened to it?

With arch humor he bowed, permitting the blazing creature to leave the car first. "See you around ... or around you," he riposted. She never even turned to acknowledge his quip, walking lithely away with her tantalizing dancer's stride.

"She don' like men, that one," broke in the colorfully woolly-headed old Negro elevator operator, showing a mouthful of pointed teeth. "I seen lotsa menz in dis heah hotel tryin' to sweet talk dat missy, but she don' give no eye to none o' dem nohow."

"Thanks for the tip," Bond said lightly. "Here, old timer." The old man grinned at the two Luci Baines dimes Bond had placed in his pinkish palm. A nice enough old fellow, but no CORE member, Bond surmised.

She *was* a smasher! Bond thought again. But he'd sensed something strange, a man-hating look he'd noticed in certain bizarre bistros with an offbeat clientele. Lesbo? Well, if she was, he'd—in Warren Harding's classic phrase—restore her to "normalcy"!

At the desk he asked for any messages.

"Uh, you're Mr. Bond in Room 1818, correct, sir?"

"Yes." (He'd insisted on that room number this time; no fool he!)

"Here you are, sir."

The brief message, in Arabic, read: "I'd ride a Camel a mile to smoke an Oasis."

What the hell was this? Bond frowned, his cruelly dark handsomeness becoming even more attractive. More than one woman had been driven wild by that frown.

Camel? Oasis? If these were code words, they were certainly not in his master book. "Clerk, are you sure this message is for me?"

"Oh, I beg your pardon, sir," said the clerk, reddening. "This is for the gentleman in 1817, the room next to yours. Mr. Jew."

Mr. Jew? Bond thought hard. "Sounds rather familiar. What's the gentleman's first name, clerk?"

"His first name is Achmed. Just checked in an hour ago. Strange sort. When I asked him to register, he just gave me a blank look as though he didn't understand what I was saying. He shoved a piece of paper in front of me that specifically requested he be quartered in the room next to yours. I thought the fellow was a friend of yours, so I saw no harm in assigning him 1817."

No sense making the clerk suspicious. Bond snapped his fingers as though in recollection. "Of course! My old buddy Achmed Jew! Slipped my mind completely. He and I golfed together in Jamaica last winter. He shot a seventy-four as I recall it now. Nice chap. Glad to have him aboard."

He thanked the clerk with a handful of Hubert Humphrey nickels and walked out onto the porch to give the matter some thought. Achmed Jew! And in the next room! Where was *he* from? Jordan? Kuwait? Saudi Arabia? Whoever he was he must be a dunderhead, indeed, to pick an on-the-head last name like "Jew" in order to blend into the crowd at this kind of a hotel. And to use his first name yet! What a faux pas! What Arabic stupidity! Or arrogance, rather, to think a name like Achmed would go unnoticed. No doubt, Mr. Achmed Jew felt uncomfortable in this totally alien environment. Well, he'd have to make Mr. Achmed Jew feel right at home—with a little welcome call late tonight.

A burst of classical music brought him back to reality. It was from a transistor radio held by an old man in Bermuda shorts sitting in a rocking chair reading a Yiddish newspaper.

Bond attempted a little friendly chit-chat. "That's lovely. One of my favorites. What do you think of Tschaikovsky's 'Swan Lake'?"

The old man waved a deprecating hand. "It's not so hot. I stayed there last year. Food is terrible. Myself, if I could afford it—the Concord." He went back to his newspaper.

In the Leni Lenape Lounge, decorated with Eastern American Indian motifs—somewhat at variance with the Polynesian theme of the Kahn-Tiki—Bond spotted the man he thought was Angelo Saxon.

"Saxon?"

The tall, weedy blonde who wore a baggy (and rather gamey, Bond's nose reported) brown woolen suit, sipping a Tom Collins, turned to him. "Why ... uh ... yes. Bond, is it? Sorry for my seeming impertinence, old man, but I'd heard you were in public relations like me. Thought you'd try to con old Loxfinger into some shady promotion or other. Had no idea you were ... uh ... in your type of occupation. Drink?"

How tactful, Bond thought. Taken down a few pegs, he wants to be friendly. All right. We'll join hands on the friendship trail for a bit. "Yes, thanks. Bartender, a Lhasa Lizard, please. Just a soupçon of mildly rancid yak butter in the bottom of the tumbler ... the right eye of any domestic lizard—iguana will do nicely ... one ounce of Gallo Wine—from the first squeezings of the grapes, please ... three crumbs from a Drake's Yankee Doodle cupcake. Shake well. Now, how much? Sixty-five cents?" Bond's chin shot out indignantly. "Good grief, man! Lhasa Lizards are never more than forty-five cents in the most elegant Manhattan posheries! The management will hear of this."

Nevertheless, he left the mixicologist some gleaming Bobby Baker pennies. Wasn't the man's fault actually. He didn't set prices.

"Now to business. What happened, Saxon?"

Saxon took out a pack of Marvels, stuck one in his prim mouth. It figures, Bond thought. Wears a brown, sweaty woolen suit in a glittering Catskill hotel cocktail lounge, so naturally he smokes Marvels.

"It happened rather quickly, Mr. Bond. Dr. Loxfinger—he's been a 'doctor,' of course, ever since that honorary degree from Brandeis University—was exhorting the crowd in the Kahn-Tiki's main ballroom to double their pledges to the UJA ... not the United Jewish Appeal ... this one's a new organization which is seeking enough money to put Israel in the Nuclear Club. It stands for 'Unleash the Jewish Atom'..."

"Yes, yes, go on," said Bond.

"Well, that's when this wiry, Levantine-type, who'd been masquerading as a busboy, dropped his tray of dishes, whipped out a revolver and fired point-blank at the doctor. I, of course, had seen the gun in his hand and made a lunge at the filthy little cretin. I missed. But strangely enough, so did he. I suppose my lunge unnerved him. Then he fled. Tell me ... did you get him?"

"Yes, the matter was taken care of on the Quickway."

"Good show!" said Saxon, but there was something deep in his eyes Bond could not fathom as yet, but did not like. "This little gunman ... did he talk?"

"No, he died without talking, I'm afraid." Was that a gleam of triumph in Saxon's eyes? "Well, tell me, Saxon, what else happened when the shot was fired?"

"Naturally," said Saxon, sipping his drink, "all hell broke loose. The loudest cries, it seemed, came from the hotel owner, Mr. Kahn. The 'busboy' had ruined forty-eight dollars' worth of genuine East Side Fiesta dishes when he dropped the tray. In the confusion he fled. You know the rest."

Time to put the screws on. "Frankly," Bond began coldly, "I'm shocked at the general laxity around here. Has there been no guard assigned to the doctor up to now? Remember, this man is the greatest thing that has happened to Israel since Leon Uris. He is beloved by world Jewry, vastly respected by non-Jews. Wrap up Albert Schweitzer, Ringo Starr and Shirley Temple and you have Lazarus Loxfinger. This man must be guarded! What a blow to our prestige, our hopes and dreams for a better world if he were to be taken from us! Especially since the impact of the 'Plowshare Papers' upon most of humanity."

"Oh," Saxon said, his eyes widening with concern, "but I agree. Fully. The doctor does have a bodyguard, you know, quite a formidable one. You will meet him later. He's a mountain, not a man ... a sort of Neanderthal, really. The doctor found him working on the docks in Marseilles, took pity on him and made him part of our entourage. This creature is the product of a rather hasty mesalliance between an American soldier, a nigger ... oops!" He winked. "Sorry for that. One does have to be 'liberal' these days. Uh, an American soldier of ... sepian hue, shall we say, who consorted with a white Scottish barmaid in Glasgow during World War Two. The issue of this one-night stand is our bodyguard. His name is Macaroon. Wanted by neither parent, he was shunted from orphanage to orphanage. Grew to be amazingly huge and powerful. He must be seven-foot six if he's an inch. Makes one rather wish slavery were back; I'd sell him to the New York Knickerbockers for a million bucks and they'd pay it gladly to get a 100-point a night scorer. Macaroon's specialty is karate. I've seen this simian shatter a twelve by twelve with one chop of that monstrous hand."

"Why wasn't he around to protect Loxfinger when he was needed?"

"Simple. He'd been drugged. Someone, the 'busboy,' no doubt, had spiced his haggis and chitlin's—that's all he eats—with a powerful sleeping draught."

Bond inhaled. "You mentioned 'entourage.' Who else is in this charmed Loxfinger circle?"

Saxon winked again. "Besides Macaroon and yours truly, there's one other ... his personal secretary, Peepee. You appear to be the sort of man who appreciates good womanflesh, Mr. Bond. You'll find Peepee quite a mouthwatering sight."

"Peepee? What kind of a gibbering, infantile name is that for a grown woman?"

"Those are her initials, P.P. But here she is now, Mr. Bond. I'd asked her to join us. Hope you don't mind."

Bond's eyes rose—then popped. Peepee was the fascinating, unreachable minx he'd struck out with on the elevator. Still wearing the same fetching costume she had on when last they met she ... she oozed ... that was the word ... oozed across the lounge, those Junoesque breasts pointing to only heaven knew what mystical horizons, that frigidly wonderful, sullen face ...

She faced him now, those frosty lips opening, spitting out word icicles: "Mr. Bond, I presume? My name is Poontang Plenty. Mr. Saxon here insists on calling me Peepee. You may if you wish. I don't give a flying f—"

"Well, now," Bond laughed, cutting her off diplomatically. "I rather like your given name ... Poontang Plenty. Fraught with promise."

Her top lip curled into an adorable sneer. "Forget it, he-man! The name is all that's been given."

The bitch has spirit! "Drink, Poontang?"

"What are you creeps having?"

"Mr. Saxon here is Tom Collinsing. I'm enjoying a rather far-out little libation with the picturesque nomenclature 'Lhasa Lizard.' One takes the right eye of—"

"Oh, crap!" she said in a blasé tone.

"The way we're cutting each other off, Poontang, this whole conversation is turning into a circumcision!"

"Cheap one-liner, Mr. He-Man. And badly delivered."

This girl's got me backtracking, he admitted inwardly. And she knows it.

"F.Y.I., Mr. Bond, I've been drinking Lizards since I was six. And ..." she looked at his drink "... no iguana eyes, either. It's got to have the right eye from a Siamese rain forest chameleon or it's utter, utter garbage."

He tried to keep his admiration for her out of his voice. "You've been around, Poontang."

Saxon yawned. "I'll leave you lovebirds to peck out each other's eyes. So long, Peepee, see you later." He bent his gaunt frame to buss her cheek.

"Put those Tussaud Waxworks lips on me and I'll kick you right in the—"

Mumbling an insincere farewell, Saxon exited hastily. Gratefully, too, Bond thought. At least the fish-eyed P.R. man was no competition.

"That water lily!" Her voice was pure cobra venom. "I hate him, him with those putrid eyes and that stinking suit—eeech!" She shuddered, toying with something in her right hand. Whatever it was it made a clicking sound like two marbles tapped together.

"Ah," said Bond, resorting to his usual lighter-than-air touch. It's as good as any other gambit in this game d'amour, he reasoned. "Ah, Captain Queeg! Playing with your balls again, I see."

"That's right, buster," her voice came up hard and gritty. "Know what these are?" She thrust her hand dramatically into his face, opening it. Two marbles, deep highlights radiating from their exotically striated cores, lay in her palm.

"Why, yes, Poontang. Marbles, aren't they? Some childish carryover?"

"Think marbles is a childish sport, Mr. He-Man with the faggot sandals?" A smile, but hate-filled. "Care to ... uh ... take me on in a little game, maybe?"

"Oh," said Bond, taken aback a trifle. "I don't know if ..."

"You gutless bastard!" Three words scourging his pride. "Just like the rest of your oafish breed. Nice shoulders on you, Mr. Bond. Trim waist. That romantic scar. I'll wager a carload of matzoh-stuffed matrons have rolled over in the clover for that combination, right, Mr. Bond? But you're gutless. Yellow—like all the rest."

Smile, Bond, smile. You're stung, but you can't show that to this adorable hellcat. Can't let her hear your teeth grinding in rage. He dragged on his Raleigh.

"Care for legends, Poontang? No? Oh, you'll like this one. Any girl who psychologically craves balls would dig this one. It's all about brave little Peter, the Dutch boy who saved his homeland by sticking his finger in a dyke. Remember? Well, Holland has long since forgotten Peter, but, you know something ... that dyke is still crazy about him."

Now it was her turn to be stung. She bit her marvelously red, full lips. "Your seamy little allegory wasn't lost on me, Mr. Bond. I've heard the same old tired insults before from other alleged 'men' who can't make the grade with me, so they hurl smutty charges. No, Mr. Bond, I don't let men into my life—or anything else. I'm smarter than any man I've ever met, stronger than most, and in that one little childish pastime you deride—marbles—I can best any man I've ever known." She tensed defiantly. "Care for that game, Mr. Bond?"

His eyes gleamed. "What's in it for me if I win, Poontang?"

"Win? WIN?" She exploded into helpless, thigh-whacking laughter, the first Bond had ever seen on that sullen face. My, she's homely when she laughs.

"Win? You stupid, prideful bastard! I'll show you who's really got balls at this table, Bond. I have. Right in my hand. The neatest shooters you ever saw smack a marble on its ass and send it flying!"

Bond looked into her eyes, deviltry dancing in his own. "Let's say the impossible is possible, Poontang. And I win. What's in it for me?"

She stood up regally, extended those staggeringly desirable mounds to within an inch of his twitching lips. "Yes ... they're yours! Yours! And everything else that goes with 'em! Gladly! But you'll never outshoot me, buster. And to make it interesting for me, I'll relieve you of some of your long green. Shall we say twenty bucks for each captured marble?"

"So, Her Nibs digs mibs, eh?"

"That's the size of it, lover boy. I'm throwing the gauntlet right in your craggy, cruelly handsome face and I hope to hell it drives your blackheads clear through your cheeks!"

He spoke. The charm was gone from his voice now, she noticed. Good! She'd made the goodlooking bastard shook up.

"You're on, Poontang. Marbles it is. Noon tomorrow, any place on the hotel grounds you want. But I'd make it far from the main building, though. I don't want the folks to be upset by your screams when I ..." He could hold back the sound of his gritting teeth no longer. In his passion a wisdom molar crumbled into chalk.

"Brave words, buster. But you're on. Tomorrow—noon."

5
The Terror from the Top of the World

"Israel Bond," the voice said stoically. "You're insane. Crazy. Demented. Mesheega in gontz."*

He did not take offense. After all, the voice was his own, coming from the dark face in the mirror, thickly lathered with Rokeach's new mentholated cream. His hand clutched the razor which housed the super-keen Cuckoo stainless steel blade, superior by far, according to *Better Beards and Blades*, the authoritative shaving magazine, to G—, P—, even the W— from Great Britain.

"You are insane," the voice continued, "because you've gotten yourself tangled up in a comic opera thriller out of 'Graustark' by 'The 39 Steps,' $7.80, $5.60 and $3.20. Consider:

"You are here to guard a Kosher Croesus named Loxfinger, who among other things wants to end constipation and war, not necessarily in that order.

"Tomorrow at noon you are to play marbles with an equally deranged, albeit winsome, Lesbian.

"Somewhere on these grounds is an alpine mulatto named Macaroon, who cracks boards with his hands and eats haggis 'n chitlin's.

"To top it off, in the very next room is an Arab thug named Jew, who is here for the express purpose of putting an inglorious end to your obscene, womanizing existence.

---
* Crazy in totality.

"And how did you prepare for all of this ... by getting blotto from a concoction whose component parts include the eye of a loathsome lizard?

"You are insane, Israel Bond. Crazy, punchy, wacked up. End of lecture."

Thanks, friend, Bond said, throwing a salute at the reproachful face in the glass, but I've got some business to attend to tonight. Mr. Jew, par exemple. (In moods of cynical ennui Bond often thought in French.)

His nerves raw from the tension he had undergone ever since the whole chaotic skein of events had started to unravel in Miami Beach, Bond gulped down one of Mother Margolies' favorite relaxants—M & M, Manischewitz & Miltown. It would ease him into a peaceful late afternoon catnap from which he would emerge refreshed and ready for the grim tasks ahead. He stripped down to his Fruit of the Loom spun Egyptian cotton shorts (you had to hand it to the warmongering bastards; they *did* grow splendid cotton), lit up his 198th Raleigh of the day (I've smoked enough for a clip of .45s at least, he exulted) and lay on his bed. A little soothing music, perhaps, to hasten the advent of sweet slumber. He switched on the radio.

"... moving right up on the chart, teens and queens, is No. 1,892, Vinnie Vee Vermin and the Vandals and their big ..."

Without even thinking, his muscular arm swept up the radio and hurled it out the window. It landed 18 floors below on a patio table where boniface Schuyler Kahn, his Estrellita and their guests, Lennie and Sali Heller of Roseola, Michigan, sat, scattering four hands of Jewish pinochle. Kahn shrugged: "That's the 35th radio to come flying down this week. Lay you 13 to 1 whoever threw it was listening to Rockin' Robby Robbins."

Bond's eyes were closing now, but there was one more chore. "Operator—get me Milton Bond in Trenton, New Jersey. Area code 609, IMport 7-8898."

He waited. "Milt? Your Israeli brother. Listen, Milt, I'm practically asleep, but I need a favor damned fast. Look through my old things in the attic, the junk I stored before I went to Eretz in '48. Still got it? Good. Now, I must have these things no later than noon tomorrow. Got a pencil?" His voice droned a list. "That's the whole schmear. Fly 'em up to the Kahn-Tiki Hotel, Loch Sheldrake, in your Piper Cub. Leave 'em at the desk. Love to Lottie and the kinderlach. I'm so damn sleepy I ..."

The receiver fell from jellyfish-weak fingers. Bond was out cold.

Cold.

He was cold. Shivering, freezing cold.

He smiled in his sleep. The smell of salty fish permeated his dream. Lox? Loxfinger? Herring? Yes, a *gooten shtickel* pickled herring, the way his mother used to make it back in Trenton, his birthplace in 1930. Momma! His warm-hearted, crafty, typical Jewish mother, who had dreamed of a profitable career for him in medicine. "Study hard, learn," she had said in her careworn way. "Someday, son, you'll be a famous abortionist with a big practice and a country clubber in Stockholm." She was smiling at him now in this loveliest of dreams. Hello, momma. I miss you.

How she had saved and scrimped for the education that had never panned out due to his wild, adventurous streak. At the butcher's she had insisted on buying the cheapest cut of bone. He could remember her even now, hiding a nickel here, a dime there, a quarter there, a cunning smile on her face. All for him! And after she had died, they had searched into all her little hiding places and found a total of forty cents. Momma, I miss you.

He knew he was dreaming, but, ah, it was divine! There was his poppa, olav hashalom, tearing up herring on his *Daily Forvartz*, handing the kiddies the choicest tidbits. My, that fish smells good. So strong, so near it might just as well be on my bed.

The cold salty fish is moving over my body, he smiled. I'm in a Catskill hotel and a cold slimy fish is crawling over me!

Crawling?

Fish don't crawl!

He sprang into consciousness—something wet, cold, slimy, furry, impossibly huge was advancing on his body. Something was—Gottenu! The pain! Something with a fetid, fishy breath had sunk its teeth into his shoulder—the bad one.

Two red eyes were glowing in the darkened room, part of something enormous that was crushing him, mashing his ribs, his chest. Pinned to the bed like a butterfly on a card, he stared into the enraged face of a polar bear!

Bond screamed, unashamedly. He tried reaching for the mezuzah with a hand already puffing up horribly from the mashing. Gone! The bear's claw had ripped the chain from his neck. Blood from the reopened shoulder wound raced lava-like down his body.

He was virtually on the verge of fainting. The swollen hand was all that remained to combat this one-ton terror from the top of the world. Its growl sent chills down his bruised spine. He could imagine the not-so-stupid Mr. Jew next door in 1817, his ear pressed to the wall, laughing gleefully at each of Bond's screams. No, Mr. Achmed Jew was not the dumb bunny he had thought him to be. While he, Bond, had talked a good game, Mr. Jew had acted! Somehow managing to smuggle his murderous Arctic aide into the Kahn-Tiki.

Only the thought of that cackling anti-Semite bastard next door kept Bond going. A rage, every bit as towering as the polar bear's, swept over him. His mashed fingers found a shoe under the bed, touched a spring in the heel. A knife sprang out. Now it was in Bond's demoniacal clutch, driving down toward the bear's exposed neck. No! Wait! Stop! He knew from the extra-light feel of the knife and its dull edge that it was a milchig (dairy) knife. Sacrilege! To kill a meat creature with a dairy knife. He dropped it, felt for the mate to the shoe, found its spring and drove the flayschig (meat) knife again and again into his adversary. Blood—the bear's now—was gushing out like an oil strike from an oversexed Icelandic volcano. With one tormented roar, the bear rolled over Bond again, inflicting more indescribable pain, then fell ponderously to the floor. It would lurk no more in the Kahn-Tiki Hotel.

He had met his greatest challenge—and won.

Gottenu! What pain! Pain! Pain! Tension! Tension! Tension! He would give the world for one Excedrin now!

Gingerly he felt for the phone. He had to make sure this terrible thing was indeed premeditated. In his heart he knew it was, but his Double Oy training dictated total surety. He heard the polite voice of the friendly desk clerk he'd talked to previously.

Though his body screamed in a million agonized places, he forced himself to make his voice as dignified as possible. "Bond, 1818. Tell me ... uh ... have there ever been any ... uh ... polar bears inside this hotel before? As guests, visitors, in any capacity at all?"

"Definitely not, Mr. Bond!" The clerk sounded highly insulted. "A polar bear in the Kahn-Tiki? Never, sir! We only get a family crowd."

"Thank you," said a thoughtful Bond. He hung up. Then there *was* a score to settle!

6
"Oasis Calling, Mr. Jew"

The phone rang in 1817.

The wiry, Levantine-type dropped the all-purpose Gideon book of worship provided by the management (Old Testament-New Testament-Koran-Kama Sutra), reached for the phone with some apprehension. He had not been expecting any calls. For a moment he debated the advisability of answering. He felt for the Sphinx-77 in his shoulder holster, patted it reassuringly and lifted the receiver.

"Meester Achmed Jew?" A harsh, thickly accented voice.

"Yes."

"The Oasis is pleased at the death of the Camel."

A sigh of relief escaped his throat. Ah, a fellow member from the Yemeni Elite for Nullifying Traitorous Zionists. YENTZ! The caller could be no other; he had used the key code words aptly.

"Who is this, please?" One still had to be cautious.

"Mr. Jew, this is Gamal Goy, your superior from the El Nakid Sidi section. I am calling with further instructions."

"Of course, excellency. But your name ... Gamal Goy. It is unknown to me."

"Fool! It is a pseudonym as is your own, Achmed Jew. Which incidentally has a uniquely Arabic touch of humor. I congratulate you on dispatching the Jew, Jew. It was handily done, by the beard of the prophet!"

"Allah Akbar!" Achmed cried. "There is none but Allah and Mohammed is his servant. But tell me, how did you learn of the matter?"

"It is not for you to question Goy, Jew. Be satisfied that we have observed and are pleased. How did you manage to introduce the creature into this inhospitable Zionist stronghold?"

"Simple, excellency." Achmed Jew's voice was tinged with self-importance at his cleverness. "I brought it in a refrigerated truck which stops regularly at the Kahn-Tiki kitchen after, naturally, disposing of the driver and his cargo. Then I led it up the freight elevator. The stupid operator was made to believe it was a tipsy guest heading for a private masquerade party on the eighteenth floor."

"You show hidden fires, Achmed Jew! Splendid! Now you will meet me at the indoor pool adjacent to the solarium. I have instructions regarding the Israeli philanthropist."

"By the nose hairs of Nasser!" Achmed cried delightedly. "Am I to be given the signal honor of destroying this dog?"

"Silence! Son of a pock-marked pickpocket! You will learn in good time. Saalum aleikum." The caller hung up.

The tense YENTZ agent could hardly believe his ears. He let go an irrepressible squeal. Surely Gamal Goy must think he, Achmed, was worthy indeed to have proffered such a monumental assignment. He chortled merrily at the name—Gamal Goy. And who said we Arabs lacked subtlety? Then he realized something else! Virtually the entire conversation with his superior had been conducted in English, a language Achmed was totally unfamiliar with. What a magnetic man Goy must be to draw a foreign tongue out of me!

Moments later he stood by the poolside, his nostrils assailed by the stench. Then he recalled he had been told it was filled with Mother Margolies' Activated Old World Chicken Soup. Stinking Zionist offal!

It was dinner time. The pool was deserted. A creepy feeling pervaded him, his own footsteps echoing against the moist, steamy walls gave him a sense of unease. Lighting a Rameses, he waited.

He pricked up his ears. He heard other footsteps reverberating through the man-made fog. Then silence.

"Achmed Jew!"

The harsh voice, sounding strangely disembodied. But from where?

"Goy?"

"No Goy, Jew! This is Jew, Goy!"

That voice! Achmed whirled, his hand sliding into his coat. Dreck! Dreck!

Two slugs from a Tzimmes-88 tore past him, missing by a foot. But in spinning to answer the misdirected shots with his

Sphinx-77, Achmed slipped on the wet tiles, his head cracking the pool deck. Stunned, his temporal parietal area gashed badly, he toppled into the pool. For a few seconds there was a strangling, gurgling sound. Then his struggles ceased.

A cold smile on his face as he watched the bloody eddies mingling with the tender bits of plump Rhode Island Red fowl, Bond came down from the high diving board, his vantage point for the shooting. The Tzimmes-88 still smoked in his swollen right hand. Justice had cried out for a chauvinistic killing with a good Jewish gun this time. Nothing fancy. Just a plain good Jewish killing. His lips spoke mockingly to the bobbing body of the drowned Yemeni: "Gamal Goy greets his desert brother, Achmed Jew. May there be many dark-eyed houris to greet you in your warriors' heaven—all of them with yaws—you bastard!" (But I really must get back to the practice range, he warned himself once more).

Flicking off an imaginary dust spot on the lapel of his Dino tuxedo, the model favored by leading stars of stage, screen and television, Bond took out his Nippo, lit a Raleigh and watched the smoke become part of the pool's mist. He pulled the wick out, placed it in his ear and spoke into the bottom of the lighter.

"Zvi?"

"Shalom, Oy Oy Seven."

"Have you disposed of the bear's body?"

"Yes, Oy Oy Seven. It has been sliced into bits. Every cat in the Catskills will have an unexpected treat tonight. And as you requested, I am having the skin made into a coat. How are your wounds?"

"Better, thank you. The hotel doctor dressed the lacerations, thinking he was ministering to a very poor skier. As for the pain, it's bad, but bearable. The Excedrins are definitely helping. You see, I had this pain that felt like two billygoats were pulling my head asunder, so in a case like this when I need big relief..."

Zvi's voice cut in: "Yes. But what shall I tell M. about our friend from YENTZ?"

Bond's grey eyes gleamed as his quick mind prepared to hurl one of his famous jests.

"One can say," he paused for telling effect, "that Mr. Achmed Jew is definitely in the soup!"

7
"This Can't Be the Regular Group!"

For once, disposing of a body had proved relatively simple for Bond. Zvi, who had left the Cafe Aw-Go-Go-Already to come to the Catskills and work more closely with him, had wangled a part-time job as an animal trainer with the Ring-A-Ding Barton Brothers & Bill Bailey Circus and Smoker ("The earthiest show on earth") touring nearby and had brought over a starving Bengal tiger, shoved it into the pool and calmly watched it dine on the Levantine.

Bond, a Raleigh dangling from his lips, commented: "You can always count on fast action, Zvi, when there's a tiger in the tank."

Grinning, Zvi again was overwhelmed by Oy Oy Seven's trigger mind. How does he do it? And why?

"Boy, that tiger is doing a real job. I don't think Agent D. could have handled this any better." Then he bit his tongue.

"Agent D.?" A sharp look of interest was on Bond's face. "Who is Agent D.?"

Zvi stammered. "Forget I ever mentioned Agent D. Please, Oy Oy Seven, please forget it. Means nothing really."

Agent D.? Zvi apparently had gleaned something from one of M.'s top secret missives. But Bond decided to press the matter no further. His confrere was obviously embarrassed enough.

"Say, Bond," said Zvi, changing the subject as quickly as he could, "how come you got all duded up in soup 'n fish to bump off this guy? What's with this whole fashion plate bit anyway?"

Bond looked at him with some asperity. "Look, Zvi. This is a rotten business I'm in ... killing, maiming, stealing, bribing. But damn it, man, there's no reason why I have to go through all of it like a slob!"

And he spun angrily on his heel, an unfortunate maneuver which released a knife that whizzed by Zvi's head, lopping off an ear.

"Iz ... I'm sorry I offended you, old friend," Zvi said to Bond's departing back, the pain of thoughtlessly hurting a chum far exceeding the minor irritation emanating from the spot where his auditory appendage had been ensconced.

Understandably aggravated by Zvi's vulgar diatribe against his wardrobe, Bond nevertheless shrugged it off. Zvi, a mere 113 rank holder, could not appreciate men of Bond's class. Bond's own idol had been Oy Oy One, a suave, nattily attired operative who had met the fate all Oy Oy holders were destined for—the end of an Arab rope. And faithful to his gentleman's code, Oy Oy One had insisted that the Egyptian hangman use a Windsor knot. Truly a man to emulate, Bond vowed.

Ten minutes later, reverting to his cover role, Bond found himself delivering the speech to the organization mentioned in M.'s communication and then found himself dragged into yet another conclave by a spry, surprisingly powerful old matron in gold lame evening hip-hugger slacks and blouse, matched regrettably with brown and white saddles. He had given an abbreviated version of his speech to the group, the Molly Picon Golden Age Political Action Club, and with another of his typically gallant (and basically good-hearted) gestures—"Waiter, a bottle of your best Geritol for every lovely lady in the room"— had gained applause and reverence.

Still pain-racked from his mauling, the bored Oy Oy Seven strolled into the Litvak Luau Room where, before a jam-packed audience, West Coast comedy sensation Henny Benny Lenny was holding sway at the microphone, tossing glib patter:

"... geez, what a quiet bunch! I've gotten better reaction from a Schick test!"

(Nervous, somewhat light laughter.)

"My God, let's all hold hands and try to communicate with the living!"

(Even lighter laughter.)

"Are you sure this is the regular group? So this guy falls off the Washington Monument and the cop says, 'What's goin' on here?' and the guy says, 'I don't know. I just got here myself!'"

(Nervous rustlings; no laughter.)

"This can't be the regular group! Well, let's try the hip, sophisticated, topical humor right outa today's front pages, huh? Viet Nam? That's affecting all of us in these troubled times. Well, these two South Vietnamese soldiers are sitting around in a foxhole under fire from the Commies and the first one says to his pal, 'I just bought me one of them Italian sports cars—a Cosa Nostra. Underneath the hood is a hood!'"

(Barely audible rustlings.)

"Uh, let's talk about civil rights, which is affecting all of us in these troubled times. So this NAACP picket meets Roy Wilkins and he says, 'Geez, Roy, is my wife neat! I got up in the middle of the night to take a leak and by the time I came back she'd made the bed!'"

(SILENCE.)

"No civil rights bits, uh? This must be a KKK crowd—Kosher, Kishkes and Kreplach. That was a fastie I just thought up. I wish I hadn't."

(Even lighter silence.)

"Uh—automation. We're all affected by automation in these troubled times. So the first robot says to the second robot, 'I'm bowlegged; my old lady is knockkneed; when we stand together we spell OX!'"

(   )

"Well, I guess this ain't the hip, sophisticated crowd that digs topical humor right outa today's front pages. Well, if that's the case, let's get back to the old jokes, folks. Hey, I made a rhyme—jokes, folks! Geez, I'm a poet and don't know it. But my feet show it. They're Longfellows!"

(Some response this time ... of a sort. A ringsider vaulted onto the stage and hit the funmaker across the mouth with a whisky bottle.)

"Well, goodnight, folks, and God bless youse. Youse have been a wonderful audience and I just wanna say I'm a veteran, with three sons who are Rabbis, who loves his mom, America and all she stands for, and my old dog, Timmie. My dog is so old that his fleas just went on medicare. Nothing, huh? Well, goodnight!"

And the peppery comedian walked off to the strains of "I Know That You Know," grinning, spitting out his teeth and whispering to a stagehand, "Tough crowd at first, but I finally got 'em."

Too bad, Bond thought. He was a hilarious chap. The frequent cabareting Bond had been exposed to as part of his P.R. role had made him rather an expert on funnymen. This one was first-rate. But the crowd had been impatiently waiting for a message from Dr. Loxfinger, who had agreed on a brief personal appearance to show an anxious Jewry he was alive and well.

Bond, too, felt a stirring at the prospect of hearing one of Loxfinger's messianic pronunciamentos. He had seen the seventy-six-year-old savant in the newsreels, of course, even there experiencing the galvanism of the man. Now he would feel it first hand.

The honor of the introduction rightly belonged to porcine Schuyler Kahn, now on stage beaming beatifically.

"Ladies and gentlemen ..."

As though a needle had been lifted from a phonograph, the murmuring ceased abruptly.

"My lovely wife, Estrellita Kahn, your co-host at the Kahn-Tiki and the only woman I'll ever look at ..." there was hearty applause; the love between the Kahns was well known to their regular patrons. (Estrellita rose, shouted, "I feel the same way about you, Schuyler, sweetie!" which triggered another wave of applause and laughter.) "Estrellita and I feel truly blessed tonight. Our hotel, the Kahn-Tiki, your Jewish haven in the hills, where homebodies can dance, sing, love, and eat like—you should pardon the expression—pigs! (riotous laughter) at reasonable, God knows, rates, which next year will have the Catskill Mountains' only individual handball courts and sauna baths in each and every room (lusty cheers) ... our hotel has been granted the esteemed honor of hosting a giant of Judaism this day. He has graced our magnificent Wahine Dining Room with his presence, the only dining room in the mountains that features high-calorie saccharine (more cheers) and—and a French mother dee!! Well, I ain't up here to plug (chuckle) the Kahn-Tiki, your second home. I'm here to humbly present the greatest Jewish gentleman I ever seen—and, believe me, Schuyler Kahn in his role as owner of the best Class B hotel in the mountains has met them all... I have become personal, intimate, best friends with all of them... Al Jessel, Georgie Jolson, Sophie Bryce and Fanny Tucker, those ice-cold mamas... the Ritz Sisters, those wonderful Marx clowns; Frodo, Bilbo, Dildo, you name 'em, I know 'em. I say the greatest Jewish gentleman of them all is the gent I'm gonna present now. Without further ado, here is Dr. Lazarus Loxfinger!"

There was a glass-shattering roar. Bond looked blankly at the shards in his hand and the ice cubes in his lap.

Lazarus Loxfinger, trailed by a huge mulatto wearing a plaid kilt and a T-shirt with the letters "In my kilt I kill" and carrying a board on his shoulder, walked slowly onto the stage. He stood motionless during a fantastic, ten-minute standing ovation, hearing his name screamed over and over again: "Loxfinger! Loxfinger! Loxfinger!"

Several women fainted during the unimaginable din. An elderly matron next to Bond shrieked: "A Messiah he is; he should only live another thousand years! Now I know what the Catholics feel when they see their Pope!"

Then Loxfinger raised his right hand stiffly, palm out. The throng stilled.

Macaroon suddenly crossed in front of his leader, swung the board off his shoulder, held it by the end with his left hand, and with a frightening blur chopped his right hand down on it. There was a sharp crack; gasps sounded through the ballroom; the board, split in two, fell to the stage. Then the monster lumbered off.

And Loxfinger began to speak.

8
The Brave Bullring

Now it was two in the morning and Bond, still beset by the sense of unreality that had begun the instant he heard the voice of Lazarus Loxfinger, found himself unable to sleep. He lit a Raleigh in the dark, indifferently watching the flames from his tossed match creeping up the blanket toward him.

No doubt of it, the man was a spellbinder. In a few words he had reduced the crowd to tears, proclaiming he would never rest "until Israel has achieved the destiny I, Lazarus Loxfinger, envision for her."

There was something unearthly about Loxfinger, the way the harsh, guttural yet strangely soothing music of his voice was seemingly able to lift his auditors to heights beyond the known, the way his incredible blue eyes blazed. Not imposing physically, he nevertheless seemed to grow before one's eyes with each word, each gesture.

He had assured them the shooting was "the handiwork of a poor misguided unfortunate, a creature of the Creator as are we all, worthy of our pity and concern. But I have no ill effects," he stated. "I shall go on as I always have until I find a final solution for Israel and her neighbors."

At the end of his speech, Macaroon had reappeared to shock the crowd with another wood-splitting feat and led the doctor away to the accompaniment of another ovation.

The man can set people afire, Bond reflected. In fact, I'm on fire now.

As the flames licked at his swollen hand and singed his mangled shoulder, Bond phoned the desk. "My room's on fire."

"I see," said the imperturbable clerk. The chap in 1818 was certainly proving an extraordinary guest. No doubt, he chuckled, the fire had been set by a polar bear!

"I'll see if I can rustle up some help for you, Mr. Bond. In the meantime please make an inventory of all destroyed furniture and bedding—in triplicate, if possible. They must be charged to your bill, of course."

His charred hand paining him, Bond, now dressed in a powder blue iridescent suit, Panama hat, string tie and Venetian bedsocks, pushed his way past the bellhops trying to contain the blaze to the 18th floor and went down to the lounge. There the dirty stayups were carousing to the pulsating rhythms of the Calumet City Five Minus Four, the lone bandsman a triangle player with limited musical conception.

Elbowing his way through the dancers, he spotted at a corner table Poontang, Saxon, Macaroon, smashing boards with terrifying grunts, and yes ... Loxfinger, the old fellow cuddling with a sultry, Nordic-type blonde, well upholstered, too, a shocked Bond noted.

Unthinkable. This saintly figure pawing, grasping, insinuating his hands into her cleavage. It was a blow to Bond's image of the man, but he supposed that Loxfinger, too, was only human.

"Hello, Bond," Poontang said in her typically hostile manner. "Come down for some night life?"

"Had a slight fire in my room and couldn't sleep. Matter of fact, burned my hand. I thought I'd ease the pain with a little nightcap."

"Oh," she said with a sneer. "Hurt your hand, eh? Your shooting hand, no doubt. I thought you'd find some way to cop out on tomorrow's match."

"I'll be there, Poontang, so don't worry your sick little head."

And to the waiter: "A very, very dry Majorca Martini, the olive from the personal groves of Francisco Franco, a simulated pearl onion on a toothpick of Pacific Plywood."

"You forgot to tell him the most important ingredient, buster. The pinch of Indian Ocean kelp taken from the belly of a pregnant female manta ray."

"Still competing with me, eh Poontang? Who's the young lady with the good doctor?"

"Some cheap little cocktail hostess named Eve Brown. He can't keep his hands off her. I'm afraid you're late, Mr. Bond. The old lecher has beaten the young lecher to the prize."

"You mean he beat you to it?" Bond shot back.

"Still nasty, eh buster? We'll see how nasty you are tomorrow after I take away all your mad money." Dashing her drink into his face, she hurried off, her breasts heaving.

Saxon leaned over. He was very drunk. "How's the Kosher cop tonight? Shoot any more baddie waddies since I saw you last?" He was still wearing the same brown woolen suit which seemed even sweatier, gamier, and baggier— if possible.

"Tell me, Saxon, who's your tailor? Pillsbury?"

Saxon's face purpled. "You f— Jew bastard!" He started a right hand punch which Bond's superior reflexes deftly enabled him to block with the point of his jaw.

"I'll overlook that, Saxon, because you're blind, piggish drunk."

"You snotty kike!" Saxon swung again wildly, missed and fell against an artificial palm tree, knocking himself out. He slid to the floor.

Bond looked at the unconscious P.R. man. "Macaroon, take this sot back to his room and sober him up."

His carbon eyes glowering, Macaroon muttered, "'Tis a bonnie moonlicht nicht, yo' mothah frigguh." He tossed Saxon over his shoulder as if the man were a feather and steamrollered out of the lounge.

Turning to Loxfinger, who also seemed on the verge of collapse, Bond said gently: "Bedtime, sir. It's been a long day for you. I'll take you back to your suite."

The doctor, who had been whispering endearments to Eve Brown in his thick drunken voice—"Eva, mine schatz, Eva"— looked at Bond with a trace of suspicion, then nodded his assent. "Yah, I go now. You are Mr. Bond, the security person." He clicked his heels fatuously, then swayed. Bond caught him, led him on a tottering path to the elevator. They got off at the ninth floor, Bond continuing to guide him toward the suite.

"You are very solicitous, Mr. Bond. But then, we sheenies have to stick together, right?" He winked confidentially, nudging Bond's ribs.

Saxon was up, partly sober, soaking wet and still bellicose. 'That Jew bastard made fun of my suit! And that stinking nigger ape threw me in the shower! My suit is ruined, ruined! I'll kill him ... and that f— kike, too!"

"Now, now, Mr. Saxon," said Loxfinger placatingly. "Your good doctor will buy you another one. May I bid you goodnight, Mr. Bond?"

"Good night, sir," Bond said. "And shalom."

In the corridor Bond let the fury he had suppressed in Loxfinger's presence roll out of him. He kicked a passing bellhop in the leg, savoring the man's yammering and sobbing.

How he had yearned to smash those epithets back into Saxon's foul-smelling, bigoted mouth. And why ... why had Loxfinger, a fellow Jew, said nothing when his aide spouted them? Did Saxon have some strange hold over the philanthropist? I've got to do some thinking.

Something else occurred to him. He decided to play a hunch. Returning to the lounge he smiled his most inviting smile at the hard-faced blonde, Eve Brown. She sized up his trim physique, the dark cruelly handsome face. She decided it would be worth her while to smile back.

Her moist cornsilk hair in strands against his pillow, the girl looked with adoration at the tawny, steel-framed Apollo who had just taken them both to the very heart of the sun.

"Geez, Mister. You're the living end."

He smiled, slipping in one of his irresistible shafts: "Your end is the livingest, too, Eve. Tell me, how did you get entangled with the celebrated doctor tonight?"

Naturally he had made love to her in hopes of eliciting some information, but that task had somehow become secondary the moment he had torn away her pitifully sordid little evening dress. (He would, of course, send her a Simplicity pattern and three yards of material.) And when he saw her golden thighs he'd heard the same old song in his blood ... the song of sex, each corpuscle a shimmering note, each vein a string waiting to be plucked, his heart the maddened metronome which would start the symphonic cadence. And the ever-ready baton.

Bond, he berated himself, you're impossibly horny. I think you'd get aroused by a navel orange. He'd once been sent by M., who knew of his amorous propensities, to a famed Viennese psychiatrist but he had disgustedly given up the therapy one afternoon when he learned the irritating noises in the darkened room were made by the analyst sucking his thumb. Anyway, the maturity accrued by the passage of time had helped him put sex in its proper perspective. It was the most important thing in the world.

"Oh, the doc," she said, her words derailing his train of thought, sending him back to the job at hand.

Nestling in the crook of his muscular arm, she related how Loxfinger had given her the once-over twice in the lounge. "I knew he was famous, of course, but I never thought he'd ever dig a cheap, flashy little number like me. And it's funny, when I told him my name was Eve Brown he sorta flipped. Like he'd seen a ghost or somethin'. All the time he was coppin' a feel he kept whisperin' crazy things like, 'Eva, it's been so long ... so long since we splashed in the pool together, watching the sun glinting on the snow-capped peaks ...' stuff like that. I swear, Mr. Bond, I never laid eyes on him before—or nothin' else. And my name's Eve—not Eva."

Bond knitted his brow with a frown of concentration. Then realized he'd made a mistake.

"Geez, you're handsome when you frown!" she said with breathy excitement. And she pulled him down to her, the old song swelling up again.

Gottenu! he thought. If I'd registered this song with ASCAP I'd have a million in royalties by now. But he surrendered to its strain, as he knew he always must.

"Zvi," Bond said in a low voice over the Nippo. "I want you to contact Monroe Goshen at CIA. Tell him I'm sending some photos of Saxon, Macaroon and Poontang. I want him to check them out. There's something going on here I don't like. And tell M. I'm making these inquiries."

"Is the doctor safe, Oy Oy Seven?"

"For the time being, yes. Shalom."

Poontang! The mention of her name had made him remember the marble game at noon. And his hand, mauled by bear and fire ... how in the name of heaven would he be able to hold a shooter in those grotesque caricatures of fingers?

He held it in a sinkful of icewater until the swelling reduced enough for him to try a few feeble shots with a cat's-eye he'd induced one of the hotel's younger patrons to give him, after having to beat the kid up badly.

Satisfied that the hand was at least serviceable, he took the contact lenses off his eyeteeth (standard with M 33 and 1/3 personnel), extracted the microfilms from the tiny cameras built into the enamel, developed the negatives in a can of Mother's Chicken Soup (it was ideal for "souping up negs" as well as eating) and airmail specialed the prints to Goshen. He, of course, had been snapping pictures of the Loxfinger party in virtually every conversation. The ones of Poontang, he knew, would drive Goshen out of his Boston bean.

Lighting a Raleigh, he laid his plans for the coming match. It's about time, he said to himself facetiously, that I laid *plans!*

The day of the game dawned bright and clear.

Bond, dressed in a sporty one-piece Air Force-type jump suit, walked over to a spot about a mile from the Kahn-Tiki's main wing after receiving a terse call from Poontang. His hand felt considerably better after repeated soakings and an injection of Hexaphilonovademocaine, a new drug invented by an Israeli, Dr. Bernard Amster, which was highly effective in reducing swollen tissue, but in a few rare cases produced an unpleasant side effect —it grew hair on the kidneys and spleen. Dr. Amster himself was one of the unfortunate few to suffer these effects. Twice a year he had to be opened surgically and shaved.

The secret agent was a bit apprehensive. There was no package from Milton at the desk. Got to play it by ear, he decided.

Poontang, all business, was wearing a sweatshirt on which were emblazoned the letters "Kansas City, Mo., Jaycees Marbles Tournament Champion 1954-55-56-57" and a pair of faded jeans that did not entirely hide her wicked silhouette.

She's trying to "psyche" me, Bond thought. All right, I know she's a good marbles shooter. But there are a few things she doesn't know about me, which I'll tell her in good time.

Pine trees and thick clumps of bushes encircled the brown patch of earth she had selected.

"Buster, I think we'll start off with a little game called 'in-the-hole.'"

"That's how it may end up, too," Bond jested lightly.

Preferring to ignore his quickie, she said: "You're an Israeli and I don't expect you know much about our games. But I'll teach you this simple one. I've dug a hole over there"—she indicated a depression about four feet away—"and over here I'll make two parallel lines about three feet apart." She busily drew them in the earth with her sneaker tips. "Now we stand on this line and trawl—throw the marble—to that line. One closest to the line goes first. He, but it's gonna be she, buster, then shoots at the hole. So does the second player. One closest to the hole gets the next shot. Object is to get into the hole first 'cause then you're eligible to shoot at the other guy's mib. If you hit the mib, it's yours. Or rather it's mine, Hercules. And it's twenty smackeroos for me. Here—take a shooter."

They stood at the first trawling line, peering intently at the second. She wound up like a baseball pitcher, then with startling delicacy let it fly. It landed about two inches from the second line. "Trawl," she said with a pleased expression. He did so. His landed six inches away.

"I'm first!" she cried triumphantly and for a moment she was the rock-hard sophisticate no longer, just an eager young girl with wind-blown hair on a spring day in Missouri.

She knelt, holding her blue marble in the V of her forefinger, shoving her thumb forward. It skittered along the loam, straight into the hole. On the first shot!

Lucky, Bond mused, particularly because of the way she shoots. It's a fairly accurate style, but not basically powerful.

"I'm in, buster! Now you're in trouble. Either you've gotta make the hole on the first shot or stay away. Because I'm now eligible to knock the crap out of your aggie."

Sticky situation, he conceded. He bent over and duplicated her shooting method, affixing his red alley in the V-position, fired toward the hole. It stopped about two feet away.

"Spansies! Spansies!" she bubbled in delight. "That means, Richard the Chicken-Hearted, that since I'm in the hole already I can take the span of my hand, either once or twice, and move my shooter closer to yours. That's one of the privileges you get when you're in first. And," she paused dramatically, "I'll take double spansies—if you please."

Her two hand lengths placed her within inches of his red alley. She shot. Click! Her aggie drove his spinning ignominiously into a bush. "Twenty *schmolyeres*, buster! Cough up!"

Expressionless, he peeled a twenty from his roll, paid up and went into the bush to retrieve his shooter. He nearly stepped on the soft, plump hand of Estrellita Kahn, who was writhing passionately on the ground with Henny Benny Lenny, West Coast comedy sensation. They did not notice him as they gyrated their locked bodies in animalistic fury, the little laughmaker whispering, "Speaking of sex, this married couple, Abie and Becky, go to a motel and ..." "Shush with the goddam jokes and swing!" she moaned. Henny Benny Lenny was a sensation at something, obviously, Bond thought.

He found the marble and returned to a smiling Poontang, his eyes radar-scanning the sky anxiously. Where the hell was Milton?

Poontang repeated her victories in the next six games, following the same pattern. She was now 140 dollars ahead. "Want to quit, he-man, and admit she-man shot the pants off you?"

Then he heard it. The motor of a small plane. Milton's Piper Cub! Soon it was just ninety feet above them and Bond could see his brother waving frantically. An object dropped out of the Piper, thumping near his feet. With another wave, Milton was headed back home.

"What kind of a tinhorn gimmick is that?" she said angrily. "Trying to rattle me, Bond?"

He lit a Raleigh, looked into her eyes with disdain, but pitched his voice low.

"My dear, I'm going to give you a short, but highly informative lecture."

"Do go on, Mr. Bond, if you think it'll help you—and it won't."

"Poontang, in ten minutes you're going to undergo the most traumatic experience of your life. Know ye this, Miss Plenty; it's a fact that I'm an Israeli, but by choice, not by birth. I saw the light of day first in Trenton, New Jersey, where as a boy I played this game at a certain intersection—Market and Lamberton Streets. Mean anything to you?"

"Not a damn thing," she said. But her voice was guarded.

"There is a vacant lot there—or was, before urban renewal changed things around—owned by one Butsi (Heavythumbs) Colodny, the butcher. And on that lot, my venomous pet, I learned the art of marbles from the greatest of them all—one Sonny Jo Washington, better known in the annals of marbles as Sonny the Schvartzeh. In fact, Sonny Jo once told me I was the best white player he'd ever encountered. No, I never beat him; no white boy ever did. But I came so close to doing it on several occasions that Sonny the Schvartzeh, as a token of his esteem, gave me this."

From the object dropped from the Cub, a burlap bag, Bond extracted a marble from a leather bag in which he found a note: "Iz, sorry I'm late. Weather was bad. Thought I'd just hedge-hop around until I spotted you. Zai gezunt—Milt."

"This, my sweet, is Sonny's own shooter, the immortal 'Potbuster.'" He let her feel it; she seemed entranced as she held the black and white beribboned aggie which brought back to Bond memories of great duels to the death under the Delaware Valley sun.

"And while we're at it, Poontang, let's dispense with this 'in-the-hole' crap. We both know it's for babies. The real test of marbles is the five-foot bullring. Here's a string with the exact measurements. Put it on the ground and trace around it while I change into my outfit."

For the first time she knew uncertainty ... even fear ... but she set about etching the five-foot ring. Bond disappeared behind another bush, slipped off his jump suit. So intent on revenge was he that he scarcely took notice of Eve Brown's cheery "Hello, Mr. Bond!" which seemed to annoy the grunting Schuyler Kahn who was making vigorous love to her. "Shut up and pump!" the hotel owner snapped grumpily.

When Poontang saw Bond reappear her blood ran cold. In his new garb, which had been among the items in the bag, it was frighteningly clear that Israel Bond was—a shark!

The difference between a shark and an ordinary marble player could be likened to that between a gimlet-eyed Dodge City hired gunslinger and a homesteader.

Bond was wearing knickers!

With reinforced kneepatches!

And on his right hand was a dirty glove with the fingers cut out, affording protection to just the knuckles!

Worst of all, he wore a red corduroy shirt and a beanie whose letters read: "ORPHAN ANNIE AND SANDY DRINK OVALTINE. SO DO I."

His killer eyes boring into her own, Bond said coldly, "It'll be one hundred bucks a marble now, Poontang. Strict rules of the Asbury Park World Tournament. Now put ten of your mibs in dead center of the bullring ... bunch 'em up tight ... no stragglers ... now add these ten of mine. We'll trawl for firsties."

His eyes in deadly slits, he casually flipped his shooter from the trawling line. It landed squarely on the second line. "Your trawl." Dazedly, she trawled. A foot off the mark.

"My firsties. And, incidentally, watch the way I hold my shooter, Poontang."

Now her worst fears were realized. Previously he had copied her own V style, but that had been a ruse, she now knew. For this time he was positioning his shooter the shark's way, aggie held between the topside of the thumb and the tip of the forefinger.

I asked for it, she thought helplessly. Now he's "psyched" *me!*

Bond cocked, shot. The "Potbuster" whizzed, crunched into the twenty bunched mibs like a missile, scattering them to the four winds. With a single shot he had knocked ten out of the ring! And worse—his shooter had "stuck" in the middle.

"Time for a little pot-clearing, Poontang, but I may leave you a couple just to see your bullring technique."

With a series of short powerful shots Bond blasted eight more out of the circle. Then he deliberately closed his eyes and missed.

He's toying with me now. And I deserve it.

Two forlorn marbles were all that were left to her in the bullring which seemed as vast as Shea Stadium. Her shot didn't even come close to either, barely making it across the ring.

"You inched,* Poontang! You inched!" His voice was a whiplash of contempt, melting the wax in her ears. "And with all your inching, you just about made it across. Watch this, Poontang."

He did not assume the kneeling position this time, but stood straight, firing his shooter from his hip. It dive-bombed on one of the survivors, driving it fully six feet past the line.

My God! she thought. A drop shot! Who alive today could zero in on a mib from three feet up with a drop shot? Oh, Bond, Bond, she whispered, you're incredible. And a strange song, one her body had never heard before, began to sing in her inner marrows.

"Your shot, Poontang."

Now he isn't even looking at me when he speaks. He hates me. I love him and he hates me. The Lord has punished me for my false pride. At least I'll show him I can get across the ring faster. She gave her arm a push from the elbow as she shot.

"Cowhunching,** Poontang? COWHUNCHING?" His contempt knew no bounds now. "No real power, so you throw your aggie, you bitch!"

Cowhunching! The foulest crime. And he's right—I cowhunched.

---

 * Illegally moving your hand and shooter closer to the pot.
 ** No real power, so you throw your aggie across the ring, you bitch!

With a last flourish he backed three feet away from the ring to show the true power of a shark, aimed the "Potbuster" and walloped the last aggie. It did not go out of the ring. But he felt no shame. His shooter had cracked it in half!

Bond looked down at his hand, which throbbed terribly, red rivulets pouring down his fingers. The hatred was gone from him now. "I'm surprised you didn't pull the lowest trick of all, Poontang, switching your shooter for a steelie."* But he sounded as though he didn't care anyway.

"Oh, your poor, poor blessed shark's hand! It's bleeding. And you shot with a hand like that ... with pain like that? Just for the sake of my damn stupid challenge? Oh, Bond, Bond! I'm yours!"

She stood naked before him, her trembling hands having stripped off her garments. "Have you any strength at all left in that golden hand?"

"Yes," he said dully. Fatigue had formed on that dark, cruelly handsome face.

"Then take that magnificent agate, that 'Potbuster' of yours, and shoot it at me ... my breasts, my thighs ... shoot it at me!" Her voice rose to a frenzy.

"Don't forget you owe me two thousand dollars," he said. "Shoot! Shoot! Shoot!"

Bond took aim, letting the "Potbuster" fly again and again. Circular red welts mottled her heavenly nakedness.

"Now!" She pushed him into the bushes, clawing off his clothes like a mad woman. "Take me, Israel Bond! Take me! I love you! Take me!"

"Yes, for God's sake, take her!" roared Schuyler Kahn. "This damn bitch I'm balling is so excited she can't concentrate on *me!*"

"And this schnook comic ain't paying no attention to me either!" yelled Estrellita Kahn from another bush. "Take her already!"

Bond whispered to Poontang. "Yes, darling, you're ready for my kind of love now. Because you've lost *all* your marbles."

He took her.

---

* The substitution of a steel ball bearing for a traditional mib.

9 M.

Dusk over Manhattan. Two teenaged gangs doing a ballet in the street below. A Salvation Army major imploring an AWOL captain to return to the fold, the captain ignoring him and trying to sell a trombone to passersby. Poontang lying in the arms of Israel Bond, sipping (from a cup balanced on his lean, hard navel) Eight O'Clock Coffee, the brand served exclusively at the Ansonia Hotel.

Their steel-mill hot affair was now in its seventh day. "Happy seventh day, darling," she whispered. "You know, the Lord rested on the seventh day. You're my lord of love. Is my lord going to rest on the seventh day?"

For an answer he stilled her kittenish teasing with his hungry mouth, leading her to another dazzling pinnacle of fulfillment.

But there was something in his face ... his dear cruelly dark handsome face ... pain in the grey eyes.

"What is it, my life, my own?"

"Your coffee burned my groin," he said softly.

"No," she said. "That's not it. You're unhappy, Israel."

"All right," he said. "I'm unhappy. I love you but it's no good. You're a gentile girl, a *shikseh*. And I swore to my mother that I would plight my troth with a daughter of Zion."

"Oh, Iz, Iz, you fool!" She was laughing but tears streamed down her drawn cheeks. "I'm a Jewish girl, you ninny! Not very observant maybe, but Jewish all the way. I'm even circumcised."

"Don't josh about things like that."

"It's true, darling. Daddy was born in Kenya to Polish Jews who had gone there to start a new life. Zaydeh, my beloved grandfather, used to go around to all the native shambas in an old Mack truck sharpening spears with his grinder, while his wife, my Bubba, sold them colorful house dresses for which they gave her colorful beads. When Daddy was twenty-one, they arranged a marriage with a fine, *haymischeh* girl from Krakow, my Mums. Since Daddy practically grew up with the Kikuyus, he adopted many of their mores, melding them with his own Judaism. Thus, I was circumcised on the eighth day. When the Mau Maus erupted in the early '50's, we all went to live with relatives in Kansas City. I'll admit life there wasn't conducive to a Jewish upbringing, but you can't deny my roots."

He inhaled a Raleigh, and pressed it to her lips. "I'm so glad, so glad!" His own eyes were wet now ... rain, he told her, but she smiled in her wise woman's heart. She knew better. They were indoors.

Nestling in the crook of his bronzed arm, she told him of life in Kansas City, a Mark Twainish tomboy life with marbles, weenie roasts, apple pies cooling on window sills, girls in blue sashes, brown paper packages tied up with strings. "Yes, darling, these were a few of my favorite things."

Then a secretarial course at the Middle Missouri Valley Land Grant College of Mining, Farming and Baton Twirling, a stint with the Peace Corps in Argentina where she and other shining-eyed young idealists had gone to answer a crying need and build a Howard Johnson's in the middle of the jungle. While there, she recounted, she had met Loxfinger, already fabulously wealthy due to shrewd speculations, and had accepted a post with him. It was she to whom he had dictated the notes that were later to become "The Plowshare Papers."

"Where does Saxon fit in?" queried Bond.

"He was already on the scene when I joined the doctor. But if he's a public relations man, I'm Marjorie Main."

"You're far more exciting than Marjorie Main, my sweet," Bond said gallantly. Which is true, he thought. It was something he felt he could honestly say to any girl. "Why are you suspicious of Saxon?"

"I once asked him if he'd ever worked for B.B.D.&O. and he said in that superior way of his, 'Hell no! Those railroad jobs are just for niggers and dumb Irish Catholics.' Now, what P.R. guy wouldn't know about B.B.D.&O.?"

"And Macaroon?"

"He came later. We picked him up in New York when the doctor first went to America to accept the Brandeis award."

"New York? Saxon said he was a part-Negro, part-Scotch waif Loxfinger found in Marseilles."

"I don't know why Saxon's been telling you these things, darling. The ancestry part is okay, but he was recruited in New York."

Three black marks for Saxon! The brown woolen suit that no P.R. man in his right mind would ever wear, his ignorance of the advertising field, his blatant lie about Macaroon. I hope Goshen's checked him out good. But, again, why would Loxfinger employ such a man?

As they dressed for a last big night on the town before the flight to Israel on the morrow (the doctor had accepted an invitation to vacation at a kibbutz in the Negev), Bond kept trying to solve the puzzle. But he had promised Poontang a memorable farewell blast. I'll think about it later.

He slipped into a fawn-colored pair of tapered Benito Brioschi slacks, a crisp Harry Cotler roc's-egg-white shirt, a neat regimental four-in-hand from Tie City, a dashing Jack Paar-type boating jacket with gold braids, doffed a visored commander's cap and boffed Poontang once more for luck. As he put on his cufflinks, the Grecian drama-masks set, each link showing a face of a little Greek boy being abused by another Greek boy, one smiling, one weeping, he looked at Poontang and was forced to chuckle.

She was wearing a very small townish brown and blue gingham checked skirt, middy blouse with a ribbon, red wedgies with ankle straps (definitely passé), and athletic socks. She's such an adorable hellcat square, he thought. That outfit was fine for a coke 'n aspirin Saturday night date at a Kansas City ice cream parlor, but hardly suitable for a New York evening. He had a glamorous friend on Sutton Place, who would gladly teach Poontang the whys and wherefores of haute couture. That would be Glynda, of course, the Wicked Bitch of the East Side, an acknowledged fashion pace-setter, perennially on the ten-best-dressed list, and one of the town's most widely respected call girls.

"Poon," he said. "There's been quite a stir about a drama called *The Deputy*. I've two tickets in the eighth row center. Shall we see it?"

"Oh, Iz," she said. "Let's not waste our last night in New York on a stupid Western. Let's go on the town!"

She wasn't kidding about her lack of Jewish consciousness, he thought. But, what the hell! She's a wholesome cornball kid, so let's have a wholesome cornball evening, make the whole wide-eyed tourist bit. Might be fun at that.

He found something touching about her naiveté, her basic stupidity. Quite a change from the chic, brittle, rootless New York girls he had dated in the past. Stephanie St. John-St. Jill, tall, poised, and filled with wanderlust. She had fallen in with a group of right-wing extremist beatniks (they showed their contempt for the world by showering every hour and dressing well) and had taken Bond to Harlem one night where she stood outside the Apollo Theatre on 125th Street picketing with a brazen sign:

LET'S HAVE MORE POLICE BRUTALITY.

And Judith Lockwood, the stunning yet subdued librarian he had picked up at the main branch on Fifth Avenue, where he had gone to pick up *The Philosophy of Hugh Hefner*. That frustrating evening in his parked Kaiser under the August moon on a Peekskill lover's lane. "Baby," he had said fervently, "we're both mad for it. For God's sake let's let ourselves go!" And her answering: "Sh-h-h, please! You're disturbing people in other cars trying to make love."

Enough of reminiscences. This evening was Poontang's.

They launched a Cook's tour of the bright lights of Manhattan. First, the Ratfink Room atop the Roundtable, where host comedian Jackie Kannon was reading selected works from a classic his firm had published, *Poems for the John*, tickling the jaded roués with his expert nonsense.

Then a movie at a Greenwich Village art house, which proudly advertised that it soon would carry the Natalie Wood Film Festival. Its present offering, however, was a "new wave" flicker, *Hamlet Beach Party*, an attempt to fuse Shakespeare with rock 'n roll to make the Bard more palatable to the teen set. It starred Bobby Vinton as Hamlet, Deborah Walley as Ophelia and Clay Cole as Polonius. It was reasonably faithful to Shakespeare, he admitted, even to the last scene when they all perished by falling off the surfboard.

She fell madly in love with the Village, its quaint shops, cut-rate art galleries (where she got quite a buy on an unpainted Picasso; it had his signature on the canvas; the rest was up to her), and its infinite variety of people. There had been one unpleasant incident when Bond spotted a thin, well-dressed man clucking his tongue in sympathy at the sight of a woman being ravished by a gang of toughs, who had practically stripped her naked.

"It's terrible," the man said, puffing his pipe. "Terrible."

"My God, man! Who is that poor woman?"

"My wife," said the man. "Look what those hooligans are doing to the poor thing. It's just terrible!"

"Why are you standing here doing nothing?" an irate Bond snapped. "She's your wife, man, your wife!"

The man shrugged. "I just don't feel I should get involved."

These callous New Yorkers! Bond thought. Well, if he doesn't want to rescue his own wife, why the hell should I? And he steered Poontang down Bleecker Street.

"Look!" she exclaimed. "A Star of David! It's a synagogue. Oh, let's go in, Israel. I feel sorta ... religious tonight."

"I'd rather not," Bond said. "It's strictly for Village Jews. It's called B'Nai Gay. I was there one Purim and I'd rather forget the whole thing. Such scratching and biting ... they all wanted to be Queen Esther. Finally had to hire a Lesbian to play Haman."

Then a ride back uptown on the IRT local. Bond noted one particularly clever subway advertisement:

YOU DON'T HAVE TO BE JEWISH
TO ENJOY CHUN KING CHOW MEIN.

The usual subway philosophers had covered it with scrawls, some obscene. One, patently a progressive jazz fan from Texas, had written:

LYNDA BIRD LIVES!

They were back in his suite, Bond's Raleigh smoke drifting up to the power-packed General Electric bulbs he demanded in all his hotel rooms. "Poon, I almost forgot. A little present for you ..." He opened his closet, unwrapped a huge parcel and handed the contents to her.

"Iz! It's lovely! What a lovely, lovely, super-fab, white fur coat! Oh, darling!" And she kissed him repeatedly. "What is it, ermine?"

"Better than that... genuine Arctic polar bear." Good old Zvi, an ex-furrier, had turned the skin into a masterpiece.

"Oh, darling ... it must have been so expensive! Cost you an arm and a leg."

"Well, a hand and a shoulder anyway," he said, indulging himself in an "inside" joke. "Now take off your clothes and lie on it. Nanook of the North wants to ride again! Mush!"

He took her.

EL AL AIRLINES.
YOU SHOULD ONLY LAND
AND BE WELL.

The sign on the sleek jet warming his heart with its folksiness, Bond, dressed in his Don Loper cape and Bermuda shorts, flashed his M 33 and 1/3 security card to the hostess: "Let's see the passenger list, please."

He scanned the names. It was good solid security technique. With Loxfinger aboard, every passenger was a potential threat. He read:

—Len Fischman, New York City, storm window and aluminum siding salesman. (That would definitely be worth checking; they were a ruthless breed.)

—Mr. and Mrs. Marvin Habas, Moonachie, N.J., he the manufacturer of a popular breakfast cereal, Sugar Prizes. No cereal, just candy-coated little toys.

—Rose DeWolf, Ong's Hat, Ariz., a classless society columnist for the *Daily Worker*. (He put a check by her name.)

—William Blitman, Buzzard's Bosom, New Mexico, president of Gila Monster City Development Corp., "The Southwest's Answer to Cape Coral."

—Rosalie, Dave, and Neal Gomberg, known professionally as the folksinging trio of Peter, Paul, & Mounds.

And so on ...

One name jarred him: "Kismet Ali Herzl, Cairo, Ill., flying carpet merchant." And in the seat next to his! So they were playing that game again, were they? Cairo, Ill., indeed! Cairo, Egypt, more likely, his trained sixth sense told him. He'd be on his guard.

And, of course, the Loxfinger party, the old man, Saxon, Macaroon, Poontang. He'd told her to play it cool, maintain her usual frigid reserve in his company. But the adorable little hellcat, hopelessly lovesick, had made a salacious grab for him as he passed them; Saxon had seen it, whispered something to Loxfinger.

With a whine, the jet rose majestically. It had taken less than thirty seconds to go up that many feet.

On the intercom was the pilot:

"Shalom and welcome aboard Flight 78, El Al Airlines, nonstop New York to Tel-Aviv. I am Captain Tevyeh."

(Bond had met the pilot in the lounge earlier. Tevyeh was the sort of flippant, devil-may-care "flyboy" that one felt confidence in. He had been a hero of the air during the war in '48, having suffered grievous head wounds in a dogfight. The eyepatches over both eyes gave him a dashing appearance.)

"Our airline is a friendly, informal operation, so just relax, have a ball, a matzoh ball, of course. (Tevyeh chuckled at his play on words; Bond, jealous, wished he'd thought of it first). Don't be hoity toity ... introduce yourselves to each other ... sing, talk, laugh, tell a hearty joke. Our lovely hostess, Miss Tigerblatt, will be around with tea in a glass and a lump sugar for between your teeth. Our dinner menu is great tonight, sweet and sour sweetbreads, three different kinds of boiled chicken, salad with *Two* Thousand Island dressing—we don't stint on El Al—raisins with almonds, the whole ethnic bit. Later we'll all line up in the aisle and Miss Tigerblatt will teach us the hora. For your amusement we'll have continuous showings of *The Jolson Story*; it'll tear out from you the heart. Or if you like canasta, join us here in the pilot's cabin ... we'll set 'er on automatic control and play for any stakes you want—the plane, if necessary. Later, when we're over the Middle East you'll all get a real thrill watching us bombing the Suez Canal. But for now just settle back and read your complimentary copy of Harry Golden's wonderful book *Enjoy! Enjoy!* I did, and, believe me, I enjoyed it, enjoyed it!"

Bond gazed into the hostile eyes of the wiry Levantine traveling under the name of Mr. Herzl. "Hello," he said pleasantly. The man thrust something on Bond's lap, hissing, "Die, Israeli jackal!"

Bond's heart pounded. A black widow spider crawled onto his bare knee, sand shifting into the bottom of the tell-tale red hourglass on its obscenely swollen belly laden, he knew, with excruciating poison.

Counteraction 12! The old words of the service manual rang a bell in his mind. There was a rebuttal for this loathsome thing on his kneecap. He unscrewed one of the large gold buttons of his cape. Out sprang a praying mantis!

Removing its little prayer shawl and yarmulkeh, the mantis gulped down the arachnid with one bite of its awful jaws. "Good show, Mendel!" he whispered to the mantis. Not all mantises were as devout these days, Bond knew. Some of the younger ones were out and out atheists, but they all retained good Jewish hearts, and that was what mattered.

Counteraction 13! As the Levantine reached for his gun, Bond's ring sprayed fiery *chrain* (horseradish) into his face. He drove his meat knife home into the blinded Levantine's innards. The man slumped dead against the window.

His head spinning with tension, Bond applied Counteraction 14. He fainted.

Minutes later he revived and dragged the man down the aisle with an apologetic, "My ol' buddy just can't take that schnapps," to the hostess. Inside the lavatory Bond lifted the seat and stuffed his victim into the bowl. Thanks be to heaven he's lanky, he thought, pushing the "flush" button.

"Takes just one good flush to get rid of a four-flusher," he said casually, wishing that Zvi had been there to guffaw at this latest Bondism.

Back in his seat he rifled the man's attaché case, no mean feat with the end of a rifle. Mr. Herzl, he discovered, was a member of the Cairo Legion Armed Police. But who had put him onto Bond?

But there was no more time for pondering. A favorable sirocco wind had brought the craft in nine hours ahead of schedule. Lydda Airport twinkled its lights below. "Fasten your seatbelts. Smoke if you wish," said Miss Tigerblatt.

Eretz Israel! At last!

He lit up a Raleigh and watched the last few moments of the picture.

"Asa, you're home from Broadway just in time," a tear-stained mother on the screen said to the black-faced vaudevillian on his knees before her. "Poppa is very sick, Asa, very sick. But before he goes, he wants to know ... this Colleen McCarthy the papers say you're going to marry. She's a Jewish girl?"

Bond's eyes were wet. He'd seen the picture fifty-six times on many El Al flights. Still it had the power to tear out from him the heart.

The wheels jolted against the soil of his adopted homeland.

He bade farewell to Loxfinger and his retinue. "We'll be meeting again, doctor. I'll probably be assigned to your kibbutz."

Those unbelievably blue eyes focused on him. "Of course, Mr. Bond. We ..." again he nudged Bond's ribs conspiratorily ... "sheenies must stick together." His breath was alcoholic.

Bond felt a strange chill as he watched Loxfinger and the others depart in a waiting Rolls-Royce. For an instant Macaroon had stood before the plane defiantly smashing another board as though he were challenging the great bird whose bowels had quartered him.

The secret agent tossed his Raleigh into a pool of fuel near the jetliner and hailed a cab. Soon he stood in front of the gleaming yellow one-story factory.

THIS IS THE HOME OF MOTHER MARGOLIES' ACTIVATED OLD WORLD CHICKEN SOUP.

And under the sign, one of her proverbs:

I AM THE MASTER OF MY FATE; I AM THE CAPTAIN OF MY VOLLEYBALL TEAM.

It was grand to be back at the same old stand. Now he could drop his cover role for a while and devote his full thirty percent effort to being just Oy Oy Seven.

As he entered the modernistic structure, he heard the familiar lamentive strains of the violin evoking memories of another era in the Jewish saga. His eyes looked up. Yes, the fiddler was still there on the roof.

"Welcome home, Oy Oy Seven!" said M.'s bewitching private secretary, Leilah Tov, flicking her tongue at him alluringly. It had been a long time since he and Leilah ...

"M. wants a full report on the double."

He quickened his pace, zipping past the Chicken Soup division, the Mushroom & Barley section, the Blueberry Blintze room. He stopped in front of a door.

MOTHER MARGOLIES

He knocked. The sweet, quavering old voice he loved so well said, "Come in, Mr. Bond."

Her back was to him and he could hear the rocker creak and the assiduous click, click, click of her omnipresent knitting needles. What was she making now? A sweater for the prime minister? Socks for Abba Eban? Or was she still knitting that lovely, multi-hued doily she had started two years ago? Someone will certainly receive a splendid present when she finally gets that thing done, he thought. But it should be someone who can really make good use of it, someone with a fifty-foot ashtray.

The rocker spun around and the kindly, wise old eyes of Mother Margolies were on him. Dear, dear Mother, the wonderful lady whose factory it was and who had permitted a secret portion of the building to be utilized solely for the dark manipulations of M 33 and 1/3.

For a very good reason. M. stood for "Emma."

Dear old Mother Emma Margolies was—M., No. 1 in the Secret Service of Eretz Israel!

10
"You'll Like Mara, Mr. Bond"

"Let's have it already," said M.

Bond opened his carrying case, dumped a mound of Raleigh coupons on her desk. "Four thousand, three hundred and eighty-two, M. How's that?"

She sniffed. "Just so-so, Oy Oy Seven. Oy Oy Nine really gave us a full measure of devotion when he was with us. More than six thousand."

"Was with us?" Bond said. "You speak as though he...."

"He is," M. said flatly. "We buried him yesterday. Lung cancer, emphysema, smoker's heart, and a particularly bad case of adenoids." She sighed. "Very clumsy at judo, botched up codes ... but, *vay tzu mineh yooren*, could that boy smoke! We got seventy-five walkie-talkie radio sets from his last batch. Which reminds me ..."

Her gnarled but nimble fingers touched a knob on the master control box under her yarn pile. He wondered what station she would try to contact. Station A—Asia? E—Europe? P—Pacific Area? But he should have guessed.

"........ so, toe-tappin' teeneroonies, avast let's blast with Castro and the Cuban Heels and their big, big ..."

It was Station RR (Rock 'n Roll). At heart old M. was a "toe tapper." Worse, a Rockin' Robby Robbins fan.

Bond lit a Raleigh, offered her one.

"Are you crazy?" M. said indignantly. "You can die from that garbage. Now let's have the report."

He began with the Miami Beach affair, relating fully everything that had happened since, placing emphasis on certain puzzlements that had occurred during the Loxfinger phase of the assignment. "My capsule opinion: It's a weirdo setup. I'd like your permission to snoop around."

"Granted. Snoop. But you should be extra careful. The doctor is more important than ever to our country's well being. You were on the plane, so I guess you didn't get a chance to read these."

She held out a bunch of newspapers from all over the globe. "The top one is particularly interesting."

It was an English edition of the United Arab Republic's propaganda mouthpiece, *Scimitar 'n Feather*, with this bannerline:

"ISRAELI LOXFINGER'S PEACE OVERTURES MULLED
    BY OUR GOVERNMENT."

Impossible!

He read the lead story. In essence it was straight-away reporting on Lazarus Loxfinger's "Plowshare Papers" with liberal quotes from them. The story was not favorable, he noted, but more significant, not unfavorable. Something big was in the wind. It had to be. For in the past a peace proposal from Israel would have drawn reams of ridicule, sarcasm and the tired old call for a "jihad," holy war, to rid the Middle East of "these Zionist bandits, blah, blah, blah."

Just as eye-opening were the organs of the other Arab nations, all noncommittal, but nonbelligerent.

The non-Arab papers had the freedom of speculation, pointing out that this was the first time Arab journals had ever carried an Israeli declaration without abusive comments.

"BREAKTHROUGH IN MID-EAST AT LAST?" asked the *Manchester Guardian*. "LOXFINGER PAPERS GET HARD ARAB LOOKSEE"—*Chicago Sun-Times*. "MID-EAST ACCORD HINTED"—*Bombay Bomb Bay*, organ of the Indian Air Force. "ARABS HINT END OF HOSTILITY TO JEWS"— *Paris Match*. And predictably:

"METS' ROOKIE HAS HANGNAIL!"
"V-DOLL AND COP LINK BARED (AND THAT'S NOT
    ALL!)"
"COMMIES SEEN THREAT TO RUSSIA"
"Mid-East Talks Peace."—*New York Daily News*.

I've been an ass, Bond realized. I actually had doubts about a man who might crack the nerve-racking stalemate that has hamstrung my country for seventeen years. Just because he drinks a little, mauls blondes and uses a few foolish ethnic slurs.

And who are you to point a finger, Israel Bond? You, the rake, the womanizer, the dimestore dandy...

"And yet," thinking he was still talking to himself.

"And yet," M. chimed in with a knowing smile, "you still have some doubts. Then go to Loxfinger, guard him and while doing so satisfy those doubts. Keep your eyes, ears, nose, and throat open at all times."

He knew she was about to favor him with one of her proverbs, which would afford him a guidepost to understanding.

"Remember," she said, purling a difficult hound's-tooth stitch, "give me the mind of a child until he is eighty-three and I will dominate him."

She'd hit the nail right on the point again! Good old M.! "I'll get down there posthaste," he said.

"I don't care how you go, as long as you get there fast," M. said. "You will be working alone ... unless something extraordinary comes up. In that case, you will be contacted by Agent D., only if necessary."

Agent D.! Again the mention of that shadowy figure behind the scenes.

She anticipated his next question: "Do not ask me about Agent D., Oy Oy Seven. Now go."

One more stop—the quartermaster's where he would receive any equipment he needed, reload the mezuzah and requisition an automobile.

He walked into the office of Lavi HaLavi, quartermaster and inventor of diabolical espionage devices. There was a plaque on the wall with one of Mother's sayings. Each office had its particular favorite. This one read: "ON THE HIGHEST SLOPE OF MOUNT KILIMANJARO IN AFRICA THERE WAS DISCOVERED THE FROZEN, DRY CARCASS OF A PATTERNMAKER FROM A NEW YORK CITY GARMENT CENTER FIRM. NO ONE HAS EVER EXPLAINED WHAT HE WAS DOING AT THAT HEIGHT OR HOW HE GOT THERE."

HaLavi hardly looked up from a diagram he was sketching.

"Shalom, Oy Oy Seven."

Behind him was Oy Oy Two, a grizzled veteran of many dangerous missions into enemy territory, testing a powerful new flamethrower. "It works," he told HaLavi. "The tip of the cigarette is definitely smoldering."

"Good," said HaLavi. "Bond, look over there. You'll be driving that baby to the kibbutz."

The grill of a gleaming new MBG grinned at him. A Mercedes Ben Gurion! And a powerhouse, too, Bond guessed.

"She'll do 375 poods per dunam, but that's not all," HaLavi chuckled. "Sports some fairly interesting features, triggered by this row of buttons ... sixty of 'em ... on the dash." He licked his lips, an enthusiastic schoolboy showing off his collection of dead Japanese beetles. "This one ... you press it and a 125-mm. machine gun slides out of the right fender. This one ... a similar gun slides out of the left fender. Then they open fire—on each other. Needs a little work there."

"Fascinating," Bond purred.

"This one ... converts your ashtray into a Lazy Susan. Here ... windscreen and windows that become completely opaque in case you're driving and don't want to be seen. You can't see either, but it's a sacrifice you'll have to make. This little button makes the dual exhaust pipes blow bubbles ... more of a fun thing than anything else, Oy Oy Seven. Radical new turbojet motor. Runs on any liquid whatsoever. So drink heartily, old man. Homer radio signal planted in the horn. It lets you pick up signals from a similar device planted in the rear axle. And this one ... I love it... the new Sunbeam laser beam. Shaves you without a blade ... or a razor. Then the master button ... this red one ..."

"Yes," said an interested Bond.

"Only, I repeat, only to be used in the direst emergency. Chips down and that sort of thing. Press it and the whole car converts into one big goddam button. Frightens the deuce out of anyone who's ever seen it."

Bond glanced at the diagram on HaLavi's work table. "This looks very complicated, Lavi. What's it all about?"

"Oh," the quartermaster smiled shyly. "It's a highly involved and frankly unproved theory of mine. May never have a practical use at all, but who knows? It's an old pet project... the vacuum-voids mystery. Basically, it's this: How many voids could we get into an unfilled vacuum? There's a lot of spatial-time continuum calculating needed here."

"I can imagine," said Bond. He could see HaLavi working himself into a burst of enthusiasm. It would do well to bolster it. HaLavi brought a zeal to his work that needed constant sympathy and praise. "No doubt, you've got it licked, Lavi."

"Well, not quite but I'm getting close," the quartermaster admitted. "My reasoning goes thusly: If we assume that there is total emptiness in a vacuum and that such a vacuum is infinite in terms of dimensions—that is, if we even *knew* that a vacuum or vacuums—and there could be an infinite number of *them*, too—if we knew a vacuum or vacuums actually was or were infinite— and, if indeed, it ... or even they actually *had* dimensions—for if vacuums, presuming there are more than one, and we don't know that either, to be perfectly truthful—well, if vacuums are infinite, how can we say that they are bound by dimensions? For would not a dimension which bounds an infinite vacuum of necessity itself be infinite? So ... can the infinite enclose the infinite? That's why we must find out all we can about vacuums before we even go into voids. For after all, voids, too, are just mere emptiness. Are voids then also infinite, without boundaries, uncontainable? If they are, how many voids can we fit into vacuums? But if, as I suspect, the reverse is also true, why can we not cram vacuums into—pay attention now—into voids?"

Bond lit a Raleigh.

"So the problem seems to be," HaLavi continued with scholarly eagerness, "the shoving of one kind of total emptiness into another kind of total emptiness. Wait!" He slapped his forehead with a self-deprecating hand. "Bond, you're looking at a horse's ass! Why should there be just *two* kinds of total emptiness? Cannot the number of total emptinesses themselves be infinite? Or at least isn't it feasible to suggest that there is at least a third kind of emptiness unit that could accommodate both vacuums *and* voids? Presuming, of course, that this third force, so to speak, is *itself* boundless and capable of that kind of magnitude. So you see, Oy Oy Seven, it all boils down to one question: Where's my blanket? I want my blanket! And if I don't get it I'm going to make a big *caca* all over the floor."

Bond, who had seen this coming and had whispered a few words of alarm into the Nippo, waved the three husky black-hooded men into the room. They swept HaLavi into their arms and carried him off, but not before he got in a parting scream: "Memorize the master list of buttons, Bond! The right button could save your life! Listen to me, Bond! Bo—." The door slammed with finality.

Poor chap. Bond had noticed his increasing nervousness of late. Between his arduous tasks for M 33 and 1/3 and his own private researches, he had suffered too much mental strain. Bond hoped HaLavi would return to his post someday. If not, his absence would leave the service with a void that would be hard to fill. Or could it be filled? Even with a vacuum? For if a void ...

I'm getting the hell out of here, Bond said.

Even as the MBG sped deep into the desert, Bond pondered HaLavi's last pitiful scream ... something about the right button. It was a typical Negev day ... unbearably hot. The sun shimmered off the rippling mirages, blinded his eyes, caught the rocks in a crystalline flash, dropping into a Wadi for a ground rule double, scoring Maris and Downing, who had come in to run for Mantle.

Five hours later he swung the vehicle down a tiny road one would have great difficulty finding on the map. Indeed, Bond had experienced six kinds of fits trying to find the map.

The unpaved road led him past an encampment of nomads, some on camels. It recalled to him a plaintive advertisement he had once read in the *Jerusalem Post*: "Having left my Bedouin and boardouin, I, Ayesha Kassim, am no longer responsible for any debts or diseases unless contracted by myself."

Then a sudden patch of green, incongruous in this tan-colored nowhere, and Bond knew he had come to the kibbutz, K'far K'farfel, which was playing host to Loxfinger & Co. He motored past groves of lemon trees. Lovely, he mused, with flowers very sweet. But he knew the fruit of the poor lemon was impossible to eat.

K'far K'farfel was one of the newest yet most famous of all the kibbutzim, these brave little desert settlements. It was here that the great Dr. Saul Rossien, the French Jew, had done some of his most illustrious work with hybrids, cross-pollination and the like. He had crossed a date palm with a breadfruit plant, getting a tree that produced nothing but date-nut bread. A New York City restaurant chain, Chock Full O' Nuts, had willingly underwritten the expense.

Under the shade of that very tree sat the dreaded Macaroon, who obviously found the sun too taxing for his usual display of karate. He seemed content to sit and split popsicle sticks with his pinky.

"Hello, Macaroon," said Bond affably.

"Why ye not lay doon anna die, yo' mothuh humpah?" said the mulatto with an unfriendly growl.

"If you're to use that phrase at all, it's 'mater-violator,' at least in my circles," Bond snipped back. He'd taken all he was going to from this creature.

Then he heard Saxon's voice, just a snatch of it, as he pushed open the noisy screen door.

"...taken care of ..." and something that sounded like "my" ... then "furor."

Saxon and Loxfinger froze, ceased their palaver at the sight of Bond. "You were not expected here so soon, Mr. Bond," said the doctor somewhat accusingly. "Mr. Saxon was just telling me about the furor my 'Plowshare Papers' have created in the world and the highly salubrious reaction among Arab leaders. I have further news, Mr. Bond, which as a security person you'll doubtless be told of eventually. The Knesset has given me permission to stage top-secret exploratory peace talks with two key Arabs. We shall convene on a dhow in the Red Sea very shortly. Around the Passover season, I believe. Confidential, of course."

"Fantastic!" Bond could only shake his head in wonderment.

"Yes, my friend, these talks could yet achieve that final solution to this nation's problems which I see just beyond the hills of doubt and confusion."

A twinge in Bond's cheek, mirroring something horrible stirring deep down inside. Something as yet nameless.

"In fact, Mr. Bond," Loxfinger went on, "I hope this meeting ..."

But he could be heard no more. Hundreds of children, bronzed and glowing kibbutzniks wearing costumes of antiquity, burst onto the scene. Rushing to the doctor they began filling his hands with hamantaschen, the three-cornered pastry of the Purim holiday. "The song! The song!" one shouted. And they began boisterously:

> *Oh, once there was a wicked, wicked man,*
> *And Haman was his name, sir.*

"What in the world is this outburst?" Loxfinger, nonplussed and a trifle irritated, asked Bond.

"Why, sir. Surely it's slipped your mind. It's Purim, of course, and the little ones are serenading you with a traditional ditty about Haman, an evil potentate who long ago tried to destroy the Jews of Persia. The cakes are hamantaschen. But you know all this, sir."

> *He tried to murder all the Jews,*
> *And they were not to blame, sir.*

Loxfinger was shaking ... violently. His pasty white face was being invaded by an angry red flush.

One of the children stepped out of the pack, handed a bouquet of desert wildflowers to Loxfinger, and in a halting recitation said: "Dr. Loxfinger, oh blessed one of Eretz Israel. You are living proof that no Haman, be he ancient or modern ... uh ... shall ever again threaten your people with ..."

"Be gone, brat! Go! Go!" Now the face was stark black. I do believe he's going to hit the kid, an amazed Bond thought. The child fled in tears and his playmates, silent and afraid, drifted after him.

"Dr. Loxfinger," Bond began. "I ..."

Saxon broke in quickly: "Go, Bond, go! I've seen this happen to him before. The sight of children reminds him of past unhappiness in the bad times. I'll take care of him. Please go!" The P.R. man led the muttering philanthropist away. He seemed to be in a hypnotic state.

Bond was totally agitated himself. Poontang! He had to talk to Poontang. "Where's the girl?" he asked the giant.

"Comin' through the rye, ofay fool," said Macaroon. The ugly incident seemed to have invigorated him. He picked up one of his ubiquitous boards, brought the calloused right hand down. It exploded into splinters.

The exhibition had no effect on Bond. He had heard the beeper from his MBG. Someone was trying to reach him. "Bond here."

"Bond? Monroe Goshen. Listen, I'm in Israel. No time for explanations. AAA Priority. Meet you at Tel-Aviv Sheraton."

AAA Priority! Was Israel in danger from the Arabs? The American Automobile Association? He did not dare guess. Bond started the motor, but suddenly Lazarus Loxfinger reappeared, his dark mood gone, strangely smiling now. "You must forgive the eccentricities of an old man who has seen too much sorrow, Mr. Bond."

"Of course, Doctor."

"Mr. Bond," he said in that confidential tone. "We sheenies stick together, don't we?"

"Not as much as non-Jews think, but we try, sir."

"Uh, Mr. Bond." The voice halting, about to divulge something delicate. "I am a man with great human frailties. Women the greatest one. I gather from your dalliance with my secretary that you, too, are a man of the world."

"You know about Poontang and me?"

"Of course, my dear boy. And why shouldn't you? She is a splendidly constructed type who will give you fine sons for soldiering, tall, blonde sons whose marching feet will crush the mongrelized enemies of ... Israel, of course."

From the back of the house came Saxon in a Volkswagen bus, speeding past them down the road to the main highway without so much as a glance at either of them. "Poor Saxon," the doctor said. "I'm afraid my little tantrum upset him. He's gone for a ride to clear his head. Getting back to the subject of women. Could you do me a favor, Mr. Bond? There's a Bedouin camp not far from the kibbutz."

"I passed it, Doctor."

"Ah, yes. Well, Bond, I rather took a fancy to a well-proportioned young nomad there by the name of Mara. She should be waiting for me in a rendezvous spot not far from the camp." His lips glistened lasciviously. "Please go and fetch her for me. You would be doing an old man a great favor. And I will reciprocate by bringing some sweetness into your life—like so!"

He clapped his hands. Macaroon appeared with a jug and in a lightning move dumped its contents on Bond's head. Something sticky and thick dripped from the top of his skull down his white linen suit. Some of it touched his lips.

"Honey!" Bond cried. "But ..."

"Has it not always been in our Jewish tradition to cover the things we love with honey, Mr. Bond? Our children's first primer of the alphabet—the aleph, baze—so that they may associate learning with sweetness? Our chopped-up Passover apples? You see, I have come to love you, Mr. Bond, because of your dogged devotion to my well-being. Is that not reason enough? Now go, Mr. Bond, and fetch the supple Mara. You'll like Mara, Mr. Bond. She has a bite, a tang you'll never forget. In fact," he winked, "I wouldn't be surprised at all if she were taken with you instead of an old codger like me. But go get her quickly!"

As he drove away from the kibbutz, Bond felt a sticky crawly feeling. It's not just the honey, he thought. It's from a personal beeper in my soul, "danger ... danger ... danger." He lit a Raleigh, last one in the pack, and was so unnerved he threw it away without taking off the coupon. Gottenu! I really must be rattled to do that.

A bit past the encampment of striped tents, he spotted a likely rendezvous site. A small bluff rose above him. He parked the MBG.

"Mara?"

His voice echoed off the wall.

"Mara?"

"Mara is here, Mr. Bond." A mocking, sinister female voice. "Your Mara. Mara Bunta!"

Pain seared his head, face, body. A stream of evil, biting things poured down the cliff wall, tearing at his flesh.

"Mara Bunta, your Mara, you Jew bastard!" Saxon's voice, unmistakably. "Mara wants you, darling," said the girl's voice. It was

Poontang's. Was she in on this too? Was her "eternal love" vow part of the plot?

He now knew what the black stream tumbling upon him was. Marabunta! South American soldier ants! Each an inch long, voraciously hungry, stimulated into a frenzy by the honey. And in five minutes Israel Bond would be a skeleton bleaching in the Negev sun!

11

"Eat, Eat, Mine Kindeleh"

Every pore was on fire from the overwhelming onslaught of the tiny fiends. He clawed at them futilely. No use! There must be thousands of them. He'd be a goner in short order. Short order. "One order of Israel Bond on toast... these army ant anti-Semites have done me in," his brain said sardonically, flinging out the last great Oy Oy Seven witticism – at his own expense

His brain! The list! The last shred of his reason was telling him something. The master list of defense mechanisms that poor HaLavi had warned him to memorize. "The right button may save your life," a voice from ten million light-years away echoed.

He'd remembered one bizarre item, chuckling at it with a what-will-Ha-Lavi-come-up-with-next wonderment. Button 27! Pushing at the ants with his bad hand, screaming as their tireless jaws ripped into his bad shoulder, Bond, lungs whistling ("Heartaches," the immortal Elmo Tanner solo), staggered to the MBG and with a badly nibbled forefinger pushed Button 27 with his final atom of power.

There was a whoop-whoop-whoop-be-boop-boop-be-boop-boop sound and for a pain-racked second Bond thought he was back in America listening to Lambert, Hendricks and Ross on Symphony Sid's all-nighter on WJZ.

The MBG's trunk popped open. Six insanely shaped South American anteaters, every bit as voracious as their prey, popped out, their gluey tongues ejecting from their banana-like heads. With a gratitude he could never express, he felt those magnetic tongues clean away the marabunta. His body empty of the foe, the creatures sprinted to the bottom of the canyon and swallowed up the remaining hordes. "Great going, lads," he whispered to his sextet of allies. "If you can't join 'em, lick 'em!"

He ignored the blood pouring from the innumerable openings in his devastated body and haltingly climbed the rise. There was Saxon pulling away in the Volkswagen bus. It undoubtedly had carried the crates of hellish cargo to the cliff, where he'd unleashed them on the secret agent. Convinced the marabunta had done their work, the sweaty Saxon was not even looking back to check.

And Bond found something else. His heart stopped.

Poontang, lying in a pool of blood, a knife between her shoulder blades. Saxon!

"Iz," she smiled bravely. "Was hypnotized ... made me do it ..."

"Don't talk, my sweet. There's a doctor at the kibbutz. A real doctor. I'll ..."

"Lazarus ... the legend of Lazaru-u-u ..."

Poontang Plenty was gone.

Standing silently over her body, Bond dug the "Potbuster" from his pocket, shot it tenderly into her face and then placed it in her hand. "There'll be big beautiful bullrings where you're headed, my mixed up darling, where pretty, cornfed circumcised kids from Kansas City, Missouri, with windblown hair never miss. Knock out all twenty mibs with one shot."

He dug a grave, unmindful of the heat, the wounds, and placed her in it with all her belongings—except the 140 dollars she had taken from him in their game. But that seemed chapters away now. "We'll meet there some day, you and I," he swore to the mound of sand, "and then you can pay me the two thousand you owe me."

Weakness flooded him. *It's been too much. My body can't take it.* He used his Nippo to contact the closest agent in the vicinity, Edward Brown, 116, who was working at a Mediterranean port on one of the tiny democracy's most vital secrets, the conversion of salt water into taffy. Brown's helicopter ferried the emaciated Bond to the factory and an anxious M.

"Israel, mine boychikl, what has happened to you?" M. cried.

He collapsed at her feet, the point of her sturdy Daniel Green Comfy slipper mashing his ant-chewed nose.

A stinging medication, jolting him back to consciousness, was applied to his countless wounds by the cool, assured hands of Dr. Howard Friedman, the personal physician of M 33 and 1/3 personnel, the man who had invented the phenomenally successful combination suppository and thermometer with a menthol tip.

Dr. Friedman's nimble fingers worked swiftly, efficiently. Bond stirred.

"Got to think things out ... put the pieces together fast," the agent said through torn lips. Monroe Goshen stood at M.'s side, fear and consternation on his American Gothic face, highlighted by the field of corn that had suddenly shot up around him.

M. spoke: "The fool eats the cheese cloth, but the wise man waits for the cheese."

Bond smiled faintly. Good old M.!

Her eyes gleamed. "I know what must be done now, Oy Oy Seven. There are things deep inside of you that must be purged ... things we must know in order to complete this insidious puzzle." And to Goshen: "Tell me, my goyischeh friend. What means 'insidious'?"

"Better you shouldn't ask," retorted Goshen. Life among these warm, basic Israelis was changing him for the better.

"You will go to sleep and have a dream sequence, Oy Oy Seven," said M. "A bad dream. I'll make it so it should be a bad dream caused by overeating, gas pains, that burning sensation. Bring the works," she ordered her ever-at-hand assistant, Major Ari Rutkoff de Camp.

Aide-de-Camp de Camp returned with a tray piled high with food.

Now her bony fingers, fingers that had created the world's finest foods, pushed vast quantities of it down his craw. Deliberately greasy London broil, great gobs of carp, sturgeon, Kem-tone-tinted roe eggs, cold (ugh!) chicken soup, schmaltz, sour pickles, badly burned cholent, a moldy onion roll, pistachio ice cream (a definite violation of the traditional dietary laws, but this was an emergency), plus the powerful knockout drops, Schloofen-22.

"Eat, eat, mine kindeleh," said the soothing voice of the Secret Service chieftain. "Eat. And dream." He passed out.

12
Oh Hell, the Gang's All Here

Phantasmagoria!

He was diving into the bottom of an endless cornucopia, horrendous sights, sounds, phantoms, jagged patterns from the cosmos of his mind. "I want to sleep with my mother, but, oh, you id!" His own voice?

HaLavi flashing by, pushing a vacuum cleaner; "Got to vacuum up the voids, Iz. Can't leave any untidy, limitless voids around, can I?" A good man, HaLavi.

Ten tons of lead in his stomach ... nausea ... hot flushes. M. flying by on a broom: "Got to see the wizard. He'll give me a new tin heart, some brains and ..."

Macaroon skipping merrily down a yellow brick road, his hand slashing Bond's brain with a blinding bolt: "Lay Lorna Doone, ye ofay mothuh ..." Saxon: "Spin on, Jew boy, spin on." "Mara's here," said a cool sinister voice. Poontang. She turned into a gigantic ant and started chewing at his marbles. Blue eyes, incredible blue eyes, opening into sneering mouths: "Sheeny! Sheeny! Sheeny!"

Loxfinger? Yes, Loxfinger!

That name screamed over and over by hard-eyed, brilliant-eyed sycophants. "Loxfinger! Loxfinger! Plowshare Papers! Furor! Furor! Loxfinger! LOXFINGER!"

They had changed into baboons, leaning on knuckles, snuffling. Brutal hairy faces screaming: "Loxfinger! Loxfinger!"

Hot waves of nausea. Bond retched, came to. There was a queasy feeling in him and it wasn't the food. It was from the dream, and what it meant.

"I've got it all now," he croaked. His mouth twitched into an uncertain smile. "I'll tell it to you straight."

M. and Goshen chorused: "Tell us."

13
The Answer

"LAZARUS LOXFINGER IS ADOLPH HITLER."

14
"I Am Agent D."

M. said, "So what else is new?" A brave attempt at casual humor, but Bond knew his bombshell had gotten to her. She inserted her needles into the bowl of soup on the tray and started to crochet the noodles.

"Monroe hasn't heard the full story, M., so let me review it from the beginning." And he recounted everything that he could remember since the night he had faced the menacing gun of the Syrian in the Miami Beach hotel, every nuance, every scrap of conversation. It all poured from his tape-recorder mind with stereophonic clarity.

"We all know the Loxfinger legend. How some years ago he came from Argentina to Eretz Israel, pledging his fealty to Zion and vowing in that first interview at Jaffa that he'd spend his whole six million if need to be make our land a better one. I need hardly remind you of the significance of the six million figure. A filthy little inside joke of his.

"His money, he said, had been acquired by judicious investments in a new Swiss cartel that manufactures bows and arrows, William Tell & Tell. I have checked with several highly informed members of the brokerage world. The company, hastily formed about the time Loxfinger showed up, has been losing money from its inception. How then could he have made millions from it?"

(Bond, in truth, had some key connections with the New York Stock Exchange but generally made it a point to stay away from them ... ever since the day he had gone to Wall Street to check on Dreyfus Company's mutual funds and had been clawed by a lion emerging from the subway.)

"His money, incidentally, did come from Switzerland, but I'll get to that later. I also checked very recently with a leading archivist. The name Loxfinger has never appeared on the rolls of death camp survivors. As for the alleged Polish town of Muzak, which he said was his birthplace, there is no such town.

"But we weren't checking this man as we should have. So bedazzled were we by his generosity, his way of endearing himself to us with every filthy dollar he spent, that we let our usual security go by the boards."

M. said, "Go on, Oy Oy Seven."

"It's obvious that Der Führer never died in the bunker. One of his many doubles undoubtedly was torched up with his mistress, Eva Braun. Oh, and remember that name. It also figures in.

"What probably happened was this: He saw the end coming and was smuggled out of Berlin, probably in an Allied soldier's uniform, those lethal eyes disguised by incredibly blue contact lenses. A sub took him to Argentina with a few trusted confederates. And as for money, Switzerland, yes, but it came from a Swiss bank account established for just such a getaway. The Swiss never question who dumps the money in their banks.

"Years in the jungle, a plastic surgery job probably. Someone tutoring him in English, Hebrew and Yiddish, the essential languages he'd have to know to pull off this stunt. A concocted story about an escape from a concentration camp, a new name, forged papers, a built-up reputation among the Jews in Rio ... he threw a few bucks around there, too, to ingratiate himself ... and then he was ready for his brazen trip to Israel.

"Consider this: In his celebrated 'Plowshare Papers' Loxfinger never said anything that some of our would-be peacemakers haven't been saying for years—with negative results, of course. Why then were the Arab leaders suddenly positive? Because ... they're in on the whole devilish plot! I'll swear to heaven a tiny clique of Arab bigshots knows exactly who Lazarus Loxfinger is. That's why they pretended to swallow his proposals."

"Then the attack on him at the Kahn-Tiki," broke in Goshen. "A phoney."

"Of course," Bond said. "No pro killer would have missed point-blank, rattled or not, unless he was trying to miss. It was Loxfinger's hope that we'd dispose of the 'busboy' before he could spill the beans, which we did on the Quickway.

"That night at the Kahn-Tiki was enlightening, however. Well in his cups, he spotted this blonde Germanic-looking hustler, Eve Brown, and for a moment the mask slipped off. Her name threw him. For a moment he thought he was with Eva

Braun again! Eva he called Eve, remember? And the reference to the snow-covered peaks. Their trysting place at Berchtesgaden, of course.

"His slurs in my presence. 'Sheeny,' he called me, and derived some twisted pleasure knowing I'd have to swallow it. But when Saxon used similar language to me and Loxfinger, as a supposed fellow Jew should have made him shut up, he said nothing. Nothing. I still don't know yet where Saxon and that monster Macaroon fit in but ..."

"I do," Goshen said quietly. "But continue."

"That snatch of conversation between Saxon and Loxfinger at K'far K'farfel ... the words 'my,' then 'furor.' Knowing I'd overheard it, the doctor tried to palm it off as the word 'furor,' f-u-r-o-r, the excitement caused by his overtures to the Arabs. A lie. Saxon was saying 'my führer!'

"Loxfinger's unrestrained rage at the poor little kid's retelling of the Haman parable at Purim time. The doctor, I suppose, must have nearly gone mad on the spot, quite logically identifying himself with Haman, his spiritual ancestor, especially when the kid said that all Hamans were doomed in the end. Monroe, you fill in some blanks right now."

"I will, Iz," said the solemn CIA man. "And thanks for spelling out the word 'furor.' It helped me a lot with this *New York Times* crossword puzzle I've been doing while listening to you."

Bond shrugged. "Nothing really."

"Those photos you sent me sure paid off," said Goshen. "Saxon popped out of our files as Lincoln Faubus Madison, a key goon in the American Nazi Party. He probably was instructed to link up with Loxfinger in Argentina and coordinate a host of Nazis, right-wing loonies and cranks who would crawl out of the woodwork and support the doctor when the time was fortuitous. Macaroon is a Black Muslim terrorist from their elite branch on Madison Avenue. His real name is Brand X. The Muslims, you know, have an affinity for the Arab cause due to their shared religious beliefs. Go on."

"I will," said Bond. "By the by I owe Saxon and Macaroon quite a lot, Saxon for killing Poontang, my love, and Macaroon for the honey job that set me up for the marabunta. No doubt Loxfinger had seen these horrible insects at work during his years in the jungle. He brought a few colonies of them here, waiting for the chance to see some Jew eaten alive. Incidentally ..."

Way ahead of him, M. cut in: "It's been taken care of, Oy Oy Seven." She was the cool pro again. "We left a skeleton at the site. If they ever go back to check, they'll think it's yours. So now you'll have a free hand to smash these monstrous *pascudnyaks*."

Bond nodded his approval. "They killed poor Poontang because they knew she was in love with me and they didn't feel safe with her around any more. Now some addenda—Loxfinger is seventy-six years of age. History books tell us Hitler was born in 1889—seventy-six years ago. Never conceiving we'd ever get onto him in a million years he arrogantly used his right age.

"The very name 'Loxfinger' ... another slur. To Der Führer all hated Jews have fishy hands. And, Monroe, he takes a rap at your parish, too, mocking your New Testament. Remember Poontang's dying words? 'Lazarus ... legend ...' She apparently had overheard something just before they hypnotized her. You remember the story of Lazarus?"

"He ... he rose from the dead," said a stunned Goshen. "I see. Hitler is telling us that the allegedly dead Führer has been resurrected."

"Precisely," said Bond. "And here's the capper ... the phrase that made me wince during Loxfinger's speeches. I didn't know why at the time. I do now. Can you guess it?"

Dazed by the complete unreality of his whole monologue, they were unable to answer.

"The 'final solution.' Remember Eichmann's phrase? Well, still obsessed is Der Führer. He's still after that 'final solution' —the destruction of Eretz Israel."

M. broke in again. "Now I shall tell you boychikls a few things only I and our highest officials know. We've swallowed his scheme, all Loxfinger, stock and barrel of it. We've even planned a ceremonial meeting with the Arabs at Eilat to show our good faith, during which a rifle will be broken to symbolically indicate our plans to disarm. Loxfinger will be there, some Arab muckamucks, our own P.M. and his aides. It'll be on the first day of Passover, just a few days away. If we cancel, we'll tip our hand. They'll know that we know something isn't Kosher. Then they'll say we are, indeed, aggressors with no wish for peace whatsoever. They'll murder us with propaganda."

"Yes, but if we follow through don't be surprised when on that first joyous Passover day an Eretz Israel, its guard down, is overrun, their armies pouring on us from all sides like those damned marabunta," said a bitter Bond.

"I've got to make a very important phone call in the next few minutes," said Goshen from taut lips. "A tall man of the West with a mournful hound-dog face must be told of this evil plot."

"What the hell good can John Wayne do at a time like this?" snapped Bond, morose, his eyes seeing the annihilation of his people.

"If that phone call is to whom I think it is," said M. shrewdly, "go make it, young man. And don't call collect. We'll pay for it. Of course, if you could make it station to station ... after 9 P.M. ..."

Even now, she's trying to save my poor little country a few pennies, Bond thought. What a magnificent old woman! Then he snapped his fingers. "M.! Loxfinger told me he was clearing the way for peace with a secret meeting with some Arab moguls on a dhow in the Red Sea ... around Passover. That would fit in with the ceremony. They'll probably be making final plans for the invasion. I've got to get on that boat, hear that conversation."

"Don't be a fool," M. said. "You'll never get within a mile of that boat. They'll have frogmen, sonar, the whole *gedilla*. Besides, it isn't necessary. Agent D. will handle it very nicely."

Agent D.! Again that name!

"M.," said an emboldened Oy Oy Seven. "Nothing should be withheld from me at this stage of the game. I've been in it from the start. I broke the case. Now ... who is Agent D.?"

"Only three people know that—the P.M., a certain scientist, and me. That's how it must stay, Oy Oy Seven. Now get down to Eilat, disguise yourself and be ready for anything. Big things will be happening in a few days. And at the right time, Agent D. will make his ... or her ..." M. said cleverly, "presence known to you. Now go kill and be well."

Bond and Goshen sat on the terrace of the Sheraton, which had an outstanding view of the terrace of the Hilton.

The Israeli, who had bummed one of Goshen's cigarettes, inhaled deeply on the Benson & Hedges. "Too much Benson, not enough Hedges," he said glumly, his mind far away.

"You're thinking about the girl," ventured Goshen softly.

"Yes, the girl, me, but most of all, Eretz Israel. In a few days we'll all be under the heels of Adoph Hitler and the Arabs."

"Look," the CIA man said sharply, "I have just been in contact with the most important phone number in the world. The very heartbeat of the capital of the United States."

"You got through to Johnson City, Texas, huh?" said Bond, his eyes aimless, beaten. But they narrowed to cold, furious slits at the sight of the waiter, a wiry Levantine, who entered with two tall cool drinks on a tray. Bond said, "Scramble, Ramble, Mountain Rocky! Knuckle, Buckle Down Winsocki!" Goshen's alert ears caught the signal. They both rose casually, yawned, and hit the waiter from both sides, hurling him over the railing onto a bus ten stories below. It later developed the poor fellow was an Israeli, having recently arrived from Morocco, but the two cloak-and-dagger men were in no mood to take chances in these last spine-tingling days of their greatest adventure together.

"Hey, Iz," said Goshen peering at the panorama of bustling Tel-Aviv. "This town has me buffaloed. How do I get around?"

Bond flipped him a copy of Joel Lieber's authoritative *Israel on $5 a Day*.

"Can you really see this burg of yours on a finski a day?"

"It can be done," Bond said, "if your guide happens to be Golda Meir." (Bond himself had written a travel book that had not been successful, *Levittown on $5 a Week*.)

They walked over to Dizengoff Square and watched the diverse types that make up the tiny democracy passing in review. Old Orthodox Jews in yarmulkehs with curly payis (sideburns) ... darker Jews from Arab nations ... an occasional Druse leading his camel into a movie theatre (Although Israel had no discriminatory laws, it was generally agreed that camels should sit upstairs in moviehouses.) ... trim, lovely Sabra girls dancing horas and singing "Hava Nagila" (Oh, Come Let Us Double Our Jewish National Fund Pledges), the song written many years ago for the new nation by Willie The Lion Smith... tourists, obviously American, gazing with reverence upon a famed monument depicting the heroes of the War for Independence, Paul Newman and Sal Mineo pointing their rifles defiantly while Eva Marie Saint dressed their wounds. So many types, Bond thought. Would they be taking the sun, bathing in the green Mediterranean a few days from now? Or would the carefree melody echoing in the square be "Deutschland Über Alles?"

The knowledge of impending disaster hung over his head like the Sword of Damocles. Well, at least there's one man who's getting a little happiness out of this ugly mess, he knew. Damocles.

Aware his confrere in espionage, "the great game" as Kipling had called it, was still in a funk, Goshen barked: "Snap out of it! At least we know the score. And Loxfinger thinks you're dead, that he's still got your government bamboozled. So you can play a lone hand undisturbed. Leave Saxon and Macaroon to me; they're U.S. citizens so they're my pigeons."

He patted Goshen's back fondly. Good old Monroe! A man couldn't have a better pal. He'd have to get Goshen laid again sometime.

"After all, Iz," Goshen said. "Times have changed. This bastard can't make the world go *sieg heil* any more."

The Israeli looked up quickly. "What did you say?"

"I said, he can't make the whole world go *sieg heil* any more."

"That's it!" Bond nearly jumped off the park bench. For the first time in days Goshen saw that cruel, darkly handsome face light up. "You're cracking, Oy Oy Seven."

"Like hell, Monroe, but you just gave me the world's greatest idea." He whispered heatedly into Goshen's conch shell of an ear. Goshen nodded.

"It's crazy, but it might make it. I'll fill M. in on the bit, pronto! You get down to Eilat!"

Now the MBG's petrol pedal was jammed down to the floor and Bond, a sharp new Robert Hall Westerfield suit on his back, was racing to Eilat, the frontier-like boomtown at Israel's southernmost tip.

Beersheva, Shivta, Avdat, Mitspe Ramon sped by, then a long stretch of desert, today's nothingness that could tomorrow be bursting with green shrubs and Greenbergs, he thought wistfully—if I can keep Israel free!

A sign: "Eilat." Nestling on the shores of the Red Sea, where thousands of years ago a hard-hearted Pharoah and his minions had perished by a miracle as they pursued the Children of Israel into its waters. Are there any more wondrous works in that bag, Sir?, Bond asked looking skyward, seeking some message, some sign. He saw one: "DRINK COCA-COLA"—in Hebrew. The skywriting pilot (unless he was an Israeli) probably was going stark, raving mad flying the plane from right to left.

On the outskirts of Eilat, he pulled off the road, changed into a laborer's uniform, affixed a moustache, and got back into the MBG. Her tank read "empty," but Bond's was full; he had sensibly downed four quarts of Gallo on the way. True to HaLavi's word, the MBG roared anew and he continued on. I'll have to come out with my own brand of petrol, he quipped. With a motto: "Puts a Pish in Your Pishtons!" I've got my celebrated wit back, the secret agent laughed with boyish merriment. Things will be all right!

M. had arranged a new temporary cover role as a laborer with Gillespie-O'Day-Dameron, an American company which had been granted a concession to drill for oil offshore. Herby Zoster, the beefy, pimply-faced straw boss assigned him the task of hauling supplies to the company barge. It would be an ideal spot from which to keep an eye on the large Arab dhow, whose sails could be seen faintly a few miles away on the calm waters.

He lit a Raleigh, an eager-for-action sentinel in the sun, which was all a-sizzle. Bond paid it no mind. Why should a Jewish boy fear anything named Old Sol?

A shifty-eyed Arab sidled up to him and whispered with a licentious mouth: "Monsieur, would you like to purchase some interesting American postcards," his voice dropped confidentially, "with dirty zipcodes?"

For a second Bond felt like smashing the filthy beggar. But—wait! Could this man be one of ours? Agent D.? Or one of theirs? He'd find out. "The prune in the spoon sings a Frank Loesser tune."

"But the man who must hum will find rum in the drum."

"Who are you?"

Whipping off his headdress, the Arab said, "Shalom, Oy Oy Seven!"

"My God! Zvi! What's up?"

"Nothing as yet. But I want to tell you that M. has okayed the use of the three hundred young pioneers you requested. They'll be down here in a few hours, dressed just the way you want 'em."

"Good," Bond said. "Meanwhile, take this knife."

"Why, Bond?"

"It's a salad knife. I want you to keep your eyes peeled at all times."

Zvi laughed uproariously and disappeared.

Now Bond was apprehensive. The days had slipped by, one after another—a logical sequence of which he fully approved. But now it was the day before Passover and he had seen or heard nothing. No visitors to or from the dhow. Could that advertised meeting be a red herring, too? All he had seen was a happy-go-lucky dolphin skimming through the sea, doing flip-flops.

It was now in the afternoon as he stood on the deserted beach. The sun was at its zenith; the clouds at their Motorola. Then he saw it. A cabin cruiser heading toward the distant dhow. He caught a glimpse of a huge dark head. Macaroon! Then Saxon! The same brown woolen suit. It could be no other. And—Loxfinger! Sitting in a camp chair with a pith helmet atop his dome as the others fanned him with large palm leaves.

For another hour he watched, waited. Then three more hours. It was beginning to darken. Apparently the principals were going to talk for a long time.

The dolphin he'd seen earlier sliced through the sea, leaving a smooth wake behind it, and swallowed a bright red and white angelfish as it neared the shore.

It was quite close to Bond now, rolling its hilariously squinted eyes at him, that perpetually sly grin to be found on all members of its species, causing him to forget his grim mission for the moment.

"Looks like you're having—you should pardon the expression—a whale of a time, big fella," Bond called to the dolphin. I'll start talking to trees next, he mused.

In the next second he was stunned as though from a mighty clout on the head.

Out of the mouth of the dolphin, in perfect Yiddish, came: "Putz! I heard all about you with the bad jokes. Enough, already! You think I can spend all damn day rolling my eyes at you? You want I should be picked up for soliciting? Or get astigmatism? I am Agent D.!"

15
Parting Is Sweet

"Look," said the dolphin matter of factly. "Light up a Raleigh. You look like a ghost altogether. I'll make a long story short. I am Agent D., Duddy the Dolphin. I am M 33 and 1/3's secret weapon. I speak Yiddish because the very clever scientist who taught me to speak speaks it. Incidentally, so clever he's not; I can already beat him in chess three out of four times.

"Now, for many years marine biologists and psychologists have thought dolphins were intelligent. They understated the case. We're positive geniuses. They always dreamed that one day we could be taught to talk. Well, now it's happened. I fell in with a Dr. R. Nathan Axe of the Israeli Marine Institute and started working with him. He was rewarding me with a barrelful schmaltz herring a day, which no other dolphins are getting, so I figured I was ahead of the game and I cooperated. Until that time, I was just bumming around in an aimless life. Oh, a Timex Watch commercial here and there, but nothing steady. I just missed getting my own TV series when Flipper, my cousin, got the part. You know how? He slept around. So I came to Israel. When your M. heard of my accomplishments she naturally figured I'd be perfect for certain situations you other operatives couldn't handle. Like snooping around Arab boats, which I've been doing all day. I got the whole poop on the Loxfinger business."

Bond stared at the grinning maw. "A fish that talks!"

"Look, schnook, I'm no fish. I'm a mammal like you. Use your head for something more than a dandruff holder. You can swim. Does that make you a fish? Certainly not. Now—let's talk shop. I've been floating near the dhow all the time. They're speaking German, which is close enough to Yiddish, so I can pick up most of it. Tomorrow is the first day of Pesach. They'll all be together at the ceremony, Hitler, his two flunkies, two high-ranking Arabs, your brass, foreign dignitaries, the press, TV, etc. They'll make a few speeches and when Der Führer proposes a toast to unity, friendship and all that *chauserai*, it'll be the signal for an all-out attack. You'll get it from every which way ... ground troops, naval batteries, Soviet-built jet bombers. In the confusion, Loxfinger will be flown by chopper to some Arab hideout. So now you know. Don't stand like a klutz; do something. The ceremony starts at 3 P.M. tomorrow. I won't be far away, so look for me."

And Duddy spun and swirled off.

Bond, using his Nippo, spent the balance of the night contacting M., Goshen, the Defense Ministry. Monroe's news was encouraging:

"Iz, three American nuclear subs, the Hazel Bishop, the Allen Funt and the Martin Luther King, will be lying off the Mediterranean coast, each carrying sixteen missiles, Polaris tipped with Lavoris. No reason an H-bomb can't smell kissing sweet. They'll be launched if necessary. That's a promise from the tall Westerner I spoke to an hour ago. In addition, an entire SAC wing will fly—very ostentatiously—over the entire Middle East. That'll give any would-be aggressors some second thoughts. Twenty thousand marines, gyrenes and saltines will be airlifted here by an armada of jet transports, cargo planes, B-56's, 47's, 36's, 29's, 17's, Cessnas, Fokkers, Spads, Macy's Thanksgiving Day parade balloons, the Spirit of St. Louis ... anything we can get in the air. In addition, I hear that one division from Fort Bragg is trained to stick big, feathery wings into wax molds on their shoulders and fly that way. If they don't go too close to the sun they've a chance of making it."

"Great!" enthused Bond.

"There's more. An hour before the ceremony each of the Arab embassies in the U.S. will get a note from our State Department, informing them we know all about Loxfinger's identity and that we will not hesitate to intervene militarily, if need be, to preserve freedom, peace, tranquility, and our oil holdings in the Middle East. I am personally going to contact the two Arabs at the ceremony and inform them we're hip to the plan. They'll cop out, don't worry, when they learn it's in their best interests to do so. We'll promise the Arabs we won't reveal their part in the plot if they disassociate themselves from Der Führer—publicly."

"Then there's nothing left but to wait. See you tomorrow, Monroe."

"I'll be there, Iz, in disguise. Good luck!"

With a little time to kill, Bond wandered into a cafe where they were staging a Passover Seder. It touched him to see these big, brawling veteran frontiersmen of Israel singing the songs of Pesach and eating matzoh, the unleavened bread, with unleavened margarine, charoses, karpas, and the other traditional foods of the Seder plate. He sang the songs he had learned as a child, "Adeer Hu," "Had Gad Yoh," and "Eliyohu Hanovee." Since he was the youngest there, they insisted that he ask the famous Four Questions, beginning with "Wherefore is this night different from all other nights?" It was only something that could happen in Eretz Israel, a secret agent licensed to kill stammering the Feer Kashes as older men listened intently and graded his efforts. "Better you should be a Unitarian," said one oldtimer.

The day of the war dawned bright and clear.

To symbolize the fact that the Arabs, too, were prepared to meet the once hated Jewish state half way, the ceremony was to be held virtually on the line that divides Eilat from its Jordanian neighbor town, Aqaba, from which the gulf derives its name.

Indeed, the rites would start in Jordanian territory, the first time in Israeli history that its officials would be recognized on Arab soil. Workmen from both nations were putting the finishing touches on a large reviewing stand, and facilities for the press and TV. The latter would carry the momentous program via Lady Bird satellite to all nations of the world. The major networks had agreed on a pool coverage with Walter Cronkite, who spoke all languages and understood all things, as the anchorman. Dignitaries from all the world would attend, except for Red China, which in a blistering radio attack had berated the Arabs for attempting a modus vivendi with "the tool of Western imperialism, Israel." They had threatened to cut off shipments of mah-jongg sets, already forbidden to Israel, to the Arabs as well.

As the time approached and various officials began to take their seats in the stand, an American Dixieland group, the Canal Street Bordello Band, serenaded the ever swelling crowd with music carefully selected to give each side equal representation, alternating "The Sheik of Araby" with "Bei mir bist du schoen."

In the offices of Gillespie-O'Day-Dameron, straw boss Zoster told his workers, "As far as I'm concerned this is just another working day. I don't give a damn what them wild-eyed Yids and Ay-rabs is up to. Now," and he bent over a geological map, "Dr. Huer feels there's an excellent chance of a rich deposit of oil-bearing shale right about here," and he indicated a point offshore on the Israeli side. "We plant the stuff here 'n here 'n here ..."

Now there was an earth-shaking roar as Loxfinger, with Saxon and Macaroon at his sides, walked onto the scene with the two burnoosed Arab potentates, the Israeli P.M. and his deputy, two members of the United Nation's Commission on the Middle East, and Dorothy Kilgallen.

As the sun flashed brilliantly off their washboards and kazoos, the Canal Street Bordello Band rendered somewhat haphazardly along with 15-year-old singing star Bobby Ricky Danka (just as haphazardly) the national anthems of the many nations involved. But there was one person in the crowd who "dug" young Mr. Danka—M., disguised as a discotheque doll, her wrinkled limbs quite flagrant in the bikini she had chosen. Bond could see a wordless "yea, yea, yea!" on her lips.

A tall, distinguished man stepped to the microphone. "Good afternoon, friends of world peace. I am Ned (Good Driver) Reamer, your All-State Insurance spokesman, sponsors of this international telecast. In deference to the solemnity and significance of this occasion, my sponsor has instructed me to forego our usual commercial messages. They merely wish me to say that whether you're from the state of Israel or the state of Egypt, you're in good hands with All-State. Thank you."

A muezzin and a cantor chanted prayers; the invocation was spoken by Oral Graham Vincent, renowned tent evangelist who had a brief and nearly catastrophic lapse of memory, calling for onlookers "to fill up that tambourine for the blessed Master." Mme. Dominique Dardeaux, a French starlet, recited a work entitled "Peace in the Holy Land Can Be a Living Reality If Mankind Truly Desires It," a one-word tone poem composed by a neo-existentialist rapist whose philosophy had gained favor in certain Kantian circles in Paris. (Bond himself was a devotee of Kant. He long had considered himself the biggest Kant man in Israel.)

The starlet concluded with a few halting, unrehearsed yet totally sincere words of her own about her latest picture for Joseph E. Levine, *Perversion—Pakistani Style*.

A murmur went through the throng as the Arab and Israeli representatives alternated short speeches, each a cool, diplomatically correct presentation. If there was no love—at least there was no hate.

Bond, nervously inhaling the forefinger he had lit, glanced about. Good! The three hundred young pioneers from K'far K'farfel were on the edge of the crowd, all clad in long black raincoats. They had been well rehearsed by Zvi, he knew, and would play their part upon his signal.

But where was Monroe? Aha! There he was near the podium in disguise. A hastily thrown together one, Bond realized, and all wrong for him. He was wearing trunks and a sweatshirt and bouncing a basketball. Bad cover, Bond mused; Goshen's only five feet four, sure as hell doesn't look like a cage star. Worse, he noted, the letters on the shirt read:

HARLEM GLOBETROTTERS.

But his thoughts were interrupted by a mighty din. Loxfinger was approaching the podium. Bond could imagine fingers tightening on triggers all over the Middle East, pilots smoking Turkish cigarettes ready to scramble into their jets, tank commanders inside their steel leviathans.

Loxfinger, in highly formal attire, was at the lectern, rustling his notes, as one of the U.N. aides was preparing to introduce him. He glanced at his Arab colleagues. They seemed to be in a heated discussion with an American athlete in red satin shorts, dribbling a ball as he spoke. Suddenly the Arabs looked at Loxfinger, shook their heads in violent disapproval, ran their forefingers across their throats in an unmistakable sign. They walked quickly to their limousine and drove off.

It was all too plain. The dogs! They were abandoning him for some reason. Untrustworthy Arab schweinhundts! Then he would take another tack, reveal to the crowd that he, Lazarus Loxfinger, had uncovered last-minute evidence of an Arab scheme to invade his homeland. That would touch off the powder keg just as well, he thought with grim pleasure. This time I shall call for a *Jewish* holy war. It will serve the same end ... the "final solution."

Bond had also seen the Arab run-out. Goshen got to them! Good old Monroe! But Herr Doktor will try anything now to start a war, he reasoned. Got to alert the young pioneers. He ran toward the young men of the kibbutz.

"... who more than any other man is responsible for our being here today ... the Twentieth Century's greatest man of peace, who should win the Nobel Prize because he is noble ... Dr. Lazarus Loxfinger!"

Smiling confidently as he acknowledged the acclaim, assured of his powers to mesmerize, to send people into battle with a willingness to die gladly, those incredible blue eyes afire, Loxfinger began: "My friends, I had hoped today to be the giver of peace. But just minutes ago I received information that ..."

HEIL HITLER!

Three hundred young men, who had shed their raincoats, stood before him. They wore brown uniforms, armbands with swastikas, arms outstretched in that rigid tribute he had adored in the good years. His godlike name was crackling from their throats. He was ...

HEIL HITLER!

... at Nuremberg now, a lone colossus walking down a wide aisle, fifty thousand pairs of eyes burning in adoration. He was ...

HEIL HITLER!

... dancing a jig on the corpse of defeated France. He was ...

HEIL HITLER!

His right hand shot up. "Yes, Heil Hitler! Heil me! I am Adolph Hitler, your Führer, resurrected! I am ..."

And pulled his hand down quickly, but too late. All had seen it. He was unmasked before the crowd, the television eyes of the world.

"My God!" cried Bill Link of the AP to Dick Levinson, NBC-TV. "It's Adolph Hitler! That voice! He's alive!" Velvel Fierverker of the *Tel-Aviv Trumpledor* nearly fell into the arms of Mo Pascucci, veteran reporter of the *Christian Science Monitor*. Regina Prior of *Women's Wear Daily* shrieked: "Got to get to a phone!"

Loxfinger flashed a baleful glance at the young "Nazis"—then saw their leader, a cruel, darkly handsome man in a laborer's coveralls. But that moustache, dangling from one side of his lip. And that scar! Bond! Israel Bond, the security man. He has been the cause of my downfall.

"Kill the sheeny swine, Macaroon, kill him!"

Saxon fired a machinegun burst into the midst of the young kibbutzniks, several falling wounded. "Die you Jew bastards! Die!" The crowd scattered in screaming panic.

One of the shots tore into Bond's shoulder—the bad one. Another zinged, burning the bad hand. He froze, hardly caring about the pain. For Macaroon loomed above him, dark, menacing, that horrible killing right hand cocked. The mulatto pulled a board out of his sequined shirt, brought that hand down. It shattered.

When that calloused rhino-hard hand comes down on me it's the end, Bond thought. But I'll get in one damn lick. He hunched into Position 75, basic judo, swung a muscular leg and drove his toe into the giant's stomach.

Macaroon's face almost turned white. Confusion, bewilderment, pain crossed it, in that order.

Elated, Bond swung into Number 45, leaping superhumanly, chopping his hand down hard on the Muslim monster's neck. Macaroon went down like a torpedoed freighter. He pulled up his bulk slowly, picked up another board, brought that awful hand down. It cracked—but barely.

Now it seemed to him there was a vicious hornet named Israel Bond, stinging him in a million places with kicks in the groin, chops to the neck, a two-finger poke into an eye. It spurted blood.

The half-blinded mulatto reeled. He picked up another board, chopped at it. *Thump!* It did not break.

But his hand did.

Hot tears flooded his brown cheeks.

And then Bond realized, with a wild laugh bubbling out of his throat, what was wrong. This big son of a bitch only knew how to break boards. He'd never learned how to use karate—on people! Probably thought no one would ever challenge him after once having been terrorized by his board smashing.

"I've got you now!" Bond roared, a demon unleashed. He slashed again and again at the tottering giant. There was bloody pulp on his hand.

"Inferior nigger *schwein!*" Loxfinger screamed. He brought up a Luger, blasted his failing strongman three times. Macaroon fell with a thunderous crash against the first row of the reviewing stand, cracking it completely. In death he had split his last board.

Poor bastard, Bond thought. But now a Luger slug smashed into his own body ... the bad shoulder again. He was alone, unarmed. Loxfinger and Saxon were lunging toward him, eyes hot with hatred.

Got to run. Where? Another slug nicked his hand—the bad one.

The tall, distinguished man appeared suddenly with his microphone. "You know, ladies and gentlemen of the world audience, when sudden disasters like this can strike, isn't it wise to call your All-State ..."

A screaming Luger slug sent Ned Reamer to his final reward. Bond hoped the man's policy would leave his widow in good hands.

But there was no time to worry about anyone but himself. The enraged Nazis were at his heels, their fusilade sending sand flying into his eyes.

"Oy Oy Seven! Over here! You should shake a leg!"

A voice near the shore! In Yiddish! Agent D.—Duddy the Dolphin! May heaven send him plankton with whipped cream, six times a day!

"On my back, hurry!" commanded the dolphin.

He leaped upon Duddy, who launched into a frantic dive deep into the Red Sea. Truly it was the Red Sea now, Bond's claret staining every inch of it.

At last the doughty dolphin had to surface for air. *"Gevaldt!* What a mish-mash this day has turned out to be. But we're clear of 'em."

Zig-a-zig! Zig-a-zig!

Two bullets from a powerful Maquereaux, with silencer attachment. Bond glanced back. It was as he feared. The cabin cruiser manned by Saxon was bearing down on them, Der Führer's hand clutching the smoking French automatic.

"Faster, Duddy, faster!" he implored. "Just three hundred yards more and we're safe on the shore of Eretz Israel, old mammal!" He could see Israeli soldiers waiting for the cabin cruiser to get in range so they could blast it into perdition.

Zig-a-zig! Zig-a-zig!

One slashed through Bond's right arm. He fell off the dolphin, choking on the salt water and his own blood. "Duddy! Duddy!"

A thickening circle of blood next to him. Duddy!

"The second one got me," the dolphin grinned. But then, dolphins always grin. Bond knew his ally had suffered a mortal wound. The courageous Agent D. thrashed, murmured *"Zol zein mit glick,* Oy Oy Seven. I'm sorry ..." and went under.

I'm done for now, he knew. Shot up ... can't swim. The boat will cut me in twain.

It was close enough now for him to see the hideous faces of the two Nazis, the arch criminal and his all too eager New World disciple. He could hear Der Führer's high-pitched screams. "Die Israel! Die Israel!"

I understand now, he told himself, as he foundered in the warm water. I am Israel Bond, but to the psychotics bearing down on me I am Israel—period. If they get me they will experience an insane orgiastic release. Their sick eyes will show them the whole Jewish nation dying ... all two and one-half million going under.

He began to say the *Sh'ma Israel.*

The cabin cruiser was just a few yards away. Bullets sang a dirge all around him. Israel's greatest secret agent was on his way out.

Then—a sudden blinding flash!

Then—a roar, louder than anything he had ever heard!

The Red Sea opened!

His face fell into wet sand. His unbelieving eyes saw the sea rolled back on two sides, leaving a pathway to the shore of Israel. He pushed his pain-wracked, bullet-riddled frame. "Run!" The wet sandy path sucked at his feet, tripping him time and time again. Fifty yards now, forty, thirty, twenty, ten, five. Touchdown! He fell into the arms of two Israeli infantrymen.

Forced to abandon their cruiser when the parted waters left it beached in a trough, Loxfinger and Saxon were running an aimless pattern on the sandy strip, cursing, screaming, shooting without purpose, two stunned drunken beings going nowhere.

Then they saw the divided waters surging back!

Two gigantic waves, their white-foamed tips looking like the jaws of a mad dog, roared down on them.

Then ... then there was just the Red Sea ... eternal, peaceful, unconquerable as of old.

16
Top-Drawer Secret

"He'll live ... I don't know why, but he'll live," said Dr. Friedman, with a clamp in his expert hand. It held a Maquereaux slug, one of two he had dug from Israel Bond's mangled shoulder. "But I doubt if this ... this man will ever do your section any good again."

M. inhaled a Raleigh. Until Oy Oy Seven came back—and he would, she prayed—she herself would assume the burden of coupon gathering. And since it did seem sinful to buy the cigarettes just for the coupons and then chuck them away, she had begun to smoke. I'm an old harpy, she told herself. A few cigarettes a day won't harm me at my age. She was on her 80th smoke of the day, one for each of her richly spent years.

"He's moving," said Leilah Tov, M.'s beauteous secretary. Her heart pounded hopefully. Perhaps someday she would nestle again in the crook of Oy Oy Seven's muscular arm. The only man she would ever love.

With a shout, Zvi Gates rushed into the Secret Service infirmary, a bundle of newspapers under his arm. *"Gottenu!* It's the biggest thing that's ever happened to Israel since ... since ..." he struggled for a fresh simile ... "since canned beer!" Without Oy Oy Seven around to spur him on, Zvi's humor tended to be a bit archaic. "Gevaldt! Look at these headlines!

'ISRAELI SUPERMAN DESTROYS MAN BELIEVED TO BE ADOLPH HITLER! SAVED BY RED SEA OPENING AS BIBLE MIRACLE IS REPEATED!'

Here's another!

> 'WORLD TV VIEWERS SEE MIRACLE IN RED SEA AND DEATH OF HITLER! ISRAELI HERO CLINGS TO LIFE!'

"What did the *New York Daily News* say?" asked M., a shrewd smile on that infinitely wise old face.

"Here," said Zvi, handing her the gutsy big-city tabloid:

> METS NIPPED BY JINTS IN 11-3 SQUEAKER
> LIZ, DICK SHARE HOTDOG AT HARVEST MOON BALL FESTIVAL
> Hitler Dies in Red Sea.

He switched on the TV. "... for the 98th time, Chet, in answer to the flood of phone calls to the station let's rerun that tape shot from our NBC-TV helicopter on that fantastic business at Eilat. Here we see the Israeli agent stumbling as he makes it to shore. And now the waves smother the man believed by many to be ..."

M. snapped it off. "Better we should regain a little sanity in this organization."

She turned on Station RR: "... and moving right up there is Number 1,003, 'Long Lean Lena' by Hairy Harry Haircream and the Harelips:

> Long Lean Lena is the girl that we've adored,
> Whenever we go surfin' we use Lena for the board!
> Long Lean Lena, yea, yea—

"Oh read this!" Leilah Tov shrieked. "They want to do his life story in the movies! And Cary Grant wants to play Oy Oy Seven! Cary Grant!" She fainted and was tenderly borne away.

"What's the matter with me playing my own life? Though Cary *is* great, I'll have to Grant it!" Bond, his eyes barely open, a slight grin on his cruel, pale, darkly handsome face, had said it. One of my weakest jokes, he thought, but the best I can do in this condition.

"Everybody out!" M. commanded. They scurried from the clinic, casting warm glances at the wounded secret agent.

"Israel, mine kindeleh," said M. softly. "You're all right."

"Yes, Mother," he said. There was a fondness in his tone, not the fondness of a secret agent for his superior, but that of a secret agent for his mother.

Please, dear Lord, don't let me show my own weakness, a weeping M. pleaded. This is a cold, hard business. I can't get sentimental over a boy I wish had been my own son.

"Oy Oy Seven, you did a fairly competent job. But we must rule out the ... uh ... divine aspects of your escape. We all know now that the Red Sea parted because of a row of strategically placed high explosives detonated by the oil company at the exact moment you fell off poor Duddy's back. We don't need miracles, my boy."

"Our land *is* a miracle, M."

"Exactly. I'm happy to see you haven't lost your deftness with a phrase, Oy Oy Seven. But there can be no publicity, no personal interviews. If you are to remain with the Oy Oy .section you must slip into anonymity immediately. We will release a report that you have died from your wounds. Your friend, Goshen, will be told the truth, of course. You two may be forced to share another assignment some day. One question: Do you think you can ever be strong enough to return to the M 33 and 1/3 section? Make your answer truthful, no heroics. We've had enough of them, God knows. Remember, a crippled agent is a danger to himself and to his organization."

Bond lit a Raleigh, scratching the match on his shoulder cast. Some of the section people had written on it in ink: "Get well, Oy Oy Seven." He was touched. As a rule, M 33 and 1/3 personnel were necessarily an unsentimental lot. Or, so he thought.

"I'll be all right in a while," he said. "Can I at least write the screenplay of my own life? Maybe I can get a few bucks out of this affair for my trouble."

"No," M. was unrelenting. "Complete anonymity."

"You're the boss, M. I can't give up my Oy Oy rank. It's my world. Without a smoking gun in my hand and a broad in my kip, I'm better off dead."

M. smiled with satisfaction. "Good. As to the latter ... uh ... pursuit, Leilah Tov is anxiously awaiting your recovery. But, remember, Oy Oy Seven, the wicked man will enter heaven more easily than a righteous man pushing a needle into the eye of a camel."

"I'll remember, M. And you remember this: Whenever my land is threatened by the forces of injustice, I want to be called in. With every breath in my body I vow this—Bond's for Israel!"

Healing sleep overtook him.

Good lad! Good heart! Good soldier! M. thought. If only the *shmegeggi* could shoot straight.

Walking back to her cubicle, M. paused to think for a moment. She nodded to herself, her mind made up.

Switching on the factory-wide intercom, she snapped:

"Now you should hear this! Now you should hear this! This is M. speaking to all personnel. You are to promulgate a report that Oy Oy Seven has died. Repeat—has died. It is not true, but you will do so. Make sure in all interviews with press, TV, and magazine people that the true facts of Oy Oy Seven's admittedly meritorious exploits in the line of duty are disseminated fully. Minus any fanciful allusions or analogies concerning our faith's ancient history. *Dos is alles. Dos is alles. Shalom.*"

Just the facts, she told herself. Just the facts. She was a great believer in hard facts. One could not run a top-flight Secret Service on fairy tales.

But there was one little fact, she decided, that she would withhold. It was totally irrelevant, meaningless. But she would sit on it for the sake of peace and quiet.

She opened the top drawer of her desk and looked at an object —a buoy marker which had been placed coincidentally in the Red Sea at the spot where the waters had first parted when the initial TNT charge went off. It had been blown onto the beach at the exact spot, again coincidentally, where Bond had fallen into the arms of the army boys.

A very simple, nondescript buoy marker really. Too small to permit the full name of the oil company, Gillespie-O'Day-Dameron, to be imprinted upon it.

But large enough for the initials of each member of the firm.

She had other important things to do. So she would not let herself dwell too long upon those three initials.

MATZOHBALL

DAGHOSTAN

DEDICATIONS

(This includes the half of the U.S. population not cited in the dedications to *Loxfinger**)

CELIA LEVINE
In Memory

DON AND SANDY BARNETT

JUDGE PHILLIP FORMAN

SAM AND ANN RABINOWITZ & FAMILY

PAUL GRAY
the "International Humorist'
and
MARK RUSSELL
the "Washington Wit"
who are sorely needed as regulars on the TV "talk" shows

ISRAEL (COKE) RUBIN

MICKEY DANER
...had he not loved honor more,
he would have loved it less

RON & CAROL AXE DR. RALPH ROBBINS
... "dream doctor," healer of the sick,
the Sandy Koufax of Miami Beach

SANDY KOUFAX
on general principles

DR. DAVID J. SILVERSTEIN
Of Lancaster, Pa., who has taught his Pennsylvania Dutch clientele to know vot good is

RON & JEAN FRIEDMAN

---

* Pocket Books, Inc., 1965, $1.

BELOVED UNCLE H. J. SHERMAN
Of Sherm's Deli, Long Branch, N. J.

BELOVED TANTEH RIVA ROSENBERG
JACK AND DORIS SHERMAN, JACK AND MARY SHERMAN, JACK AND FRANCES ROSENBERG, JACK AND SOPHIE ROSENBERG, JOSH SHERMAN, SHULAMITH AND LEO RUTKOFF & FAMILY, MR. AND MRS. DICK AXE, GAIL COATES, JACK CURTIS OF THE LATIN CASINO, LOU AND RUTH DELIN, JOHN DELBRIDGE, DR. KEN HENRY, AARON LENOFF, STAN AND MINDY LEDERMAN, GIDEON AND ELISHEVA GLAZ, BOB LANE, JAY LAWRENCE, DICK MATHEWS, BOB NESOFF, DON PALMER, MIKE ROSENFELD, DR. JOHN E. TURNER, ALICE HELGESON

ABEL GREEN
to whom Variety is the spice of life (and the bread)

EARL WILSON
and his B.W., B.M.L., T.W.A., R.C.A., M.I.T., etc.

SGT. MICKEY BRANNON, JERRY GAGHAN, "RED" BENSON, LEON BROWN, FRANK BROOKHOUSER, SANDY OPPENHEIMER, EMIL SLABODA, BIFF HOFFMAN, HERB RAU, LARRY KING, PHYLLIS BATTELLE, JANET CHUSMIR, MIKE McGRADY, THOMAS W. LIPPMAN, YUDEL SUSSMAN, CHARLIE SCOTT, DON SCOTT, FLORENCE (CHOO-CHOO) BLOCK

SYLVIA AND LIPPY EISNER, SCOTT SHUKAT, JANET AND BETTY EISNER, BERNIE SOHN, HARVEY AND HARRIETT BLATT, ALLAN DELIN, BENNIE AND JENNIE LINDENBAUM, SANDRA AND ARNIE SIMON, MILTON LEVINE, BOBBY AND MONA COURTNEY, CAROLE AND ARNIE BERNSTEIN, DORA KAPLAN, EDDIE AND ALICE GREENBERG, RONNIE AND STEVIE GREENBERG, LOUIE AND YETTA CRAVITZ, ROSIE, RICHARD, AND ELYSE RUDOW, SAM AND CEIL CRAVITT, HANNAH AND LENNIE ROTNOFSKY, SAUL AND HELEN ROTNOFSKY, LENNIE AND RUTH MARKOFF, TANTEH EVA LINDENBAUM, SIDNEY AND CHARLOTTE LINDENBAUM, YOUIE AND CHARLOTTE CAPILUPI, MARVIN AND NORMA GATES, PHYLLIS FISHMAN, CY AND MALVINA

VOGEL, MARVIN AND MARSHA ROSENBERG, BOB AND JANE AMOROS, FREDDIE AND JOSIE TRAUM, HERB AND RAE STEIN, MEYER AND BESSIE GRUSMARK, ISADORE AND JENNIE KRAKOWER, RABBI AND MRS. WILLIAM FIERVERKER, SID AND RUTH SHUCKER, LEO AND FLORENCE FEINMAN, GENE AND JOYCE KONDASH, MOLLY LEVINE, LENA LEVITSKY, SYLVIA WEINSTOCK, MARTY AND MIRIAM LAIBOW, WALT LAMOND, MARV AND ERICA LAZOFF, MORRIS AND ADRIANNE BERENBAUM, FRED AND NETTIE BERK, GEORGE COHEN, MAX YOUNG, RUTH GOVER, RON AND JUDITH EDELMAN, OWEN LASTER, DENNIS PAGET, ESTELLE RAE ADLER, "DOC" GREENE, MARK BELTAIRE, SHIRLEY EDER, ED FISHER, BOB GOLDMAN, NORMIE LAYTON, MAX ASNAS, BILL GAINES, AL FELDSTEIN, NICK MEGLIN, JERRY DE FUCCIO, JOHN PUTNAM, LENNIE BRENNER, the "boys" from MAD MAGAZINE.

MICKEY MANTLE
Who hits 'em 500 feet

JOE E. LEWIS
Who hasn't walked, that far in thirty years

And...
NANCY BROWN
Of Plainfield, N. J.

Table of Contents

1 The House of Good Taste	125
2 Rotten Roger: The First Call	127
3 Marriage of Steel	135
4 "There Will Be No Third Striking"	146
5 The Tender Teach-in	149
6 Rotten Roger: The Second Call	156
7 The Eyes And Thighs Of A Fawn	157
8 Rotten Roger: The Third Call	166
9 "The Silent One" Strikes	168
10 "Ah Got De Blues"	179
11 Poems To Touch The Heart, Turn The Stomach	186
12 A Good Skate	192
13 Herbie	196
14 Summit Conference	202
15 David And Goliath	208
16 Rotten Roger: The Last Call	214
17 Roll, Roll, Roll Your Ball	222
18 It's All Over But The Shooting	233
19 Flash In The Pan	236

"Remember, Mr. Bond, a house divided is a split level."

—M.

1
The House of Good Taste

"Plain or egg matzoh?" asked the gash of a mouth under the thick, neatly trimmed Mandarin moustache.

There was no answer from the bearded patriarch three feet away whose soft brown eyes were riveted to the blue-black metal object in the right hand of the questioner.

"Again, my dear, dear Rabbi, I shall put the question to you. Plain or egg? And remember... a single ill-advised motion on your part, and one squeeze of this"—the Walther PPK Reuther automatic in the corded right hand dipped in a mocking bow—"will transport you instantly to some far-distant Talmudic academy where your sainted predecessors, Rabbis Hillel and Akiba, are doubtlessly waiting to engage you in some wearisome polemic regarding a fine point of Mosaic law."

Again there was no response from the stoop-shouldered clergyman (possibly he was too engrossed in parsing the sentence), but the slightest of tics in the right eyelid did not escape the cold, proficient, Volga-blue ones of the gun wielder, Colonel Sergei Svetlova, owner of the professionally bored voice. Inwardly the stocky Russian seethed with exultation, an emotion betrayed by the pale pinkish tongue which licked at the wet woundlike gash of a mouth. For the colonel was on the verge of pulling off a stunning counterespionage thrust for the KGB, intelligence apparatus of the Soviet Union.

"For shame, Rabbi," the colonel bantered. "Surely you are a poor representative of Israel's famed hospitality. A Soviet official interrupts his important routine to pay a courtesy call upon your nation's esteemed housing exhibit and there is no solicitous hand to proffer a cup of tea, a mouth-watering Israeli sweetmeat. Ah well, no matter," the colonel sighed with resignation. "The scion of a Don Cossack learns early in his life to be resourceful. I shall take my own repast, dear Rabbi. Now, what would you suggest? The roof? Possibly a shutter? Or the door, that portal to Jewish learning and understanding? Yes, the door."

Colonel Svetlova's left hand touched the door lovingly, then dug the nail of the index finger into its silvery exterior and, with a quick deft slash, peeled away a gleaming six-inch whorl. The finger jabbed at the interior. There was a loud snap. With a gouging lunge, the entire left hand came away from the door with a jagged section of white-and-brown-flecked board; bore it to that gash of a mouth. There was a crunch as the teeth of Colonel Svetlova closed upon it; the voice emitted a grunt of satisfaction.

"Plain, I should say, from my limited knowledge of the Judaic tradition. Is it all plain or is there perhaps some *egg* matzoh in the other sections of this wondrously constructed, prefabricated ranchhouse of yours? Come, come, dear Rabbi. It is fruitless to delay or prevaricate further. The evidence in my hand and mouth should clearly indicate to you that Operation Matzohball is blown. Not only is it blown, but I have bagged, certainly, the world's most famous ghost in the bargain!"

2
Rotten Roger: The First Call

It had been a humdrum day for Colonel Svetlova (a pen name derived from his family's inordinate fondness for perspiration) in his top-floor office in the dull brown three-story edifice on Ulitza Ouspenskaya, the building talked about only in furtive whispers by the average Russian in the street. With good reason: it is the headquarters of the dreaded KGB.

He had leafed through the overseas cables, sorting through the usual run-of-the-mill stuff filtering in from all over the globe. New York: "We have sketchy reports of a new American missile, the IRTBM, which is designed to carry a 10-megaton payload to Moscow, after preliminary stops at 14th Street, Penn Station and Times Square." Jakarta: "The Chinese have bested us in an important psychological battle to ingratiate ourselves with Sukarno. Their gift subscription of *Playboy* arrived before ours." (That damned slow-witted Major E. B. Yevomat! He would have to pull the major out of his cushy Indonesian assignment. But there was still a chance to recoup. If prima ballerina Tamara Villbebetta would make a hasty trip to the dictator's private quarters and let him paw *de deux*....)

Then the call had come... four sentences delivered in a matter-of-fact voice, suggesting that the caller thought as little of betraying his country as he would dispensing weather information.

Shocked, Colonel Svetlova had stood mute for a moment, then allowed an unthinking "My God!" to escape from his trembling gash. And a tactful, "Who does not exist, of course," in the event his secretary, Sergeant Toma Treshkova, might note in her daily report that he had let slip a decadent religious expletive.

An old hand at KGB politics, Svetlova was positive Sergeant Treshkova had been planted in his office by his superior in the section, General Gregori Bolshyeeyit, who would stop at nothing, he knew, to discredit him.

"Sergeant Treshkova," he said with ill-concealed annoyance. "Let us hear the playback of that telephone call."

The sullen face said, *"Da,"* and Sergeant Treshkova, with some effort, extricated her lumpy body from her straight-backed chair and waddled across the room. Svetlova noted with amused disdain her oaken calves encased in the new patterned stockings favored by Western women, and recently introduced into Moscow society. They represented her lone desultory bid for femininity, he realized, but merely transformed those legs into two disgusting rolls of varicosed chickenwire. Her feral odor, that of a newborn sloth, made his nose twitch; he was further revolted by her toadlike expression, the generously pocked complexion, her damp weedy strings of lusterless blonde hair, the pendulous sacklike breasts reminding him of a wheat shipment from Canada, the warts on her nose, eyelids and gums.

As she pushed a doughy finger against the playback button on the huge tape recorder which occupied an entire wall, she whistled through her harelip a snatch of a tune she had been enamored with of late, a melody of American origin entitled "I Feel Pretty."

There was the pht-pht-pht of scraping tape, then an almost inaudible beep, which brought a wry smile to the Svetlova gash. It meant, naturally, that his telephone was bugged, the listener quite obviously General Bolshyeeyit. Svetlova knew this to be so from his conversations with Corporal Anna Annatevkah, the general's long-legged, dark-eyed secretary and Svetlova's own plant. With Anna's connivance he had managed to place a miniaturized camera in the flower bowl on Bolshyeeyit's desk. In the colonel's secret file were dozens of close-ups of azalea petals, whose value Svetlova could not as yet ascertain. But he threw nothing away.

He forgot all about his internecine warfare with the general when the voice on the tape broke in.

"Colonel Svetlova, this is Rotten Roger Colfax with information of the most vital import concerning a plot, instigated against the Soviet Union by the State of Israel, known by the code name

'Operation Matzohball.' The model house assembled by Israel for display at the Moscow International Home Show in the Institute of Architecture is made entirely of matzoh—its exterior cloaked by a capitalistic substance known as Reynolds Wrap so that you will be led to believe it is aluminum siding. It is the plan of M 33 and 1/3 to dismantle the house at the conclusion of the show this evening and disseminate pieces of the matzoh to key leaders of Jewish communities throughout the Soviet Union, each particle stamped with the Hebrew words, 'Take Heart; You Are Not Forgotten'; thus reviving the kinship between the Zionist nation and its brethren here and breeding further discontent with life under your rule. In addition, the man posing as the spiritual advisor of the Israeli delegation at the Home Show is no rabbi but, in fact—"

"Colonel Svetlova. A word, please."

The last words of the sentence were smothered by the deep bass of a lean hawk-faced man in the uniform of a general who had poked his head into Svetlova's office: General Bolshyeeyit, commander of the Internal Affairs Section of the External Affairs Division of KGB.

"*Da*, Comrade General!" barked Svetlova, leaping to attention. His stiffened hand smashed the portion of skull above his right eye in a smart punishing salute. Pain flooded his face; an angry red flush crept over the bulletlike bald head. He staggered for a second; clutched his desk to steady his swaying body.

General Bolshyeeyit refrained from permitting a grin to purse his thin ascetic lips. The general knew quite well that there was a steel plate in Colonel Svetlova's head, the result of a terrible wound suffered on a dangerous mission behind the German lines in World War Two, when a tiny vial of nitroglycerine secreted in the sexual organs of a female Gestapo agent had gone off during an exhaustive search by the colonel. He also knew that his deliberately frequent appearances (with the concomitant necessity for saluting) would someday cause the colonel to drive the plate into a highly vulnerable portion of his brain, destroying himself on the spot. A confidential surgeon's report on Colonel Svetlova's monthly head X rays had apprised him that precisely one hundred more of those enthusiastic salutes would achieve the desired result.

"Colonel, how do you plan to counterattack 'Operation Matzohball,' as our colleagues in the Israeli secret service have picaresquely named this amusing little venture?"

Svetlova's mouth dropped open. "How did—?"

"I know all things, colonel," the general cut in brusquely. "That is why I occupy the office I do."

"Comrade General," Colonel Svetlova began, "I should enjoy the privilege of smashing this Zionist plot myself. After all, the telephone call from this Rotten Roger Colfax, obviously a pseudonym used by a traitor in Israel's M 33 and 1/3, came directly to me. The caller knew the correct telephone exchange, which is highly classified, proving he, indeed, has access to material of the most delicate sort. He, no doubt, is aware of my special background in Jewish matters."

"Granted," said General Bolshyeeyit, dragging on an expensive Mother-of-Pearlman cigarette holder. Svetlova noticed with surprise—and satisfaction—that there was no cigarette in it. Excellent, he thought. This superior of mine is not infallible at all. I shall yet hold his job someday.

The general inhaled again. "You have my leave to crush this Zionist conspiracy. But take heed. If your informant, this Rotten Roger Colfax, is correct, the so-called rabbi may be an exceedingly difficult man to deal with. Have you men you can trust?"

"To be sure," said Svetlova. "I have sent for two very tough, capable men, Nikolai Federenko and Alexei Norelco. They will accompany me and stand watch outside the Institute."

General Bolshyeeyit's brow wrinkled. "Federenko I know of. An absolute brute and well-fitted for this kind of work. I, however, am not acquainted with Norelco. You can vouch for him, I trust?"

"*Da*, General. I have known him since he was a little shaver. Stupid, but massively constructed and doglike in devotion. He would lay down his life for me."

"I hope that will not be necessary," said the general. "Well, *chorosho!* In that case I shall wish you a speedy conclusion to this absurdly pathetic Israeli affair. *Dobri noch** Colonel."

"I shall not fail you or KGB, Comrade General," the Svetlova gash twisted in sheer fervor. And, as though a Jack-in-the-box touched by a spring, he leaped to his feet and once again brought that rigid hand to his brow in a rapier slash of a salute,

---

* Good night.

exploding a white-hot ball of agony in his skull. He moaned aloud.

Again General Bolshyeeyit managed a straight face. That one must have taken a terrible toll of Svetlova's tortured tissue, he reckoned. "Ninety-nine, Colonel Svetlova," he said softly, and, returning the salute, strode off in his usual measured step.

"Ninety-nine?" Svetlova was puzzled. "Ninety-nine? Now what in the name of Father Lenin did that ice-blooded martinet mean by that?"

Slowly, gingerly, he let his fingertips steal across his churning, pain-smitten head. It must be ignored, he told himself; time to work. "Sergeant Treshkova!"

She reappeared at the door. "Bring me the dossier of this *Ivriski Shpion**" he snapped, scribbling a name on a pad and handing it to her.

A deep hearty laugh made him look up. "Imagine, dear Colonel. I have forgotten my gloves, ha! ha!" It was General Bolshyeeyit whose white suede gloves were quite safe in the deep pockets of his trenchcoat.

"I shall find them at once, Comrade General," said Svetlova, who, of course, could not, despite several frantic seconds of overturning pillows, peering under chairs, shuffling papers.

"Ah, well, the GUM department store, I am sure, has another pair in stock. Again, *dobri noch*, Colonel." The general's hand flicked a casual salute, compelling Svetlova to return it. This time the jolt of pain sent him reeling into the wall. General Bolshyeeyit, preferring not to notice his fellow officer's suffering, offhandedly remarked, "Ninety-eight," and left the room.

To Svetlova it seemed his skull was crisscrossed with a network of barbed wire. To steady himself, he lit a Kemal, a superior Turkish cigarette which combined the finest, most aromatic tobacco leaf with a blend of the choicest halva. Inhaling and letting the tranquilizing smoke invade his lungs, he forced himself to pore over the folderful of material pertaining to the Hebrew agent in question.

With an American-made Bic pen, which operated somewhat haphazardly on paper, but was excellent for writing on ice, he underlined a Hebrew word, "mezuzah," a word which meant

---

* Hebrew spy.

the tiny cylindrical symbol of the ancient faith worn about the neck by all observant Jews. It contained a portion of the sacred scrolls.

But not this man's mezuzah!

"This religious artifact," he read from the dossier, "has been transmuted into a murderous device. By pressing the Star of David on its front it releases a sharp needle upon whose tip may be found an instantaneously acting nerve poison called Molochamovis-B. The Hebrew word Molochamovis is Biblical in origin. Let the agents of our service beware. It means 'The Angel of Death!'"

As though he were in mortal peril that very moment, he reached into a drawer, pulled out the Walther PPK Reuther, shoved a clip into it and placed it in his shoulder holster. He remembered something else. From another folder, this one containing various miscellaneous materials dealing with Jewish history, customs, peculiarities, he removed the present year's Jewish calendar. He looked at his Russian calendar; matched it against the corresponding date on the Jewish one.

"Ah... ha!" he said. "According to this, the Passover holiday is a week away. Rotten Roger's data seems to fit in perfectly. It certainly would take a few days for couriers in Moscow's Jewish community to ferry the matzoh to their coreligionists in other cities. And the International Home Show does conclude this evening. What an innocent, natural thing for the Israelis to do, dismantle their sample house quite legitimately; then make arrangements for transporting it to the airport by truck. Of course, there would be a terrible misfortune between the Institute and the airport. An accident, perhaps. Or a theft. And, alas, the prefabricated house would disappear. I cannot let such a thing come to pass."

He ruminated upon the eye-opening telephone call from Rotten Roger. An unbelievable pseudonym! What was the man's purpose? Money? He had no doubts that Israel's secret service, working on the most insignificant of budgets, was underpaid. Yet, he had never before come across a case of defection concerning M 33 and 1/3 personnel. A grudge, perhaps? Failure to be promoted? Then a negative thought occurred to him. Could this "traitor" be sending KGB up a blind alley to obfuscate some even more devious Israeli plot?

Colonel Svetlova had been compelled to revise his opinion of Jewish determination and fortitude after reading the dossier of the Israeli operative whose snapshot lay in his hand. It had been taken by a seemingly harmless vendor of Italian ices near the famed Fountain of Levi, a bustling landmark in Rome's Jewish quarter, where, legend had it, good fortune would come to him who tossed three Cohens into the azure waters. A series of regrettable drownings had made the *carabinieri* crack down on the traditional practice. The vendor, one Ronzoni Sonoboni, a paid KGB agent who took these pictures as a matter of routine, had snapped it with a tiny camera secreted in his lemon-ice scoop. The face was dark, cruelly handsome; the eyes cold and gray; a sensual mouth set in a hard line of decision; the total effect: the countenance of a man deep in the throes of some murderous thought.

This man, Svetlova reminded himself, is bad business. He holds an Oy Oy number in M 33 and 1/3, which grants him a license to kill! I must exercise ultra caution. To still his nerves, he pulled the cork from a bottle of kvass, kvenched his thirst kvickly and pressed the buzzer.

"Send in Federenko and Norelco immediately."

They entered, both clad in shabby black suits, with bellbottom trousers, covered by dirty trenchcoats. Federenko was first: a tall, swaggering, strong-arm man of about forty-five, an expert in karate, judo, aikido and ring-a-levio; then Norelco: short, squat, with enormously muscled arms which when applied in a bear hug could splinter an opponent's vertebrae. The little man paused to gaze longingly into the face of Sergeant Treshkova who had ushered them in. "You... hee hee... very beautiful woman." A simpering blush stole across his vacuous peasant face. She also reddened and, flashing a warm inviting glance back at him, left the room whistling. "I want that woman, Comrade Colonel. I not see beautiful woman such like she back on farm."

"And you shall have her, if all goes well tonight, my dear Norelco," Svetlova assured him. "I am told she is very exciting in the bedchamber, my friend. Now," and the levity left his tone, "we visit our Middle East neighbor's extraordinary dream house."

Athrob with tension, Svetlova's chunky legs pistoned him into the darkened street. Thump! He collided with a figure in the shadows. His hand flew to his holster; the gun was out completely when a familiar chuckle aborted his action.

"Would you slay your superior, whose only crime is a relaxing stroll on this bracing April night, my dear Colonel Svetlova?"

"Forgive me, Comrade General. For a moment I thought—"

"But there is no time for thought, Colonel. You have a hard day's night ahead of you. I shall not detain you further. Again, *dobri noch.*" The hawk-face crinkled its friendliest smile and the general saluted.

So did Svetlova.

General Bolshyeeyit, knowing his face was hidden by shadows, did not suppress his grin this time as he watched Federenko and Norelco prop up Svetlova, whose knees had buckled, and drag him into the car.

Blowing a smoke ring, he said tonelessly: "Ninety-seven."

3
Marriage of Steel

This was the prelude to the drama now being enacted in the cavernous Institute of Architecture, whose sole occupants were the bald Russian officer and the stoop-shouldered holy man upon whom he trained his automatic.

An excellently crafted disguise, Colonel Svetlova conceded. The face composed of sunken, desiccated flesh, muddy-brown eyes (contact lenses, of course); a typical rabbi's shiny, dark-blue gabardine suit exuding odors of tobacco, schnapps, and herring; payis—the curly forelocks of the Orthodox Jewish set, the Mea Shearim, dangling disconsolately; faded white talis (the prayer shawl) with Mogen David wine-purple striping draped about the bent neck; the full-blown, unkempt black-tinged-with-grey beard; and the literally crowning touch: the yarmulkeh, a black skullcap.

Prior to entering the side door to the Institute used primarily by the departed janitorial staff, Colonel Svetlova had seen the sample homes trucked away by workmen of the countries involved. Next to last to go had been Nigeria's, which had featured its new mud-brick hut designed by the famed American builder of mass housing developments, William J. Levitt. The soon-to-be Nigerian Levittown would see thousands of low-cost huts springing up under the equatorial sun. It would engender a vastly different way of life for the Nigerians who would become typical suburbanites, commuting to Lagos, the capital city, on the 6:15 water buffalo, bitching about gardens invaded by "that goddam swordgrass," lazing on their patios at sundown, watching the hyenas drag off the Avon lady.

When only the State of Israel's gleaming ranchhouse remained, Svetlova had stationed his thugs at the loading platform and startled the rabbi with his drawn weapon. Then he leveled his accusations.

The rabbi's eyes blinked in agitation. "Sir, I am at a loss to explain the unique composition of this house. And this curious reference of yours to the 'world's most famous ghost'... what do these bizarre things mean? I am but a humble servant of the Lord, mine and yours, though your society has chosen to reject Him."

"Ah," the colonel said wearily. "I had expected more intelligence from you, Rabbi. Or should I say more accurately—Oy Oy Seven? To utilize a poor pun from your own holy works, why beat about the burning bush? The game is up. A compatriot of yours, in fact, a member of your espionage branch, has told all. Or does the name Rotten Roger Colfax mean nothing to you?"

A tremorous hand stroked the beard in wonderment. "I have truly never heard of that name, sir." Then the hand began to stray slowly downward, still stroking the beard, sliding toward the neck.

"Stop!" the colonel snarled. "Touch that mezuzah and I shall present you with a third eye. I'll relieve you of that, *Rabbi*," the appellation spat with hatred. Svetlova's left hand shot out, ripped the chain brutally from the old man's neck and hurled it upon the asphalt-tiled floor. His right jackboot stomped upon it again and again, the impact splitting asunder the cylindrical symbol of the rabbi's faith.

"Blasphemy! Blasphemy!" screamed the old man. "To crush the sacred scrolls as though they were a cigarette! What do you hope to accomplish by this inhuman outburst?" The gnarled hands vibrated in righteous anger.

"Just removing the viper's sting, dear Rabbi," and the colonel bent down and felt among the pitiful wreckage for the needle. There was none. He unrolled a mashed scrap of paper in his free hand. There were Hebrew letters imprinted upon it.

And it was the colonel's turn to wear a puzzled look. "But... but..."

"I shall demand an immediate apology from your government, sir. This barbarous conduct against a man of God...."

"Silence, man of God! You are now in the enlightened milieu of Soviet socialism. We need no hoary legends to sustain us.

But," and his voice took on its coloration of cunning again, "let us see if you are truly what you claim to be. We shall commence by—" the left hand sprang out—"by tearing off this handsome, albeit false, beard."

From deep down came a volcanic, tormented roar. *"Gottenu!* spare me from further indignity. Better let me die now." Tears glistened in the eyes. Svetlova, rattled, uncertain, tugged at it again; then the forelocks, the hair.

"They are... real." The gash of a mouth had lost its hauteur. It now twitched with indecision. "And the eyes... filled with tears. Real tears. How could contact lenses produce such a phenomenon?"

The rabbi, heartened by Svetlova's rapid loss of composure, had regained his own. "Why are you doing this to me, sir?"

Svetlova looked down at his boots. "My dear Rabbi. My dear, dear Rabbi." There was genuine penitence in his speech now. "It appears that I have made an unforgivable mistake. You are, after all, a guest in the Soviet Union, Rabbi, uh... Rabbi..."

"Rabbi Chair. Spiritual head of Congregation Bethel Leslie, 354 Georgie Jessel Boulevard in the port city of Haifa. Graduate of the Moses Maimonides School of Rabbinical Training and Fund Raising, 1924. Author of several well-known treatises on Jewish lore and law; among them: 'The Stage Delicatessen—A Look at the New Judaism,' 'The Negev Desert: World's Most Frightening Sand Trap,' coauthored with an American named Arnold Palmer, and my latest study, 'Should Religion Be Allowed to Intrude at a Jewish Wedding?'"

"Impressive credentials, indeed," muttered Svetlova, who jotted down the data in a black leather notebook as the rabbi intoned them. "Your first name, please, Rabbi Chair."

"Morris."

"Of course." He closed the notebook. "Now, I do not think there is anything to be gained by your lodging a formal protest about my admittedly..." he sought to inject the proper adjective... "uh... untoward methods of interrogation. I apologize for them personally. The fact remains," and he reverted to his officiousness again, "that innocent dupe though you may be you are nonetheless guilty indirectly of complicity in this shameful plot to foment unrest among our... uh... respected—and quite happy—Soviet citizens of Jewish lineage."

Rabbi Chair's mien was thoughtful. "My dear sir. I, of course, had no knowledge of this 'plot,' as you term it, but I am bound to tell you that morally I must align myself with its aims: If one of them is to make the Passover matzoh available to Russian Jews, I am in full sympathy with it. This stratagem would have been quite unnecessary in the first place if your State Baking Trust was not deliberately ignoring the need for matzoh during the coming holiday period. In general, Russian Jews would not be so restive if they were permitted to carry out a full-fledged program of Jewish activities, both religious and secular... if your book publishing agencies would print all the prayer books required by a Jewish population of three and a half million, instead of the pitiful few they do... if your building inspectors would cease their deliberate policy of condemning Jewish synagogues on trumped-up pretexts and then never reopening them nor permitting new ones to be constructed... if Jewish criminals mentioned in your newspapers were simply termed criminals, minus the sly references to their religion, a technique which cannot help but restoke the ancient coals of anti-Semitism which have bred pogroms at worst, hostile attitudes at best... if Jews were allowed to emigrate or at least travel to other countries, policies permitted by any humane government... if—"

"'If, if, if, if'..." an impatient Svetlova waved his hand as though to wipe away each item on Rabbi Chair's bill of particulars. "I fear, Rabbi Chair, that you have been victimized by a pack of vile falsehoods emanating from the Jewish press of the West, the selfsame bunch of greedy usurers who pour their ill-gotten shekels into the swollen coffers of the artificial Zionist state. Jews of the Soviet Union are content, fulfilled. They are tolerated almost everywhere. They are even to be found in the highest strata of our lower echelons. But we are wasting our time with this fruitless dialogue. One thing is sure—'Operation Matzohball' is blown. I shall see that this wretched house of yours is smoldering on a garbage dump in ten minutes."

"One question, sir," said Rabbi Chair. "Let us go back to your initial belief of my identity as someone other than myself. What is the mystery all about?"

"I may as well tell you, Rabbi, since it will not be helpful to you in any event. Rotten Roger, our enterprising caller, stated that you were the legendary Hebrew superhero who electrified the world with his derring-do in that overglamorized business a year ago. You, of course, recall the affair of the infamous Lazarus Loxfinger."*

His eyes widening, the rabbi laughed. "You thought that I, sir, was..."

"Israel Bond," Svetlova cut in. "Or Oy Oy Seven, as he is known to your secret service. It was reported he had died of wounds incurred during the climax of the affair in the Red Sea. We naturally tended to doubt such reports. Yet, you are plainly not he. Perhaps he did, indeed, go to that reeking Jewish heaven of yours and is presently strumming the songs of David upon his golden lyre. Enough exposition, Rabbi Chair. I shall now proceed to crumble Israel's paltry scheme to bits as one crumbles matzoh in one's hand. Too bad; it was a most interesting house. Before I order it razed, why not show me around? A Cook's tour, as our capitalistic friends would call it."

"It would be my pleasure," said Rabbi Chair with a grave smile. "And since it is a Cook's tour, let me make a small pun of my own. A Cook's tour is best begun in the kitchen." And he held the front door open with the studied politeness of an Intourist guide.

"Droll, Rabbi. The kitchen, of course." Svetlova moved quickly about the kitchen, sniffing here and there, breaking off pieces of matzoh from walls, chairs, the table and nibbling them. On one end of the table was a covered dish. He lifted the checkered cloth. "Ah, what is this?"

"Plastic representations of the ethnic foods to be found on a typical Jewish table. See, here is a bottle of Tab. This is lox, the smoked salmon... here is cream cheese... and here," his finger indicated a round varnished object with a hole in its center, "a bagel. Oh please, sir, do not remove it from its base. It is anchored to the dish by a wire, as are all these representations. We did not want visitors to disrupt the display."

"What does it matter now?" asked Svetlova. If it would upset the rabbi to rip the bagel from its moorings, he would do just that. He gave the bagel a violent yank.

A bell rang, shattering the stillness of the deserted street outside the Institute of Architecture.

If one had tried to trace the source of the ringing, one would have been frustrated, indeed, for on this street there were no public telephones or fire-alarm boxes. It was coming from a most unlikely place, the handle of a mop in the hands of one of

---

* See (and buy) *Loxfinger*, Pocket Books, Inc., 1965, $1, the definitive depiction of espionage.

a pair of shabbily attired women street cleaners, the type to be seen all over Moscow.

"It's the bagel," said the mop wielder in a rich baritone voice.

"Then it's got to be trouble. The bagel only goes off when the wire is severed," answered the other woman in an even deeper bass.

"Let's get the hell in there!" cried the first crone. "It's blown. He's in trouble."

"Hold it! The two gentlemen trying to look so casual near the side entrance... KGB boys, if I ever saw any. I can smell 'em a mile away."

The possessor of the acute olfactory sense was, of course, no woman at all, but Israeli agent Zvi Gates, he of the piercing eyes and the artificial ear.* Zvi Gates, 113 in the branch, licensed to wound. Street cleaner Number Two was young, personable Itzhok Ben Franklin, 276, licensed to drive.

Hampered somewhat by their unfamiliar, cumbersome garb, they had slowly moved about the street cleaning the same spots time after time, always keeping the Institute in view. Never had the street, nor the five sleeping drunks they had scrubbed a dozen times, gleamed so. Itzhok had proposed using a liquid cleaner of no mean repute, but Zvi, the older hand, vetoed it. "It's all right for the small jobs, but if you want to do a big job—like a street—you have to dilute it in water and it loses its power. Nah, we'll use something made to be *mixed* in water. Spic & Span."

They began a measured shuffle toward the two Russian goons, Federenko and Norelco, who leaned against the loading platform, puffing strong Gorki Cigarettes with one-inch gork tips.

"*Dobri noch,* gentlemen sirs," said Zvi, bowing obsequiously as a cleaning woman would before her superiors. "My, they are two very handsome gentlemen sirs, are they not, Sonyushkah?"

"*Da,* to be sure," croaked Itzhok, eyes twinkling with allure.

"Be gone, you stinking old carrion!" Federenko commanded. Russian women! Clods they were, clods! Give me a tawny, uninhibited *fräulein* any time, thought Federenko, who had performed many missions in West Berlin. In his mind he

---

* The loss of 113's ear is described in *Loxfinger*, Pocket Books, Inc., 1965, $1, a splendid Chanukah or Christmas gift to promote interfaith understanding. It can also be given to mark Arbor Day, National Blotter and Stylus Week and President Polk's birthday.

revisited Liselotte Gerhardt who had used her passionate teeth to bite her address and phone number into his neck.

"Oh, *nyet*, Nikolai. Not sending them away," pleaded the hassocklike protege of Colonel Svetlova. "They very beautiful women. I not see women so beautiful like these back on farm." Norelco, a simple-minded field hand, was bursting to experiment with the strange stirrings that of late had been disturbing his young body. So far his only experience along those lines had been a disappointing five minutes in a fetid barn with a bored cow. A prostitute at that.

"Let them stay if it pleases you, *muzhik*,"* shrugged Federenko, shivering as his fingertips tenderly caressed his neck and "56-B Krupp Strasse, 8765" in reminiscence.

"We clean spot right here, eh, Sonyushkah?" said Zvi. Itzhok nodded and they set about mixing a powder into the battered pail of milky water. "Better use strong powder; plenty dirty pavement here," admonished Itzhok. Zvi poured the powder into the pail, humming "Moscow Nights," but at the same time he let slip from under his petticoat a small green cube, crying "Pinch nose!" The mixture fizzled for a second; then burst into a green gaseous ball. The two women, forefingers and thumbs squeezing their noses, held their breaths. Norelco fell forward, his head striking the side of the platform, blood spurted from a pulsating fountain of a wound. "A trap!" Federenko screamed. Coughing, choking, he barreled past the two women into the Institute.

"This piece of matzoh," said Svetlova. "I wrenched it from a bedroom closet door. It's different from the others." He and his rabbinical host, the tour at an end, stood in front of the house watching the floodlights flash rays off its silvery skin.

"Matzoh is matzoh," the rabbi said mildly. "I can't imagine there being any difference at all."

"Thicker. Yes, definitely thicker. But why?" He began to knead the fragment in his hand. Crumbs snowed upon his boot tips. And then something else fell to the floor—a shiny black sort of ribboned material. He picked it up, held it to the light. "Microfilm!"

---

* Peasant.

"Ah, yes," said Rabbi Chair. "That, I suspect, would be one of the microfilms of the holy prayer books, reduced in such a way that a few rolls contain the entire liturgy."

And suddenly Colonel Svetlova realized that the stoop-shouldered savant had straightened up. He shoved the rabbi back with a flailing left hand, dug into his holster for the Walther PPK Reuther with the right, extricating it with the lightning draw that had earned him a reputation in the KGB as "the fastest gun in the East."

This time it was not fast enough.

Even as Svetlova shoved him back, Rabbi Chair's right hand made a mercurial maneuver of its own, whipping the yarmulkeh from his head and sailing it at his Soviet guest with the power of an Outback aborigine hurling a boomerang.

Five sounds fought simultaneously for dominance in the Institute of Architecture.

—The frightening, whirring sound of Rabbi Chair's yarmulkeh jetting toward its goal, a short exciting marriage.

—*Qang!* The marriage: steel-lined yarmulkeh to its eager waiting lover, the steel plate in the head of Colonel Sergei Svetlova.

—*Strike! Strike!* The characteristic sound of the Walther PPK Reuther blazing in the misdirected right hand of the falling KGB bigwig.

—"It's a trap! Tra... !" The gas-blasted, nearly unconscious Nikolai Federenko stumbled onto the scene, a crippled deer with its foreleg shot away.

—His tortured "aaa-eee-iii-ooo-uuu" scream gargling in his throat, torn open by Svetlova's two slugs.

Then, to the rabbi, the sweetest sound he'd ever heard. The sound of silence.

Two men lay on the floor of the Institute of Architecture in slowly widening pools of blood, faces contorted in the attitudes of sudden violent death.

Israel Bond, alias Rabbi Morris Chair, dazedly wiped the coursing streamlets trickling from his brow into his eyes. Sweat, thank God, and nothing more. His Type-A blood had not been shed this time.

He pulled out a crumpled pack of Raleighs from a vest pocket, stuck one into his lips and scratched an Ohio bluetipped match on the door of the house. He let the smoke curl in sensuous spirals out of his mouth, nose, and ears. Footsteps clickclacked behind him, Zvi and Itzhok chugging in still in their old-maidish costumes. The heavy lisle panties had fallen around Zvi's ankles.

"Clean it up, *boochereem*,"* said Oy Oy Seven, his famed scar livid on either his left or right cheek, now that his long tapering fingers had stripped away the rubberoid hands and mask that had transformed him into a sexagenarian.

Zvi spoke. "Oy Oy Seven, sorry this one"—he kicked the sole of Federenko's shoe—"got away. Gas got the other, but this guy had a little extra staying power. And our KGB luminary in the tunic... what got him, Bond?"

Zvi, of course, was hurling a challenge at his idol, Oy Oy Seven, whose ability to inject scintillating humor into even the most perilous circumstances was well-known to all his acquaintances. And basically ignored. Except by the jocular Zvi, who loved a hearty joke and always stood like a tittering maiden in the presence of a movie star, awaiting Oy Oy Seven's next gem.

Bond knew this too well. *Gottenu!* he thought; I'm exhausted, enervated. My kingdom for a good Robert Orben jokebook right now. But there's none handy. This'll have to be *my* rib-tickler.

He smiled weakly; threw his Saturday punch. (Bond's commitment to Judaism was an integral part of his make-up.)

"What got Colonel Sergei Svetlova, dear Zvi? He made one fatal mistake. He used his head."

Zvi purpled, a soft wheeze escalated into a howling hurricane of laughter. Slapping his knee, he lost his balance and fell against the point of Federenko's shoe, bloodying his nose. "Used his head! Oh, *mommeleh*, what a mind! Dig, Itzhok? He used his *head!*"

Itzhok said politely, "Oh."

"Okay," grinned a satisfied Bond. "Fun and games over. Get this house dismantled and into the truck. Your contacts are meeting you at the Reese-Schapiro Bridge at midnight. Get cracking!"

As the two younger Israelis loaded the matzoh segments onto the rickety old E. B. White truck, he gave them a brief perceptive rundown on his minutes of torment at the hands of Colonel Svetlova.

---

* A Hebrew word for "boys."

Bond glanced down at his fallen foe again, the gash of a mouth congealed into a frozen Z, glazed eyes like bloodshot marbles caught in a ghastly white light. *"Russkoyeh sveenyah, vui!"** Then he looked at the tunic, snapped his fingers.

"Boochereem, they'll be searching high and low for Rabbi Morris Chair for sure. They know—" He cut himself short; he would not bring up the matter of the traitor at this crucial moment in the plot—"uh, I have a feeling they might be looking for the rabbi when the colonel doesn't check back in. But here's my passport out of this Godforsaken people's paradise. His uniform."

"Real Oy Oy thinking, boychikl," enthused Zvi. "Take his papers, his car, the whole schmear. Who the hell will have the guts to stop a KGB titan?"

"Another, bigger KGB titan, you schnook," said Bond with severity. "They'll all be out looking for him, especially General Bolshyeeyit, the section boss. But if I can just grab a plane out of here...."

Minutes later, Bond was resplendent in his borrowed military togs—beard and payis shaved away by Zvi's .22 Remington. The only jarring note was the trouser cuffs which ended at his knees.

"The bodies, Oy Oy Seven," said Zvi. "What about 'em?"

Bond's eyes were mischievous. "Watch, lads. We're going to make the bodies disappear. And as an added fringe benefit, a hundred-million-dollar installation, the Institute of Architecture."

Zvi's eyes blinked. *"Gevaldt!* How?"

Bond picked up the prayer shawl; kissed it reverently. He felt for the fringes on the right side of the shawl, pulled one out to a length of some twenty inches. "The fuse, gentlemen. The entire talis is woven out of explosive *plastique*."

"HaLavi, huh?" Zvi asked, answering his own question: Lavi HaLavi, quartermaster of M 33 and 1/3, creator of diabolical devices for espionage, such as the yarmulkeh.

"Colonel" Bond lit another safety match, touched it to the elongated fringe. "Let's leave it to the angels, *boochereem*, and get the hell out of here. It's now fifteen minutes to boom time."

He climbed into Svetlova's staff car, pressed the hands of Zvi and Itzhok in fond farewell.

---

* "Russian swine, you!" (A term of dislike.)

"You know," mused Zvi, "that colonel's suit looks kinda sharp on you, Bond."

Bond smiled. (He'd been saving this bon mot for Zvi.) "Well, I'll tell you, Zvi. I always was crazy about... Russian dressing."

Zvi's body shook convulsively. "Oh, *mommeleh!* I think I wet my pants!"

That Zvi! Bond cackled all the way to the airport, where he was sure he could pull rank and somehow con his way onto a jetliner to the West. Ah, the West! No matter what its faults, it stood out as a bright beacon in the eyes of all free men.

Even as that refreshing metaphor crossed his mind there was a robust Russian answer to that bright beacon. It came as a red flash that split the cold darkness of the Moscow night, accompanied by a thunderous rumble that shattered the windows in Svetlova's 1963 Karamazov sedan.

Bond dragged on a Raleigh. "Well, there goes the Institute. Even Frank Lloyd couldn't put that building Wright!"

And desperately wished Zvi could have been there to hear *that* one.

4
"There Will Be No Third Striking"

Rumors flew like U-2's around Moscow concerning the explosion and fiery destruction of the Institute of Architecture. The Red Chinese were the culprits, seeking revenge for the latest Politbureau blast at Mao Tse-tung, some claimed. Others pinned the disaster on counterrevolutionary elements trying to overturn the Soviet regime and place Anastasia back on the throne. A CIA job. Albanian terrorists. Rasputin—no one in Russia believed he had really died. Ayn Rand practicing her own philosophy.

To A. Schlepin, shadowy security chieftain of the Soviet Union, General Bolshyeeyit had been compelled to tell the truth, at least *his* version. "He deserved to die, the stupid glory seeker," said Bolshyeeyit, "tackling a man like this Israeli with only himself and two others."

"Nevertheless, General, we have suffered a humiliating defeat: the matzoh is on its way; three of our men are dead. KGB's morale has been shattered to the breaking point. We must have a stunning victory immediately. That is an order."

From the glacial quality of the interview Bolshyeeyit knew he must improvise a way back to Schlepin's good graces at once.

"Comrade Minister," he began guardedly. "What... what if KGB could revenge itself upon the Zionist state for this outrage?"

"How, General, without admitting to the world that little Israel was able to wreak an act of monumental havoc upon the proud Russian bear in the very heart of his capital?"

"True," Bolshyeeyit nodded. "But the world at large does not know of Israel's daring. Perhaps our world, the world of intelligence, knows by now, and it is that world we can impress, by destroying the very Israeli who was the death instrument of Svetlova, and the bomber in the Institute job."

"Israel Bond," Schlepin gave a cool, reflective blow on his pipe, sending the bubbles on an upside-down pyramid to the ceiling. And Bolshyeeyit knew he had temporarily saved his spurs by the spark of interest in the minister's eye.

"Israel Bond," Bolshyeeyit echoed. "Think of our restored, even enhanced, prestige when the great intelligence bureaus of the world —America's CIA, England's M.I. 5, the French Surete, Netherland's KLM—learn that KGB has brought down the great secret agent at the height of his gaudy career."

"How would they know it was KGB's handiwork?" "Easily arranged, Comrade Minister. As you know, there was recently opened in Lisbon... 'The Espionage Capital of the World' as its Chamber of Commerce proudly states on its letterheads... a new hotel, the Hilton Spy, whose clientele consists solely of undercover agents. I myself have spent a relaxing weekend in its Colonel Rudolph Abel Suite, which, of course, has red carpets. Now... what if someday the famed killing mezuzah of Israel Bond was tacked upon the bulletin board in the lobby for all spies to gape at in awe, with a message beneath: 'From Russia With You Know What. Let This Be a Warning to All Who Would Harm the Soviet Union.'"

"I see the merit of your proposal," Schlepin remarked. "But I tell you, General Bolshyeeyit: this is your last chance to redeem yourself. If Israel Bond is not destroyed...." his hands made a gesture conveying finality. "Our American friends have a proverb derived from their national pastime—basketbowling, is not? They say, 'Three strikings and you are a dugout.'"

"There will be no third striking," responded Bolshyeeyit, whose knowledge of Americana was easily as comprehensive as his chieftain's.

"What will be your death instrument? I am told that Professor Gletkin of our weapons research division has concocted a particularly agonizing poison cigarette."

"It will not work on this man, Comrade Minister. His dossier indicates he has been smoking an American brand called Raleigh for many years. No, I shall employ Israel Bond's greatest enemy against him, one that lurks within the confines of that lithe muscular body. Sex. German measles has not attacked as many women as he has. Sex will be our death instrument against Israel Bond."

5
The Tender Teach-in

At the precise moment General Bolshyeeyit was outlining his plan for retaliation, Bond, a strange softness on that dark, cruelly handsome visage, was gazing fondly upon the innocence of an oval feline face, running a forefinger across the pouting baby mouth.

They were the property of Rowena Rosenthal, blonde and eighteen, who slept trustingly in his arms on the superior Beautyrest mattress ("Reminds me of a best seller," he had jested as he took her, *"The Silent Spring"*) which cushioned the oxblood-stained Belmar, New Jersey, driftwood bed in his luxury suite at New York City's opulent Ansonia Hotel.

An hour ago, fresh off the London-to-New York BOAC super fanjet, his tension-triggered perspiration blown away by the gentle fans, Bond had restively prowled Manhattan's upper 90's in search of *divertissement,* some escapade to blot out the unbearable strain from his grim sojourn in the Soviet Union. Dressed with expensive casualness in a Rudi Gernreich coral-tinted burlap-weave suit, Esquire socks held up by sporty *TV Guide* garters, Lazy Possum hush puppies by Thom McAn which squeaked Nina Simone songs as he walked, V-taper Jimmy Van Heusen shirt with the white-on-white musical note pattern and a clip-on Franklin Pangborn paisley bowtie, he sauntered up Broadway. He considered taking in a movie; there were several small cinema palaces in the area. The Thalia's marquee advertised Walt Disney's *Harlow,* about the fifth or sixth filmic attempt at capturing the true meaning of the tempestuous sex goddess' life. And the best so far, according to one critic, since it was a full-length cartoon. The Symphony was exhibiting a horror masterpiece, one of a number of such vehicles starring the screen idols of the 1930's who were making comebacks in films of a macabre vein. The new shocker was *Die! Die! Good Ship Lollipop!*, starring Shirley Temple as the deranged host of a kiddie television show who plastered the little tykes' faces with lye pies. The twinbill at the Midtown held no appeal at all: *I Passed for White*, with Ossie Davis, a truly splendid actor, miscast terribly as a substitute quarterback who comes off the bench with 1:09 left to lead Rockne's Fighting Irish (played by William Buckley and the Yale varsity of 1921) over Southern California, with his aerial bombs; and its cofeature, a science-fiction potboiler about a mutant three-hundred-foot rye bread that escapes from the kitchens of Jennie Grossinger to terrorize the world, *The Beast That Came From the Yeast*.

He stopped at a newsstand for his copy of the spicy, informative *National Enquirer* (the lead story this week blared: "I CHOPPED MY MOTHER INTO A THOUSAND BITS AND SPRINKLED HER OVER MY WALDORF SALAD"), and a pack of Raleighs. "Sure you wouldn't like to come on over to the L & M side, Mr. Bond?" said affable proprietor Don Dewsnap, offering him a snowy filter-tipped smoke.

"Sorry, Don," he grinned back. "Not until they give me coupons with 'em." Would that he could have told him, "Don, there are four hundred Mystery jets sweeping all hostile invaders from the skies of my beloved Eretz Israel. That kind of hardware doesn't come for free, Don. Each jet costs my plucky little nation three million coupons."

Then he had strolled into an espresso joint on 96th Street, The Maxwell House, unofficial hangout of America's new radical left. There he had met the fetching Rowena and her boisterous claque at the bar as they exulted over their latest triumph, the desegregation of a previously all-white house of prostitution on Lexington Avenue. "We did it!" she cried. "Made 'em take their first CORE whore!"

She had rejected Bond's initial advances after a sullen size-up: "We new yoot of America frankly distrust anybody over thirty. You're Establishment, *status quo,* smug mugwumps, bourgeois liberals... sell us out every time." Master of improvisation that he was, Bond had baited a clever trap using her own jargon. He lured her to his suite under the pretext that he was going to conduct a "teach-in."

Once there, all pedagogical pretense was abandoned. Ripping away her faded jeans, bra and panties, all of blue denim, and her Patrice Lumumba T-shirt, he crushed his cruel sensual mouth to hers, steering her into a dizzying orbital swing among the stars of fulfillment.

Rowena aslumber in the crook of his muscular arm, Raleigh smoke filtering through alert, vigilant nasal hairs, he recalled the events that had plunged him into that heartland of intrigue, Soviet Russia.

"Operation Matzohball" had been one of two schemes handed to the strategy board of M 33 and 1/3 by HaLavi. The alternate, "Operation Reunion," a brazen bid to spirit away all of Russia's Jews, had been scrubbed by M. "There is, I fear, no Russian highway, nor any other," M. had said wisely, "that can accommodate a three-mile wide, four-mile long bus." But "Matzohball" had won M.'s top priority. "Russia's Jews sorely need an injection of the Jewish feeling. Without some sign of external concern they could well become as spiritually destitute as the Jews of America and Israel. There is only one man with the leonine courage to spearhead this mission. Bond. I am told his shoulder and hand wounds are healed."

Bond had undergone a grinding program of physical training, running six miles a day across the golden beaches of Ashkelon on the Mediterranean under the watchful eye of frail peach-whiskered Nochum Spector, a nephew of M., who held a minor code clerk's post in the service. Healing sunlight had bronzed that pale bullet-gouged body once more; applications of Mother Margolies' Activated Old World Chickenfat had toned the skin, and selected isometric exercises, the diligent pitting of one muscle against another, had given him new strength and elasticity—and pitted muscles. Evenings he spent with the real Rabbi Morris Chair, polishing up his cover role, copying the sage's stooped stance, gentle speech and self-effacing gestures. His beard and forelocks had grown at an amazing rate, the result of hormones injected nightly by Dr. Lewis Hirsh, trail blazer in accelerated hair growth. It was jokingly reported the doctor's preparation could grow hair on billiard balls. Bond, shooting a little friendly game of snooker in the doctor's gameroom one night, could attest to that. The pockets of the table were jammed with hirsute spheroids that would not go down.

HaLavi's final touches. "You must work this job 'clean,' Oy Oy Seven. Your mezuzah weapon must be left at home. I'm sure it is no secret to Soviet intelligence anymore. If you are frisked its discovery will uncover your cover. You'll wear a real one. The same logic, I'm sorry to say, applies to your heel knives. Regular shoes, Bond. Your eyes will be changed to brown by contact lenses; an old trick, but we will add a refinement. Two strands of that beard will in actuality be wires attached to tiny ducts at the side of each eye. If some playful Russian gives your impressive bush a pull, fluid will be released. Your eyes will weep."

"But, Lavi," Bond said ruefully, "I'll be entirely without weapons. I don't know what's waiting for me out in the field. Whatever it is I can't face it defenseless. Remember, I am licensed to kill."

Thus, the QM had relented, fashioned the *plastique* talis and the killing skullcap with its hidden rim of razor-sharp Swedish steel.

Finally the big night had come, the confrontation with Svetlova. Thank God for his insistence on weapons and the creative powers of HaLavi!

At the airport he had arrogantly shoved his way aboard a British European Airlines jet for London, bumping off one Fedya Zhivago, an osteopathic veterinarian, who had quailed at the flashed KGB card and gratefully fled the plane. All during the flight he had played the overbearing no-nonsense role of the colonel to the teeth, slipping just once when the overawed passenger next to him had timidly ventured, "Comrade Colonel, you must be very proud of that red star on your uniform. Who presented it to you?" Bond, his mind elsewhere, had answered: "Texaco." His eyes had peered into the velvety blue, picking out from the myriads of stars the constellation known as the Big Dipper, a pattern of celestial bodies which, when connected by the imaginary line of the mind, formed the face of Wilt Chamberlain.

Then a bump... the jet's wheels caressed the free soil of Great Britain. At the airport with a change of clothes was Judah Ben Gay, a British liniment manufacturer who also happened to be 456 in the service, licensed to rub. And a dash for the BOAC jet and, six hours later, New York.

Rowena moaned, stirred in his arms. "I'm naked."

"You're very observant," said Bond, his lips curved into a suave, humorous smile.

"Who are you?" she said incuriously, rubbing the sleep from her Booth-hazel eyes. "Oh, yes," a worldly wise smile on the baby mouth. "The teach-in. M-m-m... it was... enlightening. I think I'll go for sixteen more credits." Her plump arms pulled him down to the rose garden of her body. Bond, ever the green thumber, took it from there.

Rebellious, but a wonderful kid, he thought, as she hurried away to start a rent strike at the Essex House (where she lived). He would stop in at the Gene Baylos Boutique and have them send Rowena a little token of his affection, perhaps one of their charming hand-tooled pot-holders. He was certain she smoked it.

He slipped into his Ralston lounging robe, the colorful checkerboard square pattern set off tastefully by a Timmie Rogers "Oh Yeah" ascot, let his electric toothbrush play over his firm, even white teeth and rich red gums. Then a five-second session with the latest oral appliance, Westinghouse's new electric toothpick which deftly ferreted out the insidious particles between those dazzling molars. He was finishing his third gargle with new improved Listerine, relishing the dying screams of a million throat bacteria, when the phone burred.

"Long distance, Mr. Bond," squeaked the hotel's operator, Miss Gloria Halfon, who was fascinated by Bond but too shy to make any overtures beyond leaving a nude photo of herself in his mailbox. "Tel Aviv, Israel, calling. Mother Margolies on the line."

Mother Margolies? Calling direct? His steely left fist clenched, the Speidel watchband snapping off in his anxiety. It was unthinkable of Mother to make a personal call unless a Code 3-D condition existed—Danger-Doom-Disaster! It signified to any truly astute Israeli "op" that something was amiss.

Mother Emma Margolies, known to an adoring humanity as the kindly wise soul of eighty-one golden years whose renowned cooking (Betty Crocker asked *her* for recipes) was savored by lipsmacking gourmets from somewhere east of Suez to China 'crost the bay. Her celebrated chicken soup graced the elegant tables of presidents, kings, Indian rajahs, British rock 'n' roll stars. Yes, she was everybody's Jewish mother (even Dan Greenberg's), dispensing equal dosages of gastronomic delights and straight-from-the-heart proverbs of universal understanding, such as: "You can't teach an old dog new tricks. But you *can* teach an old dog to teach a young dog *old* tricks." (Pundits of every major religion and philosophy were still probing for the inner meaning of that one; only the Dalai

Lama was even close.) Once she had whispered to the American ambassador at a glittering state reception: "Remember, mine dear Yankee—the enemy of my enemy is my enemy's enemy." Bond himself had felt a catch in his throat when Mother had once remarked after his return from a hazardous outing: "Live each day as though it were your last because, if it really turns out to be your last, you will have made it last as long as a last day can last." He had gleaned most of the import of those words; only the last part had thrown him.

Yes, this was her image to everyone but the little band of brothers who comprised M 33 and 1/3, the men and women who slithered in the dark jungle of espionage. They knew her as M., Number One! She had allocated a small wing of her chicken soup factory for their nefarious activities. There they schemed, trained for mortal combat with their hostile Arab neighbors, conceived idealistic operations such as the one he had just completed.

"*Shalom*, Oy Oy Seven," her voice pierced the crackling static of the overseas cable. "How was your Slavic interlude?"

"The sale was transacted. However, three directors of the rival company were taken off the board. And one of their factories was destroyed."

"So I have been reading in the Moscow papers. Unfortunate."

"I must inform the office that one of our salesmen has been wooed away by the rival firm. He has been selling them information about next year's line."

In Tel Aviv, Mother sucked on a piece of rock candy clamped in her dentures; sipped, from a glass hot tea at her elbow. A traitor! "Who is the unethical salesman?"

Bond bit on the Raleigh between his own teeth. "I cannot say. But I feel he is one of the sales task force which accompanied me to Moscow. We can better discuss this problem when I return home for the first Passover Seder night, five days hence."

"I am sorry to disappoint you, Mr. Bond. A distressing sales problem has come up in our branch office at Station WI. Detailed information will be available from Ben Bon Ami, whose address may be found in the Spanish edition of our catalogue. There is a plane leaving tomorrow at 8 A.M. from JFK. On it will be the other three members of your 'Matzohball' team—Gates, Franklin, Spector. You will need all the assistance you can get. And, perhaps during the course of your next enterprise, you can unearth the identity of our unethical salesman. *Shalom*... and remember the fool plays his cards close to his vest, but the wise man has a marked deck and five aces *under* his vest."

Long after M. had rung off Bond stood silent, his handsome dark face caught up by a frown of deep concentration. Rotten luck! This Passover would find him far from his beloved Israel, involved in heaven alone knew what kind of assignment, the whole mess compounded by a queasy feeling that one of his teammates was a turncoat. Well, that was an Oy Oy agent's lot, danger and double-dealing. Don't go soft, Bond, he sneered at himself. It's got to be done. Now let's look at the Spanish edition and find out where we're heading.

From a thick black Spanish "catalogue" titled "Soup y Sales" he extracted a slim pamphlet hidden in the binding and unrolled it. His fingers skimmed the contents. "Station WI." The West Indies. Under that category he found the name Ben Bon Ami, 41 Cinco de Finko, Vera Hruba.

Vera Hruba! Good God! The capital city of the sinkhole of the world! Israel Bond was going to the pestilential, revolution-racked, murder-ridden Caribbean island of—El Tiparillo!

6

Rotten Roger: The Second Call

Even General Bolshyeeyit's favorite program on Soviet TV, *The Man From UNCLE Vanya*, could not erase what had been a most distasteful day for him.

To begin with, he had sweated through his monthly tryst with Sergeant Treshkova, a sickening, teeth-grinding affair as always, consummated in the back of a covered Red Army lorry at 2 A.M. since he would not permit her to be seen with him in decent society during daylight. The thought of her harelip pressed greedily against his mouth caused him to shudder. And her harsh voice cooing, "Say pretty things to me, my dear General lover... tell me I am lovely...." *Bozheh moy!* Yet it was a necessity. Money could not tempt her to perform the vital chores he required from her from time to time, things he could not trust any of his other underlings to do. In her case, love was the key that opened the door to snooping, listening, reporting. But how he wished that her lock would be satiated by another key!

And headache Number Two, a call from Minister Schlepin:

"What has happened to your campaign to rid us of this dirty *Zhid*,* Israel Bond? I am growing impatient, General."

"It is progressing nicely," said General Bolshyeeyit. "Already my agent is on the way to make contact with him." A blatant lie. The general had no idea where Bond could be at the moment;

---

* Jew.

his world-wide alert to all full-time agents and stringers had not uncovered the Israeli's whereabouts.

In this irritable frame of mind he had exploded when the timid switchboard operator said, "A thousand pardons, General, but I have a long distance call from a person who is not on the master list of those permitted to get through to you. Yet he claims he has highly significant information for you and you alone...."

"You stupid bitch! How dare you bother me with crank calls! I shall have you tortured, shot, hung from Chapaiyev's statue...."

He was just about to hang up when he heard her sobbing voice say, "I am sorry, Gospideen Colfax. The general cannot be—"

"Wait!" he thundered, then tried to soften his voice. "I have been a little harsh... unnecessarily, Comrade Ponyebratzie. I shall take the call." Fool that I am! He thumped his brow in self-anger. Colfax! The very man who might extricate me from this mess.

"This is General Bolshyeeyit."

"General, this is Rotten Roger Colfax. I have some information which may be of use to you. But this time it will cost you."

"How much, Gospideen Colfax?"

"One million rubles. To be delivered by tomorrow. It must be left with a Dr. Nu at the Temple of Hate on El Tiparillo. Your people on that unhappy island will know of the establishment. If it is delivered, I shall call many more times with tasty items... at a price, of course."

Bolshyeeyit, a man used to making decisions of paramount importance in a hurry, said, "I accept your terms. The money will be there, I promise you. Now, what is the information you have now?"

"By now you have guessed that I am attached to M 33 and 1/3. I was part of the band that perpetrated the killing of your colonel and his two aides and the blowing up of your Institute. The leader of that strike was Israel Bond, our beloved secret agent here."

Was that apposition cast in a sarcastic vein? This man must have a personal vendetta against Bond. It can be highly useful to me.

"Where is Bond now?"

"He leaves 8 A.M. tomorrow, New York time, on Southeast Accident Airlines. The plane will make a stop at Miami at 10:14

A.M., also New York time. Since that airline does not go to El Tiparillo, he will be compelled to take the only line that services the island, Tailspin Tannenbaum's Flying Aardvark Airways. It leaves at 9 A.M., Miami time, the following day."

"I am most grateful for that information, Gospideen Colfax. Am I correct in assuming that any... uh... misfortune that Bond might incur would not displease you a great deal?"

"You are."

"Excellent. I have assigned a very beautiful courier to arrange for the misfortune. Now, how can I contact you for further data?"

"You may leave word at the Temple of Hate. *Dosvedanyah*, General." And Rotten Roger signed off.

General Bolshyeeyit pounded his fist into his palm. *"Chorosho!*" There is time. It will be close, but there is time. Israel Bond, prepare to meet your maker."

---

* Russian for "good"; like many Russian words and phrases, constant repeating of these guttural sounds can be useful in clearing your sinuses.

7
The Eyes And Thighs Of A Fawn

In the speeding cab to Kennedy, Bond sorted through the mail that had piled up in his box at the Ansonia. Most of it the usual junk mail.... "You may have already won an evening with Lenny Bruce or Pearl Williams in the Imperial Margarine Date-A-Dream Contest".... "The Schlockmeister Organization is a progressive mutual funds agency which takes what it deems to be sensible risks in purchasing only the most promising blue-sky stock".... and that accursed rejection from the cartoon book syndicate: "We feel that your idea does not have the general appeal, etc."

Stupid, shortsighted bastards! He had thrown a multimillion-dollar bonanza in their gray-flannel laps and they had been too myopic to realize its value. Some months ago he had suggested that since they were already making stupendous profits with Superman and Superboy, why not go all the way and milk the idea from its logical beginning? "The new character would be called Supersperm, the adventures of Superman from the moment of conception," he had written. "Surely, even then there must have been all sorts of hair-raising episodes in the womb for the Sperm of Steel. Think of the possibilities, gentlemen! The doughty infinitesimal dot, clad in red cape and blue leotards, fighting off hosts of fanatical germs launched by Luthor, the Mad Spirochete! Supersperm refereeing a race to the death in the stomach between Anacin, Bufferin and aspirin! Supersperm battling the swollen yellow forces of cholesterol in a last-ditch effort to keep his mother's arteries...."

The hell with it! he thought bitterly.

An accent textured with thick Brooklynese broke the silence. The cab driver. "You know, buddy, I ride around dese here streets all day, meetin' all kinds of people; some rich, some poor, some black, some white, some tall, some short. And, you know, buddy, I kinda developed me own philosophy on duh vicissitudes of life."

Gottenu! thought Bond, another hackie-philosopher. Spare me, Lord. "What's your name, my good man?"

"Friedrich Nietzsche."

Perhaps, Bond mused, this man would be worth listening to. But now there was no time for timelessness. Ahead lay JFK Airport and the Southeast Accident superliner for Miami. He wisely tripled the amount of his flight insurance naming Mother Margolies as his principal beneficiary, with ten per cent allocated to the Espionage Tzeddukah Charity Fund, set up to provide black mink coats for the grief-stricken widows of Israeli operatives.

He sat watching the trucks pump the enriched Humble Company gasoline into the plane's hungry tanks. An odd name for a Texas product, he reflected. In his many visits to the Lone Star State he had never found anything even remotely humble.

On his way to the first-class Golden Circle area he spotted Zvi, Itzhok and Nochum but professionally gave them no glance of recognition. They were ensconced in the twelve-seat-across tourist section, appearing somewhat cramped and unhappy. Rank hath its privileges, he admitted. An Oy Oy holder deserved the luxurious touches befitting his station. Golden Circle travelers dined on Sea Isle, Georgia, pheasant under Chagall stained glass, swigged chilled Jive 7 wine in ice buckets, served by bright-eyed slinky stewardesses in crisp topless uniforms. For the tourist crowd it was a box of Nabisco fignewtons and orange Kool-Ade, served by hostesses who looked like Blanche Yurka.

Yes, there they sat... Zvi, Itzhok, Nochum, three lads who had helped him tweak the nose of the Russian bear. He could not believe even now that one of them was the traitorous Rotten Roger Colfax. Which one?

Zvi and Itzhok had done the lugging and the strong-arm work; Nochum had acted as liaison and kept in constant telephonic contact with the main office. Telephone! He could have been the caller! But then, any one of them could have stolen a moment to buzz Svetlova.

What did he know of them anyway? Zvi, Jake-of-all-trades, master of disguises, who had joined M 33 and 1/3 several years ago. He knew Zvi longed for a higher designation than 113. "You get all the glamorous assignments, Oy Oy Seven," Zvi had once jested. Was he insanely jealous deep down? And would such envy impel him to treachery? Zvi Gates with his artificial ear,* a tragedy caused by Bond's carelessness. Could that have triggered a resentment which turned to all-consuming hatred?

Itzhok Ben Franklin, a new appointee. He doesn't chortle at my rapid-fire jokes. That certainly makes him suspect, The young *Sabra* (native-born Israeli) was a taciturn sort; he was, Bond knew, an honor graduate of the Technion Institute, which turned out Israeli's scientific brain power. Did he consider the low-grade chores allotted to him beneath his intellectual merit?

And Nochum, M.'s nephew, a laughable elf who had failed miserably in a succession of difficult government posts so, thanks to the intercession of his aunt, he had been placed in intelligence. He had more than once begged, "Please, Oy Oy Seven, teach me to kill and grab broads and order food just like you do!" Bond had snickered. "Nochum, stay safe in the playpen. This game is for big boys." Perhaps I was thoughtless at the time. Would that remark have turned Nochum against me and Eretz Israel?

He became conscious of a rustling in the next seat, a pair of astonishing legs sheathed in Lady Damita Jo hose, followed them up past taut thighs, a bewitchingly tucked-in waist, two full jutting breasts straining to liberate themselves from a satiny-black Tuesday Weld-model bra, to a face... and what a face! Piquant, amusing, with two ebony eyes dit-dotting an unmistakable SOS for SEX. Hands smooth, ringless, fingernails tinted tastefully with Revlon's new Annette Funicello pudgy-pink shade. The hair, also ebony, in a chic Shetland pony tail, neatly tied with a Pabst Blue Ribbon.

"Hello-o-o-o," he began. A traditional opener; he'd play it by ear. "Traveling together, are we?"

"We are on the same aircraft. It is a distinct possibility."

---

* Once, after the accident which is described in *Loxfinger* (Pocket Books, Inc., 1965, $1, and well worth purchasing), he had said to Bond, "Look at my new ear, Oy Oy Seven. You can hardly tell it from the real article." And Bond, flashing a light into the ear and spotting the drum, had riposted: "Gee, dad, a Wurlitzer!"

There's a keen mind to go with that loveliness! "May I introduce myself?"

"You may as well. I can't do it for you."

Another flash of wit! I could, he told himself, fall in love with a girl like this in twenty seconds. "My name is Bond. Israel Bond."

"Mine is Connery. Fawn Connery." And she glanced at her watch, mumbling "eighteen, nineteen, twenty. Kiss me."

Four lips (divided fairly, evenly between them) fused in a searing instant outside the boundaries of mortal time and space. One of Bond's gold inlays slipped like a molten stream down his windpipe.

Jet motors vibrating, the swan neck of Fawn Connery in the crook of his bronze muscular arm, Israel Bond stared vacantly at the earth below. Already the houses were beginning to look like cigar boxes (they were actually, the plane had not taken off yet). But, finally, up it went, soaring over Long Island, Northern New Jersey, Camden in South Jersey (his eyes picked out the huge sign atop the Campbell's Soup Factory: THIS IS THE HOME OF POP ART) and now they were hurtling southward at five-hundred-and-thirty-five nautical knots per unit of Greenwich median time.

"Is it possible that just one... ?"

"Yes," she said. "It is love. Order me something to eat."

He beckoned for the stewardess, pinched her buttocks and began to order breakfast for two. "We'll both have," he said, a trained eye scanning the menu, "the *filet* of Neolite sole, medium burnt, with a dash of lekvar *flambé*, two strips of Spam, the dark meat only, from selected Iowa corn-fed Poland China sows, titmouse à la Benedictine on Hollywood Diet bread, the bread of all trim figure-conscious stars, and—uh—I think just a smidgen of the poached raven. Suit you, Fawn?"

"Sounds super," she said. It was good to be with a man who knew how to order confidently for a lady without stammering like a schoolboy.

"And we'll share a bottle of Napoleon Solo Brandy. I've always preferred the '38, don't you?"

"The '38," she smiled and found herself running gossamer-winged fingertips across his lean navel. This, she knew, was a man.

"What brings you aboard, my sweet?" Bond probed.

"Oh, business in Miami. Then a vacation on El Tiparillo."

The gray eyes narrowed. "What in God's name would a lovely thing like you do on El Tiparillo? The whole island is sheer madness."

"Maybe I need a little sheer madness," she whispered. "Your kind, Bond." Her hand again skipped across his groin; a kidney stone shattered into powder.

"There'll be a long layover in Miami before tomorrow's plane to El Tiparillo, my Fawn with the fawn eyes. Enough time for a long layover, if I've made myself clear," he said huskily.

"I just might buy it, Israel."

Midnight, read the hands of the Baby Westclox cooing in its layette on the bureau of Room 1818 at Miami Beach's Palmetto Roach Hotel. She lay naked, her lips brushing those of the sleeping Israel Bond with butterfly kisses. She looked at the bronzed body which, melded with her own, had taken them flying to the moon where they played among the stars. She recalled with bitterness the other men she had known, piggish sweaty clods such as Colonel Svetlova, General Bolshyeeyit and the rest. How they had used her as a man uses a tissue, crushes it and throws it into a litter basket! Never had any of them struck the spark that releases the fecundity of a woman. But this man, this wonderful man, the man she had pledged to destroy, he had cracked open wide the dam in the reservoir of her being. And she realized with stark frightening ecstasy in his arms that she had enough within her to irrigate the Gobi Desert.

I do believe this wonderful fool is in love with me, she thought. True, he is a killer; yet there is a boyish quality of trust on his cruel face that tells me he cares. I'm trembling, she thought. A man has made me tremble! And *Bozheh moy!* he is the man I must kill!

From her handbag she took a tube of lipstick and twisted it. Out slid the cosmetic. She had only to press it between those sensual lips and he would die of cyanide poisoning in a few seconds. Her hand moved slowly, closer to the lips of Israel Bond.

"No!" Was that her own voice screaming? "I can't kill you! I can't!"

Bond was now an uncoiled spring; his body lanced out, hand tearing into his jacket for the tiny Paul Derringer. He stopped. Her face was cupped in her hands; an anguished moan heaved her breasts. "I—I can't kill you. I love you, Bond."

He put two Raleighs into his lips, torched the ends of both with a waxy Mexican match which he ignited with a sweep across her buttocks. "Take one now, voyager."

Still snuffling, she inhaled gratefully.

"Now," he began coldly. "Let us have the facts. Obviously you are not a simple vacationer. You were sent to kill me. By whom? And how?"

"KGB," she whimpered. "And with this." She handed him the lipstick, looking away.

He sniffed it; made a grimace. "Cyanide!" And smirked: "The true lover's bouquet."

"You will not believe this, but I love you. I loved you from the moment I sat beside you on the plane, the moment you ordered my *filet* of Neolite sole, the moment you entered my body with your curious admixture of brutishness and tenderness." She looked away from those gray eyes. "You slept serenely, my love. I could have inserted the lipstick at any time."

"True," he acknowledged. "But is this perhaps a ploy to gain my further confidence, Fawn... or whatever your real name is?"

"It is Anna Annatevkah, Corporal, to be precise, acting under the express orders of General Bolshyeeyit who has vowed to repay you for that episode in Moscow. Oh, you fool!" The tears streamed anew. "Can you not see that in betraying my cause I have sealed my own death warrant? I was to have called him tonight with the news of my completed mission."

"Forgive me, Anna," he said, holding her next to a heart moistened by a woman's tears. "I have existed so long in this dirty game that I tend to forget people have true feelings. And now, if you are recovered somewhat, may I offer you a little B & T?"

"B & T?"

"Brutishness and tenderness, dear heart."

Eyes ashine, she whispered, "Yes, oh yes. Oh yes!"

And the Bondian moon rocket tensed again and zoomed them into Orbit Two.

Now the Baby Westclox said 7 A.M. Its functional face watched Bond and Anna, carrying their luggage, leave Room 1818 for the airport. The Israeli looked at the room door for a second; the ghost of a memory etched a faint smile on his lips. It was in this very room a year ago he had courted death and a sinewy Oriental charmer, Nu Kee.* This memory had drawn him back to boniface Schuyler Kahn's Palmetto Roach Hotel after he had first checked in with Fawn at the Fontainebleau. But they had not found their room conductive to love-making; the sight of the naked dead girl on the bed, covered from head to toe with gold paint, had all but dampened their flaming urge. So it was back to Mr. Kahn's pink-and-brown stucco pleasure palace. "Glad to see you back, Mr. Bond," the portly little owner had beamed. Poor Kahn, it developed, was having his problems with a new hotel across the street, Horowitz's Hidalgo Hacienda. Seeking to lure Kahn's patrons away, unscrupulous Horowitz had started an odious rumor that sharks had been sighted in Kahn's Olympic-sized swimming pool.

Holding hands like two prom daters, Bond and Anna huddled in the cab, their bodies brushing as it zigzagged its way along Arthur Godfrey Road, Jackie Gleason Drive, and Belle Barth Alley. He caught her peeking at the twinkling new garnet ring in its delicate Freestone peachstone setting setting on her third finger left hand. And they matched the warm contented smiles of lovers who have pledged eternal vows. He had procured it for her from Ben Melzer, a chum of his who handled only the choicest of semiprecious stones. "Damn near a tenth of a carat, darling," he said with pardonable pride. "Only reason Bennie gave it to me so cheap is because it's got a flaw—but he says it's a *perfect* flaw."

Then the reality of their situation came back to him. "You mentioned danger to yourself, Anna."

Those dark eyes clouded. "The general surely will send another 'courier,' Israel. That is why I must go to El Tiparillo with you, to spot him, to warn you in time. I know well the faces of all his henchmen." She hugged him impulsively. I will protect this man at the cost of my own life.

---

    * See Chapter One of *Loxfinger* (Pocket Books, Inc., 1965, $1, and well worth the price. A thoughtful and well appreciated *Bar Mitzvah* present, or gift to a dying enemy.)

8
Rotten Roger: The Third Call

"She... she is in love with him?"

The voice at the other end in Miami was venomous. "Of course! She cannot keep her hands off that athletic body. You disappoint me, General Bolshyeeyit. Did you think that any woman could be immune to the blandishments of our Hebrew Hercules? No, General, Oy Oy Seven has literally balled up your works. And your works loves it. But here they come. Good-bye, General. On to El Tiparillo!"

And Rotten Roger Colfax clicked off again.

Bolshyeeyit gnashed his teeth; brought a fist down upon his desk, upsetting an inkwell. "Treshkova, you pig, clean up this mess!" And he flung the heavy glass fixture into her face.

"Oh!" she cried. "My General wants to make love to his adoring Toma again!"

A bullet nicked her skull and she decided, no, this was not the propitious moment.

The hawk-face hardened into a look of hideous hatred. Anna! In the arms of this *Zhid*, willingly yielding every inch of her tantalizing, throat-catching magnificence to this... *Bozheh moy!*

He screamed over the intercom. "Treshkova! Bring me the complete A-file at once, you monstrosity!"

She reappeared; tearfully placed a bulging folder before him.

Despite his shock, he had retained some of his professionalism. If my love-smitten corporal is his concubine now she will recognize my next messenger of death; she will warn him. This will have to be handled by a man outside KGB. In the A-file (A for Assassins) would be such a cold-blooded kill-for-hire individual, one who sold his murderous talents to the highest bidder.

He leafed through the file. "Niles Gillingham-Pishtepple, forty-eight, ex-British colonel in the Ahmsopur detachment... cashiered out of the service in 1953 for cheating at Old Maid... developed a hatred of the British upper class... offered his services to Communist China in 1954... worked with a renegade kangaroo smuggling out documents in the latter's diplomatic pouch... assassinated pro-British Rajah of Cooch-Dancer by placing botulinus virus in royal swimming tank... comment by investigating officer: 'Dirty pool.'" He saw a footnote: "Gillingham-Pishtepple was shot to death in 1962 by an incensed Outer Mongolian merchant, Hee No Khan Do, leader of the Arctic Secret Society, the Ice Tong, who discovered him trying to erect hotels on Community Chest in a Monopoly game."

Bolshyeeyit, as noted before, a man used to making key decisions with the snap of a finger, said to himself: "He won't do."

Within five minutes he had weeded out all potential assassins, save one. "Of course! This is the only one worthy of consideration. This defection of Anna's has rattled me, else I would have gone to him from the start. Sergeant," he said in a softer tone. "Wipe the blood from your misshapen skull and tell me what you think of this man."

She looked at the documents. For the first time in his recollection he saw her blanch.

"*Da*, Comrade General. He is your man. May I say that truthfully I pity his victim. I would pity anyone, no matter what his crime, whose path crosses that of Torquemada LaBonza."

9
"The Silent One" Strikes

"Here is your money, *Señor*, ten thousand *habaneras;* your passport and photographs of the man and woman you are to kill. She is one of ours who has defected. He is an Israeli secret agent. The general requests that you remove the religious symbol from his neck after it is done and present it to me here a week hence as proof of your success. Are you clear as to your mission?"

The swarthy man in the flamboyant purple- and yellow-hued gypsy costume nodded. With fastidiousness he smoothed out the thick roll of bills; placed them into a purse in his hip pocket. Then he grabbed the bottle of *viñ scully* by its base, smashed the neck off against the table's edge and let its contents flow down his throat. He rose to his full height, five feet two inches, bowed with a baleful smile that revealed a blindingly brilliant mouth and a garlicky breath, and walked out of the cheap *bistro*, the Alter Cockatoo, at soixante-quatre Arnold Cinq Boulevard in the Algerian quarter of Paris.

Shuddering, the KGB contact man, Vice-Consul Piotr Durak, swallowed his own Pernod as if to wash away the evil miasma he had felt in the man's presence.

"Do not expect LaBonza to answer you," the general had explained in his telephone conversation. "It is not for nothing that Torquemada LaBonza is known as 'The Silent One.' No one has ever heard his voice, except his victims. And they have all died in a bizarre manner, laughing insanely even as their life's blood ebbed from their torn bodies."

He recalled the rest of Bolshyeeyit's briefing. "We know very little about LaBonza, my dear Durak. We know that he is about thirty and was born out of wedlock to Maria Elena Smetana, a Basque gypsy, and Benvenuto LaBonza, an itinerant Corsican vaudevillian, in the back of a caravan wagon. His mother died at childbirth and he was raised by his father and a succession of paramours. The father, a chronic drunkard, eked out a beggarly living as a third-rate impressionist of American motion-picture stars in seedy theatres throughout Europe. He was killed in a knife fight when the boy was twelve, the rearing of the youth left to one Zorba the "Geek," a carnival performer. Thus the foundation for an embittered life was laid. As yet we neither know how he became an assassin nor why he does not speak. We do know of his work the last five years, the killing of the Yugoslavian *provocateur* Wsldz Ljmc by acid, the poisoning of the entire Katangan Board of Trade by curare mixed in their Junket, that curious death of the Frenchman, LeVoisin, who 'fell' off the freighter S.S. Tateleh in the Indian Ocean... many others. He has killed for the Union Corse, the Union Sicilone, the Union Teamstere and, most recently, for the Terrorist Union for Suppressing Hebrews."

"TUSH!" Durak had whispered, scarcely daring to speak the dreadful name.

"Yes, TUSH! He can be found usually at..." and here Bolshyeeyit had given Durak the name and location of the squalid cafe. "One thing more. He is easily recognized when he smiles. With his ill-gotten fees he not only had his rotting teeth replaced but also gilded his entire mouth structure. He is also known as 'The Man With the Golden Gums.'"

Filthy business, Durak said to himself. Thank heaven my duties for the fatherland rarely involve contacts with such amoral beasts. His connection made and the formidable Mrs. Durak safely accounted for at the beauty parlor, he decided he would spend a pleasant hour with a Mme. Denise Shtoomei, a curvaceous young circus acrobat at the Hotel Pierre DeSalinger, who, he knew from previous appointments, would, for a packet of francs, bend over backwards to please him.

"That's it, chums," said the jolly pilot. "Down there to your right. El Tiparillo."

Israel Bond, his forefinger idly dawdling inside the belly button of Anna, looked out of the window of the old sputtering B-17, flagship (in fact, the only ship) of Tailspin Tannenbaum's Flying Aardvark Airways. A solicitous sun sent a shaft through the mist, illuminating the mint-green Caribbean below. He checked his map; that guitarlike island to the left was Sal Salvador; to the North the odd land mass arranged in the general outline of a dollar sign, Costa Livin, and, yes, the cigar-shaped island Tannenbaum had pointed out—El Tiparillo!

"What is that golden stretch of land that cuts the island in two, Tailspin?"

"That's the famous no-man's land called The Band. Divides East El Tiparillo from West El Tiparillo. Or EET and WET as we call 'em for short."

Good man, this Tannenbaum, Bond thought. Knows his apples. He had spotted a few in Bond's lunch box, identified them rapidly. "That's a Delicious... those two are Macs... little bugger's a Winesap... the round orange thing's an orange."

Tannenbaum, Bond had learned during a pretakeoff chat, was one of those flying bums who once having had a taste of the wild blue yonder during the war could never again adjust to life on terra firma. He'd bought the shell-scarred B-17 from a war surplus warehouse at Key Luke on the tip of Florida, painted it a snazzy coral and pink and launched his one-man air service to the Caribbean. "Don't worry about this baby, Mr. Bond," he had chuckled between a continual crooning of "Comin' In On a Wing and a Prayer." "You're airborne with ol' Uncle Sam's No. 1 air ace. I shot down six Zeroes in the last big show."

"Six... that's a fair to middlin' number, Tailspin, but I've heard of guys who bagged twenty to twenty-five."

"From a Link Trainer?"

Bond had maintained a judicious silence from then on.

Besides Anna and himself, the only other travelers were his Israeli trio and an extremely tiny wild-eyed half-breed of some sort sporting a Dick Van Dyke beard and horn-rimmed glasses, whose spidery little body was clad in a tight-fitting pair of Jack-lemon slacks and matching suede sandals, set off by a leopardskin cocktail pull-over and a crimson beret with pompons. He did not seek conversation; seemed content to mutter from time to time and make notations on a pad.

Before Bond could ponder further on the unknown passenger, Tailspin cried: "Buckle up for safety, folks. We're coming in."

The next thing he knew he was roasting in midday tropical heat, his hand pumped vigorously by a moonfaced man in a Panama suit. "*Shalom*, Mr. Bond. I am Ben Bon Ami, Israel's consul on El Tiparillo. We will converse in my vehicle."

"Let's hold up on that until I drop the lady at a hotel. Can you recommend one?"

"One has been already arranged for you and your team. I was not expecting the lady."

"She is with me," Bond said. "Let me get her situated first."

Bon Ami, with great skill, guided his fire-engine-red fire engine through narrow, bump-filled streets replete with native markets, vendors selling tacos, the inevitable corner salesmen crying, *"Lotteria! Lotteria!* Win a million *marichals! Lotteria!"*

"Gambling is the passion here, my friend. These people will bet on anything," said Bon Ami, wiping cascades of sweat from his glistening temple. "Cockroach fights, the bulls, *jai alai*, beisbol, and so on. The men even bet on their sexual prowess."

"How interesting," said Anna, the first words she had spoken since landing. "What does the contest consist of?"

"It is perhaps too indelicate a subject for a lady's ears, *Señorita*. The concept of *Machismo*, virility... manhood, is uppermost in men's minds in these Latin islands. They flock to sexual betting parlors of Vera Hruba called 'los humpos' where... ah, but we have arrived." And Bon Ami seemed grateful for the interruption of his narrative.

The consul pulled into a driveway, chattered away in Spanish to a bespangled bell captain. "This is Bell Captain Belli. He will take the lady and her bags to a fine room in this estimable hotel which is the Nino Valdez. You gentlemen will join her later after we have our little talk. *Shalom, Señorita.*"

"This, gentlemen," said Bon Ami, back in his office and very much the assured diplomat in his own surroundings, "is El Tiparillo." His pointer touched a dot on the wall map. "As you can see, we are in Vera Hruba, the capital city of West El Tiparillo, some 15 miles from The Band which, by agreement after the armistice in 1963, cuts this woeful isle in twain."

"Armistice?" asked Zvi.

"I was coming to that," said the consul.

Bond's ears, carefully tuned into the exposition he knew was coming, had caught something else. A buzzing. Circling around the overhead light set in a crystal chandelier was a wasp.

Bon Ami spotted it too. "One of the innumerable pests in these parts. Now, in 1962, leftist elements, Castroites, Muscovites and Pekingites, ceased their internal struggle for power long enough to call a temporary truce and unite behind a Russian puppet, General Umberto D. Obratsov, who attempted to take over the island from a foundering regime. The forces backing democracy got behind a moderate, General Wesson y Oyl, and thus a bloody civil war ensued. The United States backed Wesson y Oyl, sent in money, arms, materiel, freedom fighters—guerrillas who had been trained in leadership for this type of warfare at a CIA-sponsored camp in Shaker Heights. All was going badly for Wesson y Oyl when a sudden stroke of luck tipped the balance. The CIA guerrillas were wiped out to a man in an ambush set up by Peking's man here, that master of guile, Vi Teh Minh. Bereft of this leadership, Wesson y Oyl found himself compelled to wage his own battles, of which he won the next six, driving the leftist coalition troops to their half of the island. Both sides were vitiated by then and ready to call it a day. The UN negotiated a settlement in which the island was halved; set up The Band which its truce commission patrols. So at least half of the island is run by a democratic form of government. Am I boring you, Oy Oy Seven? I see your eyes are wandering elsewhere."

"Don't move, Bon Ami. Just keep perfectly still and do what I tell you," said Bond in a low tense voice. He had seen the loathsome thing crawl out of a crack in the adobe ceiling and make its way to a spot about a foot over the consul's head.

It was a tarantula.

Black, hairy, big as a dinner plate.

Bond felt his body shaking. Only M. and the section psychiatrist knew of his Melmacophobia, a fear of awakening in the dead of night to find dinner plates crawling all over his body.

The wasp had seen it as well; zoomed near it.

"I think Dame Nature will resolve our problem," said Bond, his hand clutching the front end of his wing-tipped Florsheim cordovan, which he had planned to use to squash the huge arachnid. "The wasp and the spider are mortal enemies."

But the combat never came. The wasp alighted next to the tarantula. The two creatures undulated their feelers, actually touched. As though it had received some message, the wasp made a beeline for the open window and disappeared into a hibiscus bush.

"Kill the goddam, filthy, ugly thing, Bond! Crush it... squash it to smithereens!" It was little Nochum Spector, white as a sheet done by new-improved Blue Cheer. He saw the quizzical expression on Bond. "Damn it, you phony hero! Scared of a spider? I'll kill the f— thing myself!" Nochum jumped on a chair; swung his own shoe violently. It caught the lifted front legs which bared the fangs. The tarantula thrashed about in its death throes, fell with a plop into the corner of the room. "Kill it! Squash it!" screamed Spector again and lifted his pipe-cleaner of a leg to administer the quietus.

"Hold it!" Bond snapped. He pushed Spector away rudely; coldly watched the spider's ever-weaker struggles. Pulp oozed out of its side.

"Don't be so impetuous, Nochum," he said. "I do believe we should look at this first." He made a sudden pinching movement, wrested something from the top of the crushed tarantula.

Said Bond, scrutinizing a tiny disc about the size of a jellybean held between his forefinger and thumb, "I saw something on its back catch the light and gleam as it fell. This. What do you make of it, Itzhok? We can use that Technion know-how of yours right now."

Ben Franklin took the object, held it up to the light. A low whistle left his lips. "You won't believe this, gentlemen. It's a tiny transistorized listening device!"

"Geez, I'm sorry," Spector said. "I can't stand those damn hairy things. I wanted to crush it into a paste." Contrition was on his peach-whiskered baby face.

Bond did not comment on his apology. *"Gottenu!* On this damn island even the bugs are bugged!" And heard Zvi's appreciative bellow.

"An interesting problem and I wish we had time to delve into it further, Mr. Bond," said Bon Ami. "But you lads have been called in for a reason, a damn important one. Let us continue."

Bond lit a Raleigh; made an effort to push a few stray thoughts he'd been gathering out of his mind for the present. "Go on, Consul."

"Our country's problem is here." His hand fanned out on one side of the island. "This is WET, West El Tiparillo. This Star of David represents Israel's Peace Corps facility, Camp Kuchalein, which, as you see, is perilously perched on Mount Maidenhead, overlooking the jungle-covered Valley of the Blind. There is a famous motto coined by our own M. about this place. 'In the Valley of the Blind an optometrist shouldn't set up an office altogether.'"

"The old biddy's always coming up with crap like that," Nochum butted in.

Bon Ami ignored it. "The problem is this: We were asked to send a Peace Corps unit by General Wesson y Oyl because of the impressive record our people have made in Africa and Asia. For a while things went well. The natives, a poverty-stricken, superstitious lot, at first accepted us. We helped them grow food scientifically, tended to their sick, set up schools, cousin's clubs, dance studios, garment factories; in general, made our presence welcome on West El Tiparillo. Until a few weeks ago. Then scurrilous rumors began circulating throughout their villages that we were there to exploit them. An old native man who died of natural causes despite the efforts of our Dr. Marvin Browndorf was said to have succumbed to evil magic. Three of our volunteers were wounded by nocturnal snipers. Our potable water was spoiled by poison dumped into a well. Thank heaven, we had the foresight to put in an ample supply of seltzer. The worst happened two nights ago. A little boy was kidnapped from near his village; this note left behind. Read it, Bond."

It was a rough piece of parchment: "You will never see your Pablito again, Mr. and Mrs. Garcia. His blood will be offered to our pagan god as part of a Passover ritual. Be thankful that we of the Israeli Peace Corps have chosen his body to sacrifice on the altar."

Bond's chin pulled up belligerently. "Damn it! It's that vilest, basest of those pristine anti-Semitic canards! The lie that we must spill the blood of a non-Jewish child for Passover. Who's behind this, Bon Ami?"

The moonface shrugged its brows, "Anyone of the groups I mentioned—Peking, Moscow, Castro. They all have a deep interest in undermining us. We've shown the poor people of the *barrios* that progress can be made without the dear old hammer and sickle being shoved down their throats. Naturally, the Reds don't love us for that. Take a closer look at this map; you should become well acquainted with the terrain around Camp Kuchalein."

"What's this cross near the Peace Corps camp?" quizzed Itzhok.

"That's a convent, OLEO. Our Lady of the Eastern Order. Nice folks. They've been working unofficially with us on many projects. It's right on the top of the peak, if you'll notice. Halfway down is this point, cc, a summer colony for mediocre artists and musicians called Camp Camp. Weirdos. We don't bother with 'em too much. And here is the valley..." the pointer tip rested on a representation of a pagoda. "Stay the hell away from this place."

"Why?" said Bond.

"It's a bad place, the Temple of Hate. Run by a Chinaman named Dr. Nu. Quite unique, really. He operates a year-round resort for hate groups from all over the globe. 'Come here to hate at a special rate,' he advertises. All the pariahs pop up at his place: the Birchers, the KKK, Black Nationalists, some neo-Nazi groups from Deutschland."

"Our trouble could be coming from there, you know," Zvi said thoughtfully.

"Maybe. But until we know for sure stay away. Now, you boys will head out for Camp Kuchalein in the early bright. You can join a burro supply train that leaves from in front of the consulate at 5 A.M."

"Son-of-a-bitch!" Bond was in action again, hurling his cordovan at a black thing that skittered up through the crack and out of sight. "Another one of those creepy eavesdroppers! Bugged just like the spider. It was a roach this time, big bastard, about three inches long."

"Now hold on, Oy Oy Seven," said Bon Ami with annoyance. "They can't all be wired for sound."

"I'll bet my *tuchas* it was," said Bond. "Whoever is behind this now knows where we're going. I smell trouble."

Bon Ami smiled, a teacher patronizing an excited kindergarten pupil. "Maybe. But I want to talk to you alone for a minute, Bond. You'll excuse us, *boochereem?* See you tomorrow at 5."

Alone, Bon Ami turned to Bond, a serious shadow on the dark side of the moonface. "I have some bad news. This came for you." He pulled a large package from a closet. "It's from Lavi HaLavi. Came in this morning's pouch from Tel Aviv."

"What's the bad news?"

"HaLavi. He's gone off the deep end again."

"Oh, *Gottenu!* No!"

"Afraid so, Oy Oy Seven. According to a communication, he had just finished assembling this package for your personal use when he started to foam at the mouth. But here's the dispatch. Read it yourself."

"To Oy Oy Seven: Subject—Lavi HaLavi.

"At 8 P.M. yesterday the QM of M 33 and 1/3, who had just completed a number of combat devices, walked into M.'s office unannounced and began to berate her for not giving a laxative to an overstuffed chair in the corner. 'It is in pain,' he said. 'Badly needs a cleanout.' He then accused her of refusing to accept his 'brilliantly simple' plan for protecting our nation against any attack. It was, he said, the installation of a geodesic dome over the entire country with an elaborate air conditioning unit underneath. 'Not only will our land be safe from intruders, but we will never have another soccer game cancelled by rain.' At this point, M. pressed Alarm Aleph and three men in black hoods took him away to our branch's rest home, Foam Rubber Acres, in Galilee for treatment and a long period of seclusion.

"Yours truly, Dr. Hans Pippikel, section psychiatrist."

Bond's head rocked left-right-left-right with incredulity. Poor Lavi! Wacked out again. Easy to understand why. If I had to conceive the fantastic weapons and missions he does, I, too, would be bouncing around at Foam Rubber Acres every six months.

But Lavi had given the last ounce of his brain power on Bond's behalf. This was no time to wallow in pity. Whatever there was in this package was for use by a man licensed to kill.

"*Shalom*, Bon Ami. You'll be hearing from me." And he walked into the steaming street.

Heavy of heart, his mind troubled by the new developments, Israel Bond, HaLavi's package under his arm, trudged down Calle Cugat on his way to the Nino Valdez. I'm in for it now, he thought sardonically. Now I must tackle the whole damn Communist world, rescue a kidnapped child from God knows where or the Peace Corps will be subjected to a Latin blood bath, and ferret out a traitor. He'd had some thoughts about that last item during the consul's briefing. Nochum? "A phony hero" he called me. Does he hate me that much? How anxious he was to mash the spider! And that crack about M., his own aunt, "an old biddy." Is all this enough to pin the tail on the donkey? Then there was Anna, lovely, wanton, constantly inflaming his every red corpuscle. Could she really be trusted? And, if so, what's in the cards for her and me? Marriage? But I have sworn to my late sainted mother to stand under the traditional wedding canopy with a daughter of Zion. Would Anna convert? And is the Paradise Wedding Hall in the Bronx all booked up?

This whole damn thing sounds like a teaser for next week's *Peyton Place,* he told himself. Back to work, Oy Oy Seven.

At the intersection of Calle Desi-Lu and Cinco de Virginia Mayo he saw a boisterous crowd pushing its way into a large, obviously new, building. A neon sign flashed on and off: "FREEZERIA."

Bond quickly realized what the place was. Freezerias—the mushrooming slumber palaces in which reposed the recently dear departed.

The concept of freezing the dead, until that glorious day when an ever-improving medical science could discover the curse for the various maladies that had shuffled them off this mortal coil, then unfreeze and cure them, was spreading all over the world. He had once read an article on the subject which listed a price range of $8,000 to $50,000 for the cost of freezing your dear Uncle Seymour a few hours after clinical death. It was like anything else in life, he imagined. You get what you pay for. For eight grand, he reckoned, the best you could expect would be to have Uncle Seymour thrown in with the Sara Lee cheesecakes at the local A & P. But for fifty big ones... ah, then you got the individual freezer with fresh flowers placed on the chest everyday, the weekend outings by a family come to see that all was well ("Mummy, he's smiling".... "Why not, precious? He's just sleeping until the big Reveille Day, that's all"... "Gee, you know, Syl, I think he actually gained weight. The old boy looks good"), the plug guard (for that kind of money surely one was entitled to have a man guard the plug; who could tell when some enemy who owed Seymour a bundle would yank it and leave Uncle to rot?) and the emergency generator in case of power failure. And, Bond surmised, today's four-letter obscenities would have no sting at all in fifty years. The truly shocking four-letter words of future generations would be "melt" and "thaw." And the most despicable epithets—"mother-melter," "father-thawer."

Death. It's on my mind. Why? asked Bond of himself. There was an answer from his inner voice: Because this lousy island smells of death.

The smell of death was in Anna's nostrils, though she did not recognize it as such. It encroached slowly upon the scented bath powder she had used to sweeten her body in preparation for another lunar field trip with this darkly handsome Israeli of hers. While dusting the peaks of her fine breasts, she became aware of it. Garlic. The odor of garlic.

Then she saw the grinning golden mouth in the mirror. Just as she was about to scream, she heard the voice: "You are going to die, my lovely one." And even though terror-stricken, she began to laugh, irrepressible peal after peal.

The hand squeezed the trigger twice. Anna, still howling at the top of her lungs, fell dying, blood spurting from her stomach on the plush Gulistan Saroyan carpet. The door opened, startling the little man in the gypsy garb, who pushed through the drapes and bolted down the fire escape.

"B & T time again," a cheery Bond called; then froze in horror.

She was still laughing when he found her. "Golden gums... that voice... golden gums... hee hee ha ha....." And she died in his arms.

10
"Ah Got De Blues"

"From all you have told me," said Bon Ami, with honest sympathy, "it adds up to Torquemada LaBonza. The eerie death laugh, her dying reference to 'golden gums.' Yes, it was LaBonza the 'Silent One,' the 'Man with the Golden Gums.'" And he proceeded to fill Bond in on every scrap of information in his file relating to the infamous slaughterer. "I think you've had it on this assignment, Oy Oy Seven. I'll wire M. for another Double-Oy immediately."

"No. I'm seeing this one through... for Anna," said Bond. He sat on the consul's terrace looking at the million and one lights of Vera Hruba. "She got what was intended for me. This is KGB revenge all the way; I can sense it." He crushed his fragile wineglass in his hand, not feeling or caring about the wetness trickling out of his palm's lifeline.

"Please allow me to take care of the final arrangements for Anna."

"Thanks, Bon Ami. And please, put this in the coffin with her. It's my picture. She would have wanted it. Wait," he said, his voice cracking. "Let me write a little something on it."

"Of course."

He scribbled, "To Anna, sincere best wishes, Israel Bond." Then to his host: "I loved her, you know." And he pressed his bloodied hand in Bon Ami's and walked out into the indifferent night.

Ill-tempered, loaded-down burros braying, the supply train wended its way at a crawl through the green hell of the West El Tiparillan jungle. Snow-capped Mount Maidenhead lay six leagues and three chukkers away. Already their clothes were drenched with sweat powerful enough to turn their nylon-fibre garb back into coal, water, and air.

"Must be one hundred and thirty in the shade, for God's sake," grunted Zvi.

"It's one hundred and thirty-five in the shade, to be exact," responded the precise Itzhok Ben Franklin, consulting his thermometer.

"Gottenu!" exclaimed Bond. "I'm afraid to even guess what it is here in the sun."

"Ninety-six."

He slapped at a botfly trying to bore into his neck. "These damn burros are slow as hell. Can't they go any faster?"

"I doubt it," Zvi said. "They're carrying one hundred sacks of matzoh meal, two hundred pounds to a sack."

"What the hell for?" Bond fired back.

"The Peace Corps plans to throw a gigantic Passover Seder meal for the poor in a couple of nights."

"If there's a Peace Corps, you mean. We still have to find little Pablito."

Good lads! he thought. They, of course, knew all about Anna and were trying to make light conversation to take his mind off the awful night. Except Nochum, that little snotnose, who rode ahead, his face an insolent mask.

When the sting pierced his right shoulder he first thought some giant jungle bee had dive-bombed him. Then he saw the puff of smoke and heard Nochum's anguished cry: "Ambush!"

Down dove Bond, flattening his body in the rotting vegetation. "Take cover!" Then there was a sound that set his adrenal glands flowing in terror. The sound of a miniature sort of thunder... and the pounding, earth-shaking sound of a stampede. He knew what it meant.

Buffalo leeches!

The filthy bloodsuckers were on him now, drinking deeply of his claret which poured out of three dozen punctures from ankle to thigh. *Gottenu!* don't let them go higher!

The sound of their munching was drowned out by a sudden horrible scream that trailed off. Nochum! And yells through the green, impenetrable rain-forest walls. "You meet your maker, Israeli dogs! We cut out your tongues, Jews!" Now a strident falsetto: "Marine, tonight you die! Marine, tonight you die!"

An ex-Jap *soldat*, no doubt, fighting the wrong war, he mused, but no less malevolent. *"Banzai gezunt,* Tojo!" he screamed in rebuttal.

"Bond! Over here. I'm hit!" Zvi! His hands frantically trying to cover a dark stain spreading over his shirt front.

"How bad?" said Bond, manfully ignoring his own shoulder wound and the gnawing below.

"Chest. *Oy vay,* it hurts! I was trying to reach poor Nochum. He's had it."

"How?"

"I rode..." Zvi coughed... "up to him when the first shot went off. It's awful, Bond, awful! He's lying face down in a pit... must be a hundred spikes through him."

Bond lit a Raleigh, pressed it to Zvi's blood-flecked mouth. "Poison, too, I'll wager. This must be Vi Teh Minh and his China boys. It's their kind of show. They're jungle fighters, you know."

Zvi inhaled. Thwack! He pitched forward. Now there was a second stain between his shoulder blades. "The last little joke for an old pal, Oy Oy Seven..."

Bond gulped, fighting back scalding tears. "Well, Zvi," he grinned weakly. "You got it in the chest... you got it in the back... and with all that you still haven't had a bellyful."

"Oh, *mommeleh*... I haven't got a bellyful. What a f— mind on that bastard! Oh, *mommeleh*..." his laugh and life gurgled out. Lovable Zvi Gates was dead.

The scum! The f— scum! "All right, you dirty yellow slant-eyed bastards! Uh, no racial derogation intended, fellows." He tore at a ring on his belt. "Let's see how you like a pineapple in your Chink faces." He stood up, cocked his arm, let the pineapple fly square in the face of an oncoming guerrilla. Its spines drilled into his eyes; the rotten insides squirted into the man's mouth. The marauder gagged and ran off vomiting. Good! But at least you'll live, you bastard! It's just a goddam shame it wasn't a grenade, Bond thought.

Wait! HaLavi's package! He raced back to his burro and cut the bundle loose with a slash of his machete. Tearing away the paper, he pulled out a half-dozen jars containing bright red gelatinous matter. "Mother Margolies' Old World Boysenberry Jelly," the labels read.

He tucked the jars into his coat jacket and slid on his belly through the brush, a Jewish fer-de-landsman bent on revenge. Five of them! Grouped about a mortar, one of them about to pump in a shell. "Here, you bastards! Let's have a jam session!" He hurled all six of the jars into the Vi Teh Minh quintet. They went off simultaneously, merging into one red ball of flame. He heard their screams, smelled barbecuing flesh.

"It must be napalm jelly... 'cause jam don't shake like that!" he shouted.

"Bond, over here!" Itzhok now! Was he cashing in his chips as well?

"You all right, kid?"

"I think so. Something's got my foot."

Bond leaned over. "It's a Malay snare. Got your ankle. Don't move. There may be poison on the thorns." He cut it away but, as he did, he noticed Itzhok's face was already bluish in pallor. He slit the *Sabra's* trouser leg, saw a telltale pinprick of a hole near the calf.

"I feel numb, Oy Oy Seven."

"Hold on! Hold on!" He finished cutting off the thornstudded vine. But Itzhok was not answering. And never would again.

I've lost all three... in one swell foop. My gutsy little team is gone. I'm alone in a scorching emerald wilderness, with no men and four dozen stinking burros carrying twenty thousand pounds of matzoh meal. He began to laugh wildly. Any second now he expected a bullet between the eyes. But aside from the hum of insects and the jabbering of howler monkeys, the jungle was silent. Looks like my jelly broke up the traffic jam, he thought. Zvi, would that you could have heard that one, old comrade.

He was starting to feel the loss of blood; heat, hum and howl combined with the moldy odor of the jungle to set his head spinning. He fell into the muck.

Pain! Something sticking in his shoulder.

"Look, angel," he croaked. "I know you have to fasten on my wings, but for God's sake—you should pardon the expression—use Scotch tape. That f— safety pin is killing me."

The figure in white looming above him said, "He's coming out of it, Sister. More sulfa, please."

Bond opened a cautious eye. His angel was a bulky man with warm brown eyes. In a white smock. A doctor! "Who are you?"

"Ben Kildare I ain't. My handle's Marv Browndorf, doctor attached to the ill-fated Peace Corps camp. This lady is Sister Kate. And no shimmy jokes about her. She's heard 'em all."

"Ill-fated?"

"Yes, a column of them hit the camp at the same time the advance guard ambushed you. We heard the noise and came down."

"Where am I?" He reached for a Raleigh.

"You're in a bed at the convent OLEO. They very kindly gave our remaining corpsmen refuge. We've only got six left out of twenty. You, I'm afraid, have none left."

"I know," Bond said. "I saw two of my boys get it. And Spector?"

"There was no time to pull him out of the pit. Besides, there are a couple tons of scavenger ants cleaning up down there. And we had to get you up here fast. Wounds fester like mad here in the tropics. By the way, the monks got your burro train up here. The matzoh's piled up in a nice cool cellar, so don't worry about it."

"That's the least of my worries. But what the hell are monks doing in a convent?"

Dr. Browndorf probed his Johnson & Humphrey Q-tip again into the wound, causing Bond to cry out. "Go ahead. Yell all you want. What are monks doing here? Well, there are some heavy chores around here the sisters can't handle. Besides, these monks are in their sixties. Nice old coots, Brother Thelonius and Brother Julius. I like 'em."

Bond pulled himself up. "Those goddam buffalo leeches...." He looked at his legs, dotted with minute scars.

"Used an old Burmese trick to get rid of 'em. Touched 'em with a lighted cigarette and they fell off. Funny thing, though, I used one of your cigarettes on a single leech and the rest of 'em fell off, curled up and died without even being touched. What do you smoke, anyway?"

"Look, Doc, I've got to get the hell out of here. That kidnapped kid must be found or Israel's name will be mud in El Tiparillo and all of Latin America."

Dr. Browndorf frowned. "You nuts? You've lost blood and you're weak as a kitten. It's beddy-bye for you, Bond."

"Like hell!" and he inched up painfully. "See, I'm standing. Now, get me a horse. I want to nose around this area and there isn't much time."

"It's your funeral," the doctor shrugged. "But good *mahzel* and good hunting, Oy Oy Seven!"

In no hurry at all, and not about to be pushed, was scraggly Old Kemtone, the bag of bones and alleged horse he had borrowed from the considerate monks.

Deliberately it picked its way down the rocky trail to the valley, stopping now and then to nibble the fragrant top of a locoweed bush, whinnying as it chomped the stuff down.

"Well, here I am... on my high horse," he sallied. "Come on, you glorified dachshund. Speed it up."

Old Kemtone answered by rearing up. Bond felt himself flying backwards. Splash! He was up to his neck in a brass monkey-cold mountain stream, ears rocked by the strident lovecalls of the brass monkeys.

As he stood shivering he heard a voice through the roar of the torrent. A sweet and low voice, crooning a soulful old blues song:

> "Ah got de blues; oh Lawd, Ah got de blues,
> Ah said Ah got de blues; oh Lawd, Ah got de blues,
> Oh yeah, Ah got de blues; oh, Lawd, Ah got de blues."

He recognized it in a second. It was one of the great blues torchants of jazz history, titled "Guess What Ah Got?" And that voice? So familiar! Didn't he have a recording of that voice doing that very ditty? Of course!

As he tried to squeeze the information from his fogged mind, he saw near a tree two sensationally formed brown legs, just an enticing flash of thigh... and then he heard a deep growl. There was something tawny and spotted moving out to the end of the tree limb.

Tigre! A powerful jaguar, undisputed king of Latin-American jungles. He heard a tiny frightened "oh" behind the tree. The blues singer was quite aware of the deadly stalker above her, crouched to spring.

Bond waded hip-deep into the frigid waters, unarmed; yet prepared to take the brunt of the snarling cat's lunge. Damn fool! I left HaLavi's new rifle in Old Kemtone's stirrup.

Three hundred yards away was another rifle at the ready, an angry eye pressed against the telescopic lens, the back of Israel Bond's head split neatly in the T-sight. A cheap Delicado cigarette dangled from the lips of Torquemada LaBonza.

He squeezed the trigger just as the *tigre* roared and zeroed in on Bond. The Israeli bent as the cat's paws ripped his shoulders, the foul breath from the decayed flesh in its teeth nearly causing him to pass out.

It was the brow of the *tigre* that was stove in by the soft-nosed bullet from the barrel of the high-powered Tanaka rifle. *El tigre* sank, was borne away by the rushing stream.

"*Merde!*"* groaned LaBonza. His target was now behind the tree, out of range. He climbed back on his rented quarter horse, slipped another quarter into the metered coin box strapped to its neck and rode off. He would bide his time. Another opportunity would come.

"You can come out now, my dear," Bond said. His shoulders ached terribly. The cat's claws had torn into each one. Luckily the epaulets on his Ramar of the Jungle pukkah-sahib jacket had been thick enough to absorb most of the gouging. But he knew from the hot streamlets rolling down each shoulder that *el tigre* had left a partial souvenir.

"One moment more, please." A sweet, well-modulated voice from the other side of the thick foliage. "Well, here I am, sir, and my heartfelt thanks for your selfless act of heroism in saving my unworthy life. My daily bath is rarely interrupted in such a dramatic manner."

Heavenly, utterly heavenly was the face that emerged from behind the tree, that of the most gorgeous Negro girl Israel Bond had ever seen. Two gentian-violet eyes in a finely chiseled setting, chin, nose, lips of classical proportions. All this he noticed moments later. It was her clothes that stunned the exhausted, panting secret agent. His new fascinating companion of the El Tiparillan rain forest was a nun!

---

* "Bad show!"

11
Poems To Touch The Heart, Turn The Stomach

Now Bond's memory came through for him.

"That face, that voice, that song. I remember now. Sid Mark Jazz Disc 190009-V, my most prized waxing. You are the former Sweetcakes Simmons, the world's top jazz *chanteuse,* who deserted the smoky niteries of Manhattan a few years ago to take the vows."

"Yes," she smiled. "Your memory serves you well and it is flattering to be remembered with such warmth. I am that woman, now known as Sister Sweetcakes... more popularly by the public as the Swinging Nun."

"The Swinging Nun!" He could not keep the admiration out of his reply. "Truly, Sister, you have not lost one whit of that puristic sultriness that made you the undisputed queen of the blues. Why did you give it up for this Godforsaken island?"

"You have answered your own query, sir. You said 'Godforsaken.' That is precisely why I am here. There is a burning need for the Lord of Hosts on El Tiparillo. But come. We shall talk as we return to OLEO. You, of course, will be my guest for dinner."

He suddenly lurched, fell forward, his body snagged in the tree.

"Oh, but you are hurt badly. I see blood on your shoulders."

He did not answer. For the second time in as many hours Israel Bond was unconscious.

"Wiseguy, Mr. Supersecret Agent Know-It-All. How damn long can you go on abusing that mighty body of yours?" It was Dr. Browndorf again, hopping mad, yet unmistakable pity showing on his face.... Sister Sweetcakes, her cool fingers on his fevered brow.

"This man is a secret agent, Doctor?"

"Yes, Sister. He is Israel Bond of Eretz Israel. Don't let that boyish look delude you. He kills for a living."

"Oh, dear!" the nun looked horrified. "Such a fine-looking man and so well-spoken. I find that hard to believe."

"It is true. Look after him, Sister, for a while. I must treat our six Peace Corps survivors."

"Then your camp is finished."

"Yes, overrun, burnt to the ground. Perhaps by the same people who snatched poor little Pablito and spread that filthy rumor about the Passover bloodletting."

"Do not worry, Doctor. I shall tend to him."

Bond moaned. "Brandy, Sister Sweetcakes... served in a decanter of Ezra Stoneware at a room temperature of 73.1 degrees."

"There is none, I fear," she said. "But the good brothers do have some homemade wine." She held a goblet to his lips. It was a bitter brew, aged the old Lombardy way, in deep dirty ashtrays. "If you are hungry there is some food, simple, but nourishing. Cheese and bread."

"Monks' Bread, 111 lay you ten to one," he jested, the sight of this amazing woman reviving his zest for life.

"As a matter of fact, it is," she laughed charmingly.

"I can't figure you out, Sister. Beauty, poise, sensitivity. And yet you bury your loveliness in a cowl and habit. Why?"

She pressed a Raleigh into his swollen lips, scratched a match on the heel of her thick black shoe. "It is a dreary story, Mr. Bond. I was at the height of a dazzling career, appearances in the smartest supper clubs, records selling phenomenally, the quarry of rich men of all races pressing diamonds and chinchillas upon me.... I drank too much; indulged in meaningless affairs with men I did not love. A life without purpose or form. I awoke mornings with the taste of dissolution in my mouth."

"I myself have found that Listerine—"

"Then," she went on, not noticing his helpful interjection, "I met a wonderful man, Cardinal Musial, a prince of the

Church, who convinced me that my life could yet have meaning. I became a nun, forsook my empty, glittering, twelve o'clocktail lush life. I have found serenity and hope here at OLEO. Would that my tormented half-brother could find the same."

"Your half-brother?"

"Yes, Beaster Simmons, a man of rare insight and creative genius, who, alas, has been psychologically warped by his hatred of white people. He has changed his name to Baldroi LeFagel and is a leading poet and playwright of the so-called angry school."

"Yes," said Bond. "I seem to recall one of his novels. I have it in a paperback. I found it soul-searing, unsettling. For a moment I was ashamed of being a Caucasian. However, I did purchase a Moms Mabley album. And I took out a subscription to *Muhammud Speaks*."

"What a coincidence!" she brightened. "Baldroi is its night club editor. As a matter of fact, he is—"

"He is here."

There in the doorway was the little bearded man Bond had seen on Tannenbaum's plane. The secret agent's orbs bulged in disbelief. Baldroi LeFagel stood posed like a ballerina, a toe pointed daintily at Bond. He wore an attractive, white Courrèges middy blouse and skirt, with black buttons and piping. His little feet were jammed in that fashion-setter's famed boots. He pirouetted over to Bond's bedside and flicked his hand across Bond's face in contempt. Sister Sweetcakes gasped. He paid her no mind, began to recite:

> *"You negate my existence, Mistuh Charlie Whitey Man,*
> *You have held me in chains since the world began.*
> *You have bruised my flesh and, worse, my psyche,*
> *Let me tell you, Whitey, yo' black slave no likey!*
> *From out of the ghettos there comes the roar,*
> *Of a new black man who knows the score.*
> *We will seethe in your streets, sound trumpet and drum,*
> *I promise you, Whitey, we shall overcome!*
> *And now you're frightened, Mr. Charlie White 'fay,*
> *Of our new-found strength which burgeons each day,*
> *Yes, now you wanna make up for yo' chains 'n' dogs 'n' whips,*
> *I'll make up, yes, on my terms—kiss me on the lips!"*

"Baldroi!" Her voice scourged him. "Mr. Bond is wounded and burning with fever. And he is my guest. Let him be!"

"One sweet kiss?" whimpered LeFagel.

"Begone! You shame me!"

With a wink and "see you later, Whitey, sweetie," the poet exited.

Oy Oy Seven lifted himself. "I must find the boy, Sister. And you must help me."

"Please lie down, Mr. Bond. You must rest."

LeFagel popped back. "Here's my latest, you adorable bitch," and he darted his tongue at Bond. "Dig this, sweet pappy:

> "I have a pet cobra named Alger,
> On his sweet fangs I give him a kiss,
> When I tell him 'bout them bad white folks,
> You should hear Alger hiss!"

The telephone at his bedside erupted. "It's for you, Sister Sweetcakes," Bond said. "Long distance from New York. Somebody named Marty O'Marty from Rock of Ages Records."

"Ah," she smiled. Was there the tiniest trace of longing for the old days in her violet eyes? "Dear Marty. He was my agent and now owns the record company that keeps after me to record a religious album. I may yet yield, Mr. Bond. Our parish here is quite low on funds and Cardinal Musial has given me permission to do it—if it is done tastefully and reverently. It might amuse you to listen in, Mr. Bond."

She placed that divine head next to his and for a moment Bond forgot her sacred calling. What a woman! He could fall in love with a sublime creature like this in twenty seconds. And easily be faithful to her twice as long. Already the memory of Anna, that slattern, was beginning to fade.

"Hiyah, Sister!" The high-pressure voice of a real New York "go-getter."

"Hello, dear Marty."

"Look, Sister. We ain't had a hit album on the charts for two years. Whadda yuh say yuh break down and cut one for good old Rock of Ages, huh? Something with class, naturally, but with an appeal to the wonderful kids who are the principal record buyers in today's market."

"Well, Marty, I—"

"Great! You'll do it! Actually you don't have to pray *that much*, do you? I mean, uh, well, couldn't you maybe cut one o' them lesser masses? I mean, what the hell— uh, no offense, Sister, I'm a good Cat'lic meself... well, you should hear the tunes that me and my A&R man picked out for the date. Dig these, Sister. 'Forget the Baubles 'n' Bangles—Just Give Me the Beads'... that's class... 'I Love Parish'; we kinda rewrote one of them Cole Porter things. He can't sue us now anyway. 'Paul or Nothing At all,' 'I Married an Angel,' 'Nun Domenticar'... somethin' Eyetalian always adds that *distingué laplume de ma tante,* if yuh know what I mean.... 'There's No Place Like Rome,' that's like for the family crowd... old folks buy records, too; I don't knock 'em, believe me.... 'It's Gettin' To Be A Habit with Me'—there's a grabber, a pun 'n' cuter than hell... again, no offense, Sister; I personally got three kids enrolled in the CYO... and we'll send down our hot new group, A Man Called Peter and the Padres, for backgrounds; they'll do the oo-wahs under the melody... plus technicians, equipment... you got a real jungle down there, ain't you, Sister? With birds and monkeys and all that? Maybe like we could even work in some of them in the background with the oo-wahs and rang-a-langs, like the Martin Denny sound, huh? And dig the title of the album: 'I Love Him, Yea, Yea, Yea!' The album cover has you in the nun suit, except you're in a Rolling Stones' wig, see? With a look of reverence on your sweet face, of course; don't get me wrong. So it's all set. The whole bunch, singers, sound men, will be down there in a chartered plane in a day. Uh, if you can spare a moment from divine contemplation... and, God knows, that's important... I ain't knockin' it... uh, maybe you could like rehearse some of the jungle birds and beasties. They'll get union scale, of course. Or we'll donate to any charity dear to your wonderful heart. I'm personally gonna direct this session myself, Sister. Maybe we can get a photo spread outa *True Magazine.* Or maybe even Jim Bishop could come down and write a human interest thing: 'Nun Swings, So Little Children May Walk.' Nice tide, huh? It's got heart. I'll throw to Jimmy; he might dig it. Anyhow it don't hurt to have a Bishop on our side, does it, Sister? Ha! Ha! Little inside joke there. See you soon. Don't take any wooden idols!"

Sister put down the phone, quite dazed. "He's a hard man to say no to, Mr. Bond."

"Wonder if he's interested in a group called the Rocking Rabbis? Or four Anglican caretakers... the Beadles?"

"You have a unique sense of humor, Mr. Bond," the nun observed.

"It's you, Sister. You bring out the best in me. But now to business. I've got to find that child. Any leads for me?"

"Yes. One. The last time he was seen he was playing in the vicinity of that godless place, the Temple of Hate."

"Then that's where I'm going tonight."

"No!" she cried. "In your condition? And even if you were healthy, you can't go wandering about this unfamiliar jungle at night."

"Perhaps," Bond suggested, "you would guide me there. I'd be glad of the company, Sister, especially yours."

Her eyes grew soft. "I can't let you stumble in there alone. Meet me in front of OLEO after evening vespers."

He pressed her hand; then on an impulse lifted it to his lips.

"You mustn't..." she said in a tiny voice.

"Tonight then. The Temple of Hate... and Dr. Nu."

12
A Good Skate

A far more tractable beast under the familiar guidance of the nun, Old Kemtone clopped his cantrece nylon hooves at a leisurely clip, Bond and Sister Sweetcakes wedged in the deep trough of his swayed back. So emaciated was the horse that Bond thought he was sitting upon a xylophone and indeed, by certain posterior movements he was able to play "I'm Walking Behind." Both he and Sister were silent, though they felt the mysterious beginnings of a subtle electricity between them. This incandescent creature, his heart told him, was the supreme example of womanhood. Could Corporal Annatevkah at her best ever have matched this magnificent specimen of physicality and soul? He felt in his shirt pocket for the garnet ring he had very sensibly taken from Anna's dying hand. Life and love must go on, Bond, he told himself, and one doesn't splurge on nearly a tenth of a carat every day.

Halfway down to the Valley of the Blind, the strains of a familiar operetta filtered through the liana vines and odiferous *johni-johni* trees.

"It is from Camp Camp," she informed him. "Each night the artists and musicians put on some kind of a production for their guests. Usually, they take some well-known musical work and augment it with highly modern touches."

Bond's powerful field glasses were trained on an open air stage. "I know the music. I see a mezzo-soprano singing an aria from Oscar Straus' *The Chocolate Soldier*."

"'My Hero,' I believe," Sister added.

"Correct. 'My Hero' it is. Only she is singing it to a gigantic Italian sandwich cradled in her arms."

They heard the cries of the audience exhorting the singer on to new artistic heights: "Let's go, mezzo! Let's go, mezzo!"

"From this point on it can be dangerous, Mr. Bond," she said. "There are many guards in the vicinity of the temple."

I won't worry, he thought. HaLavi's new rifle looks to have the firepower of a whole regiment. It was strapped to the horse's side, 75 Melba rounds in the magazine. Bond glanced at its unusual stock, four times wider than any he'd ever handled. He knew why and grinned. That HaLavi genius!

I could use that genius tonight, he conceded. This mystery and my problems are mushrooming by the minute. Where is the boy? Which of the three dead Israelis had masqueraded as Rotten Roger Colfax, the traitor? Or was Roger none of them at all? Who is this Dr. Nu and why has he chosen to make money out of the bigotry in this world? That shot that killed *el tigre*... was it fired by LaBonza? And Sister Sweetcakes... does she know what I feel for her? Could she give up this ennobling but barren way of life and take my hand forever? Will the cost of the Annatevkah woman's funeral be deducted unfairly from my salary?

"We are here," the nun whispered.

"Stay here with this noble steed. Or better still, Sister, get thee to thy nunnery. It's my show from here on in."

"May God go with you, Israel Bond."

"See you in church, Sister. Mine, I hope."

Pushing two branches aside, he got his first glimpse of the Temple of Hate bathed in the whiteness of a full moon that imparted a chalky patina to its gangrenous green-grey walls.

It was approximately two hundred feet tall, he estimated, with Byzantine-style minarets standing like spears at each of its four corners. From a number of windows light blazed and drunken voices sang cursed and shouted. The hate set is having a wingding tonight, he thought. Pretty soon they'll be swapping all the "Jew-boys" jokes: "Hey, Abie, vash der toilet paper; der landlord says ve got to move." Yes, Bond, you try to push the brotherhood bit all your life, go out of your way to fit in, but you meet rejection wherever you go. But what else can you expect from *goyim*?

Drop the philosophy of alienation bit, Oy Oy Seven; there's a job to be done.

He tied handkerchiefs over his shoes to muffle his footsteps and walked into a large paved area between the edge of the jungle and the temple. For cars? No, there were none around. A place to land a helicopter, more likely. As if to confirm his suspicion, he heard the chopper far off and flattened his body in the shadows cast by the pillars of the main entrance.

It came down a minute later. Out stepped a short man in a sporty Tyrolean-type Adams hat with a sprig of edelweiss stuck into the brim and a black trenchcoat, his face hidden by its pulled-up collar. Two Orientals in ski-type outfits, rifles slung over their shoulders, walked out of the doorway to greet him. Then up went the chopper in a swift vertical climb.

Whoever the visitor was he seemed to be accorded the highest respect. Bond could make out the guards' voices now.

"A pleasure to see you back, Rotten Roger, sir. Dr. Nu has been anxiously awaiting you. You'll be pleased to know that the Russian courier dropped off the million rubles today."

Rotten Roger Colfax! So there he was. And obviously not one of my poor dead lads, thank heaven!

The trio walked into the temple but, just before the door slammed thunderously, he heard a fragment of a sentence. "... greatest terror organization the world has ever known" and something that sounded like "Spector."

Spector? Were they making some callous jibe about little Nochum's agonizing end in the stake-lined pit? Wait a second, Bond. "Greatest terror organization the world has ever known." Could it be true? Yes, you dunce. There are *two* words pronounced like Nochum's surname and one of them is spelled— SPECTRE! Then the fabled organization of infinite evil was a reality! Naturally, it would have been the diabolical agency behind Pablito's kidnapping, the attack on the Israeli camp, the murders of Zvi, Itzhok and Nochum. Paid handsomely for these foul services by the Russians (he had already heard of one Russki payoff) and probably behind every significant act of terrorism and revolution on this benighted island. No doubt the Chinese and Fidelistas were kicking into the SPECTRE treasury, too. It made sense. If anything ever went awry there would be no proof of their involvement in these heinous undertakings.

If he had not been so engrossed in unraveling the puzzle, he would have seen the six-inch isosceles scorpion coming down the door, springing onto his neck and—arrgh!—its venomous sting flaying his wounded shoulder. He brushed it off with a shiver, ground his heel into it until it was a mashed heap of protein. Except for the diamond-hard black disc in the middle of the mess. Another transistor 'bug'! They know I'm here; *Katz* is out of the bag!

An alarm sounded in the temple, sending a bevy of uniformed Orientals vaulting out with brandished carbines. Shots echoed through the night, one of them kicking up a chunk of cement and hurling it into his face, opening a gash on his cheek. He kneeled, aimed HaLavi's rifle.

Zetz! Zetz! Zetz! The Moishe Dyan model spoke its message three times; that many guards fell screaming. Good! Now three from Column B! But more were swarming out as the alarm went off again. He saw a flash, felt a hot projectile skin his ankle. There were two dozen of them now, lined up between Bond and the edge of the paved strip. Beyond it lay the safety of the thick jungle. How to get past them? No time to stop and pick them off. Too many!

Israel Bond's brain clicked out a solution in a microsecond. His finger jabbed at a button in the huge rifle stock. Four wheels slid out of the wood and Bond was now standing atop a skateboard!

He crouched low over it, pushed his toe into the cement, kicked out to pick up momentum and smashed through the first line of guards. He felt nails futilely tearing at his face as he bowled them over. Now he was ramming into the second line, the Dyan firing automatically, ripping ankle bones and insteps, as the skateboard sped on.

A few feet more and freedom! But at the jungle's edge he saw a figure slip out from behind a *yeki-yeki* bush. It kneeled in the classic rifleman's position, bent a finger.

Bond ducked. In time to save his life; too late to avoid being hit altogether. Torquemada LaBonza's Tanaka sang its *saki! saki!* One slug creased the dark, cruelly handsome forehead and Bond went down face first in the cement.

The last thing he remembered, before a blessed Ken Murray blackout, was lying on the airstrip looking blearily at a pair of elegant brocaded Chinese sandals with curled-up toes.

And a mocking voice: "Welcome to the Temple of Hate, Mr. Israel Bond. My leader and I have been expecting you. I am Dr. Nu."

13
Herbie

"I shall give you a capsulized history of my illustrious life, Mr. Bond," said the cool articulate voice of Dr. Nu to the bound Bond, who sat in a chair, blood dripping from his shoulder, ankle, and head into a pool on the floor, a feast for a herd of buffalo leeches and a vampire bat on a silken tether, the other end tied about the Chinaman's right hand. "Drink sparingly of this rich Jewish blood, my beloved bat, Masterson," the doctor said fondly to his pet. "Too much and you'll get diabetes."

"I don't think I'm particularly interested in your life," Oy Oy Seven said with a stiffness that matched that of his ripped aching body. "So get on with whatever you've dreamed up for me."

"Not interested, Mr. Bond?" Dr. Nu's rebuke was mild, which made it all the more menacing. "Topjob, put our celebrated guest in the proper frame of mind for history."

Gottenu! A bludgeon split the side of his cheek, reopening the wound. It was the calloused side of a hand swung by a stocky Asiatic in a loose-fitting white robe.

"Meet my personal bodyguard. Topjob, so named because his favorite libation is an American liquid detergent of some potency. Like myself he is half-Chinese, born in Korea, and extremely adept at karate. He holds a black belt. Everyday he practices for an hour, chopping those awesome hands into Del Monte's creamed corn."

"How in hell can they get so callused from hitting creamed corn?"

"It is still in the can. Excellent work, Topjob. As a reward you may eat the leeches and Masterson. *Sayonara,* old bat."

Bond took his first good look at Dr. Nu. He was an unbelievable caricature of a man, bigger than life; from the tip of his curled-up toes to the green velvet Mitsubishi hat he must have easily stood six feet six inches. His face jarred Bond. Only one of the eyes was slanted. And his hair was a most un-Oriental ash blond. The bean pole body was clad in a dazzling long coat of Cantonese silk and black pajamas. On the coat were superb Hakusai water colors of great moments in Far Eastern history; Genghis Kahn playing handball off the Great Wall of China, a sad-eyed Buddha contemplating his navel, obviously having no ball, and another depicting two giant mastiffs with the remains of a Baptist minister in their cruel jaws, which Bond guessed was a depiction of the Boxer Rebellion.

"I," began his captor, "am the son of a Singapore opium merchant, Nu Nu, who sold the flower juice of happiness from his boat outside the jurisdiction of the British harbor police. The craft was known throughout all Southeast Asia as 'Nu Nu's Junk Junk.' My father, whilst on a business trip to London, fell in love with a buxom English music hall dancer, Tessie Watts; bedded with her. I am the illegitimate product of that night of shame, named for both of them. My name is Watts Nu.

"My father hated me from birth when the evidences of my mother's lineage, the unslanted eye, the blond hair, began to crop up on my body. I spent a dismal childhood, scorned by people of both races... a *chi-chi*, as the British call half-breeds... an outcast. Though he loathed me, my father, traditionally responsible as all Chinese fathers are, did see to all my wants and had me educated at the Jean Hersholt College of Medicine in Hopei. So highly was I regarded by my professors that they convinced the DuPont Corporation to underwrite my experiments with a new type of chemical aphrodisiac which even today is selling by the millions. You have no doubt purchased it yourself upon occasions. Erectex?"

"Yes," said Bond. "With the slogan 'Better Loving Through Chemistry.' Go on, Doctor, I now find your story fascinating."

That's it, Bond, use your chicken noodle. Flatter this maniac; gain precious time to figure a way out.

"But mere wealth meant nothing to me, Mr. Bond. One thing alone kept me groping through a hostile environment that denied me love, affection and understanding—the thought of revenge. Revenge upon my father, my mother, the whole rotten structure of mankind."

"Was there no one to give you sympathy?" asked Bond, genuinely touched despite his predicament. "There are many fine therapists who might have helped you make an adjustment, find some beauty and meaning."

"Charlatans! Amateurish dabblers in a mystery too profound for their shallow minds! But there was one," and a strange mist came over those incongruous eyes, "who might have helped. I poured out my heart, my frustration, my fears in a thirty-eight-page letter to her. A letter that began 'Dear Abby'... and when she did not deign to answer," his voice rose to a crescendo of fury, "I knew I had squandered my valuable time on a moment of weakness! I pulled up stakes and came to this island where I purchased this broken-down pagoda and turned it into a resort for hate groups, wisely deducing there was a market for this kind of enterprise. At last there is a place where the world's malcontents, with whom I feel a camaraderie, can come for two weeks at a time and rest up for their campaigns. It also serves as an excellent front for a terror organization—"

"SPECTRE," Bond said.

"Ah, you have overheard something you should not have. But it will be of no benefit to you, Mr. Bond. Yes, that is the name. And it is headed by an unique individual whom I met in..." he paused, "I don't think I'll tell you where... but it was a year ago. He is an acknowledged master in the intelligence field and I defer to him because of his organizational genius. His hatred of mankind surpasses even mine, my friend, and together we have made a joint pact. Our goal comes nearer with each passing day."

"What is that goal, Dr. Nu?"

"To rule the world, what else? And we shall! Our organization consists of three-man teams in key spots in every land, people who are totally corrupt and ruthless, who believe as my leader and I do. Among them are three top television executives and three professional football scouts in America, three used car dealers in Canada, three ex-members of Mosley's fascist party in Great Britain, three South African penny whistle players in Jo'burg, a trio of French waiters in Lyons, three rapacious ski instructors at Saint Moritz, three scientists who defected from Red China and are working on a bomb with the destructive force of one hundred wontons (Bond shuddered)... but I could go on all night."

"Have you ever considered that your Communist paymasters have their own vision of world domination and might not take too kindly to you if they found out about yours?"

Dr. Nu's smile was one of superior unconcern. "That possibility has been considered. But they do not know of the scope and purpose of our organization and believe we are content to foment these insurrections for mere money. They are unaware of the bomb we soon will have at our disposal and our even more powerful weapon, the world's most formidable army which I have created. You have already been thwarted by their espionage."

"The insects?"

"Yes, you see..."

There was a scream and two of the sinister Oriental guards came into the room, a struggling hooded figure dragged between them.

"A snooper, Dr. Nu, discovered by one of our centipede sentinels outside the temple," said one with deference.

"You see," Dr. Nu chuckled. "Our allies are ubiquitous, Mr. Bond. Let us see who has blundered into our net." And he lifted the hood.

It was —Sister Sweetcakes!

"Sister, you sweet fool! I told you to go back to OLEO! Take your hands off her, you damn yellow swine!"

"Release her. She cannot cause us harm," the doctor stated placidly.

"Mr. Bond," she started; then let go a sob. "I could not let you face this alone." And buried that ethereal face in her hands.

Dr. Nu looked at her for a moment. "Your entrance, Sister, coincides with one of my daily rituals, not as devout as yours, perhaps, but far more interesting. It is time to make Herbie happy."

"Herbie?" Bond hoped the doctor would not sense the alarm in his query.

"Yes, one of my dearest friends from a singularly isolated sector of jungle in the heart of the Amazon Basin. But come let us meet Herbie, dear guests."

A guard's cutters nipped off the biting strands of Anaconda Copper wire that bound his legs to the chair. (And I own fifty shares of the damn stuff, he thought, with justifiable bitterness.) He felt the blood slowly circulating again, squeezed his toes together to facilitate the process.

They were led by the guard and their giant host down a dark corridor; then up a winding flight of stairs to a door marked "Laboratory."

It opened to reveal a gleaming white laboratory. There were lab tables containing test tubes of various sizes, complicated machinery, something Bond took to be a computer, and a huge circular conference table topped with vases of heady jungle flowers.

"I shall explain that machine to you shortly, Mr. Bond, after we pay our respects to Herbie."

At the end of the laboratory was a door. "It is quite aromatic in there, my friends, but you will become accustomed to it quickly."

He opened it. They were in a huge greenhouse, moist and laden with the pungent smells of rain forest plants of which there were an exotic variety.

"This," said Dr. Nu, pointing to a green snake of a rope potted and tied to a long stick, "is the Malaysian death vine which claimed one of your Israelis, I believe. The genus *tutti cammarata,* as it is known in Latin. Do not go near the thorns. You have already witnessed their efficacy. They pierce the skin, injecting a derivative of the *larosa semolina* toxin. And this—" he bent to pick up a small clay pot—"holds a tiny species of Jamaican flora called the night-blooming day shade. From its seeds can be made a drug that draws the color out of the skin, nerves, and vital organs, a necessary first step toward achieving the state of invisibility. There is a minor drawback, however. The bones are turned kelly green. The only practical use I have discovered for it as yet is selling skeletons for Irish Halloween parties. And," the round eye twinkled to its slanted partner, "here is Herbie."

It was a plant, even taller than the doctor, and, as they approached it, it came alive! Several leaf-covered tendrils began a seductive swaying as though they were the enticing arms of a belly dancer.

"This is as close as all of us but one shall get," said the doctor.

"All right," Bond said. "It should be dancing at the Roundtable. Nu, Dr. Nu? I'm getting sick of this charade."

"I could not agree with you more, Oy Oy Seven," Dr. Nu said. "But Herbie's accomplishments go beyond simple manipulations of his handsome arms. Herbie is, incidentally, a nickname. His full moniker, as they say in those cowboy and Indian thrillers, is *herbis homnis fressoris*... man-eating plant."

From somewhere deep in Herbie's green depths came a rumble... and something that sounded like a slurp!

"He knows why we are here, Mr. Bond."

"Oh." Sister sagged in the arms of the guards. "Let it be me—not him. Let it be me."

Bond's voice was a tremulous choke. "All right, take her away and get it over with, you fiend! Don't subject her to any more of this."

"But, Mr. Bond." The polished voice held a note of surprise. "You completely misunderstand. I am going to take Sister up on her offer. It is she who will furnish Herbie with his banquet tonight. I have something subtler in mind for you." He turned to the guards. "Throw her in!"

"I'll kill you all, you—" Bond roared, a red ray of anger across his eyes. He closed the fingers of his bound hands into one fist, brought it up savagely under the jaw of one of the Orientals, experiencing a sweet fierce joy as the fist drove the man's teeth through his tongue. The other, however, had side-stepped his desperate rhinolike charge and brought the butt of his Wembly-Vicar automatic against Bond's head. Oy Oy Seven fell woozily on all fours, felt himself being dragged out of the greenhouse, knees rubbed raw by the Armstrong mosaic title floor.

His last, despairing look was on Sister. Screaming, she was enveloped in three of Herbie's tentacles, a primordial sucking sound coming from heaven alone knew what part of that revolting anatomy.

Then the door shut. And there was only Dr. Nu, arms folded, eyes aglow with a dreamy madness as her screams grew fainter, then ceased.

14
Summit Conference

There were new bonds for Bond now. The wire was gone; in its stead were Fibreglas straps around his wrists, chest, and legs restraining him in a high-backed chair. *Electric? No, I can't believe this is the subtlety to which the maniac alluded. There's something a damn sight more devilish in that crazed brain.*

The room was the white laboratory adjoining the greenhouse where adorable Sister Sweetcakes... *but there's nothing to be gained by thinking about her now*, he reasoned. *Steel yourself, buddy boy, it's your turn.*

His wounds had been dressed (modishly, in the latest Johnson & Johnson flesh-toned Band-Aids) by the doctor, who apparently had lost none of his medical skill. Dr. Nu reclined in a contour chair of Skelton-Red leather set in the center of the circular conference table. A bottle of Ballantine, the spirited beer, was at his side; he took frequent gulps from it and drags from the tube of a carved ivory hookah, blowing out three connected rings at a time. Topjob, who shot malicious glances at Bond, knelt at his master's feet, rubbing them with Dixie Peach Pomade.

"You are to be accorded a rare privilege, Mr. Bond, and this is because I have learned to hold you in utmost respect for your courage and derring-do. Singlehandedly you have killed three of my security force, wounded several others. But your foolhardy foray into my affairs was doomed from the start."

"What is this privilege, Dr. Nu?"

"That of witnessing my unparalleled genius. I want you to meet another friend of mine, one of my own making." A yellow index finger pointed to the computer, which stood like a silent soldier, its memory banks and switches ready to do its master's bidding. "This is IPECAC."

"What?" Bond's ears refused to believe what he had heard.

"Insect Programmed Electronic Computer for Analyzing Conversation. In short, Mr. Bond, I can talk to insects."

"Now I know you're mad, Dr. Nu. I am willing to admit that 'bugging the bugs' is a unique method of obtaining information. One would never suspect the wayward roach, the frolicking June bug to be spies. But—"

A slight nuance of contempt crossed that composed face. "Mr. Bond, you are tough, resourceful, and clever... up to a point. Yet your mind fails to comprehend the spheres in which my work leads me. I shall give you a demonstration that will save me thousands of words."

He flicked a red switch. A light glowed; Bond's ears suddenly felt a sharp pain, heard an unearthly electronic atonality. "You will find the pain subsiding in a few seconds as your ears adjust to the frequency." He spoke into a microphone. "Sectional commanders will report to the conference table on the double!"

I am as *tzoodrayt* as this yellow Eiffel Tower of a nut, Bond told himself. I must be. I see a parade creeping over the floor, a line of insects! Crawling, hopping, flying low. I hear humming, chirping, buzzing... they're making their way up the legs of the conference table, aligning themselves in set positions... the doctor has pushed another switch... miniature microphones are popping out in front of each bug... and name plates... "JAPANESE BEETLE," "CICADA," "LOCUST," "MOSQUITO," "TSETSE FLY".... *Gottenu!* This looks like an insect—

"Summit conference, Mr. Bond," said Dr. Nu with a pleased smile. "That is what you're thinking, isn't it? Before we proceed with the agenda, I'll just"—he turned off the red switch—"cut the frequency so they cannot hear us. In précis, here is the theory that led me to this marvelous discovery and IPECAC.

"As you know, I am a scientist, the world's greatest, you now must concede. As a friendless unwanted child I spent countless lonely hours. Time hung heavy upon my hands, but even at that stage I possessed a boundless intellectual curiosity about my environment. I spent many hours stretched out upon the carpet of the great forest observing nature's littlest creatures scuttle about, make love, kill, die. And I began to notice that all of them would pause momentarily in the presence of their own or other species to move their feelers, antennae, palpi or rub their legs together. This, I deduced, was some kind of language based on sound. Sound that could be heard, as in the case of the crickets; sound that couldn't, i.e., worms, beetles, aphids, termites, etc. Since various insects made certain moves, displayed certain attitudes in the presence of others, I further reasoned there must be an insect Swahili, a lingua franca, known to all such creatures. It was an interesting theory but one I put aside in some dark recess of my mind for future reference. Three years ago I recalled it; launched a series of experiments to validate it. The key word, let me repeat, was 'sound.' Yet, as I stated previously, not all of their sounds were audible, at least to my normal aural range. So I hit upon the felicitous idea of using the most sensitive sound reproduction equipment ever assembled, which could not only discern sound thousands of decibels below human hearing but boost it to our level. You will be surprised to learn that the only equipment capable of this most delicate pickup and boost is to be found solely in the chassis of a 1949 Muntz television set. Now that I could distinguish the sound I began to observe, as I had in my childhood, the different moves of insects, correlating sound and action, until I discovered the fact that though each insect had its own distinct sound it also had a universal one. Thus I began to construct their common language after many months of observing, note-taking, cataloguing. And IPECAC was born. It can do many things, Mr. Bond, because its memory banks have been fed enormous quantities of information about the major orders of insecta. IPECAC hears, reproduces sound to my level, feeds sound to its banks, translates into all major human tongues—I have pressed the English one for your benefit and mine—and reverses the procedure when I wish to communicate with them. But I will show you." Switch back on, he cried: "Hello, little friends!"

Israel Bond thought, I'm mad for sure. For in response to the doctor's salutation he saw the waving and scraping of insect appendages commence in unison; heard them—sing!

> "Hippity hop, hutsut, rainbow roo,
> Siboneyeh skippity, we love you.
> What 'ere you ask we'll gladly do,
> 'Cause we sure love you, Dr. Nu."

Unbelievable! Scores of insects chanting a childish doggerel to a beloved Romper Room teacher! What's next? he wondered. Will they pull out tiny copies of *My Weekly Reader* and find out if Dick and Jane are pummeling Baby? And that Spot has rabies? And has been making it with Robin Hound?

"Thank you, my creatures," said the doctor benignly. "And now we shall open our seminar with a discussion of how you can help your dear doctor and his leader take over this earth. First, may we hear the scout reports?"

The lighted name plate "HONEYBEE" went on. "I have been buzzing around the convent, Dr. Nu. The Israelis have been given shelter by the monks. They are without weapons, ripe for attack."

"Excellent!" cried Dr. Nu. "I shall contact the main Chinese, Fidelista and Russian Forces in EET and order them to infiltrate tomorrow night across The Band. They will launch a three-pronged attack and wipe out the remaining Israelis and the convent as well. These sanctimonious swine have been a stumbling block and a divisive influence with their insidious good deeds."

HONEYBEE flashed again. "Doctor, I have a distressing personal problem. These continual long-range spy flights have decimated me. My wings are worn to a frazzle, my strength gone."

"Fly over here, little friend," Dr. Nu said kindly, and HONEYBEE made a waspline toward him. "Here," he opened his hand and placed a pill in its palm with the other. "Eat this. A vitamin to restore your health."

"What did you give it?"

"What else, Mr. Bond? Bee-complex."

"Of course."

Now there was a beep as name plate "TICK" lit up. "Doc, will you please tell that goddam CANTHARIS to keep his horny legs off me? You think he gives a crap for our conference? To him it's just an excuse to ball, ball, ball...."

"CANTHARIS, please desist from these unwholesome activities at once!" the doctor ordered.

"Doc," CANTHARIS pleaded. "I got this Spanish fly built in. Can I help it?" And the voice grew suggestive. "Hey, GRASSHOPPER, that's a sweet leg you got there. Let me bite it, baby."

Bond heard a scream from GRASSHOPPER. "Please... no! No!" Dr. Nu's forefinger poked a button. There was a puff of smoke. The "CANTHARIS" name plate and microphone disappeared. "I regret the disruption," said the doctor, "but we all will agree that CANTHARIS, due to no fault of his own, had to be eliminated. Such as he have no usefulness in this organization."

SCORPION cut in. "Doc, that Israeli trussed up over there... ain't he the one that squashed my poor cousin, Jethro, a while back? Let me give the murdering bastard the back of my tail... a little sting-a-ding-ding-dingaroonie!"

"Leave his fate to me, my little ally from Durango. I shall see to it that your kind is revenged in full."

"Say, Doc." LOCUST was speaking now, and Bond could detect a touch of wariness, even hostility. "What's in all of this for us? All I can see is we're the patsies... the guys who die like flies, you should pardon the expression, flies, while you get this globe handed to you on a plate."

"I had anticipated that very natural question from one of you," said the doctor with the pleasant air of a lecturer about to make a point. "It is true that I shall benefit from your labors, dear insects, but you, too, stand to do the same. For instance, you, LOCUST, you and your brethren, shackled by a ludicrous tradition, only swarm once every seventeen years. Why, pray tell, waste those sixteen in slumber? A triumph for me insures you a free hand—or wing—every year at mankind's bursting granaries, wheat fields, canebrakes untroubled by meddlesome humans with their killing pesticides. HOUSEFLY, would you not enjoy unfettered flight in any human domicile, knowing that those sticky ribbon deathtraps were gone forever? CARPET BEETLE, think of it... the world's fattest, juiciest woolen rugs, thousands of warehouses filled with them, and all at your disposal. MOTH, would it not give you the most exhilarating sensation to gorge yourself on Jerry Lewis' three hundred mohair suits? You see, we have a mutuality of interest here."

"I cannot agree to this thing."

Shocked, all eyes, human and insect, focused on the illuminated name plate "JAPANESE BEETLE."

"Prease to accept humbre aporogy, but cannot be a party to destruction of my beroved Dai Nippon. I go now in peace, yiss, Dr. Nu?"

The answer was a terse, "No."

JAPANESE BEETLE met the same fate as CANTHARIS. A yell of agony, the sickening odor of singed beetle flesh, and it was over. "That also was necessary," the doctor sighed. "If there are no further items, we shall conclude with the singing of our stirring anthem, 'Larva Come Back to Me.'"

As the insects propped themselves up into a humanlike posture of attention and shrilled their song, Bond's thoughts were off his pain-racked body. That computer! If only I could get to it! The seed of a scheme was germinating in his brain.

Dr. Nu watched his horde slink and fly off.

"Can you deny now, Oy Oy Seven, that you, indeed, have been accorded a rare privilege?"

"No. I suppose I shall pay for it in some equally diabolical manner, eh, Dr. Nu?"

"Yes, Israel Bond. Your moment has come." And he clapped his hands. "Topjob! Activate the WC!"

15
David And Goliath

"Is this to be my fate, Doctor? Drowning by immersion in a water closet? Really, it is unworthy of your salt."

"Silence, unthinking fool! Did you think I would squat to such a plebeian level? WC is yet another device, Mr. Bond. It stands for Will Chiller. I had not planned to destroy that muscular body of yours which seems to have an extraordinarily high tolerance of pain. Besides, I can utilize that body in our organization. You will work your valorous deeds for us, Mr. Bond."

"Never!"

"Oh, yes. But first there is the matter of breaking your indomitable will, bending it to our purposes. And this the Will Chiller will do. Ready it, Topjob."

The doctor's aide grinned wickedly at Bond, revealing bloodied teeth filed to a point. He took something out of his robe pocket and munched on what Bond took to be one of the bat, Masterson's, wings. Then he wheeled over a machine on rollers that seemed to be some sort of television set. On its front was a large glass screen with two large buttons below. One was marked "WD," the other "WR."

"Plug it in, Topjob. I can see you are trying to figure out the abbreviations, Mr. Bond. The first is 'Will Destroyer.' When it is switched on and the subject exposed to the images its built-in tapes bring to the screen, that unhappy person will find his senses departing from him in five minutes. At that juncture, the power is cut off because any further exposure would leave the subject a useless mental vegetable. WR is 'Will Restorer,' built into the machine for my own personal use while I was testing the system. It saved my own life, Mr. Bond, when I carelessly let myself be exposed too long. With my last microdot of sanity I pushed it and became rational again. But we are wasting time. Topjob... the WD button, please."

A pinpoint of light danced on the screen; then spread into a white intensity that flooded away the black.

"Shucks, Jed Clampett. You don't mean ter tell me thar's oil in that thar land?" The speaker on the screen was a scraggly-haired woman in a calico dress. Her question was followed by howls of laughter, from an unseen audience. "What's so funny about that? Bond wondered. "Yup," said a rural-type man with a sunburned face. More uncontrollable laughter; another puzzlement to Bond. "Well, I guess we-uns is rich!" chortled the woman, smacking her backside with a good-natured flourish. More audience laughter; one of the women was shrieking at the top of her lungs.

It faded, supplanted by a pert snub-nosed charmer whose moist lips kept repeating: "Dippity-Do.... Dippity-Do.... Dippity-Do."

From another world he heard Dr. Nu: "One minute."

Now the face on the screen was that of a jolly, bespectacled little man in a pin-stripe suit and straw hat. "What makes you think you're worthy of being our Queen of Misery today, Mrs. Ruth Kurtzer of Buzzard's Bladder, North Dakota, any more than Mrs. Ray Abney, our hunchback from Rufus Jarman, Tennessee, or Mrs. Hilda Shivers, the plucky but hopelessly braindamaged housewife from Cooze Corners, Maine?" "Well, I'll tell yer, Mr. Nelson... I crawled here on muh arthritic legs all the way from Dakoty, with them cars runnin' over my poor chilblained hands, jes' so's I could tell yuh about my spavined son, Chesley, who is feelin' po'ly and needs an operation real bad so's he can harvest the crops in time to make the mortgage payment to hard-hearted Squire Taliaferro." "What do you think, audience?" cried the little man. "Is she the queen?" Booing and catcalling broke out; a brick thrown on-stage smashed the woman in her old grey head. "Guess not," shrugged the little man. "Let's bring on our last contestant, Mrs. Louise Wieczorek of Chauquatauchauqua, Oklahoma, our thalidomide-taking mother who fears that..."

"Two minutes," said Dr. Nu, inhaling his hookah tube.

An emotion-packed voice. "Yes, this fall you'll thrill to the dramatic series of a man searching for himself, Shelley Keats, a new face that will haunt your memory forever, in the role of Flapjack Huggins, a Texas medico-scuba diver with amnesia and incurable conjunctivitis, falsely accused of leaving his comrades to die in the Alamo, a Dallas motel, in 1959. Ride, walk, and swim with Flapjack Huggins and his laughable side-kick, Waco, as he seeks for thirty-nine or seventy-eight episodes the man who smeared his name. Thrill to every episode of *Branded Forgetful Underwater Intern Who Rides, Walks and Swims for His Life.*"

Bond's cruelly handsome face was undergoing a startling transformation into a clownish moronic simper.

"Three minutes," said Dr. Nu.

"Geez, Gidget." The gawky young teener on the screen fought to keep the tears from running into his pimples. "You mean you forgot you promised to go to the prom with me and now you're going with Barney Kincaide, the smartest, handsomest boy in the class... even after I drove my hot rod off the cliff to impress you 'n' ever'thing?" More riotous laughter from nowhere. "Well, I... I..." stammered the pixieish blonde sweetheart of Wollstonecraft Junior High. "Did I do something wrong, Daddykins, did I?" A man in a tweed smoking jacket puffed his pipe. "I don't know, sweetheart. I'm just your schmuck of a father. Ask mommy. She knows everything. She'll pull you out of this jam like she does every week on this matriarchally oriented situation comedy show."

"Four minutes," said Dr. Nu. Bond's eyes were rolling around, tongue sliding in-and-out. "You may unbind his hands now, Topjob; he has been rendered harmless. I don't want him to lacerate his wrists on his straps in his frenzy."

"Certs is a candy mint." "No, Certs is a breath mint!"

"Let Certs Hertz you in the driver's seat!"

"You mean to say that if the cobalt bomb destroys the world, you'll still cover my losses? H-m-m, John Hancock, huh?"

"How'd you like a nice Hawaiian punch?" Pow! "Fruit juicy, fruit juicy, Dippity Do, Dippity Do..."

The face of Bond was frozen into a mindless ear-to-ear grin. His thumb was on his nose, four fingers waving in cadence. He was humming "The Doublemint Gum" song.

"Ten seconds more, Topjob, and Secret Agent Israel Bond will be our unwitting tool."

With a sob and a rush of breath a hooded figure leaped between them; jammed a finger into the WR button.

On the screen—a handsome man in a well-cut Jackie Gordon suit, his face full of urbanity, tenderness, intelligence, wit—all the qualities present in the best of Twentieth Century man—smiled: "Good evening. This is *Open End* and my name is David Susskind. Our panel discussion tonight is on the subject, 'Will Automation, Carried to the Extreme, Throw Millions of Computers Out of Work?,' and to probe this unique problem of our times I have asked the following panelists to appear tonight—Leonard Bernstein, Arthur Fiedler and the entire Boston Pops Orchestra, Nipsey Russell, Arlene Francis and, for comedy relief, Hugh Downs."

From the first outpourings of that mellifluous, cultured voice of sweet reason, Bond had felt the horrible banalities of button *WD* fleeing his brain like frightened Lucky Thompson gazelles in the path of a Kenya brush fire. And those intellectual names! Bernstein! Francis! Russell! Each one a torch of truth and knowledge, burning away his torpor.

He was a steely spring again, lashing out with cast-iron hands on the jaws of the nonplussed Topjob, sending the killer karateist crashing into the wall.

A cold grey eye snapped a photo of the enraged Dr. Nu struggling with the slight hooded figure who had saved Bond from insanity. He battered the doctor's midsection, fists flailing with devastating potency. Dr. Nu said, "Ugh!," doubled up in agony and fell over his contour chair.

Bond swept the hooded figure into his arms.

"Israel! Israel!"

He looked down into the face of Sister Sweetcakes!

"My darling! Alive, but—"

"Hurry!" she cried. "We must find a way out!"

He carried her to the first door he could find, slammed it behind him, secured it with a bolt.

"Oh, Israel! You've taken me into the greenhouse again."

"*Gottenu!* We're in another pickle! I hope it's Kosher this time. But, my OLEO angel, how did you escape the clutches of that chlorophyll horror back there?" He gazed at Herbie, heard the rumble of hunger. A tentacle shot out, fell a few feet short of his leg.

He could hear a groan of frustration. "Eat your heart of lettuce out, you green son-of-a-bitch!" And to Sister: "You haven't answered me, my nun turned wildcat."

There was a mischievous sparkle in those violet eyes. "Israel, think it out for yourself with that keen mind I admire so."

"I see," Bond nodded. *"Herbis homnis fressoris.* Our Celery Cyclops only eats—"

"Men. Just as his generic name states. He really was quite flustered upon discovering I was what I was. Expelled me from his interior in an instant."

"Damn fool, that Herbie." And the grey eyes searched her violet ones and in a burning moment of revelation found something there—the reflection of grey eyes. I shall kiss her now, he told himself; my lips will start to home in on paradise. *Gottenu!* There was a staggering blow on the back of his neck. Sister screamed.

"It's another bug! Oh, heavenly Father... it's enormous!"

Bond spun, fell to the floor just in time to avoid another blow from a thing with the buzz of a light plane motor. A beetle with a horrifying seven-inch circumference and the black hardness of coal! It swooped back, rammed its body against his temple. He somersaulted under a table. Overhead it droned, seeking its prey.

"It's after me, Sister.... Goliath beetle," he panted. "Biggest of its breed. Comes from Africa."

He felt the welts rising on his head and neck. Damn thing has the kick of a mule! And those pincers! They can tear out two inches of flesh!

"Sister," he said tensely. "Give me a handkerchief, *tout de suite!"* * She tossed it to him, fearful eyes looking upward.

Bond reached into his pocket. He found what he had hoped to find. A handful of Israeli coins, five of them, three *agorot* and two *escargot*.

He folded the handkerchief into a triangle, grabbed one point in his right hand, put the five coins in the fold. Then he drew himself up boldly.

"Come, Goliath. A son of the House of David awaits thee."

Buzz-z-z-z-z! A sound from the far corner.

It was ready to meet his brazen challenge. Down it zipped in a black blur. Round and round swung tho muscular arm of Israel Bond. The Goliath was coming fast now... ten feet away... nine... eight... seven... six....

---

* Sound your horn for the Sucaryl.

Five coins left the improvised sling, slicing through the air like tracer bullets strafing a train. They crunched into the Goliath. Two buried themselves in its back, smashing through the hard shell, biting deeply into its insides. One ripped off a leg; two more chipped out eyes with their ridged edges.

It fell to the floor with a thump, flopping about madly. Bond, his rage abated now, stubbed out the last vestige of its life.

He turned to Sister, whose eyes were filled with candid adoration.

"Borrowing a term from your old days in jazz, Sister: when it comes to fighting a Goliath, it don't mean a thing if you ain't got that sling!"

16
Rotten Roger: The Last Call

"The door! It's glowing!" she wailed.

"Damn it!" Bond growled. "While I'm giving myself the *Croix de guerre** those babies out there are still at it."

They backed off, watching the metal of the door change from dun gray to pink, to a warm red, to a hotter white. The heat rolled over them like a Saharan wind.

"They're using acetylene torches on the metal. They'll be through in another minute. Sister, this way!" He picked up the table and flung it through the glass wall of the greenhouse. "Through that hole on the double!"

She passed through the ragged opening which caught at her habit, tearing it.

Content that she was safe for the nonce, he stood halfway between the door and the back wall, tensing his battered body.

With a shower of sparks the door fell.

Two of the guards rocketed through, made a grab for him. Bond lurched to the side. Their momentum carried them by him. He turned to face their next rush but they did not charge back.

They had gone too far beyond him! And into the grasp of Herbie!

He shuddered as he watched them vainly trying to free themselves of those greedy arms. One was lifted high into the

---

* Star of David.

air kicking and screeching; then dropped into the loathsome depths. He heard a crunch, saw two boots and a helmet spat out. Bond picked up the man's carbine and put his partner out of his misery. Better a bullet than....

Gottenu! Something smashed into his arm; the carbine was sent clattering to the floor!

Topjob!

Fool that I am, I turned my back. Now my arm is dangling like a subway strap. I must combat this mass of Oriental sinews with one swollen arm.

The karateist circled Bond with a malevolent grin, those pointed teeth clicking with excitement, the mouth slobbering for the kill. He'll make it a slow job, a top job, will Topjob, Bond knew. Crack every bone in my body with one well-placed chop after another to the vulnerable spots.

One chance! Back slowly away, Oy Oy Seven... slowly... let him advance inch by inch, savoring every moment of your fear... your whimpering is as delicious to this ape as a mouthful of leeches or a bat's entrails... "ooooh"... that's it... moan a little... his grin is widening... you're almost there, but for God's sake as soon as you feel the first prick—freeze! And pray to the Lord of Israel that your shirt is thick enough to keep the tip from going into your epidermis....

His back made contact with the tip.

"All right, Topjob, do your worst, you f— gook!"

Topjob snarled and made his run at Bond. His hand speared into Bond's shoulder as the Israeli leaped to the left. The karate specialist's follow-through sent him sprawling into the Malaysian death vine!

Bond gnashed his teeth as the pain spread through his torn shoulder. He opened his eyes and met those of the Korean, whose own were slowly being overcome by dullness. Topjob's hand moved toward Bond's neck. It's the moment of truth, thought Bond. Has he got enough left to deliver the final death chop to my esophagus? If he has, I can't stop it.

The hand brushed Bond's neck but the blow was powerless. Topjob started to fall slowly like an oak severed from its base by a handsaw. He tumbled to the floor, shook in a cataclysmic paroxysm and lay still.

Bond rolled the Korean on his back with a shove of his foot. From his armpit to his thigh Topjob was pierced with a row of thorns.

Sister Sweetcakes had quietly returned through the crack in the glass wall. "Israel. What... what happened to this man?"

He fished into his lapel pocket with his usable arm; stuck a Raleigh into his lips.

"Topjob was tough all right, Sister... damn tough. But he ran into a Jew who was a thorn in his side."

"Oh, Father in heaven, you're hurt again!" she cried. "Your arm..."

"Broken, I'm afraid. But there's no time for tears now, Sister. I've a little date with that machine in the next room."

She helped him make his way into the lab. "This is IPECAC, Sister. What it does I'll explain later. But don't think me dotty when I talk to it. I know what I'm doing. Flick that red switch. And when I stop talking, flick it off."

She complied.

Bond spoke into the microphone. "Attention, Rotten Roger, my leader. Those stupid insects are prepared to follow my instructions blindly. They will help us take over the world. Then when they have accomplished our task for us, I shall destroy them to the last bug! Ha-ha! The fools! They do not know that I, Dr. Watts Nu, have invented an insecticide so potent that it makes Black Flag and Raid seem like Breakstone Cream Cheese. Roger, Rotten Roger, and out." tie dragged on the Raleigh again. "That should crack the unholy alliance wide open. Every bug within five miles has heard Dr. Nu's plan for betrayal. Now, to find the man behind all this, Leader Colfax."

They trod the corridor lightly, Sister in the lead steering the limping secret agent as best she could. She again felt that disturbing electricity as his long tapering fingers enclosed hers.

In the darkness Bond stumbled, banged his torn shoulder into the wall.

There was an ear-piercing ring.

"Damn it! The wall... it's wired to set off an alarm when touched. We're in for it again, Sister."

At the other end of the corridor a door opened and three of the Orientals came tramping through.

"Sister, run! I can't make it! Save your pretty neck."

"No, Israel," she whispered hotly. "Try, please try...."

She yanked at his sleeve and they began to run. As they traversed the corridor they saw a number of doors with slivers of light winking out. "These must be the rooms rented by the

Temple of Hate to its vacationing clientele," she said. "Quickly... into this one!"

They found themselves in the rear of a large dimly lit hall. In the front was a hideous potbellied idol with red eyes that bored into their very souls. A little man with a messianically maddened face sat in the cross-legged style of the East, addressing a group of dark-hued men in loincloths.

"Oh, my brothers! I have good omens for you. Last night a jackal cried on my left, a baboon defecated on my right. They are a sign for us mother Thuggees who have lain asleep for, lo! these past fifty years. Rise again! Take up your strangling cords and kill!

> *"Kill lest ye be killed yourselves!*
> *Kill for the love of killing!*
> *Kill for the love of Kali!*
> *Kill! Kill! Kill!"*

The nun shook. "Israel, who are these people?"

"Thugs. The murder cult of India. They worship Mother Kali, goddess of blood. Look! See their leader? He is about to offer Mother Kali a sacred golden melon in homage. Listen, he's going to chant the centuries-old ritual to her."

They strained their ears and caught the thin reedy voice of the high priest kneeling before the idol with the melon in his outstretched palms.

> *"Here's another melon, Kali, baby,*
> *Cuddle up and don't be blue...."*

Bond nudged Sister. "Let's get the hell out of here."

They were back in the corridor. There was a guttural cry in Chinese. A guard had observed the sudden burst of light in the corridor and was shouting for reinforcements.

"Into this room." Bond said. And they pushed open another door.

The sign on the Speaker's rostrum read:

> *DON'T BUY POLISH HAMS!*
> *DON'T EAT HUNGARIAN GOULASH!*
> *DON'T LISTEN TO JAPANESE RADIOS!*

"Good evening, friends of the Western Colorado Chapter of the Vigilante Defenders. My name is Robert Forrest, the national chairman, your keeper of the flame." The tall rickety-thin man waved a greeting. He wore a green-and-white Sears seersucker suit, a white shirt with brown stripes, red-and-blue tie with a painting of Trigger, Roy Rogers' stallion, on the front, Army-Navy Store khaki socks and Father & Son brown brogues.

"It is wonderful to see so many fresh, fine, smiling American faces imbued with the fervor for the Vigilante Defenders' philosophy of life. You know, I've been involved with VD for many years now... I think VD, I sleep with VD, I try to spread VD... and in the course of many travels across our great country, from the towering skyscrapers of New York... 'course some of us have good reason to call it Jew York..." his audience tittered... "to the sunny shores of Californigh-ay, where things are so liberal out there that you can't even call a spade a spade,"... boisterous laughter and prolonged clapping... "in my travels I've noticed the evil fingers of the Communist octopus extending into every American home. Did you know, dear VDers, that many of the toys our blessed tots play with are made by—Marx? Here's a little truck in my hand..."

"Enough," said Bond.

"I think so," Sister agreed.

Back into the corridor. "Let's try this door." Bond opened a third; it squeaked loudly. The room was very small. A naked bulb cast a pale yellow light on the shabby walls. Little piles of plaster dotted the floor.

"Oh, you must help me! You must!" A huge, truck driver of a hand was crushing Bond's throbbing shoulder. "My name is Lawrence Talbot."

He was a large powerful man with a sad yet appealing type of horse face. He wore a dirty white shirt open at the collar, slacks held up by a knotted rope. He was in his bare feet.

"How can I help you, sir?" said a sympathetic Bond.

"There is a curse on me," the man said in a morose voice. "Soon the moon will be full..."

"It is now," Sister said helpfully.

"Oh no!" He sat on his unmade bed, his head in his hands. They heard his muffled voice; saw his shoulders shaking. "I have the mark of the beast upon me. When the moon is full I become one myself and kill! kill! kill!"

"You'd be a hit two doors down. Ever think of becoming a Thug?"

"Don't laugh at me! You don't believe me. Nobody believes me," the anguished man croaked.

"I—uh—rather think I do." Bond was edging toward the door, Sister's hand in his. He had seen the man's finger- and toe-nails growing. "Incidentally, I'll stop around when you're feeling better, Mr. Talbot. I'll give you the address of a fine gypsy woman in Vasaria. Name's Maleva. She knows about these things. Quick, Sister!"

He pulled her roughly out into the corridor and slammed the door into the face of the man, who had charged off the bed, his bared canines framed in a mask of hair.

"Well, none of these doors has gotten us anywhere."

"There is another one, Israel. With a gold star on it at the far end."

They approached it cautiously. Bond's heart pounded as he saw the sign. Journey's end!

"ROTTEN ROGER COLFAX."

And underneath: "Society for Promulgating Every Conceivable Type Of Rottenness."

Israel Bond let a sneer curl his lips. "Sister, you're looking at the bloodiest fool who ever walked down the pike. I let my romantically-febrile imagination lead me down the garden path. I am guilty of ignoring the obvious for the fanciful."

He put his ear to the door.

"... payable in cash or equivalent value in diamonds, Premier Chou. Our organization will see to it that the American geologists are constantly harassed. Killed, if need be. Thus, the way will be paved for your People's Republic of China to be greeted with open arms. You are agreed to these terms? Capital! This is Rotten Roger Colfax—"

"Signing off for the last time." Bond spoke his gritty sentence as he walked through the door. "The game is up, Nochum."

"Bond!"

Sister shrilled, "It's Pablito! What have you done with him, you horrible little man?" She raced to the side of a little boy in raggedy sweater and shorts, whose dried tearstains had formed tributaries on his dirty pinched cheeks. She took a letter opener from Nochum's Allandale mahogany desk, worked it behind the boy's back. "You're free now, little angel," she wept as the strands fell to the floor.

Bond's gray eyes held a gleam of menacing amusement "Nochum, you are no dummy—literally."

Nochum Spector bit his lip, then raised it in a pout of contempt. "That's correct, Mr. Super-Jew with the low-grade wit that everybody's supposed to turn cart wheels for. I had you fooled real good. By now you've guessed that the Vi Teh Minh men placed a replica of me in the pit. I was in the lead; so I simply rode behind a bush, made a few heart-rending noises and they did the rest."

"Yes, they did. They murdered two of your countrymen."

"Hacks! Third-raters! Water boys! They must always perish when they get in a great man's way, Oy Oy Seven. You were my real target; you've always been. But I see that your angel has been sitting on your shoulder again, you lucky, bumbling, overrated, thickskulled—"

"Why, Nochum? Just for the record."

"Why? Remember what you once said to me—'Stay in the playpen. This game's for big boys.' Well, I sure as hell played it like a big boy, Israel Bond. I organized the world's most diabolical terror organization with the help of that wacked-up Chink and his gadgets. I, little bitty Nochum Spector, the forgotten nephew of the great M., the old broad with the wisdom of the ages and that *fahkokteh* chicken soup. Do you know what it meant to be the nephew of M.? How the big shots in M 33 and 1/3, including yourself, laughed at 'poor little Nochum, helpless little Nochum... he'll never get anywhere... he'll ride to his pay check on his *tanteh's* I. J. Fox coattails.' But I fooled you all. Even though I never got the glory assignments and the booze 'n' broads that go with 'em, I wasn't wasting my time. 'Poor little Nochum' was listening, learning and, one day, betraying. Small jobs at first... little tips here and there to Jordan or Syria for a few hundred pounds... then I branched out big in Russia, stung the comrades for a million rubles. Now the Red Chinese are coming through with twenty million *sunyatsens*. And with my Chink No. 2 and his bugs and the wonton bomb I'll make the world grovel at my feet!"

"I could kick myself—"

"I wish the hell you would," snarled Nochum, that baby face puckered into an abhorrent glare.

"I overheard your name mentioned, thought you to be dead and concluded the terror organization in question was spelled S-P-E-C-T-R-E. When I referred to that name in my interesting dialogues with Dr. Nu he naturally thought I was referring to *his* affiliation with the Society for Promulgating Every Conceivable Type Of Rottenness. Incidentally, what colossal conceit, Nochum! Surely you must have known one of your old section mates would figure out those initials someday."

"By then it would have been too late to matter."

"It's all over now, little man with big dreams."

"Not yet!" And Nochum shot through the floor!

"A chute!" Bond cried. "And here on the desk... a button! The little bastard pressed it while waxing so eloquently. God knows where he is now. We've got to get up to the convent and warn the folks. There's an attack coming. They'll be wiped out in the morning!"

17
Roll, Roll, Roll Your Ball

After reuniting Pablito with his overjoyed parents in the village of Pupi Campo (Mrs. Garcia covered Bond with tear-soaked kisses of joy; Mr. Garcia shook his hand with awe and picked his pocket), they made their way up Mount Maidenhead on a winding obscure trail known only to Sister Sweetcakes and the Keystone Automobile Club, slipping time and again in hidden mudholes, their faces raked by spiny (though nonpoisonous to Jews and Catholics) *rikki-tikki* shoots.

Once he stopped in his tracks, put a warning finger to his lips. "Mamba." A reptile snaked across their path, followed closely by several smaller ones. "Mamba's Daughters."

At the halfway point to OLEO they heard another melody from the Camp Camp loud-speaker. "Scallopini's Symphony in DC for Congressman and Kickback," he said authoritatively. "The largo de cascara passage has always moved me."

Sister brushed a gila monster off her leg. "Israel, what can we do about the impending attack?"

"I don't know. We have no weapons up there. They'll have mortars, grenade launchers, machine guns. They don't even have to scale the mountain. They can just pop at us from Camp Camp and blow the convent to bits." As though his last sentence had decided something for him, he turned to her, a curious tenderness on his cruelly handsome face. "Sister, I'm not letting you go a step further."

"Israel, I must go back. OLEO is my home."

He was fighting an emotion now, one that made him clench and unclench his fists. His watchband again snapped in two; so did his rolled Bethlehem Steel I.D. bracelet.

"Sister Sweetcakes, I love you. There is no one in this world quite like you, your gentleness, your selflessness... damn it, Sister! Renounce your calling! Renounce your faith and take mine!"

Lashed by a passion he would no longer fight, he told himself: I shall kiss her. Our bodies will lock and sway in a kiss that will teleport us to a golden meadow bending in a warm, murmuring wind, where lambs and lions and friars and optimists and rotarians lie together in peace on the banks of a clear, sweet brook containing natural fluorides whose waters will gurgle "The Indian Love Call."

Eyes closed, sweet surrender written on his dark, cruelly handsome face (in both Hebrew and Latin), his lips sought hers—but found a rigid hand pushing them away. "It can not be, Mr. Bond."

"You called me Israel one otherworldly moment ago. Why this change of heart? Why, why, why?"

"I'll tell you, I'll tell you, I'll tell you," she stammered.

He lit a Raleigh. "Sister, is this to be the farewell speech, the verbal Dear John the Baptist letter?"

"Yes, Mr. Bond. You ask too much of me. Give up my nun's garb; give up my faith. Why did you not ask me to give up my color as well?"

"Actually, you really could. There a an in California by the name of Earl Scheib who promises that for $29.95..." He bit his lip, realizing the horrible option he had just give her. "You know that doesn't mean a damn thing to me. We don't *have* to live in a decent neighborhood."

Her hands fluttered. "At a time like this," she said, "I wish I had not vowed to give up smoking. I have already broken one vow by even thinking of you in a secular way. I shall do penance for it, Mr. Bond, if the cardinal is understanding. Believe this, Mr. Bond. If ever I had again wanted the company of a man, a man's man, it would have been you. What woman could resist that courage, that strength, that passion, and those great one-liners?"

"Manifestly, you are that woman, Sister." His words were tinged with bleakness.

"Yes. And I will tell you why. When I saw the tragic innocence on the face of Pablito, I realized there were so many, many thousands like him on this island, children of the poor who need me more than you do, Mr. Bond. To give them succor I must deny that part of me which is all too human, the part that remembers too well the feeling of personal abandonment with your kind of man."

"Sister,"... the tears were falling like rain on a case of Hunt's Ketchup... "I have been"... his voice faded... "a rotter."

"Oh, no, dear Mr. Bond," and she wiped each one away with the tail of her habit. "For a person who kills as readily as you do, you are the most sensitive tender being I have ever known. Come, let us be firm friends forevermore."

"That would be my dearest wish," said Israel Bond. "But I would ask—no, beg—for one favor."

"Name it, Mr. Bond. It is yours."

"Please, please never mention to another living soul that you saw a secret agent cry."

Dawn came to El Tiparillo, one of many English girls who had taken advantage of the low seasonal rates.

Early risers, the comical *balagoola* birds darted from tree to tree, their raucous "peterpee! peterpee!" rousing the denizens of the jungle. A bull chameleon's sticky tongue scored its first direct hit of the day on an unsuspecting *colavito* fly. Under the canopy of the trees, where no light shone, snorting Gillette razorback hogs dug their tusks under rotted timbers searching for succulent grubs, severing the head and tail and eating just the grubsteaks. The heat, already soaring, caused a fungus mold on a log to burst into pure penicillin. And in a pool, its surface painted brownish-green by algae, a piranha and electric eel thrashed about in a fight to the death, the latter's Ever-Ready battery losing power as they exchanged vicious bites.

Israel Bond stood on the precipice looking down into the Valley of the Blind at the Temple of Hate. His field glasses caught the sun glinting off bayonets and throwing knives. He saw Spector, in the uniform of a field marshal, and Dr. Nu walk into the paved area and the soldiers lift their rifles in salutes. He had counted five hundred of them.

His unrequited love for the nun shoved into a deep corner of his mind from whence he might extract it someday and weep about it into his egg-drop soup, Bond was very much the cold unfeeling Oy Oy Seven again.

A feathery touch on his arm made him turn. Baldroi LeFagel. "Oh, your sweet body is all cut up. Let me rub it down—with mine."

"Damn it, LeFagel! This is no time to flounce around. There are five hundred guys down there who'll be shooting up this place any moment now, guys who can blast the head off a pin, who blend into the jungle and strike like rattlers, who can kill you with one karate stroke."

"Oh, worry not, you heart-stopping thing. I'll protect that precious Herculean body of yours. I have a black belt in karate myself."

"So have they."

"Mine has sequins."

The six survivors of the Israeli Peace Corps, two on crutches, all bearing the scars of the sneak attack, came to the cliff's edge. In their eyes he could see trust and hope. He knew they looked to him for leadership in this hour of tribulation. By thunder, he would give it to them!

He lit a Raleigh; let his eyes rest on each face for a few seconds. "At a time like this when our backs are against the wall, I'd like to pose a simple question: Any of you guys ever hear of George Gipp?"

From the lack of recognition, even disinterest on their faces, he knew he'd taken the wrong tack in resurrecting The Gipper. He would start again, this time with a more whimsical approach.

"*Boochereem*, it looks hopeless. I just learned the convent's telephone line to Vera Hruba has been cut. I can't get through to Bon Ami for men and ammo. But don't despair. I'll get us out of this somehow."

Five of them smiled grimly, but he saw their faces set into masks of determination. Stout lads! They'll give a good account of themselves. But a sixth dropped his crutches, climbed over the low retaining wall girdling the convent and jumped three thousand feet to his death.

"If he's going to show bad faith like that we can bloody well do without him," Bond said stonily. "Brother Thelonius!" The monk looked up from his beloved yellow billyrosebush. "There'll be one less for breakfast."

"Hey!" shouted one of the corpsmen. "We got company! Look, a dozen guys coming up the mountain."

Bond's heart leaped. Could Bon Ami have somehow learned of their plight and sent men and guns? Hot damn! With the right weapons we could hold off that army until real help comes.

Over the wall popped a red sweating face. "Hi, folks! The Rock of Ages Records' caravan is right on the ol' schedule! Tell Sister Sweetcakes to sound her A a few times. Marty O'Marty and the boys are in town!"

Down went his heart, pierced by an arrow of futility. *Gottenu!* Of all the times to record a religious album... with death from international Communism staring us in the face. "We who are about to die salute you, Mr. O'Marty." And taking the recording executive aside he gave it to him straight.

"I better tell the fellas, Mr. Bond." O'Marty beckoned to A Man Called Peter and the Padres, four thick-mopped musicians with Selmer harps, and the technicians who puff up the path bearing the tools of the trade. "It's all off."

"Hey, man?" said A Man Called Peter. "You mean like we ain't havin' no session?"

"Kid, don't you realize that the Vi Teh Minh men, the Russkis and Fidelistas might be here any second?"

"Screw them other groups, daddy. You signed the contract with *us*."

"I shall personally lead our onslaught upon the convent," said Nochum Spector. "You will be at my side, Dr. Nu. I'm sure it will gladden your heart to see our bullets cut down these dogs."

"There is just one of them who interests me, my leader. Israel Bond. I shall have my revenge upon him. I want him staked out naked on a bed of ground glass in the tropical sun, watch his lidless eyes burned black by its rays, hear his screams for mercy as I place bamboo slivers under his nails and light them."

"I shall leave the fate of the great Oy Oy Seven to you, my good Doctor. Are your insects prepared to soften them up before we move in?"

"I outlined our plan over IPECAC a few minutes ago. They will swarm over and into the convent, biting, tearing, stinging. Our job should be what the Americans call 'shooting fish in a barrel' after that."

"Excellent! Let us move up the mountain. The first barrage is at 1300 hours."

Around the table in the dining hall of OLEO, served by the solicitous nuns and Monks Thelonius and Julius, sat Bond, the Peace Corps boys, Baldroi LeFagel, Dr. Browndorf, and Marty O'Marty's retinue.

"Delicious, absolutely delicious," said the doctor. "What is it, Sister Butterball?"

The plump little nun blushed. "It's what the Americans call 'fish in a barrel.' We nuns put mackerel, holy mackerel, of course, in a barrel and..."

"Bond! I've got my transistor radio working," called out O'Marty. "At least we can get some news of the outside world." He turned a dial. "Hey, a Miami station."

"... identified by White House security men as the leader of the protest against our involvement in Viet Nam was Rowena Rosenthal, eighteen, of Manhattan. Miss Rosenthal said she would urge young men not only to set fire to their draft cards but also to their draft *boards*. And in Viet Nam itself, American B-52's plastered the North Vietnamese hamlet of O Feel Yah for the third straight day. Aerial reconnaissance photos, according to an Air Force spokesman, showed that our bombers—quote—knocked out fifteen thousand trees, which will never again threaten the freedom of the South Vietnamese people, at least six small hills and a very sullen swamp—unquote. From the politically torn island of El Tiparillo comes word of new civil war this morning. West El Tiparillan forces were rushed to The Band, that neutral zone that divides the island, to meet the forces of General Obratsov from EET which launched an attack late last night. Said General Wesson y Oyl of WET—quote—We shall never, never surrender and, if we do, it will be with dignity—unquote. Early stock market reports show Calvert up a fifth, International Nickel down a quarter, International Quarter down a nickel, and Made-A-Wee Diapers unchanged. And that—"

"Turn it off, Marty. We heard the news all right and it's lousy," said Bond. Revolution in El Tiparillo! And WET's army committed to the border. No, there'll be no in-the-nick-of-time cavalry charge for us, Gunga Din.

OLEO shook violently as the first barrage whined over the wall into its side. Nuns screamed, sank to their knees in prayer. Bond looked down at his hand, sliced from heel of palm to pinky tip by a spear of a shell fragment. Dust choked his nostrils. He felt his rubbery legs giving way.

Sister caught him. "Mr. Bond, you're hurt again!"

She tore off a strip of her garment and wound it around his gushing hand. "It's the best I can do, my poor friend."

He patted her hood. "You always do the best you can, Sister. Anybody else hurt?"

"Brother Julius. A slight scratch. But what are we to do?"

"Sister, only God knows. I had not foreseen this hopeless siege. This is not a slickly planned affair with predictable moves and countermoves like Operation Matzohball."

Matzohball!

Say it again, he screamed at his brain. Say it again!

"Matzohball!"

"Brain, you used your head," and he laughed harshly, triumphantly.

"Mr. Bond, you are acting in a highly irrational—"

"Matzohball!" he whooped in a fierce boyish joy. "That's it! Sister," and he hugged the bewildered nun, "have you any large kettles?"

"Kettles? Adversity has at last unhinged you, Mr. Bond. Would you throw kettles at these murderous, heavily armed, godless barbarians?"

"Come, come," Bond chided. "No commercials for our religious beliefs. We both know that God helps him who helps himself. Kettles?"

"Only a small one or two for making tea. The soup and the stews are prepared in the cauldrons."

"Cauldrons! *Oy mommeleh,* cauldrons! Let's get 'em!"

She led him into the kitchen. "There." On top of the old-fashioned stove were a dozen four-foot-deep cauldrons.

"Tell every able hand, man and woman, to get cracking! I want them in here on the double!"

A minute later they stood hushed before him.

"You haven't got time to tell me how crazy I am. You've just got time to do what I tell you to do. I'm going to work all your asses off—pardon me, Sisters and Brothers—and you won't stop. Dear ladies, get me boiling water. And I want every man jack of you to follow me to the cellar. Let's go. It's time to start the ball rolling!"

"I see smoke coming from the roof," said Dr. Nu. "Our last barrage must have set it on fire. We shall not have to wait too long now, leader of SPECTOR, Spector."

Nochum growled. "Where are your insect allies? They should have overrun the place by now."

"Perhaps there has been some misunderstanding, SPECTOR leader. But I feel sure—"

"Misunderstanding?" Spector's voice was icy. "You know what the penalty is for failing SPECTOR."

Dr. Nu almost turned white. "My leader, I'm sure that—wait! Listen! Tell the men to stop firing."

Spector held up his hand. The shooting stilled.

"Hist!" cried Dr. Nu. "Can you not hear them?"

From far off they heard a drone. One solid sound at first. And then, as it came nearer, they could distinguish individual noises, buzzing, chirping, the crackling of dead leaves under billions of insect feet. Now, there unfolded a black blanket, spreading over the horizon as far as the eye could see. Uncountable hordes of ants, scorpions, tarantulas, crickets, beetles, centipedes... all manner of crawling things... and, hovering above them, their winged cousins in air-borne legions that for an instant blotted out the sun.

"They are coming to me," Dr. Nu smiled.

"It's quiet down there," said Dr. Browndorf. "Something's fishy."

Bond put down his field glasses. "No, buggy. Look, Doc."

The medico put them to his eyes. "My God, bugs! Ugh! Billions 'n' billions 'n' —"

"Don't get panicky, Doc. I've a feeling they won't be coming here after all. Are the boys doing the job?"

"Yes. The cauldrons are lined up by the wall. And one of the boys got a brainstorm. He tore down all the rain spouts, tied them together and formed a sort of pipeline to the kitchen. We'll get a continual supply of hot water from the hot water taps."

"*Tov m'oad!* And the stuff?"

"They're opening it and boiling it as fast as they can."

"Make sure it's packed as tight as a witch's tit. Use just enough hot water to make it firm and bouncy. A soggy one won't go fifty feet."

"Roger."

"Don't ever say that name again," Bond said savagely. "It's lost its charm." Idiot! You had to open your sensual mouth! Now the doc's looking oddly at you. Can he suspect that M.'s own nephew is a traitor? No, of course not. Nobody knows but you and Sister. And it must stay that way out of respect to the grandest old dame you'll ever know.

"Oy Oy Seven!"

Bond's morbid spell was broken by one of the Israeli boys coming up the path, running, in fact, from Baldroi LeFagel who nimbly skipped after him.

"Baldroi, leave the kid alone or I'll—"

LeFagel said gaily, "Look, it's all over my hands." He held them out, revealing a gummy yellow covering. "I've been helping those *superb* young men pack it. I tasted it, incidentally. It's delicious. Jewish delicacy, no? But then all Jewish delicacies taste delicious. You're Jewish, aren't you, Bond?"

Bond sent the little poet spinning with a backhanded cuff. "Get lost, you— or I'll tan your hide. Uh—sorry, LeFagel."

"You had to make it a racial issue, right, Whitey?"

The young Israeli, whose name was Neon Zion, said, "We're ready to roll, Oy Oy Seven. Give us the word."

They were silent as he approached them, even the nonstop talker, O'Marty.

"Did you knock out a big enough section of the retaining wall?"

"Didn't have to," piped up Brother Thelonius. "They did it for us with their last mortar barrage."

"O.K.," Bond said hoarsely. "Now we push it."

"Like hell!" It was A Man Called Peter. "Look, baby, I came up here to go-go, yea-yea-yea, wail, swing, rock. Ain't nothin' in this Local 802 union book says I gotta do donkey work."

"I'll shove that book down—" Bond made a move toward him.

"Cool it, daddy. You're looking at a scab."

Shots skimmed over their heads. "Rifles," said Bond. "They must be planning to come up now. Doc, give me back the field glasses."

He adjusted the zoom-in lens. Camp Camp, he saw, was gone! Smothered by the hellish hordes of insects. Their first phalanx was now moving on Spector, Dr. Nu and the Vi Teh Minh men, Russkis and Fidelistas. Dr. Nu bowed formally, bent down to speak to the leaders of the various species.

He saw the Oriental's mouth agape. My God, the man must be screaming his head off. They're on him! The yellow is disappearing. He's turning black... with insects! Now there's just a blob writhing on the ground. *Sayonara*, Dr. Watts Nu! You and SPECTOR wanted the world to crawl... and now the crawlers have had their revenge.

Spector! Where was he? He's left his Oriental genius to be gnawed to the bone. He's fleeing down the mountain. You know damn well what's on his mind, Bond. The helicopter! A quick flight to EET with all the swag he's stashed away in the temple and he's back in business with a newer and more dangerous Society for Promulgating Every Conceivable Type Of Rottenness. You can't let that happen, Bond.

"Heave to, everybody! Push, push, push; let's get the ball rolling!"

Sweat rolled from muscles pushed to the bursting point. Men and women grunted, swore, prayed... in vain. Nothing happened.

The hell with it, thought Bond. Smashed, lacerated shoulders or no I'm throwing them to the wheel. He backed off, shouted, "Get out of the way!" and broke into a trot, revved up into a sprint, his head and shoulders hunched up a la a blocking back about to cut down a safety man. And he rammed into the stupendous yellow thing.

Ten tons of matzohball shuddered, rolled over the lip of the precipice!

Down, down, down plummeted the yellow avenger, bouncing from ledge to ledge, gaining incredible speed. It crushed hundreds of thousands of insects with a single bound; then bounced up, up, up in the sky; then down again into the panicking soldiers, strewing them about like tenpins, and down, down, down into the airstrip.

Bond's glasses picked up Nochum Spector, a briefcase in his hand, looking up in horror. Then Spector fell to his knees and began to pray. Too late for that now, you little bastard! The matzohball bounced and came down upon him. Bond saw Nochum and the helicopter disappear under the yellow avalanche. There was a rumble, the sound of magma loosening the bowels of the earth. The matzohball careened into the Temple of Hate. A pillar toppled; then another. The minarets at the roofs corners cracked, fell into the lot. And with a roar the Temple of Hate collapsed into a pile of green debris. Under it were the shattered body and dreams of Nochum Spector, Dr.

Nu's IPECAC and the Will Chiller, insatiable Herbie and the Malaysian death vine, plus assorted bigots from every land. Bond, a Raleigh in his lips, had a strange feeling that only Lawrence Talbot got out in time.

"*Kinderlach.*" He grinned shyly at his flock, who fixed worshipful eyes upon him. "You can never be sure about dice, but when you roll a matzohball you've got a natural winner!"

18
It's All Over But The Shooting

Merriment reigned in Our Lady of the Eastern Order... and bravado. Now that the ordeal had rolled away like the matzohball, each one cited his own part in the fantastic, bolt-from-the-blue scheme that had destroyed the archvillains and their Communist cadres.

"If it hadn't been for the good old Rock of Ages Records' caravan, you never woulda had the man power to put together that Jewish yo-yo," boasted O'Marty, deep in his cups.

"How about my participation? If it hadn't been for my artistic touches, O'Marty, you sweet Irish bitch, that ball would not have been so round and firm and fully packed," snipped back Baldroi LeFagel, shallow in *his* cups, a black lace Mansfield bra.

"You should all be ashamed of yourselves," said Sister Sweetcakes. "We should all thank our dear Lord for sending us the Samson who destroyed the temple of the Philistines... Israel Bond."

"Amen," they chorused, and fell silent.

The "Samson" leaned against the wall near the precipice, his eyes still glued upon the holocaust below. The matzohball was beginning to come apart under the torrid midday sun. He thought of Nochum. M. must never know her beloved nephew had been the culprit. He would tell her that Rotten Roger Colfax was a Russian all along and that the traitor business was literally a Red herring to cause doubt and suspicion among the M 33 and 1/3 team. He rehearsed his speech for the tenth time:

"You would have been proud of the heroic way he met his Lord in that terrible jungle, Mother."

"Talking to yourself, Mr. Bond?"

"Hello, dear Sister. Come to say good-bye?"

"Yes, Mr. Bond. But let's make that au revoir. I hate good-byes. I know our paths will cross again someday. Now I must go back into the convent and make that long-playing record for Marty. I have asked that the proceeds be set aside for the creation of a Boys' Town on El Tiparillo. Indeed, my brother Baldroi has evinced interest in helping me operate it."

He would, Bond thought.

"Until our paths converge, I want you to have this little token of my esteem and... uh... affection. Please take this, Mr. Bond."

In the palm of his hand was a mirror framed in a lovely coral rectangle. "It is exquisite, as you are, Sister."

"Whenever you look into it, Mr. Bond, you will see my favorite person in all the world." A rose of a blush surfaced on her cheeks. She pressed his hand against her heart. Then she turned and walked slowly back to the convent. She stood at the door, waved and was gone from his sight.

"Adieu, Sister Sweetcakes," he whispered. "May the Bluebird of Happiness bring you Jan Peerce."

He looked into the mirror and saw her (and his) favorite person in all the world. And—someone else! An evil animal whose demented grin bared a golden treasure trove.

Torquemada LaBonza! The "Man With the Golden Gums!" The "Silent One!" No misnomer there. He had not even been aware of the man's approach. Good Lord! LaBonza must have been taught that soundless walk by a Mohican. He glanced at LaBonza's feet. Moccasins. And written in beaded script on each toe, "Property of Uncas."

Israel Bond, you egotistical fool! While you were basking in the plaudits of your admirers back at OLEO, thinking you'd pulled off another successful conclusion, you forgot all about the world's most feared assassin, LaBonza, whose victims die in an insane fit of laughter. Why?

He was to know immediately.

The voice of Torquemada LaBonza came out of that Midas mouth:

"Eh-h-h... what's up, doc? I'll tell you, doc. Your hands, doc. Eh-h-h, that's 'cause I got this silencer against your backbone, doc."

Bond began to laugh and laugh and laugh. It poured out of him like the blood from any of his wounds. LaBonza, angered, spun him around with his left hand and raked Bond's cheek with his gun sight, reopening the old gash.

Still Bond laughed, though the cheek smarted terribly. He could not help it, no matter what.

Torquemada LaBonza's voice was an exact carbon of Bugs Bunny's!

19
Flash In The Pan

"LaBonza, I can't help it. Nobody could. How in the world did you ever get a voice like that?"

No answer. For a moment Bond thought his query had drawn a Mel Blanc.

Then LaBonza spoke. "I—uh—guess it don't matter now, doc, 'cause I'm gonna kill you anyway and bring that hot-shot mezuzah of yours back to KGB. Pretty humiliatin', ain't it, doc? The Israeli superman is brought down by a cwazy wabbit, eh, doc?"

Though convulsed by simultaneous mirth and fear, Bond nevertheless managed to get the story.

His father was an impressionist, LaBonza pointed out, but made a meager living at it. There were many Cagney-Robinson-Cooper-Grant imitators working the cheap theatre circuit and the father was ruefully aware he had blown his talent on a surfeited market. However, LaBonza added, his father adored the cartoon characters in those delightful shorts one saw accompanying every movie in the '30's and '40's. No one was specializing in these imitations and so, almost from birth, he took Torquemada to the movies three times a week, hoping to leave the boy with a profitable legacy.

"You can't envision what it was like for me in those formative years with a tyrant for a father. Ah, phooey!" (He was Donald Duck, now, quacking irately at his rotten lot in life.) "And, thufferin' thuccotash, thir (now he was an equally incensed Daffy Duck), from the very beginning every time I'd try to thpeak normally, that thtupid father of mine would dig his thumbth into my cheekth until my mouth ached. Thoon I wath afraid to even try thpeaking like a normal perthon. And e-e-e-e-ven wh-wh-wh-en he d-d-d-died (Porky Pig had taken over the narrative at this point) I was so used to speaking like this, mouseketeers (Porky passed the ball to Mickey), that I continued on this way. I was ashamed to tell people I couldn't speak like they could and afraid they'd laugh at me when I spoke the only way I could. Kinda awful, huh, Pluto?"

"Why did you become an assassin, LaBonza?" No harm showing a little sympathy to this strangest of human beings.

"Oooh, I thawt I taw a puttycat." (It was Tweety Bird's turn.) "Why? 'Tause I hated my daddy 'tause he made my wife weal miserable. I wanted wevenge on a wotten world. I wanted to—hah! hah!—kill wots of wittle gway wabbits—I hate wittle gway wabbits —and kill even more people." (Elmer Fudd muscled in.) "But, son, why are yuh—ah say, why are yuh askin' me all these dadburned fool questions? You-all ain't tryin' ter put somethin' over on old Torquemada, is yuh? Ah say, is yuh?" (Leghorn had picked up the ball.)

"Certainly not, LaBonza. It's just that your story is so fantastic I want to hear all of it. Why the golden teeth and gums?"

"Jiminy Cricket! (Bond had no trouble identifying this one) I'm your conscience, Torquemada, so I'll answer the gentleman's question. It's 'cause your father squeezed your cheeks so often your teeth softened and fell out. And, honest, Pinoke, so did your gums. So when you killed your first man you had the whole business done in gold so's you'd be sumpin' special, huh? Watch out, Pinoke, the Blue Fairy's back!"

"Well, LaBonza, whoever put in that golden mouth of yours cheated you, buddy boy."

"Ah, *mon ami*, if you are making ze fun of Pepé Le Pew, I keel you *très* slow and easy, a bullet in ze leg, ze hand, ze rib, ze elbow, ze ankle."

Bond smiled nonchalantly. "Why should I make fun? I'm a damn serious guy when I face death, LaBonza. Now, look for yourself. Here's a mirror. If you look very closely you'll see you got the cheapest kind of gold. Maybe it isn't even gold. Maybe it's pyrite—fool's gold. See for yourself."

LaBonza grabbed the mirror. He turned it around and held it toward him, opening his mouth wide.

Bond tensed. If he had figured it out right he had one last chance.

As LaBonza's mouth opened wide the sun flashed against the generous golden expanse, the flash ricocheting off the mirror into LaBonza's eyes. He was blinded for one significant second.

Bond hit him low and hard, the impact with the man's knees sending pangs through his sore shoulders. LaBonza was hurled back, back... and over the wall. His hands clawed for a grip on a root, lost it and he fell into space. Bond heard screaming oinks, quacks, tweets, adieus... then heard them no more as the black dot bounced off a ledge and plunged to the bottom of Mount Maidenhead.

"Adieu, yourself, Torquemada LaBonza," whispered Israel Bond to the valley below. "You could have made the big 'hit' of your career if you'd finished me off. But you gummed it up!"

And now it really *is* over, he knew. This odyssey that started on warm friendly beaches, *segued* to the chill of a Moscow night and climaxed on a jungle mountain top.

Yet, he pondered, could any of it have been real? It had been an adventure peopled by a conglomeration of characters only to be found in the marred convolutions of a psychotic writer's mind.* Had any of these menaces been more than cartoons? Any of them? Svetlova with the gash of a mouth, Dr. Nu, Herbie, IPECAC, Spector, Topjob and, finally, LaBonza, a true product of Disney, Lantz, Terry?

How could he put a fitting finis on this nightmare in keeping with its cartoonish genre?

His gray eyes gleamed, the smile forming as he knew what he *must* say. Somewhere in heaven Zvi Gates, all atremble, waited. Israel Bond said: "Th-th-th-that's all, f-f-folks!"

---

* Look, booby. Don't get so damn personal with the Freudian analysis. You like that imbalanced author well enough when he's shoving hot broads into your bed like hotcakes. You could very well be replaced by a Taureg private eye.—S. W.

On the Secret Service of His Majesty, the Queen

DEDICATIONS

These include residents of NATO countries unfortunately omitted in the dedications to *Loxfinger* and *Matzohball*. What does it take to merit a mention in these towering novels? The answer is simple: Most of the people cited are not only cheerful, obedient, trustworthy and kind and never leave a national park without spraying their campfire embers with soft Culligan water, but also have gone out of their way to promote sales, thus insuring a better way of life for my fine family.

WILLIAM J. BLITMAN and NORMAN "RED" BENSON
In Memoriam.

ELLIE, DAVID (0010) and JUDY (007) WEINSTEIN
My fine family.

JOE E. LEWIS
Who once said, "Behind every beautiful woman is a beautiful behind." If the Pickled Plato is performing in your town, don't miss him.

WILLIAM B. WILLIAMS
Of WNEW, New York. To the trade: Velvet Baze Velvel.

MERV GRIFFIN
Who gave me my first break on national TV. Merv, I still insist that within my Walter Slezak-type body is a Sinatra-type voice. Dare you ignore the commercial possibility of launching a Singing Spy?

NORMAN SHAVIN
Of the Atlanta Constitution; a geeter, a finer.

GODFREY CAMBRIDGE
Who, if the Bond film people ever decide to do Live and Let Die, is the logical choice for Mr. Big.

MAI ZETTERLING and SUSANNAH YORK
Who have been my constant companions in recent fantasies— mine, unfortunately. Ladies, do with me what you will.

JULIE CHRISTIE
Take what's left.

TEX McCRARY

EARL WILSON

FRANK BOWERS

LEE J. MALTENFORT
Of *Bestsellers*.

JERRY AGEL
Of Books.

JACKIE FARRELL
Of the New York Yankees.

LEONARD KATZ
Of the New York Post.

FRANK FARRELL

WALTER WINCHELL

RON AXE & MIKE ROSENFELD
No female singer has the right to complain about the lack of good material if she has failed to record "Mirror," lyrics by Axe, music by Rosenfeld. It may be found in Vicki Carr's Discovery 2 *LP.*

LAURA LANE
A splendid song stylist.

THE NESHAMINY "N" CLUB
Of Bucks County, Pa.

ED JOYCE
Of "Expertise," WCBS, New York.

WALT CANTER
Writer and mensch.

JIM HARPER

Of WINZ, Miami, owner of one of the world's greatest picture names. ("Jim Harper, I can't ask you to go up against those rock 'em, sock 'em Cornhuskers with a knee like that. So we'll lose the twenty-third annual Okra Bowl; better that than crippling a fine young boy forever." Jim Harper flashed his pain-tinged smile and with the aid of a pneumatic drill the freckle-faced kid from Glenville began to chip the cast from his leg. "Can't let the guys down now, Coach O'Brien. Tell 'em to keep feeding me on good ol' K-34 off left tackle. I'm gonna pack that pigskin across those chalk lines until....")

RAY HASSON and LIZ TROTTA
Of NBC News.

DIZZY GILLESPIE
John, there's still time to record an album of my modern jazz pieces. Don't snicker; you didn't think I could produce top-flight thrillers, either.

GEORGE SPOTA
Of the Martin Goodman Agency, New York; with gratitude.

JOHN CALLEY
Of Filmways and the 99¢ Royal Roost. Peewee Marquette, we never forgot you.

OSSIE DAVIS and RUBY DEE
Two elegant pros.

FLORENCE FRIEDMAN
Of Meyers Stationery & Book Store, Fairless Hills, Pa. Sell, maideleh. *sell....*

REGINA PRIOR
Secretary Emeritus to Johnny Carson.

CLARENCE PETERSEN
Of the Chicago Tribune, who looked into the heart of a weary traveler and found cholesterol.

SOL IMMERMAN and BARBARA HUNTLEY
Artistic geniuses of Pocket Books.

BERNIE GROSS and MAX HUDES
Of the Carnegie Delicatessen, New York.

HARRY and JOHN HOLLAND

REGIS PHILBIN
Nobody should look that wholesome.

BUDDY GOLDBERG
Manager of the Jay Leader Insurance Team of the Levittown, Pa., Western Little League, and his charges.

JESS CAIN
Of WHDH, Boston, an explosively funny, deeply disturbed young man.

ARNOLD BIEGEN
Of Booth, Lipton & Lipton, New York.

MELVIN L. KARTZMER
President, First Florida Consultants, Inc.

TEDDI KING and DAVID ALLEN
Fine pop singers.

JAMES J. SHAPIRO
Of Simplicity Patterns.

B. J. HARRIS
President of WQXT, Palm Beach, the "lebedicker from Louisville," and his **PAULA, ALAN JON, PAMELA JOY and PEPPIE JAYNE.**

LEON BROWN
Of the Philadelphia Jewish Times.

NEAL HEFTI
Who, by his gorgeous reworking of blues, "Girl Talk," deserves the chance to do the arrangements of my jazz pieces for an LP.

JACK McKINNEY
Of WCAU, Philadelphia; seeker of truth.

SGT. NEIL ROBINSON

Of Armed Forces Radio.

DICK CAVETT and GEORGE CARLIN
Fine young comedians.

TIMMIE ROGERS
Who made "Oh yeah!" household words—in his household.

CASSIE PASSMAN, HARRY MOSES, LEN and NORA FISCHMAN, MR. and MRS. ALBERT FINKLE, FRED and NETTIE BERK, CHARLES and BELLA GREENBERG, CHARLIE GRAY, JERRY and MARY LOU GLAZE, SAMMY MORRIS, FLORENCE GRAD LONDONER, CY and CLAIRE NEIBURG, KENNY SOLMS, PETER REMENY, KENT TALIAFERRO, SANDY TIMMERMANN, MERLE RUDERFER, ESTELLE and SIDNEY LUTZKER, JANET HELD, BOBBIE WEINER, MR. and MRS. HARRY BOTOFF, MR. and MRS. NEIL LEVENSON, MR. and MRS. ROBERT KURTZER, CHRIS WINNER, STEVE PINKUS, NANCY CARTER, MENDY, WILLIE and DAVE KRAVITZ, MR. and MRS. WILBUR J. LEVINE, STEVE SCHENKEL, DR. and MRS. MILTON PALAT, DR. and MRS. GEORGE ISAACSON, TED and SYBIL COOPER, ARNOLD and ESTELLE KIMMEL, NACHAMA LEVY, IRV and LEAH WURZEL, HARRY BLAZE, MR. and MRS. WILLIAM GERVON, SY and RUTHE LEDIS, FREDRICA KIRSCHNER.

FRAN SHANKIN

EVERETT G. WALK
Of Luden's, Inc.

JESSE H. WALKER
Of the New York Amsterdam News.

BILL (Talk of Miami) SMITH
Of WKAT, Miami. Not a bad name, either.... ("You can kill me, Gestapo Chief Guttmacher, but there'll be a lotta guys like me, Bill Smith, on the way... guys with names like Tompkins n' DeLuca n' Kelly n' Weinstein... guys from Glenville, Sioux City, Brooklyn n' Levittown... peace-lovin' Joes who never asked for this war but when their Yankee dander's up will show you how to finish a fight. Hear those engines overhead, Guttmacher?")

DICK WEST
Of UPI, witty but dewlapless.

OSCAR BROWN JR.
A delightful addition to anyone's record collection.

LES ROBERTS
Bright young writer.

HORACE GREELY McNAB
Of WBCB, Levittown, Pa.

RON POLAO
Of the unforgettable face.

LARRY DeVINE
Of the Miami Herald, who, alas, never knew Yudel Kaplan.

DONALD HAMILTON
Whose Matt Helm books never let the reader down.

"IAN STUART"
Sir, please kvetch out another Satan Bug, Black Shrike, *etc.*

JUDY EDELMAN and RUTH GOVER

ROBERT MAGAZINER JR. and JIM WILSON
Of Ocean City, N.J., officers of the first and probably last Israel Bond Fan Club.

ROGER PRICE
Of Grump *Magazine.*

JUDITH RASCOE
With admiration.

WILLIAM H., JoANN and TERRI LYNN PETTIT
Of the Burlington County, N.J., Times

FRED E. WALKER
General manager of KYW-TV, Philadelphia.

On the Secret Service of His Majesty, the Queen

NORMAN, MARGIE, MARSHA, SKIP and JANET WEINSTEIN
No relation, but worthy of inclusion due to sensible choice of surname.

WEINSTEIN'S DEPARTMENT STORE
Of San Francisco. Again, no relation, but the sign just made me... kvell... all over.

NATHAN WEINSTEIN
Of Mystic, Connecticut.

MARYLOU SHEILS, BILL and LIL HOLSTEIN, FRANK and SUSIE MARRERO, ARNIE and PAT SOMERS, DR. HARRY LEVINE of 6360 Wilshire Blvd., Los Angeles, Calif., AL LEVINE of LONDON ASSOCIATES, Chicago, MAC and SHIRLEY ENGEL, EVE REMENY, JUDY SPIEGEL, MARY JANE HIGGINS, MARETTA TUCKER, MR. and MRS. HAL SINGER, NORM LEIGHTON, NANCY HELPERN, MONIQUE VAUGEL, DOLORES MIRANDA, BERT and IDA ENGEL, STEVE PIERINGER, MIKE, SUSIE and TOMMY STUDNIA, STAN EARLY, ROSS HIRSHORN, NORVIN NATHAN, MR. and MRS. WALTER WARREN, MARVIN and PHYLLIS HABAS, MR. and MRS. SAM MELMAN, DAVID and ESTHER ZWEIG, LEONARD, HELENA PAVLOVA, LINDA, KAREN and SHERRY BOGARDE, JEAN BERNSTEIN, LINDA BILLINGTON, MARGIE, BERNIE and STEVIE HIRSH, DOLLY COHEN, MARY MILLER, SEYMOUR GINSBURG, DAVID and HOPE WISNIA, CARMELA CANDELA, BARRY SINCO, DAVID O'MEARA, TONY ROIG, CLAUDE and HEATHCLIFFE TRENIER, NANCY PALMER, pretty JAN and passable STAN FEINTUCH, LINDA LATZ, Bat Lady of San Francisco.

FRIAR BOBBY GORDON, MR. and MRS. FRED KANTOFF, PHIL WEISS of FRIEDMAN, ALPREN & GREEN, MRS. NATALIE FULTON, SELMA LITOWITZ, ALAN, GRACE, LEIGH, CORY and TOD BRESLAU, SAUL MILLNER, MURRAY HORNICK, MORTON SPITOFSKY, CHARLES CHARNE, ALLEN DELIN and the rest of BRONX COMMUNITY COLLEGE, NEWMAN and IRENE HOFFMAN, MR. and MRS. HAL LEFCOURT, GENE D'ANDREA of Andrea Motors, Morrisville, Pa., GEORGE and SARAH GORDON, PRISCILLA SLOSS, JAMES E. MAGEE of New York Life Insurance.

BILL HART

Of WCAU-TV, Philadelphia, who once slated, "No man is an island." He also said, "No hockey puck is a dirigible; no telegraph pole is a pencil box." Bill has this flair for correctly identifying things.

CEIL DYER

ANTHONY LaCAMERA
Television critic, friend of Norman Shavin.

GEORGE F. BROWN and EDDIE LOPEZ
Of the San Juan Star.

DAVE DUSHOFF, DALLAS GERSON and JERRY KATZ
Of the Latin Casino, Cherry Hill, N.J.

TONY BEACON and MARY MURPHY AIVAZIAN
Of the San Juan Diary.

WOODY ALLEN
With admiration.

LEON, CLAIRE and KIRK NUROCK
The last named an amazing young jazz player, arranger, composer. Record companies please note.

DON THOMPSON
Of the Rocky Mountain News.

CLEVELAND AMORY
With gratitude.

HARRY NEIGHER
Of the Connecticut Sunday Herald.

WALTER BORENSTEIN
Of the North American Review.

JACKIE PETTYCREW
Of the Arizona Republic.

BEVERLEY GITHENS
Of the Eureka Springs, Ark., Times Echo.

DOLPH HONICKER
Of the Nashville Tennessean.

RUTH JACOBS and SHOLOM RUBINSTEIN
Of The Jewish Home Show, *WEVD, New York.*

SUE NAPIER
Of the Lexington, Ky., Sunday Herald-Leader.

RICHARD CROKER
Of the Georgia State College Signal.

CHARLES McHARRY
Of the New York Daily News.

JERRY GAGHAN
Of the Philadelphia Daily News.

FRANK BROOKHOUSER
Of the Philadelphia Bulletin.
In Philadelphia, nearly everybody on the Bulletin *reads* Mad Magazine.

HERB RAU

HERB KELLY

LENNY MEYERS
Of WHDH, Boston.

BILL and STUART BLUMBERG

JULIE DANE
Of WHDH-TV, Boston. Noch a mool, the Name Game. ("What? Chili Chuvalo, the Chilean Spitfire, walked out on the Blofeld Follies of 1935 ten seconds before the opening curtain just because I wouldn't let her two-year-old brother conduct the orchestra? Well, that does it—one million bucks down the drain!" Kindly old Pop Abel Green looked up from his tattered Variety. *"Now, hold on there, Mr. Florenz Blofeld. Maybe you are the world's greatest showman and I'm just a broken-down old hoofer who sweeps up backstage, but there's a lovely*

young kid right under your nose, little Julie Dane, our script girl, and she's got a voice like an angel and she knows Chili's part by heart and....")

HOWIE TEDDER
Of the Trenton, N.J., Times, *who got me into this business. Blame him. (Ginmill comics who need shtik should contact him.)*

CARL GEORGE
Of KABC-TV, Los Angeles.

NICK SERUBY
My old barber.

ELLEN WILLIS
Of Fact.

PAUL CONDYLAS
Of KABC, Los Angeles; "The Voice of the Tigris and Euphrates."

MIKE JACKSON
Of the Los Angeles Herald-Examiner.

BOB KENNEDY
Of WBZ-TV, Boston.

BRUCE McCABE
Of the Boston Record-American.

HERB KENNY and GEORGE McKINNON
Of the Boston Globe.

ROBERT TAYLOR
"The Roving Eye" of the Boston Herald-Traveler, *a likable, perceptive chap hamstrung by a prosaic name. Drop it; use Spangler Arlington Brugh.*

HELEN HESSEN
Nurse Parker at Duh Fontenbloo.

IRV KUPCINET

SAM BUTERA and ROLLY DEE

HARRY HARRIS, ROSE (SAM) DeWOLF and TOM LIPPMAN
Of the Philadelphia Inquirer.

GENE PACKARD and ART MILLNER
Of WKDN, Camden.

SAM GYSON

BEN McELVEEN

BEN BOROWSKY *Of the Bucks County, Pa.,* Times.

DAVID ROTHFELD
Of E. J. Korvette, Inc.

DEE CARUSO

ROBERT V. COX
Of Pepsi Cola.

DR. HOWARD S. FRIEDMAN
One of Philly's finest.

JAN MURRAY

KENNY DELMAR

ADAM WADE

JOHN WINGATE
Of WOR, New York.

ERNEST SCHIER
Of the Philadelphia Bulletin.

RAY JOHNSON and CHRIS GRIECO
Fine pianists.

MILTON THE FLORIST
Of Times Square Subway Florists, Inc. (IRT Division)

HARRY YAVENER, DOROTHY CANTWELL, ED "DUFFY" RAMSEY, BUS SAIDT, LOU GUNKEL, HERB BLACKWELL, JOE LOGUE, EDDIE HOFFMAN, STEVE MERVISH, PATTI PRINCIPI, GEORGE MOLDOVAN
Of The Trentonian, *Trenton, N. J.*

ART THOMPSON
Of the Delaware Valley Advance, *Bucks County, Pa.*

BOB LANDRY
Of Variety.

MIKE CONNOLLY

WALLACE COOPER
Of the Associated Negro Press.

TOM STORY and DON BARNETT
Of American & Drew Furniture.

LADDIE SCHAEFFER, BERNIE COSNOSKI, BOB GOLDMAN, DICK BURNS and TOM DURAND
Of WTTM, Trenton.

PEG MacEACHRON
Of WJNO, West Palm Beach.

WARD WILSON, MARY NEMEC and BOB WILSON
Of WEAT-TV, Palm Beach.

GEORGE WHITE and his SCANDALS—TOM ANDERSON, BILL GORDON and SANDY LECHNER
Of WPTV, Palm Beach.

JAMES GARRETT
Of the Cleveland Press, *a nice man, even though he's the brother of the polecat who gunned down Billy.*

GEORGE BARBER
Of WPBF, West Palm Beach.

On the Secret Service of His Majesty, the Queen

PAIGE PALMER
Of WEWS-TV, Cleveland; Mrs. Strength and Health.

JOEL DALY
Of WJW-TV, Cleveland.

ED FISHER
Of WJW, Cleveland.

THE LINDELL A.C.
Of Detroit.

MARY MORGAN
Of CKLW-TV, Windsor, Ontario.

CAROL ANDERSON, FRED SHAW, MICHAEL THOMPSON and
JACK KASSEWITZ (a friend of Norman Shavin)
Of the Miami News.

DOC GREENE
Of the Detroit News.

MARK BELTAIRE
Of the Detroit Free Press.

LARRY JONES
Of WWJ, Detroit.

SHIRLEY EDER
Of WJBK, Detroit.

DICK OSGOOD
Of WXYZ, Detroit.

DICK DESAUTEL
Of WJLB, Detroit.

HAL YOUNGBLOOD, LEE MURRAY and JIM LAUNCE
Of WJR, Detroit.

THE SU CASA
Fine Mexican restaurant of Chicago.

JACK WALLACE and WALTER BLUM
Of the San Francisco Examiner.

EDDIE HUBBARD, JACK BRICKHOUSE and JACK ROSENBERG
Of WGN, Chicago.

JACK EIGEN
Of WMAQ, Chicago, who does a trenchant, hilarious impression of Mike Nichols.

LEE PHILLIP and JUDY McKEOWN
Of the Lee Phillip Show, WBBM-TV, Chicago.

DICK BAKER
Of WCIU-TV, Chicago, America's greatest comedy team.

DUKE ZIEBERT
Of Duke Ziehen's Restaurant, Washington, D.C.

IRA BLUE
Of KGO, San Francisco, the controversial gentleman for whom I demonstrated my quicksilver ad lib ability by composing an original song on the spot: "Ira Blue... Ira Blue... ain't these tears in muh eyes tellin' you?"

BILL GORDON
On the Scene at KGO-TV, San Francisco.

OWEN SPAN
Of KGO, San Francisco.

HILLY ROSE and BOB VAINOWSKI
Of KCBS, San Francisco, members of SPECTRUM.

JOSEPH P. MUNIZ
Of Thom McAn Shoe Co.

DON RIGGS and MARCY LYNN
Pittsburgh's "Wakeup Kids."

GEORGE BOURKE

On the Secret Service of His Majesty, the Queen

Amusements Editor of the Miami *Herald*.

JAY BUSHINSKY*
Of the Miami Herald.

LARRY KING
Of the Miami Beach Sun.

JOHN HAMBRICK and BOB HILL
Of KHOU-TV, Houston.

RIC RICHARDS and BOB KELLY
Of KTHT, Houston.

ARNOLD ROSENFELD
Of the Houston Post.

CHARLIE JOHNSON and ALAN JOHNSON
Of KPRC, Houston.

JEFF MILLAR
Of the Houston Chronicle.

BOBBY BROCK and BOBBY BRUTON
Of WFAA, Dallas.

DON DAY
Of KXOL, Fort Worth.

ED BARKER, WES WISE, JIM UNDERWOOD and FRANK GLIEBER
Of KRLD, Dallas.

JACK GORDON
Of the Fort Worth Press.

ANN TINSLEY
Of the Fort Worth Star-Telegram.

---

* A non-person.

SID MARK, GEORGE LYLE, STEWART CHASE, JOEL DORN, VINCE GARRETT, RICK FRIEDMAN, JOE ZAWACKI, GENE SHAY, RON TILDON and ART (Bagels and Lox) RAYMOND
Of WHAT-FM, Philly's 24-hour-a-day jazz bastion.

BERNARD PEIFFER JAZZ TRIO
(Peiffer, piano; Johnny Coates Jr., vibes; Gus Nemeth, bass. Fellas, I wrote these jazz pieces, you see....)

CHARLES W. ADAMS
Of Coca-Cola.

LEO ARYEH ATTAR
Sportsman of Israel.

HUGH M. HEFNER, A. C. SPECTORSKY, JACK KESSIE, SHELDON WAX, FRANK ATLASS, HY ROTH, BOBBIE ARNSTEIN and TANIA GROSSINGER
Of Playboy. "Hello, I'm your Bunny, Berigan."

DOUGH CHINA, JAY STEVENS and MERRITT HADLEY
Of WGBS, Miami.

BERT WEILAND and JIM WHITTINGTON
Of WIGO, Atlanta.

FRANCIS RAFFETTO
Of the Dallas News. (Recipe for a foileh verenik furnished upon request.)

VIDA GOLDGAR
Of the Southern Israelite.

TOMMY THOMPSON
Of WSB, Atlanta.

NATE ROBERTS and BERNARD BROWN
Of WGST, Atlanta.

HAL PARETS
Of KTTV, Los Angeles.

DAVE (The Pure American Voice) WEBSTER and MARY McGRAW
Of WQXT, Palm Beach.
OSCAR PETERSON and LUCKY THOMPSON
Two great jazzmen just a furge of a fifkin away from immortality, who could achieve it merely by recording an LP of my... the hell with it! I'm sick of begging.

******

And, of course,
NANCY BROWN
Of Plainfield, New Jersey.

(If your name wasn't mentioned, there were valid reasons. Maybe you were a Don't-Bee, 'stead of a Doo-Bee, a Goofus and not a Gallant. But you have another chance because there's a fourth and final Israel Bond thriller in the works. So take that Dial shower every morning, warm the world with your tingly MacLean's smile and support your area National Educational Television station. I'll hear about it, don't worry. 'Cause you see, P. F. Flyers fans, Uncle Sol really loves you. He just wants you to come up to his standards, that's all.)

Table of Contents

1 A King's Secret Shame	261
2 TheBitch Of Schweinbaden	264
3 Trenton, I'm Coming	270
4 "My Boys, They're Killing My Boys"	278
5 Those Vines Have Slender Shapes	282
6 "The Martini Gave You Away..."	287
7 Candy, I Call My Killer Candy	292
8 Dark Pool, Sweet Pool	296
9 Where Love Has Gone	300
10 Tell Me, Where Can I Go?	301
11 There's Something Strange In The Heir	303
12 A Strong Man Weeps	309
13 Gas, Meter Of A Traitor	315
14 Call To Greatness	325
15 A Score In The Sky	329
16 Dee Dee, Da, Da, Da, Da, Dee Dee	335
17 Let's Do The Tryst	338
18 Blood And Sand And Blood And Blood—	342
19 Shivs, I'm Here!	351
20 This Pond's Minus Honey And Almonds	356
21 For "The Clipper" And "Mighty Mick"	361
22 Good Old Sol*	368
23 First Things Second	373
24 Sermon On The Mount	377
25 All's Fair, In Love And "La Guerre"	383
26 The Tale Of The Little Princess	388
27 Ain't That A Kick In The Glass!	394
Epilogue	401

"Don't Quote Me"—Bartlett

1
A King's Secret Shame

"Ben-Bella Barka."

The plea tugged its way past the swollen, blackened tongue through the desiccated lips.

The Grand Vizier of Sahd Sakistan looked down with pity upon the sprawled body of the man in the red Macadamia lizard nightshirt whose sweat-drenched head lolled against the virginal softness of the Doris Day foam rubber pillow.

"Yes, my King, O son of jasmine, honey and saccharin, blessed shining scimitar of ten thousand righteous disembowelments."

"Ben-Bella Barka, I am dying."

Ben-Bella Barka glanced at the fever chart stapled to the foot of the Bengalese ivory bed made of Consumers' Union-approved tusks from selected elephant graveyards. The jagged red line was at 119 degrees, the very top of the chart, and ended, still on an upward trend, at a notice which read: CONTINUED ON NEXT CHART.

"I fear as much, leopard of Araby. As it comes to all men in this uncertain world, so must the black camel of death come even to a king."

"Look, schmuck. Cut out the Westbrook van Voorhis *March of Time* documentary crap and listen to me," the king muttered. A sudden fit of coughing sent a trickle of blood down the right corner of his mouth. "Speak truthfully to me, Ben-Bella Barka, I command thee. What will befall my country upon my passing?"

Ben-Bella Barka winced at the king's choice of language. My master has been too often among the infidels, he thought. He tried to avoid the monarch's eyes as he answered. "Anarchy, O Lord of the Thighs, giver of pleasure to many concubines. You leave no heir. Thus, the Kurds and Wheys will be encompassed in a divisive power struggle, leaving Sahd Sakistan easy prey for the colonel in Cairo and his agents here. The mystery rider will do her best to save us, but who will listen to a mere woman?"

The king sighed. "Sarah Lawrence of Arabia, the beauty whose face no man has e'er seen unveiled." He coughed again more violently and groaned. "Ai! May Allah spray uncut Clorox upon all carriers of germs! That last spasm split my truss. The end is nigh, my Grand Vizier. Is that cold fish of a German doctor within the walls of this room?"

"He is in the hallway beyond hearing, O roaring lion of a hundred Tom & Jerry shorts. Speak freely."

"Draw close. I shall divulge to you a secret which I have kept locked in my heart for twenty-seven years."

Ben-Bella Barka moved quickly to the king's side.

"I have a son."

"You jest, O panther of the bulrushes."

"Nay, I speak the truth. Listen well: Years ago when I was a young man given to wildness and adventure I heeded your advice when you told me to discard my royal raiments and go among the common people as a lowly seller of myrrh and frankincense so that I might learn something of the world outside the palace. I learned many things, Ben-Bella Barka, among them the fact that nobody in my kingdom knew what the hell myrrh and frankincense were and cared even less. In my absence you attempted to seize the throne and I was forced eventually to return and lop off your ears. Do you recall that episode, Ben-Bella Barka?"

"Louder, sire. As you know, I do not hear too well."

"During that one-year hiatus I became a merchant seaman on a charter boat carrying prostitutes from Calique to New York."

"Yes, sire. A tramp steamer."

"Good! You remember. In Manhattan, under the pseudonym of Bernie Seligman, I lived with a handsome, lusty Negro wench named Caldonia Simmons in a boisterous, fetid tenement at 117th Street and Madison Avenue, which, when it was finally condemned by the Board of Health as totally unfit for apartment dwellers, was converted by the city into an elementary school. Those were the happiest, freest days of my life, making uninhibited love to her three times a day and leaning out the fifth floor window to observe the colorful activities of the storied, high-powered Madison Avenue way of life; those distinguished men in smartly tailored grey flannel suits carrying attaché cases filled with heroin. But I digress. Caldonia and I had a love child, a boy named Beaster who has since taken his mother's name. I would have remained with her always except for her damnable stubborn streak and, thus, one night in a fit of pique I deserted them. She since has borne children by other men, according to our ambassador who was ordered to keep strict surveillance on the boy. A few years ago we lost contact with him. Yet, I know he lives. My son lives! And by the laws of succession he is the king. Find him, Ben-Bella Barka, and see he is rightfully seated upon the throne. Swear this by the beard of the prophet, Allen Ginsberg."

"This I swear, potentate of the pomegranates, master of ribbon-cuttings and shopping center openings."

Peace and resignation appeared on the shrunken face. "Ai! It is sworn, and should you abrogate this sacred vow Allah will dispatch myriads of locusts to clog thy giderum. In a little teakwood box under my pillow you will find more information pertaining to my son. As for me, Ben-Bella Barka, because I am an enlightened monarch, let my funeral be devoid of ostentation. I shall be buried in a plain platinum box and laid to rest inside a towering pyramid 10,000 cubits by 12,000 cubebs which need not be built by the blood and deaths of thousands but rather can be ordered prefabricated via the Spiegel catalog. Beside me will be my wives, bedecked in their finest Ceil Chapman black silk VC pajamas, my Cadillacs, gold and jewels, my stereo, my complete set of the works of Harold Robbins, and, for the love of Allah, please put in a humidifier. Ah, my faithful old jackal, I grow weary... the light grows dimmer... and yet I see a spectral face of infinite sweetness calling to me...."

His voice grew faint. Then he pulled up his emaciated frame and stared across the room as though beckoned by a vision from another time, another place.

"Caldonia! Caldonia! What made your big head so ha-a-a-a-r-r-rd!"

He fell back.

Ben-Bella Barka, according to ancient Sahd Sakistani ritual, placed an Oreo cookie over each of the king's eyes and bound them to the skull with Tuck Tape.

King Hakmir Nittah Chinek, defender of the faith, protector of caravans and president of Mecca Records, was dead.

2
The Bitch Of Schweinbaden

Like an atomic fireball expanding in slow motion, the sun came out of the darkness, painting the Gulf of Aden gold. What had been a gloomy, foreboding shape by moonlight was transformed into a sparkling white villa on the shoreline of the Road of the Feculent Figs in the tiny enclave of Sahd Sakistan which clings to the southernmost tip of the Arabian peninsula.

The villa, ringed by hundred-foot high walls of Masonite-Dixonite, is known to the madcap international jet set as Shivs, the world's preferred gambling casino. Once the fifty-room estate of a sheik, it was confiscated by the Sakistani government during a revolution that saw the sheik flee to America and eventually become a paid consultant for the Joyvah Halvah Company. King Hakmir, desperate for funds to feed his people, sold the white elephant to Hosmer Crenshaw and Montpelier Melon, the safflower oil cartel barons, who, when they were expelled from an exclusive London gaming club for not being able to recite Kipling's "Boots," launched their own in retaliation. Under the Crenshaw-Melon stewardship, Shivs began siphoning away the action from the London club as well as Monte Carlo, Vegas and Ocean Grove, New Jersey.

In the prime of their adventurous lives disaster struck these hearty, Rabelaisian men in 1962. Their stylish two-seater went out of control during Sahd Sakistan's fourth annual Soapbox Derby and hurled them over a bluff into the sea. Because they had been the very spirit of Shivs, it was assumed the casino would fold. It was saved on the day of their funerals when the grieving widows, in a graveside transaction marked by recriminations and a few well-placed blows with wrenched-off coffin handles, sold Shivs to Heinz and Gerda Sem-Heidt, the husband-and-wife co-chairmen of a mace-and-chain syndicate. The Sem-Heidts mainyained Shivs' high standards while at the same time broadening its scope to add skat, catch five, knucks, and pisheh-paysheh to the list of attractions which included "the big five,"—chemmy, baccarat, roulette, craps and, of course—*la guerre*.

No matter how scintillating the play in the casino's other parlors, the patrons were drawn by irresistible impulse at night's end to the *la guerre* table. The moment of truth was here; all other forms of wagering paled into insignificance. Only the truly affluent are found in the La Guerre Room, for its membership is limited to holders of Account Numbers 1 to 350 at the Suisse Bank de Legumes, which guarantees personal cash deposits of no less than 500 million Bolivian *quasars* or 750 million Ruthenian *colodnys*, and any banker will tell you these are the two most stable currencies on earth.

At 11 A.M. the doors to the conference room at Shivs swung open, admitting nine of its ten directors. They seated themselves in plush Jamaican poisonwood chairs with matching ottomans and lit aromatic Muriel cigars. There were two places at the head of the table for the co-chairmen—one empty, the other more than amply filled by the corpulent bulk of Heinz Sem-Heidt, who signaled for silence.

"Since our voices can be heard on the sound system in the cellar and my wife can converse with us, we will proceed with the agenda. Herr Zentner?"

A tall blond man with watery eyes stood ramrod straight. "I have the pleasure to report that King Hakmir is dead." There were murmurs of approval, even handclaps. "We, of course, have sent word to the palace that the directorship of Shivs offers its heartfelt condolences (laughter) and regrets that the valiant efforts of our physician, Dr. Ernst Holzknicht, to save His Majesty, were to no avail. (Louder laughter.) It was most fitting that the good doctor should have attended the king, for it was he who placed the *sivana bacillus* in the king's Diet Pepsi in the first place." The directors gave a standing ovation to the smiling doctor, who shook his head with self-effacement.

"A minor but hardly insoluble problem has evolved. From a listening device planted on the fever chart we have learned there is an heir and that Ben-Bella Barka has been ordered to seek him out and enthrone him. The Grand Vizier will be shadowed, of course, and Hakmir's son eliminated by some regrettable accident. We foresee a rulerless enclave beset by a vitiating power struggle between the Kurds and their traditional enemies, the Wheys, enabling our client from the U.A.R. to take control. Our fee will amount to 900 million *quasars*, plus 10 percent of the royal treasury."

Herr Zentner sat down to sustained cheering.

An iron voice cut through the collective self-satisfaction and their smiles vanished as though wiped off by an artist's brush.

"What about the mystery woman? I want her eliminated!"

Heinz Sem-Heidt blanched. "Mein liebchen, Gerda, we are doing all in our power to end her disruptive tactics. I swear to you by Himmler's pinky ring that before long she will be rotting in the sun."

The iron voice in the cellar was cold, dripping with malice: "This Sarah Lawrence of Arabia, as she calls herself, for the last year has been preaching unity between the Kurds and Wheys, appealing for an end to antipathy for the sake of Sakistani nationalism. She has led them in sorties against U.A.R. infiltrators. She even urges them to enter upon friendly relations with Israel." A stream of curses followed. "Who is she? Why is she here? Is she in the pay of the Zionists? I want these answers and the issue resolved immediately!"

Heinz Sem-Heidt collapsed in his chair, his obscenely fat jowls shaking. "You have heard my wife, gentlemen. Put a Condition Black priority on Sarah Lawrence of Arabia. We will hear other reports. Herr Krug?"

"Fellow directors, I wish to report that our fee for capturing Hebrew Secret Agent Moe Zambique, Oy Oy Five, taken in Damascus and brought here for questioning by Gerda, will net us twenty-five thousand Straits dollars when we turn him over to Syria."

"Twenty-five thousand Straits dollars?" There was rebuke in Heinz Sem-Heidt's retort. "A pittance. The capture of an ordinary Double-Oy from Israel's M 33 and 1/3 is worth easily five times that figure. And if we had taken Oy Oy Seven, well...." His hands made a sky's-the-limit gesture.

Stocky Herr Krug puffed his Muriel. "Yes, but this should be considered what the Americans term a 'loss leader.' Let the Syrians have him for that price. They will soon become so highly dependent on TUSH, our Terrorist Union for Suppressing Hebrews, that we can safely raise the ante on each succeeding job."

There was a long trailing scream from the cellar. As inured to violence as they were, the nine men shuddered.

The iron voice returned: "Gentlemen, let us not concern ourselves with the piddling Syrian payment. Oy Oy Five will be of no use to them now. Please delay any further items until I come to the conference room."

They heard the whine of the elevator, then the doors opened and a wheelchair bearing Gerda Sem-Heidt was pushed across the green-and-black swastika-patterned carpet by a dwarf in a dunce cap and a medieval jester's outfit with tinkling bells on his pointed shoes.

Gerda Sem-Heidt fixed her mustard-yellow eyes upon her twitching husband, then let them scan the other directors. She was a wizened crone of seventy-three who bore a startling resemblance to the witch in the cartoon *Snow White*. Her hands were bony, clawlike, empty of rings, with extra-length fingernails which the dwarf set about honing to razor sharpness with sandpaper. Her face was chalk white, which made the yellow eyes and vein-blue lips appear even more hideous. Virtually bald, she concealed her few wisps of yellowish-white hair with a fiery orange-colored muskrat wig. Her cadaverous body was covered by a red and white J. C. Penney housedress and her unstockinged, bean-shooter feet were ensconced in Kitty Kelly's Mexicali Rosen *huaraches*. And there was something else on her body, revealed by the deliberately opened housedress.

As the directors saw it their sullen Nordic faces turned a sickly greenish hue. She watched their reactions with a smile. No matter how many times she displayed it, they could never become used to it.

Gerda Sem-Heidt was the proud possessor of a plastic heart.

Dr. Holzknicht alone was undisturbed as he viewed with clinical detachment the exposed components in their transparent styrene housing, the action of the atria and ventricles, the unoxygenated blood changed to bright red by the lungs. It was he who had installed the device after a seizure that left Gerda paralyzed in both legs and close to death. The plastic heart drew its power from an external electromagnetic coil hooked into a transistor battery that never left her lap. The same coil toasted her English muffins of which she had a constant supply in her pockets. Now she grew bored with her shocking little game so she closed her housedress. "Let us continue, gentlemen. I want to hear Dr. Holzknicht's summation of 'Operation Alienation.'" To the dwarf: "Locksley, a muffin, *bitte.*"

Dr. Ernst Holzknicht, a slightly built man with a bland face and the large forehead of the scholar, cleared his throat. "Fellow directors, as you know, I am not only a surgeon but a diplomate of the Schisselzelmknist Institute of Advanced Psychiatry. It was my good fortune to assist occasionally our Führer (the men's right hands shot up in a robotlike heil) during those phases of the war that called for an understanding of the mentality of the Third Reich's enemies. When our beloved co-chairmen, Heinz and Gerda Sem-Heidt, whom we all served with unquestioning loyalty in those glorious, fulfilling days at the Schweinbaden Concen—er, Detention and Cultural Rehabilitation Center—asked me to mount a plot against the *Juden*"—several of the directors growled; Gerda spat into Locksley's puckered apple of a face—"I accepted their challenge with strength through joy. In our previous sessions we have discussed the psychological factors which are involved in 'Operation Alienation.' Now it remains only to carry out the physical extirpation of these installations"—his hand swept across a map of North and South America and Western Europe containing thousands of locations denoted by pins—"and Phase One will be complete. Then in a few days we should begin noticing the inevitable results. Thousands of field men will be taking surveys on synagogue and Jewish organizational attendance, United Jewish Appeal contributions, Catskill Mountains and Miami Beach resort bookings, El Al aircraft and Zim Line cruise ship reservations, etc. I have not the slightest doubt that we shall witness a drastic decline in all of these activities. Now I shall yield to Heinz Sem-Heidt, who will outline the personnel problems."

Heinz Sem-Heidt pushed his hands down hard on the armrests of his chair to hoist up his three-hundred-pound body. "There are no personnel problems, mein lieber Doktor. In this world, happily, there is never a shortage of Jew-haters. (Laughter and applause.) It was a simple matter for our sub-agents who combed the locations marked on our map to find disgruntled individuals willing to attach a Calgonite charge to the wall of a Jewish-owned business. There are five thousand key targets on the three continents, which means the total cost to TUSH, at one hundred dollars Amerikanische per incident will be approximately a half-million dollars. My winnings at *la guerre* alone should cover that cost.

"It is an ingenious plan and we are beholden to our dear colleague. The repercussions felt by the State of Israel will avenge TUSH for many indignities, not the least the murders of our dear Führer (the men heiled again) and our top assassin, Torquemada LaBonza, at the hands of Secret Agent Israel Bond. Our stock will rise on the Espionage Exchange when the Arab world observes that we have caused the virtual withering away of Israel and Judaism without resorting to armies, nuclear weapons or germ warfare. And, as a not inconsequential subsidiary benefit, we shall enjoy the destruction of M 33 and 1/3, the Israeli secret service, and M., the disgusting old harpy we now know is its Number One. And who knows? If Wotan and Thor are smiling down on us, Oy Oy Seven will also be found in the rubble. Gerda, my sweet, do you have any comments to make?"

"Put the plan into being." The blue lips smiled, but there was no mirth on the face or in the mad-dog yellow eyes. It has been a most satisfying day, she mused. A Jewish agent hangs from his thumbs dead in the cellar; my dear doktor has crafted a plot to bring the verminous Jewish state to its knees. A most satisfying day....

For a moment she seemed years younger, "The Bitch of Schweinbaden" of the happy, rewarding days. It was not for nothing that those few who escaped her clutches to tell the tale never referred to her as Gerda. To them she was and always would be "Auntie" Sem-Heidt.

3
Trenton, I'm Coming!

Executing a picturebook LeMans turn, he swung the majestic old 1938 Vance-Packard, the automobile of true status seekers, over the instep of the CITGO attendant, shouting, "You're a gasser!" as the man fell stricken against the high-test pump (the witticism, he knew, would do much to assuage the pain from the mashed foot) and headed out of the restaurant stop onto the New Jersey Turnpike. Destination: Trenton, New Jersey, place of his birth.

Israel Bond was going home.

The meal had been as exciting as a Blue Barron recording of "Tiptoe Through the Tulips." There was no doubt in his mind; the world's safest job was that of a foodtaster for Howard Johnson's. No, don't be smart-alecky, he scolded himself. The dessert, frozen baked beans on a stick, had been first rate, the coffee rivaling Horn & Heartburn's best, and the painting of the waitresses' faces orange and turquoise to conform to the general decor a cheery touch.

A surge of power from the Vance-Packard, whose 24-cylinder, 8.6 axle ratio, short-stroke, tall-coxswain engine was revved up to maximum cruising speed of 118.9 hectares, sent a chill pulsating through his being. With no strain it hummed past two Cadillacs and an Imperial (all parked on the shoulder for repairs), its 12-ply Firestone tires purring a symphony at that most crucial of the world's rendezvous—where the rubber meets the road.

Bond stuck a Raleigh between his sensual, Chap-Sticked lips and adjusted the magnifying glass on the Vance-Packard's visor to entice a goodhearted cosmic ray to veer from its endless course toward galaxies unknown and zero in on the cigarette's tip and ignite it.

His two-week vacation after the El Tiparillo affair[*] had not been prosaic. An old love, Charlene Krosnick, had stolen away from her husband and children to share a night of bliss with him in New York. He took her to see *The Bantu and the Bubby*, the musical comedy sensation by top songsmiths Manny Sheldon and Sheldon Manny about a sweet Jewish grandmother who convinces South Africa to abandon its odious policy of racism and appoint a sensitive Negro goatherd as its new prime minister. They dined at romantic, candlelit Nedick's where a strolling gypsy comes to your table to play your favorite *chansons d'amour* on his tambourine as the waiter pours the orange drink over ice shavings. She then insisted he take her to see *Thunderball*, the popular spy movie. "Gosh, Iz," she sighed as she gazed into the mocking yet tender grey eyes of the secret-agent hero on the billboard. "He kind of looks like... you. Are *you* really some dashing spy, Iz?" She giggled at the thought. "I hardly think a guy who promotes Mother Margolies' Activated Old World Chicken Soup would be a swashbuckler, though, would you?" And on an impulse and to tease him she kissed the figure on the advertisement.

"You're making me jealous, Charlene," Bond had jested. "But I'm better than he in one place," and he whisked her via subway to his luxurious suite at Manhattan's regal Ansonia Hotel where he whispered, "Let there be no puerile shame, no holding back. *Every pore must score.*" As their bodies fused in *score de combat*, he crooned into her fragrant apricot of an ear an aphrodisiacal song based upon the Kama Sutra.

> "I'll be loving you, all ways...
> "With a love that's true, all ways..."

But he had become bored with matchless ecstasy so he had accepted two part-time freelance jobs. The first had been a puff. Through Seymour Feig, an old drinking buddy, he was engaged by a Mr. Farraday to fly to Los Angeles and bring back a certain package. He went there without incident via the "friendly skies of United" (Pan Am's were indifferent; TWA's downright hostile, he had been told) but coming back a charming girl

---

[*] *Matzohball*, Pocket Books Inc., 1966, $1. It contains certain insights no Ian Fleming novel could ever hope to match.

in the adjoining seat turned out not so charming after all, covering him with a Chase-Manhattan .38 Banker's Special and expressing an interest in his attache case. He had been compelled to drive the case against her lovely jaw, breaking it and disabling an operative from the second leading weekly news magazine in America. Back in Manhattan he delivered the flat parcel to the soft-spoken, pipe-smoking Farraday, an agent for the Number One such publication.

"Capital, Mr. Bond! Now, until we release it ourselves, the secret of who will grace our magazine's 'Man of the Year' cover is safe, thanks to you."

He had refused Farraday's sizable check. "I cannot in good conscience accept payment. My people owe you an everlasting debt. Your magazine's recent, heralded Essay on Judaism with its generally favorable tone has done more to secure recognition and acceptance for my people than any document since the Ten Commandments."

After a lump-in-the-throat silence during which he realized he was in the presence of a unique human being, Farraday said, "Is there anything we *can* do that might please you, Mr. Bond?"

"One trifling favor. Have your Show Biz editor do a nice, lengthy feature piece on the gentleman who has taken it upon himself to be my Boswell and chronicle these adventures of mine. And now, sir, may good *Fortune* attend you and may you have *Time* to enjoy it!"

Farraday cracked up. "Geez, that's hilarious!" and when Bond, eyes atwinkle, zinged in a topper, "Of course, don't play fast and *Luce!*" he'd literally fallen on the floor.

Assignment Two had been no piece of cake, his torn shoulder testified graphically.

"There's a frightened kid holed up in the Hotel Bogaslovsky on West 46th Street," Bond was informed on the phone. "He's promised to work for us, but if he steps out of that room for sure he'll be killed."

"Who's after him?" Bond wanted to know. It was the kind of question a real top-drawer agent asked.

"There are undercovermen in town representing cliques from Dallas, Minnesota, Philadelphia... many others. They're ruthless men and if they can't have him, they swear nobody else will. They tried once in Chicago, even killed his guard, but he slipped 'em. Deliver him to us alive and usable and there's twenty grand in it for you. Use the code words 'Flood Formation' and he'll let you in."

The terrorized tot, Bond discovered, was one Casimir Predpelski, aged twenty-two, six feet six, 275 pounds, from Hamtramck, Michigan. Bond spent the better part of a day calming the thumb-sucking Gargantua in Dr. Denton pajamas with a medley of Polish love songs, which included "A Glass of Beer, a Bowling Ball and You" and "Keep Throwing That Dart, in the Dartboard of My Heart."

A chunky little room service waiter named Paulo Gunty brought matters to a head. As Bond noticed with relief from the third-story window the van that was to take him and Predpelski to freedom, the little waiter held out a huge candy cane to the lad. "We always bring some sweets and goodies to our younger guests. It is a policy of the hotel."

"Candy! Candy!" the monster cried with a childish eagerness that made Bond smile a parental smile.

Click!

In a hideous second of revelation Bond knew the truth. Two feet of naked steel shot out of the cane brandished by the little man in the monkey jacket who had played the servile fool until his victims were lulled into complacence. Gunty shouted a fanatical "From Green Bay with hate!" and thrust at Predpelski with the classic *coup de murville.*

Bond hurtled his frame between swordpoint and bobbing Adam Nowicki's-apple on Polish throat, incurring a nasty slash as it ripped through the trenchcoat epaulet down into his right shoulder. But he'd yanked out the Chris-Keeler, squeezed the trigger and heard the characteristic, silencer-muffled *slut! slut!* and saw two angry holes pop up in Gunty's forehead. There was an insistent hammering at the door and someone shouted, "Break it in."

Undoubtedly there were more of Gunty's cohorts in the hallway, perhaps far too many to handle.

When he saw the stuff in the corner, an inspiration flashed through his mind.

It was piled up in an odiferous mound.

Kielbasa!

The Polish sausage the kid loved best. Links and links of it. Holding his nose, Bond tested the links. Good-o! They were bound by solid, dependable Bangalore twine.

"Here's our escape route, buddy boy," he told the whimpering leviathan. "Tie one end around the bedpost and throw the rest out the window."

He put two more slugs through the door, exulting in a scream. He heard a voice: "Jesus, he just killed the chambermaid."

Bond looked down. Predpelski had already shinnied down the thick, greasy chain of sausages with amazing agility for one his size and was bolting into the back of the van. Bond started his own descent, his long, tapering fingers around the links in a viselike grip. He was at the second story now, pausing just long enough to chance upon a disrobing brunette and take her phone number, when he spotted the trio of hired killers racing up the street to the van.

Swegroes!

They were the flaxen-haired, lapidus-lazuli-eyed, chocolate-hued descendants of Swedish mariners who decades ago had impregnated the willing women of West Africa's Hullaballuba tribe. They wore Libby's split-peajackets, nail-studded Levi Strauss Levi's and crepe-soled Aleutian bedsocks. Once, on a psychological warfare mission into Jordan where he had dynamited a theater showing an Omar Sharif movie, Bond had come in contact with a Swegro, disguised as an usher, in the employ of the Jordanian league for actors-in-espionage, Mosque & Wig. It had been a hellish minute of combat that left the Swegro decapitated and quite incensed about it and himself with a dirk in his shoulder. A mean lot, Swegroes, far worse than Bulgars, and now he had to get past three of them!

They saw him immediately. Shots rang out, one of which skinned his gun hand and he dropped the Chris-Keeler into the street. *Gottenu!* Unarmed!

There was one chance. He kicked out against the sign HOTEL BOGASLOVSKY, MANHATTAN'S PREMIER RESIDENCE FOR DRIFTERS AND INDIGENTS and, releasing the chain, fell through the roof of the van, crying, "Go! Go!"

Miles away, the van parked at Yankee Stadium, the driver handed Bond the twenty Big Ones. "You've pulled it off, Mr. Bond, but then, it's what we'd expected of a man with your reputation. As for you, Predpelski, sign here on the dotted line. Thanks to Israel Bond, young fella, you are now the middle linebacker for the New York Giants."

There could have been a third freelance gig, for even bigger money, but Bond had no desire to tail the president of General Motors.

A burst of song from the Vance-Packard's custom-made Atwater Kent UHF-CIO radio drove the perilous Predpelski affair from his mind. It was a composition that had moved the hearts of Americans from coast to coast and was certain to capture the annual Larry Hart Award for the most meaningful lyric of the year.

"*Batman!*
"*Batman!*
"*Batman!*
"*Batman!*
"*Batman! Batman!*
"*Batman!*"

Unforgettable!

For variety's sake and Abel Green's as well, he switched stations.

"... on record against this evil manifestation of man's inhumanity to man. Mass murder is bad business. It is degrading to its victims. It by no stretch of the imagination does anything to dignify the mass murderer. It removes from society people who have a vast potential in many areas. It causes resentment, economic dislocation, suffering and sorrow. Mass murder must end and that is the unequivocal policy of Station WDULL here in Metuchen, New Jersey. You have just heard our fourth radio editorial condemning mass murder. Of course, any responsible spokesman with an opposing viewpoint will be given equal airtime to reply."

He changed stations.

"... extraordinary series of events. Following the mysterious explosion that leveled Wishnevsky's famous bagel and bialy bakery under the Jerome Avenue El in the Bronx come reports of like explosions or bombings—though no deliberate criminality has been yet proven— throughout the country. Two famous Kosher wine companies have had their Brooklyn distilleries blown to bits with three known dead, seven missing and scores injured. Traffic in that unhappy borough is backed up all the way to Michigan City, Indiana. In Manhattan two prominent show business delicatessens on Sixth Avenue went up, hurling tons of sour pickles and tomatoes through a stage door onto the Rockettes at Radio City Music Hall. In Coney Island a convoy of trucks transporting Nathan's immortal hot dogs has been wiped out on the Belt Parkway. Chicago's contribution to the holocaust has been several explosions at bakeries, wine warehouses, dairy product plants and three huge corned beef and pastrami processing centers. Windy City police said the sky there looks like Mrs. O'Leary's cow is back in business again. Here's more: like events are occurring in Philadelphia, where a cream cheese plant and dozens of small delicatessens and a number of catering houses were blown up; St. Louis, Detroit, San Francisco, Cleveland, Denver, New Orleans, Miami Beach, the last named a shambles... in short, every major city in the U.S. Reports of additional explosions in all of these cities are coming in so fast the news wires are running behind. There are further reports, unconfirmed, that several major cities in Canada, Western Europe and South America have experienced disasters at the same sort of establishments. A freighter of Panamanian registry, the *Hispianola Roll*, en route from Halifax to New York, radioed news of an explosion and a raging fire in the hold. Coast Guard vessels are steaming to the rescue; helicopters have airlifted seventeen wounded. We will interrupt for further bulletins. Now back to William B. Williams and more of that great WNEW sound of music."

For the next half hour Bond relaxed as William B., he of the humorous, dulcet voice, spun some of the Chairman of the Board's greatest vocals from albums dedicated to young lovers, swinging lovers, medicare lovers, liver lovers, etc. If he had not been so enchanted by the music he might have surrendered to a nagging voice inside (or possibly outside; one could not be sure where nagging voices came from unless one were hopelessly married) that urged him to think, think, think about the bizarre newscast, seek some grand design in the widely spread catastrophes.

The sign on the Trenton Freeway bridge said "SLIPPERY WHEN WET," followed closely by one that said "NOT SLIPPERY WHEN DRY." The on-the-ball New Jersey Highway Department would let no driving condition go undescribed, an impressed Bond thought.

He pulled into the driveway of his brother Milton's town & country clubber at 1919 Starling Dropping Drive in the heart of Trenton's opulent Hiltonia section, and parked behind Milt's snappy 1966 Sherpa-Hunza. He banged the solid brass Rusty Warren knocker against the massive Pacific Plywood door. It opened and he was bathed in the love and warmth of home, the not-too-sister-in-lawly kisses of Lottie, the whoops of leaping Rickey, twelve, and a mushy buss from adorable, six-year-old Praline. Milton himself stood strangely apart; a questioning look said: We've-got-something-to-discuss, younger brother.

4
"My Boys, They're Killing My Boys!"

"LET HE WHO IS WITHOUT SIN BEGIN SINNING BECAUSE HE'S MISSING FUN! FUN! FUN!—Mother Margolies."

The long queue of sun-baked tourists waiting to be admitted into the various divisions of Mother Margolies' factory outside of Tel-Aviv noted with approval one of her typical Old World proverbs emblazoned on the main gate. "Gosh, eighty-four years old and she still comes up with those golden thoughts," said a B'nai B'rith president from Wisconsin, fanning his pink, flushed face with Joel Lieber's authoritative *Israel On $5 A Day*. "I wish we were in there already," responded his wife. "I'm dying to get hold of her personal recipe for Mother's Activated Old World Clam Chowder." Her husband snorted. "Don't you know the first thing about the dietary laws? Clams ain't Kosher; they don't chew their cuds...."

In the private, sealed-off wing of the factory M. watched the throng on her closed circuit TV as she knitted what soon would be Oy Oy Seven's new paisley shoulder holster. A *geeter boychik*[*] that Israel Bond, a little sex crazy sometimes and maybe a little too clothes conscious, but when it came to murdering and maiming, a fine person altogether. Oy, such a dirty business this cloak and dagger stuff! What a shame good upstanding fellows like Bond and the rest of the Double Oys had to expend their talents on these nefarious activities when they could be raising families and studying our holy works. But nations must have security forces or they succumb to predators. It's the way of the world, I suppose, she reflected. I've lost my own dear nephew, Nochum, in this filthy enterprise.

---

[*] Good boy.

M. was worried, deeply so. With the exception of Bond, who was on leave in the United States, all the Double Oys were unaccounted for. Oy Oy Five had gone to Syria to track down a lead on these TUSH people and had failed to call in. If he'd been taken by TUSH and that... that *thing*, Auntie Sem-Heidt, heaven help him! In M.'s way of thinking, TUSH was as dangerous to the survival of her nation as the American Council for Judaism. Now Double Oys Two, Three, Four and Six were missing—and right here in Israel! They had gone to that little bureau near the Ministry of Defense in Jerusalem to renew their licenses to kill... and never returned! She'd sent the new lad, Neon Zion, to investigate. Where *was* he?

And what was the meaning of these explosions bannerlined in this morning's Tel-Aviv *Trumpeldor*? They all seemed to have occurred at Jewish establishments in both the Old and New Worlds and many of them were somehow related to eating and drinking. Certainly, food for thought.

All in all, it was a gloomy day, she thought, putting aside the completed shoulder holster and starting on a trenchcoat for Lazar Beame, her chief of operations; for Israel had just lost a potential friend, King Hakmir of Sahd Sakistan. An Arab, true, but not one of the diehards. Through his Grand Vizier, Ben-Bella Barka, he had made overtures of a peaceful nature to Israel's ambassador in Paris.

The day wore on. She watched the tourists, Americans for the most part, meandering through the Potato Latke division, the Hall of Kishke, and the new Schaveria and shrieking with delight at the automated conveyor band carrying pots of fresh-made beet soup—"The Borscht Belt," as Oy Oy Seven had named it. What a wit that lad had!

The buzzer sounded. "M., it's Quartermaster HaLavi to see you, sir," said M.'s beauteous secretary, Lilah Tov. "Shall I send him in?"

"Yes."

"Oh, sir. Have you heard anything about the Double Oys? Op Chief Beame is most concerned."

"As yet, no. But the one you're personally concerned with—" M.'s TV focused on Lilah's blushing loveliness—"is safe, Miss Tov. Oy Oy Seven will be back soon."

Lavi HaLavi walked through the door. "Shalom, M. I have come to discuss some new devices for the field." He was an intense, nervous little man with fidgety eyes that seemed afraid to look into hers. The white-laboratory-coated QM had been back in harness just a few days, having spent the last six months at Foam Rubber Acres, the Service's rest home for distraught personnel. "Oh, I can't stand it in here!" he cried. "This cold air drives me insane."

"Patience, HaLavi," M. said in a tranquil tone. "It will be quitting time soon."

"I have added some new modifications for Oy Oy Seven's car, the Mercedes-Ben Gurion." He spread open a chart. "You will notice this, Button 71-a. If Bond is being tailed he has only to press it and a movie screen rolled up in a rear bumper springs out, a camera emerges from the roof and projects a series of... uh... shall we say 'art films'... which cannot help but distract any members of the 'oppo' in the car behind, thus giving him time either to eliminate or capture them, as the situation dictates. The films were taken by me at Bond's request and deal with his summer-long escapade with the Countess Tracy Di Terrazzo-Crotchetti at Portofino. Ever the sexual perfectionist, he uses them as training films to study techniques, manipulations, and so forth. They would make a ballistic missile come to a dead stop."

HaLavi lit a Raleigh and tore the coupon from the pack, placing it in a receptacle near her desk. "My ninth contribution of the day, M. You should soon have enough for that nuclear reactor. To continue; Button 95 releases a mist of Colgate's 007 cologne to freshen both his face and any wilting carnation in his lapel. And I rather think the Colgate copywriters missed out on an obvious grabber of a slogan that would treble their sales: 'Use 007 Products and You, Too, Will Get Pussy Galore.' Button 96 pops a piece of Danish into his mouth; 97 converts the MBG's front grill into a barbecue pit into which 98 flings filet mignon for two, seasoned, to be sure, with Accent; 101 converts his license plate into a hilarious sign that says 'CHICKEN INSPECTOR'; you know Oy Oy Seven's far-out sense of humor... and 105 converts any *shikseh* riding with him into a member of our faith by a tape cartridge containing recorded instructions for instant proselytizing and a spray symbolizing a ritual bath. Oh...." he pinched his nose. "This air conditioning...."

"Go on, Quartermaster HaLavi."

He dragged on his Raleigh. "I have taken the liberty of sending Oy Oy Seven several new portable devices in care of his brother in Trenton." From a pocket he fished out something.

"This is my new anti-homer capsule capsule. If Bond suspects an enemy has swallowed a homer capsule, he needs only to introduce the anti-capsule capsule into the other agent's body and it will nullify the first one immediately. Here's a little toy he will find invaluable." HaLavi held up a length of metal. "It is a device which can be strapped to his leg. I have urged him to carry it at all times. Made in my laboratory by a fantastic new process of freezing ore at one million degrees below zero, its ridges can slice through any metal known to man. The new metal, by the bye, is called Instant Processed Cold Rolled Extra Strength Steel."

"Excellent, QM!" She nodded. "Now you may take a breather from the air conditioning. Shalom."

Gasping, his nostrils flaring in his anxiety, HaLavi fled. Then a chill shook M.'s body as she heard Lilah Tov cry, "3-D! 3-D! 113 is back with a 3-D!"

3-D! Danger, doom, disaster!

Neon Zion, 113, was a pale young blond ghost as he slunk through her door. "Dead. All dead... Oy Oys Two, Three, Four and Six. They were in a cab on Ben Yehuda Street after leaving the license bureau. It blew up." He sobbed and buried his face in her shawl.

"My boys, they're killing my boys," M. said, keening, close to fainting.

At that moment the homeward-bound receptionist, rummaging among the coats in the front-office cloakroom for her own, found the thing under M.'s silver-blue mink, ticking, ticking, ticking....

5
Those Vines Have Slender Shapes

Milton Bond at forty-five was twelve years older than his Israeli brother. Like all the Bond men (there was a third brother, Ragland, forty-one, a Jonny Mop quality control inspector—"Rag" to everybody), he was blessed with the familial dark, cruelly handsome visage, his bloated a trifle by dietary indiscretions. The Bonds were Russian Jews who had settled in Trenton after a decade in London's East End where the father, Solomon, was employed by the local branch of Youngtwerp of Antwerp as a rhinestone cutter.

After the passing of their parents and the departures of Israel and Rag Bond for their own careers, Milton had wooed and somehow won Lottie Vine, one of the lithe, leggy, desirable daughters of industrialist Oleander Vine, and with the father-in-law's backing opened a successful catering house in West Trenton, the Pinochle Royale, where upper-class Jews staged their various social and sometimes religious functions.

Throughout Lottie's sumptuous meal Milton remained uncommunicative. She noticed this and attempted to brighten the occasion with light banter. "Trying some new things tonight, Iz. Mrs. Paul's frozen fishsticks, Mrs. Paul's frozen shrimp, Mrs. Paul's frozen mythical kraken suckers...."

"What's the next thing she's going to freeze? *Mister* Paul?" It was one of Bond's better jests, yet he noted Milton's face held no smile. Something wrong there. Milton normally would roll on the floor for that kind of a one-liner.

"Okay, big brother, noble patriarch of ye Clan Bond." It was a few minutes later and he was emerging from a bracing shower with Mione Soap, its haunting flavor permeating through Milton's bedroom. "Let's have it, stoneface."

Milton sat on the edge of his Frida Kahlo-designed Xochitl tostada bed, puffing doggedly on a 95-cent Dutch Master. "Your face. It looks like hell. And your body—bruises, welts, slashes. It's like this every time you come home for a visit. What the hell are you doing for a living, Iz? And no crap."

Bond inhaled a Raleigh, blew a figure eight the hard way—four twos. He looked into those grey eyes, so shrewd and hard like his own. "You know what I do, Milt. PR for Mother Margolies. These"—he ran his hands over the purple and yellow blotches—"are the result of a car crackup."

"That scar on your shoulder?"

"If you want to know the truth, Adolph Hitler did it to me. With a Luger."

"I said, cut the crap. I've had the feeling for a long time you're in some kind of... well, undercover stuff. PR guys don't get chopped to pieces from parroting the praises of chicken soup to adoring women on seven continents."

Seven. Milton said *seven*. My number! Does he know even more than he's suggesting? Of course, there *are* seven continents; he would have been idiotic to say "twelve."

Bond's face stiffened. "Why don't we just watch a little TV, huh?" He flicked on the Zenith portable, giving an affectionate pat to as many of the superior, hand-wired circuits as his long, tapering fingers could locate.

When the buzz died down an Indian chief, hatred blazing from his lined face, spoke: "White man steal Apache land, white man slaughter buffalo, white man make Injun loco with firewater, traumatize him, emasculate him, steal Indian nuts, leave him rootless without something of value. Now, white man—die!"

The rangy trail boss did not flinch. "Hear me, Running Abscess, mighty chieftain of the Trocadero Apaches. You and your braves massacred the peaceful homesteaders at Lamprey Landing, took many scalps, burned homes, schools, churches, trading stamp redemption centers. And now you expect the Great White Father in Washington to put your likeness on the new nickel after *this*?" He drew the trembling woman in calico to his breast. "I'm savin' one bullet for you, Miss Lucy. I seen what these murderin' redskins do to white women." She cringed. "What—what do they do, Lonestar?" He looked at his boots in embarrassment. "They... they violate 'em, Miss Lucy." She screamed: "Yoo-hoo, dear sweet Apaches! Over here! Over here! Take your goddam hands off me, Lonestar...."

Milton turned it off. "Iz, I want you to do me a favor. I want you to see Lottie's sister tonight. She's been asking about you."

A pang triggered a sonar ping in the soul of Israel Bond. Liana Vine! Youngest of the desirable, leggy, lithe daughters of Oleander. She remembered.

They had been "The Sweethearts of Trenton High" and, on a few hundred fumbling occasions and seventy distinctly competent ones, lovers. Cool, lissome, blonde Liana. Probably there had been three or four prettier girls that year... Phyllis Rosenblum, the cattle dealer's daughter; Monique Introlligator... mischievous Felice Pixie Berman. But there had been something special about Liana, something you couldn't put your finger on (it was rare in that respect). Her painfully shy smile? Perhaps the gliding carriage of a ballet dancer? Or maybe it was the protective urge she evoked in him, the way she made him feel she *needed* him as he posed her for pictures against the gate of her father's hundred-acre plastics factory.

It might have come to something, but then erupted the trouble in Palestine. Young Israel Bond, steeped in intense Jewishness by his parents, heard the call for deliverance from across the world. He had long been involved in Jewish National Fund collections, he belonged to Young Judea, Trenton's YMHA,[*] the Allenby Club and A.Z.A., a fraternity for Jewish high schoolers with mathematical interests (Angle Zide Angle).

With alacrity he joined a kibbutz[**] near Hightstown, N.J., where Zionist-minded youths were being trained to endure conditions approximating those in Eretz Israel, fabled land of Milk and Magnesia. Realism was the keynote at K'far K'Near, once the potato farm of McSorley Shinn, a taciturn Baptist. The eager kibbutzniks slept on straw mats in barracks swarming with scorpions and pit vipers (imported at great cost from the Holy Land), tilling the soil under fire. (The kibbutz had advertised in a rural weekly for men who wanted $1.25-an-hour work shooting through barbed wire at Jewish boys and girls. K'far K'near had been overwhelmed by the generous response from the surrounding community. Many had expressed a willingness to perform this service gratis, proving, as a highly

---

[*] Young Men's Hebrew Association.
[**] Farm settlement.

complimentary article in the kibbutz newspaper pointed out, that brotherhood was no myth.)

The war. Awful moments on mountain roads pocked by mortar shells. Hand-to-hand combat with bestial mercenaries of Glubb Pasha's Arab Legion. His rapid rise in the informal yet deadly Palmach* to the rank of water carrier. A flair for recklessness and conspiracy noticed by an astute colonel in the Shinbet,* leading to an eventual post with M 33 and 1/3, the coveted Double Oy number and a license— to kill!

Eighteen years away from Liana. Still she remembered.

There was a small PR chore to get out of the way, a speech before the Histamine, the ladies auxiliary to the local chapter of the Histadrut,** which met each month at the Pinochle Royale. Then the decks would be cleared for an evening with Liana. Her voice was silky, teasing, on the phone. "Mother and Daddy are in Aruba, so it's just you and me, Iz. Wear something casual."

"Like my skin, dearest?" He prayed she would not hear the juvenile pounding of his heart.

He donned a pair of Botany 1,000 nankeen stretch pants and Shropshire Argyle bedsocks, and pulled a buff-colored cashmere T-shirt over his rippling torso. He completed the ensemble with a multiflowered Korvette's luau car coat of guazeroy and went downstairs, six steps at a time, to meet Lottie's admiring, "Wow! Is someone I love very much duded up sharp to meet someone else I love very much!" The oval face softened. "Iz, be kind to her."

There was Praline to kiss goodnight, but not before she recited a poem she'd memorized "just for you, Uncle Israel." Whereupon she launched into Robinson Jeffers' "Roan Stallion," faltering here and there as a tyke might, but giving it a generally knowledgeable reading. "Off to bed, you rascal!" and he whacked her saucy behind. For Rickey, who was above that sort of thing, a catch with the lad's new Superball, a five-minute tutoring session on the New Math ("X can lift 60 tons of potash; Y can lift twice as much potash as X; Z can lift only half as much as X. Question: Why is Z avoiding his social responsibilities?"), a hearty handshake and "keep studying for that Bar Mitzvah, fella."

---

* Army of Israel.
** Zionist Labor Organization.

A good kid, Rickey, with the usual problems of adolescence. "Uncle Iz. Dad's kinda corny about some things, so can I talk to you about, uh..."

"Don't do it, Rickey lad. You'll go blind and eventually insane. You shouldn't be troubling us oldtimers for advice, anyhow. That's the kind of thing you should be learning on the streets. Tell you what, fella. Uncle Iz'll send you some Superman color slides that'll explain the whole thing. These were made in pre-Castro Cuba. 'Night, Rickey."

In Milton's Sherpa-Hunza they made some safe small talk about cars, politics, suburban life. "Pretty quiet out here," said Milton with satisfaction. " 'Course we did have our little excitement last summer. Guy next door's power mower went mad. One minute it was breezing along chewing up the crabgrass; next minute it whacked out, ate up three poinsettia beds and somebody's pet Schnauzer. When it went for a Volvo we got scared, called the SRS... that's the Sears Rescue Squad... and they shot the poor bastard dead on our lawn."

"Any of that wife-swapping bit going on out here?"

"Nah, old hat. The real hippies are swapping their mistresses. Hey, Iz, did you read Jim Michener's new book?"

"You bet, Milt. Damn fine. I saw him in Jerusalem while he was gathering *'Source'* material."

From Milton's outraged "ooooh" and his howls of hilarity Bond knew the ice of early evening had been broken.

Chums again!

6
"The Martini Gave You Away..."

He finished the speech before the sweet old matrons, any one of whom could have been fated to head the Secret Service of Israel, so much like M. were they. Having won Mother's products a few dozen more lifelong supporters, he rejoined Milton in the latter's modernistic office with the genuine Tupperware spittoons which were gaining favor with busy executives.

"Come on, Iz; I'll take you through the joint."

He led the Israeli through the Pinochle Royale's rooms, explaining their functions. "You see what it is, Iz. Jews have become so jaded; they just won't buy the oldtime ways any more. You gotta give 'em that ol' show business pizzazz in every area of existence. Now this," and Milton's eyes were humorous, "is the Slice O' Life Room."

No further explanation was needed as Bond watched the rite of circumcision performed upon an eight-day-old squeaker in a room whose walls were a montage of *Life* Magazine covers. "*Noch a Yid!*"[*] Bond said with fervor. "Amen," Milton chimed in. As the *mohel* worked, they saw the child's cowering father, his arm before his face. Not so the mother, who coolly applied a tape measure to the pink monkey feet.

"Real Jewish mother," Milton commented. "Already measuring him for corrective shoes."

After they passed through three kitchens ("Kosher, non-Kosher, Kosher-style," Milton informed him), they came to a masculine den upon whose knotty pine walls hung pennants of Midwestern universities and photographs of elephantine football players with grim expressions (Bond spotted Casimir

---

[*] "Another Jew!"

Predpelski in the togs of Michigan State). "This is our Big Ten Room."

"For old grads and such?"

"Hell, no. This room is for the *minyan*.* Hence the name. Clever, huh? The Tanteh Claus Room is undergoing repairs so we'll skip that one."

"*Tanteh* Claus?"

Milton stripped the tinfoil off a 95-cent Chano Poso cigar. "Well, you know how our kids feel sorta deprived when Christmas comes around. So I dreamed up a great *shtik* that's made this place the talk of the East, maybe the country. We have this little old lady in a red dress and white beard sit on a throne in that room and the kids come in and tell her what they want for Chanukah. If they've been real good, she says she'll drive up from her big Lincoln Road toy shop in her Cadillac, which is jammed with goodies, and leave 'em Chanukah gelt and toys for eight straight nights. The parents are wild for the idea 'cause this way we work in religion. Now, my magnum *epis*."

They walked through nutria-lined swinging doors into a vast nightclub setting crowded with raucous people in furs and evening wear. "It's bigger than the Copa, huh, Iz? This is the Club Thirteen, my room for post-Bar Mitzvah receptions. Got a dilly tonight for multi-millionaire Keefe Barrington's kid, Whitney. Getting this shindig was quite a plum in my compote. Every fency-dency catering house in the East was after this one."

On stage at the microphone an animated little man in a flashy Crawford Clothes Po Valley mohair suit was gabbing.

"Good evening, ladies and germs. Welcome to Whitney Barrington's Bar Mitzvah reception. You know what a Bar Mitzvah is. That's when a Jewish boy reaches manhood. And a motel is where he proves it!

"And speaking of San Francisco... I just wrote a song called 'I Left My Heart in San Francisco and My Sinuses in Arizona.'"

He spoke through a cupped hand to the musicians. "Notice how the hip material never makes it? Well, back to the dreck, by heck. My wife is a lousy cook. She has to call a repairman to fix a TV dinner.

"Jesus, it's *all* dying tonight. And is she square? She thinks a condominium is something a guy buys in a drugstore.

---

* A Jewish religious service requiring a minimum of ten adult males.

"Speaking of spies, they got a lot of spies on TV. There's a new spy called Blue Light, but he's got troubles. Whenever he drives his car they won't let Blue Light cross at the Red Light until they give him the Green Light!"

Marvelous, marvelous, Bond thought, envying the clever construction. Why aren't these fools laughing? And haven't I seen this little funmaker before? Yes. It was Henny Benny Lenny, West Coast comedy sensation. His mind wandered back to a night at the Kahn-Tiki, the leading Class B hotel in the Catskills, and pain twisted the cruelly handsome face as he recalled the wonderful girl who had been so enmeshed in that electrifying Loxfinger caper,* the girl who now slept under the eternal sands of the Negev. Poontang Plenty. Something cried out from the core of his being with the profoundest sincerity: *Better her than me.*

"Speaking of sex, did youse hear about the Greek who found true love by accident? He backed into it. Oh no, this can't be the *regular* Bar Mitzvah crowd. I love rock 'n' roll. My favorite song is 'I'm Too Tired to Rock Around the Clock, So Let's Just Walk Around a Watch.' Forget it, you f— rich-bitch bastards!"

Wow! Bond enthused. What a great powerhouse of an impromptu shock line, designed, of course, to win back the blasé celebrants; but they continued to ignore the scintillating monology that could have been theirs. He jotted down as many of Henny Benny Lenny's gems as he could remember.

Henny Benny Lenny's triangular head hung in defeat.

"And now," he blared, "the real star of this show, Master Whitney Barrington!"

As the 25-piece band crashed into a pounding, frug-beat version of "Mahzeltov!" the crowd broke into yells at the entrance of a small boy with an incurious, bored demeanor who walked down a red carpet toward the stage flanked by six dazzling young women in extra-tight diamond-encrusted miniskirts. At a signal from Henny Benny Lenny six cages descended from the ceiling into which the maidens sprang.

Whitney Barrington, resplendent in his midnight-blue Dean Acheson diplomatic trousers with sateen stripes and regimental Martin Agronsky patent leather loafers, squeaked out of his world-weary face from a voice box whose nodules were pimple-stippled:

---

* *Loxfinger*, Pocket Books, Inc., 1965, a magnificent overture to this unsurpassable series—S.W.

"My Bar Mitzvah speech."

Bond nudged Milton. "Bet his dad's grinning from ear to ear right now."

Milton grimaced. "The old man ain't even here. He's an Ethical Culturist. It's the *shikseh* he married who insisted on the Bar Mitzvah."

Something odd happened. After his opening line, Master Barrington's voice suddenly became rich and dramatic as the lips moved hesitantly, droning on about "my sacred commitment to the faith of my fathers"... "this memorable day in which I take my place among...."

"Hell," Bond grunted. "That's Richard Burton's voice. The kid is lip-synching his speech."

"Family's got money, Iz." Milton shrugged. "Whose voice do you think sang the selection from the Haftorah[*] in synagogue this morning? He lip-synched the tenor voice of Jan Peerce."

Whitney Barrington's proclamation of his covenant with the ancient faith concluded, Henny Benny Lenny raised his hand and the band hit a fanfare; the girls frugged tigerishly in their cages.

"Now, ladies and germs, the presents! Will the gentleman from Price Waterhouse please come forth... or even fifth..." (the sharp ad lib died) "... with the envelopes?"

Bond left somewhere between the 500 shares of AT&T from Uncle Giles Rivkin of West Palm Beach and the "12 points, Whitney, 12 points in Uncle Morris Barrington's Shalomorris Hotel in fab-yew-louse Lust Ve-e-e-egaa-a-as!" Weary of it all and sorry for Master Whitney —it's all downhill for him after tonight, he thought—Bond needed a drink, but not here in this Fellini orgy scene. "Try any of the kitchens; there should be someone around. Place's full of part-time help tonight," Milton said.

The man behind the service bar in the Kosher-style kitchen was tall, powerful and very blond, very cruelly handsome, too, Bond noted. He looks like a Gestapo *me*.

"Hungry, old chap? Or thirsty?" The accent was slightly German, the English colloquially good. "We have just the sort of fare that will appeal to your discriminating taste buds, Mr. Bond. Gold-speckled-with-mauve bayou heron eggs, scrambled, not shirred, *pommes de terre Chevelle*, piping hot Chase & Sanborn Coffee—and remember, sir, what Mr. Chase didn't know about

---

[*] The additional reading from the prophets.

coffee, Mr. Sanborn didn't know, either—served with Domino Sugar's Vitali-style cubes cut to geometric exactness by Cal Tech-trained technicians...."

Bond lit a Raleigh. "How did you know my name was Bond? And that my tastes are so extraordinary?"

The blond man smiled. "You must admit, sir, you look remarkably like the entrepreneur of this establishment. And you hardly seem the sort who'd order Skippy peanut butter on white bread."

"You're very perceptive. A Montessori Martini, please."

The man set about making one. "Beefeater Gin made from potatoes crushed by the feet of exceedingly bright Italian orphans, a Samuel Bronston lemon, and a little shake...."

Bond's heart was about to burst through his splendid chest. He smelled it on the man's large, corded hands. Calgonite! The thoughts piled up like blue chips on a *la guerre* table. Calgonite. Bombing. A Calgonite-scented man in a Jewish establishment. Jewish establishments being bombed left and right. And the last three words....

He smiled in spite of himself. "The martini gave you away. Martinis are *stirred,* never shaken. Anyone who drinks 'em shaken is a social misfit. And I saw the tattoo on your wrist when your tuxedo sleeve moved up... the symbol of the SS jackboots kicking naked buttocks. You're from TUSH."

7
Candy, I Call My Killer Candy

"Sessue Hayakawa!"

The Nazi spat it from his sneering mouth as he hunched into the ping-pong stance of the karate expert.

It's started, Bond thought. He's attempting to "psyche" me with a stream of vitriolic Japanese words that will bring on panic, terrifying images of him as the star pupil in the Ginza studio of Sensayuma, "The Cobra," master of unarmed combat.

I must "psyche" back, guttural word for guttural word, hissing curse for hissing curse, until he, too, is beset by devilish eidolons of me as a holder of the Black Belt in the top half of the twelfth Dan, in my red Dan River karate robe, the star pupil of Moto of Kyoto, the only man alive whom Sensayuma fears. And I must be *all* Moto; a mere quasi-Moto will not intimidate him.

Hunching into a similar pose, Bond snarled:

"Ginza! Osaka!"

"Nagasaki! Hiroshima! Hirohito!" The TUSH man's rejoinder was disdainful.

Gottenu! Three Japanese words in a row! Does this kraut really know the lingo? No, Bond, don't use "lingo" when you yell back. It isn't even close. He'll die laughing of contempt.

"Ko-Ko! Yum-Yum! Nanki-Poo! Saki! Sedaka! Glocca Morra!" There, Hun! Six straight! But those last two... true, they *sounded* legit, but will he accept them? Or insist on the strict rules laid down in Admiral Yumekimi Meshuga's definitive *Pre-Karate Combat Cursing?*

The TUSH agent yawned, a great comical yawn.

Gottenu! He treats this as though it's a kindergarten exercise! Is he *that* confident? There is an unnatural stillness in the air, the moment before the black funnel springs out of the west to carry away the Kansas farmhouse, Dorothy, Toto.... Interntally, he said, "For god's sake, don't say 'Toto'!"

In a quicksilver instant the German cried: "Zero!"

Just as quickly, Bond responded: "Mostel!"

Oh, *Gottenu!* The response had been mechanical, unthinking. "Zero," the Japanese airplane, was a legitimate entry, but "Mostel," star of *Fiddler on the Roof*—no way. Israel Bond, you stupid son of a bitch! You fell into the oldest trap in the game. He knows you can be had. Round One to the killer from TUSH!

The smell of victory in his nostrils, the blond titan soared off the balls of his feet, his stiffened Commando's cutting edge of a right hand smashing down on Bond's torn shoulder... screaming: "Fukuoka!"

Bond fell back growling a savage, "Same to you oka!" but his paralyzed shoulder was a useless instrument. A brutal savate kick to the stomach almost bent him double and sent him crashing into a service stand, spilling a trayful of dessert over the marble floor; another to the same spot and it was all over. He lay groaning, conscious of two Flagg Brothers pebble-grained brogues planted at each side of his neck. One sickening thought kept pushing through the red haze in his head:

I've been taken by a man who wears nine-dollar shoes!

Standing over him like a Colossus of Rhodes was the scarcely winded man from TUSH. Why doesn't he end it? Stupid question, Oy Oy Seven. These TUSH people are never content with a mere "hit." It must be accompanied by the infliction of total degradation. I know what he has in mind for me.

"It is finished, Oy Oy Seven. I had long entertained the hope of ending your career in this fashion but the co-chairmen of my organization had already contracted to furnish Torquemada LaBonza to the KGB to do the job. Alas for him, happily for me, he was not equal to the task. In a few seconds I shall kick your head off its trunk, then plant a 50-zis Calgonite charge that will blow this Jewish pigsty to oblivion and 300 sons and daughters of the Chosen People with it, including your beloved brother. It is the kind of thing I have been doing for the last twelve hours in New York as part of Dr. Holzknicht's magnificent 'Operation Alienation.' As an added fillip, I may leave another 50-zis at your brother's house. His sweet children will enjoy the ride. And now, the crowning touch, *Judische-hund*...." There was a clicking sound of cubes. "Drink your martini—shaken!"

He'd known it was coming, but that didn't make the ignominious, nauseating stream of ice and liquid on his lips any more bearable.

But there was *something* bearable, something with prongs pressing into the small of his back. Something that could be a weapon. He must keep drinking the martini to glut the TUSH man's appetite for sadism. He felt his gorge rising but he kept swallowing. His left hand was inching under his back. Now!

"Fork you!"

It tore out of his throat with maniacal fury as his left hand drove the fork into the TUSH man's ankle, savoring the awful wail as prongs chomped through skin, capillary, gristle, marrow, cockle, mussel and bone. The German was howling like a banshee, writhing on his own back now like an animal in a trap. Bond yanked at the fork. Stuck too deep! His hand closed on a hard, cold object near the spilled tray and he drove it into the horrible O of the screaming German's mouth, past the palate, hammering it with his elbow far back into the throat, snapping off six gold-filled teeth in the process. There was an eye-rolling paroxysm, the face turned a revolting purplish-blue, the hands flopped at the sides.

Out of curiosity Bond forced open the jaws and extricated the object that had killed by strangulation. A thin smile hardened the cruel, sensual mouth. To no one in particular he remarked mildly, "There's nothing like a frozen Milky Way to take those snotty Snickers off a face."

Oblivious to the swelling on his head, the gushing shoulder wound and the fire in his kicked stomach, he frisked the German, found a plastic I.D. card:

"James Bund, 43, Ulbricht Allee, Schweinbaden, D.D.R."[*]

So this was James Bund, Number Two in TUSH's murder gang and one of the Schweinbaden camp ghouls as well. Bond found an interesting notation elsewhere on the card:

"Religion, Dryad."

As a man not only licensed to kill, but also to perform a memorial service over the victim (when possible), he felt obligated to perform the latter function, even though the man had been a swine about the martini. But... Dryad? He summoned to mind the only appropriate liturgy he knew to cover this situation. He whispered:

---

[*] East Germany.

"I think that I shall never see,
"A poem as lovely as a tree..."

Then the martini finally got to him and Israel Bond was very sick.

8
Dark Pool, Sweet Pool

He found the Calgonite in a Volks in the Pinochle Royale's darkened parking lot, shoved the corpse of James Bund into the back seat and drove deep into the woods of nearby Titusville. With a makeshift fuse of Bund's shoestrings he touched off the Calgonite, and from a hill a half mile away watched the blast sear 300 feet of scrub pine. The "pineys," those moonshiners of the forest, would be blamed for the explosion, he was certain. He could almost hear some rural sheriff cackling: "Them stupid bastards made the white lightnin' too damn powerful that time...."

Using his European heel and toe walk (which he had been taught by a European Olympic champion with but one heel and one toe) he ate up the six miles back to Liana's house in twelve minutes, using the time to reflect on the fast-moving events since he'd heard the newscast. The phrase "Operation Alienation" kept bedeviling him, but for the second time in the same day he repressed an analysis which might have led him to something concrete, for he was now standing before something very concrete, the Vine mansion at the corner of Lazy Lazarushian Lane and Molting Macaw Road. It was a fabulous edifice designed in the Early Bonanza ranchero period with effigies of notorious outlaws Billy the Kid, the James Brothers, and the Hole in the Wall Gang hanging from the saguaro cacti on the front lawn.

The door was open. A silvery voice said, "In the kitchen, Iz," and he tiptoed across the Dacron-Orlon-Leon rug (the latter no miracle fibre—the manufacturer wished merely to immortalize his son) and....

There was Liana Vine.

Naked.

She stood braced against the Progressive Furniture Company's Totie Fields model table, proud, unashamed, fully cognizant of the effect of her wondrous physiognomy upon him. "If anything's to happen, dearest Iz, it should be in here. No matter how rich we get, we Jews still live in the kitchen."

"I'm hungry," Bond said. "Did the special pie I ordered from Maruca's come yet?"

Without warning she began to cry, her creamy shoulders shaking. "Oh, it's all wrong. This whole thing I had in my mind... seeing you after eighteen years... and I'm naked... and all you're interested in is some damn pizza pie...."

He slapped her hard. "Sorry, *ketzeleh*, but I don't dig hysterical broads. Not even one I love with all my heart." The last sentence, pitched in a low, throbbing tone, seemed to snap her out of her funk and she dried her face on a rich-textured, high-pile Hudson napkin. "Besides, Liana, you're a Trentonian and you know damn well we call it *tomato* pie, not pizza. And only Maruca's of 119 South Olden Avenue refuses to pander to commercialism by utilizing provolone or mozzarella, two flat, uninspiring cheeses when cold, let alone melted. The Maruca boys, Pat, Jake, Spike and Slippery Joe, top their pies with their own secret formula, the only other copy of which is in a Curia safe in Vatican City."

"You've changed, Iz." Her smile was sweet yet grave. "You're so sophisticated 'n' all." Her warm, finely fleshed but not disgustingly plump arms encircled his neck. "Were there any others, Iz?"

His fingers caressed the silky Chemstrand hairs at the nape of her neck. "Don't throw up smoke screens, my pet. The question isn't what *I've* been doing. I'm a man. How about you, *maideleh*? Simon pure all the way?"

Her breath titillated three of the 1,917 erogenous zones on his left ear. "Just once, Iz. It was back in '57 and I hadn't gotten a letter from you in nine years and..."

"Tramp!" He shoved her against the wall. "You bitches! You're all alike. Who was it?" His slaps turned her cheeks blood red.

She bowed her head. "A guy I met at the John Cage Music Festival in Poughkeepsie. He was the third player in the coal scuttle section. Short, fat, morose fella... kinda reminded me of comedian Jackie Vernon. I was just sorry for him, Iz, 'cause everybody was dancing with a girl and he was dancing with a cello, and I guess I was sorry for myself, too. Nine years without...." Her voice cracked.

His nose rose, pushed up by a snarl of loathing. "And now you want your old lover boy to swing for you a little, eh, bitch! By heaven, I'll take you as callously as I took..." He reeled off four thousand different names, each one a dagger in her heart, he knew.

Arms flailing like a John Deere thresher, he threw his clothes to the floor, the cool sensuality of the Armstrong tiles causing insensate emotions on the broad, excitable areas of his bare soles. He was in a shimmering mist, nothing mattering but the pitiless defoliation of this adorable hellcat who had brought her soiled body to mark their reunion. His cruel, sensual lips parted, the liberated teeth laughed with barbaric glee and sank into her neck.

"Oh, Iz! Iz!"

Her own teeth were busy beavers hewing a scarlet path on his shoulder, reopening many of the wounds he had suffered in the field. Breasts swollen to aching mounds of desire crushed his chest; her thighs, taut, supple, greedy, pressing his, hothouse hands searching, finding the wellspring of life and love and godhead and it was springing —and well. Her tongue tip was a mine sapper roaming his ears, gums and throat for buried caches of erogeneity; his long, tapering fingers responded, kneading, cosseting the holy labyrinths causing tactile sensations of indescribable karma, dharma and shawarma.

From that kitchen radiated the unstoppable impulses of their incendiary liaison to the alarmed sensors of an unprepared world. Several stallions went berserk at a Cheyenne rodeo, bucking off their riders into the gravel. A seismograph at the University of California at Berkeley shuddered, registering an unbelievable 71.4 Richter which hurled the leadership of the Free Sex Movement into a Newman Club seminar on "The Shining Shield of Abstinence," then attacked an aroused Sperry Rand satellite tracker. In a cold-water flat on Greenwich Village's Morton Street an orgone box glowed with a white-hot heat that sent beads of perspiration rolling down its galvanized sides—and there was no one within. Through it all the song of sex roared unabated in the obsessed body of Israel Bond; sparkling glissandos intermingled with ernie durandos; fugues swelled into fullblown rizzutos, and her thighs were yielding to his, revealing concept and cosmos, bread and wine, death and transfiguration, port and starboard, David and Lisa, night and day, day and night for she was the one and she was Earth Mother, releasing at last the boiling life-force in her depths, and he was taking it, reshaping it, selling it to Goodwill Industries, for he was Earth Father and father knows best and he was in the clutch of a centrifugal force, surrendering to it and his head slipped down, down, down into a pool... sweet, dark... so sweet, so dark....

9

Where Love Has Gone

She helped him pull his head out of the bowl of chocolate pudding on the kitchen table. He had failed her.

"Well, how was it, Iz?" she said with ill-concealed bitterness.

"MY-T-FINE."

10
Tell Me, Where Can I Go?

Once again Israel Bond's rapier wit saved the day.

For ten minutes Liana Vine laughed her adorable hellcat head off. "Iz, what a stupendous pun you just made!"

He chucked her under the chin. How had he ever stayed away so long from this warm, bewitching, understanding girl? He would reward her patience for he knew that she must still be seething like a tidal wave which can find no coastal town to obliterate. The rapier would become the rapist!

Before he commenced his second onslaught he was struck by an inspiration. If laughter and love were so inescapably intertwined for Liana and him, why not combine the two? Poking about, he found an Allan Sherman album chock full of the chubby little fellow's devastating song parodies and placed it on the stereo that serviced the entire Vine manse with music.

So it was that, accompanied by Sherman's "gift of laughter," he took Liana Vine once more; this time it was no cold, furious exhibitionism, but mature and rich, a love of giving, not sadistic taking, and they melded soul-searing climaxes with guffaws at the comedian's rib-tickling punchlines. Fortune was with them, the funniest bits, "Sarah Jackman" and "Drapes of Roth," issuing from the speaker at the exact moments of fulfillment in their sexual congress.

Congress was in session a long, long time.

"Think you'll ever forget that third coal scuttle player now, my dearest angel?"

"Don't ever go away again, Iz. Stay. Marry me, live with me. I don't care which." Then she said, "Ouch!"

"Did I hurt you, *schoendeleh*?"

"No, dearest. I'm sitting on an ant button. But you haven't answered me.

"Hold on thar, Miss Liana. Thou has fain tempted me, fair damsel, but it can't be done that quickly. I'll have to ask out of Mother's, maybe help train another agent—uh, salesman, to fill my 10-D wing-tipped Florsheim cordovans."

Her hand flew up to her mouth. "Oh, my God! I meant to tell you...."

"Meant to tell me what, my funny valentine who makes me smile with my heart?" He saw her strained face and his heart ceased smiling.

"Forgive me, Iz. The thought of seeing you again, doing this... it just drove everything else out of my brain. Iz, there's no need for you to go back and resign. You're out of a job."

He pulled himself up. His voice was harsh. "What the hell do you mean by that?"

"I heard it on the radio just before you came in. A bulletin from Tel-Aviv. Mother Margolies' Activated Old World Chicken Soup factory... it's been blown up!"

11
There's Something Strange In The Heir

London?

Israel's secret service handed what could be a knockout punch and Op Chief Beame was ordering him to London?

Beame had been quite dictatorial about it on the phone. "This is a Mem Echod, repeat, Mem Echod. Rendezvous with 113 at Point WCH, Station Benny der Graiser, for further instructions. Shalom."

"Are you in Foam Rubber Acres yourself, Op Chief? Zvi is—"

The line went dead.

He shook his head. Beame's off his—and despised himself for the cheap play on the name at a catastrophic time like this. Well, Beame *was* off his beam, damn it! 113 had been Zvi Gates' designation and lovable, laughable Zvi Gates was gone, buried in some Godforsaken spot in the green hell that was the El Tiparillan jungle, with only kindly Sister Sweetcakes, "The Swinging Nun," caring enough to stop by sometimes and place a portion of boiled beef on his grave. No, Beame isn't the type to go off the deep like HaLavi. There's a logical explanation, idiot. A new 113. He felt a childish resentment toward the man already and cursed himself for being unjust.

Wait! Mem Echod!

Gottsedanken!

Mem is Hebrew for—M! Echod for—One! Mother was alive! Benny der Graiser was Yiddish, the *lingua frankel* of the truly cultured "in" of the world. Benny the Great, the Big, or Big Ben... London, his next stop.

Now HaLavi's new gear was in his bags and he was looking out the window of an El Al jet 31,000 feet up and he wanted a woman.

A strange symbiosis of sex and air travel caused a continual disquiet in the body of Israel Bond, dreamy local sensations caused by the hum of the engines, perhaps, or the clouds that suggested tremendous, fleecy mega-breasts. This merger of lust and altitude had grown more pronounced of late on his many jet excursions. (He would fly nothing but pure jets because of his Electra complex, a fear of turboprop planes.) And it was becoming peripheral. Sometimes he would feel the stirrings in a cab on the way to the airport, other times while telephoning for airline reservations, and once even in a supermarket where he saw an item whose very name seemed to spell out the linkage—Airwick.

To quash the feeling he busied himself with *The New York Times*. There was a wrapup on the explosions, minus the one at Mother's which had broken too late to make the edition. The FBI had been ordered to investigate the 178 deaths at 4,000 disasters; dozens more were dead in South America and Europe. As Sahd Sakistan mourned King Hakmir, Grand Vizier Ben-Bella Barka had flown on a hush-hush mission to London. New York's Mayor Lindsay had been offered a plan for a new police review board which would review the decisions handed down by any civilian review board; the mayor had promised to review it. Andorra was on the verge of detonating its first H-bomb, but its nuclear researchers were hesitant about doing it on their own territory; not to set it off would mean loss of face since a belligerent Lichtenstein soon might have its own bomb; to set it off would mean saving of face but loss of Andorra.

"Coffee, tea or LSD!" chirped voluptuous Shoshanna Nirvana, the curvaceous, black-eyed Yemenite stewardess. "The latter," Bond requested, popping the cube into his sensual mouth; for three hours he was afloat in a reverie that enabled him to see music and hear Marcel Marceau's entire act. He came out of it as the pilot, Captain A. B. Nathan, announced the descent into London.

Point WCH was code for the William the Conqueror Hotel.

"Cabbie, take me to 1066 Hastings. Do it in less than ten minutes and there's a handful of farthingales, forepence and jujubes for you." On the way to Cheapside they passed what had been a delicatessen, its windows blown out; on the sidewalk lay salamis and tongues in the appalling rictus of death.

"Gar! Fifteenth bloomin' one I seen like that todye. Someone's got it in for the bloody Yids, they 'as." Bond cut four farthingales from the bigot's tip, kicked holes in the cab's rear tires with his heel knives.

He paced the room hour after hour, each new disaster aired by the telly deepening his concern. He looked at the two-foot mound of Raleigh stubs and berated himself for the habit. Maybe the coupons would cover the lung operation, he smirked. Swallowing 103 Luden's cough drops to alleviate a slight sore throat, he moved to the door when the rap sounded, opened it wide and was driven back by an agonizing blow to his tender stomach by the muzzle of a .44 Serenata-Holmes.

"Just put your hands behind your neck." The speaker was a sandy blond with a bandage on his forehead. He was slim, of medium height, wore a black Haly's M.O. windbreaker, khaki ducks and white hush-puppies. With his left hand he removed the outsized Italian wraparound sunglasses that blocked off a third of his face.

"Neon! Neon Zion! You damn fool kid! Don't you remember the Matzohball caper?"*

"Stow it, mac. The quick brown fox jumped over the pickled lox."

A rage shook Bond. This damn snotty punk, an ex-Israeli Peace Corpsman who owes his life to me, is pulling guns and demanding countersigns as if I'm some runny-nosed recruit. There was no choice but to play along:

"Folks who live on Quemoy are known as Quemoyim,
"And all these Quemoyim, for damn sure, are goyim."

The breath whooshed out of the kid and Bond realized how nervous he must have been. "Thank God it's you, Oy Oy Seven! I had to do what I did. Orders."

"What the hell is bugging Lazar Beame? Doesn't he know who I am?"

Neon lit a Raleigh. "Mr. Bond, since it happened, nobody knows anything any more or trusts anybody. Sure, you look like the man I grew to worship on that terrible isle, but you could have been a TUSH-y** with a plastic surgery job." He closed his eyes. "Here's the scam: Somebody disguised as one of the tourists left some Calgonite, at least 200-zis' worth, in the front wing of M.'s factory. It went off at 5:30 P.M., just missing the

---

* Described in *Matzohball*, I think, but maybe it was *Loxfinger*.
  Why take a chance? Buy both. In huge quantities.—S.W.
** An agent of TUSH.

departing tour group, and that was a break, at least. Imagine the stew we'd be in explaining five hundred American deaths to the State Department."

"They weren't really after the Yanks. We were the target."

Neon slammed his fist into his palm. "Yes, but how in hell did TUSH know the factory was a cover for M 33 and 1/3? Another thing... with the exception of Oy Oy Five, missing, presumed captured, and you, sir, all the Double Oys are dead. It's foolish to suppose TUSH hadn't heard of you. But how did they know who the others were?"

Bond bit his lip. He knew, but that could come later. "Who got it at the factory? How bad is M.?"

"Crippled. In a wheelchair. I was next to her when it happened. A hundred cases of Mother's Activated Old World Kosher Charcoal Briquettes fell on us. Got my head banged up, but that's all. Uh, you and Lilah were kinda close, I take it...."

Bond sprang at Neon, dug his long, tapering fingers into the lad's shoulders. "Lilah! What about her?"

Tears streamed from 113's eyes. "She wasn't as lucky. It hurled her into the gefilte fish vat. It was boiling."

"The others?" He let go of Neon and stared into the London night. In his rage he whipped out the Chris-Keeler and fired through the window into Berkeley Square. The nightingale fell dead. "The others?"

"Aide de Camp de Camp, gone... Section Psychiatrist Pippikel, gone... Mendel the Mantis, gone... a few dozen factory workers, too...."

"HaLavi?" Was the little genius of weaponry out of it, too?

"He's O.K., sir, s-s-s-ort of. He had just stepped out for a breath of hot stale air—he can't stand air conditioners, you know—and he was knocked down. But he came out of it kinda funny. I was the first to get to him. He'd been hit a glancing blow on the head by a board with one of M's immortal proverbs painted on it, which said 'HELL HATH NO FURY LIKE A PLYMOUTH.' He looked at me and said, 'You know, Neon, if you keep feeding massive doses of iron to Persian lambs, you might very well get steel wool.' I didn't say anything to that, but then he said, 'Lord, if I don't do something quick they'll die!' And he pulled these shoetrees out of his lab coat and...."

"Say it," Bond commanded.

"He took out these shoetrees and started to *water* them with a sprinkling can. Then Lavi got real worked up. He started to tell me about some theory of his. 'You know, Neon, if it is theoretically possible to engrave the constitution of Israel on the head of a pin is it not also possible for the entire *Knesset*[*] to meet on it as well? In a land as small as ours space is a precious commodity. By moving the building onto the pin, or, perhaps, even all of Jerusalem....' and that's where I called an Alarm Aleph and Op Chief Beame took him away."

Bond was pulling on his trenchcoat. "We're wasting time. Let's get the hell home." He swore to the mocking moon over the church spires: I'll get revenge for all of this. The insolent moon jibed back: *"I'm from Manakoora. You Gotta Show Me."*

Neon dragged on his Raleigh. "You're not going back, Oy Oy Seven. Mem Echod order. You've a job that starts right here in London town."

Up your foggy day, Bond grumbled to himself.

"And..." Neon moved to the door... "if I'm not mistaken it starts this second."

A bronzed, gaunt man in a double-breasted sharkskin suit with rakish fins protruding from the armpits entered. His face was distinctly Arabic, proud, barbaric, distinguished by a hooked nose. A yellow fez perched atop his grey locks. "Israel Bond, I am Ben-Bella Barka, Grand Vizier of Sahd Sakistan. Please come with me. Your duties commence at once."

"Goddamnit! What the hell is going on in M 33 and 1/3? Are they trading me to the Arabs for Suez and thirty oilfields?"

Neon smiled. "Something like it, sir. M. has consented to have you act as the Secret Service of Sahd Sakistan on a temporary basis. You are to guard King Hakmir's son who is in a ticklish spot, untested and surrounded by enemies. The new monarch was specific in requesting you. Ben-Bella Barka found him living here and contacted our P.M., who agreed to the deal."

"Deal?" Bond kicked the wall, dislodged three coats of Sherwin Williams and a cheap reproduction of a Kim Novak painting. "This is lunacy! The big show's going on in Israel; they're bumping off our Double Oys, crippling our Number One, and I get sent on some f— tinhorn assignment! Listen, Ben-Ball Breaker or whatever your name is... what's in this for my country?"

The mouth was taut and cold. "A great deal, Mr. *Boor*. In return for guarding His Majesty, Sahd Sakistan, a believer in *realpolitik*, is going to be a force for your nation's welfare in

---

[*] Israeli Parliament.

the United Nations. Our alignment with you on key issues will lure the Asian states from their ties with the Arab bloc and perhaps even convince our Middle Eastern neighbors to end their unprofitable obduracy. There is more at stake for you in Sahd Sakistan than in Tel-Aviv, no matter how horrendous your present tragedy."

"He's right, Oy Oy Seven," Neon asserted and Bond knew it. "M. says I'm to be your assistant."

Bond's shoulders slumped. "Where is His Majesty?"

"He is having his fitting for the coronation. Come with me, gentlemen."

Ben-Bella Barka's block-long Rolls took them to an address in fashionable Mayfair and parked in front of a glittering salon on Darn Cat Mews. They got out and walked the block to the entrance. Several English shopgirls with delicate tea biscuit complexions tittered and blushed as the darkly handsome Israeli favored them with a cavity-free grin, an elegant bow and several sure-fingered probes. "His Majesty is in Monsieur Pierre's suite, gentlemen."

And in Monsieur Pierre's arms, it developed. The designer, clad in a purple toga and hunter's-green Jamaicas, held the tiny monarch to his heart. *"Mon roi, mon amour... je t'adore...."*

Then a wild eye caught Bond's bemused face and a spidery hand pushed the Frenchman's face aside cavalierly. "Split, you disgusting Frog! Here's the real stuff in life to cling to—my sweet Super-Jew...."

Sahd Sakistan's new monarch looked like the cat about to swallow the aviary. With a frenetic series of ballet leaps he vaulted to Bond and threw his fragile arms around his neck. "Oh, blessed spirit of Oscar Wilde, it's the beefcake bonanza, the Eldorado of erectility, the mother lode of musculature, and it's mine, mine, mine...."

Bond had groaned as soon as he had been able to take a good look. His heart hit his heels as he recognized the elfin Negro with the Dick Van Dyke beard, horn-rimmed glasses and Courrèges dress and white boots, who had been tapped by destiny to rule a nation.

Baldroi LeFagel!*

---

* Brother of Sister Sweetcakes, the "Swinging Nun." Buy *Matzohball*, Pocket Books, Inc., 1966, $1.

12
A Strong Man Weeps

"I will *not,* I will *not,* I will *not!* Let Israel be overrun by Egypt, let the sky fall in the sea, let banks fail in Yonkers. I will not!" Bond stormed.

Then his patriotism triumphed and he consented with utmost reluctance to take Neon's quite sensible advice.

"If you're going with His Majesty tonight to the night club, it ill behooves you to look out of place. He may already be shadowed by TUSH, Mr. Bond. You must not look as though you're guarding him. You must appear to any tag* as one of LeFagel's companions."

So Bond put on the dress.

After the first shock of seeing the smart Cecily of Sicily two-piece electric blue Jersey knit cling to his lithe, muscular frame, he found the freedom of the skirt somewhat refreshing. After all, Scotsmen wear these kilt things all the time, he reasoned, and certainly no one finds the Scotch unmanly. And the blonde wig... well, hadn't Harpo Marx worn one like it during his career? And Harpo had never been suspect. As for the shaped Cuban heels, doesn't Jose Greco—

Knock it off, Bond; stop the rationalizing.

You're afraid of what you're wearing, afraid you might like it.

Hadn't a renowned observer of mankind once said, "There's six percent of latent homosexuality in every man"? Who was it now? Freud? Jung? Oscar Wilde? Of course, it had to be Oscar, who once mused, "Boys will be boys"... and that's what made Oscar Wilde!

---
  * An espionage term meaning one who is employed to "shadow," "tail" or "trail."

And, Mr. Bond, his inner self continued, what man taking a shower at the Y has not looked at the man in the next shower and said to himself: "That's another man taking a shower there"?

He thought: We all have hangups, hidden fears. I was in LeFagel's room a few minutes ago and he showed me a picture he'd taken of New York City's Chrysler Building with its gleaming needle top. He was positively misty when he looked at it. I know what it represents to him, of course. Looking at it from my standpoint, it made me feel sexually inadequate. And imagine a poor bastard who's hooked on junk... to him it must seem to be the mother of all fixes and he'd die happy if he had a 1,500-foot arm and a 200-foot-wide vein.

Snap out of it, Oy Oy Seven! The philosophical mood, not the dress. There's a job to be done for M., Eretz Israel and the ruler of Sahd Sakistan. You're on the secret service of His Majesty, the Queen.* Thank heaven Neon's working out all right. Smart young kid, even suggested he'd go on ahead and case the joint because we shouldn't be seen together.

Bond finished with the base makeup and Maybelline eye shadow. Not bad. I could never be one of those truly *beautiful* girls, but I'm undeniably... *interesting.* A touch of Tangee on my cruel, sensual lips and it's off to Soho with Baldroi LeFagel and an evening at King Baldroi's own nitery, the Gayboy Club.

LeFagel was a vision in crinoline and lace when Bond stopped by to fetch him. "I feel so Scarletty O'Hara tonight... magnolias by moonlight... warm winds whipping whatever part of the slaves ol' Massa missed in the afternoon...." He suddenly stared at Bond.... "Why, you've turned, you've turned! *O mirabile dick, too!* Glory, glory...."

"Cool it, LeFagel. This is just a disguise. Don't get your hopes up."

LeFagel winked. "I'd much rather get *your*... hopes up, you bonny, brawny thing." He clasped his hands in a prayerful attitude.

Gottenu! Bond sighed. The double meanings start already!

As the cab rumbled through the night a blanket of fog lent a sinister touch to the city. Good-o, Bond thought. It'll be hard to be tagged in this pea souper. He felt his purse, heavy with the comforting weight of the metal object inside, hoping he would not need to use it.

---

* Possible title.

"Say, LeFagel, what's with the Old-South-by-moonlight getup? A man who's written such violent anti-white power structure novels like *Up Your Blue Toilet, Mister Charlie* and *Burn, Whitey, Burn in the Fire Next Time* has no right to look like a 19th Century plantation owner's imperious daughter."

LeFagel put an orange-tipped Phyllis Morris between his lips. "Oh, I'm over that phase. Not that I'm unsympathetic to my people's problems, you understand, but if they haven't got enough sense to better themselves by inheriting Middle East kingdoms the hell with them. Anyway I'm much too involved these days with the real movement, Bondikins."

"Call me 'Bondikins' once more and I'll kick your tail."

"And I'll accept it gladly, as a prelude to better things, of course. The real movement is typified by *One* Magazine, the organ—you'll pardon the expression—of the most vigorous of all the ethnic groups— us."

"I've seen it. It takes One to know One."

"Touche! Well, they haven't gone quite far enough, so I've initiated a One World movement of which my Gayboy Club here is the opening gun. Next, *Gayboy* Magazine, our slick entertainment-jammed periodical which will feature our Gaymate of the month—and what a coup it would be if the first centerfold attraction was Hugh Hefner... naked!" The tiny ruler shivered at the very thought. "It'll also feature our own comic strip heroes, Fagman and Birdie. In our version they'll *both* be named Bruce. And if the Fagphone should ring, they'll just never answer it, that's all. Oh, it'll be the wildest thing in publishing, sweet Samson, highly departmentalized, too. Our dear senior citizens will have their own section called the Gay Nineties. There'll be contests on 'Why I Switched' in twenty-five words or less with grand prizes like wrestlers and truck drivers. Oh, we're here."

Bond felt a sharp pain aft as he guided LeFagel toward the lavender-blue Dilly Dilly door of the club and turned to see an evil grin on the ruddy cabman. By thunder, the man had pinched him! Only his Double Oy training constrained him from punching in the brute's face. Then Bond smiled. The man had pinched *him*, not LeFagel. No matter which scene I make, it's *me* they're after, and he felt somehow reassured and waved back at the driver.

Down winding steps they went, into a dimly lit cellar crowded with tiny circular tables, no bigger than hula hoops, around which were clustered little knots of Gayboy regulars, their lively faces illuminated by candles stuck into Clorox bottles. At a small bar a fierce-looking, mustachioed man smashed his hand in front of the bartender, spilling drinks onto the sawdust floor. "I can lick any man in the world!"

"Our champion, Joan L. Sullivan," whispered LeFagel. "Superb, no?"

In a pinspot on a miniature stage was a heavily rouged, marceled blond sitting on a stool, his legs crossed. He wore a lavender shirt made of live death's-head moths, the ends tied at his waist, and the tapered red-satin slacks so popular in this milieu, Transves-Tights. He was singing in a throaty German accent.

> "When we crawled in bed one night last week,
> "I found we had the same physique.
> "You brought a new kind of love to me."

Sighs and moans ensued. "Willi, you're fantabulous!" cried a plump onlooker.

"She *is* chi, isn't she chi?" the admiring king said.

"Who is she?"

"I'll certainly find out." LeFagel exchanged a whispered conversation with the plump onlooker, then turned to Bond. "That's a new one I've never heard of. Willi Marlene from East Berlin. She asked my maître d' if she could go on tonight. Far as I'm concerned, she can go on *any* night."

"Damn it, LeFagel! Enough with the *fakokteh* innuendoes already."

"Jealous, jealous, jealous. Admit it. Cat got your tongue? Lucky cat."

Bond paid him no mind. He was thinking. Willi had asked to perform, Willi from East Berlin. King Baldroi, we may be in trouble right off the bat.

As Willi did a medley of bittersweet songs obviously dear to his enrapt audience, "Blowing in the Wind," "My Nancy With the Laughing Face," "Mad About the Boy" and a slow, specialized rendition of "Stouthearted Men," Bond scanned the layout. On the wall back of their table was a gallery of photographs of world-famous celebrities. "Are they... uh... special, too?"

" 'Course, silly Semitic sweetness. The squares would die if they knew. See that one of the big-league ballplayer? He's a switch-hitter off the field, too. And the nuclear scientist? Right now he's working on something for us, the Gay-Bomb." LeFagel pointed a finger. "Like that mural?"

It depicted one of the heroic moments of antiquity, a homosexual holding off hordes of Mongols singlehanded to protect his Greek city-state, the immortal *Fellatio at the Bridge*.

Willi demonstrated his versatility with a collection of risqué stories which had the audience in titters (one of them with a rhyming punchline, "faggot maggot," wasn't bad at all, Bond conceded, writing it down in his notebook) and ended his turn with a rousing yo-ho sea shanty whose lyrics fitted in harmoniously with the general theme of the Gayboy.

Throwing kisses to all, stopping to bestow special favors on a few, he made his way to LeFagel's table.

"Your gracious, gracious liege, heartbeat of Swishdom, defender of man's unalienable right to be alien," he purred and knelt to kiss the blushing king's hand.

As he genuflected, Willi Marlene's right hand slipped into the back pocket of his Transves-Tights, Bond's eyes on it all the way.

Bond's fingers were without prehensility, it seemed. He couldn't get the damn clasp to open, cursing himself for not having tried a few dry runs with the purse.

Willi's right hand came out with a curved *kris*, its wicked silhouette standing out in the candlelight.

Bond swung with all his power and smashed Willi across the throat as the dagger moved toward LeFagel's heart. Willi Marlene fell softly on his back, a broken rag doll.

LeFagel was screaming from the top of a chair now, hurling the Clorox bottles all over the club in his hysteria. One of the candles touched off the stage curtains and it flared into a sea of flames.

Bond stood looking down at Willi Marlene's body. How good it had all been before tonight, he thought. The glorious killings by Moshe Dyan rifle, the Tzimmes-88, the frozen Milky Way, the ten-ton Matzohball. Now I'm at the nadir of my career.

To look at it from a professional viewpoint, he *had* done his job, the weight of the gun inside crushing Willi Marlene's windpipe. For now, Baldroi LeFagel was safe.

But he couldn't keep the enormity of *how* he'd done it out of his head.

I have just killed a man by striking him with a purse.

He turned his face aside so that he could not be seen.
Israel Bond wept.

13
Gas, Meter Of A Traitor

LeFagel snapped him out of it.

"Mr. Bond! Mr. Bond! I'm on fire!"

So now it's *Mr.* Bond when you're up against it, eh, King Baldroi? He resisted an urge to cry, "Burn, baby, burn!" and pulled the screaming ruler from the table top, beating out the tongues of flame with his hands.

The wild fire LeFagel had set off by his outburst of irrationality was spreading like... well, wildfire. Not a bad line, either, Bond thought, and jotted it down as he hacked and wheezed on the smoke.

Bond put the tiny fellow on his torn, aching shoulder and barreled through the clawing, howling Gayboy customers to the street, the cool air a godsend to his scorched body.

Depositing LeFagel in a trashcan, he raced back into the inferno three times, snatching twelve more trapped customers, dumping them all on the sidewalk.

"Oy Oy Seven!" There was a bleat from one of the blackened faces in the third batch he'd taken up.

Neon!

"Are you okay, kid? And where the hell were you?"

"Backstage. I just came to a minute ago. You've saved my life again, Oy Oy Seven. I wish to hell I knew how to—"

"Forget it, boychikl. That's what Double Oys were made for. Why were you backstage?"

Neon choked for a minute. "Goddam smoke... it's damn near burned out my lungs. Got a cigarette?" Bond slipped him a Raleigh. "I told you I was going on ahead to snoop and I found something." He looked rueful. "Trouble is something found me, too. I'd spotted this Willi Marlene actor making up in the dressing room and I saw one of those symbols on his wrist."

"TUSH?"

"Well, sort off. Naked buttocks were being kicked all right, but by high heels."

Bond snapped his long, tapering fingers. "TUSH's special department for killer homos. He was in the Gayfia."

"Well, I guess he'd seen me in the mirror or something, because when I turned around I got coshed real good." He rubbed the back of his head. "Sorry, Oy Oy Seven. I loused up my first big job and he got away."

Bond gave the youngster a friendly jab to the mouth, which split it and sent three teeth flying into the gutter. "He's been taken care of, fella." Several of the Gayboy patrons ran screeching down the street. Bond grinned. "See them running. I guess that's what they really mean by drag racing."

"Oy, mommeleh!" Neon's eyes bulged out and he was in the grip of an uncontrollable fit of laughter. "Damn, that's funny! *Drag* racing!"

Hey, Bond thought, looking at young Neon with new respect. The kid's a *laugher!* Hell, he laughs more than Zvi Gates ever did. 'Course, I'm sorry for what happened to Zvi, but....

Back at the William the Conqueror he called for a parley.

"We've got to get the hell out of here. TUSH has a boatload of agents in London. But we'll throw 'em a curve. Instead of Sahd Sakistan, our next stop'll be Israel."

"I suppose I should thank you for saving my royal life, Bonderooney," said a subdued Baldroi LeFagel. "It was precious of you. Mayn't I reward you in my own sweet way?" His eyes burned into the secret agent's.

"Yes, by acting like a king. Now go pack."

"Take this, Mr. Bond. It's a special edition of my new book of verse, *We Should Think About Spoons and Other Poems*. Bysie for a whilsie, luscious long, lean Litvak of my heart."

LeFagel flounced out and Bond signaled for Neon to follow him. He opened the fragile, scented volume whose text was printed upon cerise ScotTissue. He read the title poem.

> "We should think about spoons,
> "On haunted parapets kissed by beaks of owls.
> "Spoons, spoons, silver thighs of hate-love,
> "I pressed his thighs with molten spoons,

"He slid down the mountain on his giderum.
"Too short the peacock's sugared toes,
"Too short, one long, dit-dit-dot, dit-dit-dot."

Bond's cruel, darkly handsome face was filled with sorrow. The little bastard has talent, by thunder! He reread the line about "the peacock's sugared toes." Real talent, sensitive imagery. And LeFagel squanders it on this awful sexual aberration. Why, with a little toning down and some strict discipline Baldroi could very well be doing verses someday for Hallmark Cards. Sure, some of those ivory tower chaps might look down their noses at Hallmark Cards, but, by God, when you got a Hallmark Card you knew where you stood! He vowed: I'll straighten out this pint-sized pansy, make a real *mensch*[*] out of him yet!

As he did his own packing he looked with regret on the electric blue Jersey knit dress that had served him so well on this grim night. Seems a shame to throw it down the incinerator, he thought. I'll take it along. There might come a day when I'm just bugged by everything else in my wardrobe and....

Ben-Bella Barka's chauffeur took them to the airport, Bond keeping a rear window watch for any tailing cars, his hand clamped around the purse.

At the airport he bought them all insurance, including the new policy that covers death by plane crash in the waters of a holy shrine—sold only by Lourdes of London—and settled back to do some hard thinking as Neon and Baldroi snoozed. The London *Times* had more explosions to report, a total of 4,999 on the three continents. The Pinochle Royale would have made it an even 5,000, he reasoned, adding 4,999 and 1 and coming up with the inescapable answer.

The *Times* noted that in every instance but five the bombings had destroyed edifices which had some relationship to food and drink. The exceptions were five Halifax-to-New York freighters. Were these just random, unrelated incidents? Or part of the TUSH plot in some unrecognizable way?

James Bund's oblique references came back to him. "Operation Alienation." "Dr. Holzknicht." He'd have to tell M. and Beame immediately. Then a great guilt pervaded him. He'd also have to tell them that he had covered up the sordid betrayal of Eretz Israel by weaselly Nochum Spector, the little man with

---

[*] Man.

the big dream of world domination in the Matzohball caper.**
Nochum had been M.'s nephew; Bond had not wished to hurt the old woman. But his silence had cost Israel almost 60 dead, including his buddies, the Double Oys. That part of the story intrigued him the most, the blown-up cab in Jerusalem after they'd gone to renew their licenses to kill.

It was obvious. Someone in the license bureau had fingered them in some way.

He would pay that bureau a friendly little visit.

Two cartons of Raleighs later, the El Al jet circled Lod Airport and angled downward. It touched the soil of Eretz Israel and tears rolled down his cheeks. He whispered:

"This land is mine. God gave this land to me."

The unloading took a bit longer than he'd bargained for. His personal effects occupied just twelve suitcases, but there were 86 others stuffed with Raleigh coupons to get through customs. Enough for a medium tank, if M. bargained right, to help keep Israel free!

Lazar Beame was waiting in the Citroyenta, the ugly but gutsy little car produced in Beersheva by a French-Israeli cooperative. Beame was a short, stocky man of 55, with a tanned, stoical face. He was an ex-Double Oy himself who had moved up when he reached field-combat retirement age of 45. He'd begged for a two-year extension, but M. had turned him down: "You don't know what the really good wines are any more, your thickened waistline makes you unattractive to women and your golf game is way off. Worst of all, you can't work that hair-across-the-doorway trick any more. You're bald. Come in out of the cold, Lazar."

Beame's teeth were serrating a White Owl, and he paused from time to time to spit out bloody feathers. "You wouldn't happen to have a cigar on you, would you?" When Bond shook his head, Beame said brusquely, "We're in Emergency Site Zaddik-Iyan-Gimmel-Gimmel-Yood ever since...." He bit through the cigar in his anger.

Z-I-G-G-Y. Ziggy's! The popular Kosher restaurant on Jerusalem's Bezalel Street. Was that the new cover? Was fat, wisecracking Ziggy Gershenfeld, the Max Asnas-Toots Shor-Duke Ziebert of Israel, a big cog in the Secret Service?

"Surprised?" Beame said sotto voce so that King Baldroi and Neon, seated in the rear, could not hear. "I can hear your

---

* In the Matzohball caper; *Matzohball*, 1966, $1.

brain clicking. Yes, it's Ziggy's and, yes, he's way up in M 33 and 1/3; has been for years. There are some things you never learn until you get up to my level, Oy Oy Seven. Actually the Kosher restaurant front is fine for M. She'll be hidden away in the kitchen and besides it gives her a chance to cook while she's planning counter-operations."

They motored through the Judean hills, harsh and beautiful. Somewhere along the line three of the Citroyenta's four tires fell off, but the doughty auto chugged along with spirit. "These little babies can really take it, Bond," said Beame. The rear end dropped off at Jaffa Road and Bezalel Street, the motor fifty yards from Ziggy's, yet the sturdy frame made it right up to the door.

From the restaurant he could spot the Old City, which lay in Jordanian territory, and the words of an old Israeli spiritual rang in his head:

> "Ah looked ovah Jo'dan and what did Ah see?
> "Comin' fer to carry me home....
> "A band of Ay-rabs was a-shootin' straight at me
> "Comin' fer to carry me home...."

They were hustled through the service entrance, down a hallway rampant with odors of pickles, stuffed cabbage, and *chili con carnage,* into the kitchen.

There was M.

She sat in a wheelchair, her slight legs made tree-trunk thick by yards of bandages. There were bruises on her forehead and cheeks and a plaster sticker on the tip of her nose. But her eyes had lost none of their keenness.

"Shalom, Oy Oy Seven, 113, and honored guest, King Baldroi."

After a round of salutations, M. suggested that Neon take King Baldroi to the front for a bite and seemed bewildered by the little ruler's arch response.

"The King has a bizarre sense of humor," Bond said, apologizing. He then unloaded his terrible secret from a heart that was bent into accordion folds by it.

Beame's reaction was instantaneous. "You stupid bastard! Nobody's feelings should ever be spared in this game. There's a ton of blood on your head, Mr. Bond. If I were you, M., I'd take away his number and throw him to the wolves."

M.'s answer took a long time in coming. "Op Chief Beame is correct, Oy Oy Seven. You have done a terrible thing." Bond bit his elbow in shame. "And a noble thing. I must be condemnatory in my official capacity, grateful for your concern in my human one. I disagree with Op Chief Beame's solution, however. It is unrealistic. Oy Oy Seven is perhaps our last hope, Mr. Beame. He will finish this assignment at least, before any departmental inquiry is held. The king still must be protected and this TUSH junta smashed. Maybe God will again strengthen Israel Bond's hand so he can redeem himself. Now, Mr. Bond, a detailed report on your experiences in Trenton and London, and your theories."

So that's it, Bond thought. This is my swan song. The folds in his heart gave way at the seams and the whole mess collapsed into his stomach. Popping ten Rolaids into his mouth to neutralize it, he recounted in an unemotional manner the whole story.

M. and Beame registered shock at his mention of Dr. Holzknicht.

The former pressed the pilot light button on the stove and in five seconds Ziggy Gershenfeld waddled into the kitchen, wiping his hands on his apron. "I heard Oy Oy Seven's report on these—" His forefingers touched his hearing aids. "I was wondering when you'd call me in." He was a round little man with bright eyes in a face that was a dead ringer for Harry Golden's. "If Holzknicht authored this thing it's something dark and deep. Certainly gives me food for thought."

"How odd, Z.," said M. with a nervous smile. "That very phrase 'food for thought' went through my mind when I first heard about it."

"Invert it! Invert it!' Bond was screaming.

"What the hell do you mean?" thundered Beame.

"Think about food! Think about food! Can't you see it?" Then Bond spoke slowly, as though recalling something from a dream. "Liana said it. 'We Jews still live in the kitchen.' She said it."

"Liana who? And what's it got to do with this whole...." Beame started.

Z., Ziggy Gershenfeld, spread his arms. "Everything. She must be a smart cookie, your Liana. Now what ingredients have we got? TUSH... a sharp, perceptive psychiatrist like Holzknicht... and he's great, I got to say it about the *Deutsche momser*... the destruction of food and drink outlets... 'Operation

Alienation'... your friend's knowledgeable observation about Jews and kitchens... there's a pattern in the whole thing."

Bond cut in. "Let's add some more elements. The preponderance of these disasters occurring in America's cities with big Jewish populations... others in South American and Western European cities also with big Jewish populations...."

Z. twisted his apron in his hands. "I got to make some calls, lots of calls. I got a theory. I say we all meet here in three days."

Beame stuck out a belligerent jaw. "Can we wait three days, Z?"

"It's got to take at least that long to get hold of all the people I need to talk to."

M. nodded. "You shouldn't waste a moment then, Z. Oy Oy Seven, you'll keep an eye on LeFagel. Op Chief Beame, you'll give Z. any help he needs. For me there's a whole new factory to design. Someone give me a slide rule, pencil and some brown butcher paper. I'll start to *potchke* with it a little."

Bond had Neon spirit LeFagel away via *sherut*[*] to a Negev kibbutz, K'far K'farfel, where an old friend, Dr. Saul Rossien, was experimenting with the old chimpanzee-typewriters theory in comparative obscurity and safety. Some scientist had once claimed that if you set a thousand chimps before the same number of typewriters one of them might by accident duplicate some classic by Milton, Homer, Shakespeare, etc. So far the best thing Dr. Rossien had noticed was the work of one chimp who had laboriously pecked out: "One thousand chimps at one thousand typewriters."

For the next three days Bond moseyed around the license bureau, a shabby little office in the cellar of the Menasha Skulnik Building on Ben Yehuda Street. The office manager, Sharett Pincus, was one of those officious, small-fry bureaucrats who nursed his own little bailiwick jealously, but at the sight of Bond's hard face and gold security card he dissolved into a quivering mass of fear and cooperated to the fullest.

Besides Pincus, there were three others in the bureau, all clerks and all Jews who had fled from oppression in North Africa. They even looked a great deal alike—short, swarthy, with black moustaches. Pierre LaToole was from Morocco; Hassim Moonlight-Bey and Shofar Ben Blue refugees from Cairo. Naturally, their records were quite in order.

The sign was the first clue.

---

[*] Hired taxicab.

"Who authorized your bureau to put this up?" Bond said, his finger indicating a placard over one of the windows: LICENSES TO KILL.

Sharett Pincus stammered, "Mr. Bond, sir. There was a memo from the Ministry of Defense. I never ignore memos."

"Damn it, man! You should have ignored this one," Bond said.

Pincus paled. "I'll follow your policy and ignore all memos in the future, sir. But could you send me a memo on that?"

It was clear to Bond now. One of the three (he'd pretty well discounted Pincus) had forged a memo on MOD stationery, which was easy enough to obtain, dropped it in Pincus' box and the man had complied. There's no sense asking which one. They'll all deny it and two will be telling the truth, he thought.

Bond suddenly became jovial. "Sharett, you people do a lot of good work down here. My superiors would like to sort of express our appreciation. You and your good lads are invited to dinner at Ziggy's internationally famed restaurant tonight as my guests. It's all on the house." He slapped the man's back. "See you at eight."

Back in Ziggy's his face hardened again. "M., it goes like this: They knew from Nochum's tips who the Double Oys were, but they added an extra touch. They knew damn well that a Double Oy spotting a sign 'LICENSES TO KILL' would naturally walk to that window. The four Double Oys made the unfortunate mistake of going for renewal in a bunch. That was as sloppv a security mistake as mine was. So the plant in the bureau tipped off his bomber. When they all left the bureau in the same cab... sitting ducks."

M. sucked on a piece of rock candy. "How do you propose we smoke out the plant?"

"They've got some kind of food warfare mounted against us. Let's turn it on them. This is what I want."

At 3:30 P.M. Ziggy's was closed to the general public. A sign on the door said "Death in the Family."

M., despite her imprisonment in the wheelchair, was a dynamo in the kitchen. She knew just what Oy Oy Seven had in mind. "Lazar, put extra onions in the chicken soup, the hot Spanish kind. On the gefilte fish double the chrain;* no, triple it. Use the red cabbage around the meatballs, not the green. The pickles should be from the bottom of the barrel, the briniest

---

* Horse radish.

ones you got. And throw some pepper on them; it wouldn't be such a crime. No margarine in the potato *kugel*;* it's not strong enough. Mix in a jar of my Activated Old World Chicken Fat from contented capons. Use the cream soda; it's got more bubbles than the root beer, and serve it warm."

At 8 P.M. Sharett Pincus and his three clerks walked into Ziggy's. They were greeted by Israel Bond in a brilliant silver dinner jacket with half-dollar-sized Tahitian pearls for buttons, an Arrow Gordon Dover Taper Glenn shirt with a Lash LaRue leather whip tie, Jantzen's black velvet evening swimtrunks, and Esquire Old Frontier bedsocks with the Norman Rockwell painting of Quantrell's Raiders wiping out a wagon train on the sides. Mr. Bond was charm personified on this gala occasion, a master of amusing badinage (his joke about a "faggot maggot" scoring resoundingly); in short, a hail fellow well met all the way.

And that glorious dinner!

"Mr. Moonlight-Bey, you've only eaten nine pieces of kugel! For shame! Little clerks with hollow legs need lots of nourishment. Come on, Mr. LaToole. Surely you can stand another pound of that gefilte fish! Mr. Ben Blue, open wide and nice; Mr. Bond'll give you another spoonful of relish...."

Ninety minutes later the dinner was over. "Golly," said Bond, "I guess that was just about the niftiest meal I've ever had." He rubbed his tummy. "What do you lads feel about the dinner? Give me your honest opinion."

"*Merci*, Monsieur Bond. It was *formidable*." This from Pierre LaToole.

Shofar Ben Blue shook his head in disbelief. "Amazing. Amazing."

Bond lit a Raleigh. "Mr. Hassim Moonlight-Bey?"

Mr. Hassim Moonlight-Bey patted his own stomach. His full lips opened, revealing firm, strong teeth. From that mouth came a belch, no ordinary belch, but a mega-belch, one that sounded like the ten-second buzzer at Madison Square Garden combined with the horn on a 1931 Model A Ford.

Israel Bond smiled. Then he hurled his bowl of Mother's chicken soup into Mr. Moonlight-Bey's leathery visage with all his strength, squashing the aquiline nose to jelly. He dove like an avenging falcon on a lynx that has raided its nest, pinning

---

* Pudding.

the man to the floor and driving his fist against the man's solar plexus.

He stood up. Beame and Z. came out of the kitchen wheeling M.

"There's your goddam spy. Your gassy belch, Mr. Moonlight-Bey, so traditionally the Arab mode of expressing satisfaction with a meal, gave you away. Sweat him, Op Chief Beame, sweat him good so he'll talk. From this point on we're back in the old ball game!"

14
Call To
Greatness

Z.'s three days were up.

What was left of the battered Secret Service of Eretz Israel looked with hopeful eyes upon the restaurateur as he shuffled his notes. Op Chief Beame made the introduction.

"The Arab had some interesting things to say, but they can wait until Z. is through."

Z., obviously nervous, put down his notes, walked over to M. and began shuffling her notes. Bond, with one of his gallant, uncalled-for gestures, sprang to the table and brought M. Z.'s notes to shuffle.

Neon Zion, a 113 and unauthorized to take or shuffle notes at top-secret meetings, took out a deck of cards and was about to shuffle them when he caught Beame's stern eye.

Z.'s opening statement of his peroration was blunt:

"TUSH is trying to alienate the Jews of the Western world from Israel by destroying the one element it thinks is holding that relationship together—Jewish food."

Beame, who had been shuffling Neon's cards, glanced up at Z., swirled his forefinger in a circle around his ear.

"I am not crazy," Z. said with no rancor. "Dr. Holzknicht was the key to the puzzle, of course. During the last three days I have been in contact with those who knew him at the Schisselzelmknist Institute and they concede he is warped but a genius. As an illustration of that genius let me say that in 1955 he performed an unauthorized operation upon Gerda Sem-Heidt at the Konigsborgen Clinic. It was too delicate an operation for him to do alone so he enlisted the aid of two Rosicrucian chiropractors. One of them talked to me. Holzknicht gave her an external plastic heart and it works."

There were gasps from all but M., who made a notation on Z.'s notes, then handed them to Beame for further shuffling.

"The good doctor has made a thorough study of Jewish life, according to one of his old colleagues, and, I'm sorry to say, is more familiar with the milieu than most Jews. Undoubtedly, because he speaks our languages, Hebrew and Yiddish, he has been among us in disguise for many years in many places. He has noticed the shameful indifference of huge numbers of Jews toward Jewishness in recent years, which has been manifested in many ways: the rising rate of intermarriage, divorce and alcoholism, the slackening of synagogue attendance, dwindling affiliations with Jewish organizations, the weakening of respect between children and parents, the burning rush to change names, bob noses—this trend has been arrested for the moment by Barbra Streisand's celebrity, but it may surge again.

"He saw a phenomenon so common to us that we wouldn't give it a second thought. Have you ever noticed how Jewish we become, even the most disaffected of us, when we sit down to bagels and lox, corned beef, pastrami, kishke, borscht with sour cream, M.'s insuperable chicken soup, Manischewitz Wine, sour pickles, et al? In a twinkling of a boiled potato's eye that vestige of the emotional side of our heritage pops up. With each bite of the schmaltz herring we become ghetto philosophers; each bar of cream cheese sings the score of *Fiddler on the Roof*; each piece of rye bread—and suddenly we're fighting for the varnished heel with the union label again—makes us hum 'bum-bai-biddy-biddy-bum-bai!'; the sweet moments spent with the dear departed, the Mommas, Poppas, Zeydahs and Babas, are relived in a kitchen of long ago, and you now can appreciate the wisdom of Mr. Bond's lady friend, and, in short, we feel Jewish, and... and this is important... *charitable* to other Jews, to Israel.

"This is why Dr. Ernst Holzknicht destroyed the sources of food, many of the leading establishments where Jews congregate to eat it, and so forth."

Bond raised his hand. "I'd like to go to the bathroom, but tell me this. How does the bombing of the five Halifax-to-New York freighters fit in with your theory, Z?"

Z. laughed, "Schnook, you answered your own question and you don't know it. I'll help you. Where is Halifax?"

"In Nova Scotia." Israel Bond's face was flushed with shame. "I see. They were all carrying Nova Scotia lox."

"*Vu den?*[*] You see, just thinking about food has me talking Yiddish!"

Beame seemed half-convinced. "Let's assume everything you've said is true. But there's been no sign of any campaign against the Jews outside of North and South America and Western Europe. Don't they figure in?"

"No, because Holzknicht knows they don't count for a tinker's dam. You've got three and a half million Russian Jews who are in *drerd*[**] and they can't get out; you have a few more in the Arab countries isolated in medinas with no money, education or status; in the Far East you ain't got enough to buy a booklet of Hadassah raffle tickets. It's the Western Jews he's after. These are the ones who support Israel, don't you see? Remember, this thing is called 'Operation *Alienation*.' If the Jews of the West fail to buttress Israel in these crucial years when we should be growing we'll be so weak we won't be able to withstand attack... and all because some guy isn't getting his bagels and lox on Sunday mornings any more.

"Dr. Holzknicht knows it'll take years to rebuild the massive food structure TUSH's Calgonite planters have leveled these past few days. And by that time so many 'marginal' Jews will have left the fold that it would never be the same again anyway. For all we know, the damage is already done.

"I made some spot checks in every big city concerned. There's been a decline in these related activities already. The tourist bookings to Israel—down. UJA donations—down. Synagogue Sunday breakfast meetings—down."

M. turned to Beame. "Here, your trenchcoat is done. I'll shorten it later." She looked at Z. "Do we just sit on our hands? Is there no way to counterattack this monstrous thing?"

"No, it's bad for the circulation. Yes, there is one chance. If we could get hold of any one of TUSH's big three, Auntie Sem-Heidt, Heinz Sem-Heidt or better still, Dr. Ernst Holzknicht, and make him confess this terrible scheme to the world, get the master plan, the list of all people paid for the bombings. With the proper exposure on TV, press and radio we could show the world what's happened and, incidentally, make our fellow Jews so mad they'll start going to daily services again and maybe buy some Israel Bonds, too. The question is: Who will shake these rats out of their nest and get the evidence?"

---

[*] What else?
[**] Hell... or Russia. The terms are interchangeable.

Operations Chief Lazar Beame answered him for all those present. He walked briskly to the bathroom, flung open the door and cried: "Israel Bond, come out and save Judaism!"

Bond slammed the door. "Now?"

"Yes, now!"

Bond emerged.

The grey eyes were cynical. "I thought I was just about all washed up with M 33 and 1/3."

"It's all changed." Beame said tersely. "Now I'll tell you all what the Arab said, from least important to most. One, Ziggy's was to be bombed. I intercepted the guy with a 100-zis charge. He's out of business for keeps."

Good-o! Bond thought.

"Two, he didn't know anything about the master plan; he's too small to be trusted with that info.

"Three, he does know where TUSH is located. The Sem-Heidts are operating a gambling casino as a front.

"Four, it's in the very place you're heading, Oy Oy Seven. Sahd Sakistan. So this is your chance to wipe the slate clean."

The slate? a peevish Bond thought.

"Go in there, Oy Oy Seven, smash that filthy cabal, get the documents, capture one of the big ones and make him talk, save the king from assassination, save Eretz Israel from disappearing into oblivion."

"Hold on, Op Chief. You're going too fast. I think I ought to make some notes."

15
A Score In The Sky

It started its nerve-racking attack on his system the moment the Air India jet roared down the Lod airstrip... the old feeling.

Israel Bond, the most monumental task of his career awaiting him, lit a Raleigh and tried to stifle the libidinal monster inside clamoring for release by poring over the bulky report M., Z. and Beame had compiled for him.

"Sex Sexistan"—steady there, Oy Oy Seven; your eyes are playing tricks. Push this depravity from your mind. "*Sahd Sakistan*"— that's better—"is a territory about the size of Assault-Lorraine." *Alsace*-Lorraine, you pitiful, sex-haunted wretch!

It was then Miss Mookerjie, the olive-skinned, ebony-eyed hostess in the filmy red sari, a blue dot on her forehead, walked by his seat. "Can I be of service to you, Mr. Bond?" the sweet mouth spoke its polite singsong.

"I think not, Miss Mookerjie." Somehow his long, tapering fingers were closing around her willowy calf. He forced himself to read on.

"It has been playing both sides of the Cold War fence with adroitness. To illustrate, the Sahd Sakistani flag depicts a red, white and blue eagle clutching a hammer and sickle, beneath which is the motto, IN GOD WE TRUST—IF THERE IS ONE. Its principal exports are oil and malaria."

His hand was up to the butterscotch softness of the back of her knee, her breasts exuding Mumbai Madness Mist that rocked his libido into overdrive.

He could stand it no longer, slamming the report to the floor. "Miss Mookerjie! Follow me quickly or I can't be responsible for my actions!" He clutched at his throat and stumbled into the alcove between first-class and tourist, where the stewardesses prepare food and drink. Once inside, he pulled the curtain shut and pointed to an I.D. bracelet on his right wrist. "Read... read...." and fell gasping against the sink. Miss Mookerjie looked at the inscription on the bracelet, then into the tormented grey eyes, and smiled. "Of course, sir." Her nimble fingers flew to their appointed rounds and in five seconds her appointed rounds were revealed by the falling of the sari to her slender ankles.

With the unruffled efficiency of a trained servant of the air, she stripped Bond's Levi Strauss one-piece skydiver Score-Suit from his lithe, hard body and allowed a bronzed, muscular arm to draw her head against his chest.

"My name is Israel, O solicitous daughter of the Ganges," he said through cyanotic lips.

"Indira," she breathed. "Indira."

"Look, baby," he snapped. "I know *where*. I've done this before."

"No, Mr. Bond—Indira—it's my *name*."

Now they knew each other's names and that made it so real, so right, and his sensual lips, red once again, were sipping the bee nectar from hers. "Drink this." His command was hoarse, his body charged with expectation, as his hand bore a vial of desire-igniting Gallo Wine to her lips, setting her afire, and they began a fantastic flight pattern to fulfillment 150 miles an hour faster than the jet was going, making a mid-air adjustment to correct any weightlessness, and they collapsed onto a carpet of something green and cool, spent and content.

"What's this sticky green stuff, Taj Mahali dolly?" He prayed she would find favor with the sparklingly conceived internal rhyme.

"We are reposing upon the Royal gelatin which was to have been the dessert on this flight."

Two jetstreams of Raleigh smoke misted the window. "We made it on Royal gelatin, eh?" His grey eyes twinkled with levity. "I guess this is what they mean by a Royal—" but he aborted the witticism in an uncommon fit of good taste. He would not cheapen the moment this magnificent jewel of the East had granted him. "That blue dot on your forehead, Indira; it's gone."

She tasted his Raleigh. "Yes, I am a member of on erotic Hindu caste and that blue dot always disappears after I make love. With any luck, it will come back soon," she said, eyes a-twinkle.

Back in his seat he was disgusted with himself for employing the old I.D. bracelet gambit. He held it up to the light. "I am afflicted with a rare phenomenon known as *sat-air-iasis* and must have sexual contact lest I go into convulsions that could prove fatal to me and possibly result in misfortune to the aircraft."

Bond pulled up the collar of his expensive yet tasteful Hill & Range tweed trenchcoat ("It's what today's teeners would call real 'boss tweed,'" his midtown Manhattan tailor had assured him) and drew pleasure from the label's claim: THIS GARMENT, IF PERFECT, WOULD BE AN IRREGULAR.

King Baldroi, his eyes two malicious darts, leaned across the aisle. "I saw that little bit of hanky panky with the hostess, Bondy bitch. Come now; tell me. What did you two do in there? Did she force you to commit natural acts?"

"Knock it off, LeFagel!" He regretted the phrase. The little bastard would sure as hell twist them into his own frame of reference.

To his surprise, LeFagel did not, flipping a sheet of scrawled-upon yellow paper into Bond's lap.

Poetry.

"Tiger, tiger, burning bright,
"In the darkness of the night,
"You've made an incredibly stupid bungle,
"You've set fire to the whole damn jungle."

Good-o! LeFagel's showing a definite move away from the aridity of his homosexual orientation. Though I wish he wouldn't pet Neon's head quite so often. Well, I guess Rome wasn't built in a day. Although Levittown *was*.

When the jet dipped over the Gulf of Aden he saw the name U.S.S. *Jew* on the side of the mighty aircraft carrier whose decks were laden with neat rows of Chickenhawk jet fighter-bombers. Sound psychology, Bond admitted. America already had one called *Wasp*; the new boat would make a lot of swell folks feel a genuine rapport with the Great Society. But what was a carrier doing anchored off Sahd Sakistan?

He found out as he stood in the customs shed watching the MBG lowered by crane to the sandy soil. "Mr. Bond?" An inspector nudged his elbow. "You are wanted in the inner office."

Beckoning for Neon and LeFagel to follow, he walked through a passageway to a door, spitting upon it as his trained Double Oy eyes reported it was made from Cedars of Lebanon. When he felt the object dig into his back his mind clicked out Position 71—from the old manual he himself had authored for M 33 and 1/3 personnel, "Simultaneous Sex and Self-Defense"—and he fell to his knees with a slick, showy maneuver and whispered, "Don't shoot; I beg you, don't shoot."

The laugh held a note of admiration. "Okay, Oy Oy Seven. I see your reflexes haven't dulled one iota. On your feet."

That twangy New England accent! So redolent of B & M Baked Beans in dark brown jars; raucous gulls swooping out of a stormy sky to carry off stray Portuguese children; the Splendid Splinter, Ted Williams, at Fenway Park, taking two, then spitting to right. By thunder, it was....

"Monroe Goshen! You old lobster lob! You Penabscot putz!" With delight he hugged the sawed-off man with the dour Puritanical visage whose slight frame was draped in a herring-scented Gloucester nor'easter trenchcoat... Monroe Goshen, operations chief of the Central Intelligence Agency's Mid-East Section, who had spent with Bond in Eretz Israel those last spine-chilling hours of the Loxfinger caper.[*]

Pouting at the physical manifestation of fellowship, LeFagel said, "Well, that about tells the story, you heartbreaking Hebrew! It's the *'fay* fags who turn you on, right, Whitey? The *partzehs* on *schwartzehs* aren't good enough for you."

Bond pushed the querulous monarch away. "Look, your highness. This man's an old fighting chum of mine. I suspect he's here for the same reason I am, to keep your hide intact, so drop the green-eyed monster bit."

Goshen introduced himself all around. "True, your highness. My men and I came here on a carrier, ostensibly as part of a goodwill tour, but we've definite orders from the Tall Texan to keep you on the throne. If Sahd Sakistan goes Commie, we could lose a billion barrels of oil a year. Let's continue this discussion at my embassy. You'll all be my guests for dinner. Don't worry, Mr. Bond; CIA agent Brown will deliver that razzle-dazzle car of yours to the palace."

When the customs inspector observed that Goshen's black Simulac limousine with the United States seal on its plates was well on the way to Baghs-Groove, the capital city, he picked

---

[*] *Loxfinger*, Pocket Books Inc., 1965, $1.

up a telephone and dialed an unlisted number. He spoke for a minute, then quaked as the iron voice issued instructions. "Ja, mein lieber Gerda."

He walked to the spot where the Mercedes Ben Gurion had been deposited by the crew. "One moment, gentlemen. I must affix Mr. Bond's temporary Sahd Sakistani sticker to his license plate," which he did, with an exaggerated show of grunting diligence. As the left hand smoothed out the sticker, the right was touching the magnetized end of a metal cylinder to the underside of the Alcoa bumper.

It was a homing radio.

Wherever the MBG was going, so was a tiny sentinel from TUSH.

Two minutes later CIA Agent Brown, a towering Negro in a trim Ray Charles trenchcoat, stepped out of the office and was about to start up the MBG when he saw the red sedan pull into the parking lot. "1965 Togliatti," he told himself. "Let's look at the little old manual." He opened a pocket-sized book titled "Oppo Autos" and read: "Togliattis are manufactured in the Communist-dominated Italian town of Fiore by the Roberto Scinto dynasty, known ultra-left sympathizers. It is no coincidence that Togliattis are always registered to members of SMERSH (a contraction of the Russian words 'Smert Shpionam'— 'Death To Spies'), SAMBO, the newest top-secret surveillance cadre organized by a distrustful Moscow, whose initials stand for Smersh Also Must Be Observed, and TUSH. SMERSH and SAMBO invariably use Dagroes as drivers, opining that Swegroes, Spigroes and Bulgars are too dimwitted to manipulate the vehicle. The latter breeds, however, may accompany Dagroes as strong-arm men. TUSH, most imaginative of these clandestine networks, *will* use a Swegro as a driver if he has passed a driving test administered by a Dagro, mutation Bulgar or a Spigro with no less than 25 percent Dagro blood."

No doubt of it, Brown reckoned. The Togliatti is here to tag the MBG. Might make things a bit sticky later on for Goshen's Israeli pal with the bigshot reputation. I'll have to see that Mr. Bond gets an edge on these scum!

"Hey, boys!" He called to the usual gang of ragtag Arab urchins pestering the deplaned tourists near the taxi stand for cigarettes. He waved a pack of Waterfords and they raced to his side. Brown spoke to them in Sakistani, distributed the cigarettes, and watched them as they sprinted to the Togliatti, sportively climbed over and around it until the swarthy, hatchet-faced driver, whose woolly poll, thick Negroid lips and Sicilian curses stamped him as an unmistakable Dagro, shooed them away.

When the red sedan started up and headed toward Baghs-Groove, Brown got into the MBG, turned on the ignition and heard the beep, beep, beep of the homer planted by one of the boys under the Togliatti's license plate.

Brown smiled. *We're ahead of the game now.*

Not knowing he'd merely evened it.

16
Dee Dee, Da, Da, Da, Da, Dee Dee

As Goshen's Simulac rumbled through dark, narrow streets there came from a lofty minaret the ululation of the muezzin and they saw the faithful prostrate themselves in the age-old tribute to Mecca, holiest of Islam's shrines, then heard a second cry from the chanter that held a definite note of annoyance.

Bond smiled. "I'll translate. He's crying, 'No! No! You fools! Mecca is *east, east!*"

"This, your highness, is the native quarter, the fabled Cissbah," Goshen broke in with the Fitzpatrick narration. "It's so named because—well, look for yourself." There were burros and their riders making their water, as all good beasts and men must, against a dank, moldy wall. "Your father, King Hakmir, was quite science-minded. Well aware of the traditional usage of that wall, he had his researchers cover it with a gigantic sheet of Tes-Tape to create a sort of instant health diagnosis. As you can see, the third rider on the right and the fourth burro on the left are incipient diabetics."

"Can't we get any more speed out of this, Mr. Goshen?" said edgy Neon. "We're going at a snail's pace."

Not quite, Bond thought. He'd been clocking a snail that had started all even with the Simulac on the Via of the Hairy Houris and was outpacing it by at least one-sixtieth of a kilo per nonnautical dunam. They began to pass mounds of rubble that contained entire families, the fathers puffing pipes, children diving in and out of the debris in merriment, mothers at the bottom of the piles with old-fashioned papyrus brooms sweeping them together.

"Your late father's public housing project, sire," Goshen pointed out. "Before he instituted it, the *fellaheen*[*] had no debris to call their own and slept in sewers, puddles, marshes, etc. See how happy they are now? Generosity was an integral part of Hakmir's nature. He often told our ambassador, 'I've made my pile; now let my poor unfortunate subjects make theirs.'"

From the look in LeFagel's eyes, Bond knew Sahd Sakistan's new ruler had been touched deeply. Good-o! Perhaps King Baldroi will yet be—

The first volley stitched its way across the Simulac's windscreen[**] and he hurled LeFagel face down upon the Du Pont 501 orange and black Cottage Club carpeting. From the front seat he heard Goshen moaning. "I'm hit, Oy Oy Seven. Save the king...."

"Monroe!" Bond's muscular right arm lanced out, pulled the CIA op chief over the seat and deposited him next to the sobbing LeFagel. "It's an ambush, Neon. Right in this narrow alley and we're caught like rats in a trap."

"Say, Oy Oy Seven, that's a sharp simile you just came up with, that rats-in-a-trap business. That one of your originals?"

"You bet, Neon," Bond told the worshipping 113. Maybe I'm off base lying to the kid, he thought, but what the hell—Neon's under enemy fire right now and it's no time to start shattering the kind of illusions that make men happy to fight, to die, if need be. "How's Goshen?"

"Shoulder wound. Not too bad. Who's the 'oppo' out there?"

Bond shouted over the next barrage. "About fifty Kurds in black burnooses blocking the alley. We're in for it, I'm afraid."

Bond could hear the twanging of Neon's crossbow and from the occasional screams at the end of the alley he knew the kid was giving a good account of himself. Time to start doing the same, Oy Oy Seven, he chided himself. He worked the back door open and dove into one of the piles of debris, the impact sending stones cascading down its sides. The patriarch at the top of the mound hurled a deep-throated insult at him: "Home wrecker!"

His long, tapering fingers slid inside his Neiman-Marcus shoulder holster and liberated the ice-cold Colt 45. He yanked off its pop top and let the bracing malt liquor run down his parched throat. An excellent beverage, he knew, but no substitute for the weapon I need at this vital moment.

---

[*] Peasants.
[**] Britishism for windshield. Thrown in to give this book a touch of class, which it needs.

When he heard it he thought: I'm losing my mind. I'm lying next to a shot-up limousine in a fetid alley, slugs whistling by my dark, cruelly handsome face, and I hear music! And it's so familiar. *Dee dee, da, da, da, da, dee dee.* Yes, the first eight notes of the main theme from the motion picture *Lawrence of Arabia*.

The music swelled, came closer and the shooting ceased. He could hear utterances of awe from the band of attackers: "She comes! She comes!"

Bond got up and looked down the alley, blocked no longer by the Kurds, who had opened a pathway and were kneeling along its sides. Through it bobbed a woman on a white camel from whose neck hung a black box whence emanated the music—a tape recorder, he guessed. She wore a gold robe whose effulgence was doubled by the Arabian sun. A red tarboosh with a golden flyswatter for a tassel sat upon her head. Only two glowing coals, a pair of indescribably piercing eyes, could be seen over the top of her black veil.

When the white camel snorted, a cool, mellifluous British voice calmed it. "Be still, Latakia. Thy mistress commands it." The dromedary obeyed.

Those wondrous eyes swept over the grim faces of the Kurds, who held their smoking Bunning slider-carbines in their gnarled, sun-blackened hands, the pained expression on the wounded Goshen, the wide-eyed Neon Zion, the trembling, lip-biting elfin king, and then found Bond's unflinching grey eyes. For 120 seconds black eyes and grey eyes locked in a duel; then Bond's cruel sensual lips parted in an arrogant grin of desire and he knew somehow that under the veil her own lips were framed in an answering smile.

"Welcome to Sahd Sakistan, your Highness." There was respect in the voice, but no submissiveness. "I was a friend of your late, beloved father, King Hakmir, and have sworn to uphold his successor. Why these misguided tribesmen have dared to fire upon their rightful ruler is a mystery I shall endeavor to unravel."

LeFagel's composure returned. "We owe our lives to you, gracious lady. Who are you?"

A white-gloved hand reached under the camel's neck, touched a button and the *dee dee, da, da, da, da, dee dee* strain issued forth again. "You will always know I am here to protect you, sire, whene'er you hear the opening eight notes of my traveling theme music. I am Sarah Lawrence of Arabia."

17

Let's Do The Tryst

As the mystery rider interrogated the Kurds, Bond promised the pale CIA Mid-East Op Chief, "This'll stop the bleeding," and he unscrewed his belt buckle to remove a tube, squirting its contents on the hole in Goshen's left shoulder. "It's cherry salve. My mom used to *schmear* it on every wound we kids ever had... burns, knife slashes, boils, even a deep puncture I received once when I fell from a window and was impaled on a rusty fence post." Directly upon application the cherry salve drew the bullet from the flesh with a loud pop and the ragged edges began to knit. In a few seconds every trace of the wound disappeared, including an adjacent vaccination mark and a tattoo, I'M A BOSOX FAN.

"You missed your calling, Mr. Bond," the mystery woman remarked. "Those long, tapering fingers should be healing men, not ending their lives with karate blows."

Bond, placing Goshen in the rear of the Simulac, said, "You seem to know all about me, Miss Lawrence, which gives you an advantage, since I know nothing about you." The grey eyes challenged hers again. "And I'd like to—very much."

"Mount Latakia and ride with me, Mr. Bond, and we can discourse as I guide your auto out of the Cissbah."

Ordering Neon to take the wheel, Bond accepted a white-gloved hand and with the fluidity of the high hurdler sprang onto the veiled beauty's mount.

The cool, musical voice was deferential. "You seem to be no stranger to a hump, Mr. Bond."

"That expertise, Miss Lawrence, is something I hope you'll have complete knowledge of someday," he sallied, and drew an appreciative chuckle from her.

"You have a rapier wit to match that lithe, muscular body, Mr. Bond." She touched Latakia's ear and whispered, "Onward, noble ship of the desert." Latakia moved forward with an undulating motion that lulled them both into a state of euphoria. As they rode, Bond encircled her waist, his fingertips tingling with a strange sensation never before known to him. *Gottenu!* he thought, now it's happening on *camels!*

"I am a twenty-fourth cousin by marriage of the famed Lawrence who changed the face of Mid-East history," she said in her clipped, precise British manner. "As a little girl on our ancestral estate, 'Guanay's End,' which is situated in the center of the triangle formed by Saxonshire, Normanshire and Brokenshire, I was regaled by Pater's tales of my cousin's exploits in Arabia and vowed to make a pilgrimage to the area one day to retrace his glorious footsteps. A child's silly longing, I suppose, and I more or less had forgotten it because of the multifarious activities afforded members of my class. Pater was an M.P. for the constituencies of Sussex, Wessex and Essex and—"

"Perhaps," Bond interjected, "you'd be interested in the benefits of a locale very dear to me, My Sex?"

"Capital, Mr. Bond! You *are* an amusing chap! To continue: As the daughter of landed gentry I went through the usual rounds, riding to the hunt with my trained pointers, Alpo and Thrivo, humdrum semesters at the exclusive Miss Fenton's School for the Bored, where I majored in ballet, fencing, art and class hatred. There was never a shortage of dashing swains for the beautiful, accomplished daughter of an M.P., Mr. Bond, and I was constantly turning down marriage proposals from such eligibles as Ronald Duckblind, Brenfleck Coddingfeather, even Britain's most sought-after young gallant, Sir Marvin of Throneberry. Despite the flattering attention I sensed the innate emptiness of this decaying way of life. My ennui did not escape the shrewd eyes of Rector Justin-Thyme Mother, spiritual leader of our Anglican parish. Father Mother, when he heard the dreams of an impressionable girl, said, 'Then go to the Middle East and take up the tasks left undone by Lawrence of Arabia.' However, there was much to be learned before I could come here—the art of riding a camel, for instance, which I mastered after many months of practice riding on a carousel in Blackpool. England's most renowned female armorer, Lady Major Ruthboyd, taught me to handle rifles, side arms and medium-range rockets; I was schooled in the many dialects of Arabic by

Ibn Tard, dean of the Institute of Middle East Languages and Intrigues; dressed for the desert by Muslim Dior and taught to exist on a mere handful of tanna leaves a day. I came to Sahd Sakistan a year ago and introduced myself to Hakmir and the leaders of the Kurds and Wheys, meeting first with rejection, until I had the presence of mind to play my theme song. Having seen the picture, they were convinced I was, indeed, Lawrence's kin. It was this hard-won admiration, Mr. Bond, that made the Kurds halt their attempt to assassinate King Baldroi back in the alley. The Kurdish chieftain told me he had received a report that LeFagel was an impostor, a false pretender to the throne, and that a *real* pretender to the throne was about to arrive in Baghs-Groove."

"This smacks of TUSH handiwork all the way, Miss Lawrence," Bond said. In the next few minutes he gave her a recap of his adventures, including the showdown with James Bund, detailed descriptions of the episodes with Liana Vine and Indira Mookerjie, and threw in for good measure the Loxfinger and Matzohball cases, plus his entire sexual history.

As she stirred in his arms during certain portions of the narrative, he thought, Good-o! She's all worked up. Before long this captivating creature will be mine evermore. What a find! Beauty, warmth, a "class broad" from Great Britain with a tony upbringing. She's the only woman worthy of your love, name, number and license to kill, Oy Oy Seven. A man needs to sink roots some time, and maybe I'm too far over the hill to stay in this racket any longer—I've already caused the deaths of almost five dozen good folks. This magnificent woman in my arms can redeem me, uplift me and maybe, since it's obvious she's loaded, set me up in my own high class shoe salon (nothing but I. Miller's and British Walkers) on Kings Highway in Brooklyn. True, I've sworn to my sainted mother that I'll never place a wedding band on any finger except that of a Daughter of Sharon; yet, that too can be worked out. I know the moment I take Sarah Lawrence of Arabia in a way she's never known before, she'll see the ultimate value of Judaism and convert with celerity. Wonder if Milton'll give me a 25 percent discount on the wedding at the Pinochle Royale? He should, really—I'm his brother, and besides I saved the joint for him and I think I'd be justified in telling him so.

He was already under the traditional canopy with Sarah Lawrence of Arabia, the rabbi intoning the sacred marriage contract, when her scent nudged him back to Sahd Sakistan. "It's driving me wild, Miss Lawrence. What is it?"

"A special blend, 'Evening with Profumo,' made for me by Maitland of Moreland Street. I am pleased at its effect on your olfactory sense. But we are at the Road of the Feculent Figs and I shall take my leave."

He slid off Latakia and motioned for the car to halt. "Shall I see you again, Sarah Lawrence of Arabia? There are things a man and a maid must talk of and they are best said by moonlight."

For another 120 seconds black and grey eyes flashed fire and desire into two another, his crossfire causing the rim of her veil to smoulder, hers turning his Talon zipper into red-hot mesh, charring his Arrow briefs. "Some aim high for happiness, Mr. Bond, while others...." She left her proverb unfinished, but its corollary proposition was quite clear.

"You haven't answered me, Miss Lawrence." His voice was husky, his hands betraying his febrile state by abrasive rubbing that expunged the lifelines from his palms.

"It is my wont to be each night at 9:30 at the Oasis of the Sheik's Spear to commune with the spirits of the desert. Good day, Mr. Bond."

"One thing more, Miss Lawrence. Learn Hebrew. You'll need it the rest of your life because, Miss Lawrence, from this moment on, it's you for me, babe... only two for tea, babe...."

Was that a sigh breaking through the glacial Pommy reserve? He was not to know. She issued a command and Latakia loped off into the distance, the sun transforming her into a golden figurine.

Well, Oy Oy Seven, he thought, she's named the trysting place. An oasis by moonlight—in the company of a heaven-sent woman. It can be the kind of cataclysmic joining of kindred souls to be found only in those Kathleen Winsor reprints you keep buying.

Gottenu! he breathed, and to somehow dispel the unendurable passion surging through his marrows, he swung his bronze, muscular arm and struck Neon Zion in the face, splitting open his startled subordinate's lips. "Someday, Neon, when you're a man of the world, you'll understand."

113 made no reply as he searched the haunted grey eyes of Oy Oy Seven for a clue to the outburst. There was none, save the curious word repeated over and over by the panting lips. "Moonlight... moonlight... moonlight...."

18
Blood And Sand And Blood And Blood —

"I have composed another verse," proclaimed LeFagel. Bond, hoping desperately for another artistic indication of a turnabout in the king's psychological makeup, squeezed his fists in expectation. The animalistic fury triggered by the dramatic eyeball-to-eyeball confrontation with the mystery rider had receded when the first puff of his Raleigh brought back the sordidness of the real world. Goshen drove on, immersed in some memory of his New England childhood, muttering, "Happiness is a harpoon in a white whale." Neon Zion, possessor of youth's happy resilience, was on his seventies in paddle ball, the puk-puk-puk of the ball furnishing a surrealistic punctuation to LeFagel's recitation.

> *On a ghostly night of yore,*
> *A man tapped on my chamber door,*
> *It was cold out, so I granted him a haven.*
> *He said, "Kind sir, my name is Poe,*
> *And I've been searching high and low,*
> *Tell me please, sir, have you seen my f— raven?*

Good o! Bond thought. Not a dot of deviation in that one. In an irrepressible gesture of goodwill he jabbed his potent left at LeFagel, drawing two fonts of claret from the ruler's mashed nose. LeFagel grasped the significance of the heart-felt demonstration and returned a shy smile that held no suggestion of effeminacy whatsoever. He seemed content to just sit, bask in the warmth of Bond's feeling, and bleed a great deal.

But the air of camaraderie flew away like a frightened sparrow when Bond, leaning out of the rear window, spotted the white edifice at the very end of the shoreline road. "Is that it?"

"Shivs." The CIA op chief made it sound like a four-letter obscenity, although it was actually a five-letter word. He saw the old deadly look on Bond, the sudden lust for battle that imparted a murderous glow to the grey eyes and the dark, cruelly handsome face.

I know what's on his mind, Goshen ruminated. He's thinking the enemy's in there, the ghoulish krauts who've killed and crippled his comrades, blown up his people's vittles... and my ol' fire-eatin' buddy's dying to go in there and have at them. But I spoke to M., Z. and Op Chief Beame via the carrier's Ship N' Shore Blue Denim Network and I know what the odds are of getting the goods on TUSH— maybe a million to one—and even Oy Oy Seven, the man I and the whole world have come to idolize, won't get out of there alive. I'm an atheist—the only day I take off all year is Madalyn Murray's birthday —but if I were the praying kind I'd offer one now for Eretz Israel, the Promised Land, where there are there Cohens in every fountain, and Secret Agent Israel Bond, the neatest guy I'll ever know!

They were cruising through the modern section of Baghs-Groove, passing Young Moussa Koussa's Spy Secrets Exchange, Farouk's Bargain Souk with a 40% off sale on borth whirling and non-whirling dervishes, and Loew's Hosni, the art movie house where Dennis Morgan in *The Desert Song* had been packing them in since the 1940s, and finally the Simulac swerved into a palm tree-lined driveway up to the entrance of the US Embassy.

Waiting for them with a pasted-on smile was a weedy, sun-reddened man in a Sy Devore orange Eden Roc-weave tropical suit and Redd Foxx safari beret, who introduced himself as Tender N. Callowfellow, the ambassador, with a promise of a dinner "fit for a—" he began to giggle—"king." So it was, the braised sloth paws in flavored *eau de Conigliaro* parve fluoridated sauce a revelation to even the most jaded tastebuds, washed down with *vin scully* '24 from the vineyards of Chavez Ravine, and "of course, your Majesty, Ambassador Scotch—" he chuckled again—"on the rocks," and he poured it over the dolomite chips.

"I think," said Ambassador Callowfellow, pulling a bell rope, "it's time for After-Dinner Mintz. Ah, there you are, Mintz, my man." A short, white-haired oldster entered and served them pungent circles of Certs on red hot coals.

Goshen and Bond spent the next hour discussing the job at hand, while Callowfellow and the king retired to the former's study for a chat about the upcoming coronation.

"I've splendid news," beamed Callowfellow, re-entering. "His Majesty has consented to have America host his coronation at the Sahd Sakistani embassy located in the Empire State Building in New York. It will serve to remind the world of the unbreakable link between our respective nations, and will have the benefit of our superior news coverage. I'm terribly excited about it."

"I, as well," retorted the bright-eyed monarch pressing the ambassador's hand in fond farewell, and then departing for his new home.

Built by John McShain from a design based on a collect phone call from Frank Lloyd Wright's widow, the palace of the late Hakmir was an up-to-date Alhambra of harrylimestone, upon whose slanted roofs rested alternating cupolas and parabolas. In the front, lined on two sides by proud rows of Afghani opium poppies, was an immense pool on whose surface floated sprigs of wolfbane and spiderwort nibbled at by chattering les cranes, fred robins, and a rare merv gryphon. Overhead winged a brilliant red herb jeffries flamingo like a flame in the sky, flying over the enclave to its lover nearby. Near the entrance was a pewter statue of the late monarch from whose nostrils came a continual spray of provocative Vegamato, the essence wafted to the Middle East by the thermal air current originating in New York's Wall Street known as the "Underwriters' Wind."

"Iz," said Goshen, "for heaven's sake, don't try anything foolish. As far as the world knows, Shivs is a perfectly respectable outfit that pays its taxes and keeps its nose clean. You can't go in there like Gang Busters without proof. Anyway, your first job's keeping his Majesty here safe and sound; we're all agreed on that. I'll be in touch. See you later, fella."

"Wouldn't think of it, Monroe, you ol' Rockport chowderhead," Bond pledged, throwing a salute to the departing CIA op chief. Once inside the royal suite, he told Neon, "Keep Tabs on Baldroi—or regular Coke, if you're not watching your calories," and was rewarded by 113's prolonged laughter. He showered with distilled Culligan rain water, applied No Sweat, the deodorant that checks unseemly perspiration by destroying the glands that produce it, to his virile armpits, removed his beard with the super-keen Schlock blade that gives a man twenty slick shaves and thirteen bloody ones, donned a heavy-duty Haitian Papa Jacques-strap, Chantilly lace sunslax, a Krishna Menon waistcoat of bleeding madras (LeFagel saw it, meowed, "I go for men who use Menon" and was cursed at by Bond for backsliding), Royal Blakeman Andalusian bedsocks, slung on M.'s paisley shoulder holster with one of Lavi HaLavi's deadly new inventions inside the Instant Processed Cold Rolled Extra Strength Steel device. Bond put on the Korvette's luau car coat and swallowed six Excedrins (there might be agonizing pain ahead) and twelve Benzedrine tablets (if there was to be pain, he wanted to stay awake and enjoy it to the fullest; it was, after all, as much a part of life as pleasure) and a homer radio capsule whose signal could be traced by any "friendly" with a standard M 33 and 1/3 Ribicoff-Javits bipartisan receiver-transmitter-juice blender, then inserted one of the new anti-homer capsules into his belt buckle compartment under the cherry salve ointment he always toted for wounds and infections.

"You're going on a job, Oy Oy Seven, against orders." A shocked Neon said it.

"Just forget what you've seen, kid," Bond snarled. "I'm going to take the MBG for a little spin. If I just happen to lose my way and it just happens to stop at Shivs, well...."

To save time he slid down the copper rainspout outside the king's window to a rear courtyard and walked into the empty garage which once had quartered the thirty Cadillacs now sharing Hakmir's eternal rest in a mass grave. Grinning at him like an old chum was the grill of the MBG. She roared her delight at perilous adventures in the offing when he put her in reverse, depressed the accelerator, and zoomed out, the armor-plated rear deck killing the tethered sacred white elephant with a pulverizing smash to its side. He got out, clucked in sympathy, and pressed Button 5, whose concealed acetylene torch emerged. He used it to slice the tusks into portable sections, which he heaved into the back seat. Tough luck for Mr. Pachyderm, he thought, but what's done is done and there's a grand (or even more) piano in it for me.

As the exhaust from the MBG's quadruple pipes singed the Portland Cement driveway to the main road, the Togliatti that had been parked behind the garage for two hours eased out. The beep-beep-beep of the homer on the MBG made the four swarthy men exchange evil grins.

From 1000 feet up in a helicopter, the two cars seemed to the giant CIA Negro agent like insects, Bond's a silverfish, the TUSH vehicle a beetle. The flapping of the huge sign being towed by the chopper was a disturbance Brown had long since gotten used to. It told the people below: YOU ARE ONLY 8126 MILES FROM FLORIDA'S FAMOUS STUCKEY'S, THE HOME OF DELICIOUS PECANS, SOUVENIRS AND PASSIONATE PAGAN LOVE RITES BETWEEN SEMINOLE INDIANS AND GIANT ALLIGATORS. A perfect cover, he knew; Stuckey's advertising was famous the world over and no one would question its presence in the Middle East.

Brown had been sitting by the chopper on the roof of the U.S. Embassy when he heard the gleep-gleep-gleep from the transistorized device in his hand. It was one of the cleverest items ever created by the CIA weapons unit and would never arouse the suspicion of the "oppo" because it was not shaped like a cigar lighter, fountain pen, pillbox, et al. It looked like a radio. Goshen's orders had been succinct: "I've just left Bond at the palace to guard the king but he's got the smell of fire and brimstone on him, and I know damn well he's going to Shivs. Tag him by chopper."

Brown's binoculars caught the MBG shooting away at 87.9 blazing kiloknots. Wow! Plenty of Passover horseradish in that engine!

When the hatchet-faced Dagro at the Togliatti's wheel heard the beep-beep-beep (picked up by the powerful antenna on the front fender and fed into the dashboard receiver) begin to fade he also increased his speed, sliding the syncro-dynaflush transmission into Forward Speed Six.

A Raleigh waggling in his sensual lips, Bond sped down the shore road eager for the hand-to-TUSH combat that could mean either life or death for his adopted country. Ahead lay Shivs, its sun-splashed windows twinking a brazen challenge: *We're here, Oy Oy Seven, the whole rotten Nazi bunch of us. Take us—if you can.*

Got to hand it to the krauts, he thought. For sure they've cleaned those windows with Windex and can see 100 miles in any direction—a pro touch all the way.

Engrossed in fantasies of revenge he did not pay proper attention to the fork in the road, berating himself as he saw he'd veered off the shoreline drive onto a bumpy spur whose route shunted the unwary driver into the hellish furnace of the desert.

"You stupid, albeit dark, cruelly handsome, bastard!" he railed at himself, but the self-deprecation faded from his lips when he saw the blinking red light on the power ashtray whose interior secreted his radio hookup. He pressed Button 175, the ashtray swiveled, hurling two dozen Raleigh butts into his lap, some still smoldering, but there was no time to grouse about petty discomfort, for the radio was in full view, a tiny vleep-vleep-vleep coming from the cantilevered coils.

Forget the "stupid," make that modifier "lucky," he grinned, kissing his reflection in the mirror. That right-hand turn had been providential. He had picked up a homer concealed on some car in the area. If he'd stayed on a straight course, he'd never have noticed it. And he blessed the slipshod, amateurish side of his nature that so often had stood him in good stead.

He gave the MBG's gas pedal the full weight of his right Andalusian bedsock and she escalated to 156.6, her extra-grip Firestone tyres[*] more than a match for the sucking sand. With dismay he heard the vleep-vleep-vleep dying out and on a hunch made a 45-degree angle turn off the spur onto the desert itself, gunning her up to 176.2. There was a squashy sound; he looked back at the mangled donkey and its nomadic rider splayed out under the merciless sun. His forefinger punched Button 200 and he saw the canteen of water and the medical handbook jet from the rear into the poor fellow's broken hands. Good-o! Beggar's got a 50-50 chance of survival now, he exulted.

Alarmed by the diminution of the MBG's homer the trailing TUSH-y two miles back also played a right-hand-turn hunch, a hideous smile splitting the hatchetface as the beep-beep-beep pulsed back.

Goshen's airborne tag shook his head with incredulity at the scene below, two high-powered chargers whipping up dust storms as they tore madly around and around in a three-mile-wide circle. It was clear now—the MBG also had been "homered," without his knowledge. Time to end it. He switched on the special channel used by the CIA and M 33 and 1/3 to contact one another. The gents in the Togliatti might hear it too, but unless they had a scrambler, which was unlikely, they would get gibberish.

---

[*] Manufactured in Great Britain.

"Brown Shoes and White Bread to Rozhinkehs Mit Mandlen*... Brown Shoes and White Bread to Rozhinkehs Mit Mandlen... come in please...."

Bond understood the recognition signal at once and listened to the CIA tag's analysis of the dilemma on the ground. "Good-o! Brown Shoes and White Bread. Rozhinkehs Mit Mandlen acknowledges. Out."

He halted the MBG and clambered up the burning side of a powdery dune. He could see an arrow of dust streaking his way, estimated the Togliatti's arrival time at 90 seconds, 93 if its driver wore a Timex. From the shoulder holster he liberated HaLavi's scaled-down version of the Anna Sten gun, touched the eraser on his Ticonderoga pencil, which split it into a tripod, and mounted the weapon on it with his left hand, sliding the cordovan Hickok belt out of the loops of his sunslax with the right. He reversed the belt. Its hidden side contained 100 notches, in each nestled a steel-jacketed denizen of death.

Better take a closer look, the CIA man thought, and he brought the chopper down 750 feet. Yup, the crazy bastard's spoiling for it, like Goshen said. Gonna take on four of 'em by himself. Guess he's everything he's cracked up to be. Better get down there and backstop him.

The glint of the sun on the MBG's silvery roof tipped off the Dagro in the pursuing Togliatti. He braked it 50 yards from the dune and the doors flew open, the four occupants diving into the sand. Bond, feeding the Hickok belt through the Anna Sten, opened up and heard screams from two of them. The Dagro grabbed at his chest and pitched forward on his face; a second, whose racial stock was unrecognizable for the moment, was also out of it, blood gushing from his forehead. He gave the remaining duo, without question Swegroes, a long burst. From the thumps he knew he'd put at least ten slugs in each. Not good enough, buddy boy, not good enough. It takes a damn sight more than ten slugs to stop a Swegro, he knew.

The Swegroes jabbered at each other for a second, then began a steady crawl toward the dune, leaving dreadful crimson trails on the white sand. He emptied the belt, certain he'd pierced Swegro flesh again from the howls of vexation. But they kept coming. And he was out of ammo!

From his vantage point he could see them dragging their riddled bodies inch by inch up the dune, their eyes malevolent

---

* Raisins with almonds.

jewels. "Don't come another step closer or you'll regret it!" Bond cried. "I was never inoculated for chicken pox."

Their answer was contemptuous laughter; they dug their octopuslike hands deeper into the white powder: "By yumpin' yiminy, we gwine cut you..."

They hit the top at the same time, their tentacles tripping Bond and sending him tumbling down the dune. His head struck the MBG's rear fender. It's all over, he thought bleakly as the Swegroes loomed over him, their faces widened by triumphant smiles. There was a flash of something metallic and the point of a knife bit through his luau car coat into the waistcoat.

Suddenly the Swegroes were upright no more. Both were on their knees clutching their guts, still yelling defiance. Five feet away stood a powerful Negro, his lips in a gelid grin, bluish smoke rising from the muzzle of a Lucky Thompson submachine gun. "Stay down, Mr. Bond!" The Thompson chattered again, planting 50 slugs in each Swegro, driving them to their backs. The smaller of the Swegroes looked up at the gunner in sorrow. "You could yust stop it. I tink I bane die now, baby." And the brown eyelids rolled over the blue pools.

The second shook a fist, continued to scream defiance and, back on his feet again, made a rhinolike charge at the CIA man, the steely fingers gouging into the man's throat. Bond could hear the newcomer's frantic grunts and he ignored the claret streaming down his side, pulled himself into a sitting position and snatched at a gun in the dead Swegro's hip holster. He put five bullets into the attacking Swegro's back, heard a groan and saw the man topple.

"You all right, buddy?" Bond said, then: "Watch it!" The CIA man spun to meet the Swegro's second charge, sidestepped it and retrieved the Thompson.

The Swegro turned, screamed, "Defiance! Defiance! Defiance!" took a round in the heart and lungs, clawed futilely at the CIA man, then muttered to himself, "Why should I do all the f—ing work?" and fell on his face again.

"Don't go near him," Bond shouted. He staggered to the MBG, took a fragmentation grenade from the glove compartment and waved his ally away. He pulled the pin and shot-putted it onto the Swegro.

A minute after the explosion, the CIA man sniffed at the remains.

"Well, there's a little fight left in him, but damn little, Mr. Bond. Let's make sure."

From the sleeve of his trench coat he wrested off a button and placed it in the Swegro's mouth. He folded his arms and waited.

"That's it. There was enough cyanide in that button to kill a hundred and forty thousand people, the population of Bremerhaven, Germany."

Then their eyes popped. The gutted mound that had been a Swegro stirred, and the mouth said, "The latest census puts Bremerhaven's population at a hundred and fifty thousand. Defiance! Defiance! Defi— " They heard a throat rattle. Then all was still.

There was no doubt now; the Swegro was dead.

19
Shivs, I'm Here!

Bond inhaled his 519th Raleigh of the day. "He was a tough one."

His rescuer nodded. "Swegroes usually are. Frankly I don't know why the other one copped out so easy. Let's give a look." He gave the corpse a meticulous examination. "Look what I found in his back. A knife and I'd say it was in at least six inches. Yours, Mr. Bond?"

"Hell no."

"Wait, there's a name on the hilt. 'Property of Colonel Stuart Bentall, M.I. 5.' I remember him; British agent. But he's been dead for ten years. Which means this baby's been toting a pigsticker in his back since 1956 or earlier. I guess one of our bullets must have driven the point into a vital organ."

Bond was kneeling by the two dead men near the Togliatti. "Not a mark on the Dagro. He must have succumbed from fright. Dagroes can't take it too well. Other one looks like a Bulgar or maybe a Bulgro. I got him all right. My initials, I.B., are in his forehead."

"Hey, Mr. Bond! You've been hit."

Goshen's giant saw Bond touch the sticky mess dribbling from his side and a profound sadness humanize the cruelly handsome face. "It's my waistcoat, made of bleeding madras," Bond said. "It took the brunt of the knife, saved my life." He cradled the garment in his muscular arms. "Any plasma in that chopper?"

"Sorry. No."

Bond walked over to the shame-faced CIA man. "Not your fault, buddy boy. You couldn't have known. Anyway it's too late." He knelt, scooped a hole in the sand and placed the waistcoat inside. "You know any decent words to say in Hindi or Urdu? No?

Well, I'll just say something from my heart, that's all." He looked at the forlorn little mound of sand. "You were a good waistcoat. If there's some kind of a Laundromat for waistcoats where gentle pro-Semitic laundrymen never use harsh detergents, I hope that's where you're headed. Shalom."

He picked up his Hickok belt and Korvette's luau car coat. "Since I owe you my life I guess introductions are in order, partner. But you know me already." His grin was boyish, guilty. "Goshen didn't trust me, huh?"

The rugged CIA agent shrugged. "Well, you know Goshen." He proffered a shovel-sized hand. "Name's James Brown, CIA Agent Seven-Eleven. The bigot who assigned me that number said it was a *'natural'* because so many of my people are expert crapshooters."

"Makes no difference to me, Jimbo," Bond said. "I read *Ebony* Magazine all the time; Willie Mays is my favorite ballplayer, and if a fine, cleancut Negro moved next door, say a Diahann Carroll, Nancy Wilson, Lena Horne, Barbara McNair, or a Leslie Uggams, I sure as hell wouldn't go running to a realtor with a 'for-sale' sign in my hand."

"You're an okay 'fay." Brown's initial wariness was gone, dissipated by the Israeli's frank, hardhitting clarification of his liberal philosophy, a potent display of his peerless decency.

"And you're okay too—in spades," Bond flipped back, drawing a hearty cackle. "You look like a real specimen, Brown. About six-three, I'd say, 225 pounds. Hell, man, you look like you ought to be full-backing for some pro team at six yards a carry. How did you get into this lousy business?"

Brown lit a Waterford and sighed. "Man, that's real water! Well, seems the CIA had sort of a sociological problem. As you know we're divided into White and Black categories, the former signifying the people in desk jobs, the latter the rough-stuff boys. Someone noticed there wasn't a single black in the Black, so they started shopping around for a token operative. They'd been impressed by the undercover and often violent aspects of the job I'd been doing in civilian life—registering Negro voters in Mississippi. And the guy who made me Seven-Eleven said, 'Now we got a *real* shadow for the tag jobs.' Let's skip that for now. So you're really going to bust into Shivs?"

"Got to," Bond said, his jaw muscles bulging. He filled James Brown in on the caper, including his showdown with James Bund, threw in the *Loxfinger* and *Matzohball* sagas, but left out the detailed descriptions of the episodes with Liana and Indira and his entire sexual history. No sense cluttering up Brown's head with irrelevant information, he reasoned.

"I can't say as I blame you. But I hope you don't mind if I backstop you again. Orders."

"You might come in handy, Jimbo. I've a homer capsule in mah chit'lin's. Can you track me from outside the walls?"

"Sure. I've got a gadget. If I hear your beep go to sleep I'll assume something's awry."

They got into the MBG. Bond used Button 61 to lob a brace of Calgrenades, 3/4-zis force, which blew the Togliatti and the helicopter to bits. "Can't leave a messy desert, Jimbo. Let's go."

"Hold it, Bond. I have some data on the joint that might prove helpful. When your people told Goshen of the TUSH setup here he thought we ought to find out more. So I went pub-crawling in Baghs-Groove last night and the fourth dive paid off. I found a Hungro pretty well in his cups."

"A Hungro?"

"Part African, part Magyar. They tend to be moody, weepy types, big boozers. I got a manual on 'Oppo Mixed Breeds' that has all this crap, incidentally. Well, this one was a room service waiter at Shivs and he just couldn't stand confinement any more so he sneaked out through the rear gate, possibly by bribing a Bulgro... they're always on the take, you know... and went on a bender. 'Course I helped him along with a few shots of *zuki;* that's the native beer made from stagnant well water and decomposed Chevy fan belts. And earlier today I took these from the chopper." He took a manila envelope from his trenchcoat, opened it and spread some aerial photos on the front seat. "The Hungro said the top floor here is for the personal use of the Shivs directorate. There's a conference room here and the rest are individual suites for Auntie and Heinz Sem-Heidt, Holzknicht, and the other seven. Third floor's for the household guard and the service corps. Second's for selected guests, big spenders who get free lodging and eats—no bargain 'cause Shivs gets it all back and then some in the casino, which is on the first floor. Heinz runs the LaGuerre Room. He wins big, too. Seven other krauts run the rest of the gambling. Only Auntie and Holzknicht are never found in the casino. God knows what she does. He's got some kind of a lab upstairs where he fools around. One bit of good news—there are no Swegroes inside Shivs 'cause they might scare the customers away and the help, too. Bulgars,

Bulgroes, Mickgroes, Spigroes, Spigars... they do the strongarm work. And then they have the dogs."

"Dogs?"

"Yup. Hohenzollerns."

All right, buddy boy, Bond excoriated himself. So they have Hohenzollerns. And maybe more awful beasties that go bump in the night. You didn't think you were going in there to hear Ronald Reagan do readings from Zane Grey, did you?

"In front of Shivs is the guest area, swimming pool, patio, bar, etc. As you can see it's rather small in comparison to the rest of the grounds. It's closed off by a twenty-foot-high Papuan ironwood fence. I guess the management doesn't want them snooping around the rest of the estate. As for internal security, you just must assume the rooms are bugged and that every non-guest hasn't got your personal interest at heart. I have, though. If I can't hear your belly beeping 'I've Got You Under My Skin' I'm coming in."

CIA Agent Brown's account of the horrors within those walls cast a pall over both of them as they motored silently on, their eyes peering through the mist along the shore for the first glimpse of the witch's lair.

"Stop 'er, Mr. Bond." Anxiety constricted the voice, robbed it of its robustness. "We're about two hundred yards away. Close enough."

Israel Bond lit a Raleigh and noticed with a sardonic smile that it was the last one in the pack. An omen? The last Raleigh he'd ever smoke? Some people wouldn't consider that prospect the least bit alarming, but they weren't secret agents walking into the mouth of hell. "If I don't make it, Jimbo, you'll find a couple thousand cigarette coupons in the trunk. See that M. gets 'em. And tell her I went out smiling with a Raleigh in my sensual lips. So long, big fella."

He stepped out and saw the brazen windows in the upper floors twinkling a new message: *Come into our parlor, Oy Oy Seven. The spiders are very hungry today.*

Up your glass! The epithet blazed back at them from the grey eyes.

When Bond heard the truck grinding along the sandy path, he crouched behind a clump of spiny *Sarajevo* cacti. As it puttered by, he saw the sign on its side, HAJI'S LAUNDRY, and then saw it stop at the rear gate.

Praying the squish, squish, squish of the Andalusian bedsocks on the sand would not be heard over the idling motor, he raced to the back of the truck, his Vicks 44 in his right hand, put the point of it against the lock and blew it off, the Silentium Silencer muffling the discharge. He dove into a pile of something white and fragrant and closed the door behind him, his trained Double Oy nose telling him he had landed on a Rinso wash. Good-o! I've made a clean start!

Bond heard the driver and the guard, the latter's soft, slurring speech indicating its owner was a Bulgro, exchange a few jokes, one of them with the punch line "faggot maggot," and he tore up a Jackie Kannon towel in anger. Goddamnit! That one was getting around too fast! There was no time to pencil the joke out of his notebook of goodies, for the truck was moving again. He heard the ominous clang of the closing gate.

OK, Shivs. I'm inside, he thought. I ask no quarter and I give no quarter.

Then he snickered at his Gung Ho-Don Winslow-Captain Midnight bravado. Big deal! These days, what the hell can you do with a quarter?

20
This Pond's Minus Honey And Almonds

Through a small window in the rear door he could see they were passing through an area darkened by trees and thick foliage. He flung the door open and sprang onto a cobbled roadway, the impact sending a jolt of pain through his Andalusian bedsocks. He heard the clatter of the truck die. All was still, save for the humming of bees, the chirping of "katydid! katydid!" from one part of the forest, a scornful answering, "dirty stoolpigeon!" from another.

The squeak of wheels coming up the path sent him on a headlong dive into the nearest bush. He cursed himself for his precipitance, for he'd landed in a *chipango* plant whose spearlike shoots cut open his right cheek. The smell of his type-A blood sickened and frightened him. What if the dogs scented it?

A spasm went through his body when he heard the doggerel crooned by the iron voice.

> "Fee, fie, foe, foo,
> I smell the blood of a lurking Jew."

He was looking into the mustard-yellow orbs of Auntie Sem-Heidt.

She sat in her wheelchair, her chalky face looking as though it had been fashioned from a thousand grave-worm bellies sewn together. Her clawlike fingers stroked the life-giving battery on her lap with a repulsive fondness. The wig she had chosen this afternoon was algae green, matched by a similar tint on her lips and a green-and-black housedress. "There is someone in the forest, Heinz."

"Nein, lieber Gerda. A small animal, perhaps, or the wind." Her mate stood by her side, stuffing schnitzel dumplings into his cave of a mouth, his profane blimp of a body garbed in a Bavarian mountain climber's costume, white-lace dickey, red-velvet shorts and suspenders, the piano legs in lederhosen and red-leather Mary Jane sandals. "Let us continue our constitutional."

"Nein, we shall stop here for a moment. Locksley, a muffin, bitte."

The dwarf in the jester's outfit seemed pleased at being able to service his wardress. He took a muffin from her pocket and inserted it between the electromagnetic coils. Its scent filtered through the shoots to Bond's nose, enticing at first, then acrid, and he heard Auntie Sem-Heidt's invectives. "Cursed gnome! You have burned my muffin! Heinz, my knout!"

The scrawny arm lashed out with surprising power, the metal tip of the knout thudding against Locksley's back.

"Enough, Gerda. You will kill the creature," Heinz said. "A good dwarf nowadays is hard to find."

She acknowledged his wisdom. Locksley expressed his gratitude for the cessation of the flagellation with a cartwheel, during which he clapped his hands several times. It drew a whinny of approval from his mistress.

"Your gyrations have pleased me, dear little freak." The claws patted the puckered apple of a face. "I shall reward you with a chance to see Auntie Gerda's little toy. Behold!" She spread open the housedress and the dwarf did a triple cartwheel this time.

Gottenu! The Israeli's grey eyes did cartwheels of their own. Z.'s voice echoed: "He gave her an external plastic heart and it works."

If his own heart had not been pounding so stridently he would have heard the rush of air and the snarling "baa-a-a" just before the thing hit him like a bullet. *Gevaldt!* He could not stifle the cry as the teeth and horn penetrated his right shoulder. "I was correct!" the iron voice called. "There is an intruder! The dog has flushed him."

A 135-pound steel-ribbed Hohenzollern, the part-German shepherd, part-German sheep bred by the S.S. during the '40's in the Mordegruppe Research Center in the Black Forest for sentry duty and ferreting out downed Allied fliers, was worrying at his throat, the foul-smelling saliva now mixed with Bond's blood dripping from the fangs. He could see the orange and black coat and the thick white mushroom of wool on its skull, the hard lance of a unihorn—Hohenzollerns, nervous, unstable, as apt to tug out a friend's throat as an enemy's.

Man and beast were rolling over and over, both raked by spines and shoots, the former's right elbow taking the fury of the teeth. Bond's left hand grasped the stem of the woolen mushroom and pulled it over the creature's mad-dog eyes, blinding it for a vital second, then with a superhuman effort drove the animal against the trunk of a tree. There was a yelp and the spine snapped.

Ignoring the claret pouring out of his mangled arm and shoulder, he ran deeper into the brush, for a chorus of baa-a-as told him the whole pack had been set loose on his bloody trail. There was a thrashing sound, a slurring Bulgro voice: "He went this way!" An angry Dagro's, "No, you stupid bastard, the other way."

Gottenu! Fire ants, crazed by the odor of blood, were sliding down little poles and swarming out of their hills. He brushed a loathsome phalanx off his body, not before the industrious pincers had carved out another chunk of shoulder.

"Bear left!" It was the gravelly command of a Bulgar. Bond ducked behind a tree and saw a hawklike face emerge over the foliage and stiffen into a sneer when a Spigar voice somewhere piped out: "No, he doubled back, you — clod!"

It was quite apparent these hired thugs despised each other. By thunder, he'd use that ill feeling against them!

He sent out a slurring shout. "Hey, man, where you come off callin' me a stupid bastard? I don't take that — from nobody, 'specially a lice-ridden Dagro!" He pitched his voice higher. "Ain't no stinkin', garlic-chompin' Spigar gonna tell us Dagroes what to do. We got the brains in this outfit, man; you ain't nothin' but meerkat dung; you ain't fit to sleep with a Swegro; you lower than a Bulgar's bunions; you smell like a Hungro sittin' in nine-week-old goulash." He simulated a gravel-throated tirade next: "Who dares compare a pure Bulgar with the rest of you half-breed carrion? Death to Spigars, Hungroes, Spigroes, Dagroes! Mere total paralysis to Bulgroes, who at least had enough sense to be born part Bulgar!"

Full-scale insurrection broke out in ten seconds. He could hear vile imprecations and knew his stratagem had worked. The hunters had become the hunted! Dagro knives slashed Bulgar bodies; Spigroes clubbed Bulgro heads; Spigars and Hungroes traded blasts with sawed-off mortar pistols. Everywhere was the smell of cordite, Woolite, bauxite and death.

But he heard the baying of the Hohenzollerns and he trembled as he pushed his torn body through cacti, thornbushes, and Wilkinson swordgrass, his Korvette's luau car coat in shreds. The terrain grew soft, then—splash!—he was knee-deep in a slimy pond, its muddy brown slowly stained red by his dripping wounds. Brown, red... and now— silver! A silvery mass darting across the water—Gottenu!—voracious yellow teeth were ripping into his legs. He fell to his knees, took another bite on his hand which severed his beloved 30-year-old Irving Caesar Sing a Song of Safety Club ring. It fell into the murky waters, lost forever.

Somehow he managed to stumble to the other side, avoiding the snapping jaws of a jacare, the Brazilian crocodile, which he dispatched by emptying all of his Vicks 44 slugs into its eyes. There was no time to skin the creature to compensate himself for part of this ordeal by treating himself to a fine pair of Amazonian bedsocks (150 quasars retail if they were a farthingale) because the red-eyed, steel-fanged Hohenzollerns, six of them, came through the thicket to the opposite side of the pond. "What a croc!" he said, looking at the body of the slain jacare with regret, and turned to meet the new challenge.

Though they growled and thrust at the air with their unihorns, they did not charge across the pond. They know what's in there, he thought. Got to make 'em mad enough to come over. Another psychological warfare bit?

"You yellow, lily-livered Deutsche hunds... come and take a Jew—if you can! Come on, krauts. I've seen chihuahuas that could kick the crap out of the whole bunch of you." One braced to spring; an older, wiser head bit into its tail to restrain it.

Bond spoke a flat, pedantic sentence. "According to the better trade magazines, the Renault outperforms the Volkswagen in every way."

Now there was no holding them back. The impetuous one left his tail in the older Hohenzollern's mouth to lead the charge, blood gushing from his hind quarters. They followed suit, eyes rolling with insensate hatred, coming on for the kill. They never reached him. One by one they were savaged by the silvery mass, howling in agony as they went under; again the water swirled with red and pink.

Pieroghana! the flesh-loving Polish devilfish of the Vistula River, known to drag down careless fishermen, pleasure boats and, in three recorded instances, left-wing governments....
"Dobzheh, dobzheh!"[*] He collapsed.

---

[*] Good, good!

21
For "The Clipper" And "Mighty Mick"

It was the iron voice somewhere close by—"Heinz! Release the birds!" —that told him he dare not linger another second. He staggered blindly into the forest again until—thump!—his head rammed into something hard, the Papuan ironwood fence James Brown had indicated to him on the map. Beyond it he could hear brittle laughter and splashing. He knew the relative safety of the guest area could be his, if he could scale it.

How?

Fool that he was, he was leaning on the answer—a bamboo tree. He jerked one of its stems back and forth until it cracked explosively. Balancing it between his hands he backed off about thirty feet. There came the whirring of wings; he turned to see a formation of diving condors, then the mesmeric yellow eyes of Auntie Sem-Heidt as the wheelchair pushed by the straining Locksley came into view. Her hand flicked out, the knout's steel tip catching Bond between the shoulder-blades, but he was rushing toward the twenty-foot-high barrier, thrusting the bamboo pole into the earth, arching his body over its top as talons and bullets reached for him in vain. He was soaring up, up, up over the ironwood stakes, whose discolored points meant certain death by curare, fugu or snail snot if they scratched the tiniest hole in his epidermis. He was vaguely conscious of the fact that he had broken the world's pole-vaulting mark by a foot or more (with an old-fashioned bamboo pole, not one of those hopped-up Fiberglass jobs) but he put the feat out of his mind, for now, the black-green netherworld behind him, Israel Bond was descending into the opulent section reserved for the big spenders; well-manicured lawns, flowerbeds and a circular pool around which sat potbellied men in the company of tanned, supple goddesses in bikinis being served drinks by dark little men flashing obsequious, gold-toothed smiles.

His feet thudded into a pudgy back, sending one of the male guests sprawling into the pool, the klonk of skull against diving board fortuitously smothered by the splashes of frolicking guests, and Bond flopped into a Jivaro lounging chair next to a splendidly proportioned auburn-haired enchantress who did not look up as she commented in an offhand manner, "That was my husband, Count Amontillado Di Terrazzo-Crotchetti, you just knocked into the pool. He cawn't swim, y'know."

"Pity," Bond said. Then—"Tracy! Tracy!"

The face was bored no more. "Iz! Iz, my darling!" The wonderfully wanton jet-setter who had shared that memorable summer with Bond at Portofino buried her fine, white teeth into his shoulder, the torn one. "Oh, my darling. You're hurt. And what are you doing here?"

One of the poolside waiters came to the table. "*Pardonnez-moi*, Countess. This gentleman—" the lips smiled; the eyes were hostile—"is a friend of yours? You are cognizant of the by-laws of Shivs regarding non-members and interlopers."

"A very dear, dear friend, Valdespino. This is Mr.—" She felt his urgent hand upon her thigh, saw a signal in the grey eyes—"Mr. Dalby, Larrimore Dalby, of Dalby & Ross, my suture future brokers. Good man to know if you're trying to corner the suture market, Valdespino."

The eyes remained suspicious. "I have a sorrowful announcement, madam. The count has drowned."

"A tragic loss, Valdespino. Let's have a round of drinks to his memory. I'll let Mr. Dalby order." She shot Bond a challenging glance.

Still wants to know if I've got the old expertise, he mused. He looked at his watch. "Well, Valdespino, it's 4:30, too early for the Dom DeLuise '17 which must never be served in the heat of the day, too late for the Armand Ruderman '25, which is at its effervescent best only between 9 and 11 A.M., and then only if served within four hundred miles of either side of the International Date Line (her eyes were filled with veneration, the mouth moistening with lust) so let's just make it two Good Old 'Arolds, with either the Lavagetto '38 or the Cavaretta '40, spiced by Sneakee Pietro, favored by all derelicts of good taste. That meet with your approval, Valdespino?"

"Oui, monsieur. The *drinks* meet with my approval." He went to fetch them, his cold eyes still on Bond.

He practically italicized the word "drinks," Bond thought. (He could not know the italicization was literal.) They meet with his approval, but I don't. He kept looking at the blood on my shoulder. I'm going to have trouble with this little man.

"Bless you for the little white lie, dearest Tracy." He painted the oval cheeks red with an affectionate squeeze of his bloody hand.

"Oh, it'll cost you, Iz, don't worry." She ran her cool hand over the corrugated muscles of his navel. "What are you doing here anyway, Mr.... uh... Dalby?"

"Freelance writing job. Sneaked in to get some data on a piece to be called 'Gambling, Armageddon of the Soul,' which I hope to peddle to *The Watchtower* Magazine."

"You're lying, Iz—uh, Larrimore. I've suspected for some time you're one of those secret agents... those nights in Portofino when the shoulder holster pressed against my body as we made love... the times you'd jump up from some nightmare yelling 'SMERSH! SWISH! TUSH!' and start firing that damn gun all over the place. I never told you about the killings of bellhops and cleaning women I had to hush up with my husband's money."

"Okay, so you know. Keep it down, bright eyes. There are mikes hidden all over the place."

"If you're here to probe the evils of gambling, my pet, why don't you take a gamble and discuss them with me at full length... on my full-length bed? Room 25, second floor."

"Logical way to get into the subject," Bond jested. "Let's away, shall we?" First he took out his Inca-Dinca silver cigarette case and fumbled with a Raleigh so he could keep it open a few seconds longer. The interior mirror caught Valdespino behind a palm tree, popping a capsule between the white and gold teeth. Planting a homer capsule in himself like mine, Bond realized. Señor Valdespino is going to tag me all over the joint. Bet somebody in Shivs at a master controlboard right now is getting a beep-beep-beep on the personal frequency assigned to Valdespino, which tells him Valdespino suspects something. "Second thought, Tracy, I'll meet you at the room a little later. Keep stoking the home fires, you adorable hellcat."

"They are now," she panted. "Don't you dare forget me, you motherstoker."

Bond walked toward the villa, smiling at the oafish klomp-klomp-klomp of footsteps behind. A clumsy tag job... you never tag a man in cheapo Father & Son croco-mocs, Señor Slewfoot.

He nodded to the blah guests on the porch, went inside and found the Herr O' the Hund Cocktail Lounge to the right of the main desk. "Seven and Seven," he told the sleepy-eyed Bulgro behind the bar polishing the Dixie Cups.

"Fourteen." Then the man, suddenly aware of the fact he was not being given a math quiz, blushed in the adorable way that all rattled Bulgroes do. "Sorry, sir. I'll make one up right away."

"Better make that two Seven and Sevens. I've got a friend coming in. Hi, Valdespino," he said with an airy wave. "Join me for a little drinkie-poo?"

The sheepish waiter decided to brazen it out. "If you wish, sir, though it is against Shivs' policy for the help to fraternize...."

"No buts about it, old man. I insist. About time hard-working little waiters got waited on themselves, huh?" Bond picked up the two drinks, letting the anti-homer capsule capsule fall from his palm into Valdespino's. "Down the hatch, fella." He experienced a thrill as the man drained his drink. He started to down his own when the Bulgro said, "That'll be three quasars and six, sir." Bond dug out a five-quasar note and walked over to the bartender. "Keep the change. And here's an extra colodny just for the way you blush."

The mistake was turning his back to Valdespino, long enough for the little man to place a pellet into Bond's half-finished libation. Bond came back to belt it down, said flippantly, "Nice talking to you lads," and went back into the lobby. He ambled down a corridor into the casino past a number of guests in Bermuda Schwartz shorts, hot-eyed degenerate gamblers who stuffed farthingales into a battery of machines. One screamed, "I hit! I hit!" and Bond saw the man's shaky hands receive a pack of Luckies.

He did not know what made him turn his head; intuition, perhaps; whatever it was, it saved his life. The knife whistled by, burying itself into the heart of a rose on the damask-covered wall. His hands flew to his mezuzah, the cylindrical symbol of his faith on a chain around his neck, and, with a long, tapering finger on the Star of David, he aimed it at Valdespino who was pulling another knife from his cummerbund. But the second knife fell from the man's hand, the Molochamovis-B tipped needle from the mezuzah flew far from its intended mark, killing the unfortunate chap who'd beat Shivs' one-armed bandit for the cigarettes. Bond and Valdespino were doubled up, their hands clutching their stomachs, water streaming from their eyes. They began a frantic race toward a door with a painting of a haughty cavalier on it, cursing and shoving each other aside. Then they were in the room, felling two elderly gentlemen about to go into the stalls with hammer blows, and, at last, in the stalls, Hickok belt and cummerbund falling to the floor. From the groans of Valdespino and his own Bond knew they had both been victimized by anti-homer laxative capsules of similar potency.

"Truce," he gasped and heard a weak, "Oui, monsieur."

He lit a Raleigh. "Smoke, Valdespino?" He heard a grunt he took to be yes and shoved one underneath the partition along with a blue-tipped Ohio match.

"Merci."

"That's quite a device you put into me, old man. A Dr. Holzknicht special?"

"Indeed, sir." Valdespino sighed. "And—oooh—may I compliment you on the efficacy of the one you placed in my drink, sir."

"Fella named Lavi HaLavi's responsible for—" He could not finish the sentence.

Some time later, the fight and everything else drained out of them, they were engaged in an amiable chat. Bond admiring the Polaroid photos of Valdespino's wife and three children his former adversary had passed to him. "Nice young 'uns, Valdespino. Though I'd hate to entrust their future to the kind of megalomaniacs you've thrown in with."

With one of his trenchant analyses of the political forces shaping the world's destiny, coupled with an offer of a CIA job for 25 percent more than TUSH was paying (plus hospitalization, old-age benefits and a tour of Disneyland; he was sure Goshen would make good on all counts) he persuaded Valdespino to change sides. As they washed up, he told the waiter, "You won't be sorry, old chap. The CIA can always find a spot for an ugly, clever little knife-throwing fanatic."

"Mon Dieu!" Valdespino was suddenly pale. "I have been guilty of the worst sort of amateurism." He made a hasty search through the cubicles. "Look, Mr. Bond, in each roll of ultra-soft, irritant-free Delsey. Listening devices. In Shivs, sir, even the stalls have ears. They have heard my betrayal. It is all over for me. Get out while you can."

Gottenu! Bond slapped his forehead. "I've also forgotten. My buddy, CIA Agent James Brown, is out there. Now that he isn't getting the signal he'll be barging in."

They headed through the casino to the lobby. Through the loudspeaker they heard shouts in a sort of doubletalk Bond assumed was a code for Shivs' personnel.

"Mr. Bond, they are ordering their men to get the guests back into the casino on some pretext or other—-free hot milk and Malomar cookies, I think. Which means they don't want witnesses around when they open the front gate to admit your friend, whom they have spotted. He, too, is a goner. They will cut him down. I have just heard my name mentioned as well, sir, in a most unfavorable light."

"Got to warn him, Valdespino. Is there any—"

Valdespino would be of benefit no more. He fell on his face, a machete vibrating in his back. Down the corridor flew a trio of Shivs' house police, two Bulgars and one that looked like a cross between.... What does it matter *what* breed he is, you idiot! Bond swore at himself. Run! Run!

He lurched back into the lobby, firing the mezuzah's auxiliary needle into the desk clerk's cheek, the nerve poison doing its job in 1.9 seconds. He crouched behind the front desk, discovered some bars of Camay on a bottom shelf and jammed them into the pockets of his Korvette's luau car coat. No reason why a secret agent has to have rough, red hands, unless, of course, he's an Apache, Bond reasoned. When he pushed the bars into the right-hand pocket a long, tapering finger hit the round, hard thing.

Little Rickey Bond's Superball! Damn it, he'd forgotten to give it back to Milton's kid after that swell game of catch in Trenton... sixty billion lightyears away. Without knowing why, he let his mind wander back to that catch. He'd seen how Superball, the latest toy sensation, could outbounce by a 50 to 1 ratio the ordinary balls he'd used as a youngster.

He knew now how to warn CIA Agent James Brown, but it might prove fatal. The hell with the risk! With his "Old Wrangler" Ralston Cereal Tom Mix Straight-Shooter knife he cut a message into the ball: TRAP! STAY OUT! BRING HELP! BUY AN ISRAEL BOND! In his mind's eye he saw the front porch of Shivs facing the front gate, perhaps 600 feet away, and himself as a fourteen-year-old would-be Joltin' Joe D. back in Trenton, hurling his moth-eaten tennis ball against the porch of his Union Street home in the game known variously as "pinnerball," "stoopball," or "porchball."

He knew they'd be waiting for Brown; so they were, their gimlet eyes at the sights of Manicottis trained on the gate. There would be time for one drive only against the "pinner" or point of a porch step. Now! He charged down the steps and stooped into position. "Der Jude! Take him!" The iron voice... he tore his grey eyes away from the horrid yellow ones and swung his usable left arm on a downward slant, felt a grand old-time tingle as the ball kissed the point and took off like an angelic thing, up, up, up, a black dot tickling the underbelly of a cloud, then over the hundred-foot wall around the casino with plenty to spare, the tape measure blast of all tape measure Ballantine Beer blasts, a Yankee Stadium roof-clearing thing of beauty, and he could see in the center of the explosions in his head the faces of DiMag and Mantle smiling a "well done, fella" and hear his own stammered reply: "That one was for you, Clipper, and you, too, Mighty Mick," before the half-dozen rifle stocks clubbed him into limbo.

22

Good Old Sol*

To his amazement the voice was not iron, the eyes were not yellow, but brown, intelligent, almost sympathetic.

"Let us talk quickly, Oy Oy Seven. There is little time. Even now Gerda is dressing for the extraordinary occasion of inflicting—ah, let us say testing, some unusual devices upon the catch of her lifetime, Secret Agent Israel Bond. Undoubtedly she is putting on her finest housedress and practicing upon Locksley, her dwarf, with a whip she has sworn will be used only upon you, a cat o' twenty-seven tails presented to her by Der Führer (The speaker's hand shot up in a heil) himself. Cooperate with me, Bond, and I will save you from unimaginable suffering. I want to know how much M 33 and 1/3 knows about 'Operation Alienation,' how deeply the CIA is involved, what plans both have for counterattacking, how the new king can best be gotten to and eliminated, as well as a few items to sate my personal curiosity."

Bond, his hands chained to the wall, saw a bland face and the high forehead of the scholar. His questioner was a man of medium height with a military crewcut who wore a white labcoat. Of course—Dr. Ernst Holzknicht, whose mild appearance belied his status as the evil genius behind all of Eretz Israel's woes.

"Where am I, Holzknicht?" He would not give the kraut the courtesy of "Herr Doktor," no matter what the cost. "And remember, under the terms of the Geneva Convention I can only give you my name, rank and Diners Club number."

---

* The chapter title just happened to work out this way. But I can not quarrel with the sentiment.—S.W.

Dr. Holzknicht blew a mouthful of Muriel smoke into his face. "You are in the cellar of Shivs, the very room where Oy Oy Five met his end at Gerda's claws, so you see there is no regard for Geneva's niceties here."

Bond inhaled the foul air. "And if I cooperate, then what? Autographed pictures of David McCallum and Robert Vaughn?"

"I will reward you with a quick, painless death, an injection of *diathorenzymesheckeygreen*, and say that you died of your many wounds, which, if you'll notice, I have treated. I have no personal interest in torturing you. It would serve no scientific purpose."

"You're not like the others, Holzknicht. You're a genius of medicine and psychiatry, you don't enjoy sadism, and I see you're wearing a pair of fifty-colodny Dr. Joyce Brothers bedsocks, which means you have a fully developed artistic sensitivity; yet you align yourself with these ghouls. Why?"

"That is a long story, Bond. Ja, I agree; the Sem-Heidts are quite mad. Heinz is a fat-swollen sybarite who lives only for calories and the cheap thrills of the *la guerre* table. Gerda is a monster who must cause some kind of misery every day of her life or she finds life meaningless. I regret that a man of my intellect and taste has been forced to seek alliance with them, but TUSH has power and the finances to underwrite my researches."

"Can't those researches be conducted for some democratic country? I'm sure your past indiscretions would be forgiven."

"You do not fully understand, Bond. The main reason I am with TUSH is because I concur with its ultimate goal. Even as a young scientist I was far ahead of my older, allegedly wiser colleagues in understanding the monumental problems facing mankind. Long ago I foresaw the great upheavals arising from awakened nationalism in the former colonial territories, the impact of the population explosion, the terrible food shortages, automation, water pollution, the threat of attack by aliens from other planets and the ever-growing possibility that the sun may die in five billion years, leaving earth a cold, shriveled, dead mass of rock. With my logical, dispassionate scientist's mind, I arrived at one incontestable solution to all these problems."

"And that is?"

"We have got to destroy all the Jews."

"Well," Bond said uncertainly, "if you put it *that* way"—then he was furious at himself for a momentary weakness—"no, damn it, no! I won't play ball, kraut. Do your worst."

"So? A pity." The doctor sighed. "In that case I shall leave you in the capable claws of Auntie Sem-Heidt. First, however, we shall soften you up." He walked to a corner of the cell and slid open the lid of a screened cage. "Good day, Bond, and goodbye." He was gone.

From the cage came a soft scratching sound... then, one by one, out came an abhorrent line of crawling brown things, each about six inches long, with countless little feet and curved claws at each end. Israel Bond felt the hair on the back of his neck—rising!

He was about to be attacked by a miggle of millipedes from the Lesser Antilles.

They moved inexorably toward him. He could pick out the pinpoints of red that were their eyes. Their bites might not mean death, at least the instantaneous kind, just simple agony that would turn his fine black hair white and the dark, cruelly handsome face into a Dorian Gray After within seconds.

In his terror he twisted at his manacles, rubbing huge patches of skin from his wrists; they held. Something clanged against the floor and he realized that in his straining desperation he had snapped the Tuck Tape that bound the Instant Processed Cold Rolled Extra Strength Steel tool to his body. Alas, it was six inches (the exact length of the filthy stalkers) from his feet. Might as well be six miles, he lamented, as the line of millipedes moved on, now less than a foot away, their claws held high to lance into flesh. He closed his eyes, whispering, "Hear O Israel, the Lord Our God, The Lord is One." He waited for the first prickle of millipede feet on his legs, the first claw squirting venom.

What was taking them so long?

He opened his eyes.

They had stopped in their tracks, deploying in battle formation toward the steel-barred opening that served as the cell's only window.

Crawling through the bars, caught by a shaft of fading sunlight, was the enormous, hairy arachnid of the desert, a solpugid, searching for food.

"Solpugid. Sol. Sollie baby." Thrice he entreated the new arrival in a voice cracking with emotion. "Help me, Sol. Help one of your own who's up against it now. Don't stop to polemicize about Orthodox, Conservative and Reform differences. *Ich bin a Yid,* Sollie. *Du bist aichit. Helf mir!*" (I am a Jew... you too... help me!)

The arachnid seemed to comprehend. It quickened its pace, furry legs impelling it into the midst of the enemy, the terrible jaws scoring direct hits time and again. Three of them were cut in twain, the severed halves thrashing in death throes. But Solpugid had been slashed damagingly by two of them hitting it from both sides in a prearranged pincer plan; its vital juices ebbed from the bites. It drove back at the two attackers, pulling them within the area of the jaws. Bond heard the crunch of the jaws into their carapaces. One left!

"Sol! Behind you!" It spun to meet the sneak attack—too late—and the claw laden with excruciating poison struck home. Solpugid shook the millipede off its back with a mighty heave, which sent it banging into a wall, then chomped it into jagged bits.

Gottenu! Bond thought. It's saved me. Then he felt a new thrill of horror as he heard the elevator whine, bearing, he knew, the Bitch of Schweinbaden.

That damned tool! So near, yet so far.

He looked at the barely alive Solpugid.

"Sol, that hunk of metal. If you've got anything left—push it over to me."

A few of the eyes blinked dully. It's so damn shot through with poison it can't hear me anymore, Bond thought.

Solpugid got up.

With its last atom of power, it staggered up on three of its eight legs (the rest, no doubt, were numbed by the circulating venom), geared itself for a final rush and smashed into the chunk of metal, which, Bond deduced, must have outweighed it 150 times. The tool skipped over the stone, coming to rest against his ankle just as the elevator hit bottom. Bond was in action, kicking off an Andalusian bedsock, pinching the device between his toes, kicking up and catching it with his even, white teeth. He ignored the claret oozing from the corner of his cut sensual mouth, bit harder into the tool and with a series of nods worked it against his chains. He smelled the burning metal shavings as the IPCRESS file ate its effortless way through the links, and suddenly he was falling on his face as they gave way. No time to crow (he was a poor birdcall imitator anyway)— the squeak of the wheelchair down a cellar corridor and the harridan's cackle were broadcasting a message: Run! Run! Live to fight another day when the odds are better.

"*Olav Ha Sholom,*"[*] he whispered to the dead Solpugid, then scraped the IPCRESS file against the bars which crumbled before its ridges. He was halfway through the window when the cell door swung open. "Stop him, Locksley! Stop him!" Her new whip laced Bond's back but he was beyond feeling. With a vicious backward kick he hurled the dwarf, who was attempting to bite his leg, into the wall. Outside, he looked down and balled up his right fist and shook it at the yellow eyes, which gave way for the first time to his grey ones. "You gutter bitch! You'll have a real heartburn before Eretz Israel is through with you!" He fled into the sultry night.

---

[*] Rest in peace.

23
First Things Second

On the sound theory that TUSH would expect him to hightail it as far from Shivs as his battered frame could take him, Bond walked coolly up the porch, through the lobby now bustling with guests about to start their night's run at the tables, and, shunning the elevator, went up via the service stairs. His object: the fourth floor and the documents that would incriminate the heinous junta before the whole world.

As he reached the second floor landing he saw a shadow and cocked his left fist for a killing blow. There was a sob and warm arms fell upon him. "Tracy!"

She was naked, atremble; demented eyes rolled in the oval face. "I've been waiting, waiting, waiting! Oh, Iz, Iz, Iz! Hurry, hurry, hurry!"

Well, they say all good things come in threes, he thought, and let her drag him down the hallway into Room 25. It was apparent she had been champing at (and for) the bit quite awhile. A pile of Viceroy stubs spilled out of an ashtray onto the Du Pont 105 throw rug, the blankets on the Mr. Greenjeans hide-a-bed were tossed to one side, the phonograph was playing DePussey's "Afternoon of a Nymph."

It was matchless ecstasy for Tracy, so much so that on her roller coaster ride to fulfillment she bit through and tore off from her arm her black mourning band; not for Bond, whose wounds prevented him from reaching that exalted realm, though he did settle for a fuzzy area's fuzzy area between sublime rapture and divine consummation.

"Iz." She was sleepy-happy, her oval face glistening with the contentment of a baby who has just guzzled Gerber's Strained Scotch. "Don't leave me ever."

"I must—for now, darling. I've got a big job ahead of me. Sleep and dream of that summer in Portofino. Incidentally, sweet, I've films of that interlude. Would you mind terribly if I had them exhibited at some of the better men's clubs? Gladly share the net receipts with you after the distributor's take."

"Do anything you...." She was asleep.

Sweet kid, Tracy. A *shikseh*, but that could be altered. Man could do worse than end up with her, especially since she was now the sole heir to the count's squeegee empire. Stop the dawdling, Oy Oy Seven, and get up to the fourth floor!

It was deserted, the directors and Heinz Sem-Heidt downstairs running the games. At the conference room door sat a dozing Spigar with a Wickersham-Freehan antelope gun on his lap. From the smell it was obvious the man had been at the *zuki* keg and it was an easy matter for Bond to take the weapon from his hands and bash his head in.

The room held nothing of interest for him except for a few Muriel cigars in a bowl, which he took. He ransacked eight of the directors' suites, again finding nothing rewarding, eschewed a ninth, obviously the doctor's, when he heard the bubbling of some chemical or other. But he received a jolt when he eased open the door to the tenth suite.

She was in the wheelchair, the yellow eyes masked by chalk-white lids on whose surface were branching green and red veins; snores gurgled from the thin nose and blue lips. Her hands rested on the jester's cap of Locksley, who slept in a barbed-wire crib next to the wheelchair, his thumb in his mouth.

Bond tiptoed across the threadbare rug, kicking aside strewn-about housedresses, his grey eyes darting into nook and cranny for the documents. On the walls he saw shelves lined with her personal library—*A Child's Garden of Perversion, Jayne's Fighting Whips of the World 1965-66, Flay Your Way To Contentment, De Sade—He Really Knew How to Hurt a Guy*—and a pennant, SCHWEINBADEN, CAMP OF THE MONTH FOR THREE STRAIGHT YEARS.

And then he found it—behind her ermine-trimmed iron Maiden Lady—the safe. He prayed the tom-tom that was his heart would not rouse the hag as he pulled the sandpaper from his hip pocket and sensitized the tips of his long tapering fingers. Click! The first tumbler —five minutes passed—click!— the second—good-o! He glanced at the radioactive dial on his shockproof Kissling. Nine-twenty. In another ten minutes the safe would yield its treasure. By nine-thirty the proof of the existence of Operation Alienation would be in his hand.

Nine-thirty!

Gottenu!

She would be at the oasis at nine-thirty, his own and only true love, Sarah Lawrence of Arabia!

Well, Oy Oy Seven, what comes first, your personal happiness or the destruction of the powers of darkness?

Certainly, he told himself as he bounded down the stairs and through the lobby, the papers would be there tomorrow, none the worse for a good night's sleep, possibly the better for it, because an old, sleepy-eyed, grouchpuss set of documents wouldn't be disposed to divulge anything significant.

He chopped down on the doorman's neck with his stiffened left hand and commandeered a Lincoln Continental convertible, flattening the front gate, two Bulgroes and a Russgro on his juggernaut jaunt to the desert.

A million jewels hung suspended on the black velvet night. Somewhere the Norman Mailer Choir sang a Norman Luboff arrangement of "Stairway to the Stars" to the accompaniment of the Les McCann Trio. One thought plagued him. Would his hot Baronevkeh *shtetl* blood so recently cooled by his encounter with Countess Tracy be revived with a flash from the dark eyes of the mystery woman? Or would he prove a dismal failure and break her heart? *Gottenu*, he prayed, my kingdom for six dozen oysters laced with Gallo Wine!

He need not have worried, for as he parked the MBG under the palms he heard the tender *dee dee, da, da, da, da, dee dee* theme – this time a scat version by Joe Carroll; she had cleverly changed tapes for a new dramatic effect – and his body began tingling in all the right places, even in a few new ones he had never dreamed were zones of Eros, the tips of his Andalusian bedsocks and the loops of his Hickok belt.

The white camel poked its nose over the dune and the cool musical voice said, "Come, Mr. Bond. My desert is waiting." No second invitation was required. He crashed through the windscreen, paying no heed to the new cuts and bruises, and slid down its bonnet to the lukewarm sand. Now he was on Latakia, enclasping her waist, thrilling to her whispered: "Blue heaven and you and I."

"And sand kissing a moonlit sky," he breathed. "Miss Lawrence, will you convert to my faith, marry me and set me up in a corner news stand business?"

"Yes, yes, oh yes!"

He hurled her off Latakia into the dune. His sensual lips brushed her eyes and found to his delight her lids were spiced with Murine and ginger nut cookie dust. "Take off your veil, Miss Lawrence, and let me see the seventh heaven of seventh heavens."

The voice was pleading. "Nay, let us preserve the illusion of this first night between us, Mr. Bond, I pray you."

"I accede, my sweet. Does that restriction apply to your golden robe as well?"

She trembled. "It is yours to do with as you wish. Lift it."

"Miss Lawrence, not that it matters since I am a man of the world, but will I be the first?"

"Would that I had saved myself for you, dearest. Alas, no. There was one other, a ship that passed in the night just once. In America some years ago I went to a John Cage Music Festival in Poughkeepsie...."

Bond scowled. "The third coal scuttle player?"

"Yes. But how...."

"Button your lip, you f— loose-moraled wench! Let's make it!"

He heard his childish, spiteful words echoing in his fine, intelligent ears and was ashamed. "Forgive me, Sarah Lawrence. It doesn't matter. I love you."

His long, tapering fingers drew warmth from her thighs.

"One question, Israel Bond. I know you love me, but why do you want to climb upon my body?"

It came out of him with passionate conviction.

"Because... because it is there."

A modest moon blushed and slipped behind the dune, and, as his thighs conquered hers, she emitted a last heated word.

"Ra-a-aw——*ther!*"

24
Sermon On The Mount

He awoke with the first heat of day to find the note pinned to the belt of his sunslax.

"My dearest, dearest, adored one. How can I ever convey the gratitude of a girl who has been taken beyond the boundaries of all sensation that is a woman's to know? There is an old proverb. 'Every five hundred years the great *ookaloptishman* bird flies out of a secret passage in the tomb of Nofkeh-titi the Ninth and devours a single grain of the Arabian Desert's sand, then disappears back into the recesses of that sacred burial place. When that bird has eaten the desert's last grain of sand and is taken to the Great Academy of Medicine at Khartoum for a high colonic, then one second of eternity will have elapsed.' I shall love you for *all* of eternity, Israel Bond. Until that glorious day when we are made one under the traditional canopy of your faith... and I have already committed to memory the Aleph-Baze and three of the five books of Moses... I remain yours completely — Sarah Lawrence of Arabia."

On the way back to the palace an elated Israel Bond sang the joyous, innocent songs of his childhood, *I Took My Girl to the Enginehouse, She Was a Lulu, Country Boy, Country Boy, Sittin' on a Rock*, his heart pumping the electrifying news: She's mine! She's mine!

In fact, those were the first words he cried as he saw Neon Zion and Monroe Goshen sitting by the great pool, their heads down, their eyes those of beaten dogs.

"Congratulations." Goshen's comment was dry, insincere.

"Come on, Monroe. You can do better than that for an ol' buddy about to kick the bachelor habit. How about you, 113?"

Neon turned his face away from Bond and kicked a Great Northern Hotel auk to death.

"Iz," Goshen said with resignation. "While you were running off half-cocked and unauthorized after TUSH and your lady fair, the king was kidnapped."

Gottenu! Bond slapped his forehead. "How?"

"Bunch of guys in white burnooses, the Wheys, stormed in with guns and took him to a court of judgment at their camp. 'Pears someone told 'em he's a phony. They're going to try him, then behead him. I don't think even the Lawrence dame can get him out of this one."

Back in the MBG, Bond wallowed in self-loathing as Neon and Goshen continued their "Coventry." I've done it this time, he thought, fouled up the assignment, failed to get the goods on TUSH. Beame was right; I've had it with M 33 and 1/3. Win, lose or draw, this is the last caper, Oy Oy Seven.

Only James Brown, at the wheel, had a friendly word. "Man, that vitamin-enriched ball of yours saved my tail, Mr. Bond. I read the good word and made tracks fast—to get help. But when we came back in force, you were off the grounds. TUSH was very cooperative, very, but they'd never heard of you, of course. All traces of your visit had been cleaned up. And while we were there, the Wheys took LeFagel."

Brown had the MBG at an impossible 289.7 hectares, liquefying the road surface, until he pulled into the encampment of a thousand white tents. They got out, arms held high judiciously, covered by stone-faced sentries with RK-47s, Roskolnikovs built in Russia. "Take us to the king," Bond demanded. "There is no king," one spat, "just an impostor. Follow me, infidels."

More inflammatory TUSH agitprop, Bond figured. Thanks to Sarah, it didn't work on the Kurds, so now they've poisoned the Wheys.

In the center of a circle of thousands of men in white burnooses sat LeFagel, his hands fluttering. "Save me, Super-Semite, save me!" An aged warrior, obviously the muktar[*] of the tribe, called out scornfully. "What is the judgement of the Wheyan people?"

"Death! Death! Death!" The verdict rasped out of thousands of throats. *Gottenu!* Bond thought. If I had the Luden's cough drop franchise I'd leave this enclave a multimillionaire.

---

[*] Balaboss.

"The pretender will be given the opportunity to make a final statement," said the muktar.

LeFagel drew himself up, a new dignity in his bearing. Good-o! Bond thought. It may be the end but he's going out like a man. My tutelage has not been for naught.

"In my final moments I have composed a poem," said the king.

> "'Looking death in the face I find something more,
> 'Than the River Styx boatman who refuses to accept my Cunard Line credit card...
> 'Or grinning skulls welcoming me to the abyss as I inhale,
> 'The joint of no return,
> 'Or dancing devil dolls by unholy firelight,
> 'Prating of unspeakable terrors to come,
> 'No, I find something more meaningful than this,
> 'I find the beanbag I lost as a child,
> 'And finding a beanbag is death.'"

Even the muktar seemed impressed as he dragged the ax along the sand, the blade cutting a furrow to LeFagel, who knelt to receive it across the back of his neck.

Now it was lifted high, its frightening symmetry caught by the sun....

Dee dee, da, da, da, da, dee dee....

Crack! The ax flew out of the muktar's hands.

Sarah Lawrence of Arabia, astride Latakia, those black eyes at the sights of a Congoleum-Nairn-516 elephant gun, broke through the circle of white-burnoosed tribesmen to reach LeFagel's side.

"Before ye dare spill the truly royal blood of Hakmir's son, I would beg for a boon," she said. "I have brought a great, wise holy man with me, who has been touring our land with his spiritual cavalcade. True, he is not of your faith, but he speaks for all mankind with a transcendent message of universality. Listen as I translate his words, then decide if you are to murder your rightful ruler." She beckoned and a little wrinkled man in a Krass Brothers white linen suit, string tie and eleven-gallon Tex Ritter hat entered on an imposing Arabian steed.

By thunder! Bond thought. It's Oral Vincent Graham,* the tent evangelist, the man who stirred the world's heart just before the climactic showdown with Loxfinger in the Red Sea! But can even *his* words still the enmity in this tension-charged situation?

Oral Vincent Graham stood in the stirrups, his keen eyes gauging the hostile mood of the bloodthirsty crowd. He would have to choose his words well. A king's life hung in the balance.

"Whomsoever gainsayeth the measure of men? Yea, whomsoever gainsayeth? Dare ye of small measure gainsay what is not man's to gainsay?"

He paused to let his statement sink in; a wave of angry muttering assailed his ears. They were stirred up! Good!

"The days of the years are as threescore and ten; to the more fortunate, tenscore and three. Wherefore walketh he who gainsayeth not? To green valleys and lush fields, sayeth the sages, yet do not even the sages gainsay and not sayeth? *Sometimes?*

"Pride goeth before a fall, yea, and so doth summer. In the winter of our years we seek the summer, gainsaying it when we can, not gainsaying it when we cannot. Who among ye strays from righteous gainsaying, who dares to number among his summers threescore and ten of straying, gainsaying, measuring and scoring?"

Bond could hear Sarah Lawrence sobbing. He knew the tears were soaking into the veil; his own cheeks were wet.

"Lest ye who would be judged e'en to the measure of the days of your years, beware! Hist! Even to thy children's children and thy children's children's children. For the sins of the father delight the father. Hist! Lest ye hist in haste! If a man walketh not alone can it not be truly said that he is with someone? Whether in vales or fields?

"Oh, my friends, hist and harken. Let it not be said, I say unto you —LET IT NOT BE SAID!" He closed his eyes. "Amen."

Even as the skies echoed the last crescendo of his wrath (bouncing his words off both vales and fields), the muktar and his people were kneeling before LeFagel, smothering his hands with kisses. "Forgive us, O glorious planter of a thousand irrigated opium fields!" The king placed his hand upon the weeping muktar's head. "You are forgiven, muktar; now go

---

* Incorrectly identified as Oral Graham Vincent in *Loxfinger*. There were numerous errors involved with *Loxfinger*, the most glaring, some felt, the decision to publish it.

make peace with the Kurds and together we shall go on with the winning of the East."

Bond's first impulse was to rush to Sarah Lawrence of Arabia's side, but he saw her riding off into the sunset, her head bowed in thankful supplication. "See you at the dune, baby!" he shouted.

The ride back to Hakmir's palace was exuberant, LeFagel leading the chorus of applause for the little evangelist, who kept insisting he had not done anything to deserve it. "Speech wasn't even mine, Mr. Bond. I must 'fess up. I cribbed it verbatim from an obscure little volume called *Thoughts for Alternate Thursdays* by some chap I never even heard of. Name of Lavi HaLavi."

Goshen put his hand in Bond's. "Guess we all owe you an apology, Oy Oy Seven. Thanks to that quick-thinking filly of yours, King Baldroi is now accepted by all of his people, which scotches at least one half of the TUSH scheme. A united people will see to it their king isn't killed; ergo, TUSH fails, its stock goes down on the Espionage Exchange. Shame you haven't been able to expose the terrible plot against your people, though. Maybe it just isn't in the cards."

Bond shook the little CIA op chief's lapels. "Yes, yes! The cards! The cards!"

"You cracking, Iz?"

"No, Monroe. You said it isn't in the cards, but it *is*—literally. What will happen if I go back in there and take on TUSH at *la guerre*, smash their organization by bankrupting it? How can they pay off their agents and run their vast world-wide network if they're broke?"

Goshen looked into those grey eyes, once again hot with the lust for battle. "You may have something there, Iz. But, my God, man, do you realize the kind of stakes you'd need to play a showdown game with Sem-Heidt? Astronomical."

Bond flashed a hard grin. "Raise it, then, damnit! Your government blows billions trying to ferret out these villains. Let me have that stake, buddy boy, and I'll wreck 'em for all time!"

A slow smile began to steal across the dour, puritanical face. "Sounds crazy, but why not? I'll have to make a call to the Tall Texan, maybe have him cancel the loan to Thailand and send the money your way."

Bond smiled. Good-o! Monroe was on the ball again. By chance he spotted the villa and the smile stiffened, for the sun was flashing another message from the brazen upper windows: *You've been lucky, Oy Oy Seven, but come in here once more and....*

"Stop the car!" Bond cried. He pressed Button 502-A and the 155-mm. came out of the floorboard.

Goshen cringed as he watched Bond, his sensual top lip curled into a sneer, fire round after round at the windows. "You f— snotty glass, you panes in the ass... take that! That! And that!" In seconds the upper windows were blown out and Goshen could see the smoke rising from the roof.

"Got every damn one of them! And I'm coming back to get the rest of you, Shivs! Let the cards fall where they will and may the devil take the hindmost torpedo...."

25
All's Fair, In Love And "La Guerre"

"I'll need," said Bond, running his fingers over his head, "at least six more coats of Beacon Wax, 113. If you can scrounge up some shellac to mix in with it, fine." Neon left the royal suite to carry out Bond's bidding.

Bond sat in his Arcaro jockey shorts, the bible of the great game, *Scarne on La Guerre*, at his elbow, as he practiced a few exquisite maneuvers, the "Richelieu Riffle," the "Buffalo Shuffle" and the tricky "Crusader's Cut."

Goshen put aside the breezy, informative *National Enquirer*, whose front page featured EDDIE SEZ: IF LIZ WANTED ME BACK I'D GO BACK, BUT NOT UNLESS DICK COULD LEARN TO CARE FOR DEBBIE and MR. ED'S SECRET SHAME. He hurled a packet into Bond's lap. "There's your stake, Iz, eighty billion quasars, which represents the advance the Tall Texan got from his publisher for *The Great Society's Genyewine Coloring Book* and *Games Texas People Play*. As a precaution, I'm coming along with my CIA boys so TUSH won't get any ideas about highjacking the dough—if you win."

Back came Neon with the ingredients. As Bond slipped into his Cy Devore *la guerre* gambling outfit—Sammy Davis blue tuxedo, Levi Strauss' "After Nine" formal Levi's and his last pair of rare, 500-quasar Carpathian bedsocks fashioned from the pelts of werewolf puppies— the industrious 113 worked the mixture into Bond's scalp. "It's hard as a rock, Oy Oy Seven."

Bond sent a stream of Raleigh smoke against the artificial plant in the corner. It shriveled, edges curling, and died. "Let's go."

His pudgy hands caressing a pile of fuchsia billion-quasar notes, Heinz Sem-Heidt looked around the table. Ach, the fight was gone from this crowd; they had been no match for his Teutonic precision. In Position One was Baroness Yvette Mimeo, a principal stockholder in the A.B. Dick Company, her sundered skull on the table, claret flowing from a deep fissure. Two and Three were occupied by the Iranian frozen custard magnates, Nassim Zolzein-Shah and his wife, the man obviously dead, the woman a babbling wreck. Four, Five and Six were vacant. The Formosan beef and bean sprout consortium, playing erratically as all Orientals do, had been wiped out early. Two had died from the rigors of the game; the third had decently blown his brains out with the Paul Bines pistol provided by the management. Number Seven, Countess Di Terrazzo-Crotchetti, had lost three billion colodnys and begged off with a headache, promising, however, that an old friend would sit in for her. *Zehr goot!* A new goose to pluck!

Shuffling the six packs of cards that go into each boot, he did not notice the entrance of the lean, dark, cruelly handsome man flanked by a coterie of mean-looking individuals, until the menacing voice shook the 4,800 ounces of flab in his body.

"Position Seven this night will properly be occupied by Oy Oy Seven. Yo challengo banco."

The words hit the crowd like a thunderclap. The bank had been challenged! In ten seconds every gaming room in Shivs was deserted by patrons rushing to witness the drama of a lifetime.

Heinz Sem-Heidt looked into the grey eyes of Israel Bond. The quasar notes fell from his hands.

"Strict rules of Scarne, kraut; triple bidding and the Foch boots. Agreed?"

"Ja." Buckets of sweat rolled down the jellyish jowls. "Herr Zentner," he said to the croupier. "The Foch boots, *bitte*."

Bond lit a Raleigh and watched Zentner place the original combat boots worn by Marshal Foch in the Great War upon the baize cloth and put six packs of cards (examined first by Goshen) into each toe. Two other Germans, Krug and Von Kreel, lugged in the caldron of steaming Cream of Wheat, another vital part of the time-honored ritual.

Zentner placed a bowl of Cream of Wheat in each contestant's left hand, a Foch boot in the right. The crowd ceased its hubbub. "*Monsieurs. C'est—*"

"*La guerre!*" Bond and his porcine foe screamed it simultaneously, hurling the Cream of Wheat into each other's faces and bludgeoning each other's heads with the Foch boots, which, as they made contact, opened at the toes to permit a pink card to fall onto the baize.

Shaking his head to clear the fuzziness, Bond spoke. "Mine has—let me see—one, two, three, four, five, six black things. Yours has; oh, hell, *you* count 'em, Nazi."

"I see three, possibly four."

"Page eighteen of *Scarne on Counting* states clearly: 'Six beats three, possibly four.' You sure it isn't three *and* four, which would give you an American Totalisator Company aggregate of seven?"

"Nein."

"I said *seven*, not nine, you f—ing kraut! Cheating already?"

When Zentner pointed out Sem-Heidt had meant no, Bond gave a cruel laugh. "OK, fat boy. Shove over two hundred forty billion quasars. Now I'm tripling the triple bid."

"C'est—"

"*La guerre!*"

Cereal and boots flew unerringly to their targets. Gottenu! Bond thought. Beacon Wax might not yellow my head, but can it take sustained punishment? I feel it starting to crack.

His finger ticked off the red hearts on the left side of the card—four. Were there more? Yes! Two in the center, which gave him a total of six. Now, if only the right side of the card—hallelujah! One, two, three, four more! Without question, he was holding a ten. No, *eleven*— another red heart had appeared! Uh-uh, buddy boy, there are no elevens. The latecomer is a drop of your type-A blood! "Switchez les boots, Sem-Heidt. Privilege of the challenger. And what's your card?"

"I count four diamonds on my card. Are there more, Herr Zentner? Nein? I have lost again."

As the men exchanged boots, Bond said in a furry voice: "That's two thousand one hundred sixty scullions, uh, billiards—"

"Billions," Goshen corrected him. "Iz, you're way ahead, but you're starting to go round the bend. Quit now before he pounds you into sawdust."

"No, no," Bond argued, his hand to his scalp. "Got to go on till he's busted. His boot was heavier, Monroe. That's why I called a switchez." To Sem-Heidt: "Another triple triple, Nazi."

Cereal flew and boots crashed, Bond trumping Sem-Heidt four more times and soon the Nazi's face was blocked from

Bond's view by the latter's mound of 15,553 trillion quasars. "Want to dip into your colodnys now, Heinz?"

"*Ja, der colodnys, judischer Schweinhund.*" Despite his staggering deficit, there was supreme confidence on the swollen face. Heinz Sem-Heidt made an undetected move with his right foot, kicking the wastebasket under the table.

With the change of currency, the German's luck changed—and he came up with seven trumps in a row, all on aces of spades, whittling Bond's pile to less than half of his original stake.

Bond's bleary eyes caught the smug satisfaction on the Nazi's inner-tube lips. Rivulets of claret rolled from his lacerated head onto the baize. Gottenu! Damn near busted—what a rotten run of luck; beaten by seven straight aces of spades.

Hold on! Seven? In a combat boot with *six* decks of cards that should have *six* aces of spades? Buddy boy, the Hun is shafting you! And I wouldn't be surprised if Holzknicht gave him some illegal head coating—metal maybe.

Bond squandered 20 billion quasars on the next hand to see how it was being done, incurring a terrible jolt that sent the last fragments of Beacon Wax sliding off his skull onto his claret-spattered Sammy Davis tux. His own boot missed badly, but on his follow-through his bloodshot eye saw the hand snake out of the wastebasket and deposit another ace of spades in Sem-Heidt's hand, good enough to beat his nine of clubs, he knew from past experience.

"I—I feel sick," Bond said and fell over the table, deliberately ramming his torn shoulder into the caldron of hot, bubbling Cream of Wheat.

"Clumsy schwein!" snarled Sem-Heidt, ducking the steaming white avalanche, then recoiling in horror as he saw it flow over the edge of the table into the basket. Soon the basket was overflowing with cereal and there was a horrible stench of something burning, a futile thrashing inside. Stillness.

A swaying Bond, steadied by Goshen and Neon, pointed a finger at the basket. "Dump it out on the table."

Gasps flew throughout the *La Guerre* Room as the basket was turned over and the cooked cereal-saturated body of Locksley, the dwarf, fell onto the baize with a spongy thump, the puckered baked apple of a face in the horrifying rictus of death.

And with the dwarf and the cascading Cream of Wheat was something else—dozens of sodden aces of spades. Israel Bond spread them out and issued a clarion cry:

"Yo declaro coup de cheato; ergo, yo conquero banco!"

"Cheat! Cheat! Cheat!" The shouts barraged Heinz Sem-Heidt's ears. "Coup de cheato!"

"Which means, Nazi, according to the rules of Scarne, the whole kit and caboodle is mine—quasars, colodnys, the five-pack of Muriel Cigars in your lapel pocket, plus any decent phone numbers in your little black book. You're out of business. I've just kicked your organization on its TUSH. Take 'em all, Monroe."

The blob began to weep as the CIA team fanned out and covered the seven other German directors. "She will kill me! If you don't protect me, she will kill me!"

Goshen ordered his men to clear the room. He gave it straight to the teary Sem-Heidt. "We'll give you the fullest protection, Nazi, if you spill the beans about TUSH's plot against the king and Judaism. Otherwise, you're free to walk out right now. 'Course, Auntie might—"

"Nein! Nein!" The piggish eyes rolled in anguish. "I hate her! I have always hated her! I only married her because of her superior family background. Ja, I talk."

"I'm going upstairs, Monroe," Bond said. "Neon, Jimbo, come with me."

In their absence the CIA team's Bell & Howell sound camera was grinding, recording for posterity fifty thousand feet of lachrymose confession. In a few hours excerpts of it would be spotlighting the newscasts of Cronkite, Huntley-Brinkley and Jennings and, via Telstar, the rest of humanity. And thanks to Seymour Feig, Bond's press agent buddy who had negotiated a fast deal, it might also end up as a one-hour spectacular sponsored by Xerox, "TUSH, The Heil-Heilabaloo World of Neo-Nazism," with possible narration by Sue Lyons and Doodles Weaver.

A helluva night's work. Goshen smiled. The cabal exposed, Sahd Sakistan secured for democracy, thanks again to the greatest espionage weapon of all time, Israel Bond.

His joy was not shared by the dark, cruelly handsome "weapon" on the roof nor by 113 and James Brown, who watched the baleful yellow eyes glaring back as the helicopter climbed over the wall. Auntie Sem-Heidt and Dr. Ernst Holzknicht had escaped.

26
The Tale Of The Little Princess

When the eye-opening call came from M., Bond was on the moon-bathed dune with Sarah Lawrence of Arabia, his head in her golden lap, his mouth open to receive the Joyvah jells and Philly Greenwald Concord grapes dropping from her fingers. Their second physical fusion had been matchless ecstasy-squared, though she had again refused to lower her veil. "Not until our wedding night, dearest. And I hope you will be pleased to learn that I have memorized all of Hillel's commentaries, the writings of Peretz, Sholom Aleichem and the Singers, and six of Alan King's best routines. I shall soon be well acquainted with the rich diversity of Jewishness."

The beeper in the parked MBG sounded a Mem alarm and the voice of his Number One in Jerusalem unfolded the shocking contents of a cardiogram—a telegram that comes from the heart—sent to her c/o the Ministry of Defense.

Dear M., my beloved enemy; soon to be, I pray, my devoted friend:
I wish to surrender myself to you personally and confess all my sins. It is all too clear that God is on your side, M. How else to explain the crushing of our TUSH by the heaven-strengthened hand of Israel Bond? I suppose I should have remained at Shivs to take my medicine, but Dr. Holzknicht, who witnessed my husband's debacle at the la guerre table via closed-circuit television, convinced me to flee with him. Since then we have parted company. I am hiding out in the Cissbah in Sahd Sakistan. Where Ernst has gone I truthfully cannot say, but I know he is planning an even ghastlier operation against the fine Jewish people, 'Operation End-All,' details of which I will be happy to furnish you as proof of my sincere contrition.

We are two old women, M., who should be playing mah-jongg together and fondling fat cherubic grandchildren instead of locking wigs in mortal combat. Let us forget the unpleasantness of the past and unite in genuine sorority. Enclosed is a map showing a suggested rendezvous point three nights hence. Please bring only one other person with you, as I shall be accompanied by my last servant, a harmless Monagro.

Hoping you'll find it in your heart to come and accept my apologies for any inconveniences I may have caused you and your People of the Book, I remain,
Gerda Sem-Heidt

When Bond arrived at the airport, Op Chief Beame, his face mirroring his distrust, was wheeling the smiling M. down the special ramp built by the El Al technicians. There's something messianic in those warm eyes, Bond noted, and it's driven away her common sense. He could hold it in no longer. "M., it's a trap!"

"Damn right," Beame said, chewing on another White Owl, this one a cigar. "I've begged her, Oy Oy Seven, but she won't listen."

M. patted their heads with her careworn hands. "Mine dear boys, always worrying about a mother. It does my heart good to see your filial agony. It's what I live for. No, *boychiklach*, I must go to this fallen wretch and redeem her. And from a security standpoint, which I'm sure you think I have overlooked in my zeal, it behooves us to familiarize ourselves with any new Holzknichtian deviltry before he has an opportunity to execute it. If it is a trap, we must take that chance. You will accompany me, Oy Oy Seven. Whatever happens, you must swear not to interfere."

He did, the vibrations from his cracking knuckles splintering the crystal of his Kissling.

Bond polished off three cartons of Raleighs during the ride to the Cissbah, placing coupon after coupon in M's hands. He could see her sweet, serene face in the mirror, an unspoken prayer on the lips. The sun was sinking and from the minaret came the final call of the muezzin: "Hey, you—yes, *you*, you snotty young Allah-Is-Dead crowd over there—move aside and make room for pray-ers, make room for pray-ers!"

Number 10 on the Street of the Jaundiced Jackals was a one-story warehouse-type edifice with YUSEF LATEEF'S SCHOOL OF MODERN FLUTE in faded letters on the door. He unlashed the wheelchair from the MBG's roof, placed M. on the seat and kicked the door open, wheeling her into blackness. Somehow he found a wall switch and flicked it, a single naked bulb casting a weak light in the empty, soundless room. On the floor he saw a large roach and he smoked it up in three mighty inhalations to allay his nervousness.

A door on the opposite side of the building creaked open and there was a squeak of wheels across the earthen floor. Now he could see two mad-dog yellow circles coming out of the blackness and a chalk-white face radiant with triumph, which told his palpitating heart that Auntie Sem-Heidt was in no penitent mood, a fear confirmed by the presence of the swarthy, grinning Monagro (a rare half-breed indeed, who came from Monaco), who pointed an updated version of the premier Russian combat rifle the Kalashnikov, known as the AK-47 ... this one, the RK-47, or Razskolnikov, which was powerful enough to blow holes in holes! It was a hideous weapon designed for one purpose – if there was a crime it was the punishment!

"So, filthy Judischer mongrels; you have come."

There was distress in M.'s face. "Those are hardly the words of a woman seeking her way back to mankind, Gerda."

"Ha-ha! You doddering fool! Did you nourish the hope that I, Gerda Sem-Heidt, would grovel before Jews? Die, Mother Margolies, die!"

"M!" Bond heard his warning shout melt the fine-grained wax in his ears as he swung her wheelchair out of Auntie's line of fire, but he was a shade too slow. Auntie's right claw touched a button on the battery in her lap. Something streaked from the right armrest of her wheelchair, a steel projectile which nosed into M.'s right shoulder. Now a pain was searing his own right shoulder; he looked dumbly at the Monagro's knife, fell to his knees. He could see the roseate glow leaving M.'s face and hear the grinding of her false teeth. Hold! Hold! he pleaded with the Poli-Grip in her dentures. Hold and preserve her dignity in her last moments!

Auntie's claws smacked together in fierce joy. "Just the first round, my Chosen People. Chosen, yes, for death. Ha-ha!" She nudged the Monagro. "A droll joke, eh, Cagliostro? Chosen for death. Hee-hee!"

Gevaldt! thought Bond; Auntie's "hee-hee!" is even more bloodcurdling than her "ha-ha!"—not that there's much blood left in me to curdle. Up, up, he expostulated to his body, up! He braced himself against M.'s wheelchair and felt the knife fall out of his shoulder, a torrent of claret hot upon its hilt. He saw M. swallow hard and press her Korvette's gauzeroy handkerchief, the one he'd given her for her eighty-fourth birthday (alas, she looked years older now) against her spouting wound.

"Gerda, I should like your permission to tell you a few things that are in my heart." M.'s request was almost inaudible.

"Ha-ha! Behold the things in *my* heart instead! Behold!" The claws tore away the housedress. Bond squeezed his eyes tight. I'm craven, craven, he told himself, but I can't stand to see it again. He could not see (a fitting penalty for his cowardice) that M. did not flinch at the mechanical wonder on Auntie's body.

"It is a fine heart," M. said. "I know it must give you a great deal of pleasure, Gerda. Now, may I tell you of the things in mine?"

"Talk, creator of vile, reeking chicken soup. It will amuse me to hear the blatting of a trapped Jew. Do not think for a moment that I shall soften my heart—" she sniggered at her inside joke—"as Pharaoh finally did for Moses." Auntie turned to the Monagro. "I can see you are impatient, my pet. Hold off yet a moment before I bestow upon you the pleasure of cutting the great Oy Oy Seven's throat."

"Thank you, Gerda. I should like to give you the synopsis of a Shirley Temple movie I had the pleasure of watching."

M. started in a shaky fashion, painting a word picture of a dear curlyhead of a moppet in a frilly frock and blue hair ribbon whose Mums had passed away, her adoring, dashing Daddy, a soldier of Good Queen Victoria, and the love they held for one another. M.'s voice seemed to regain its resonance as she described long walks through the drowsy green beauty of an English summer day, the father's eyes softening with tenderness at the sight of his "little princess" gamboling across the meadow, picking a nosegay here, petting a fluffy rabbit there, skipping across the flat stones of a clear, burbling stream. Bond, his eyes still fastened, could see it all... the glances of affection between father and moppet, the thistles rustling in a gentle breeze.

Then M.'s voice drooped. The trumpets of war had sounded to shatter the idyllic life. Daddy was called to fight with his regiment in a strange, hostile land. With no kith or kin, he was forced to leave his golden-tressed angel in the care of a boarding school headmistress who assured him the child would find it warm and friendly.

Long, lonely days for a shy little girl, unable to fit in with the haughty daughters of noblemen, lightened infrequently by letters from Daddy, which she would read a thousand times to her lone friend at the school, Singh Dennis-Singh, the Hindu who served as the dishwasher and polo coach. Then the dark day when the telegram arrived: "Your father, Sergeant Major K., of the Fifth Scottish Black Watch Grenadiers, has been taken prisoner by the cruel mountain tribes and is presumed to have been tortured to death."

"Stop! Stop! You filthy Jewish bitch!" The iron voice cut in like the Monagro's knife.

Bond, not knowing why M. had chosen this soulful narrative, awaited the worst, but suddenly he heard the Monagro's voice, heavy with emotion, intrude: "Let her continue, Gerda. Please let her continue."

M., pale and uncertain, her hand still pressed against the wound, went on.

Realizing the child was penniless, the headmistress forced her to vacate her cheerful room and take up residence in the garret, where she shared a closet with a dozen noisy shrews. "You will work in the scullery, *little princess*," the headmistress smirked, and so the golden girl toiled over pots and pans twenty hours a day, her little hands turning scabrous. In restive dreams she would see Daddy smiling. "The bloody beggars have been a bit hard on me, little princess. I've got only an eye and a leg left, but, never fear, I'll get home someday." He would, too, he would, she told Dennis-Singh who had climbed up with her gruel, "and it'll be like it was before, you'll see."

Bond heard the Monagro's deep, convulsive sobs and, without looking, knew the man's face was covered by his hands. "Goodbye, Gerda. I'm going to see a priest." The Monagro's feet pounded on the earthen floor and Bond heard the door slam.

"Come back, you half-breed cretin!" It was the iron voice. "I warned you, you Judischer scum! Now-—"

A second rocket was ejected from the wheelchair and Bond winced, expecting to hear M.'s death wail, but he heard its harmless thud into the wall and her strangely composed voice resume the tale.

On a depressing night when the golden girl lay tossing with fever, the sad-eyed Hindu at her bedside, the headmistress threatening a caning for feigning illness, there came a knock on the garret door.

"Yes, yes, yes?" The voice of Auntie Sem-Heidt, wheezing and breathy, iron no more.

"Through that garret door," said M., her own voice quivering, "came an eye and a leg wrapped in the scarlet coat of a Grena—"

"Daddy! Daddy! Daddy! It's her Daddy.... Oh, oh, oh!" It was Auntie, screeching and sobbing. "Daddy! Daddy! Da—"

A protracted hiss, the pungent smell of something burning, a ghastly strangling cough—

He could bear his self-imposed blindness no longer. His eyes went first to M., a satisfied smile on her dry lips, then to the sprawled-out scarecrow across the room. A greenish, rigid tongue had forced the blue-vein lips apart; though the yellow eyes were open, they saw not. He shuddered at the Dali-esque nightmare of the squidlike thing, its molten tentacles slowly spreading from its white-hot center. Auntie Sem-Heidt was dead. Her heart had melted.

27
Ain't That A Kick In The Glass!

"Damn it," Bond fumed. "These long tapering fingers have time and time again kept the world safe for democracy. Now they can't even push a rose into the slit of a lapel."

"First of all, Mr. Nervous *Chulairyeh*[*]," laughed Neon Zion, "it goes in by the stem, not the blossom. Secondly, you're *tzittering* like a child; let me do it."

Israel Bond *was* nervous. He was in the Empire State Building suite of Muhammud Alan-Shurmahn, Sahd Sakistan's ambassador to the U.S., and this sunny day in June was his wedding day. Minutes ago he had been on the 86th floor's open-air terrace to witness the splendiferous coronation of Baldroi LeFagel, who months back had insisted Bond share his memorable day by marrying Sarah Lawrence of Arabia immediately afterward. Hell, Bond mused, this thing is hairier than that windup with Auntie in the warehouse.

Op Chief Beame's Aleph-Priority response to his frantic beeper had saved M. and himself. He'd rushed them to the Jewish court physician, Dr. Chayim Khayam, who'd administered plasma, Mother's Activated Old World Germicidal P'chah and four vital Excedrins, plus, of course, cherry salve. Sarah paid daily visits to the recuperating pair with armloads of calf's brains lotkes and read verse to them from Bond's favorite, "Best of *My Weekly Reader*."

M., curt at first, had finally fallen under Sarah's spell. "You're a good *shikseh;* if you'll convert I'll come to the wedding." The veiled beauty kissed the fragile hand. "Smashing, M., old girl! I shall, indeed. Since I last saw Mr. Bond, I have memorized *Jews, God and History*, the songs of Shoshana Damari and Theodore Bikel, the speeches of—"

---

[*] Mr. Nervous Curse/Cholera

"Cool it, baby. M. says you're in," Bond had riposted.

With the joint news release by the Tall Texan and Ambassador Callowfellow that America was going to host the coronation of its native son turned king, the country had gone gaga. LeFagel Bagels, shaped like a crown, began popping up in every Jewish-owned establishment (they'd all been rebuilt by the Tall Texan's crash program, Operation Help-A-Hebe). Imperial Margarine had donated the royal crown (beating a disgruntled soda company to the punch) for the fete. A particularly clever tobacco firm inserted a full-page ad in *The New York Times*: "Roi-Tan Loves You, King Baldroi, 'Cause You're the Roi and You're Tan." LeFagel's *"We Should Think About Spoons"* vaulted to No. 1 on the best-seller list; he benefitted further from a commercial tie-in with 1847 Rogers Brothers Silver, which gave the book free with every 42-piece set of spoons. (People did not seem to want anything but spoons; it was considered passé to eat steak with a fork these spoon-fad days.)

LeFagel's party arrived to a tumultuous New York welcome; a lavender line was painted down Fifth Avenue by his adoring claque from the old "angry poet" days. He seemed distant in their presence, however; one spying him in bulky Julius Boros plus-fours cried: "Sellout!"

There had been a final soul-searching dialogue with LeFagel an hour before the coronation.

"Sixty minutes from now, Oy Oy Seven, I shall be king, but I'd give it all up—power, fame, money—if you'd consent to go away with me. What say you, captor of my heart?"

Bond put his arm around the little king. "You've made tremendous strides, Baldroi. When first we met, you were a screaming faggot. Step by step I've seen a miracle unfolding. Now, I don't know too much about these things, but I'd guess you have roughly 7.9 percent homo left in you, a bit higher than the permissible 6 percent in most men, but certainly manageable with a little effort. Fight it hard all the way. Your people need a man at the helm. For their sake, think manly, talk manly, do manly things."

LeFagel left him with a grim smile and Neon rushed back to Bond ten minutes later with a bulletin: LeFagel had assaulted a shapely female researcher from *Sh-h-h* Magazine.

Good-o! Bond thought. My work is done. He's a real man!

A richly humorous incident had stamped the Tall Texan's warm, human brand on the formalized proceedings. He and the king had posed for the TV cameras performing a hallowed Sakistani rite, the salting of each other's *shasheeshah* (tails of spring lambs ground up with halavah) as a sign of mutual respect between world titans. Bond had whispered something to the Tall Texan, who whispered back, "Right fine, son. I'll say it," then lifted the saltcellar and cracked up the crowd with a sly, "Come, your Majesty; let us *season* together." Bond had refused the Tall Texan's offer of a high-level speechwriter's job, but exacted a promise that the latter would give Monroe Goshen a salary hike far above the Administration's 3.3-percent guideline, which everybody was ignoring anyway.

Borne to the throne by two Kurds and two Wheys in an Abercrombie & Fitch four-door sedan chair, LeFagel, dressed in blinding white Labrador snow-goose feathers and tennis sneakers, took the crown from Ben-Bella Barka's hands and, crying out three times "Y'llella abdabeel" (Sakistani for "I am crying out three times"), placed it on his head. He then left for dinner with the Tall Texan. "Put Mr. Bond's wedding on the bill, too, huh, Prez?" LeFagel had said. Now the hundreds of dignitaries and security people were gone; only a handful were left for the nuptials. M., knitting madly, put the finishing touches to Bond's wedding yarmulke. Milton and Rag and their wives sat next to her.

And alone in the back row was Liana, lovely and brave. She'd made a pretext of fixing his zipper to talk to him. "Iz, I know she's a lovely girl, but if it doesn't work out, I'll be waiting."

"How long? Don't make commitments of fidelity you can't keep, like last time," he said a little too harshly.

"Forever."

He seemed appeased. He stood at the mesh railing looking at the breathtaking panorama of the world's most exciting depressed area 1050 feet below, waiting for his bride.

Rabbi Zalman Bindlebinder, head of the somewhat Reform congregation Temple B'nai Venuta, who had been recommended to M. by friends, was shamefully late, profusely apologetic. "Coronation traffic, you know, Mr. Bond." He waved in two workmen who wheeled the portable wedding canopy (*huppah*) onto the terrace. It was quite tall, about nine feet, and was constructed of aluminum and bedecked with thousands of posies. He had them position it at the spot where the red carpet abutted a wall. Then he put his finger to his lips and the small assemblage hushed.

Goshen, Neon, Op Chief Beame and James Brown, acting as ushers, helped the unsteady groom down the carpet as the accordion player squeezed out "Because of You," halted it after a few bars, fooled around with "Because You're Mine," stopped again, consulted a sheaf of music and then went into "Because," the onlookers aah-ing with relief. "Turn around, Iz," said Goshen. "You've got company."

She came, Latakia's soft padded feet leaving four-inch indentations in the rug. From the first notes of her theme song he knew she had made an irreparable break with her past for his sake. The notes were the same, but now the tape rolled out a special new version by a cantor: *dai dai, bime, bime, bime, bime, dai dai....*

From that moment on, his grey eyes hypnotized by her bottomless black pools peeping over the veil, he was in a dream, somehow managing to repeat woodenly what was asked of him by Rabbi Bindlebinder. A voice in the dream said, "Ring? Mr. Bond? Ring! Ring! Ring!"

He heard himself say: "Somebody answer the phone." Goshen chuckled, took the nearly tenth-of-a-carat garnet ring from his pocket and placed it in Bond's feeble fingers.

"Now," said Rabbi Bindlebinder, "the ceremonial breaking of the glass to remind us of the destruction of our temple in ancient times and the bitterness of life we must endure." Bond's eyes struggled to focus on the rabbi's hand as it placed the glass near his feet. "Break the glass, Mr. Bond," said the amused spiritual leader. Bond drove his Angora bedsock down hard and sent Goshen hopping off with a crushed big toe. "Again, Mr. Bond." Loathing himself for the simpering grin he knew marred his cruel, darkly handsome face, Bond stepped down again, missing by a wide margin.

"Iz, you dotty, frightened boy! I'm not going to be unlawfully yours a single moment more. This is a job for *Mrs.* Israel Bond." With a sparkling laugh Sarah Lawrence of Arabia Bond jumped off Latakia and lifted her well-turned leg. "No! No!" It was the Rabbi, inexplicably enraged. Down came the foot and her soft-soled ballerina splintered it resoundingly. "There, that's done. Hold me, my lovely, lovely husband. Oh, I'm going to—"

She crumpled to the red carpet. Now the smog of fear was burned off his mind; he sprang to her side and cradled her head in his arms. The uncovered part of her face was blue.

"Dear, dear. The excitement, I suppose." It was Rabbi Bindlebinder calming the shocked wedding guests. "See to her, dear people. I'll roll the *huppah* away to give the poor child some breathing room." He put his shoulders against a side and guided it toward the terrace's railing.

"Sarah, my love." His eyes hot and salty, Bond pulled away her veil to administer mouth-to-mouth resuscitation, then froze.

Sarah Lawrence of Arabia's upper lip was adorned with a thick, black, neatly trimmed military moustache. She mumbled in a dying voice, "Curse of all female cousins, twenty-fourth to forty-eighth, related to Lawrence by marriage... 'the Lawrence Lip'... imbalance of hormones... must shave daily... didn't want you know 'til married... so sleepy... so...."

The smell from the shards of glass! Yes, *gorgogga*, the pancreatic juice of the *varapapa* frog of the Honduran swamps; no deadlier venom had ever existed.

She was gone. He knew who was responsible.

"Holzknicht, you kraut fiend!"

From the *huppah*, which had suddenly acquired a seat that held Rabbi Bindlebinder, came a flash, and hot metal creased his scalp. "Die, Bond! This is Nazi Germany's revenge!"

"Iz!" Goshen yelled at the top of his lungs. "Take my gun. *You* finish the sadistic bastard." As Goshen slung the snub-nosed Tiniff .44 across the floor to the flattened-out Israeli, Dr. Ernst Holzknicht, who had so brilliantly played his part, cut the CIA op chief down with three slugs.

Then from the top of the canopy emerged rotor blades, whirring, lifting it slowly. The traditional canopy of a Jewish marriage was a garlanded helicopter!

Throwing all caution aside, Bond made it to the rising chopper in six unbelievable leaps and squeezed the fingers of his left hand around the circular steel frame to which the three wheels were attached, shoved the gun into the pocket of his Sunkist orange tuxedo and grabbed another six inches of the bar with his right. Doktor Holzknicht, three feet above him, thrashed out with his Heidelberg bedsocks in an attempt to smash Bond's fingers, scoring a glancing hit on the right hand, but he was forced to pay attention to the controls, for now the chopper was high over the terrace, fighting for altitude against the pull of Bond's weight. The Israeli felt the wind, so deceptively gentle on the terrace, become a dangerous Hydra-headed force, buffeting him this way and that, and he squeezed harder. Up went the chopper—the 94th floor, the 99th; he looked down and saw death beckoning from the street some 1200 feet away....

It was over the very tip of the Empire State Building's TV tower that the Nazi exploded his next trick. He pushed a button that jettisoned the circular frame. Now Bond was falling from the underpinnings of the craft, Holzknicht soaring away with a savage laugh.

"Auf Wiedersehen, jüdischer dumbkof!"

Gottenu! Bond fell toward the tower, then with a divine inspiration, thrust the steel ring over the slender TV tower tip and came to a teeth-rattling stop.

Ringer!

He had made himself a living quoit.

The impact bent the tower, which began to rock sickeningly back and forth, but he held fast. Close your eyes, fool! Don't look down until you've regained your equilibrium or you'll surrender to a mad urge to let go. Think about something else. He thought about the terrible reception the area's millions of TV viewers were getting this very instant because of the swaying tower. Bet the Mets *really* look shaky now, his sardonic wit told him.

There was a clatter above—Holzknicht, stunned by Bond's coup, circled back for the kill. Bond released his right-hand grip on the steel ring to fish Goshen's gun from the tux. He bit a sensual lip as the chopper zeroed in. Why doesn't Herr Doktor open up with his machine gun? I'm defenseless against it. The pht-pht-pht of the blades gave him the grim answer. A last bit of Aryan sport. Holzknicht wanted to maneuver the craft in such a way that the blades would....

Now! You'll have only one chance, buddy boy. Bond, his clothes flapping in the blade-made breeze, put a single shot into the copter. He hadn't aimed for Holzknicht; it was the machine he had to stop before it shredded him into Cohenfetti. Not a bad line, he smiled, considering where I am.

He heard the first sputter, then a violent choking sound, and knew he had hit the control box and severed vital wires.

The doctor was frantically climbing out of the chopper; smoke began to curl ominously. Then Holzknicht leaped onto the tower, but he failed to grab it solidly and began a long slide toward Bond. "Die with me, Jüde!" His feet came down ponderously on the hand in the ring and Bond screamed; his bloody squashed fingers released it. They were falling together.

Even as he fell, Holzknicht's hands moved to throttle Bond and the latter felt nails tearing at his neck, then slipping off as a crosscurrent swept the falling Nazi away from him.

The air rushed through Bond's nose and ears; he could hardly catch his breath. He fell headfirst past the 86th floor and heard M.'s heartrending cry, down, down, past the 75th, where his face was spotted by a curvaceous brunette secretary in a window, BLOCH & TACHLE, MARINE LAWYERS, whose eyes lit up in recognition. Yes, Hillary Katzenellenbogen, she of the unforgettable weekend at Brown's Hotel in the Catskills, the body beautiful who had won the "Miss Jerry Lewis' Favorite Resort" swimsuit title; be true to me, sweet Hillary; goodbye... past the 46th, KELSEY KOMPUTERS... hell, he owned a hundred shares of that! And it's going up, up... and *you're* going down, down, his wit needled him again; the 32nd... just a few more seconds, Oy Oy Seven, and that lithe, muscular body you prize so will be a stinking mess of smashed atoms on the 34th Street sidewalk... the 25th... at least the f—ing kraut goes with me; I hope you're in heaven watching him blubbering as he falls, Sarah, my darling; the 19th... hey, TANTAMOUNT PICTURES is holding a screening of *The Wind that was Gone is Back*...; not bad; I saw it at the Cannes Film Festival... the leading lady was better in my bed than she was in the leading man's... Valvolene, my darling... I'll miss you... the 12th, 9th, 5th... zooming by the 4th floor and the huge sign LEVINE 'N ROSE, LEGAL EAGLES, he heard a recorded voice of a chaneuse with an eerie resemblance to Piaf's crooning in her emotional style:

> *If you're heading for divorce,*
> *Cherie, here's your recourse,*
> *Just call Levine 'N Rose...*
> *F. Lee Bailey (Monsieur Class)*
> *Says they can save your ass,*
> *So call Levine 'N...*

"...Adieu, little sparrow," he whispered wistfully. I never did get to hear the last Rose. Last Rose of Summer? Picardy? My Wild Irish? Abie's Irish? Second Hand?

And adieu to you too, Oy Oy Seven. Here comes the cement that'll squash you into Kasha... 3, 2, 1... pain, pain, pain. Israel Bond crashed into something huge and black and his swan dive to glory was over.

Epilogue

Trivia Festival Week, that annual excursion into the nostalgia of yesteryear, was in full swing. At the Hotel Statler the Orphan Annie Fan Club crowded into a suite to sing:

> "Who's that sloppy little mess?
> "Who wears that same ol' goddam dress?
> "Who can it be?
> "It's Little Orphan Annie!"

    The oldest member, a Miss Hecate Sensenbaugh of Omaha, was given the coveted privilege of barking "Arf! Sez Sandy" at the appropriate moment in the song, not so much in deference to her golden years as for the fact that she possessed a pair of lidless, lashless, pupilless eyes. The new Lincoln Center for the Performing Seals housed a tremendous Trivia contest attended by 12,000 Triviaddicts, the very best of all an Elmo (Mr. Total Recall) Trickypepper of Shortweight, Oklahoma, who remembered that it was Tastee-Yeast who sponsored Jack Dempsey's *My Battle With Life* on the radio. At the Americana the Tisch clan hosted the Bobby Benson bunch; the Donald Meek fans, every bit as fastidious as their hero, ate watercress sandwiches on paper plates and tittered at each other at the Warwick; the Johnson Family[*] and Amos 'N' Andy Fan Clubs, gathered at Marsal's at the Brevoort, made two historic decisions: (1) to merge; (2) to accept Negro members.

    Utter solemnity, and quite fitting too, marked the Robert Armstrong Fan Club outdoor conclave on 34th Street. The president, made up and costumed to emulate the rugged film star, took off his pith helmet and led the members in the somber recital of the immortal old line: "It wasn't the airplanes that got

---

    [*] Not the stars of the Kenny Solms—Gail Parent *Great Society* LP, but a "radio family," all played by one very clever impressionist. If you recall his name, you rank up there with Elmo Trickypepper. —S.W.

him; oh, no. 'Twas Beauty who killed the Beast." They whispered "Amen" and boarded the bus in silence.

So it was that a few minutes later the sorrowing M. led Latakia and the other crushed, tearful wedding guests out of a side entrance, not knowing that Oy Oy Seven had landed upon the fifty-ton Andy Warhol-designed, foam-rubber replica of King Kong, who himself had taken the terrifying plunge off the world's tallest structure in the 1933 film classic.

Israel Bond, waist-deep in rubber and matted fur, was bloody and battered—understandably—but very much alive. There was no elation in his heart, for he had seen the warped genius who had taken his own true love's life bounce off the simian's skull into the back of a beer truck making its way toward—God only knew. His lips twisted into a moue of irony as the grey eyes saw the brand name on the truck— Lowenbrau. And they say *we're* clannish, he thought bitterly.

There'll be a day of judgment, *mein lieber Doktor Ernst Holzknicht*. We'll cross trails again.* Maybe on an Alpine mountaintop, on a burning desert, in some impenetrable rain forest (to be truthful, I hope it isn't a rain forest. My rain-forest attire is the tackiest part of my whole wardrobe), on a frozen tundra or across a crowded room. And once I have found you, I'll never let you go.

FIN

---

* In the last Israel Bond thriller, *You Should Only Live and Not Die— Altogether,* from the Papermate Pen of Sol Weinstein, a wonderful person altogether.

You Only Live Until You Die

Dedications

RONNIE AXE
In Memoriam.

SAM and CHAI SOORA WEINSTEIN, ELLIE, DAVID and JUDY WEINSTEIN, DR. and MRS. HOWARD FRIEDMAN, HARRY and BESS EISNER, STAN and RHODA EISNER, JOE E. LEWIS, DON and SANDY BARNETT, JACKIE (RATFINK ROOM) GANNON, LOUIE and CAROLE KAMER, WALT and MATTI MYERS, BEVERLEY GITHENS, LAURA LANE, SANDY LESBERG, DR. HERMAN CORN, DR. JULIUS SOBEL, IDA BLITMAN BOB BOOKER and GEORGE FOSTER, LOU JACOBI, MARJORIE RUTH BERNSTEIN, LINDA LATZ, SHIRLEY TABACKMAN, ART HOPPE, BOB and VICKI LANE. DICK and ANDY MATHEWS, HERBERT EDELMAN, SAM JACOBS, MRS. E. LAUREN HOWIE TEDDER, BOB TEDDER, WARREN RENSHAW, ALPHA EPSILON PI of EMORY U. and RABBI HERBERT HENDEL.

MR and MRS. I. (DICK) AXE, CAROLE AXE, MORT SLAKOFF, BILL LEWIS, AUSTIN MACK HANNAH GRATZ, JAMES R. LOWELL, MAX LERNER, ROSARA BERMAN, MRS. ABRAHAM E. WEINBERG, ETTA KLEINER, BILLY GARBER, JEFF KELLER, JOAN KARPINSKI, MARCELLA TRUDNAK, MR. and MRS. SID LUTZKER, TED and SYBIL COOPER, LEN and HELENA BOGARDE, DENIS P. DORSEY, LAWRENCE OKAMURA, LEO RUTKOFF, JACK and MARY SHERMAN, JACK and DORIS SHERMAN, JOSH SHERMAN, HARRY and JOHN HOLLAND, IRWIN and MARGIE WEINSTEIN JOHNNY COATES JR., JOHNNY COATES SR., BOB (SMOKEY) STOVER, IRWIN MOSES, ART SHAINES, JERRY NEELMAN, FRANK SADOFSKY, JAMES M. STILL JR., MARVIN and BERNIE BLUMENTHAL, HERB and SAM BLUMENTHAL, DANNY ROTH, BEN MELZER, STAN LEDERMAN, NEWMAN HOFFMAN, GEORGE GORDON, PAULA MELZER, JULIA HECKEL, MARILYNN FULTON and DR. BERNIE AMSTER.

EARL WILSON, SAMMY DAVIS, KARL BARRIE, MORTY GUNTY, LEE TULLY, SOUPY SALES, VIC LaVOLPE, DON and BEV PALMER, SAM PLUMERI, ROSE (SAM) DeWOLF, HARRY HARRIS, PAUL LEVINE, CLAIRE HUFF, WALT CANTER, STEVE FLANDERS, MAL WEST, MARK MONSKY, CIRO TORCHIA, KIRK NUROCK, CHUCK WIECHARD, ERIC COHEN, FRANK ZUBACK, BILL PETTIT, STEVE ("THE SCENE") PAUL, SANDY

OPPENHEIMER, BILL WINTERS and JACK (NIGHT TALK) McKINNEY. SY and MALVINA VOGEL, NATHAN A. FRIEDMAN, ESQ., MARV and MARSHA ROSENBERG, ARNIE SOMERS, STEVE SCHENKEL, FRED BERK, ALLEN DELIN, HARVEY and HARRIETT BLATT, LIPPY and SYLVIA EISNER, LEONARD G. FELDMAN, HARRIET HOROWITZ, SAM and BOOTSI COLODNY, MILTON LEVINE, BILL and LIL HOLSTEIN, MONIQUE VAUGEL, MARIO and MARGE PASCUCCI, NICK TOLKACH, ANN BOEKER, LEE J. MALTENFORT, LES ROBERTS, MIKE ROSENFELD and SUKEMASA YAGIHASHI and MICHIHIKO YAMATO, collegians.

SID SHLAK, LEON BROWN, JOE FRANKLIN, GODFREY (WEIGHT-WATCHER) CAMBRIDGE ED BROWN, JUDY EDELMAN, DEBBIE BAKER, CARMELA CANDELA, JACK CURTIS, JOEL DORN, LEN and NORA FISCHMAN, HARRY BOTOFF, BERNIE GOLDBERG, NEIL LEVENSON, DR. HOWARD LEVENSON, JULIUS (YUDEL) KAPLAN, IRWIN and HERBIE SPIEGEL, MARV HABAS, FRANK MARRERO, JIM TIGHE, DEBBIE MILLER, CHARLIE TRESKY, CHICK HALFON, FLORENCE FRIEDMAN, LENNIE WERKSTELL, FRAN SHANKIN, LILLIAN STUDNIA, WALT LAMOND, MARTIN and MIRIAM LAIBOW, KATHY MICHEL, LENNIE ORLAND, MEL (SHAKY) KUSHNER, METZ BERGER, ALVIN BERGER, SELMA FEGELSON, NORMAN LEIGHTON, BOB GOLDMAN, ARTHUR (TEN COPIES) AZARCHI, BUDDY (FLASH) MYERS, and JIM FRASCELLA of the A & P.

WILLIAM and DOLLY BANKS, JACK DASH, GEORGE WILSON, SID MARK, STEW CHASE, GEORGE LYLE, JIMMY CARTER, JOE HUNTER, BOB EVANS and RICK FRIEDMAN (all of WHAT-FM, Philadelphia), LOU DEITCH, NORMAN, PHYLLIS, MARK, DANA and JULIE SHAVIN.

CONG. CHARLES LONGSTREET WELTNER, DON TUCKER, BILL, MIKE and JEFF WILLIAMS, MR. and MRS. FORREST DUKE, LAURA TRACY, BOB JOYCE of KRAM, Vegas, DR. MICHAEL DEAN, COAST GUARD LT. COMDR. ED ARD, DR. and MRS. SEYMOUR LEDIS, BRUCE HUFF, MRS. DONALD L. RANSOM JR., PAMELA and GERALDINE LANDOU, PAUL S. HAYNIE, SID BRUMMEL, AL and THELMA BARON, CARL (KUSHELEH) ROSENTHAL, DAVID R. WEISMAN, PAUL DOBISH, RON LEVASSEUR, CHRISTIAN JACOBSEN, GEORGE COHEN, HUMPSIE and ABE FINKLE, MICKEY and HELEN DANER, GEORGE (JEEBEE) TEMKIN, LEW and EVELYN MARSHALL, KEN and CAROLE SYME, NORM and MARGE WEINSTEIN, LABRON SHUMAN (and his burnoose), and LINDA BILLINGTON.

JOE and CEIL BERKOWITZ, DR. RICHARD E. SELZNICK, LEN FEINBERG, LEON ROSENBERG, MEL (TWINKLE) STARR, IRWIN BODEE, WILLIE COHEN, MUFFY COHEN, HERBIE CLARK, NORM WISHNOW, JACK HAVESON, EUGENE HAVESON, LEN (FLOPPY) SWERDLOW, HERMAN KRAHN, HERB BRODY, JOE BELLITZ, MEYER BLOOM, JERRY HEYMAN, IRVING BUDDINE, RABBI WILLIAM FIERVERKER, ARLENE BERLIN, WALLACE WEINSTEIN, WARREN REDNOR, JERRY REDNOR, ABBIE BASH, IZZY POLLACK, RED NUSSBLATT, JOE ROGOFF, SHARKY ROSENTHAL, ACE AARONSON, TEDDY SNYDER, BARRY SNYDER, LON FRIEDMAN, GIL SUSSMAN, LOUISE STARK, ALAN HARRIS, BOB COWART, WILLIAM M. COWAN, MARC DROGIN, JEFFREY BYERLY, LEWIS LIPPIN, DR. EDWARD JAFFEE, RABBI BENJAMIN SINCOFF, CLEVELAND AMORY, ART ABRAMSOHN, JACK SHAW, and DAVE WISNIA.

ROBERT PINCUS, BILL and TURK TASHLIK, MAURICE POTOSKY, MRS. NELLIE GOETTEL, LARRY FUCHSBERG, CECE DANTZIG, MAX YOUNG, MARK, DIANA, SHIRA and MICHAEL GOLDMAN, BILL (VELVEL) SCHULMAN, BENNIE KEINER, SAMMY MORRIS, LARRY GELMAN, JACK and FRANCES ROSENBERG, JACK and SOPHIE ROSENBERG, DAVID NYMAN, DAVID VAN METER, CAROLE WOLFORD, SHYRLEE DALLARD, JOHN CARTER of A.G.A.C., VIC WOOLF, MRS. KIM MARSH, JOAN ALBERT of the Fontainebleau, PHIL ZELT, MO JAFFE and SGT. RICHARD LIPSHUTZ. PAUL GALLAGHER, EDDIE GOLDSTEIN, SAM BUSHMAN, HILDE SIMMONS, CONNIE KRATZOK, GWENDA TALENS, HAROLD (HESHY) STRAUSE, JOE and CHARLOTTE NASSAU, JERRY and MURIEL HIMMEL, JOSEPH McNAMARA, MAURY LEVY, MATT SLEEPER, MOISHE and BOOMIE SEGAL, IRV KERN, DR. LEONARD PHILLIPS, ARNOLD TOMOR, ISRAEL (COKE) RUBIN, DR. MILTON PALAT, DR. GEORGE ISAACSON, DR. ARNOLD KIMMEL, MARTIN and MINNA SAVAR, ABE and JERRY HERSH, ANDY FLAGER, BUS SAIDT, YALE RABINOWITZ, SAUL ROSSIEN, MILTON FEINBERG, PHIL (FIFEL) BLOOM, NATE, SAM and FRED MELMAN, TEDDY FLAER, PHIL MILLSTEIN, IRV DANA, NORMAN STERN, HARVEY STERN, SHIRLEY MERRIMAN, and NICK MEGLIN.

JACK (ELEPHANT BOY) WALSH, BARRY REISMAN, MELVIN KARTZMER, LEON KARTZMER, CHARLIE PAPIER, DONNIE PAPIER, BARBARA SYKES, MOLLY LEVINE, JOE CANNON, HAZEL SWEENEY, ROGER GLACKIN, CLAIRE MILLER, MR. and MRS. GERRY FINN, BENNIE MOSKOWITZ and JULES RESNICK.

MRS. HELEN MEYNER, HAROLD MAY, BOB BURTON, JIM POWERS, JACK HELSEL, J. WELLINGTON PIDCOCK, HORACE GREELEY McNAB, COUSIN DAVE GOMBERG, DAVE (OLDTIMER) HORWITZ, RON SCOTT, CHRIS WINNER, GABE ROSEN, CARL (KIVVY) ABROMOVITZ, DR. LEWIS HIRSH, SCOTTY MOSOVICH, MAYNARD BARKER, BOB AMOROS, SAM (TAMMI) KAPLAN, JACKIE and ARNOLD HODES, DAVE PITASKY, DAVE, WILLIE and MENDY KRAVITZ, JOE BERGER, JERRY, SIDNEY, MARTY, RALPH, ALFRED and IVAN POPKIN, IRV WARACH, ELI WARACH, ROBERT OLINSKY, BENNY OLINSKY, LOUIE OLINSKY, MILTON OLINSKY, IRV OLIN, CHARLIE BYER, RABBI WILLIAM, NATIE, JERRY and SIDNEY GORDON, JACKIE and WALTER HARRISON, WALT BELLAK, JACK POLLACK, PAT POLLACK, PAUL CAGAN, HARVEY SILK, MARK LITOWITZ, HARRY ZOLTICK, ALLAN and WALLY PLAPINGER, ERWIN WAINER, HYMAN (COWBOY) BALITZ, SHELDON SEAVEY, ZIGGY WALDMAN, CLYDE LEIB, EMIL SLABODA, HARVEY YAVENER, JOE LOGUE, EDDIE GOLDEN, ED (DUFFY) RAMSEY, EDDIE SOLAN, STEVE MERVISH and GEORGE MOLDOVAN. MURRAY BURNETT, BOB MENEFEE, TED REINHART, MIKE McGRADY, ABEL GREEN, NORMA NANNINI, BILL KARDALEY, ANDY ETTINGER, NATE ROBERTS, NORM BROOKS, ELAINE BELK, DURWARD EARLY, BERT and MIKE WEILAND, MARK VAN BROOKS, TOMMY THOMPSON, BETTY STEVENS, JAY (FINE SWISS WATCHES) GOLD, SYLVIA MANDELL, B. A. BERGMAN, FRANK BROOKHOUSER, WAYNE and AGNES ROBINSON, DAVID and STEVE KUSHELOFF, MURRAY, MARILYN, DEBBY and HOLLY ARNOLD, FREDERICK WERTHEIMER, AL FINGERMAN, HY and MARILYN GARDNER, FLORENCE BLOCK, DAVE WEST, CHARLIE SCOTT, EARL JOSEPHSON, MURRAY FISHER, JULI BAINBRIDGE, SHELDON WAX, ED, ROSE, WENDY and STEVEN BURTON, BOBBY DARIN, DON BARBER, TEDDI LEVISON, MICKIE SILVERSTEIN, RALPH COLLIER, BILL STRETCH, STEVE O'KEEFE, COL. CHARLES GREGG, CHARLIE PETZOLD, DON SCOTT, RUTH OLIS, FRANK MULLOY, HILDA SHIVERS, BOB RITCHIE, HOWARD MacDOUGALL, RALPH PEARL, JOE STEAD, FRANK WATRING, BOB (BOOKSTORES) CRAIG, BILL LINK and DICK LEVINSON, and SID and BUNNY SHORE.

MERV GRIFFIN and TONY GAROFALO, RUBE VERIN, BEN GRAFF, CHARLIE HERB and AL AMBERG of RUBE'S BARBER SHOP, Levittown, Pa., FRANK BISANZIO, LOU EMANUEL, EARL GEORGE of A.F.T.R.A., RON POLAO, LOU SCHEINFELD and JAY SARNO, JIMMIE (THE GREEK) SNYDER, RON AMOS, NATHAN JACOBSON, DAVID VICTORSON and MAURY, MURIEL and BRUCE STEVENS of Caesar's Palace, Vegas. JOHN HUEGHNERGARTH, artist, MR. and MRS. JERRY GAGHAN, SID SHUCKER, GEORGE BLAISDELL, JACK McCUTCHEON, LEWIS CHARLES WENDELL JR., JERRY VERBEL, WILLIAM B. WILLIAMS, FLORENCE LONDONER, DR. JULES K. LEVY, JERRY SCHLOSS, ROBERT (LAUGHTRACK) PEET, BERNARD ZELL, MICHAEL SPOLL, APRIL AARONS, ISADORE SOLOVAY, MARTY MOSKOWITZ, JANE SCHULZE, CY and CLAIRE NEIBURG, JACK and BARBARA GILL, BARBARA KELLMAN, DON PHILLIPS, TOM (CONTACT, KYW-TV, Philly) SNYDER, DONALD E. KNOX, STAN BERK, DIANE ACTMAN, JIM TATE, and DR. WALDO FIELDING, ART MOGER, GEORGE ESTES, AL SHERMAN, MILT YAKUS, MIKE REINGOLD, GEORGE ROBERTS, DAVID HOFF, IRA GOLDBLATT, RICHARD C. JACOBS, AL KORN, JESS CAIN and LENNY MEYERS of the TUB THUMPERS, Boston.

And... NANCY BROWN LEVINE of Plainfield, NJ.-Poughkeepsie, N.Y.

Table of Contents

Prologue	412
1 Mondo Bondo	413
2 The Historical Verity	427
3 "Making Rove On Me—Fast! Fast!"	439
4 Tag Day In Tokyo	448
5 "Forget About the Black Room!"	455
6 Night of Treemandous Terror	460
7 Fisherman Overboard!	466
8 A Crawler, a Baller	469
9 Kopy Enraged, Kopy Engaged	473
10 Shimon Sez	476
11 Shell Shock	483
12 "When You've Been in the Biggest Oyster There Is"	488
13 The Dane Talks	492
14 A Fitting Climax Requires a Fitting	498
15 Brolly Brawl On The Bullet	503
16 Bowling Brawl in the Bathhouse	507
17 Games Xerox People Play	513
18 Bondo Limbo	517
19 "Israel Bond Is Dead"	523
20 Mr. Tambourine Man	526
21 Not All Lox is Smoked Salmon	530
22 Loves Of A Bond	534
23 The Quest Ends	539
24 Neck Check	541
25 Dem Bones, Dem Bones, Dem Dry Bones	546
26 Now Heah de Wud of de Lawd	551
27 How to Talk to a Jewish Mother	553
Epis-A-Logue	557

PROLOGUE

We have an old saying in the Israeli Secret Service well worth committing to memory, Mr. Bond. Briefly, it is this:

If you meet a man for the first time and he discharges a pistol in your direction it could be he's a nervous, insecure person hungering for some attention or even sympathy in this increasingly dehumanized world.

If on your second meeting he makes a threatening gesture with a machete it could be a manifestation of a severe sexual aberration since, as we now know from Hollywood films, a knife is a penile symbol.

But should you meet the same man a third time and he attempts to take your life by using curare, cyanide, low-yield nuclear weapon or one of those extra-fat-drenched hamburgers sold by a firm whose name will not be mentioned here, and cries out, "Die, Israeli dog!" then such behavior can only be construed as out and out bellicosity, justifying at the very least a nasty letter to the New York Times (no more than 500 words please), or even a physical response of some sort.

- M

1
Mondo Bondo

Two hours to Tokyo, where he would rendezvous with Baron Cockimamiyama Sanka, the *ichi-ban*[*] of the *Kyodo Kikaku*,[**] Israel Bond was jolted out of a demon-haunted nap by a rapid-fire sequence of sounds:

> ... The snatch of song in a lilting, ingenuous Irish brogue:
> "Ivory liquid helps yer hands feel young again..."
> ... A horrified shriek.
> ... A metallic thump against the left wing of the Japan Air Lines superjet.

Gottenu! The realization of what had occurred cast him into utter despair.

We've collided with Mary Mild.

He awoke in a chilling sweat to find upon him the solicitous eyes of the enchanting kimonoed and obied stewardess, the maiden called Festering Wind.

"It was bound to happen sooner or later, Mr. Bond. Miss Mild's frequent, haphazard flights as a soap company's television spokeswoman through congested air corridors have endangered hundreds of commercial planes. However"—and her manner was reassuring—"it was just a glancing blow. I am confident of her ability to make it to Guam or Wake for any necessary repairs to her body or starched apron."

Quite the charmer, this Festering Wind, Bond thought; *something more than the typical, efficient JAL servant of the sky dispensing*

---
[*] Number one
[**] Japanese Secret Service

her ever-handy supply of fluffy pillows and bowls of green tea. For Festering Wind was also one of Baron Sanka's most trusted agents and under orders to accord Bond the super-deluxe treatment a guest of his stature warranted. When the Baron called for VIP service he did not stint. The jet's first-class compartment, customarily catering to sixteen people, had been revamped for Bond's sole use and closed off from the tourist section by a bamboo curtain. Its seats had been ripped out to make space for a contoured swivel-chair bed under which thrummed a Relaxacizor unit; an *ofuro*, the deep, tiled Japanese bath now abubble with lethal chunks of Blofeld blowfish; a well-stocked bar with such offbeat libations as Creme de Mousse (the tiny antlers had been removed); a massage table; and a stereo corner which had already regaled him with *Senator Dirksen and Congressman Powell Recite the All-Time Top Forty Hymns* and at present was pumping out a catchy medley, "You're the Top," "You Can Do Anything Better than We Can" and "What Can We Say, Sir, After We Say We're Sorry?" all from the new LP *The Beatles Apologize to Jesus at the Astrodome.*

In her frequent capacity as a masseuse Festering Wind had become accustomed and therefore indifferent to the bodies of magnificent men—sumo wrestlers, karate masters, *kendo* stick experts and the like—yet she shivered whenever her fingers strayed over the musculature of this *gaijin*[*] clad only in an extra-long, extra-wide Carnaby Street Mod tie (all he actually needed in the way of clothing, so generous was the amount of the tie's material). But aroused as she was by the massive shoulders, a trim waist that was more Hebraic than wasp, and long, tapering fingers, she found herself transfixed again and again by the cruel, darkly handsome face marked by a whitish scar on the left cheek (or was it the right? It seemed to be constantly *shifting!*) and the sorrow misting the gray eyes. Surely, she deduced, this man has suffered a monumental loss in his recent past.

Bond extracted a filter-tipped Raleigh from a pack Scotch-taped to his left thigh and ignited a blue-tipped Ohio match with a rub inside an abrasive furrow of skin perched atop his right shoulder, a memento of a madman's Luger bullet in the unbelievable Loxfinger business of 1965. "How long was I in dreamy Dreamsville, my pet?"

"You shuttered those haunted eyes an hour before we landed in Hawaii to refuel, Mr. Bond. I had not the heart to wake

---
[*] Foreigner

you. And Baron Sanka's orders were explicit. I am to let you rest whenever possible."

"Man, that Sanka really lets you sleep," Bond marveled.

On chopsticks whittled from the softest balsa wood that grows in the gardens of the Meiji Shrine, she fed him *hershi-sushi*, those succulent squares of chocolate-covered squid so highly prized by Japan's upper class. Then it was time for his hourly massage, and to make up for the ones he'd missed while asleep, Festering Wind decided to put something special into it—herself. Peeling off his Mod tie and her diaphanous kimono and utilizing every wile taught to her by Madam Making-the-Bird-Rise of the Nishi Academy of Sexual Stimulation and Fish Cleaning, she led him through the flowery gateway of her being, their stamens and pistils dissolving in the searing instant of their cross-pollination. *Gottenu!* he sobbed soundlessly. *I never dreamed it could be this way again. She's got my mojo*[*] *working and I love it! Oh, Sarah, Sarah, my lost angel. Forgive me again for my callous infidelity.*

An astral shape materialized over his head; two reproachful black eyes peered over a veil into his guilty, flinching gray ones. *I forgive you, Iz, my darling. But don't enjoy it too much.*

I won't, I won't, his heart pledged.

But somehow he did.

After it was done and she'd swept away the last soggy petal the ecstatic Festering Wind glided to a rack and wheeled over a load of books and newspapers. "I picked these up in Honolulu, sir. Would you care to read?"

His ebullience flown, Bond stared at his moody reflection in the Perspex and gave a listless shrug. He jammed one of the new super-length Benson & Hedges into his sensual mouth, maneuvered the tip so that it would touch a flickering candle on the bar two feet away and inhaled deeply, blowing out fifty-four smoke rings, twenty-three octagons and the word "antidisestablishmentarianism." He thumbed through the books—*The Wit and Wisdom of Lester Maddox, God's Answers to Children's Letters, No, You Can't!* (a new biography of Sammy Davis by a Mississippi sheriff) and *Frodo's Hobbit Cookbook,* discarding them as too depressing. His heart quickened momentarily as he saw under the pile the Sunday *New York Times,* of all the world's newspapers his absolute favorite. (Bond had long considered himself the perfect amalgam of brains and brawn—erudite

---

[*] Male member (Shikoku dialect)

enough to understand the Sunday *New York Times*; strong enough to carry it.) But the advertisements in the slick magazine section, so captivating as a rule, left him oddly unmoved—the dewy-eyed sylph in scanties and a judicial wig: "I dreamed I refuted the findings of the Warren Commission in my Maidenform Bra"; the dour spokesman in the rent-a-car pitch: "We'd love to make Number Two all over Number One."

Nor was there the slightest appeal in the cavalcade of inanities that constituted the front-page stories. An extremist civil rights group had made vociferous demands for "Black Power!"—at the main office of General Electric. The spirit of ecumenism continued to proliferate; a Vatican emissary gifted a prominent Jewish organization with a replica of the famous Papal encyclical on "Peace on Earth," *Pacem in Terris*; the latter had reciprocated by mailing the Holy See the ancient Hassidic treatise on child psychology, *Pacem in Tuchas*. In New Haven, a campus "mating" computer, fed data on key socioeconomic and sexual factors, had concluded that the ideal marital partner for a Yale man was another Yale man. America's urban riots would be the theme of a new Broadway musical, *Sniper on the Roof*. United Press International columnist Dick West had interviewed a Monterey, California, youth arrested for stabbing nineteen policemen and setting afire ten houses of worship. "My incarceration is illegal and an affront to creative people everywhere," the youth lamented. "What hope is there for the artist if the authorities cannot comprehend the improvisational nature of a 'happening'?"

Bond tossed the *Times* aside for the *Pacific Stars & Stripes*, the sprightly tabloid that services America's fighting men throughout the Far East.

And the bold-faced lead story lashed out at him like the tongue of a cobra.

Carrying the byline of columnist Al Ricketts, the story was datelined Kagoshima, Japan.

A Lieutenant Eno Nanonuni, commander of an Imperial Japanese patrol boat, had reported contacting an unidentified fishing trawler "violating our territorial waters. I deployed our craft so close to the intruder that I could clearly see the glazed, mad-dog eyes of the crew, who were hanging over the rail and spouting epithets of a particularly offensive nature, relating as they did to our beloved Emperor. I also saw nets laden with illegally harvested fish."

Ordered to halt and receive a boarding party, the trawler responded by raking the patrol boat with machine-gun fire, wounding Lieutenant Nanonuni and three of his men. "I replied in kind," the officer stated, "by ordering a brace of torpedoes to be put into her below the waterline. She sank at once. There were no survivors. I sent down a diver, who identified the drowned men as Caucasians and emerged with two souvenirs, the log and flag. The former indicated the vessel was the *Blintz Charming*, of Haifa registry, commanded by Captain Jacob Bar-Kochlefel, and the route of passage the Suez Canal, Indian Ocean, Strait of Malacca, South China Sea and a final entry, Kagoshima. The latter was even more intriguing. It bears the Star of David."

The *Pacific Stars & Stripes* fluttered from Bond's agitated hands to the floor. "The Bernardi," he whispered out of his suddenly taut throat. "Hand me the Bernardi."

Sensing the alarm in his request, Festering Wind flashed an enticing length of leg as she reached up to the overhead rack, unlocked the instrument case and gently deposited in his lap the violin carved out of huge blocks of vermicelli by the sixteenth-century Jew, Erschelli Bernardi, in the opinion of many the superior of Da Vinci in cartography, painting, alchemy (Bernardi had transformed gold into peat moss) and sophisticated weaponry. The second he tucked it under his sensual dewlaps he felt the cordovan-stained pasta radiating a mystical glow throughout his body. On the upper right side of the violin was the raised, two-inch copper Seal Of Bernardi, its somewhat vulgar acronym glinting in the first rays of the Eastern sun. For those of limited intellect a Stradivarius or an Amati would be quite adequate, thank you, but the minuscule handful of true stringed-instrument aficionados would settle for nothing less than a "Bernie." Alas, the floods that had ravaged Florence had buried all of the Old World's Bernardis in the muck and in all of creation there were but three extant, one owned by Heifetz, another by Henny Youngman and the third cradled in the reverent arms of Israel Bond, now en route to "the calm beauty of Japan at slightly under the speed of sound."[*]

When inexplicable events dictated a session of cogitation, Bond often found scraping the yellowed but still supple iguana-gut strings an invaluable aid in cranking up his mental processes. The gray eyes narrowed; the muscles of the right arm coaxed a spirited series of *cadenzas* and *wallendas* from the third move-

---

[*] Courtesy of the Japan Air Lines brochure.

ment of the *Emilio Largo* and he leaned back to mull over the shocking item from the *Pacific Stars & Stripes.*

Gottenu! So that was the gruesome fate of the *Blintz Charming!* It had been a mystery bedeviling the Israeli Ministry of Fisheries, who in desperation had thrown it to M 33 and the Secret Service. The trawler had been missing for weeks. No last-second SOS had ever been transmitted; no debris spotted on the Mediterranean. Now it had turned up in Japan, "The Land of the Rising Datsun," to perpetrate a senseless attack on an Imperial craft. What the hell was going on here? Soon he'd be beseeching Baron Sanka for a helping hand in tracking down Dr. Ernst Holzknicht, sole survivor of the Nazi murder gang, the Terrorist Union for Suppressing Hebrews, TUSH,[*] that Bond had wrecked in the Queen caper—Holzknicht, the diabolical genius whose "Operation Alienation" had come within a whisker of wiping out Judaism; Holzknicht, who'd metamorphosed a joyous June wedding day into horror by murdering under the canopy Bond's wife-to-be, the mysterious veiled rider of the desert, Sarah Lawrence of Arabia. And how disposed would Sanka be to lending that hand after this slap in the face from Bond's adopted homeland?

He sawed away at the Bernardi for a few minutes, coming up with an acceptable ending to Schubert's "Unfinished" Symphony—the seven notes that signified "Shave and a haircut, two bits!"— and wondered why the composer hadn't resolved his problem that simply. Good-o! His mind was clicking on both cylinders. Now he had to rid his body of its sloth. To accomplish this he handed the Bernardi to the girl, opened the bamboo curtain and commenced a punishing chain of traveling pushups, deep elbow-and-knee bends and cartwheels down the aisle of the tourist section, which would not only start the vital juices coursing again but also allow him to check out any new arrivals on at Honolulu, a solid bit of security technique always to be practiced by an agent carrying an Oy Oy license to kill.

The passengers, all familiar to him since he'd boarded in San Francisco, were dozing. Except the new one in Seat 26A.

Crooning a prayer, "O mani pod may hom,"[**] his fork-bearded chin dug into a pot of a belly, was a moon-faced Oriental in the saffron robe of a monk. His sagacious black eyes scanned Bond's intent expression and twinkled fractionally.

---

[*] Which rhymes with "push," and that means there's trouble, big trouble, in River City.

[**] Hail to the jewel in Tiffany's window!

"My son." The voice was low-keyed, irresistible. "There is a great sadness in your face. Sit by me and let me attempt to bring a little solace into your life. You have lost someone dear to you, is it not so?"

Bond, a grim smile on his sensual lips, slid in beside the newcomer. This was either a holy man blessed with acute perception or... someone in "the game."

"You seem to know much about me, holy one."

"It is my training, my son. I am the monk Aw Gee Minh, so named because my mother gave birth to me in a Hong Kong theater featuring an old Wallace Beery film. I am returning to my strife-torn land of Vietnam following a tour of Hawaii on a Rambler Foundation grant."

"Rambler?"

"I applied too late to procure one from Ford. In Honolulu I was privileged to attend the Congress of Revelations by Acknowledged Psychics, the highlight of which was the candlelight wedding of Edgar Cayce to Bridey Murphy. We toasted the happy couple with glasses of Reincarnation Milk. Now let us consider your condition. Life's vicissitudes have hurt you deeply. To revitalize your life force and start you on the road to *satori* or enlightenment, we must conduct a *mondo*, which is a Zen Buddhist dialogue between a monk and an acolyte. The dialogue may seem trivial, but it is a valid tool for probing the innermost secrets of the heart. Before we begin it will be necessary to purify our mouths of any hateful words lingering from past conversations." He produced a paper packet from somewhere in the robe's folds, slit it open with a deft thumbnail and poured some black specks into his palm and Bond's. "Let us eat them, my son. They will produce phrases of sweetness and grace."

Bond wolfed down the dots. "How spicy they are, holy one. What are they called?"

"Zen-Zen. Now the *mondo*. I shall put to you questions of an abstract nature and you will respond to the best of your ability. Question One: *What will you do if they ask you to kill the cuckoo?*"

"I shall stand in front of the clock and shield it with my body, if need be."

"Excellent! Despite your grief, you continue to display compassion. Second: *What will you do if they force you to kill the cuckoo?*"

"I shall kill them. But who *are* they?"

"Why do you ask?"

"I must know. I have a right to know. I have a feeling the cuckoo wants to know."

"Why should the cuckoo want to know? It is only a bird."

"Hath not a bird the right to know? Hath it not eyes, ears, nose and throat? If ye prick it, will it not bleed?"

They were moving ever closer to the arcane meaning of the *mondo*, the monk making cuckoo-like noises, Bond doing his obscure and difficult impression of John Byner imitating Kirk Douglas imitating Frank Gorshin, when the girl's urgent cry halted it. "Mr. Bond, please return to your compartment."

Bond, a trifle miffed, rose reluctantly. "Forgive me, holy one. My governess calls. I can't thank you enough for your concern. I've learned much about life in these simple exchanges. At least I now know that life is not a fountain."

"If it is anything, life is the Fontainebleau in Miami Beach, my son," Aw Gee Minh said sententiously. "Farewell. We shall meet again in the place where there is no darkness."

"And no cuckoo," Bond said with touching tenderness.

Back in his quarters, Bond told Festering Wind, "The interruption was quite unnecessary. He was a harmless, well-meaning old coot trying to do me some good in his own way."

"I am sorry, Mr. Bond, but the Baron also ordered me to keep close surveillance on you. A man in your profession faces constant peril. And besides, it is time for your next MacLuhan massage."

She once more removed his Mod tie and he vaulted onto the table. Her hands, of surprising strength for one so slight, were assiduous octopi on his ankles, calves and buttocks and he felt the chronic soreness fleeing these spots to settle permanently in his neck and shoulder muscles.

Suddenly he sensed tension in her hands and speech.

"All good things come in threes. Said Peter Gunn: 'You'd better muzzle that badly trained mutt who's on top of us.'"

He caught it at once, the cipher she was formulating after the key word "threes." *Gunn... muzzle... trained... on... us.*

The derisive voice said, "And what will you do, Oy Oy Seven, if the cuckoo turns on you and bites you in the TUSH?"

The silencer coughed twice and he heard Festering Wind's "Oh" and felt her hands slide off his thighs. She crumpled at the foot of the massage table, a widening stain on her breast.

Fanatical eyes aglitter, the monk pushed through the curtain. "I also understand a simple three-cipher, Mr. Bond."

Smoke wafted up from the silencer attachment on the Toppo-Gigio, the little Italian mini-Mauser.

"You needn't have killed the girl."

"A maiden who knows ciphers and has strong hands is far too dangerous to let live, my son."

"So the good, wise monk is a TUSH-y?"[*]

"Ah, my *mondo* was not in vain. You have indeed grasped the meaning of life. Now my Toppo-Gigio will impart the meaning of death."

"Who are you?"

"An old enemy, Mr. Bond. I had boarded this aircraft with a purpose. To destroy it. Imagine my glee at discovering your presence and realizing I could accomplish my primary mission and even two old scores to the bargain." The gun wielder emitted a hard, cough-like laugh that sounded like his silencer. "Part of what I told you, Oy Oy Seven, is true. I am Aw Gee Minh from Vietnam but it should not take you an eternity to conclude what half of that nation claims my allegiance. I am the younger brother of that master of Communist guerrilla warfare Vi Teh Minh, whom you destroyed on the cigar-shaped Caribbean isle of El Tiparillo.[**] Long has his spirit cried out for vengeance."

"And the second score?" Bond's query was nonchalant as his right hand inched toward his mezuzah, the cylindrical symbol of his faith dangling on a chain around his neck.

"I'm afraid that won't do at all, Mr. Bond," the monk said equably, but the mouth twisted into a sneer, the fat forefinger squeezed the Toppo-Gigio's trigger twice and it splashed its molten message into Bond's body, the first severing the chain and nicking his neck, the second hammering into his right shoulder. Bond, battered to his knees by the one-two punch, gazed in disbelief at the bloodburst from the gouged-out shoulder top. Slug Two had whistled through the furrow of skin, flattening both sides. Through the haze of pain he thought, *Well, there goes the best damn match-scratcher a man ever had. But what's he waiting for? I'm exsanguinating like a butchered steer. Where's the finisher through the heart or between my sensual gray eyes?*

"By now, Oy Oy Seven, your modus operandi is well known to us. That mezuzah and its hidden dart tipped with Molochamovis-B venom is far safer on the floor, don't you agree? To continue: The second score I shall repay involves a niece who

---

[*] An agent of TUSH
[**] *Matzohball*, 1966, $1.00.

once was one of our topnotch agents until she was subverted by your sexuality in the so-called Loxfinger affair. You will recall Nu Kee, whose cover role was that of 'Miss Vietcong' in the beauty pageant."

"Yes," Bond panted. "A fine girl corrupted by your expansionist doctrines until I inserted a large"—he paused, seeking a tactful phrase—"Hebrew point of view. What has befallen her?"

"She died by my hand after we caught her working for the Americans in Saigon. Familial feelings have no place in this business."

The blood kept gurgling from Bond's shoulder and he bit his lip to fight off the tides of darkness threatening to sweep him into unconsciousness. "This primary mission you alluded to..."

"In a few minutes," Aw Gee Minh said in a pedagogical manner, "after your demise, of course, I shall stroll into the pilots' deck, place my weapon against the captain's neck and command him to radio Haneda Airport that his plane is being hijacked by a crazed member of the Shinbet.[*] After he has made contact I shall shoot him and the copilot, set the plane on automatic control to keep it airborne awhile longer and step out of the door. My minichute will unfurl and during my descent to the Pacific I shall fire a Veery pistol so that the hydrofoil waiting for me at a certain coordinate will spot the flare and take me from the life raft presently tucked about my midsection. A hundred or more passengers from many nations will perish and Israel will be blamed for an insensate act, as the good *Herr Doktor* planned. Japan, in particular, will be outraged."

"Holzknicht again." The despairing words rasped out of Bond's bone-dry throat. "How were you recruited into this cabal?"

"Dr. Holzknicht has quite a file on those holding grudges against Israel and, more specifically, against you, Oy Oy Seven. Now the *mondo* ends. The cuckoo calls."

"Wait! I beg of you, wait!"

"How disappointing," the monk smirked. "The celebrated Israel Bond begs for his life like some common cutpurse."

"Not for myself, holy one. For humanity. Take the Bernardi with you when you jump."

---

[*] Sherutei Betahan, an early version of an Israeli intelligence force. Len Deighton's books contain loads of "inside" references like this. They also have skillful plots and meaty characterizations... if that's what you want... S.W.

The monk's brows knitted in puzzlement. "But this is extraordinary. The glorious strains filtering back to the tourist section were not recorded? You possess a genuine Bernardi?"

"On my seat. See for yourself."

A circumspect left eye followed Bond's forefinger. "It is true. Capital! It will bring no less than twenty million colodnys into the coffers of TUSH when I peddle it in Macao. Your chance remark, Mr. Bond, has earned you another five minutes of life."

"Shoot and get it over with."

"No, my friend. Pick it up and play for me."

Bond drew himself up with as much dignity as his bloodied frame would permit. He grunted a coarse biological suggestion to his adversary.

The monk chuckled. "For your information, Mr. Bond, I happen to be a pure hermaphrodite who can do and have done countless times precisely what you suggest. But you have forgotten one of the cardinal precepts of a membership in TUSH. A foe is not only to be vanquished but, when possible, humiliated to the nth degree. Pick up the Bernardi, Secret Agent Oy Oy Seven."

"I refuse. Do your worst."

He saw the slow rise of the Toppo-Gigio and whispered the *Sh'ma Israel*. It coughed; there was a buzz-saw sound and he paled as the copper Seal Of Bernardi flew off the violin into the seething *ofuro*.

"You bastard! You've desecrated a masterpiece."

"Not at all, Mr. Bond. My perfect shot merely drove the seal off its hinges. However, my next shots will crunch the violin into splinters unless you serenade me with no further delay. Pick it up. Good. Now, in this order I want you play and sing 'The Horst Wessel Song,' The Internationale' and finally the number-one song on the Southeast Asian Hit Parade, 'The Thoughts of Chairman Mao.'"

Bond positioned the Barnardi against his claret-soaked shoulder. The swine! His captor had chosen three songs calculated to turn the stomach of any Jew: the Brown Shirt hymn and its boast of impaling Jews on knives; the old Communist anthem, mocking him with its reminder of more than three million of his kin entrapped by the Jew-baiting Soviet regime; and the sycophantic paean to the xenophobic old Leninist who threatened to send the hordes of Han rolling over the world.

No matter. If by sating the TUSH-y's lust for degradation he could preserve a priceless Jewish artifact, then his personal debasement was inconsequential. He launched into the first "request" in guttural Berliner German, letting his defeated gray eyes absorb die indescribable loveliness of the Bernardi for the last time. Where the seal had been were four tiny holes, each housing one of the hinges, and he felt a profound relief. A competent metalsmith could heat the Seal Of Bernardi, pound it back into shape and insert it into the pasta with little or no visible damage. And, of course, the monk, after he'd put the quietus on Bond, would fish into the *ofuro* to retrieve it. He'd have to, to guarantee the instrument's authenticity.

Midway through "The Internationale" his body began to shake and he heard the monk snicker: "Fear pervades the invincible Oy Oy Seven?" but he ignored it. He allowed a sickly grin to crease his lips and carefully lowered his eyes to the section of the violin laid bare by the removal of the seal. A definite message carved in elegant curlicues! But in what language? Italian? Latin? No! By thunder, Yiddish!

He was playing and singing about "the final conflict," his heart thumping intricate paradiddles Max Roach or Buddy Rich never could have duplicated, while he screamed at his brain: *Translate! Translate!*

Now he was on the whining Cantonese song, one cylinder of his brain concentrating on the decipherment of the tortuous Yiddish paragraph.

> I met you in a commune
> Under a Peking moon,
> Thanks to the thought of Chairman Mao!

> *Mine bridder* Yid—*my brother Jew*—*if at this moment you are held at bay by an anti-Semite...*

> The poster on the wall
> Said in love we'd fall,
> Thanks to the thought of Chairman Mao!

> *... button on the bow...*

> We filled up jars of night soil,
> A task we found divine;

I filled mine with your night soil,
You stuffed your jar with mine!

... exposes a notch into which you may insert the iguana-gut string closest to your right hand, the pressure from which...

We sauntered through the town,
And painted the town brown,
And heard a "well done" cheer from Lin Paio!

... releases from the tip of the bow a steel shaft dipped in a compost of ingredients...

There was gladness in the eye
Of good old Chou En-lai,
And we knew we'd hurt revisionism—and how!
Thanks to the thought,
The blinding thought,
the thought of Chairman...
A good man and a fair man,
The thought ... of ... Chairman Maaaaaaaaoooo...
oh voh dee o doh!

"In truth, Mr. Bond, I have never heard it sung so well, not even by the Red Guard Tabernacle Choir. You missed your calling, my friend. Had you chosen the profession of a music hall minstrel you would have enjoyed a long, venerable life. Goodbye, Secret Agent Oy Oy Seven."

The pudgy gun hand pointed the Toppio-Gigio straight at the heart of Israel Bond.

But the drawn iguana-gut string had twanged its Nashville Sound, propelling the bow-turned-arrow from the violin-turned-bow. Deep into the right cheek of Aw Gee Minh burrowed the discolored tip of the steel shaft. The bow swayed back and forth, a maddened pendulum of death. In creepy fascination Bond saw the moon face change from yellow to a revolting purple as the still lethal venom on the shaft tip—a mixture of bizarre elements like belladarvi, hemlock paste and warlock droppings found only in that infamous region of Italy known as the Borgia Belt—diffused through the capillaries.

Aw Gee Minh's body was a Macy's Thanksgiving Day parade balloon suddenly deflated. The knees turned to rubber, caved in and he fell ponderously on his moon face.

"The poison was in the violin," jibed Bond. "Isn't that enough to drive you... cuckoo?"

The black vortex had him helpless in its grasp now and he surrendered to the inexorable tides. As he slumped against the massage table his last recollections were of his Jewish brother who'd sent him a message of salvation across the centuries; his feeble jest, "Saved by an SOB!" and the popeyed Japan Air Lines purser charging into the compartment....

During a blessed spell of unconsciousness Israel Bond found time to reflect upon the decision that was sending him winging to the exotic Far Eastern land where, the cognoscenti will tell you, the cherry blossoms best around the age of fourteen.

2
The Historical Verity

A month before, Israel Bond, at the wheel of a 1967 Nader, the world's safest sports car (it was constructed of panels of Campfire marshmallows, which upon impact would fluff up into spongy billows to cushion the driver), turned off the Strip into the driveway of Fabulous Las Vegas' newest, gaudiest address, Caesars Palace, that twenty-five-million-dollar Roman orgy with crap tables. He guided the Nader under each of the thirteen spewing fountains to gain a free car wash, then squealed to a halt at the entrance, where two collections of statuary quickly established the resort's classical motif: *The Rape of the Sabine Women* and *The Sabine Women Seen Consulting with Alan Dershowitz and Melvin Belli.*

"*Salve!*" chirped a bellhop in a centurion's uniform, who proceeded to unload Bond's Ventura-Condoli luggage.

"*Lesbia est puella,*" Bond countered, drawing upon his storehouse of Catullan maxims.

"Well, that's *de rerum natura*, I guess," the bellhop conceded and ushered Bond to Caesars Palace's preferred suite for big spenders, the Maximus Rabinowus. Waiting within, as the coded cable from Jerusalem had told him she would be, was M.'s new secretary, Lobsang Rampapport, a Tibetan who'd made a recent conversion to Judaism, her luscious, lipogenic limbs revealed by a spangled Vestal Virgin minitoga.

"We shall beat our spears into pruning hooks," the girl said self-consciously, pausing to allow Bond to complete the countersign.

"And our prunes into compote," Bond retorted. He made the bellhop's eyes bulge with a crisp two-hundred-salazar tip and two center-aisle tickets to *Cabaret* and shooed him out. "So you're M.'s new right arm? And you're all excited about this espionage crap, the passwords and such. Kid, get out of this lousy racket before you end up like Lilah Tov." His voice cracked on the adored name of the beauteous brunette who'd died so horribly in the Queen caper.

Lobsang's mouth tightened and he knew his warning had sunk in. Two of her eyes remained steadfast and clear, but her third eye wept copiously in memory of her predecessor.

In the days that followed, a legend was born along the Vegas Strip about a dark, cruelly handsome man whose grey eyes sought something on the horizon beyond the ken of mortal men... a man ferried from casino to casino in a Caesars Palace VIP golden chariot pulled by six haughty Arabian steeds and driven by a dashing charioteer named Ben Hur-Owitz... a man whose wanton gambling reduced the high-stakes exploits of Nick the Greek to Little League size.

Israel Bond... Israel Bond... Israel Bond...

His name was whispered at the Desert Inn, where he smashed the bank at *la guerre*;[*] by the dealer at the Flamingo, who quailed at Bond's icy calm: "You've just picked the Old Maid from my hand, old chap. You're done..." which meant a loss to the house of seventy-eight million dollars; and at the Thunderbird, where he fired a sizzling twelve-under-par 62 on the miniature golf course to humble the resident pro, Slammin' Sammy Schneid, who boggled at Bond's incredible curling birdie putt through the treacherous maze of Pepsi-Cola cans on the sixteenth green.

On a fateful Sunday night at Caesars Palace, fourteen distinguished men in Savile Row suitings of Phil Harris tweed clustered outside Bond's suite. They were the distraught owners of the Strip's major hotels and they'd been stung for a collective loss of seven hundred million dollars.

"Gentlemen." Mr. Tropicana opened the discussion. "This Bond guy has racked us up but good. What's to be done about it?"

"Nothing," said Mr. Sands. "I had my spotters watching Bond on the hidden TV over the Old Maid table. The son of a bitch plays like a maniac, like there's no tomorrow, but he's

---

[*] The world's most sophisticated card game. See *On The Secret Service of His Majesty, the Queen*, the third Israel Bond thriller. Its title earned me the commendation of "Honorary Homosexual."— S.W.

honest. Funny thing... every so often he looks off into space and mumbles, 'Sarah, Sarah!' over and over."

"Wonder where he got his original jackroll?" asked Mr. Aladdin. "He couldn't have run up seven hundred mil that fast without big front money. And I hear through the grapevine that he's even rejected an invitation to dine with Howard Hughes."

"I can answer that," put in Mr. Caesars Palace, inhaling his White Owl. "Before he came to Caesars Palace he'd made a killing on the market. When the Tall Texan at 1600 Pennsylvania Avenue gave a certain type of dessert his enthusiastic Good Whitehousekeeping Seal of Approval at a widely covered press conference, Bond, who'd been tipped that the endorsement was coming, moved fast, got his people at the Dreyfus Fund to corner fifty thousand shares of Minute Tapioca and came out five million smackers ahead."

"Who is he anyway?" said Mr. Sahara.

"He's allegedly a public relations man for Mother Margolies' Activated Old World Chicken Soup, the brand served in our Noshorium," said Mr. Caesars Palace. "But I got some friends in a hush-hush bureau in DC. to check him out. The PR job is a cover. He's really Israeli Secret Agent Oy Oy Seven."

"I don't give a damn who he is," scowled Mr. Tropicana. "Question is do we take our losses and get scourged by our respective stockholders or try to recoup by challenging him at Monopoly? I personally favor going for broke."

A fervent chorus of "Me, too" cinched the decision for Mr. Caesars Palace. "OK, gents." He stuck a finger into the buzzer. The door opened and Lobsang Rampapport, sleek and self-assured, bade them enter.

"Mr. Bond knows why you are here, sirs. The Monopoly board is set up; the deeds have been waxed with Esquire neutral shoe polish; the houses and hotels given fresh coats of Sherwin-Williams paint. However, he insists upon two preconditions."

"Which are?" said a suspicious Mr. Dunes.

"First, he wants to use the silver doggie as his mover. He has loved the little doggie since childhood."

"Now, wait a damn minute!" roared the reddening Mr. Flamingo. "He's got one helluva nerve! I, too, always use the little doggie. I love the little doggie and—"

With an annoyed sigh Mr. Caesars Palace trod heavily on the point of Mr. Flamingo's Corfam brogue. "Agreed. Bond uses the doggie. But I get the race car, huh, fellas?" In deference to his role as host boniface, the other hotelmen nodded their sullen assent. "And the second precondition?"

Lobsang exhaled a contrail of Raleigh smoke. "He demands that the game be representational; that is to say, the hotels on the board will represent actual Fabulous Las Vegas real estate. In short, your hotels, sirs."

The moguls froze into attitudes of blinking incredulity.

"*Gottenu!* What *chutzpah!*" cried Mr. Caesars Palace. "He's out to turn the Strip into his private game preserve. Well, gents, there are eight movers, counting his, which means if we agree to function as a consortium the odds are seven to one in our favor. I say let's take him on."

"Still wish I was using the little doggie, though," said a rueful Mr. Flamingo, flicking a salty rillet from the corner of an eye, but he followed his colleagues across the parlor-pink Du Pont 1002 carpet (twice the thickness of the 501, which was not deemed luxuriant enough for a suite as splendiferous as the Maximus Rabinowus) into Bond's bedchamber.

Their target lay in a chinchilla hammock, a soigné hot-orange pair of Foster Grants masking his eyes and a provocative Mary Quant-type minijock barely concealing his wondrous underhang, viewing on a Zenith color TV the third game in a pro football tripleheader, the Runnerup Bowl, which pitted the loser of the NFL-AFL Superbowl against the winner of the NFL-AFL Super Runnerup Bowl. On a screen a commentator in an Armour's porkpie hat was saying, "... really hitting out there, Red. You can't tell me these guys don't take postseason football seriously when we've already had three definite deaths and eight maimings. 'Course, we did have our little moment of hilarity when the rabbit ran across the field, so let's have an instant NBC TV replay of the furry little fella's antics. Ah, there he goes! Notice how Br'er Rabbit seems to slow up just long enough to make the field judge commit himself, then runs a deep post pattern between Commissioner Rozelle and Sandra Dee. Our statistician, Larry Allen, tells me it's the third time in a Runnerup Bowl that a white rabbit has interrupted play. Brown rabbits have done it twice, of course. Any comments, Red?"

Via split-screen technique the announcer was joined by the Gallopin' Ghost telecasting from the Goodyear blimp.

"Well, Lindsay, it's been exciting from up here. The one development that's come as a surprise to me has been the Philadelphia Eagles' usage of a seven-seven-eight pass defense."

"Course, that calls for twenty-two men, Red."

"Right! Oh, it's radical, no getting away from it, but darn effective. Murder on look-in passes, even when the look-in receiver has been guarded by a lookout. In general, though, I'd like to tell the fans what old 'Lonzo Stagg told me years ago: 'Red, keep your eyes on the field, 'cause in the long run that's where games are won or lost.'"

"Couldn't have said it better myself, Redhead. More pro action after this word from the all-new, all-charged-up Plymouth. Remember: *Plymouth is out to run you over this year....*"

"Mr. Bond, your opponents are here," announced Lobsang Rampapport.

Bond used his Zenith Space Command tuner to blow up the set, brushed a few burning shards from his sensual insteps and pulled himself into a sitting position. "I await your pleasure, gentlemen."

At 2:30 A.M. the impossible happend. Bond, on Connecticut Avenue and facing a staggering gauntlet of purple, orange and red properties, all with hotels, rolled his third consecutive boxcar to send him to the safety of JAIL for three turns, a throw that augured catastrophe for the Vegans. Mr. Desert Inn turned Rinso white as his snake-eyes deposited his top hat squarely on the Bond-owned, hotel-occupied Park Place and on the very next roll duplicated it to land on... Boardwalk! Then Mr. Stardust's racing car cruised to a CHANCE, his sweat-drenched fingers picked up the orange card and he came close to fainting as he read aloud its dictum: ADVANCE TO BOARDWALK.

It was all over; the consortium was bankrupt. "Quite by CHANCE," punned Mr. Caesars Palace in a noble display of wit in the face of utter defeat. One by one, the hotelmen walked over to Bond and piled the deeds to their empires in his hands.

"Vegas is yours, Mr. Bond," said Mr. Caesars Palace. "Those pieces of paper represent a few billion dollars in real estate, but they also mean thousands of jobs and the economy of an entire state. Keep Vegas humming, old man. As for me"—and Mr. Caesars Palace smiled bleakly—"it's back to selling National Shoes on Thursday nights and Saturdays until I can build up a stake big enough to take you on again."

Mr. Flamingo touched the victorious silver doggie to his lips. "Bye, little fella." His scalding tears dripped onto the Monopoly board, rusting out the Reading Railroad and short-circuiting Electric Company.

The crushed ex-owners had almost reached the corridor when Bond, his tone strained and husky, called out: "Take Vegas back! I don't want it. I want something else instead, something much bigger."

Mr. Sands spun on his heel, uncertainty and hope commingled in his expression. "What, Mr. Bond?"

Bond told them.

Mr. Caesars Palace disgustedly waved a pinky-ringed hand. "Forget it. Keep the damn hotels. Frank doesn't give private concerts in anybody's room at 3 in the morning."

"Wait!" Mr. Tropicana had grabbed Mr. Caesars Palace's lapels and aided by Mr. Aladdin was shoving him back into the suite. "You've got to ask him. Frank loves Vegas. He won't want to see his town go down the drain. Ask him, Mr. Caesars Palace, *ask* him..."

At 3 A.M. Caesars Palace exploded into mega-frenzy as the entertainment world's Chairman of the Board strolled through the main lobby, the sixty-piece Nelson Riddle orchestra at his heels.

At 3:05, the last warm-up A sounded, he held the hand-mike cockily and flashed a breezy grin at Bond and Lobsang. "Hi, Bonnie! How's your Clyde? We'll kick it off with 'My Kind Of Town,' segue into 'The Impossible Dream,' then..."

Bond's sensual jaw jutted out in belligerence. "You'll kick it off, *buddy boy*'—and the band quaked to hear someone laying down the law to the Chairman of the Board—"with 'Kick Out of You,' the exact arrangement from the *Songs for Young Lovers* LP; slide into 'What Makes the Sun Set?,' which I want done in *bossa nova* tempo; followed by 'There's No You,' 'The Music Stopped,' (Bond rattled off thirteen more titles) and take out the set with 'Strangers in the Night.'" He stretched out on the hammock, rolling the little silver doggie around in his palm, an unnatural brilliance illuminating his darkly handsome profile.

He's going to crack, Lobsang thought; *he's going to crack. And I know just when and I can't stop it.* Though all of her three eyes were now raining torrents, she got hold of herself long enough to snap off the thin neck of a vial of Schloofen-22, the Service's powerful sedative, and inject a hypodermic needle into the cloudy solution.

Her prediction came to pass at the expected moment, the coda of "Strangers in the Night," when the Chairman of the

Board poured all of his brash tenderness into the phrase "dooby dooby doo."

From the hand of Israel Bond erupted a rifle-like crack. He looked dumbly into his palm, flecked with bits of silver and blood. "Oh, Lord, look what I've done! I've crushed the little silver doggie to atoms. The doggie's dead... Sarah's dead... it's all wrong, all wrong... dooby dooby doo..." and buried his heaving face in Lobsang's creamy decolletage.

"You may go, sir," she said to the balladeer. "You have saved Las Vegas, but broken a man's heart." After the room was cleared, she found a blue tributary on Bond's inner arm, slid in the hypo... and he knew temporary peace.

"Aleph priority!" Lobsang's frantic signal got her through to M. immediately. "M., it's all over for him. He's a lachrymose vegetable. It would rend your wonderful heart to see his face cloaked in five-o'clock shadow, maybe even a quarter to six." (In Jerusalem, M. shuddered.) "And he's been going about like a slob in that scruffy Sea Isle cotton shirt and black loafers. That kind of getup is permissible for third-rate British agents, not for Oy Oy Seven...."

"Dry all your eyes, Lobsang, my child." Even over the transcontinental cable M.'s voice conveyed its curative effect. "And take one of my proverbs of universal understanding to guide you in your hour of need: 'A man may work from sun to sun, but a woman's work has been so simplified by modern appliances it's too ridiculous to discuss.' *Shalom*."

In the kitchen of the internationally renowned Ziggy's Restaurant, on Jerusalem's Bezalel Street, Mother Emma Esther Margolies —to the world, the creator of matchless chicken soup and philosophy; to a tiny coterie, M 33 and 1/3 of the Israeli Intelligence, M., Number One – ladled a pot of her Activated Old World Bessarabian Momma Ligga, the future of Oy Oy Seven weighing on her mind.

There were, to be sure, other pressing matters: the curious disappearance of the trawler, the resurgence of Nazism in Germany, threats from Egypt, Syria, Iran, and for some unexplained reason, Pitcairn Island, but the fate of Oy Oy Seven would be atop the agenda to be considered by Operations Chief Lazar Beame, her second in command; Z., the jocular, roly-polyish dead ringer for Harry Golden the tourists knew as restaurateur Ziggy Gershenfeld, and the new staff psychoanalyst, an American-

Jewish girl named Dr. Betty Freudan, whose book *Fulfill Yourself By Depriving Your Man* had caused a stir some years back. A gorgeous thing she was, too, M. thought. Why couldn't Oy Oy Seven fall for a girl like that instead of those empty-headed *shiksehs* who invariably brought him misery?

M. wasted no time as they filed in. "You should all look at the carbons of Neon Zion's report of Oy Oy Seven's first field assignment since that *gefailicheh*[*] New York business."

> TO: M.
> Subject: Oy Oy Seven
>
> *At 22:10 hours on June 5, 1967 I accompanied Oy Oy Seven to a point designated on Map Gimmel-200 as Vector Herbert, from whence Syria's border raiders, El Shikourim,[**] have been harassing our farms and water projects. From the first I noticed several anomalies in his appearance. His Hammacher Schlemmer trenchcoat, which was in need of a pressing, had a wilted carnation in the buttonhole. There were three rents in his faded Levi Strauss night-stalking commando Levi's, also unpressed, and—this I feel is important—he was not wearing any of his famous five hundred pairs of stylish bedsocks. In his Neiman-Marcus shoulder holster, whose stench indicated it had not been saddle-soaped for ages, was no weapon, but a moldy Hebrew National salami. We did not motor to the border in his Mercedes Ben-Gurion, which I am told he has not driven since his last adventure. We went by cab. He did not overtip or even tip the driver. Instead he started a petty, vociferous squabble over the fare. I cautioned him, "Be still, Mr. Bond. El Shikourim may hear us." He grew surly and withdrawn, pulled out a Polaroid photo of the Lawrence woman, looked at it and wept.*
>
> *At 22:59 we crossed the marshes, our heads under water, breathing by the old hollow reed technique. Occasionally Oy Oy Seven would stop to blow bubbles. He seemed to think it amusing. Fortunately, some*

---

[*] Terrible
[**] The Drinking Ones

braying donkeys on the Syrian side covered his puerile noises."

We lay in wait for El Shikourim about an hour under some scrub cacti and were rewarded by the sight of their red-bearded leader, Feisal Fullah-Sheik, a veteran terrorist suspected of killing several of our hydraulic engineers. During our vigil Oy Oy Seven had been drinking a very cheap, malodorous Turkish hair tonic (what a far cry from the glorious libations he ordered in the past!) and was disgustingly intoxicated. Instead of garroting the Syrian, he jumped up and shouted at the top of his lungs, "Feisal, baby! You wanna li'l taste?"

If his reason was absent, his storied luck was not. Feisal's mount, startled by the outburst, reared up and threw its rider headfirst into a wadi, where he incurred a broken neck. The other brigands, riding up to investigate the commotion, saw their leader expiring and fled in panic.

Oy Oy Seven examined the now dead Feisal and said, "I guess he got the point, eh, Zvi?"

This is the saddest part of my report. Of course, Zvi Gates, my predecessor as 113, licensed to wound, died in El Tiparillo two years ago. And the one-liner Mr. Bond threw at the corpse about getting "the point" would have been appropriate—if Feisal had been impaled by a harpoon gun or swordcane. It lacks relevance when applied to a broken neck.

My regretful conclusion: Israel Bond is no longer the world's most formidable secret agent, no longer the man I grew to worship in the Matzohball and Queen capers. Continuing him on as Oy Oy Seven would, I opine, jeopardize the entire operation of M 33 and 1/3 and his fellow agents and lower our prestige in global espionage circles.

Respectfully submitted,

—Neon Zion *(113)*

P.S. I want his Oy Oy Seven number.

A death ray from the planet Mongo could not have pierced the collective gloom, but Z. made a manful try. "The business about the bad joke young Zion puts so much emphasis on could be fixed, you know. Oy Oy Seven is mentally tired, that's all. The pressure of having to come up with a tremendous joke each time he kills has burned him out. A simple solution: We call up the William Morris show business agency in New York; they assign Jay Burton or Sheldon Keller to write Bond some fresh one-liners to cover any conceivable kind of death and—"

"That's no answer, Z, and you know it," snarled Op Chief Beame. "Neon's a nervy little *momser* asking for the world's most heralded license to kill, but he's right. Bond has had it. Hell, I've been puking at Rangemaster Rosenzweig's last few reports on Oy Oy Seven's shooting. He's been missing at three feet with a bazooka. The only thing he's hit in eight weeks is the late Rangemaster Rosenzweig."

A cluster of soup greens, which had been so crisp and lively, wilted at Beame's disclosure and fell with a disconsolate splash into a pot of chicken soup. M. pretended not to notice the mishap and said, "Dr. Freudan, may we hear the results of your psychiatric workup?"

The pert blonde crossed her splendid legs. "Before I recommended a Caesars Palace vacation for Oy Oy Seven I spent considerable time on his case. He is sound physically. The understandably severe injuries he suffered in the fall from the Empire State Building have healed in a satisfactory manner. However, he hallucinates whenever he has sexual intercourse. He sees the ghost of the veiled beauty, this Sarah Lawrence of Arabia he was to marry, standing over him, her accusatory eyes provoking great feelings of guilt."

M.'s withered face held a searching look. "How do you know he is physically sound, doctor?"

A blush stole over Dr. Freudan's cheeks. *Thank heaven I'm wearing an opaque skirt,* she thought. Her answer was a mite too defensive, she realized later. "I am a medical doctor as well, M., and I took it upon myself to examine Oy Oy Seven for any injuries that might be related to his mental state." *I couldn't help it,* her heart confessed. *There he was on the couch shivering so, the* poor dear, so I covered him with a blanket, which didn't help, then my coat, my clothes, me, and then that marvy musculature was doing insane things to me—not the sweet semi-rape women are supposed to enjoy and really loathe, but pure and lovely bruising, bashing barbarity with the right touch of Neanderthal, plus a hint of Ervin Laventhal. Oh, Iz, Iz, my shameless love for you is branded on my face and M., the dear, sweet old wise thing, knows it!

"You should do something about that burn on your face, Dr. Freudan," M. said with a cool, diagnostic smile. "An overdose of sun, hah? So, mine *tireh* doctor, what's to be done?" She, Z. and Beame awaited the summation that would close the door on the career of Israel Bond. From the damning evidence there could be no other verdict, it seemed.

Dr. Freudan lit a Raleigh. "In my researches into the qualities that make a secret agent the *rara avis*[*] that he is, I have learned one thing. When a secret agent appears to be down and out, unable to function in 'The Great Game,' it is a historical verity that he can be revived by the kind of intrigue and danger only to be found in Japan." *Oh, Iz, Iz, she grieved inside. I don't want to let you go, but it's the answer.*

Beame pounded his fist against the table. "You're crazier than Bond is. What the hell can Japan do for his breakdown? And why there? If you're thinking about putting him back into the field, let it be West Germany. Quiller didn't finish the job. Or Jordan. Let him knock off a few of these 'holy war in Palestine' nuts King Hussein can't control. Or let him check out a harebrained story I just received to the effect that our missing trawler was seen going through the Suez Canal."

"It's got to be Japan." Dr. Freudan stared the op chief down. "Japan."

It was in M.'s lap, as all major decisions were, and they knew it. M. had these famous bees in her peruke, among them an exaggerated faith in agents who believed in dressing to kill to kill, whose parents came from the Ukrainian *shtetl* of Baronevkeh. Would she allow her prejudices to becloud her usual sound judgment?

"I'll tell you something a person learns only when she's in my eight-and-a-half-double-E low-heel I. Millers," M. said. "The Shinbet and Mossad have been jealous of our little agency's status for years and have been trying to convince the PM that we're unnecessary and should be incorporated into their

---

[*] Or *rara hertz*. The usage depends on the latest ratings.

structure. One factor has kept M 33 and 1/3 autonomous—the incredible successes we've scored in the Loxfinger, Matzohball and Queen affairs, which have pulled our little nation from the abyss. And who, I should ask, is responsible for those successes? Oy Oy Seven, Israel Bond. If you all want to keep on picking up your paychecks you'll listen to me, *kinderlach*. So happens I agree with the good doctor."

Beame made a last stab. "Japan isn't even in our sphere of influence. There's nothing cooking for us in Japan."

M. clenched her gnarled fist and yelled, "Gnash! Gnash! Gnash! Gnash!"

"What's that supposed to mean?" asked Beame.

"I left mine teeth in a glass so it's the only way I can express my anger at your stupidity. If I know Oy Oy Seven, he'll start something cooking, don't worry. That lad could uncover suspense in a crate of lettuce. So it's settled. Z., you'll get Bond's friend in the CIA, Monroe Goshen, the fellow who got shot up in the Queen business, to send in Oy Oy Seven's behalf a nice letter of introduction to Baron Sanka, my counterpart in Tokyo. Beame, you'll prepare a white paper on the political situation in the Far East that Bond can use as reference material. I suggest you get in touch with the only truly knowledgeable people about that region, Sidney Toler or Warner Oland, who both played Charlie Chan. Dr. Freudan, you'll fly to Las Vegas and administer whatever therapy"—her tone was pointed—"he needs between now and departure time. Book him on Japan Air Lines, deluxe accommodations. A first-class killer should never fly tourist. And rehearse a hefty, hearty farewell for him at the airport. What is it the Japanese say? *Sy'n' Sarah*, no? My mind is made up. For the good of M 33 and 1/3, Eretz Israel and the whole profession of espionage, I decree: Send him to Japan!"

3
"Making Aove On Me—Fast! Fast!"

Somewhat dizzy from the bloodletting on the jet, Bond sagged against a wall of the Haneda Airport phone booth. "I got a bit of a break, Schlomo. Turns out that the Japan Air Lines purser who found me used to be the head surgeon at Kyoto General Hospital. He quit four days ago for the greater challenge of teaching Western air travelers the Japanese games of go and shogi. He rigged up a makeshift tubing by linking some soda straws and transfused me on the spot. Didn't have blood so he used Sacramento tomato juice. I can still hear the *plop, plop, plop* reverberating in my circulatory system."

On the other end, Schlomo Salvar, Bond's contact in the Israeli embassy, said, "I'd say it was *quite* a break, Oy Oy Seven. Damn glad to have you around. This idiocy concerning our trawler is causing repercussions. We've just been handed a stiff note from Count Iyama Pishaka of the Foreign Office. And the Sokka Datgai—that's the militant right-wing bunch—are threatening demonstrations against the 'warmongering Jews.' They've already burned down three USIS libraries."

"American libraries? Why?"

"We have none here. They've got to show their displeasure some way. Lucky thing you stopped that bogus monk or we'd also be liable for the loss of an eight-million-dollar jet, not to mention compensation to the passengers' relatives. One thing puzzles me. How did an Israeli ship ever sail blithely through Nasser's Big Ditch?"

"I don't know, Schlomo, but I do know our *Herr Doktor* is behind it. Keep Frequency Baze Tzaddik open at all times. I've got a Kral-Cain syncraphone hidden on me. *Shalom,* Schlomo."

The two-way beeper, no larger than an Alka-Seltzer tablet, was concealed in the false sixth toe of his right Tasmanian Devil bedsock, a pair of which he'd slipped on before deplaning. He'd also donned tight-fitting Sebring Pit-Stop slacks and put on a happi coat and face. Tucked into his right-hand pocket was a snub-nose Simon-Garfunkel, the six-shot persuader tooled for him by gunmaker Paul Bines of Universal Firearms Corporation, the American firm that long ago had made an arrangement to furnish M 33 and 1/3 the latest in small arms in exchange for Raleigh coupons.

"Roses are red, violets are blue..."

"Sugar is sweet, but it's a damn good thing he retired from the ring; the kids were beginning to knock his block off."

The coded salutation came from a chubby New York type in the front seat of a boxy black Cedric sedan idling near the taxi stand. Bond replied, "Hickory dickory dock... The mouse ran up the clock... The clock struck one... The mouse got hysterical... He's now in rehab."

"You're my man," grinned the driver. "It's good to look on a *poonim* with a little *taam* in it.* My name's Heshy Burg from Mosholu Parkway. Baron Sanka sent me to pick you up. Since I'm always hanging around the main drag, the locals call me Ginza-Burg. Get in. I'll stow your gear in the back."

Though the Japanese custom is to drive on the left, the loquacious Ginza-Burg kept for the most part to the right lane of the freeway to Tokyo, sending oncoming motorist after oncoming motorist swerving into poles and abutments. "Hot damn!" chortled the ex-Bronxite. "Betcha I've sent almost fifty of the little buggers to their honorable ancestors." When he saw Bond's frown, he added hastily, "'Course, the government tacitly encourages this practice. Country's bursting at the seams. They're damn grateful if you help thin out the masses now and then."

During the pell-mell jaunt Bond learned Ginza-Burg was a Jackie Mason Rabbinical Seminary student who'd ranked high in his Talmudic studies, but flunked the major courses, Nightclub Standup Comedy 1 and 2. Embittered, he'd come to Japan in search of an "indefinable something." What it was he found hard to define, he admitted to Bond.

Ginza-Burg left the freeway at the turnoff to the Assakissa section and sped through a network of narrow alleys, halting in

---

* A face with a little Jewish spirit

front of a two-story edifice at Ichiwada-ku, 4-chome, chrome-6. "We're here, Mr. Bond. Welcome to the Cathouse of the August Tea."

* * *

"Ichi! Ni! San!"

On *"san,"* Japanese for "three," the two men facing each other across the low lacquered black table unballed their right fists to reveal their choice of either one or two fingers in the age-old, intellectually demanding contest of odds-and-evens, played throughout the world and held in especial fondness by game-loving Orientals.

Each contestant jabbed out one finger.

"Evens!" An exultant cry escaped the throat of Baron Sanka, the chunky little man in the expensive *yukata* whose watercolor print depicted heroic kamikaze pilots diving their bomb-laden planes into West German camera and automobile factories. "Evens again, Izzy-san! My twelfth triumph in fifteen games."

Bond, sitting on a tatami mat in the cross-legged style of the East, knew he was playing badly. With just minimal concentration he might have been holding his own, perhaps even winning, because on Baron Sanka's playing hand there was only one finger.

To celebrate Sanka's win, the geisha Flowering Fungus let a hesitant smile play on her lips (her instinctive Eastern wisdom told her it was the correct anatomical location for such a display) and plucked a discordant tune from her six-stringed Selmer samisen, winning an approving *"Yo-I! Yo-I!"** from Sanka and the madam of the pleasure palace, a shrewd-faced old woman named Eating the Mango.

"It is a very mournful air, Izzy-san," remarked the Baron. "I shall translate as she sings." As Flowering Fungus chanted in a wavering basso profundo, Sanka said, "It is the story of a great samurai, Raykko, which in English means 'Lord of the Auto Seat Cover.' One spring day Raykko wanders into a small village, where he is greeted by the headman and his wife. They present Raykko with fish and rice cakes and bow low. Presented with this unexpected opportunity, he swings his sword and decapitates them. The headman's son, Sardo, offers Raykko green tea and Raykko responds by cutting the boy in twain. He goes into each hut and chops up the sleeping inhabitants. A party of children back from an outing to Fuji approach and trill

---

* Good! Good!

a gay song extolling the samurai's goodness. He runs amok and hacks them into mincemeat."

"I agree, Cocky," Bond said, using the diminutive form of Sanka's name. "It is a sad song."

"Oh, no, Izzy-san." Sanka registered mild shock. "To this point it has been a most jolly song, but now Flowering Fungus is singing the depressing part. Raykko looks about, but there is nobody left to kill. *Nobody.*" Was that a muffled sob from his host? "Think of it, my friend. Here is a warrior who has consecrated his life to the noble art of slaughter, and he stands there frustrated, no victims in sight. Oh, the final verse does tell us how he eviscerates a few cats, dogs and chickens, but it is just not the same."

The geisha's dirge was smothered by a raucous cacophony from an adjoining suite occupied by a group of American businessmen and the squawks of Billy Bones, a bleary-eyed parrot, who was the Cathouse of the August Tea's mascot: "Polly Adler wants a cracker—awk! Bless this house—awk! A Coorveh is not a Chevrolet—awk! Pieces of tail—awk!" *Friend parrot has been around,* Bond observed.

Eating the Mango showed her green and red waxed teeth in a smug grimace and chattered in Japanese to the Baron, who, laughed. *"Ah so des' ka!* Our honorable madam says the Yankees next door are complaining about her unreasonable price structure. She informs me she operates this house in accordance with a Western oil company slogan: 'You Expect More from American—And You Get It!' A droll comment, *hai?*"

"Dammit, Cocky!" The three Orientals were stunned as Bond brought his fist down on an irreplaceable Merciless Ming Dynasty vase, pulverizing it to smithereens. "Let's stop this hissing, bowing, *hai*ing, and *ahso*ing and get down to brass tacks. You know why I'm here. I want a piece of vital information from your organization so bad I can taste it, but I know damn well you won't give it to me until I prove my valor by locking horns with you in a battle of haiku poetry. That's the size of it, eh, Cocky?" Ashamed of his boorish tirade, Bond drove his fist into Eating the Mango's stomach in a sincere gesture of apology. At a sign from Sanka, Flowering Fungus bound Bond's mangled hand with cool mandarin orange peels, which possess blood-coagulating properties.

"Ah so des' ka, Izzy-san," said Sanka. "You have been boning up on our culture. Yes, haiku is the door to my confidence. As

you know, it is a unique form of poetic expression limited to seventeen syllables per verse. The only Western forms that have ever approached its feel, its nuances and shadings are the poems of Nick Kenny, in his Early Period, and the Burma-Shave rhymes so foolishly scorned by the Philistines of American belles lettres. Every Japanese, from the Emperor to the humblest *pachinko* ball polisher, is adept at haiku. Consider this verse by Karo, the seventeenth-century syrup manufacturer:

> *Only shrimp and eels*
> *can sate my hunger; O*
> *tempura! O morays!*

Does that not lift your heart, Izzy-san? No? Perhaps you would feel more at home with a contemporary haiku composed by the *baseboru* pitcher Masi Murakami, the only Japanese ever to have won a berth in the American big leagues, a bullpen job with the respected San Francisco Giants. Taste this instant of exquisite despair:

> *Woe! I hung a curve*
> *to Henry Aaron; they'll*
> *never find that mother!*

"Are you ready to enter the lists, Izzy-san?"

Bond's sensual nostrils fired a salvo of Raleigh smoke into a squadron of dragonflies on maneuvers around a lantern. One by one they fell dead into the courtyard pool. *Unleash your imagination, buddy boy,* he urged himself. *A good showing at haiku and Cocky-san will place his far-flung espionage network at your disposal. A bad one... well, don't even think about that.*

"Please accept this humble contribution to your art, Baron," Bond said and began to compose in a wobbly fashion.

> *"The gingko leaf, torn*
> *off by a breeze, falls, falls, falls,*
> *falls, falls, falls..."*

Gottenu! Fifteen syllables squandered and no meaningful resolution in sight. Think, Oy Oy Seven, think! A felicitous flash of creativity came to him and he had it.

"... and lands!"

Sanka's mouth widened; a mote of fear appeared in the hitherto unrelenting eyes. *Good-o! Time to press home the advantage!* Like a jaguar moving in for the kill, Bond hurled a second verse at his shaken host.

*"If 'seventeen' had
seventeen syllables, this
crap would be a snap!"*

"Superb!" breathed Sanka, applauding with his hand and finger. Bond stubbed out his Raleigh on the Baron's big toe. "Honesty compels me to admit the verse says nothing whatsoever "

"Then it is genuine haiku."

Emboldened by his successes, Bond chugalugged down a ten-gallon container of sake. "Here's a bonus, Cocky-san, a sensible Jewish rebuttal to an Anglo-Saxon's distorted viewpoint:

*You only live twice? Feh!
Fleming was wrong! You
only live until you die!"*

Sanka, though entranced by this *gaijin's* hidden fires, nevertheless said with mild severity, "It does not exactly fit the pattern. Your verse is eighteen syllables. But I find the logic incontestable. It would make an admirable book title."[*]

"Point of order, my dear Baron. What you just heard was a Hebraic form called *chai-ku,* the *chai* being our symbol for 'eighteen,' thus permitting the use of *eighteen* syllables. Now to business." Bond's cruelly handsome face assumed the animalistic look feared by his enemies on seven continents, five oceans and, by the latest Roper Poll, ninety-eight thousand lakes and forty-three thousand reservoirs.

"Where is Dr. Ernst Holzknicht?"

The sentence lashed the room like an Arctic wind.

"I would be happy to give you a map showing the locations of the Arab world's top-secret missile bases. Or a list of clandestine anti-Zionist groups being bankrolled by rightist Texan billionaires."

---

[*] I'll take it.—S.W.

"Where is Dr. Ernst Holzknicht?"

"Or Formula Pikadon Psi, our process for duplicating the Soviet's gigaton bomb at $39.95 per bomb. Or documents proving that the CIA is about to merge with the AFL-CIO."

"Where is Dr. Ernst Holzknicht?"

Baron Sanka looked away in chagrin and popped his thumb into his mouth.

"You don't know." Bond's words came out like leaden dumplings. "I broke my mental hump to master this haiku *narishkeit*,* and for what?" As quickly as it had come, the old-time combination of arrogance, tasteless humor and murder lust that had made Israel Bond the unparalleled engine of destruction he was faded away, and for a minute he lapsed into an embittered silence. "I knew this Japan mission was a sheer waste of time."

"I have dishonored our budding friendship. Flowering Fungus!" Sanka snapped a command and Bond saw the geisha blanch at the mention of a word—*seppuku*. She tiptoed to a closet and brought Sanka a huge sword.

"With this weapon," Sanka intoned, "I shall end my unworthy life. A simple crosscut from my left ankle to the right frontal lobe of my brain, then another from my navel to a spot precisely three inches above my left ear—"

"Stop!" Bond sent the sword flying out into the night with a backhanded swipe. There was a scream from the garden and a shout from one of the American businessmen: "Jesus! Somebody just killed Spotty Wassermann! Sixteen months I teach the *schmuck* to be a crackerjack Crackerjack salesman and he lets himself get bumped off by some gook."

Bond slammed the paper screen shut. "Suicide is no answer, Cocky. I want Holzknicht. I've told you about his handiwork, the murder of that sweet girl of yours on the plane, and though I can't prove it, it's drachmas to donuts he was behind that trawler deal. I want him. You're going to help me get him."

Sanka made a ceremonious bow. "I shall contact every single agent under my command, Izzy-san. However, there has been dishonor in this room tonight and only suicide can expunge its stain. Someone must die lest the gods be wrathful."

"You Japanese are really turned on by this suicide *shtick*, aren't you?"

"But of course. Dying is our way of life." Sanka wheeled suddenly, pointed a finger at Eating the Mango and Bond felt a

---

* Foolishness

chill pass through him. *Gottenu!* The Baron was giving the hag a death sentence and she was bearing it with the stoicism of her breed. She bowed low and walked into the garden to retrieve the sword.

Sanka, sensing Bond's distaste, said indifferently, "What does it matter? She is old. Now some entertainment of a robust nature far more gratifying to a *gaijin* than unappreciated wisps of poetry, *hai?* Flowering Fungus is yours tonight. Do with her as you wish."

A great honor, Bond thought. *He is offering me his personal geisha. I cannot accept out of common decency. He is, after all, my host. And she is a dog.*

"I cannot allow you to go to your *futon** alone, Baron. Are there others?"

"*Hai!*" Sanka clapped his meaty palms. "Send in the maidens!"

Through a side entrance undulated a river of pillow geishas, lithe and lissome, their eyes cast down in the charming modesty that befits a hooker. Bond's gray eyes cruised the line, then fixed on one who was tall, tan, young and lovely. "This one, Cocky-san."

She clasped her hands and bowed. "My name Ipanema."

Sanka leered. "You have chosen well, Izzy-san," he said and backed out of the room.

"You speak English, Ipanema?"

"Yiss. Spikking berry good Engrish."

Bond held the solemn, owl-eyed maiden to his breast. How weightless she was! "I'm so glad, my *goyischeh* geisha. I am a man touched by tragedy and only through such an encounter as we are about to experience can I feel the reawakening of spring. Can you appreciate the holiness of this moment in time?"

"Yiss. Spikking berry good Engrish."

She understands, she feels, his heart sang.

Her agile fingers unfastened his kimono, then hers, and they stood naked in a moonbeam. "You rooking at these hot cards, prease." She fanned out a deck of the notorious Yokohama Sex Shop playing cards, each illustrating one of the fifty-two positions of lovemaking. There was actually a fifty-third, the joker, which was quite unbelievable, he decided. *No man on earth could have deployed himself into that position. No six men!*

"You berry handsome man," she sighed, forcing him down upon a *futon* of indescribable softness, stuffed as it was with

---

* Sleeping mat.

the throat feathers of eunuch hummingbirds. Then, without warning, she held him at arm's length. "Before I roving you is matter to discussing. Money."

Bond's heart fell. "So this everlasting 'rove' is predicated on commerciality?"

"Ten thousand, fifteen thousand, maybe twenty thousand yen." She could hold back her welling tears no longer. "Prease say you making rove on me, Izzy-san. Twenty thousand yen all I got."

Now Bond was weeping himself, acceptable, manly tears of a low salt content. "You sweet kid. Of course I'll do it. And not for twenty thousand or even fifteen. Ten's plenty, plus forty-five percent of your take, OK, baby?"

"Yiss. Now making rove on me, fast, fast!"

Their flanks came together in a fiery collision and as they knew each other carnally, the evanescent spectre of Sarah stood over his shoulder, the doleful eyes proclaiming: *I forgive you again, Iz, my darling, but do try to keep this sort of activity at a reasonable level, won't you?*

4
Tag Day In Tokyo

He awoke to feel packets of thousand-yen notes thumping on his chest.

"Ipanema keeping her bargain, Izzy-san. As you sreeping I making many yen for you. Baron Sanka-san reaving this note."

It read: "I trust you are enjoying the favors of Ipanema. Later today I may have some news for you. Ginza-Burg waits below to drive you to the Tokyo Hilton—S."

In his Hilton suite an hour later Bond put the finishing touches on the questionnaire found in each folder of stationery. The usual pap: "Was your bellhop cheerful and courteous? Your chambermaid? The desk clerk? Were the meals tasty?" etc. After each query he wrote: "Disgusting," "Foul," "Swinish," and on the line designated for the guest's name scribbled a bold "Conrad Hilton." What a flap that would cause in the front office! Mass firings, morale problems, etc. Why was he engaging in this shabby cruelty so alien to his basic good nature? *Because you've been hurt*, answered his heart petulantly. *Now let somebody else, in this case a perfectly good, blameless hotel, know what suffering is!*

Sanka stopped by at 3 P.M. as Bond watched a Japanese salary man, the ubiquitous type in short-sleeved white shirt and black tie, step off the tenth-floor ledge of the adjacent Sanai-Flushai Building.

"*Gottenu!* Another suicide. Twelfth one I've witnessed since I checked in. Now, what was *his* terrible sin?"

Sanka shrugged. "Who knows? Perhaps he failed to obtain choice seats to the Kabuki for his employer. Or he might have knocked over the water cooler, which is unforgivable. At any rate, I have some information, Izzy-San."

Bond tensed, his long tapering fingers crushing a cast-iron water pitcher to paste in his anxiety. "Bravo, Cocky-san!"

"It is a small lead at best, but what is it you Westerners say— 'From little acorns come nutrition-starved oaks,' *hai?* One of my men, a fisherman named Nikko Tee-Yin, who possesses the well-known photographic mind, spotted a thug in the village of Shimonoshima, which is on Kyushu, our southernmost and warmest island. He cabled this morning that the man is a certain Skwato, a member of the despised midget people, the Pippu-Skweeku of northern Honshu."

"Why are they despised?"

"The majority of Japanese are short of stature. We must have somebody to look down to. The Pippu-Skweeku fill the bill ideally. Because of their size they make splendid undercover men. Our files show this particular one was a sub-subagent in Japan for the Terrorist Union for Suppressing Hebrews, which your evil doctor organized."

"Under what circumstances was he observed by your fisherman?"

"Skwato is attached to the retinue of a *gaijin*, a Danish archaeologist, Professor Igneous Feldspar, who has been carrying on some excavations in Shimonoshima. Feldspar has our blessing, of course, but we routinely plant a man among foreign visitors to assure that their enterprises are not inimical to our interests. Thus, Nikko Tee-Yin was assigned to the Feldspar party. Another fisherman more or less is never suspect in that territory. In the course of nosing about he came upon Skwato, who is helping the professor on his spelunking excursions into a labyrinth of caves even no Japanese has ever explored."

"This professor chap," said Bond, struggling to keep his demeanor bland. "What does he look like?"

Sanka heard Bond's hissing intake of air, saw the sensual lips pull back to expose the rich, red gums kept free of pyorrhea by five hundred Stim-U-Dent massages a day. He laughed. "I am way ahead of you, Izzy-san. You believe perhaps that Professor Feldspar and the hated Dr. Ernst Holzknicht are one and the same? I am sorry to disappoint you, but your description of Holzknicht as a man of medium height, with brown, 'almost sympathetic' eyes, close-cropped black hair and the large forehead of the scholar does not tally very well with this." He handed Bond a clipping from the Mainichi chain's English edition, banner-lined: THE GREAT DANE ARRIVES ON KYUSHU, SAYS

HE'LL DIG IT THE MOST! (*Cute line,* a jealous Bond thought.) Accompanying the lengthy article was a photograph taken at the airport in Beppu of a gigantic man with blond curls who must have stood at least seven feet and a sullen-eyed, thirtyish woman, lithe and leggy, whose fruitful charms burst every which way out of a topless hanky-kini. Bond knew that look, that of a woman sexually unfulfilled, who craved the bone-crushing foreplay, duringplay and let's-do-it-again-afterplay that only he, Israel Bond, could purvey.

"She is his wife, Magma, and they have been married just a short time. Their passports claim Danish citizenship and their credentials appear impeccable. But if you are willing to follow this slenderest of threads, Izzy-san, I shall be happy to accompany you to Kyushu, for by coincidence my next item of state business also takes me to the excavation site. In the same cable Nikko hinted that a discovery of the first rank has been made. On one of their expeditions deep into a cliff Feldspar and Skwato came across a series of scrolls, which Nikko overheard the former say are not inscribed in Japanese. Nikko asked the Dane to let him bring the scrolls to the surface, but Feldspar refused, claiming they have been hermetically sealed so long they might crumble to dust upon exposure to the elements. Nikko further said Feldspar and Skwato of late view him in a hostile light since it was presumptuous of a humble fisherman to make such a suggestion. It could be Nikko's cover is blown. Nevertheless, I want those scrolls in our government's hands. If they truly cannot be moved I shall have a portable Xerox machine brought to Shimonoshima and have them copied on the spot. Our next stop, Izzy-san, is the Xerox building, where"—the Baron's eyes danced—"a surprise awaits you. We go, *hai?*"

"Hai," Bond said. *Hell, this lingo was duck soup if a guy applied himself a bit.*

The Israeli handcuffed to his wrist an attache case prepared for him months ago by Lavi HaLavi, the quartermaster of M 33 and 1/3 whose brilliant devices so often had saved Bond from death. *Pauvre* Lavi, thought Bond in French, the language he often used in contemplative moods. *Pauvre* Lavi, under treatment *encore* in Foam Rubber Acres, the service's rest *chez* for disturbed personnel, after another of his periodic bouts with madness. Lavi's latest whackout had come during the Queen show and at present he lay in Galilee crooning fados, those soulful Portuguese songs of unrequited love, and scribbling equations far beyond human comprehension, then airmailing them to mysterious addresses all over the globe. Because of his condition, the little QM had been unable to service Bond with the usual battery of espionage gimmicks. "You will have to go it alone this time," M. had phoned. "Your main weapon will be your brains," which comment had made Op Chief Beame laugh himself sick for twenty minutes.

Ginza-Burg's Cedric was at the hotel entrance and rocketed away on another round of Burg vs. the Japanese people, the twelve-toned *thonk, thonk, thonk* of human anatomies against fenders conducted in Leonard Bernstein fashion by the lone finger on Sanka's right hand.

"I can't contain my curiosity, Cocky," Bond confessed. "How did you end up with one finger? Karate accident?"

Sanka passed Bond a Hi-Lite cigarette. "This finger is the survivor of a rather painful episode dating back to World War Two."

"And what did you do in the great war, Daddy-san? Lead some bugle-blowing, doped-up banzai wave against the Yanks on Bataan?"

"Alas, no, Izzy-san. How worthy that would have been! I was far from the site of glorious carnage when hostilities broke out. Because of my proficiency in English I was placed in intelligence."

"I notice you have no problem with the letter *l*, which so many Japanese convert into *r*, as in the phrase rots of ruck.'"

"I am aware of the joke," Sanka said wryly. "It is *hirarious*. No, Izzy-san, the *l* is quite manageable. Hist! L-l-l-inda, l-l-l-ovely, l-l-l-ascivious, l-l-l-o-l-l-l-ipop. It is the *r* I sometimes have weal twouble pwonouncing. To continue, when the decision to bomb Pearl Harbor was made, I was a student at UCLA. As you know, all Japanese went to UCLA. During my stay there the student body consisted of 99.9 percent Japanese—all in intelligence and working in disguise as gardeners—and Jackie Robinson and Kenny Washington. After the attack, the FBI struck with frightening speed, interning every son of Dai Nippon save me."

"Why not you?"

"A great piece of luck. It so happened I was the house gardener of a film-studio press agent named Seymour Feig."

"Sy? Hey, he's an old buddy of mine."

"So? Well, Mr. Feig knew the authorities were coming for me so he negotiated a fast deal. I would be free in his custody if I agreed to play a series of spitting, gold-toothed Japanese villains in his company's war movies. I had no choice. It was that or spending years in a barbed-wire enclosure in the desert. Knocking out my teeth and replacing them with gold dentures, I tackled the job diligently, albeit it was simplified by the screenwriters, who gave me one line in each film: 'Fright Rootenant Armstrong, you 'Melican pig! Where is your aircraft carrier?' which I spoke to Van Johnson in *Rip the Nip!*, *Take That, Tojo!*, *Slap the Jap!* and similar extravaganzas. I was bayoneted by Van Johnson, strangled by Van Johnson, pushed into a pit of cobras by Van Johnson and in one film lost four fingers on this hand when an alleged dummy grenade went off. To this day, although I realize he is a most worthy thespian and was only following the scripts, *I hate Van Johnson.*" The Baron's eyes were coals of fury. "Of course," Sanka added in a mitigating manner, "I hold no such dislike for Humphrey Bogart, who, as you know, did the bulk of his fighting in the European theater."

"You'll pardon my interruption of an intriguing narrative, Baron Sanka, but we're being tagged by someone who picked us up near the VIP Bar near Tokyo Tower."

"So?" said Sanka; a polite way of saying, "Pooh-pooh," Bond knew.

Bond pointed to Ginza-Burg's rear-view mirror. "Pink-and-orange two-seater, Kyushu license plates. Looks like a '67 Sony, one of those combination TV-set-and-car jobs I've seen around town. I see you're amused. This'll amuse you even more. It has no driver."

"But this is not possible, my impetuous friend." When Bond told him to see for himself, he said, "*Hai,* you are correct. Take a right turn at Tiger Tanaka Boulevard, Ginza-Burg, and we shall see if the tag stays on us."

"If we're being tagged by an agent being run by an adverse control," Bond said coolly, "we can do one of several things. One, we can lead the tag to a phony vector point. Two, we can get out of the car and make him tag us on foot. Three, we can flush and challenge him. Four, we can leave him unflushed and unchallenged, somehow contrive to get on *his* tail and tag *him*, hoping he'll lead us to his base. Five, we can lead him to a 'safe house,' 'mike' it, find out if he's working through a 'cutout' or a mailbox drop,' flush the 'cutout' and let the tag continue, unaware of the switch. Six, we can lead him into a waterfront dive, where he can do a one-and-a-half gainer."

"What the hell are you talking about?" yelled Sanka.

"That's real espionage patois," said a sheepish Bond. "I don't know what it means, either, but I thought the possibilities were worth exploring."

Ginza-Burg was on Tanaka Boulevard now, rolling past *sushi* shops, suntory bars and the Loew's Mikado, which was double-billing *Marat/Sato* and the prize-winning documentary *Hiroshima: Unspeakable Act of War or New Concept of Instant Urban Redevelopment?*

"The car is still with us," Sanka said. "Stop, Ginza-Burg."

The chauffeur braked the Cedric in front of a slanted-roof shrine dedicated to Frito, the ancient, beloved god of the corn chip. Bond looked back to find that the Sony also had halted, about a hundred feet behind. He lit a Raleigh and made a great show of relaxation designed to make their tag think they'd stopped for some social purpose.

Then his panther's body uncoiled, the pile-driver shoulders hit the side door, driving it off its hinges, and Bond was diving onto the bonnet of the Sony, his Simon-Garfunkel out and slamming its staccato *protest! protest! protest!* into the windscreen. The tiny auto was in reverse now, its wheels screaming under the burden of Bond's weight. *Dammit! Where was the driver?*

Gottenu! A gout of flame whizzed out from somewhere in the vehicle and—*thwack*—a slug lacerated its way through his happi coat into his right shoulder. He fell off the bonnet face down into the street, his enriched type-A claret spurting over the asphalt. Some drops seeped into a crack; a wayward seed was fertilized; a bunch of chrysanthemums popped up and grew to a foot in height.

Sanka and Ginza-Burg were out of the Cedric, the former shaking a futile finger at the disappearing Sony, the latter pulling Bond to his feet. *"Gevaldt!* You've been hit."

"Not really," Bond said mordantly. "The scab from my smallpox shot came off, that's all."

"You were right, Izzy-san," said a crestfallen Sanka. "I have been guilty of underestimating these people, whoever they are. What gall! Shadowing the Number One of the Japanese Secret Service in his own bailiwick!" He stammered the worst thing a Japanese can say about his own negligence. *"Shimatta!"*[*]

Bond's rejoinder was surly. *"No-shitta!"*[**]

---

[*] I have made a gross blunder.
[**] You certainly have!

Score another one for the "oppo"!

5
"Forget About the Black Room!"

In the Nisei N' Nefu restaurant, one of countless little establishments tucked away in the basement arcades that crisscross the Xerox Building, Sanka purchased enough mandarin orange peels to staunch Bond's newest wound. The Israeli, eager to try his hand at ordering native delicacies, took the restaurant owner out to the front window, which like so many Tokyo eateries contained plastic representations of the bill of fare, and leafing through *Instant Japanese,* the little booklet of basic terminology, pointed to *"this-su," "this-su"* and *"that-tu,"* his facile performance in the difficult tongue earning the man's respect. When they'd finished the repast, Bond rubbed his tummy. "I've been around, Baron, but I must admit I've never eaten better plastic."

They washed it down with frosty mugs of the soft drink preferred by 95 percent of Japan's parliament, Diet-Rite Cola, and took the elevator to the executive chambers of Xerox on the twentieth floor. Bond, a Raleigh between his sensual lips, mentally shredded the report he'd planned to send Mother Margolies' Activated Old World Products—or MOMAR, its cable designation. "I was shot up by a Buddhist bonze and a driverless car." How Neon, that cheeky little *putz,* would hoot at that one! "I told you Bond has gone crackers," he could hear Neon saying to M.— Neon Zion, whose life Bond twice had saved, and now the ungrateful punk was hungering for the Oy Oy Seven number, according to Betty Freudan, who'd leaked Bond the scam on the Jerusalem powwow. No, it would be far more sensible to inform the home office things were proceeding well and that he was Kyushu bound to track down a promising lead.

At the entrance to the Xerox suite Sanka winked. "That little surprise I mentioned waits inside, Izzy-san. But no matter what transpires, bring out that portable Xerox."

Bond's fist rocked the oaken door of the head Researchers suite, emblazoned with the Xerox motto: LET THE EMPLOYEES AT IBM THINK; YOU COPY.

A furry voice that sent desire pulsating through his lithe, muscular body said, "Come in."

She was bending over a worktable, her full lips pouting, her dazzling abel-green eyes poring over a complicated equation of five-dimensional multilinear galactic values arranged in conical plexigons of a base-ten, submicronite unit. Around her neck hung the silver chain and plunger that identified her as one of the ten members of MIT's most select scientific honor fraternity, Alta Zeyda Kapplan, which scorns any IQ under 355. The AZK frat-soror house, which carried out a humanitarian program of helping the handicapped, employed Mensa people as janitors and kitchen help, Bond knew.

The chain-and-plunger insignia was her lone concession to conventional garb. The rest of her was stark naked.

She did not appear in the least flustered by the gray eyes that toured her loosely coiffed ebony tresses, swan neck, muskmelon mammaries, awesome nether structure and rose-pink toes. *Gottenu! If the Japan Travel Bureau could guarantee regular tours like this, Europe would be deserted at the height of the season,* Bond thought.

"You must be the Mr. Bond the Baron telephoned about," she said in that provocative huskiness. "I am the head researcher here. My name is Kopy Katz."

Touché! Bond thought. How apt a name for a Xerox intellectual! What a specimen, the likes of which he'd never seen! And yet, would it do to start a love affair in a heart still haunted by Sarah?

"I'm no good for you." Bond said. "I'll take you, use you like a hot scented *oshibori* towel, then toss you into the wastebasket of broken dreams. You're looking at a man who has lost the capacity to love. I tell you all this because I possess ESP—Extra-Sexual Perception—and it's obvious to me you're longing to be violated."

"Maybe I am, maybe I'm not, Mr. Bond. Yes, I confess a sort of detached scientific interest in certain portions of your compelling body, but as for giving myself to a man I've known for less than thirty seconds, well..." Her speech ended on a brittle laugh.

Bond's right hand bludgeoned her face, leaving an angry five-fingered fan. "You bitches are all alike. You all want the little preliminaries to the game of love, don't you? Flowers, two-buck boxes of Whitman Samplers that I get at Korvette's for $1.59, friendship rings, juvenile kisses stolen on hayrides. Well, *ketzeleh*"—his cruelly handsome face stiffened, the last of him to do so—"here's a demonstration of what I can do for you, my insouciant Miss Kopy Katz. Take it or leave it."

Growling, he unlocked the attaché case from his wrist, removed the rolled-up movie screen and the alarm-clock-size projector, set them up and killed the lights. He sat back, crossed his legs and lit a Raleigh.

"THIS IS ISRAEL BOND" flashed on the screen, followed by an imaginative set of pop-art titles designed by Saul Bass, with scoring by Mancini. For the next five minutes the real scoring was Israel Bond's. The crisp narration by Doodles Weaver began:

"This is the story of Israel Bond, a man among men. Let's let vivacious Pennsylvania matron Charlene Krosnick, who often slips away from her husband and children to find unequaled bliss in Bond's arms, tell us part of it."

There was Charlene nibbling at his ear in his luxury suite in Manhattan's Ansonia Hotel. "Iz, Iz, Iz!" *Good opening sequence,* he thought. *Charlene always was an enthusiastic sort. Ah, a superbly executed Balinese three-quarter-angle stroke had made her swoon. Hope* that *melts the Mendenhall glacier in your innards, Miss Katz!*

Narrator: "And now a Catskill Mountain moment of madness..."

Mancini's musical mood was meringue; the love object Poontang Plenty; the place the Kahn-Tiki Hotel in Loch Sheldrake, New York. "Iz, Iz, Iz!" Watching Poontang's Revlon-tinted nails rip the heavy-duty Wilton carpet to tatters, he felt a pang echoing from the long ago. *Poontang, my sweet, lost love. Poontang...*

"Big-city love takes a back seat now to the kind o' down-home carryin' on in Amurrica's Midwest, as Omaha's cute-as-a-cornflower Katie Winters shows you in this silo scene." A square dance set the stage; the snub-nosed brunette snuggled on his shoulder. "Shucks, Iz. I've got a cool secret. I love yuh." *Dear little Katie Winters! If only she hadn't perspired so much.* The film rolled on.... Anna Annatefkeh, the voluptuous KGB killer in the spine-tingling Matzohball adventure, taken in *kazotsky* rhythm...

Liana Vine, his Trenton, New Jersey, high school sweetheart, succumbing to a *freilach*... Rowena Rosenthal, the teen-age "New Left" activist, joining him in a freakout to a Bob Dylan medley on a blanket made of *Ramparts* magazine covers (restless, restless Rowena! When the civil rights and peace movements had lost their spice for her, she'd moved to Mr. Rogers' neighborhood)... dozens of altar Bunnies yielding to him at Chicago's recently organized First Church of Hefner, Hedonist, under a stained-glass window depicting a frail, pipe-smoking man nailed to a circular bed: HE SWUNG TO MAKE US FREE... and, inevitably, Bond's conquest of Sarah Lawrence of Arabia on the moon-bathed dune. *Sarah, Sarah, my one true love...*

"Stop it! Stop it!" Kopy Katz's screams lancinated his eardrums.

He cut the film at the closing credit— PRODUCED BY R-K-OY PICTURES—and saw her sway against her desk. "I—I seem to sense the inchoate stirrings of a preorgasmic flush, Mr. Bond."

And he knew he had her on the ropes, helpless to ward off any onslaught. But wait! That mumbo jumbo she'd mouthed. Typical Masters-Johnson *Human Sexual Response* stuff. Of course! That was the key to copping a fast copulation from Kopy Katz, woman of science. He would woo her in her own frame of reference.

"Observe, Miss Katz," he said clinically. "My tumescence has become functional."

"Quite so, Mr. Bond," and her eyes confirmed his claim. "I myself have achieved a more than adequate state of lubricity accompanied by a pronounced vascocongestive increase in labial locations."

"Which would seem to call for immediate insertion of tumescence, Miss Katz."

"I should think so, yes, Mr. Bond. And please employ concomitant prestidigitation at crucial mons and clitoral checkpoints. Please."

They began a surging thrust that swept them rapidly past several preliminary plateau phases, the researcher moaning, "Manifest psychogenic reaction noted."

"Envelopment firm; friction mounting; all stimulative systems green," Bond reported.

"Oh, Mr. Bond! It behooves me to inform you that I'm veering at breakneck speed toward the arrival plateau. Oh, Iz, I'm arriving, arriving, arriving...."

"Quick! Join me in the Masters-Johnson cheer: Go, go, gonads! Go, go, gonads!"

But further jargon was unnecessary, for now his body was steering hers into the outer reaches of the universe, and she abandoned all diffidence and hotly whispered obscene spatial calculus into his ears during a "big bang" climax that melted innumerable Mars bars and intimidated Saturn into pawning four of its rings.

His own fulfillment was marred ever so slightly by the vision over his shoulder, who spoke through a tear-soaked veil. *Oh, Iz. You've been unfaithful again.*

I know, dearest, answered his cheating heart. *But I'm a man with a man's needs.*

"Iz." This voice was earthly. Kopy's. "I love you. But I ask no guarantees. Love me as long as you wish; then, if it pleases you, chuck me into that wastebasket."

Bond inhaled a Raleigh. "You think that portable doohickey can give us a clean reproduction of the scrolls?"

A lightning bolt fulminated out of the abel-green eyes. "You're damn tootin', buster! Xerox can copy anything, anything!"

Oh-oh. He'd hit a nerve ending there. Miss Katz appeared to be a real 150 percent, rah-rah "company" gal all the way.

"I see you don't believe me," she fumed. "Well, for your info, I've a project in a secret lab up here called the 'Black Room' where—" She bit her lip.

"What about the 'Black Room'?"

"Forget it, buster." Three word icicles. "Forget you ever heard me mention the 'Black Room.' Now, pick up that portable in the corner and let's get cracking."

6
Night of Treemandous Terror

Deep in thought and Kopy, Bond, inhaling his 1,006th Raleigh of the day, lay in a compartment on the 150-mph blue-and-cream *Bullet,* the super-express train which has made Japan the talk of the transportation industry. Destination: Beppu, the place of the geysers, via Osaka, Kobe and the Inland Sea.

There'd been a piffling matter to dispose of before he'd checked out of the Hilton, a phone call from, of all people, blond, willowy Liana Vine, half a world away.

"Iz, darling. I've just been married here in Trenton at your brother Milton's catering house, the Pinochle Royale. I didn't want you to find out from anyone else."

"Who is he?" Bond had bellowed.

"A nice Jewish fella, Sidney Glumpkin. Owns a phylactery factory in the Williamsburg section of Brooklyn. I met him at the Concord on a ski weekend."

"Well, *slalom aleichem,*" Bond said rather nastily.

"Oh, Iz, don't take it that way, please. I was so lonely and I've waited two decades for your marriage proposal. I'm way past thirty, Iz. I need someone. There'll never be another you, especially at night, but..." Liana's voice dropped. He could hear the band striking up *Shereleh,* the vibrant wedding dance, disheartening proof that she indeed had taken the vows of a Jewish wife.

"And, Iz, I've long suspected you're some kind of a secret agent. So do your brothers, Milt and Rag Bond. Be careful, darling, please."

"Now, you listen to me, Liana. You've just done a sneaky little thing behind my back, but if you're married, you're married—that's it. However, I want you to swear you won't let this bumpkin or Glumpkin or whatever his name is touch you for a year. I'll know if you've lied to me, baby. The sin will eat through your face like leprosy. If at the end of the year you haven't heard from me, consummate the marriage with my blessings and name all the children after me. Israelita will do fine for the girl." She complied and he was appeased. "Now, put Glumpkin on. Sidney? You've just heard Liana's sacred pledge. Don't touch her, understand? Anyway, you'd be a fool to try and match the sexual pleasure I've been giving her all these years." He spent five minutes describing it in substantive detail to the groom. "And if I decide to marry her, you'll pay for the divorce, plus long-term alimony, right? Good. You sound like a decent clod, Glumpkin. Now go enjoy your married life." He hung up, proud of his equitable handling of the Liana situation.

But there were more important problems, anyway. That driverless-car business. Was it the beginning of a round of shadowings and attempts at assassination? If so, who was the target, Sanka or himself? Did the "oppo" know he was in Japan on a vengeful odyssey? This Danish egghead Feldspar—was he legit? Maybe, but why enlist the talents of a confirmed *pascudnyak* like Skwato? Or was Skwato using the professor as a cover for a new TUSH assault even more sinister than "Operation Alienation," which had decimated Israel's Secret Service and razed Mother's factory in Tel Aviv? Was Holzknicht in Japan or pulling the strings from long range? Questions, questions. Even this sweet kid in his arms had her secrets. That cryptic reference about the 'Black Room'... what was it all about?

There was a screech and Bond sailed headlong into a steel wall. "What the hell..."

Sanka strolled into his compartment and pressed a mandarin orange peel onto the knot mushrooming on Bond's temple. "Someone has jumped in front of the *Bullet*, Izzy-san, a common occurrence on this run. Some three million people per annum choose the railroads as their method of self-destruction. Not everyone has the stamina to climb up a volcano, you see."

"Suicide, suicide, suicide," Bond sighed.

"As I said previously, it is the time-honored way of expiating disgrace, and the more ingenious the suicide the more honor accrues to the victim's family. Here"—and the Baron handed Bond a newspaper. "This is the English edition of the Asahi chain. One of its most widely read features is the daily column of the witty Suicide Suzuki."

Surrounded by type was a half-column photo of one of the merriest faces Bond had ever beheld.

> *Hi, neighbor* [Bond read]. *Here's old SS on the neat, all-reet Death Beat! Hariko Harumi, the Sofia University dropout, also became a* dropoff *today—from the top of the Dream Center. Old hat, Hariko; wish I could say you've a second chance.... Yoshio Dai-Ichi is getting his kicks on the River Styx, and well-deserved ones, too, 'cause his departure was a thing of beauty. He went to Haneda and walked into a jet taxiing toward the terminal. Yup, it's the best when you die Northwest!... And let's hear it for Kono Yamato, who, having failed twice to cut out from this scene, finally worked it by cutting out himself. He flung himself under one of those machines at the Toyopet auto factory that stamps out parts from sheet metal. So, death wishers, if the grill of your next car has an extra-big grin, that's Kono....*

Death, death, death. Japan was a veritable discount house of it. Would his own sensual body be added to the pile before this caper was through?

He lounged on the *futon* and expelled a perfect smoke ring from his sensual lips, lined out two jets from his nostrils which crossed in midair to form an X, and watched the O and X float upward, the O taking a clear lead until it settled into the center of a ticktacktoe board he'd etched in the fluffy dust of the ceiling. Three O's across, game and set!

They had put up (and out) for the night at a Beppu *ryokan*, the type of inn where one sleeps on the floor of a sparsely furnished room. Kopy slumbered soundly, her arms locked in a protective, maternal way around the portable Xerox. Sanka had not seemed surprised that he and Kopy were sharing digs. "In Japan we do not yet possess your guilt concerning the cohabitation of unmarried people. We also place no stigma upon nudity, which is why Miss Katz feels free to walk our streets *au naturel*. Good night, my friend," and he'd retired to an adjoining room.

Bond extinguished his Raleigh in a porcelain bowl housing a delicate *ikebana* flower arrangement. A cunning breeze brought a shy daisy in contact with a randy azalea and he decorously looked away, though his ears caught the latter's imploring "I'm half crazy all for the love of you."

For a while he read the Good Book, then closed it midway through the story of Daniel. Tough spot that Daniel was in; Bond hoped he'd get out of that lion's den. Of course, if it had been written today Daniel would have a den mother in there with him. A wonderful book, the Bible. He read it every night—religiously.

There was a restiveness in him that precluded sleep. It was useless to fight that kind of feeling, so he opened the screen further and gazed into the garden with its oddly colored rocks, dwarf trees and a streamlet burbling its happiness at being alive and wet to the sultry full moon. As he tightened his lips around a Raleigh and scratched a blue-tipped Ohio match on the candy crystal of his Necco watch, the flare picked up a shadow.

One of the dwarf trees was moving.

He flipped the Raleigh away, cursing. Goddam cigarette was producing optical illusions now!

No, by thunder, the tree *was* moving!

There was a faint rustling as it picked its way past its partners, sidestepping rocks hither and thither, and then it braced and broad-jumped over the streamlet.

Bond's heart skipped a beat, then a whole twelve bars, for a sliver of moonlight illuminated something brandished by one of the fronds. *Gottenu!* A sugarcane bolo!

Across the garden toward the *ryokan* padded the tree, its steps almost inaudible on the thick tufts of gunter grass. Bond concealed himself in floor-length drapes, his incredulous gray eyes on the leafy stalker all the way. It brushed past him; he could smell the biting essence of its blossoms. Now it was poised outside the screen to Sanka's room.

Another fingery frond eased the screen along its track until it was almost completely open. The bolo was lifted high.

"Cocky! For God's sake, get up!"

There was a scream as the bolo sliced down, but Bond was already diving against the base of the trunk. His right shoulder bulled into the corrugated folds of the bark and he felt them cruelly abrade his flesh. His flying block drove the tree through a paper wall into another room and through the gash he could see its inhabitants spilled over the low tables. Sanka, his face contorted, was trying to stem with his finger a cascade of blood from a slash on his left shoulder that had laid it open to the bone. And now he was retreating in fear, for the dwarf tree was hurtling back, bolo cocked for the final coup.

Bond shouted another warning. "Cocky, duck!"

The bolo buzzed over Sanka's head like a giant gnat and Bond could hear a string of curses from somewhere inside the tree. *Gottenu!* How in heaven was he going to stop a rampaging killer tree?

The answer was on the wall, a glass partition containing a fire extinguisher and an ax. He hammered his fist into the case, wincing as the splinters bit into his knuckles, but he tugged the ax from its rack and swung it in a sweeping arc, grunting in satisfaction as its flat side caught the center of the dwarf tree in a crippling smash. There was a muffled cry; the tree spun around and lunged onto him and teeth were worrying at his shoulder, but the bites were feeble and did not pierce. Bond's left foot lanced out in a Pone Kingpetch kick, again catching the tree squarely in its middle, and he backed off, turned the ax around to expose the cutting edge and let go with the smooth, flat swing that he'd once used to fell a Sequoia. The edge bit in and the scream was a blood-curdling thing that trailed far out into the night. The tree split neatly in twain, a bloodbath burst through the bark and the halves lay still.

"Iz!" Kopy, pale as an uncoated Creamsicle, rolled into the Baron's room on rubber legs, stared at the ghastly remains at Bond's feet and swooned. He let her slide softly to the tatami mat.

"I need a doctor, Izzy-san. Badly."

Bond's alert eyes told him Sanka would bleed to death if not tended to posthaste. *Gottenu!* His kingdom for a tube of the cherry salve that could halt the flow in a second! Or a dozen mandarin orange peels!

Wait! The old Celanese tobacco trick taught to him by Sir Hu Wu Wu Herbert, the head of Ceylon's secret service; would it work on such a grievous wound?

He dashed to his room and took a carton of Raleighs from his luggage and a bullet from the chamber of his Simon-Garfunkel.

"Cocky, bite hard on this," he snapped, inserting the slug between the Baron's gold teeth.

"How will biting on the bullet help?"

"You always bite on a bullet when someone's dressing your wound. It's tradition. Besides, if you swallow it, it makes excellent roughage, I daresay."

Bond field-stripped two hundred cigarettes and jammed the tobacco into the raw fissure, tamping it down with the ax handle. Sanka grimaced several times but bore the ordeal with the courage of his race.

The gushing slowed to a trickle, then stopped.

They exchanged smiles, two spymasters who genuinely appreciated each other's manliness in the face of peril.

Bond let go a sigh as he first began to feel the injury he himself had incurred when his shoulder rammed the abrasive covering on the dwarf tree. "I'll say this." He grinned. "His bark was worse than his bite." *(Great one-liner, his brain told him. You're not ready for the trash heap yet, my friend!)*

Sanka was on his knees beside the tree halves, his nimble finger stripping away the husk and fronds. "I regret I did not have the presence of mind to say, 'Landsman, spare that tree!' Izzy-san. We might have learned something important if we'd kept it alive." He gave a low whistle. "By the belly of Buddha! Look what lurked under this camouflage!"

It was the severed body of a man, which, if joined, could have been no more than two feet tall. Even in the rictus of death the teeth continued to grind in the slavering mouth; the eyes remained pools of unspeakable ferocity.

"Without doubt, Izzy-san"—and Sanka's nose wrinkled in disgust—"this ugly little night crawler is the thug described by Nikko Tee-Yin. Yes, my *gaijin* friend, you are looking at Skwato."

7
Fisherman Overboard!

Sanka, fully revivified, set upon the trail of the marauder, his keen eyes questing over the garden, picking up a telltale spot of crushed grass here, a bent twig there. "There is an old saying by a sixteenth-century animal tracker: 'It is easier to follow the spoor of a lion than that of a flea.'"

Bond nodded in acknowledgment of the wisdom, which came close to equaling M.'s.

A mile down the road parked under a banyan tree was the Sony. Bond plucked a banyana from a low-hanging branch, peeled off its yellow skin and munched away while Sanka conjectured.

"Now we know why we could not see the driver, Izzy-san. Skwato was so short he operated the vehicle from under the windscreen. If I am not mistaken there is some sort of periscopic device which enabled him to see the roadway and an aperture through which he put that bullet into you. The dwarf tree disguise is an old Pippu-Skweeku one for practicing the art of a *ninja* or a 'stealer-in' to commit murder. Other members of his clan have hidden themselves in umbrella stands and bowling bags. He probably shadowed us to Tokyo Station, learned our destination and drove to the Inland Sea, where he brought his car over by ferry, perhaps the very one we used."

"One thing disturbs me, Cocky. His target was you. Someone does not wish your presence at Shimonoshima. Feldspar?"

"Who knows? Let us waste no time in finding out."

On the 175-kilometer junket to Shimonoshima by rented limousine, Sanka was meditative. In the back seat, Kopy, still unnerved by the bizarre, bloody incident, held Bond to her heart.

"Iz, I've a feeling you're an Israeli secret agent. I know what Sanka's profession is and if you're chummy with him you're in the same game. Oh, angel, I came so close to losing you. A man like you has his head on the chopping block every second of his life. Maybe the next time you won't be so lucky. If I ever get you back to Tokyo alive... the 'Black Room'... yes, the 'Black Room.'"

He saw she had been wrestling with a monumental decision and patently had made it.

The air became rarefied as the vehicle climbed the road winding around a range of cliffs, rumbled through jungle terrain and past exploding *jigoku,* the "hells," which sprayed a gaudy variety of colored boiling plumes into the mist from the nearby sea. At the top of the tallest cliff they came upon a sprawling tent city, the headquarters of the Feldspar expedition, Bond presumed. They made a bumpy stop near the largest tent. "Feldspar-san," the driver said.

A massive hand covered with golden hair pushed aside a flap and the seven-foot Igneous Feldspar, ducking his head so he could ease himself out, emerged and wobbled toward them on giraffe legs.

"My dear Baron Sanka." His hand smothered the Baron's. "How good of you to have come." Ice-blue eyes in a pasty face snapped photos of Bond and Kopy. "I am afraid I have not had the pleasure of meeting these people."

"My name is Israel Bond." Bond watched for a reaction that never came. "A friend of the Baron's. And this is Miss Kopy Katz, who's come to Xerox your scrolls."

"Excellent! I had not wished to make a bothersome issue out of the scrolls, but until I can devise some safe way of bringing them to the surface I must insist they remain in the cave."

Sanka lit a Shinsei. "*Yo-i!* Then that is settled." He held something under the giant's nose. "Professor, look at this photograph. I took it in a Beppu *ryokan* moments after the subject tried to assassinate me. Do you know this man?"

"Why, it is Skwato, the little drifter I met here during the early days of my excavations, a foul-tempered, friendless being, but I took pity upon him and gave him employment. His size permitted him to squeeze into tiny crevices in search of fossils, and on one of these excursions he found the scrolls. He tried to kill you, you say?"

"Yes, but Mr. Bond thwarted the attempt. Skwato is dead."

"Then we all owe you a great debt, Mr. Bond," said the giant, shaking his blond curls in disbelief. "Ah, it seems this expedition is cursed. Skwato is the second of my workmen to meet a violent end."

Sanka's finger whirled in agitation. "The second?"

"A dreadful misfortune took the life of one of the men who supply us daily with fresh seafood. Standing too close to the edge of the cliff, he was caught by one of the unpredictable air currents that swirl between the cliffs and the ocean. He toppled one thousand feet."

"Who was this fisherman?"

"A man called Nikko Tee-Yin."

8
A Crawler, a Baller

Dinner, held out of doors and served by taciturn Japanese, was a subdued affair despite the excellence of the professor's cuisine. Bond had never tasted anything as succulent as the Da Nang pongi stake shoots doused in the Green Giant's delicately seasoned butter sauce and Camembert Kampfert cheese dip.

Sanka was unaffable, no doubt brooding over the "accident" that had cost him a first-rate *tantei*,[*] Bond thought. Who had been the convenient "air current"? Feldspar? Or one of his many aides, including some Scandinavians in long-sleeved black sweaters not given to much more than some noncommittal small talk and a hawk-faced man who spoke English in a thick Slavic accent. He'd been introduced by Feldspar as Dr. Yaynu, a Bulgarian paleontologist who'd quit his homeland before the Communist takeover.

Bond, resplendent in Takashima cultured-pearl pajamas and Alfie bedsocks which had cost him thirty quid and six buskers, quaffed his fifth flagon of Beefeater Gin and coleslaw. "Where, professor, is the charming Mrs. Feldspar? I've not seen her since we arrived," queried Bond, and he got a jealous stare from Kopy that would have snuffed out a wildcat oil fire. She dashed her *patie de marco* lungfish soufflé into his face and exited in tears.

"Magma has asked to be excused, Mr. Bond. She finds these humid Kyushu nights too taxing. Indeed, all of Japan bores her, I fear. Perhaps she will prove more companionable on the morrow. I myself have come to adore this land. Here is a sense of order and harmony I find lacking in decadent Europe and its preoccupation with television, go-go girls, *le hot dog* and the

---
[*] Spy

scandalous behavior of the jet set. I have searched my heart for a way to repay Japan for the serenity she has brought me and I think I have found it."

"But certainly the discovery of the scrolls is repayment enough."

"That is a contribution to the world, Mr. Bond, and, incidentally, tomorrow I shall reveal a portion of the scrolls' contents at an international press conference to which you are cordially invited. Working in the cave by dim kerosene lamplight, I was only able to jot down a few paragraphs, which I have transcribed into English. My gift to Japan is of a more personal nature. At my own expense I shall rebuild the Great Herrosukka Buddha, whose ruins lie a few hundred yards from the main cave."

Bond sensed the fervor in Feldspar, a man with a mission—one of construction, not destruction, as Bond's was—and for a moment the Israeli felt ashamed at his years in the seamy spy business. The Dane seemed a likable, openhearted chap and Bond hoped he was an innocent party in this affair.

"The Great Herrosukka Buddha, Mr. Bond, was literally the idol of millions of Kyushu Japanese. On holy days throngs made their way up these cliffs, some on foot, the elderly on donkeys, to place garlands of onion rings at its feet and burn joss sticks of Wrigley's seaweed gum. Then a year ago a typhoon of extraordinary magnitude struck, flattening thousands of homes, killing hundreds of thousands of peasants, destroying the sisal and jute crops, which are the staple diet of Kyushu farmers. It climaxed its assault by hurling the Buddha into the Pacific, leaving only the tattered base. The Norwegians whom you met this evening are construction experts and, indeed, one of them, Ibsen, holds the rank of Master Builder. Working from my sketch of the Buddha, they will reconstruct it in a matter of days until it again towers one hundred feet into the sky of Japan. Then will my debt be repaid. And now I shall retire to my tent to burn the midnight oil over my scroll translations. Goodnight, Mr. Bond."

Feldspar bowed and stumbled off on the giraffe legs. *Poor bastard,* Bond thought. *It's as though he were on stilts.*

Stilts!

By thunder, he'd been a maudlin fool.

There was a quick way to find out. His long, tapering fingers yanked the Bowie-Handicapper throwing knife from his right bedsock and zipped it at the departing scientist. Feldspar yelped as the tip bit into his left calf, tripped and fell over a hibachi stove, howling again as a sleeve of his Ruark bush jacket caught fire.

Bond snatched the bowl of cheese dip and used it to quench the flames. "Professor, a thousand pardons. I had to do it. I thought somehow you were Dr. Ernst Holzknicht."

"Holzknicht!" The Dane's face whitened in loathing.

"Holzknicht!" Clamping his steam shovel of a hand against his leg, he hopped into his tent and closed the flap.

That's torn it, Bond thought. *I've just knifed my host on a ridiculous, billion-to-one-shot. The man must think I'm a mindless butcher. Yet how horrified he was when I dropped the magic name. Could be my nemesis has a hold on him. You're getting into deep waters, my friend.*

On the way to his tent, some five yards from Kopy's, he heard her wind-borne sobs. Hell, another jealous broad. Just because you balled 'em and promised undying love, they thought they owned you. Let her stew a bit.

His lodging was no Imperial Hotel suite, that was certain. A cot, a blanket, a fifty-yen reproduction of the *Mona Lisa* tacked over his pillow. A sardonic smile curved his sensual mouth. Didn't they think he knew that under the *Mona Lisa's* moustache was an enigmatic smile, not an O-shaped expression? Who did they think they were fooling with, some M.I. 6 idiot? Sure enough, inside the O was the little electronic snooper, a Reddy Kilowatt bug with a Dr. Seuss-Ikon frequency range of six long-ton hectares, a standard piece of TUSH equipment. Who was the patient listener on the other end?

He ground it to jonesereens under his contemptuous heel, stripped to his E. J. Korvette parsely-patterned wallaby-skin skivvies and stretched out on the cot. From his bag he took a gallon of Suntory, the excellent Japanese Scotch, poured it into a water bucket, mixed in shredded ginger, soy sauce and a pinch of Mother Margolies' Activated Old World *lekvar* and guzzled it down. He blew out the candle, pulled up the blanket and in seconds was dreaming he was locked in a backstage room at the Copacabana, the entire chorus line begging for his sexual favors. *Well, the show must go on,* he jested in his sleep.

Something woke him.

Something on his ankle.

Israel Bond froze. Tendrils were moving up his right leg, parting the fine, grade A-1 hairs covering the blemish-free epidermis he toned each day with brisk Dannon yogurt rubs. *Don't move a furge of a fifkin, Oy Oy Seven,* his brain told him. It may be the lethal Kyushu tarantula! Or the golden Ibusuki scorpion, whose sting... Don't move a muscle! The tendrils had passed the knees he'd studiously had recapped every twenty thousand miles and were gliding toward his inner thigh, higher and higher. *Gottenu!* What if it was headed... there? And it was, dammit, it was! He couldn't let it vitiate his manhood; he couldn't....

His right hand slammed down, mashed something and there was a splintering noise and a stifled scream.

"My hand, you've broken my hand...."

He fished an Ohio blue-tipped match from his Takashimas and relit the candle.

His nocturnal visitor was a naked woman!

9
Kopy Enraged, Kopy Engaged

Magma Feldspar, the tigerish blonde whose sex-starved face had hungered for him from the newspaper clipping, writhed like a ferret in the steel trap of his hand. "I've been watching you all day through binoculars," she whispered. "I didn't dare greet you at dinner because I think I'd have torn the pj's off your lithe, muscular body then and there. For the love of Eros or any other banned magazine, take me, take me, take me!"

He released her hand. "Let's not be puerile about it, baby. A situation like this calls for a little savoir faire." On his compact Webcor he placed a spool of tasteful recordings he often used to make love by. His gray eyes sparkled a teasing challenge. "What'll it be? *The Friggin Forkful? The Muggers and the Fuggers? Swing Along with Mitch? George Beverly Shea Sings for Fundamentalist Lovers? Hava Negila?*"

"If a *negila* is what I think it is, yes, I'll hava *negila!* And you, you hava piece of Danish now!"

He sprinkled a pint jar of Nescafé on her glistening flesh (it was unthinkable to have Danish without coffee) and released the unbearable tension in her, saving the red-corpuscle-melting Siberian Steppe backflip for the joint moment of cataclysmic unification.

Sarah's face floated above him, her sloe eyes two leaky faucets. *Oh, Iz, Iz! Again?*

Forgive me, angel, but I'm a man, etc.

Thwick! Thwack! Two flashes of pain flayed his back and he whirled to find Kopy wielding a belt. "You-you rotten..." She could not finish her recriminations, choked on the tears streaming into her mouth and ran blindly into the night.

Magma lit a Raleigh. "You seem to be in demand, my Sinai stud. I don't care as long as I get my share."

Bond poured her fifteen fingers of Suntory and watched her toss it down like a dockhand. Fun time was over. Now the snap quiz. "How did you ever tie the knot with our nonswinging seven-footer? You don't look like the ivory-tower type, Mag. The basement is more your speed."

Magma threw back her hustler's head and cackled. "You've got me pegged, Bond. Iggie bores the hell out of me. I met him in Copenhagen a few months ago when I was a bar girl at the Club Elsinore. He took a shine to me, came in night after night, spent *mucho dinero*. Then he popped the question and I said to myself, 'Magma, you're not getting any younger,' so I accepted. The question was the last thing he's ever popped."

Bond ran his hand over her quivering navel. "Tough situation for a gal with your appetite."

"You said it, handsome. Hell, when I realized he wasn't going to do anything more than kiss me good night on the cheek and mess with his books and formulae, I decided I'd have to catch a little extracurricular jazz now and then. But none of 'em have been anything like tonight. Why all the questions? You some kind of secret agent?"

"Has he ever mentioned the name Ernst Holzknicht?"

Magma sat up, her mouth in a hard line. "I've answered all I'm going to. Sleep tight, tiger."

Bond bent her head with a slap. "And you've had your last tankful, Mag, unless..."

"All right, all right." She gingerly touched her swelling cheek. "Once Iggie got a long-distance call. We were in West Berlin at the time. He turned pale, started to shake. I heard him say, 'Ernst, for God's sake don't hurt the boy. I'll comply.' Shortly thereafter, Iggie said we were coming to Japan. That's all I know; I swear it."

"Toodle-oo, Magma. We'll have some more hanky-panky in your tanky real soon." He kicked her out, lit a Raleigh and reviewed the tidbits she'd contributed. The pieces of the puzzle were coming together. Holzknicht did have a hold on the giant— "the boy," whoever he was. He'd have to win the Dane's confidence and perhaps do Feldspar a good turn before this caper was ended.

Deep racking sobs rent the air. Kopy. He'd treated her pretty rough, he supposed. Time to make up. He crept into her tent and embraced the puffy-eyed researcher.

"Oh, Iz, how could you hurt me so?"

Bond stroked the ebony tresses. "It was strictly in the line of duty, *maideleh*. Remember what you said about a secret agent facing death every second? Well, what you just saw was a perfect illustration. I could have died of ecstasy from what that broad was doing to me."

Her lips were two raspberry floats brushing his neck. "Darling, you don't know how difficult it is for a nice Jewish girl. We'd all like to marry our own kind of fellas, but you Jewish boys treat us so mean. You see a Jewish girl and right away you run a mental Dun and Bradstreet on her. Is she pretty? Accomplished? Rich? Then along comes a heavy-breathing *shikseh* like that Magma and all of a sudden it's *love* with no questions asked."

"*Are* you rich?" He hoped the query sounded lighthearted.

"Heavens, yes. An Alta Zeydah Kapplan won't touch a job under one hundred thou' per. And Daddy's loaded. Made a pile pushing a line of low-cholesterol, high-protein foods—organic swamp cabbage, newt burgers, tumbleweed tea. Surely you've heard of him—'Unsaturated' Katz?"

"You bet," and his hand was sliding the nearly tenth-of-a-carat garnet engagement ring onto her third finger left hand. "You and I are for keeps, Kopy Katz. Hit Xerox for a raise. Little squeakers need tons of white booties and nappies."

Deliriously happy, she fell into his bronzed arms. "Oh, Iz! Iz!" Then slyly, "Do you think you can instigate another state of tumescence?"

Bond grinned. "I guess it can be arranged, luv." To himself: *Gottenu! In the near future I damn well better get to the first sperm bank I can find, and make a withdrawal!*

10
Shimon Sez

The Dane's aides had set up a long press table outside his tent for representatives of every leading TV network, newspaper, wire service and news magazine, plus correspondents from *Women's Wear Daily*, *The Boot & Shoe Recorder*, *Fact*, *Playboy* and *Variety*. At each place setting was a pitcher of Yoo-Hoo chocolate drink and two Mallomars. Clarence Petersen, the *Chicago Tribune's* man, nibbled his and spoke to Norman Shavin of the *Atlanta Constitution*. "Better be damn good to drag us out to this Godforsaken place. Probably some third-rate fossil find worth two graphs on the split page of the *Moline Dispatch*. Nothing's going to knock that trawler story off page one, anyway. Wonder what got into the Israelis? They've got enough trouble with the fezzes without stirring up Japan's litchi nuts."

"Yeah." Shavin nodded. "I hear the Sokka Datgai is picketing Ann Dinken's Kosher-style Restaurant and the Tokyo Jewish Community Center with signs—YIDDEN GAY AHAME. Here's Feldspar. Lord, what a long drink of water!"

Igneous Feldspar lurched on the giraffe legs to the head of the table. "Ladies and gentlemen, it was gracious of you to make this rugged voyage to an obscure village. When I have concluded my presentation I am sure you will feel it was worth the effort. I have in my hands a few golden gems of a historical treasure trove, the translated excerpts of scrolls discovered in these cliffs by my associates and myself. To preface my remarks, let me say that we are all derived from one of four major strains, Negroid, Caucasoid, Mongoloid and Trapezoid."

The CBS-TV news chief puffed his pipe. "Trapezoid? I must admit, Professor Feldspar, that the last-named group is quite unfamiliar to me, perhaps even to all of us gathered here in this strange moonscape of a setting, wondering what astonishing developments await us on this muggy day in the twentieth century, sponsored, as you know, by the Prudential Insurance Company, whose public-affairs television documentaries have—"

"Knock it off, Walter!" expostulated his curly-haired, boyish NBC-TV rival. "You still haven't learned. To keep your sentences. Terse and punchy."

"Bring back Arnold Zenker," said the other NBC-TV man.

"The Trapezoids," said Feldspar, "flourished millions of years ago and were so named because of their unusual shape. They are now extinct. Because of that shape they were unable to enter restaurant doors and thus perished of starvation. What I am leading up to is that one would have expected these scrolls to have been written in the ideographs of the Mongoloid peoples who came to Japan from the great Asian continent. They are not."

Dozens of eyebrows rose.

"No, the scrolls are not Oriental. In point of fact, they are written on papyrus."

Shavin nudged Petersen's arm. "Papyrus? Hell, that's Middle Eastern. The Nips use rice paper."

Feldspar smiled. "Correct. These scrolls are an admixture of Aramaic and Hebrew. They are the work of a diarist named Shimon, who appears to have begun recording his experiences sometime between 800 and 700 B.C., about the time the Assyrians were bidding to dominate the known world. In some of the scrolls, which I've bypassed for the sake of brevity, Shimon tells of towns being sacked by the armies of Sargon II. I shall begin where Shimon, his wife, Rachel, and their infant son, Zoomgolli, and others of their clan decide to leave the region.

SCROLL FOUR

Shambles! Dispersed by the invader, Israel is no more. Ruben the Soothsayer, seeking a sign from the Lord of Hosts, came to our tent at the instant tiny Zoomgolli spake his first word. It was not the typical cooing attempt at "mother" or "father." It was distinct—"East."

Ruben says the divine summons has been sent to us through the child. We shall go east!

SCROLL NINE
Weary of body and soul, stardust and moonglow, wine and roses, we paused to seek shelter in a village of crude huts. The inhabitants, a listless lot, sit in the sun performing some profane invocation to false gods by pressing to their lips tubes of an acrid weed whose tips have been lit by fire, then drawing the smoke into their lungs. Rachel, whose olfactory sense is keen, said, "What a mess o' pot!"

Feldspar pounded the table. "Gentlemen, can you not see the woman's random comment, altered a trifle by succeeding generations, has come down to us as... Mesopotamia?"

SCROLL TEN
I am one hundred years old today. To mark the occasion sweet Rachel baked a cheesecake from a secret formula taught her by Sarah and Leah, matriarchs of the tribe of Gad. Someday, I predict, the Sarah-Leah cheesecake will be a delectation to all mankind. Zoomgolli does not share our festivity. He remains a solemn, introspective boy of ten and has not uttered a single word since the one that impelled us onward. Does he await a new command from on high?

SCROLL ELEVEN
The word has come! Zoomgolli cried, "East!" Zebediah the Kohan [high priest] said, "Let it be done." Tonight we trek east.

"Many did not survive the march through the land of the Medes we know as Iran," noted Feldspar. "Shimon cites his increasing age; he is now one hundred and fifty, Rachel ten years younger. Zoomgolli, sixty, remains reticent. He cannot hear well, Shimon says, because of his habit of stuffing dead birds in his ears."

SCROLL NINETEEN
We are in a barren land of scorching deserts, whose denizens are sly of face, sinewy of body.

They ride horses and camels like *mishigoyim*, swooping down on our encampment to pillage and murder. On one such raid we lost Ezra the Shoemaker, but heartless Hilda the Harlot mourns him not. "Slow pay and he also made *love* like a shoemaker," spake the tart tartly. Rachel noticed the women of this place working pointed sticks into sheeps' wool to make coverings. "Why, they are knitting Afghans!" she said. Zoomgolli broke a fifty-year silence to shout, "East!" We go east.

Bond snapped his long, tapering fingers. "I'm starting to dig this stuff. Rachel's observation gave us the name Afghanistan."

A series of scrolls Feldspar touched upon in brief told of the dwindling tribe's years in Sinkiang and Mongol-ruled territories. Rachel, now 180, was ailing more frequently. "It has been many a moon since she accorded me the benefits of her womanhood," complained the diarist. Zoomgolli twice cried, "East!" The high priest expired at age 290. Shimon blamed Hilda the Harlot for his death. "She had no right to stimulate a middle-aged man as she would a stripling."

SCROLL TWENTY-EIGHT
The end is near for sweet Rachel. We have traded the last of our pottery for passage across a great sea in the boat of a merchant, Len Ox of Chee Yi Nah, who was so enthralled by it that he proposes to emulate it and name it both in honor of his country and himself. Rachel was leery of the sailship. "Good husband, you do not expect me to ride in that junk, do you?"

Enrapt at the saga, the Dane's audience was playing the game to the hilt. "Hey, she coined the name for the Chinese boat!" said *Detroit News* columnist Doc Greene.

SCROLL TWENTY-NINE
Sweet Rachel breathed her last as our boat touched the shores of this lush paradise whose mountains belch smoke and fire. "May the Lord go with thee, Shimon," she gasped unto me. "It is

unfitting for a man to be alone. Press your suit with our last woman, Hilda the Harlot. Purify her in a ritual bath and cleave unto her as a husband." I was inconsolable. Not even Ruben had a decent sooth worth saying. I went to my flesh and blood, weeping, "Zoomgolli, thy mother is dead. Comfort me." Zoomgolli said, "East." I thereupon spake in anger. "My son, hath not the Lord given thee a greater lexicon than the solitary word 'east'?" My son smiled fatuously and spake: "Lexicon." With a sinking heart I perceive we have been led, lo, these many years, by one of unsound mind.

SCROLL THIRTY-ONE

Hilda the Harlot will have none of me, disdaining my proposal in a hateful manner. "I need no doddering fool of two hundred and eighty and his idiot son for a family. My preference is Reuben the Soothsayer. He is two hundred and sixty-five and besides he is a professional man." Zoomgolli brightened and said, "East lexicon." How gratifying to witness his burgeoning intellect! We are the only people on this island, few in number and lonely. Yet we practice our ancient faith, lighting candles on the Sabbath and striving to recall the all but forgotten litanies. Oh, Lord, where hast Thou brought us?

"I have reached the scrolls containing revelations I still find difficult to believe," said Igneous Feldspar.

SCROLL THIRTY-SIX

Hosanna! A boat has crashed upon our shores! From it limped a bedraggled, seasick collection of brownish-yellow, slant-eyed souls from various parts of the great Chee Yi Nah land we traversed, who speak in tongues with which I am conversant. They are pagans who worship crickets and coolie hats. The last of us are endeavoring to teach them our belief in one God Almighty. We have built them an Ark of the Covenant and to hear them repeat the *Sh'ma Israel* gladdens the heart.

Ruben the Soothsayer and Hilda the Harlot were found dead at nightfall. Natural causes.

My loins cry for gratification, yet there is no one to cleave unto. However, one of the newcomers is a maiden, Oshima, fair to behold, whose glances signal the unmistakable message that she, too, wishes cleaving unto. Can such a thing be possible between a man of my hoary years and a maid of fifteen? Under pretext of teaching her to read and write our language I have come close to her often. I shall ask her father for her hand.

SCROLL THIRTY-SEVEN

Consent has been given! How my blood tingles! And Zoomgolli adores her. She cleans out his ears and inserts fresh dead birds every day.

SCROLL THIRTY-EIGHT

We married in the tradition of my faith. Before the ceremony I made her swear to preserve this humble history in a secret place so that in years to come the world may know of the strange destiny that befell one of the lost tribes of Israel.

Our survivors intend to intermarry with the new people as a means of perpetuating our creed. Will we succeed? Or will the pagan ways prevail? Only He knows.

On this last sheet of papyrus I record my thoughts of this promising night. She disrobes before me. I am on fire. It has been decades since Rachel's demise and I feel like a young groom about to taste the bliss of conjugal union for the first time.

"And that," the Dane said, "is the last entry of Shimon."

"*Gevaldt!*" Bond cracked his knuckles. "What a yarn and what a place to break it off! What a shame we'll never know how the old geezer made out."

The others echoed his sentiment, but Feldspar held up his hand. "I said it was the last thing Shimon ever wrote, but on the bottom of the last scrawl is a short passage, obviously jotted by the maiden. It reads: 'Old man clove, fall dead just when Oshima starting to cleave unto. Bad old man. Maybe Zoomgolli better. Oshima want cleaving very fast.'"

"Professor, I apologize." Bouncy blond Regina Tellez of *Look* magazine stood up. "I thought this was going to be one big bomb, but it's turned out to be a bombshell a thousand times bigger than the trawler incident. Oh, how it's going to shake up these islands something fierce!"

"What do you mean?" said the *Cleveland Press*'s James Garrett. "Granted it's a humdinger, great Sunday-supplement stuff, but what's the big deal?"

Feldspar wore a grave, hesitant look. "Miss Tellez' analysis coincides with mine. Can you not see the implications? This very spot, Shimonoshima, is doubtless named in honor of the two principals of that doomed marriage, Shimon, an elder of Israel, and Oshima, who may have come from China, Korea, Malaya or any of the other lands that spawned the Oriental race. Shimon speaks of the 'new people' as pagans worshiping in an animalistic mode before they were taught monotheism by a highly advanced tribe *who were here first*. The conclusion is dramatic: Though the people of Japan at present practice Shintoism, Buddhism, or variants of either, they are the direct descendants of Jews."

Bond fell back howling. "Baron Sanka, as the snake said to Mother Eve, 'How do you like them apples?' Or should I better say—Sanka*leh*?"

The laughing jag died in his throat when Baron Cockamamiyama Sanka stomped off hissing, and Israel Bond realized he had just said something for which, if there had been no one else around, the Number One of the Japanese Secret Service would have killed him.

11
Shell Shock

"Dr. Yaynu will guide you through the labyrinths, Mr. Bond and Miss Katz," said Igneous Feldspar. "I suffered a leg injury falling over a tent rope last night"—Bond gave the giant a look of gratitude for the lie—"which rules out my participation. My men have left scuba-diving equipment in your tents. I suggest you suit up as a precaution because these cliffs, due to volcanic activity, are filled with cracks into which the sea has rushed. I shall meet you at the entrance to the main cave in ten minutes. And Miss Katz, as a fellow scientist you'll appreciate my concern for the scrolls. Be ever so gentle as you Xerox them."

Sanka, cooled down and chummy again, walked into Bond's tent as he was pulling on his forever amber Lloyd Bridges Seahunt Swimslax and flippers. "More than ever, Izzy-san, it becomes imperative for my government to scrutinize those scrolls. Unfortunately I was unable to convince the news media to withhold the story and thus I fear my people will be psychologically unhinged, their cultural pride shattered. I myself believe the scrolls to be either spurious or, to be charitable, poorly translated. With all due respect to your estimable faith, we Japanese are definitely not Jewish."

Scratch a Manchu and you'll find an anti-Semite, Bond thought. "OK, Cocky-san," was his curt reply. He stopped by for Kopy, helped her strap on her scuba gear and they headed toward the beckoning Dane. The sun flashed off Feldspar's hydrofoil a thousand feet below and Bond had a thought. Was that the craft that would have picked up Aw Gee Minh had he carried out his nefarious scheme?

A Japanese workman, one of a gang of hundreds lugging materiel of all sizes and shapes up the perilous road to the cliff top, slipped in front of him and let a green cylinder clank on its nozzle against a rock. A clear liquid frothed out. "Clumsy fool!" thundered the Dane, an irate flush stealing up to his blond curls. The man cowered as though expecting a blow, but the Dane managed an insincere smile. "Be more careful in the future, my man. The men are bringing up equipage for my Herrosukka Buddha project, Mr. Bond. The Norwegians are progressing at a good pace."

Kopy wrinkled her nose. "Lox."

"And cream cheese to you, luv," Bond riposted.

"No, Iz, I meant—"

Feldspar said quickly, "And here is Dr. Yaynu, your Pied Piper for this excursion. Good morning, Yaynu."

The hawk-faced Bulgarian, wearing a black mock-turtle necked sweater and Levi Strauss jeanlets, nodded a greeting.

"No scuba gear for you, Dr. Yaynu?" Bond said.

Dr. Yaynu's eyes became hooded. "I don't believe I am going as far as you are, Mr. Bond," an averment the Israeli sifted for a double meaning.

The Bulgarian ushered them into blackness and flicked the switch on his outsize flashlight. A monstrous black billepede skittered over the cave floor and Kopy screamed. Dr. Yaynu squashed it indifferently under his half-calf Nancy Sinatras. "Here are many such creatures—scorpions, tarantulas, black widows. Mind where you place your hands."

The passageway slanted downward and they began to smell an overpowering combination of primordial ooze and the musty salt of the sea. Dr. Yaynu's beam picked up myriads of crawlies, each new one sending a spasm through the shapely researcher. Once Bond felt his front foot plunging into a crack and shouted, but Kopy grasped his hand and pulled him free. "Iz, be careful, darling. No telling how deep these things go."

When he heard Kopy gasping for breath, he said, "Let's stop, doctor, and give Miss Katz a rest."

"If you wish, Mr. Bond. Actually we are at the chamber where Skwato found the scrolls of Shimon. We had it widened to accommodate Professor Feldspar. Slide through the opening, Miss Katz, and we shall pass the Xerox to you."

Bond lit a Raleigh. "Go ahead, baby. History awaits you." She smiled, kissed him warmly and knelt at the opening, wriggled through on her tummy and took the Xerox from Bond.

"Iz!" Her voice had a hollow, faraway ring. "They're here! And they're just marvelous!" There was a whirring and clicking and her excited bursts, "Got it! Got it!"

"She will be occupied some time, Mr. Bond. Would you care to see another of the wonders of this place?"

"You're the doctor," said Bond. "Lead on."

They took a left fork and scrambled toward an ever-increasing roar. "An enthralling grotto, Mr. Bond, formed by eruptions and oceanic erosion. It is a sight you'll never forget."

He was not overstating the case. They emerged into a cathedral of nature hewn by ten thousand herculean stonemasons. Below seethed the ocean, this way and that, buffeting the walls with maniacal force.

"Is this not a magnificent place to die, Oy Oy Seven?"

Dr. Yaynu's hand sported a long-barreled Brezhnev-Kosygin.

Israel Bond's lips formed a moue of disgust. "It appears I've let myself be a TUSH pigeon again, Dr. Yaynu—if that's your name."

"It will do for you, Mr. Bond, although it once was General Bolsheeyit, one of the top policymakers of the KGB until you smashed my career by your daring foray into the Soviet Union with matzoh to lighten the hearts of the Russian Jews. It was you who murdered my assassin, Torquemada LaBonza, 'The Man with the Golden Gums.' And it was you who disposed of our bloc's top counterspy, the Bulgarian named Avakum Zakhov, whom we had lent to the Syrians to conduct a campaign of terror under the pseudonym of Feisal Fullah-Sheik." The hawk face hardened into hideous hatred. "Yes, you, Oy Oy Seven, brought me disgrace and forced me to flee Mother Russia, you filthy Zhid!" He smashed the flashlight against Bond's jaw.

Bond said through gritted teeth, "And Holzknicht reached into the grudge file and plucked you out, too, eh, Yaynu? All kinds of ghosts are slithering out of that file, it seems. I suppose you're going to kill the girl as well."

"No, my friend. *Herr Doktor* wishes the world, especially the Japanese, to see the reproductions. I am sure you noted Baron Sanka's dismay at the notion his antecedents were Jewish. Multiply that feeling by one hundred million sons and daughters of Dai Nippon and you will get the picture. Step by step—and there are even greater provocations in the works—they will be irritated into a war against Eretz Israel. I shall tell Miss Katz we went sightseeing and, alas, you slipped on the ledge and fell into the grotto. Move back, Mr. Bond. At the count of three it will be all over."

Bond took a tiny step backward.

"*Raz.*" The ex-KGB bigwig was counting in Russian, an added fillip of revenge for Bond's role in the Matzohball affair. Below, the sea issued a seductive siren's call: *Come on down! You're finished, Oy Oy Seven. Why even wait for the third count? Come on down! Take one more step back and find eternal rest in my bosom.*

His mind telegraphed back: *The hell with you, Tomon the way Dooley, Mrs. Danvers and Rebecca, too! And make that wire collect!*

"*Dva.*" Yaynu ticked off the second count.

But Bond, who'd been measuring the time between counts, was spinning in the graceful pivot taught him by the Big O of the Cincinnati Royals, and at *"Tri"*—three—had his back to the Russian and felt the bullet whang into the heavy-gauge steel of the oxygen tank. He completed the pivot to see Yaynu clutching at the spot in his guts where the slug had ricocheted. Yaynu blatted, but in a final suicidal lunge battered his bullet-like head into Bond's belly.

And they went over.

On the way down Bond was an unstoppable wild man, the crook of his bronze muscular arm crushing his foe's neck, and he screamed a beloved old Passover song into the bluish Slavic face.

"Die, die Yaynu! Die, die, Yaynu! Die, die, Yaynu! Die, Yaynu, die, Yaynu!"

How long they fell he could not be sure—two or three seconds, perhaps—and as he saw the sea rushing to meet him he twisted in midair and swung the body of the strangled Yaynu under him so that it would take the brunt of the impact. Nevertheless his own head exploded in a red network of zigzag pain patterns and he soared to the surface, affixed his face mask, started the oxygen and submerged again, for he'd got the bad news. He was some two hundred feet from the ledge with no way to scale the sheer sides of the grotto. If there was a way out it would have to come from underneath, perhaps a channel to the Pacific. If water had got in, there had to be an egress somewhere. There had to be! He'd only an hour's worth of life-sustaining air; not a pip of a popkin could be wasted.

Round and round Bond swam, examining his watery trap from all sides, his eyes straining to pierce the murky greenness. He tensed. A shadow passed over his head; wicked rows of teeth grinned at him. Barracuda! Ten muscular feet of murder whose

Gillette super-stainless cutting power could serrate him to strips. *Keep swimming at a steady pace,* his heart warned, *or it'll sense your panic and close in. Make believe you're a larger, deadlier fish, a dolphin, say. Nothing dares attack a dolphin.* He sliced toward the bottom and saw a colony of sponges, a bull and several simpering does. Pulling a razor-sharp Solingen-Helm knife from his right flipper, he slashed away at the harem, liberating the great round bull and, bouncing it off his head in the jocular manner of a dolphin at play, made some sportive 'Flipper' noises he hoped would approximate a dolphin's chuckle. It seemed to do the trick. The 'cuda backed off respectfully.

Was that a blessed glimmer of light in the distance? Yes! He gave the bull sponge a friendly farewell pat on its holey buttocks and paddled toward the light, thrilling as he felt the water turning warmer. The light became more intense and his heart leaped. Thank God, he'd found a cut-through to the sea! The current seemed inexorable, but he fought it inch by inch, until he could now see a dimly red ball of fire—the sun! *Stroke, stroke, stroke; you're almost out of here, buddy boy; thirty feet more, twenty, ten....*

The current reversed suddenly. Unbelievably. It was no longer pushing him; it was pulling him. Why?

Gottenu! The suction was damn near wrenching the mask from his face. In a frightening glimpse Bond saw the sun blacked out by something at the end of the tunnel to freedom, something yawning, two valves widening to reveal a pearly ambience. There was a last sucking sound and he was drawn into its midst. The valves snapped shut with sickening finality.

And Israel Bond knew he'd exchanged the frypan for the oven. He was locked inside that most dreaded of all deep-sea denizens, the one-hundred-foot oyster!

12
"When You've Been in the Biggest Oyster There Is"...

A swell tilted the barge sitting in the reef-rimmed Maroon Lagoon—so named because of the trillions of brownish-red microorganisms which stain its waters—sending the brooding American on the camp chair sliding toward his Japanese partner.

"Damn it, Tats, I'm getting sunburned, seasick and fed up with this whole deal, and spare me that patience-of-the-East *shtik*." So spoke Seymour "Sy" Feig, a fortyish, spindly-legged man with thinning brown hair, who wore a raffish Korvette's Acapulcowitz cabana suit—Sy Feig, the fabled, flamboyant press agent who'd discovered Sylvester Soulmeat working on a New York Department of Sanitation truck and in six months made him a rock 'n' roll star. ("Sylvester, baby, if there's one thing I know how to handle, it's *garbage*.") Of late Feig had made his mark as a producer of low-budget, quickie movies—*Born to Flog, Leather Whip Beach Party* and *Hell's Angel, Flog Me from Your Dirty Honda*—which were garnering socko grosses at a Forty-second Street theater. The *New York Daily News* critic had given them the highest possible rating—four weals.

Handsome, poised "Tats" Nagashima, the Orient's most prominent show business entrepreneur, tried to mollify his grousing companion. "Sy, we've had a few slow days, true, but you have to admit things have been looking up—literally-all day. A thirty-two-foot crayfish and a forty-one-foot 'pusfeller came out of the lagoon and Clancy got some thrilling footage. Believe me, I wouldn't have asked you to invest your dough and travel more than nine thousand miles if I wasn't sure there were some first-rate, untapped monsters down below. You saw the films I've shot from here—*It Came from the Maroon Lagoon,* T*he Creature from the Maroon Lagoon Versus Frankenstein and the Grandson of the Fly,* etc. Huge moneymakers. It's just a matter of time, that's all."

Feig masticated his unlit Dutchmaster. "Crayfish, octopussys. Passé. You can't pull the public in with crap like that no more. What we need is like a three-hundred-foot dinosaur, the biggest that ever lived—the oedipus rex, wasn't it?—dripping with slime, incensed at impious man, who has disturbed his million-year snooze by detonating a hydrogen bomb, so he comes to the surface to wreak his malice on an unsuspecting world. That's what we need. And what I need personally is that diving chick over there. Geez, what boobs on that broad! Tats, try again, huh? Ask her does she want to be in pictures."

Nagashima yelled something to the almost naked maiden in the little flat-bottomed, high-sided boat, who shook her head in negation. "No dice, Sy."

"Why is she so goddam uppity? What's she got against me?"

"It's a long story. She despises film people. Her name is Go-Down Mikimoto and she is Japan's most beautiful and celebrated pearl diver. Two years ago she was prevailed upon by our film industry to go to the States and play herself in a South Sea epic, *Shark God of Cuticura.* When she was screen-tested they decided she didn't look native' enough, so they gave the part to Raquel Welch. Go-Down suffered terrible indignities at the hands of some lupine movie moguls and swore she would never consort with *gaijins* again. You don't stand a chance."

"Want me to shoot any more calm sea-type exteriors?" said Liam Clancy, the red-faced Irishman in the studiously torn Levi Strauss Sea-Snuggies, who operated the camera and sound.

"Nah." Feig gave the girl a censorious glare.

When it swooshed into the sky Nagashima first assumed it was a waterspout. "Shoot it, Clancy. We'll work it in somewhere."

Then they saw it, the huge white bauble suspended atop the column of water and mist and the two immense blackish valves spread flat at its base. Something hacked and coughed and belched sonorously; there was a long sigh and the valves cracked together and went under.

"Mother of God!" cried Liam Clancy.

"Mother of pearl, you mean," Feig corrected. "That's a pearl, pal, biggest damn one ever. Must be fifty feet around. Hey, it's falling!"

The pearl bounced into the sea, drenching them to the skin in a mountainous spray. Clancy cursed, but stayed at his post filming away in blazing zeal. To pick up the sound of the pearl rolling over the breakers, Clancy boosted the volume and lowered the boom.

Go-Down Mikimoto was a tawny arrow diving from her dory, her supple flanks a symphony of rhythmic precision as she stroked toward the bobbing blob and called to Nagashima.

"This is incredible," said Nagashima. "Go-Down says there's a man inside. We'd better haul it in before it sinks."

"Film, Clancy, film!" With that command, Feig jumped from the barge, Nagashima following closely. They thrashed a foamy path to the girl, whose forefinger was indicating a shadow-figure lurking behind the lustrous covering. The trio, making a monumental effort, pushed the pearl in the direction of the barge, shouting for assistance. Six technicians leaped into the water and together they managed to roll it onto the barge, which rocked menacingly. "Don't tip us. I'm getting shots like you never saw," Clancy cried.

Go-Down banged an impotent fist on the pearl. "Hurry! It must be opened or he will die."

So, you can speak English, you little cocker, Feig thought, copping a fast feel that went unnoticed. "You're right, chickie. Hey, you guys, bust this thing apart."

Nagashima and his crew broke up some tables and chairs and used the legs as clubs until there was a sound of splintering, and the pearl split and in a swirl of sand and sea a man fell upon the deck.

Nagashima removed the oxygen tank and face mask.

Feig smacked his hand against his head. "*Gottenu!* Bond! Israel Bond!"

"Sy? Sy Feig, here in Japan?" The gray eyes then focused on the gleaming configuration of Go-Down Mikimoto. "Honey, help me, please. You know the legend of oysters, what they're supposed to do to people? Well, when you've just been inside the biggest oyster there is... Please, baby, please."

Simpatico were the black eyes of Go-Down Mikimoto. "Of course, sir." Wriggling through Feig's fingers, she removed her skimpy loincloth, liberated Bond from the Seahunt suit and snuggled against his chest. An "Ar-r-gh!" savage and primeval, escaped his sensual lips and he seized her with a spasm that shook the barge.

Nagashima hid his eyes considerately. Feig did not.

"Shoot it, Clancy! Shoot it! Damn it, this'll pack em in, by Skouras! Tats, you were one hundred percent right about the Maroon Lagoon. It really came through for us. What a plot!"

Nagashima looked askance at his exuberant confrere. "I concede it's amazing, but what's the plot?"

Feig laughed. "Are you nuts, Tats? A gigantic oyster surfaces, spits out the mother of all pearls; it breaks open to reveal an oversexed Hebraic Hercules who's got to hock a broad or he'll die of frustration; he lands on a gorgeous knish of an Ama diving girl and gives her the hock of ages. That's no plot by you? Hell, Tats, it's"—he strove for a metaphor—"'New Wave'... *avant-goiter!* And we don't screen this one in some *shlock* moviehouse, either. This one goes right to the art theaters."

For the better part of an hour the two splendid anatomies locked and hocked, finding desire's peak in a crystalline explosion. When it was done and the burning deck hosed down by Nagashima's aides, Bond sighed. "Sarah, forgive me. This one was simply uncontrollable."

Feig blinked. Was that a voice? *"Iz, I forgive you, darling."* No, just a keening breeze, he decided.

Bond's eyes were closing now. "Poor bastard oyster. I ruined it, Sy. It'll need a complete valve job...."

His head lolled in Go-Down Mikimoto's lap.

13
The Dane Talks

"I've been sleeping three days?"

"Yup. Like a top." Feig handed Bond a Schweppes 'n' tonic and watched his buddy down the perky quinine and Jeris. "You look like hell, Iz. Lump on your noggin, shoulder torn up, purple belly bruise. I take it you're still at the old secret-agent business?" When Bond grunted at the indiscretion, he said, "It's OK. Tats here is a close-mouthed type and I don't think this lovely creature, Go-Down Mikimoto, is going to blow your cover, either. Now, how in hell did you get in and out of that Pacific pocketbook?"

Bond lit a Shinsei and gave them a condensed version of his tribulations, beginning with the battle on the JAL jet. "Well, I'd about five minutes of air left and nothing seemed to be working. This may be the wrong adjective, but it was getting *clammy* in there. Oystery sounds better, don't you think? I spent an eternity punching at its meaty interior, then I lifted my face mask and began biting chunks out of it, which explains my shameful deportment, Miss Mikimoto. I'm truly sorry."

"It's Go-Down to you, Mr. Bond, and I'm not." She held another cool slab of shark bladder against his shoulder wound. "An old Ama remedy."

"I'd become resigned to an oystery grave when the principle of how a pearl is formed went through my mind. It's caused by a foreign body that irritates the oyster. Size-wise I was big enough to be a foreign body, yet nothing I did seemed to rile it until I remembered I had the world's most potent irritant in the compartment of my old Captain Midnight decoder ring, a pinch of Mother Margolies' Activated Old World Chrain. I schmeared it smack dab in the middle of the oyster."

"*Chrain* is Yiddish for horse-radish, folks," informed Feig. "Ain't nothin' under the sun got the bite of Mother's *chrain*. It could clear up the sinuses of the chairman of the board of Dristan. Go on, Iz."

"It had been pitch black in there, but after I applied the stuff the meaty mound began to glow. It started to choke and wheeze and then something sticky was enveloping me—nacre, the secretion which, when hardened around a grain of sand, creates the pearl. I felt the nacre solidifying, and then it decided to come up and regurgitate me. I must say, it was a wonderful transition, from nacre to naked. You know the rest. Go-Down, if you hadn't spotted me, I would have smothered inside." Bond suddenly moaned. *Smothered inside.* His fiancée was still in the fetid caves of Shimonoshima, probably dead of suffocation. "Kopy..." The sensual teeth clicked savagely. "If it's the last thing I do, I'll get Holzknicht for that—that is, after I do the screenplay for the sequences you've just filmed." He spent two hours banging away at Feig's Smith-Corona portable. "The usual Screenwriters Guild rates will suffice, Sy, and I'll meet you in New York for the voice dubbing. Now, somebody get me to Shimonoshima, *schnell!*"

"I shall row you there, Mr. Bond," said a desolate Go-Down. "Step into my dory. It is a sturdy craft designed by Horthy of Budapest."

Bond licked his lips in sheer joy. *Gottenu,* what a setup she'd handed him! "A Budapest boat, eh? I guess it's"—his flashing wit laid in one of his most scintillating one-liners—"*hunky dory!*"

As Go-Down Mikimoto churned the oars, her eyes devoured him. So this was Secret Agent Israel Bond, her lover! She had read many novels pertaining to his ruthless breed, the first-rate creations of Le Carré, Deighton, Donald Hamilton, Adam Hall, etc., and enjoyed them all, although she preferred by far the newest writer mining this vein, Sol Weinstein, an exciting, prepossessing American, in whose Pocket Book Specials paperbacks, *Loxfinger, Matzohball* and *On the Secret Service of His Majesty, the Queen* ($1 per copy; mail orders filled promptly, gratefully by Pocket Books, Inc., 630 Fifth Avenue, New York, N.Y.; no extra charge for author's autograph or body), she'd found an approach to sex and violence unexplored by the others. How cruelly handsome Mr. Bond was! He reminded her of photographs she had once seen of the young George Gershwin.

At the landing in Shimonoshima, Go-Down faced him for what might be the last time. "Shall I ever see you again, Mr. Bond?"

"Our fates will lead us to one another again, Go-Down. In the meantime, love me...Never, never change... Keep that breathless charm... Don't you rearrange it ... 'Cause I love you ... etc., I want to think of you as I saw you first, a proud untamed mermaid. I would recommend two minor alterations—Westernizing your eyes and lightening your pigmentation by drugs—but otherwise stay as you are." He kissed her passionately and stepped onto the shore.

"And I shall be ever afloat near this village should you require me," the Ama nymph said, but her pledge never reached his ears, for Bond was clambering up the path to the tent city, bowling over sweating Japanese bearing more paraphernalia on their backs, and in ten minutes he'd gained the top. He stopped in his tracks, shivering.

The Great Herrosukka Buddha regarded him from suspicious slitted eyes.

Gottenu! They'd built it up to its hundred-foot height in seventy-two hours. Palpably the Great Dane and his Norwegians were geniuses at this trade. Bond walked to the base, feeling somehow that the eyes were following his every step. At the feet he came upon a pile of bleached bones, which he nudged with his foot.

"Please do not disturb them, Mr. Bond. These are some of the remnants of bygone worshipers and their donkeys who died at the Buddha's feet after the torturous climb. I have left them as a memorial to all those who have genuflected here."

From the shadow of the Buddha stepped Professor Igneous Feldspar.

"I knew in my heart you possessed the leonine courage to survive, Mr. Bond." The giant sounded genuinely relieved. "You are destined for greater glories."

Bond lit a Raleigh. "Prof, we've got some palavering to do. Whether you know it or not, I have been threatened from the moment I neared this land by an undercover neo-Nazi organization known as TUSH." He unfolded the narrative. "I am of the opinion that Holzknicht has a hold on you. Magma told me of your apprehension for 'the boy' in a little" —he found himself blushing—"chat we had one night. Come clean, Feldspar, and I'll do my best to extricate you from his clutches."

The Dane expelled the sigh of a man who has been carrying a secret onus too long. "Yes, Ernst has a hold on me. In the late 1920's we were fellow students at the Schisselzelmknist Institute of Psychiatry and Medicine in Berlin. Even then Ernst Holzknicht was astounding his professors with concepts beyond their understanding. He was first to cure a moribund loaf of bread by massive injections of penicillin, the first to train a dog to shout at the clang of an alarm: 'Meat-bell! Meat-bell!' Ernst was a misanthrope, who despised his brother students and instructors. For some odd reason he was drawn to me; why, I cannot say—my Danish jollity or my outlandish size, perhaps. Whatever the reason, we became firm friends, although we had many a heated polemic over the ascendant Nazi philosophy which had begun to infect him. I well remember the day he told me flatly, 'The world will never be a decent place until I destroy all the Jews.'"

"I recall a similar dialogue with the good *Herr Doktor* in the cellar of a gambling casino. Pray, continue."

"Graduation parted us, although we corresponded for many years until the day the *Boche* swarmed into Denmark. I had no further wish to fraternize with a man who was using his God-given genius to further the cause of maniacs. Besides, I had married a charming Oslo poetess some years before and was immersed in the bliss of family life. Her name was Helvig Rolvig, winner of the Nobel Prize for her only published collection of poetry, a 350-page, two-couplet volume, *Reflections from the Middle Ear*. She was a great one for copious footnotes."

"Helvig Rolvig was *your* wife?" Bond's eyes softened and he recited the well-remembered lines:

> Apes and grapes
> Have dissimilar shapes.

"I've adored her poems since I was a gawking teener. How happy you must have been."

"Ah, under that hard-boiled, cruelly handsome facade is the soul of a dreamer, Mr. Bond. Yes, we were sublimely happy. But the very spirit of independence that flavored her poetry cost her her life. A Nazi officer who also admired her works commanded her to either compose a poem in his honor or die by firing squad. I shall never forget the way she drew herself up and cried:

For you?
Oh, pooh!

and her horror when she realized that in her defiance she'd done what she'd sworn not to do—compose a poem. She snatched a rifle from a guard's hands and killed herself on the spot."

"How awful."

"Luckily there is a living reminder of Helvig Rolvig, our only child, Knute, whom I raised myself. He grew to be a strapping lad and is something of a scientist himself. His specialty is graffitology, the discovery and translation of graffiti, those pithy wall scrawlings. Spelunking in the Swiss Alps, Knute discovered graffiti most certainly chipped into cave walls by early man, among them: 'Would you want your daughter to marry a Lake Dweller?' and 'The fool seeks fire from flintstones; the hippie uses a Zippo.' By this time Knute no longer needed me, Mr. Bond, and I was a lonely man craving companionship, but unable to give a woman pleasure because of a rare penile affliction that strikes old men—a monk's hood. On an aimless jaunt into Copenhagen's night life I met, wooed and eventually won the present Mrs. Feldspar. Do not be embarrassed, my friend. I am aware of her sexual need for you. To resume, we honeymooned in Berlin, where out of the blue I received a call from Ernst—after all those years of estrangement. I prayed he would be regenerate, but he wasted no time informing me he had kidnapped Knute and would kill him unless I became involved in a charade to be played out in Japan. I now see that Skwato and the man who called himself Dr. Yaynu were his minions. You probably have guessed that Dr. Yaynu killed the fisherman Nikko Tee-Yin. And it was my hydrofoil that was to fetch Aw Gee Minh from the Pacific. How happy I was when I realized he had failed. You showed great resourcefulness as usual, Mr. Bond."

"What about the scrolls?"

"They are genuine. They must be. How can I, who am so knowledgeable in this field, be mistaken?"

"Real or false, they cost a sweet kid her life. Kopy Katz."

"Oh, but she is alive."

Bond's knees buckled and he braced himself against a toe of the Buddha. "Alive?"

"When all of you were gone so long I sensed tragedy and despite my gammy leg I led a search party into the caves. We found her unconscious on the blood-spattered ledge where you and Dr. Yaynu had your difference of opinion. She had heard the shooting and rushed to your aid. She thought you had died. Baron Sanka has taken the poor child back to Tokyo."

"I want Holzknicht. Is he in Japan?"

"I—I cannot—"

"You've got to help me nail him, professor. I know what your son means to you. Israel's millions mean as much to me. If Holzknicht isn't brought to heel, unimaginable devastation is in the offing for two countries."

Igneous Feldspar looked into the insistent gray eyes. "You are right. I shall cooperate. Ernst has told me to register at the New Fujiya Hotel in Atami, where I am to receive further instructions. I shall transport you to Honshu in my hydrofoil on the morrow."

"Good Dane, Great Dane," Bond said. "If I had a can of Red Heart I'd feed it to you right now. You've earned it. But I'll do something better. I'll save you, your son and Japan and Israel."

"And save me before I go mad, for heaven's sake!" The voice, hoarse and demanding, came out of a thickly blossomed *yoni* bush. Something flew at his ankles and pinned him against the rocks. It was Magma Feldspar, naked and on fire. "Iggie, you no-score *klutz;* beat it while I make it with the King of Swing!"

"Professor, I—"

"Do as she asks, Mr. Bond. I understand." The golden curls drooped over the hurt eyes and he shuffled away on his Frankenstein-monster walk.

"There's nothing I won't do for a friend," Bond yelled to the giant, but Magma's lips, voracious and vampirish, crushed his words back into his sensual tonsils. "Screw thee and thy goddam goodness, lover boy. Let's make it."

"Up thine, baby," Bond riposted.

They made it.

Sarah cried.

No one listened.

14
A Fitting Climax Requires a Fitting

The Great Herrosukka Buddha blinked an indifferent farewell to the hydrofoil swerving around the cliff. "One positive thing has come from this deviltry," said the Dane. "The Buddha is rebuilt. My Norwegians will stay behind to coat its fiber glass body with a bronze spray. Hopefully, when you've brought this evil affair to a successful conclusion, I shall rejoin them in a few days to make a final inspection. By the next festival it will be ready to receive worshipers."

"Fiber glass. That's how you people got it up so fast."

"Bronze, my friend, is too expensive and too heavy. It would have taken years to haul a thousand tons up those cliffs and sculpt it. Ibsen's fiber glass bulk was easily transportable and malleable, and it is resilient enough to withstand any climatic conditions."

Feldspar had scheduled a conference on the scrolls at Meiji University, but he promised to meet Bond in two days at the Atami hotel. "I'll be there, too, Gray Eyes," chimed in Magma.

The hydrofoil made its elegant way past freighters and launches and put in at Pier 12, and Bond and the Dane shook hands. "Until then," said the latter, assaying a graceful leap back onto the deck, but the giraffe legs failed him and he tumbled into a cluster of his crew.

Those damn legs, Bond thought. Poor bastard has no coordination at all. What hell it must be to forever totter like a wino in a world of surefooted men.

Ginza-Burg, whom he'd phoned from Kyushu, was waiting in the Cedric. "As you requested, Oy Oy Seven, I didn't tell the Baron. It's gonna be a real surprise. We'd all given you up for lost. Maybe you can do something about these," and he dumped three English editions of local newspapers in Bond's lap.

In a front-page editorial the *Japan Times* expressed rancor at "the piratical attack" by the trawler and the contents of the scrolls. "These alleged historical documents, of which we have seen only Xerox copies, threaten the very soul of the islands. Can they be another Israeli machination?" The Yomiuri paper called for "suspension of relations with the Mideast aggressor. One can now appreciate the belligerence of the Arab states if this is what they have had to contend with since 1948." Signed by "Parker Waterman," the Asahi editorial went a step further: "A proud people must unsheath its sword, if need be, to keep from being sullied by Zionist marauders and doctrines."

Ginza-Burg, executing a slick Fangio sideswerve, forced a crowded bus into a ravine. "Gotcha, you cockers! All six dozen! That Asahi piece worries me, Mr. Bond. As you might suspect, Parker Waterman is a pen name. He's Britt Kato, the Minister of Propaganda, and you can take what he wrote as the official line. The Nips are getting a little *fahbrent*."[*]

Bond consumed seventy-six Raleighs and, when he ran out, three coupons, finding no noticeable difference. Bad business, this mounting Japanese truculence. *Herr Doktor* had once again correctly read the mentality of a nation. Under the servility, smiles and politesse skulked the old samurai war spirit, longing to be unleashed. One couldn't blame Feldspar for that martial characteristic or for the scrolls' revelations. But Shimon's scribblings, compounded with whatever new insults Holzknicht was planning, were bound to cause big trouble. The Nazi had to be liquidated before the lid blew off.

Bond had planned a grand entrance cum trumpet fanfare, but he whipped the Selmer from his lips when he heard the desperate voice of Kopy Katz in the Baron's Cathouse of the August Tea suite.

"No, Baron. Please. It's not your fault."

"I have dishonored myself, Miss Katz. Mr. Bond was my guest, his personal safety my obligation, yet I allowed him to die. Only *seppuku* can cleanse my sin. A simple slash from my right eyeball to my pancreas—"

"No, Cocky!" Bond bashed his way through the paper screen to come upon the tableau he'd expected: Sanka in a black kimono,

---

[*] Burned up

the sword held high to pierce the stocky body; a cringing, powerless Kopy. "Give me that sword, you damn fool!"

The command triggered off Sanka, who went into a posture of offensive swordsmanship and swiped at Bond, the blade leaving a long, bright gash in the Selmer's mouth.

"Iz!" Kopy fainted over the low table.

"Mr. Bond, as you being away Ipanema making berry, berry many packets of thousand-yen notes. Take them prease."

"Not now," Bond growled, but in shoving away the geisha tugging his arm he let himself be exposed to a second swipe, which drew a thin red line across his knuckles. He sidestepped a third, aimed a half-strength Oyama *bari* kick. Good-o! The tip of his Tijuana Brass bedsock mashed the stubby brown finger on the sword handle and the weapon clattered on the tatami. Sanka, his eyes rolling and maddened, chopped a calloused knuckle into the stomach bruise left by Yaynu's bullet head, which would have killed an ordinary man not possessing the steel-banded muscles Bond had toughened by one thousand pushups between his right-wing Minuteman orange juice and Wheat Chex with Alba nonfat milk each morning. The Israeli saw an opening, brought the Selmer down on the Baron's head. There was a cavernous *klonk* and Sanka fell unconscious over the inert Kopy.

"Dizzy never swung a Selmer like that," Bond said to no one in particular and when no one answered was not disappointed. He slapped Sanka's cheeks sharply and the *Kyodo Kikaku* chieftain came to, fully recovered from his derangement.

"I cannot believe my eyes, Izzy-san. You have returned from the dead. But only *seppuku* can atone for my shame lest the gods be—"

"I'm hip to this bag by now," Bond cut in. "Call in Flowering Fungus." Sanka did and the geisha scurried to his side. "Cocky, tell her to sing that ballad of Raykko once more."

Her first toneless note in the basso profundo convinced him. "Baron, I'd hoped her singing would have improved enough to warrant sparing her life. It hasn't. Let it be her."

Sanka agreed and tossed the geisha the sword. She bowed low and left the suite.

"*Yo-i!*" Bond said. "Now your deities and my muse have been placated." He splashed sake in Kopy's oval face to revive her and detailed his adventure since the cave episode, omitting the Go-Down Mikimoto interlude for the sake of her susceptibilities.

"The 'Black Room,'" she murmured. "It's got to be the 'Black Room.'"

"This is no time for gibberish, baby," Bond said impatiently. "Holzknicht is due in Atami and I've got to get to the top tailor in town on the double."

"A tailor? I do not understand, my friend."

"Baron, it is unthinkable for me to have it out with him in these rags. When you're heading toward the climax of your career as the world's *ichi-ban* secret agent you need groovy threads."

Once he saw the gravity of the situation, Sanka did not hesitate to recommend Ling Ah Lingle, a Chinese Jew from Hong Kong, whose sign in the basement of the grand old prestige hotel, the Imperial, advertised: SUITINGS FOR SPIES, IF YOU'VE GOT THE DAGGER, I'VE GOT A CLOAK TO MATCH IT.

In the window were some end-of-season specials Kopy thought darling. "Iz, I love those silken rope sandals."

"They can be unraveled by pulling on a couple of hidden knots, which gives you a reliable pair of Calcutta strangling cords. In the trade we call sandals like those 'Thug Boats.' That shorty nightie is for KGB girls; the big puffy buttons have death pills inside. Hey, that's a helluva nice Harry Palmer slip-on heat-seeking sweater. Changes from dull brown to bright orange in the presence of a passionate enemy female agent. Mr. Ling Ah Lingle has a pretty spiffy line."

The paunchy proprietor listened attentively to Bond's sartorial needs. "None of the items in my regular stock are for you, sir. They would be appropriate if you were going up against SMERSH, Phoenix, the Gehlen group or the Wackenhut Organization, not TUSH. You require what I would term 'confrontation clothing.'"

"That's the ticket." Chap knew his business. "And the finest bedsocks money can buy. The whole wardrobe can be put on the account of Eretz Israel."

"Eretz Israel? Bedsocks?" The man's butterball face split into a smile of homage. "There is but one man in 'the game' who attaches such importance to bedsocks, who slithers in the dark jungle of espionage for the Star of David. You are Israel Bond, Oy Oy Seven. This is the privilege of a lifetime, Mr. Bond. I shall outdo myself." Humming and measuring, stopping to comment how pleasurable it was to clothe such a physique, Ling Ah Lingle hit a new high in haute couture. The stunning ensemble started with Penkiovsky Paper Pantaloons, a Baby Jane Holzer minidicky, a breathtaking Georgy Girl cummerbund, a pure silk black-and-tan Gypo Nolan trenchcoat (it cost twenty pounds), and he capped it by slipping onto Bond's sensual feet a pair of virtually unobtainable Abominable Snowman bedsocks, each one three feet long, which he swore had been chipped from the feet of an actual Yetta—a female Yeti—discovered in 1921 under a Valley of the Blue Moon snowslide.

There was a moment of uncertainty at the full-length mirror; but then Bond preened and saw himself as an effulgent rainbow, each item a perfect complement to the others, and the joyous tears washed his darkly handsome cheeks.

"Oh, Lord, it's so—so—kicky! Dr. Ernst Holzknicht, you will meet your doom at the hands of the most madly Mod, switched-on spy the world has e'er beheld."

Ling Ah Lingle was still dancing when the little old lady in the blue-and-white shawl entered his shop.

"Ach, did I not see Israel Bond as I passed the Japan Travel Bureau at the other end of the arcade? He departed so rapidly I had no chance of catching him on these old legs."

"He was here, madam, but he's left for the Hilton. He—" and the Chinese stopped abruptly. He'd no business revealing the comings and goings of his clientele. "I must ask you to forget my indiscretion, madam."

"Oh, he'll want to see me, I know. *Shalom,* Ling Ah Lingle." She gave him an engaging smile and returned to the arcade.

The haberdasher lifted the receiver of his telephone. "Operator, please connect me with the message desk at the Hilton."

He had an afterthought and replaced the phone in its cradle. *She said,* "Shalom," he thought. An old lady in a blue-and-white shawl, the colors of Eretz Israel, who uses *Shalom* as her valediction...

He barked a relieved laugh and went about his business.

15
Brolly Brawl On The Bullet

The first caller was Sanka. "Izzy-san, you have forty-eight hours to clear up this affair. If you do not, I cannot be responsible for my government's actions. I have just spent a most unpleasant hour in the Diet office of Propaganda Minister Kato. He showed me a disgusting collection of hate telegrams that has been pouring in from all over the globe since those accursed scrolls were promulgated. Some of the salutations include: 'Emperor Hirosheeny,' 'Hiro-Kike-O,' 'Honorable Number One Mockyo of Tokyo'—those are the milder ones. You cannot expect Japan to put up with further affronts. I shall meet you on the train to Atami." He added a frigid *"Ohayo"** and hung up.

"Wisconsin to you," Bond raged at the dial tone.

A woman from the Tokyo Jewish Center was the second caller. "We have heard you are a public relations spokesman for Mother Margolies' Activated Old World Products. Are you still available for talks before women's groups?"

The anger oozed out of him. "Yes, my dear. I'm leaving for Atami on the 3 P.M. *Bullet*, but buzz me in a day or two. I'll be delighted to address your sisterhood."

He packed his new wardrobe, slipped into some informal attire—robin's-egg-blue Fruit of the Loom Underwonders, rose-colored Don Loper mini-Bimini shorts and cigar-brown Erik Is Here bedsocks with Viking prows on the toes—and buzzed Ginza-Burg, who gunned the Cedric toward Tokyo Central Station at his usual clip, eight dead pedestrians per block. "You'd better get in all the killing you can, *boychikl*," Bond said, "because we Hebes might not be welcome around these parts much longer. Second thought, let *me* take the wheel," which he did at

---
* Good morning

the next stoplight. Slamming the pedal to the floor, he waffled three policemen and twenty-one shoppers.

Boarding the *Bullet* with Sanka, who was nattily dressed in Ainu bearskin leotards, Bond was beset by uneasiness. Just what would Japan do if he couldn't squash TUSH? Launch a war against Eretz Israel? Surely a piddling attack at sea and a few pieces of racist literature wouldn't justify that drastic a response. The Nips might break off diplomatic relations, but that would be tolerable. Then again, they might begin supplying to the Arabs the cream of their technology; that wouldn't be. How sticky it got depended on the next demon from Holzknicht's Pandora's box. Damn it, here he was going into mortal combat with the archenemy minus a single major-league espionage device from Lavi HaLavi. Why had Lavi flipped his dandruff when he needed the little QM's brainpower so urgently?

His melancholia was interrupted by a genteel knock on his compartment door. "Mr. Bond?" One of those adorable little train girls who sell sandwiches and soft drinks smiled shyly at him. "A Western woman requires your presence in Compartment 13."

"What does she look like?"

"Very ancient, sir, and wearing a shawr. She said a strange phrase to me—'*Sharom Areichem.*' This way, prease."

"*Gottenu!* What the hell is M. doing in Japan to complicate things just as this caper is moving toward a finale? Cocky, you'll pardon me for a mo'."

At Compartment 13 he used the present month's simple door signal, pounding out a Chico Hamilton 12/9 cadence left-handed, a Mongo Santamaria bongo riff right-handed, and whistling from both sides of his mouth simultaneously the two themes from Jobim's "No More Blues."

The door slid open.

Her back was to him, but he could see the babushka atop her silver-blue Larry Mathews senior-bopper wig and the blue-and-white shawl, and the love he bore her flooded away the angry speech he'd been rehearsing.

She turned. A venomous, lined face glared at him, the metal tip of a black umbrella dug viciously into his belly bruise. "Hands behind the neck. Walk in slowly. Use your shoulder blades to slide the door shut."

Buddy boy, you deserve anything you're going to get in this four-by-four death trap, he castigated himself. *Is M. the only shawl-draped old Western woman in the world?*

One whiff of her *parfum*, "Forever Eichmann," told him all he needed to know.

"So, you are the *Jude* who killed my son."

The metal tip prodded him twice more, but he dared not retaliate. This was an all too familiar bit of weaponry. It could protect you from the rain, yes, and also spread your intestines apart with an expanding dumdum bullet. You could call it either a "brolly-blaster" or a "bumbershooter," because of the Luger built into the harmless-looking umbrella, without which a conservative Londoner would seem naked.

"There must be some mistake, madam. I am a public relations—"

"You are Israel Bond, the *schweinhund* who killed my only son. I am Frau Ilse Marlene."

Marlene! Of course, the mother of Willi Marlene, the knife-toting member of TUSH's elite branch for killer homos, the Gayfia, whose windpipe Bond had stove in during a hectic incident at London's Gayboy Club in the Queen adventure. "Madam, I—"

Blim! Blam! Her left hand smote his own windpipe. "I believe that is how you did it, *nein?*" *Splish! Splash!* Two more chops split his sensual lips and he retched on the blood pouring into his swollen throat.

"I am afraid you will be in no condition to deliver that speech at the Tokyo Jewish Center, Herr Bond. Yes, it was I who called. Like my late son, I have had theatrical training."

Grand Guignol, no doubt, Bond thought.

"How simple it was to deceive you and your tailor. A simple Hebrew phrase, a few stage props—babushka, shawl, wig—and you let your minds see what you wanted to see—your beloved M."

"The grudge file, Frau Marlene?"

"*Ja.* But I will tell you, since it will not matter in any case, that I am disobeying orders. I was ordered to tag you, but I shall not be robbed of the chance to end your derring-do for all time, Herr Bond."

"One question, *bitte,* Frau Marlene." If her answer was negative, a bobby-pin-size chance remained. "Have you ever ridden the *Bullet* before?"

A tinge of respect entered the toad face. The Jew was not going to whine for his life. "*Nein,* this is my first trip on a *Japanischer* train."

Bonds left hand edged behind him, found a steel clothes hook on the door and clamped around it with all his power. "I presume, Frau Marlene, that brolly-blaster is the same weapon that took the life of—oh, what was his name?" He assumed a quizzical expression. *Stall, stall, Oy Oy Seven!* "Colonel Onan Lemming of the British M.I. 5 in the Liverpool Airport slaying of 1964...."

The *Bullet's* screech was Mozart to his ears.

He'd been braced for the sudden stop, but the unaware hag flew across the compartment and her head caroming off the steel wall was the sweet sound of Mike Epstein's forty-ounce Louisville Schlooger kissing a fast ball into the right-field bleachers. Bond sprang onto the dazed woman, chopping down on her right wrist, and the brolly-blaster fell onto the seat. Infuriated at the startling turnabout, Frau Marlene shook her head to clear away the cobwebs and then snaked back at him, her bony claws raking his cheeks. Her left hand darted to an exposed stocking top and freed a length of silver. But before her hand could complete the deadly arc, Bond had the brolly-blaster pointed dead center at her maddened face, depressed the trigger and—*splat!* Frau Marlene had an extra mouth where her wartstippled nose had been. There was a blood-choked wail; the dirk fell from the wizened fingers and she collapsed on the floor into a bundle of old rags.

Hearing a hammering at the door, Bond wiped the blood from his lips with the back of his hand and opened it to meet the sharp scrutiny of Sanka.

The Baron examined the garbage heap that had been Frau Ilse Marlene without comment.

"Your statement came back to me when I was under the gun, Cocky. 'Some three million people per annum choose the railroads as their method of self-destruction.' One of them paid off for me. Who was it?"

Sanka smiled sardonically. "I have just seen the mangled body on the tracks, Izzy-san, with the note pinned to its kimono. Your savior was Suicide Suzuki."

16
Bowling Brawl in the Bathhouse

"Yes," said Sanka, reflecting upon the event as the cab neared the New Fujiya, "you escaped death at the Nazi woman's hands because of a magnificent act by our eminent chronicler of death. Suicide Suzuki, as it turns out, lived in a luxurious villa on a hill overlooking the New Tokkaido rail bed. His note stated that his last column contained a typographical error that resulted in the misspelling of one of the suicide's names. Instead of haranguing the printer, as he would have been well within his rights to do, he shouldered the blame squarely, apologized to the publisher and the victim's family, went to his home, donned a ceremonial kimono, took out several scrapbooks containing all the "Death Beat" columns he'd ever written, ate them in penance, rupturing his insides, then climbed to the top of his villa and hurled himself onto the tracks. A glorious way to leave this vale of tears, Izzy-san. The gods are smiling now."

Atami, oft referred to as Japan's Coney island by people who have been to neither, nestles, nestles by the Pacific behind a high seawall. On the tiny beach are piles of boulders cut into the shape of monstrous children's jacks. In the rear of the resort are bluffs and mountains from whose terraced ridges hang hotels, both Western and *ryokan*. Its narrow streets bustle with kimono-wearing Japanese on holiday, their omnipresent cameras clicking away in the national sport, the taking of pictures of other Japanese taking pictures.

The resort's newest sensation is the waterfront nightclub-restaurant, the Psyche-Deli, where the country's growing number of English-speaking acidheads congregates to eat delicatessen and dig an incongruous combination of hip American entertainment and those leave-nothing-to-the-imagination Japanese "strip shows." For an additional fee slipped surreptitiously to the crafty-eyed proprietor, Tripleader Taramuki, they will find minute cubes of LSD hidden in the greasy hearts of pastrami sandwiches.

Bond and Sanka joined the Feldspars at a ringside table. "You will enjoy the Psyche-Deli, Izzy-san," said Sanka. "Here performs Japan's *ichi-ban* stripper, Pickup Pochiko, whose control of her— ah—private region is so masterful that she is able to pick up a hundred-yen note without using her fingers or toes."

"We have one in Herzlia who can do that and also make change," Bond said. *There, Cocky-san, a little Israeli chauvinism for you!*

The secret agent, his "confrontation" clothes augmented by a shoulder holster which cuddled to its leathery bosom a five-shot Stitt-Coltrane, searched the Great Dane's face for the recognition signal that would say: *Let us make an excuse to leave the others, Mr. Bond. We have an appointment.*

Feldspar's smile said: *Not yet.*

In the wake of the stripper followed expatriate American jazzman Cassius Clink, inventor of the vibraskull, the controversial instrument that had caused him to be banned from his homeland. Clink, ranked by critics with Gillespie, Parker and Tristano as a primogenitor of the modern school, had by accident found his bag during a brawl in a San Francisco bistro, *The Starving W.* Wielding a bottle of Jack Daniels in self-defense, he discovered that human skulls had a vast spectrum of sounds—alto, tenor, soprano, bass, baritone, etc. By arranging selected individuals into a battery of "living tones" and perching himself on a stool high above them and swinging six-foot mallets, he'd created the vibraskull.

He was scheduled for a thirty-minute set but had to end it at five when in the middle of a driving, double-time passage on "You Go to My Head" three of his "living tones" ceased to be that way. "This," said a disappointed Bond, "is the inevitable result of a Cassius Clink concert. But he still deserves the unstinting adulation of the jazz world. He is the father of the head arrangement."

Two porters mopped up the grisly leavings of the aborted session and then over the loudspeaker came the cry: "Limbo! Let's do de limbo, mon!" Cheering wildly, the Psyche-Deli patrons thronged the floor for the limbo contest, the traditional highlight of the evening in any Japanese nightery from Tokyo's swanky New Latin Quarter to those dingy taverns for the *eta*, the country's "untouchable" class. Bond noted the childish docility of the patrons being led under the ever-lowered limbo stick until it was scant inches from the floor. The hands-down winner was a Tokyo University student, who accepted the trophy from his position under the rug.

The room went black; strobe lights began to wink, and so did Feldspar, slowly and deliberately, three times. Sanka saw Bond and the Dane locked in a conspiratorial glance and remarked, "Good hunting, gentlemen."

Twice on the ten-minute ride up a mountain trail the cab driver had to stop. "There is a bad knock in the motor." He could not locate the source despite a diligent investigation.

"There is nothing wrong with the motor," the Dane said. "Please drive on." His wise eyes messaged Bond: *Control yourself, my friend. Your heart is beating like a Maytag washer.* Bond sucked in a few deep breaths and his heartbeat reverted to its normal 565 counts per minute.

The journey ended in front of a building positioned precariously on a pine-tree-covered cliff. "This is the Samarra Bathhouse, Mr. Bond. I have been instructed to be on the roof garden at midnight. We have a few minutes. Let us use them in a refreshing *ofuro*."

Samarra. Bond's cruel, sensual mouth was framed in an ironic smile. What a fitting place for an appointment!

Feldspar handed a sullen cashier a ten-thousand-yen note and they were shown by lovely maidens in gym uniforms to separate cubicles. Bond disrobed and splashed about in the tub, declining his masseuse's offer of a three-thousand-yen "speciar massage."

"I believe that autoeroticism is a matter for the individual and, besides, it should only be practiced in Cadillacs, young woman."

He dressed quickly, rechecked his Stitt-Coltrane and rapped on the door to Feldspar's cubicle. "Four minutes, professor."

The Dane wore a light-blue *yukata* and as he tottered up the stairs on his giraffe legs Bond noticed his knees were circled by bands of thick grayish scar tissue. Feldspar must have had some horrible car accident, he thought. No wonder the man had no control over his gait.

At eleven-fifty-seven they were on the third floor, Feldspar sliding open a screen, and then on the roof garden. The ocean's scent was pervasive and heavy here. Hundreds of feet below, whitecaps rolled in to end their existence against the boulders and seawall.

"Ouch!" The Israeli shattered the silence by banging his toe into an unyielding mass. Flicking on his Zippo, he saw a pyramid of big black iron balls. "What the hell are they?"

"Souvenirs of the Russo-Japanese War of 1905, Mr. Bond. They are cannonballs used to sink Czarist ships in the battle of Tsushima Strait. After the war they were recovered by the thousands by Imperial divers and brought to Japan, where they are venerated as symbols of national might. It is a poor bathhouse, indeed, that does not have a similar pyramid on its premises."

"It's eleven-fifty-nine. You sure he's going to show?"

"Ernst has the Germanic obsession with punctuality. He will announce his presence at the stroke of midnight; no earlier, no later."

Bond was on a countdown, his heart doing mad flip-flops, ping-ponging off his kidneys, gall bladder and liver. Thirty-three seconds, thirty-two, thirty-one... Surely there should have been a noise on the stairs by now.

The second and hour hands embraced at twelve.

A blinding light flared at the far end of the roof garden. Under a floodlight, sitting in a wheelchair, was a man in a white lab coat, his black hair trimmed in a military crewcut.

Dr. Ernst Holzknicht.

He was not alone. Kneeling by his side and cocking a Manchester-Schlesinger rifle was a tough-looking, slant-eyed mulatto, heavily lipsticked and rouged, his wiry figure encased in a coral Pucci blouse and Braniff Airlines hostess skirt. High-heel Kitty Kelly light-opera pumps of patent leather gleamed in the floodlight. Bond knew the breed—a member of the notorious Black Dragqueen Society, the Far Eastern cult of deviate slay-for-payers. From the mulatto's obscenely curved lips dangled a long yellow cigarette exuding a sweet, acrid tang. A king-sized Chiquita Bananajuana! Just the sort of cigarette to inflame the high yellow into a yellow high—for murder!

The smirking voice that had plagued Bond in a million nightmares spoke. "Listen and do not interrupt." The mouth moved in an odd, jerky way; so did the hands. "So, Oy Oy Seven, you have come to Japan to exact revenge and quash my operation here. Too long have you been a thorn in the side of neo-Nazism. You and your Secret Service are responsible for the deaths of Lazarus Loxfinger, our god; East German Secret Agent James Bund; Gerda 'Auntie' Sem-Heidt, and a host of other TUSH patriots. Your daring feat atop the Empire State Building put me in this wheelchair with a broken body. You have induced this grotesque pig of a Dane to betray me. But you made a foolhardy move by coming here tonight. You will never leave here alive. As for you, Feldspar, you will rue the day you cast your lot with this *Jude*. I shall permit you to live long enough to see your beloved son injected with my new *barbarella* toxin. Shall I describe its unimaginable agony to you, the rotting of tissue—"

"*Boche! Boche!*" the Dane screamed and broke into his laughable gait toward the Nazi, his hands knotted into fists, the golden curls jiggling.

"Stop him!" Holzknicht commanded.

The Black Dragqueen's rifle buzzed and Feldspar seemed to hang suspended for a second as one of the slugs thudded into his leg, but his rage was as towering as his size and he lunged onward like a crazed bull. Bond's Stitt-Coltrane was out, crashing its entire clip at the Black Dragqueen, but the five bullets missed by a wide margin, blowing out a section of the railing behind the Nazi and his gunsel.

From the Manchester-Schlesinger came an unerring response; there was a searing jolt in his gun hand and the Stitt-Coltrane went flying over the roof. *Thwack!* Another M-S slug hit Bond's right thigh with a tremendous impact, driving him into the pyramid of cannonballs.

Feldspar's hands were inches away from throttling the Nazi's throat when the giraffe legs could take it no longer. He sprawled at the foot of the wheelchair, sobbing impotent curses.

Israel Bond had already made up his mind what his do-or-die tactic would be the instant his head cracked into the top ball. He summoned up his last ounce of power, hoisted the ball and went into the old Don Carter four-step the kegling ace had taught him one night at the White Horse Bowling Academy in Trenton, New Jersey. Now he was on the fourth step of the approach, then his rippling back and shoulder muscles released the cannonball in a mighty thrust.

The Black Dragqueen tittered at the puny effort, but then he froze in horrified fascination, unable to pull the trigger, as he saw the ball gaining momentum and coming at him on a thunderous roll. Before he could snap out of his panic, it was too late. The ball crunched into his ankle, hurling him on a side slant into the bottom of Holzknicht's wheelchair, and suddenly both of them were falling back through the gaping hole in the railing, down, down, down... and the screams of the Black Dragqueen were lost in the pounding of the whitecaps.

Bond forced his bloodied frame to crawl inch by inch to the edge and gazed down at the precise moment the moon scudded out from behind a cloud to bathe the seawall in silvery light. There was the wheelchair in a thousand fragments on the boulders... a white-sleeved hand disappearing under the waves.

Bond lit a Raleigh and whispered to the gasping Dane. "I made the seven-ten split—and they split, too. It's all over, professor. Dr. Ernst Holzknicht is dead."

17

Games Xerox People Play

Another stroke of luck.

The well-proportioned masseuse, into whose ground-floor cubicle Bond had dragged the giant, informed the bullet-riddled duo she was an intern who found it necessary to moonight at the Samarra to supplement her meager income. From a case she took a thin, delicate instrument, inserted it into the band of scar tissue around Feldspar s left leg and extracted the ugly, flattened Manchester-Schlesinger slug.

"Good-o!" Bond enthused. "Honey, you're a regular"—and he chuckled roguishly as he whipped in the sparkling pun—"*Yen* Casey!" (When she did not collapse from laughter, he attributed it to her unfamiliarity with top-drawer Western humor.) "Professor, it looks like you're going to be OK. I can see your eyes brimming with gratitude for the valorous deed I've just done, but save your thanks. Purchase an Israel Bond of a sizable amount to help keep the Middle East's sole true democracy hale and free and that'll be reward enough. I've got some loose ends to clear up—the safe return of your son, squaring things with the Japanese— but in the interim, you cab it back to the Psyche-Deli and tell Sanka TUSH's Mr. Big will menace his country no more. And now, honey, take that lump of iron out of me."

When they were alone, the masseuse plied her skill on Bond's thigh and so adroit were her cool fingers that he scarcely felt a twinge. What he did experience as she probed that sensitive area was a pleasurable tingle, a sudden tumescence that rivaled Everest in lofty grandeur, and then their lips were locked in an ore-smelting kiss; pores excited pores; teats teatillated teats, and they were on the verge of a climax that would have blown the long-lost continent of Atlantis out of the depths of the sea and deposited it on the boardwalk of Atlantic City, when Bond's exaltation was shattered by the materializing of Sarah in the steam of the *ofuro*.

Oh, Iz. You've been unfaithful again.

"All right, goddammit!" he swore, disengaging himself from the disappointed masseuse. He strode briskly to the apparition and shook his fist. "Baby, I'm a man with a man's needs. You've been avenged. The Nazi pig who did you in is now in Davy Jones's locker. Or, if that's overcrowded, in Peter Tork's, Micky Dolenz's or Mike Nesmith's." (*Gottenu!* Another shaft of brilliance! The block-busting one-liners were pouring out at an incredible rate!) "Sarah, I know you got a lousy break in New York. Dying can be an awfully traumatic experience. But I'm alive; my life has to go on. Certainly there must be a host of sexy shades floating around in your dimension you can certainly turn on with—Old Marley, Canterville, or if you dig kids, Casper. What I'm trying to say in the kindest possible way is—*Stop bugging me!*"

Two chilly lips bussed his cheek. *Adieu, Iz. Adieu forever.*

And that's that, Bond thought. Resuming his place at the side of the delectable maiden, he grinned. "Shall we get back to the earth-moving business? If we really make an effort we can heave Vietnam into the Bering Sea and make the world safe for democracy and Drew Pearson."

His cruel sensual mouth was bruising hers when—

"Bond! Aleph priority!" The voice of Schlomo Salvar crackled over the Krai-Cain syncraphone's Frequency Baze Tzaddik. "The embassy just received a frantic message for you from a Miss Katz. Says she's trapped in her Xerox suite by two TUSH-ys."

"I'm on the way, Schlomo. Over and out," Bond told his false sixth bedsock toe. "Honey, I know you must think you've run into an *ichi-ban* weirdo who goes around talking to clouds of steam and his toes, but there's no time to explain. Where's the phone?"

A call to Sanka produced a *Kyodo Kikaku* helicopter on the roof garden piloted by a Major Domo, a ramrod of an officer. "I am at your disposal, Mr. Bond. The Xerox facility is but a few minutes' flying time from here and its penthouse contains one of Tokyo's finest heliports."

"*Arigato domo,* Domo. Or, Domo, *domo arigato.* Or..." *Dammit! There's another powerhouse of a one-liner somewhere in that combination,* Bond thought, *but it's escaped me for the moment. Anyway, this is no time for quipping when Kopy's in danger. Why* has TUSH gone after her? And who's directing the show now that Holzknicht's out of the picture?

The copter reached an altitude of two thousand feet in a few seconds and soon the garish, tinselly Ginza section was below them. The bars would be just about ready to close by now, Bond knew. Gorgeous hostesses, who'd been lighting cigarettes for tourists at three thousand yen an hour and promising paradise in their alluring winks, would be sneaking out through the back entrances to join their musician boyfriends while the drink-befuddled John Q. Travelers were being sobered up by tabs that could have financed insurrections in eight new African nations.

"Xerox ahead, Mr. Bond. Will you require my assistance?"

"No, thanks, Major Domo. After what I've been through, a couple of minor-league hoods will be Hostess cupcakes."

The craft hovered over the landing pad, then set down gently, though the gales from its rotors flung a trio of broom-wielding janitors over the edge. Bond watched them plummet like bundles of wet wash. "Don't feel bad about it, Domo. You've just created three new employment opportunities." He cursed himself for adopting so easily the Japanese indifference to death, but pushed it out of his mind when his feet hit the gravel.

He raced through the opulent surroundings, pausing only to filch a bottle of Johnnie Walker Black Label from a table on the terrace and give his insides a good heat treatment, then vaulted five steps at each bound down a stairway leading to the twentieth floor suite.

Kopy's oaken door was ajar. (*I wonder if she has a jar that's adoor,* he thought, in yet another demonstration of his fantastic wit.)

"Kopy! Kopy!" His voice echoed through her empty office.

"Iz." Her voice, so faint, so far away.

"Darling, what have they done to you?"

"Quickly, Iz. Through the green door!"

He barreled through the suite, upsetting lamps and worktables and a Ben Shahn masterpiece, the *Mona Schevitz,* until he found the green door, turned the handle and peered into a long, dimly lit corridor. "Kopy!"

"At the end of the hall, Iz! Hurry! I can't hold them off any longer!"

A shot shook the hallway.

Bond crouched, revved up into the old Bob Hayes breakaway sprint and traversed a hundred yards in 8.9 seconds. Another scream—"Iz!"—sent a chill down his sensual, splendidly interlocked vertebrae.

He stopped on a dime at a black door over which a red DANGER sign glowed dully. Picking up the coin and pocketing it, he drove his massive shoulders into the door, cutting it down like a blocking back paving the way for Gale Sayers, and hurtled into utter blackness.

"Kopy! Kopy!"

Her voice was quite near now, curiously cool and mocking. "That's fine, Iz. Just fine."

"Dammit! Are you playing games, baby? Where are you? It's so dark I can't see my hand in front of my—"

Thump! On all sides he heard partitions hissing from the ceiling to the floor. Bond flailed his fists and met cold metal. He was in a trap. "What the hell..."

Kopy Katz's laugh rang out, frightening him with its eeriness.

There was a flash as bright as an exploding sun. Something titanic clobbered his head. Israel Bond pitched to the floor and lay motionless.

18
Bondo Limbo

"Someday you'll find it in your heart to forgive me for my little ruse," said Kopy Katz, placing the tenth icebag on the splitting head of Israel Bond. "I hated to do it this way, but, dammit, Iz, you kept ignoring my pleas."

He dragged on a Raleigh. "And you fired the shot, I gather."

"An added touch of drama, darling. It worked, didn't it? Oh, heaven, what a thrill to see you charging down that corridor like Lancelot to the rescue! My lovely, lovely knight." The raspberry lips blew suggestive zephyrs into his ear.

"Oy Oy Seven! Aleph priority!" Schlomo Salvar was back on his false sixth toe. "I've got to see you right away. All kinds of *mishigass*[*] have been happening around here. First of all, your seven-foot Danish playmate stopped in, bought a ten-thousand-dollar Israel Bond as a token of his gratitude, fed me a few shots of some wicked brandy and left for Kyushu. Then Baron Sanka stormed in yammering bloody murder. He brought a copy of a video tape that's been airmailed to every major Japanese TV network from an undisclosed source in Europe. They've junked their regular schedule of programs to play it over and over. Turn on your TV set, then get here on the double."

Kopy pressed one of a row of buttons on her desk and a wall-size Sony hummed. The white dot spread; a Japanese announcer came on jabbering harshly and waving his arms in agitation.

"I'll translate, darling. He says the event we're about to witness occurred yesterday at a Common Market banquet in Brussels. It was filmed by an observer using a portable hand camera and supplied free of charge by 'A Friend of the Great

---

[*] Craziness

Japanese People.' The man at the podium, he says, is Israel's Minister of Trade Hyman DeFlower. Recognize him?"

Bond did. "That's DeFlower, no doubt about it. *Gottenu!* He looks like he's stoned. Notice the glazed eyes, the St. Vitus-like *tzittering* of the lips."

"... able on this auspicious occasion to reveal for the first time a stunning breakthrough by a group of miniaturization specialists at our Technion Institute. Israel can now produce transistor radios of a quality far superior to anything emanating from Japanese laboratories—and cheaper, gentlemen, much cheaper. In the months to come we will reign supreme in this lucrative enterprise. Surely you cannot now deny my nation a Security Council membership in this prestigious organization..."

The Japanese commentator reappeared.

"He says, 'We shall replay the tape following a lengthy statement from Propaganda Minister Britt Kato.' Want to see more, Iz?"

"What for? Baby, as the razor manufacturer said when he accidentally dropped one of his shavers from a Cessna flying over Yankee Stadium: 'Now the Schick has really hit the fan!'"

"Iz, I'm going with you." The lovely Xeroxite replaced her silver chain and plunger with a copper one more suitable for casual afternoon wear and they took the elevator to a subbasement, where she tossed him the keys to a rakish, low-slung Castro convertible. "A wild thing, Iz. Quadruple carbs, twenty-four-volt Ruffing-Dickey battery, Sid Mark Three Pratt-Whitney engine capable of 188 nonmetric poods per dunam, and at night you can convert it into a very sexy couch."

The Castro whisked them to the embassy through streets ominously deserted. "I don't like this stillness," Bond said. "I haven't hit a single pedestrian in more than eighty blocks. Something's brewing."

A Miss Cilia Cohen, Salvar's curvaceous sabra secretary, led them to the diplomat's plush inner sanctum, where Sanka sat on a divan, seemingly under control, throwing spitballs at a large photograph of Theodor Herzl.

"Thank God you're here, Oy Oy Seven," said the short, bespectacled Salvar, rising to offer his hand. "I've been trying to convince the Baron there's been a horrible mistake but I'm afraid I haven't been getting through."

"The speaker in the video tape was Hyman DeFlower, is that not a fact, Izzy-san?"

"Yes, Baron, but he was wacked out of his *keppel*, couldn't you see that? Someone induced him to make that preposterous statement by some devilish means. Holzknicht, maybe."

"But your Danish friend apprised me of Holzknicht's death in Atami. Was Feldspar lying? Is this whole Holzknicht business a red herring cooked up between you and the Dane? The scrolls, the attack on me at the *ryokan*, all of it?"

"Dammit, Cocky-san!" Bond shook Sanka's shoulders. "Didn't I save your life in Beppu? Wasn't I wounded myself?"

Sanka sighed. "I don't know what to think, my friend. Salvar-san showed me a communication from your PM denying categorically Eretz Israel's plan to control the transistor market. But it hardly matters now. Our public is livid with rage, awaiting only the green light from the Diet to—"

Over the intercom shrilled Cilia Cohen. "Mr. Salvar! Come quickly! Look down the block! There's an army approaching the embassy."

Japanee no Jew!
Japanee no Jew!

The roar washed over the embassy.

Japanee no Jew!
Japanee no Jew!

There was a tinkling of glass. "Rocks—they're throwing rocks!" Miss Cohen was hysterical.

The four occupants of Salvar's chamber moved to a balcony overlooking the street. "The Sokka Datgai, Izzy-san," said Sanka with grim satisfaction. "They are coming in full force. I warned you my people would brook no more insults."

Bond, his gray eyes sweeping over the sea of blazing yellow faces, lit a Raleigh. "Where are the riot police?"

"They are on the way, Izzy-san. But I suspect they will not be too effective."

"You mean they'll have been told not to be too effective?"

Sanka's sneer was answer enough.

Japanee no Jew!
Japanee no Jew!

They were surging forward in phalanxes of two thousand, each preceded by a sound truck whose trained agitators were inflaming the marchers. "Hands off transistors! Japanee no Jew! Japanee are Japanee!"

A police truck pulled up, disgorged a paltry contingent of men in black uniforms and red combat hats. From the rear of the truck they pulled out four long steel riot poles and paired off into teams. They made a few halfhearted thrusts to contain the mob, grinning as they permitted themselves to be shoved back step by step.

Piff! Paff! Two rocks walloped Bond's head and in the mind-expanding flashes of agony he conceived a solution to this hairy situation.

The riot poles!

He recalled the docile, antlike behavior of the Japanese in the Atami nightclub as they'd scrambled to get into the limbo contest.

"Schlomo! I'm going down there. Send two of your best men after me, quickly! Tell them to grab one of the riot poles and pay attention to my spiel."

Bond leaped over the balcony railing to the soft, squooshy greensward, tore a bullhorn from the hands of one of the policemen and climbed onto the roof of the truck.

"Limbo! Let's do de limbo!" he yelled.

At first the demonstrators greeted his exhortation with a fusillade of missiles and he thought: *Anybody who dreams up a nutball scheme like this has rocks in his head. (Gottenu! Another gem! If he got out of this alive he'd have to phone Earl Wilson and plant it in the "Wish I'd Said That" department of the column.)*

His two embassy aides, strapping, bronzed sabras in light-blue Barbara Eden genie-jeans, had reached the scene, picked up an abandoned riot pole, stationed themselves at the ends, and the mob hushed, awaiting curiously the next move of this demented *gaijin*. Bond took advantage of the silence to bawl:

> "Whether you've got a monko or chimbo,
> Jump in de line and let's do de limbo!"

One of the agitators began to giggle. "Rimbo! Ret's do de rimbo!" The chant spread like wildfire to those in the rear. "Rimbo! Rimbo!"

"*Boocherim!*" Bond commanded his cohorts. "Move the stick away from the embassy. Where I go, you go."

"Rimbo! Rimbo!" The Sokka Datgai army was shouting and laughing now, and the first phalanx's ringleaders commenced to wiggle under the retreating pole, setting off a wholesale rush.

"Run! Move it to the next street!" Bond thundered. And to his brain: *Create, create! Keep improvising Calypso verses and this crowd is Silly Putty in your long, tapering, sensual fingers.*

> "*Whether you Japanee or Jew,*
> *De limbo is de ting to do!*"

He broke into a gallop; so did his pole-bearing sabras and the joyous, jouncing hordes.

> "*Whether you be an uncle or tanteh,*
> *Do de limbo like Harry Belafanteh!*"

(A false rhyme, his ashamed brain admitted, but, hell, even heavyweight lyricists like Stephen Sondheim and Johnny Mercer would be copping out in a desperate game such as this!)

> "*I load de bananas on de sailing clipper,*
> *Daylight come 'n' me wanna go home.*
> *But I don't work when it comes Yom Kippur,*
> *Yomtov come 'n' me wanna stay home!*"

Gottenu! He'd been running and shouting for miles, it seemed. Where were they now? Yes, Shinjuku! The road-construction gangs were dropping their jackhammers, picks and shovels to join the ever-lengthening line that was causing the most horrendous traffic jam in Tokyo's history. And still more recruits were falling into the ranks—hostesses and their inebriated clientele from cheap bistros, burly cops deserting their beats, geishas jumping from pedicabs, and the scrawny individuals who'd been pulling them.

On limboed the caravan, Bond, his two puffing Israelis and hundreds of thousands of Japanese, including the Diet, which had ceased its debate on the new trade agreement with South Korea to become shrieking, ecstatic participants.

His body pleaded for a respite, but he ignored the heartrending entreaties of his nearly rent heart, wheezing lungs, tortured gristle and blunted shoulderblades. Onward! he urged them. The flag at the Israeli embassy will not be trampled this day! He croaked through the bullhorn in a fast-diminishing voice:

> "*Mom, you made a booboo, I shout!*
> *Don't like my daddy—please t'row him out!*
> *Daddy real nasty—that swine!*
> *I t'ink dat you married Joe Pyne!*"

They'd reached the Hakone area and presently were stumbling about in pine forests and game preserves, past ski lodges, into icy mountain streams. The embassy aides finally faltered and sank to their knees and relinquished the hundred-pound steel rod to Bond, who, without missing a beat, held it a foot from the ground to allow another few thousand or so to squeeze through on their bellies, then steeled his body for the last grueling leg of the contest.

On the summit of Mount Fuji, aglow in the roseate sunset, the limbo dance ended. Bond looked at the exhausted Japanese strewn about like clothespins on the trail, turned his eyes upward to his Maker and whispered in hoarse reverence:

> "*Lord, who made me nimble; Lord, who made me quick,*
> *I thank thee from my heart for dat good ol' limbo shtick!*"

19
"Israel Bond Is Dead"

Major Domo, who'd been ordered by Sanka to track Bond from the copter, picked him up at Fuji's sixth station and ferried him to the embassy lawn. He limped past the adoring Cilia Cohen into Salvar's office, to be met by Kopy, whose abel-green eyes held a deep concern.

"Iz, thank heaven you're back. Schlomo's gone off the deep end. He started acting peculiar a while ago; a glaze came over his eyes and he sounded sort of, well, mechanical. He told Sanka he could straighten out all the misunderstanding if Sanka could get him an audience with the Emperor. Said he had new information proving Eretz Israel's innocence. He was so persuasive Sanka agreed. And he said he had a gift that would warm the Emperor's heart."

"A gift?"

"The Emperor is a marine-biology buff. Loves to add exotic specimens to his collection. Schlomo showed us a cute little tropical feller called a Ribicoff Rarity, which is spawned only in a certain stream in Connecticut, then spends the rest of its life trying to swim to the Indian Ocean. As you might imagine, darn few of 'em ever make it."

"Sounds damn fishy to me," Bond said, scoring minimally in the humor department. "I've got to get to the palace on the *double* double!"

He leaped back onto the lawn and caught Domo about to take off.

"This is most irregular, Mr. Bond. Landing on the grounds of the Son of Heaven's residence requires the highest security clearance."

"Dommit, Damo!" he swore and the hip Major cackled at Bond's rib-tickling play on his name. (Another socko ad lib! Who'd get this one? Jack O'Brian? Charles McHarry? Robert Sylvester? Even his straight lines were registering mega-boffs on the laugh meter.) "Forget the red tape, Major. If you refuse me you'll forevermore be known as Japan's Benedict Arnold."

The intensity in his expression won Domo over. "Hop in, Mr. Bond."

They came in fast over the Imperial Hotel, the palace moat, populated by huge golden-red carp, the high wall of brownish-gray boulders, then skimmed over gingkos, pines and brilliant clumps of cherry blossoms.

Crack! Crack! Bullets flew up from the carbines of a band of guards deployed into a human shield at the archway to the Imperial reception room. *Thwack!* Domo caught one in his shoulder, but bravely stayed at the controls and brought the craft to a jolting stop.

He staggered out, ignoring the blossoming patch on his jacket, and shouted something to the guards. "They'll pass you, Mr. Bond. Go!" Then he fell on his back.

Bond dropped a life-sustaining Excedrin into the gaping mouth. "Chew it, Domo." He ran through the arch down a tiled walkway, under a torii gate, and dived through a screen, landing catlike on his feet a couple of yards from the gold-and-black-robed Emperor of Japan, who was squinting into a glass tank held by the top-hatted, white-tie-and-tailed Salvar. "This, Your Majesty," the diplomat intoned, "contains—"

"Death! Caveat Emperor!" He flattened Salvar with a quarter-strength South Korean karate cut to the midriff taught him by a Seoul-brother, made a sensational shoestring catch of the falling tank and raised it high.

The cry of "Death!" in the presence of the Emperor started the adrenal coursing in Sanka, who whipped out a black Wembley-Vicar, got Bond in its sights and squeezed the trigger three times.

"Sanka, you fool," muttered Bond, pressing the long, tapering fingers of his left hand against his punctured abdomen.

With a moan he cocked the fish tank in his hand like a football and let it fly in a Bart Starr-bullet through the screen. He smiled thinly and toppled to the carpet.

A red ball artichoked into the sky; there was the oppressive smell of Calgonite, and fragments of the torii gate flew into the room.

"By the belly of Buddha!" screamed Sanka. "There was a Calgonite charge in that tank! Oy Oy Seven!" He went down on his knees before the Israeli. "The royal physician, quickly!"

"Cocky." Bond's voice was almost inaudible. "Got a last great one-liner for you, *boychikl*. It's adieu to espionage. I... just... haven't... got... the"—there was a ghost of a chuckle as he got in the punch line—"stomach for it... any more...." The sensual, vein-free eyelids rolled over the gray eyes.

Sanka felt for the pulse, caught the tiniest of throbs. Then nothing.

"Your Majesty," he said, bowing slowly and gracefully. "Your life has been saved by the greatest practitioner of espionage the world has ever known. It was his gesture of *sayonara* to you, to me and to the people of Japan. The royal physician will be of no use now. Israel Bond is dead."

20
Mr. Tambourine Man

In his Cathouse of the August Tea suite, Baron Cockimamiyama Sanka concluded his votive offerings to his household gods, recitating a haiku.

> *"I do not fear death.*
> *What I do fear is that it may*
> *not be permanent."*

"Excellent!" said his lifelong friend Count Iyama Pishaka, of the Foreign Office. "A verse of our seventeenth-century haiku master Bassho?"

"No. Buck Rogers of the 25th century." Sanka lit a Raleigh, his 10,718th since he had pulled the trigger that meant "thirty" for Israel Bond. The coupons would be sent to M. in Jerusalem so they could be credited to Bond's account. "It is good of you to stand by me in my final hour on this mortal coil. Have you prepared the sword?"

"*Hai.* I have dipped it from hilt to tip in Binaca, a Japanese potion. Your death will not only be agonizing, but fragrant. Allow me to place the ceremonial robe upon you." Slipping the richly brocaded garment over the chunky shoulders, he asked, "Have you completed your will?"

"You will find it on a scroll near the gods. The twenty-seven million yen I have accumulated from years of dedicated defalcation will fund a number of causes dear to the heart of Oy Oy Seven—the Committee for the Purchase of Israel Bonds, of course, and the United Jewish Appeal, the Jewish National Fund for the Reforestation of the East Bronx, the Joe E. Lewis Foundation for World Peace through Alcoholism, the Jewish Home for the Uninspired and so forth."

"What crosscut have you chosen, Baron? The classical style of the *daimyo** Haidan Sikko, which begins at the wisdom teeth and ends in the colon?"

"I have ruled out that one, my friend. Because of an operation I underwent two years ago, I have only a semicolon. No, I have decided upon a modern technique created by the founder of our national sound-recording system, Muzaki—from anus to larynx, from Memphis to St. Joe, wherever the four winds blow." *How Izzy-san, who had been so enamored of humor, would have appreciated that one,* Sanka sighed.

In his mind's eye he could still see the El Al jet with its sad cargo, the simple pine box wrapped in a giant-size trenchcoat (a sentimental touch requested by Miss Katz), winging to Eretz Israel, where the state funeral would be held.

Because of the unusual nature of Bond's passing and the need for complete secrecy, the simplest sort of ceremony had been conducted at the Jewish Community Center of Tokyo, attended by only a handful of mourners: Kopy Katz in a black chain and plunger, and her escort, a humpbacked, bearded man in dark glasses she'd introduced as her father; the embassy people, including a handcuffed, red-eyed Schlomo Salvar, who'd been permitted to attend by a special order from Sanka; Ginza-Burg, a yarmulke jammed over his cabby's cap, and Sanka, Pishaka and Propaganda Minister Kato, who'd been sent to express the official grief of a stunned Emperor.

Ginza-Burg had said the Kaddish, the Prayer for the Dead, and added an affecting aside. "I gotta leave real *schnell*. There's a fare in my cab and the meter's still running, but I just wanna say this. If there's a shining spot that's like a Kosher Camelot, that's where this wonderful warrior is right now. *Olav Hashalom*—may he rest in peace."

An unexpected visitor had come to the front of the chapel, a little man in a white frockcoat, string tie and thirty-gallon Pedernales River sombrero.

"Folks, I'm Oral Vincent Graham, the traveling evangelist, and it was my privilege to have known Mr. Bond during two of his adventures. When his boss lady in Jerusalem learned I was in Japan spearheading my latest crusade, she cabled me and asked me to say a few words that might comfort you in this moment

---

* Feudal noble

of tragedy. During my oration there'll be a tambourine passed among you. Any offering you'd care to make will be deeply appreciated. If you find yourselves without coins or folding money, just throw in your credit cards. We accept 'em."

He lit a long, odoriferous cigar, leaned against the casket and spoke his piece:

> "Ashes to ashes, dust to dust,
> If you don't like my figure,
> Take your hands off my bust."

He hemmed and hawed for a few seconds, clearly embarrassed.

"You'll pardon that unfortunate lapse into childish doggerel, folks. Funny how them little outhouse-wall poems come back to you at a time like this." He extinguished the cigar on the casket and resumed.

"We all came from Clay—or Muhummad Ali, if ye subscribe to another faith—and back to Clay we must go. Did not John the Baptist sayeth upon discovering a precious stone in the waters of the Jordan: 'Holy mackerel! It's Sapphire!' And, yea, unto ye I say, did not Ezekiel crieth when he saw the wheel, 'Number five on the black!'

"The Lord freed Sam Sheppard; he shall not want. Yes, let he who is without stones cast the first sin. For out of the mouths of babes comes Pablum and pacifiers. And Nashua fit de battle at Pimlico and the odds came a-tumblin' down.

"Be that as it may. Ye shall know the truth and it will make you sick.

"You've got to walk that lonesome valley; you've got to walk it by yourself. So walk on through the wind; walk on through the rain; for a rose must remain in the sun or the rain or its lovely promise won't come true. I know that Israel Bond's indomitable spirit is walking right now through that lonesome valley, the wind and the rain and those crappy waterlogged roses, and he'll never stop, though he's scorned and covered by scars, until he climbs every mountain, fords every stream and reaches the unreachable stars.

"I thank you." Oral Vincent Graham had taken the cigar butt from the casket, relit it by scratching a match on the seat of his pants and poked through the tambourine.

"Cheap crowd," someone heard him mutter.

Even the Japanese observers, who had been trained all their lives to conceal their deepest emotions, had wept quarts of tears.

A curious incident had occurred as Sanka got in the line moving past the casket to pay his last respects. Miss Katz, who surprisingly was dry of eye, shook his hand warmly, but her bent old father cursed at him and landed a sharp kick in the *Kyodo Kikaku* leader's groin. "You trigger-happy fascist bastard! When I think of that beautiful boy lying in there all shot up and all the women in the world who'll never know what true ecstasy is because of your precipitate action, I could—"

"Please, Dad," Miss Katz had said. "The Baron was only doing his duty, which was to safeguard the Emperor." She had then led the fractious codger away.

Now the sword was in Sanka's hand and finger. "Count Pishaka, please grant an old crony a last wish. Use every bit of your considerable influence to cool the temper of our people. Bond gave his life to prevent war. And while I as yet have not penetrated this mystery, I am certain his nation is not at fault. Give Major Domo the records of this case and tell him to institute a thorough investigation until the real culprits are in chains. And now, *sayonara,* Pishaka."

The men exchanged deep bows.

"Stop him!" The scream of Kopy Katz came through the paper screen.

"Let him do it already. I'm not going to make a career out of stopping this *schmuck* from doing himself in," said a familiar whimsical voice. "All right, I'll stop him. But it's the last time."

Kopy's father walked into the suite from the garden. He wrested the sword from Sanka and broke it over his knee, pulled off his beard and dark glasses, lit a Raleigh, removed his Chesterfield coat, to whose rear lining a pillow was fastened, then ignited his Chesterfield coat with his Raleigh. "Wish I could light my Raleigh with this Chesterfield" he muttered.

Baron Cockimamiyama Sanka's eyes rolled like marbles gone mad; he grasped at his throat and fainted dead away.

"Any spirits of ammonia around here, Count Pishaka?" said Israel Bond, stomping on his coat to stop the fire.

21
Not All Lox Is Smoked Salmon

A pinch of *chrain* in each nostril brought Sanka back to the land of the living, though he did not speak for many minutes. With eyes wide as those in a Walter Keane portrait, he stared at the dark, cruelly handsome, broadly grinning Oy Oy Seven.

"Sorry I kicked ye in the old *baytzim* back in the chapel, Cocky-san, but you must admit I had justification. When you run into a guy who's just killed you, you have to do something positive or lose your self-respect. Friends like you I don't need; I'd rather have nonviolent enemies." He softened and wrapped a sinewy arm around the Baron. "I'm kidding, old Nip. Truth is I've gotten fond of you. I don't blame you for seeing red. If something appeared to be threatening my PM, I'd do the same."

"I saw you take three W-V bullets in the stomach. I saw you expire. I saw you placed in a coffin and flown to your homeland."

Bond passed his pack of Raleighs around. "This will prove I'm no ghost. Here's my latest haiku. Dig.

A good sex life stops
mental illness. Fight a
crackup with a shackup!

OK, Cocky?"

"*Hai*. Only Israel Bond could be so profoundly romantic. But how—"

"Years ago in the Orient," Bond interjected, "I learned the secret of clouding men's minds from the Mongolian, Takka Ah Shonda, the last of the red-hot lamas. Oh, you tell 'em, Kopy. It's a shade too involved for me."

Kopy Katz inhaled and heaved her magnificent mammaries. "Israel Bond did die. At least an exact duplicate of him died after leading the Sokka Datgai on the limbo chase. A short time ago, I, who've been living in constant trepidation that sooner or later his Oy Oy Seven number would be up, lured him into the 'Black Room,' a secret lab in the rear of my Xerox office, and copied him—molecule for molecule, subatomic particle for subatomic particle. While Iz lay around reading *Commentary* and eating boxes of Good 'N Plenty, his duplicate was pulling off the usual Bondian superfeats. The 'Black Room' itself is the inside of an experimental Xerox that nobody in the organization, not even Mr. Sol Linowitz, knows about—the Xerox-Googol-Plex. Without going into too much detail, it utilizes transuranic elements in an instantaneous but controlled nuclear process. That's what caused the flash and gave you the headache, darling. You were in the epicenter of a mini-H-bomb explosion. It gave the Ginza section a helluva shake, but this town's always being rocked by minor earthquakes so nobody paid much attention. When I received the formula, I'd originally intended to use the 'Black Room' to duplicate another Xerox. Think of the billions I could have saved the corporation by duplicating new machines instead of building them from scratch. But"—her voice lowered—"I fell in love, Iz, and because of that I did something far worse than betray my country or my faith. I—I betrayed Xerox."

Bond ran a loving hand over the oval face. "I appreciate it, baby. But you said you 'received' the formula. You mean you didn't whip it up yourself?"

"Gentlemen and Iz, I'm no slouch in the gray-matter league. Only nine other people in the world wear this insignia." She fondled the chain and plunger. "I won't go through the whole list, but among them are the fabled little old colored shoeshine boy who wrote not only all of Irving Berlin's songs, but Richard Rodgers', too; Morris Berenbaum of Thiokol, who discovered that certain forms of German measles are caused by viruses hatched in the motors of Volkswagens; David Susskind, whose main goal is discovering his own possibilities; Yonkel Schreiber-Burns of the Rand Corporation, who is well on the way to creating eternal life, as soon as he gets over the last little hurdle—how to stop people from dying. We Alta Zeyda Kapplans keep in constant touch by mail and ham radio, swap our latest theories. The formula for the Xerox-Googol-Plex is the brainchild of the *ichi-ban* AZK of us all. Your Holzknicht couldn't carry this man's bedroom slippers."

"Who is he?" said an interested Count Pishaka.

"A man with a confirmed IQ of 666—the little devil—and, I'm proud to say, a fellow Jew. He's quite mad, of course, but he periodically breaks out of it to bedazzle the rest of us. His name is Lavi HaLavi."

Bond turned his sensual gray eyes away so they could not see the mist gathering. "I cursed him for failing me and all he's done is save my life—again."

Now it was Sanka's turn to be the comforter. "Izzy-san, this is no time to weep. This is a joyous occasion. Tomorrow we shall work hand in finger to corral these malefactors, but now let us celebrate. We shall have a feast fit for a king—an Alan King!"

Gottenu! Bond thought. *My scintillating wit has rubbed off on the Baron. He's damn near as fast on the uptake as I am.*

Sanka phoned Ginza-Burg, gave him a series of instructions and hung up. "The food is on the way, my friends. Blintzes from Charlie Mano's, mouth-watering sukiyaki from Kathy, one of the mama-sans at the VIP Bar, and a conglomeration of Ann Dinken's best Jewish delicacies. In the meantime let us make merry."

They sat in the Lotus position around Sanka's table, singing boisterously like children at a campfire. Bond and Kopy taught their hosts some jolly Stern Gang dynamiting songs; the Japanese predictably sang "Sakura"; then Sanka opened the curtains of a wicker cage and commanded a chorus of crickets to chirp in foxtrot rhythm and they danced—Kopy with Sanka, Bond with Pishaka—until they fell in laughing exhaustion on the tatami.

Ipanema chose that moment to stagger into the suite with a carton on her slim shoulder. She dumped its contents on the table, which cracked under the burden of the thousand-yen notes. "Ipanema keeping her bargain, Izzy-san."

"Who is this girl?" said an irritated Kopy.

Think fast! Bond told his brain. "A waif I used to send CARE packages to in the 1950s when she was in an Osaka orphanage. She vowed she'd work her tail off to repay me, darling."

Sanka tactfully sent the maiden away to commit suicide. "And here, my friends, is Ginza-Burg."

The cabby, his face alight in an infectious smile, sauntered through the screen bearing three large trays. *"Essen! Meer gayen essen, kinderlach!"*[*]

He set one tray on the floor and peeled off the tinfoil coverings.

Kopy's nose wrinkled. "Lox."

"And bagels to you, luv," Bond said. "Seems to me we've done this verbal byplay before. This is going to be one dull marriage if all you do is say 'lox.'"

"Silly." She held his hand. "Oh, yes, I remember now. I said it on the cliff, didn't I? But that was when that poor little workman dropped the cylinder and Feldspar got all hot and bothered. I didn't mean smoked salmon that time, Iz. Lox is also a bit of scientific slang. I meant to pursue it further, but, as I recall, Feldspar practically stepped on my conversation."

"What did you mean?" A sudden hardness was back in Bond's eyes.

"Lox means liquid oxygen. You know, the stuff they use in guided missiles."

---

[*] Chow, chow, bambinos!

22
Loves Of A Bond

"Faster! Faster!" Bond begged Major Domo, now at the controls of Baron Sanka's Lear jet.

"We are already at 650 mph, Mr. Bond. Beppu Airport has cleared us for touchdown in six minutes."

"The hell with Beppu. From there it's another two hours by car to Shimonoshima and we can't afford the time. I want you to cut your speed, come in over the cliffs and we'll bail out."

"A dicey proposition. The currents may catch you and blow you far out to sea."

"A chance we'll have to take."

"May I give my belated thanks for the remedy you forced into me in the Imperial garden, Mr. Bond?"

"Don't thank me, Domo. Thank Excedrin. And remember—only Excedrin can take away the pain caused by aspirin. Kopy, you ever jumped before?"

"Loads of times," said the researcher. "When I was a teener we lived in northern New Jersey and I belonged to the Teterboro Airport Skydiving Club. It was such fun free-falling and trying to avoid Arthur Godfrey's plane. Give me another minute, though. I haven't finished mixing the stuff."

"Are you sure it's necessary?"

"Lavi HaLavi thinks so. It's his idea. Simple but absolutely brilliant as usual. I radioed him at Foam Rubber Acres in Galilee and, thank heaven, I caught him during the five minutes of each hour that he's rational. The psychiatrist told me he spends the rest of the time riding on a rocking horse, crying, 'Half a league, half a league, half a league onward!' then looks behind and asks, 'Where the hell are the other 599? If you think I'm going into the mouth of hell alone, you're crazy!'"

An improvement at that, Bond thought. *At least he's out of the sandpile.* "What else did he say?"

"If TUSH has managed to assemble a nuclear missile under our noses, you know the target. By now Lavi has alerted the Ministry of Defense to evacuate the citizenry of the Tel Aviv-Jerusalem area, though I don't think that'll do much good. It could reach Eretz Israel in twenty-five minutes. Maybe it's already been fired. If not"—and she held up a test tube of a pinkish liquid like a proud mother doting on her newborn—"there's still a chance." Kopy unscrewed a cap on her silver AZK plunger, poured the brew into it and recapped it. "A missile uses thousands of gallons of hydrocarbon fuel piped into it from storage tanks. If I can just—"

"Shimonoshima ahead," said Major Domo. "You'll find the chutes on the wall near the door."

Bond helped Kopy into the harness, worked his way into his own chute and lit a Raleigh. By now the Baron should have rounded up his *Kyodo Kikaku Kommando* forces, a top-secret cadre of hardened battlers, and perhaps their copters were leaving Honshu this very second, he hoped. But for the next couple of hours he and Kopy would have to carry the ball alone.

He signaled to Domo to pull the door switch, yelled "Cochise!" (Bond considered himself an innovator, not a follower, and besides, he'd always felt Geronimo had been overexposed) and hurled himself into a brilliant, sun-splashed sky. Kopy picked up the cue— "Crazy Horse!" —and jumped after him.

The sentinel on the cliff picked up the pair of vanilla-ice-cream-cone-shaped objects in his binoculars and spoke hurriedly into his walkie-talkie. *"Achtung!* Two interlopers in the sky. One of them is *Der Jude."*

"Acknowledged. Deploy the men, Eisswess. Take Bond alive." In the largest tent Professor Igneous Feldspar sipped daintily from a glass of Liebfraumilch. "So," he said to the naked, sex-crazed woman thrashing about on her cot, "your hero comes like an avenging angel of the Lord. Run to him, you disgusting trollop. It will provide me a bit of entertainment."

"Bond! Bond! Bond!" shrieked Magma Feldspar and ran out into the sunshine.

Even from her dory a mile from shore and a thousand feet below, the keen-eyed Ama maiden knew it was her lover alighting on the cliff. "Those thighs, those shoulders, that cruelly handsome profile," she sobbed. "It can be no other."

Go-Down Mikimoto drove the oars toward the landing at a rate that would have left the racing shells of Princeton, Harvard and Dartmouth capsized in her boiling wake.

Bond hit the rocks first and his heart sank as he heard Kopy's "The wind's got me! Help, Iz!" A sudden, treacherous current was, as Domo had feared, impelling her seaward. "Kopy!" he called helplessly.

His ears caught the grating of feet and he spun, tearing his Hontze-Ganendel automatic from his Neiman-Marcus shoulder holster. It was one of two guns he'd hastily requisitioned from Sanka's private arsenal. The other was a Beretta, stuck into his cummerbund.

He crouched behind one of the many *yoni* bushes. Into view stalked six truncheon-wielding Norwegians, part of the bunch he'd met earlier, but they'd exchanged their black sweaters for polo shirts and their exposed inner arms bore the telltale tattoo—jackboots kicking naked buttocks. Norwegians, hell, he thought. They're TUSH-ys! And while they might be great shakes as Buddha-builders, they're without question missile technicians as well.

"He landed in this vicinity, Pieterdeter," said one of them in a Rhinelander dialect. "We need not concern ourselves with the girl. I saw her swept into the ocean. But why should he have come virtually unaided?"

"He rather fancies himself as a superhero, I am told, my dear Eisswess," said the contumelious Pieterdeter.

Bond ground his cavity-free teeth, shoved the Hontze-Ganendel back into its holster and flung himself out of the hiding place, snarling, "S for Solomon, H for Halavah, A for Abraham, Z for Zangwill, A for Abraham *noch amool*, and M for Moses! SHAZAM, you Nazi bastards!"

He crashed like a boulder into the sextet, his bronzed arms, elbows, stiffened fingers and steel shafts of legs dealing lethal blows to salient sectors of their anatomies.

Eisswess died at once of a crushed windpipe. The nose of Pieterdeter was mashed into strawberry Jell-O. A toe emasculated one Herr Hauptnerr.

The remaining threesome, who'd been less forcefully battered by Bond's Ugandan elephant charge, got in close and drummed their truncheons against his stomach and right shoulder, reopening a few of the old combat wounds in the latter location. Claret gushed forth like the geysers of Beppu, but he took a mighty breath and his chest expanded to twice its normal size, hurling them to the ground. Though he would have preferred to finish these lice by hand, he decided to conserve his fading power. Liberating the Hontze-Ganendel again, he blasted away at the whimpering Germans—the characteristic *ver gehargit! ver gehargit!* report shaking the earth as the heavy-caliber slugs blew them down. They lay splayed out in various attitudes of death.

"I must say I like your attitudes," he flipped and patted his back for the bon mot. Wondering vaguely which would hold out longer, his strength or his humor, he jogged toward the tent city, his sensual gray eyes seeking the perfidious Danish giant who'd led him down the garden path so often in this puzzling affair.

Kopy landed on her back, the weight of her drenched chute several times pulling her under, but she finally undid the harness and freed herself. Coughing, regurgitating brine, plankton and a medium-size langouste, and arching her willowy body, she began a choppy crawl to the shore. *Gottenu! It'll take me an hour to reach him,* she lamented.

Then she saw the boat. "Help! Please help!"

Go-Down Mikimoto had no intention of stopping for this *gaijin* woman, whom she had seen parachuting down in the company of her man, but she had a guilty second thought: *Perhaps he loves this woman. I cannot do anything to hurt him, although rescuing her may shut me out of his life forever.*

"Give me your hand," said Go-Down and lifted the fatigued researcher into the dory. "You are his woman, is it not so?"

The Xeroxite gave her rescuer a knowing appraisal. "You love him, too."

Go-Down did not answer, but her bobbing Adam's apple betrayed her emotions and Kopy knew it was so.

"You poor, sweet little lady," Kopy said, drawing the trembling Ama girl to her breast. "We've got to help him together. He's in there alone against—God knows what. And I've a mission of my own."

As Go-Down rowed, Kopy explained what had to be done.

"Oh, but I know Shimonoshima quite well, Miss Katz," affirmed Go-Down. "Only yesterday I was at the site of the completed Great Herrosukka Buddha. Some of the Japanese workmen are relatives of mine and permitted me to pray before it."

"And you didn't see anything that looked like large tanks?"

"No, Miss Katz. But if these evil ones are as clever as you say, they might have concealed them in any number of large caves and built underground pipelines to your supposed missile. Yet I saw no missile. The only large edifice standing is the mighty Buddha itself."

Kopy Katz swore at herself in Yiddish, then said, "I'm a fool to the tenth power, Go-Down. It's so damn obvious. The missile is inside the Buddha!"

"Then we must kill it at its source, Miss Katz. As a child I played often in the labyrinths of Shimonoshima and still remember many of the passageways. I shall lead you through them for his sake."

"You're an OK gal, Go-Down," said Kopy Katz. "Now get your stroke rate up to 150 per minute and let's go spelunking."

They smiled at each other, these two gorgeous, naked women, so different in background and appearance, but, like the colonel's lady and Judy O'Grady, sisters under the skin.[*]

---

[*] A little cheap emotion never hurts any book.—S.W.

23
The Quest Ends

Bond, crawling on his swollen belly like a deadly puff adder, racked up Nazis seven and eight in a noiseless fashion. They stood on guard several yards from Feldspars tent, smoking and chatting unconcernedly, and by the time they heard the *yoni* twigs snapping under his advancing body he'd pressed the button of his mezuzah to send the two Molochamovis-B-tipped needles whizzing into their necks.

Good-o! Ten left, counting the Dane, or rather the German, which he certainly had to be. But who was Feldspar or whatever his name was? He'd familiarized himself with the entire TUSH dossier since the organization's inception in the mid-'50s and had etched into his memory the facts concerning every one of its major operatives, all of whom had been taken in the counter-attack in Sahd Sakistan—except the late Holzknicht, who'd lammed to the U.S. None of them, either living or dead, came close to approximating the outré physique of Feldspar.

Lost in thought, he did not realize he himself was being stalked. Just as he tippy-toed to the giant's tent, there was a rush of air, the slapping of naked feet and—*whump!*—he was cut down by a flying tackle.

"Bond! I need you! I need you!" wailed the aroused Magma Feldspar, whose satiny, powerful arms were locked around his ankles.

The commotion brought the Nazi scientists on the run and the great golden hand pushed aside the flap and Feldspar lurched out on the giraffe legs, a Luger cocked at Bond's head.

"One more time!" Magma implored him, her greedy hands scrabbling at his manhood. "One more time!"

Bond said, "OK," and absentmindedly began to vocal-bop the famous coda from Basie's "April in Paris."

"No, you lamebrain! I mean, take me, take me!"

"Excellent!" said Igneous Feldspar. "You have served me well, you Danish bitch. Now, *auf Wiedersehen*." He swung the Luger around and fired. Magma Feldspar's head blew up in a red cloud.

"You bastard—killing your own wife," Bond swore and in a lightning draw aimed the Beretta at the spot between the giant's ice-blue eyes.

Feldspar did not blink an eyelash. He seemed amused. "Fire, Oy Oy Seven."

Bond squeezed the Beretta's trigger.

Nothing.

The damn gun had jammed.

"It is a matter of record that all Berettas jam in crucial situations, Herr Bond. It serves you right for selecting a ladies' gun."

Thonk! Klonk! Frick! Frack! His aides' truncheons landed on Bond's head and the secret agent was out cold.

"Welcome to BO minus forty, Herr Bond." Triumph wreathed the pasty face of Igneous Feldspar.

"Which has no connection with Lifebuoy, I bet," Bond said. He gave his pulpy head a shake. It seemed three sizes too big. His hands were clasped in front of him, turning blackish from the biting straps of saranoflex. "Forty minutes to blastoff, eh?"

"*Sehr gut.* Your mentality is unimpaired by the piddling blows. This is a shining moment in your life, Herr Bond. Your hyperactive heart should be leaping for joy."

"What do you mean, you murdering swine?"

The giant blew Muriel smoke into Bond's face. "Tut, tut, my friend. Is that any way to speak to the man you've traveled thousands of miles to confront? I am Dr. Ernst Holzknicht."

24 Neck Check

Well, why not? Bond asked himself. *There were two of* me. *Yet the Holzknicht who went over the roof of the Samarra bathhouse looked like the old, despised model. An actor? An expendable, low-grade TUSH-y made up to simulate* lieber Ernst?

"Let me begin at the beginning," Holzknicht said.

Bond had no bone to pick with that approach. It was one his own logical mind might have chosen. "Please do."

"When I fell from the Empire State Building and bounced off the foam-rubber skull of King Kong into the Lowenbrau beer truck, I suffered a multiplicity of injuries. But in the undaunted spirit of true Nazism I hung on and when the truck wended its way through Manhattan's Yorkville section I tapped on the window, got the bewildered driver's attention and paid him well to assist me into a certain apartment building on East Eighty-fourth Street."

"Fritz Kuhn Towers, no doubt," Bond broke in. "We've had it watched sporadically. Loaded with your kind of maniacs."

Holzknicht let that disclosure pass. "In my heart was a consuming hatred for you and Eretz Israel which, if transformed into heat ergs, could have turned the polar cap into a Congo rain forest. I lay in my bed, broken and spent, but my brain was as sharp as ever. It told me that you would eventually turn up in Japan to seek the kind of sinister intrigue that can only be found here."

"The historical verity," Bond half whispered.

"Ah, someone in your M 33 and 1/3 has also read every novel of espionage ever written. Yes, the historical verity. Well put."

"BO minus thirty-five," trumpeted a voice from the walkie-talkie on Holzknicht's cot.

"Why did you have to go through this elaborate folderol involving the Japanese? A few ounces of your *barbarella* toxin dumped by night into the major reservoirs of Eretz Israel would have accomplished your task."

"Too simple, Herr Bond." He sighed, a Heidelberg dean trying to explain the principles of Clausewitz to a child brought up on Bomba the Jungle Boy. "Like so many great men who reach middle age, I am afflicted by accidie, which can only be overcome by spurring on my mind to create concepts of infinite subtlety such as 'Operation Alienation,' which sought to destroy the spirit of Judaism by removing its most significant element—Jewish food."

"You damn near succeeded," Bond grunted.

"After my wounds healed and I'd decided to come to the Orient, it became necessary to alter my appearance. I administered local anesthesia to myself and operated on myself, replacing my fine German hands with these steam shovels—one at a time, of course—and adding eighteen inches to my legs by means of bone grafts. A lesser man would have been squeamish, but we of the Master Race are something more than lesser men. More or less. I softened the angular lines of my face with plastic surgery to achieve this bovine pastiness, inserted ice-blue contact lenses, let my black hair grow and went to Mr. Schatzi, the East Berlin hair stylist, who curled it and lightened it with Summer Blonde by Clairol. My next step was a change of nationality. In Copenhagen I bribed a minor official to create a new identity for me, then induced a bar slut to marry me. I knew our paths would cross, but you would be seeking Ernst Holzknicht, not a stumbling blond giant with a wife. I duped Magma into believing I was under Holzknicht's influence via a faked telephone call, for it was my plan that she fall in love with you and in an intimate moment 'spill the beans,' as the Americans say.

"It has been a game of cat and mouse, Oy Oy Seven, and I have not been the mouse. How I laughed inside when your noble heart was touched by the pathetic, ungainly figure of Igneous Feldspar and his crushing secret sorrow. Of course, Knute Feldspar never existed. And, by the bye, I was the German officer responsible for the death of your beloved Helvig Rolvig.

"I obtained the approbation of the Japanese to carry on my excavation project and brought over the 'Norwegians,' for I was determined to have an ace in the hole, the missile, should all else fail. They were former members of the *Führer*'s V-2 echelon, who escaped Europe through our underground network to eventually turn up in Egypt to work for the Cairo Colonel. I borrowed them from a secret missile base in central Egypt.

"In the meantime I set into motion a series of incidents calculated to inflame the Japanese against Eretz Israel. The first was the trawler. In a Greek waterfront cafe its crew was fed coffee into which was mixed Hypno-70, a drug which has a hypnotic effect upon the taker lasting from a day to many months, depending upon the amount ingested. The *Blintz Charming* was cleared for passage through Suez by the Colonel and made its attack upon the Imperial gunboat. My second ploy, the destruction of the JAL jet, was foiled by you because of Aw Gee Minh's petty desire for revenge. Had I known you were on that flight I would have ordered him to destroy another.

"The scrolls—faked, of course—were prepared by an Arab scholar versed in Biblical lore. Although they were inscribed on papyrus treated by a special process to make them appear pristine, I dared not let a true expert scrutinize them, so I insisted they remain in the cave. My mistake was chatting about them in the presence of Nikko Tee-Yin, whose consequent suspicious behavior convinced me he was from the *Kyodo Kikaku*. Before Yaynu eliminated him, he had already gotten word to his *ichi-ban,* who cabled that he wanted copies, so I agreed to the Xeroxing by Miss Katz.

"Once I knew Sanka's interest was aroused, I was afraid to have an intelligence operative as shrewd as the Baron snooping around, so I ordered Skwato to tag him to Tokyo and liquidate him. By this time you were his ally and foiled Skwato's attempts in Tokyo and Beppu.

"The other major provocations were also drug-inspired. One of my agents slipped it into Hyman DeFlower's borscht in Brussels. I myself gave it to Schlomo Salvar in brandy."

"Put two more foils on my tally sheet, *Herr Doktor*," Bond said. "I led the demonstrators away from the Israeli embassy, then returned to prevent the Emperor's death. I imagine the Ribicoff Rarity was a mere goldfish done up by a pop artist."

"I learned of the failure of the latter scheme when I turned on television. Instead of fiery declarations of war it was carrying such drivel as *Shogun Fight at the Kamakura Korral, My Three Samurai* and *The Dog from U.N.C.L.E.* And today's papers were peculiarly devoid of scathing editorials," the Nazi said.

"Good-o! Sanka, Count Pishaka and Minister Kato have been suppressing the hotheads. Tell me, if all these gambits had worked, how would the Japanese have reached Israel?"

"Certain circles in Red China and the U.S.S.R., who would like to see Eretz Israel go under, were prepared to wink at the squadrons of Imperial Japanese atom bombers flying over their respective territories, even to refuel them. There would have been a brief violation of Iranian air space, then they would have zeroed in over Arab states, who, of course, were more than happy to cooperate. Would they have minded the loss of a few hundred thousand out of their one hundred million if the Zionist state was at long last exterminated?"

"BO minus twenty-five, *Herr Doktor*."

"You see, Herr Bond, I wanted you to survive the murderous inclinations of Yaynu and Frau Marlene. I knew that they, like the monk, so detested you they would disobey my orders, but I also felt you would luck through in your customary fashion.

"When you became my protector," he chuckled, "and insisted upon a showdown with Holzknicht, I was prepared for that exigency, too. The 'Holzknicht' you sent over the bathhouse with the Black Dragqueen was a robot, the idea for which was suggested by the remarkably lifelike Abraham Lincoln in the Illinois pavilion at the recent New York World's Fair."

"Of course. That accounts for the jerkiness of the mouth and hands, *Herr Doktor*."

"*Ja*. I had ordered the Black Dragqueen to merely wound you as well as myself. I wanted to see how you, disarmed and bloodied, would dispose of your tormentors. Incidentally, I feel virtually no pain in these new legs." The Nazi suddenly jabbed his cigar end into Bond's cheek, held it there for a second that seemed an eternity. "A small repayment for the knife you hurled into me, *Jude*."

Though nauseated by the stench of his burned flesh, Bond kept his cool. "Why did you keep me alive?"

"Because"—and Holzknicht peeked at his watch—"in less than twenty minutes I want you to witness that which you cannot prevent, the blastoff of a missile tipped with a multi-megaton warhead, and listen to a shortwave radio account of the flash from my colleagues at the Egyptian base in another twenty-five minutes. I want to see your cruelly handsome face dissolve into that of a blubbering infant when you get a mental image of a twenty-mile-high mushroom blotting out the friendly

Mediterranean sun, the Knesset Building burning like tinder, the bulk of your population incinerated, your organization and your M.—"

"You bastard!" Bond rose, but the gloating Nazi hammered a fist into his mouth and he fell back on the cot.

"Take him to the Buddha," Holzknicht said to the TUSH-ys on guard at the tent flap.

I've mucked it up good this time, Bond thought, as four sneering Nazis laid hands on him. *Kopy's given some shark the sexiest meal of his life; these butchers are cuffing me about as though I were some harmless puppy, and Eretz Israel will be gutted in forty minutes.*

"Herr Doktor!" A technician was racing toward the giant. "The personnel in Cave Delta have seized two more intruders."

Holzknicht spoke into the walkie-talkie. "Continue the countdown, Von Werner, but be prepared to halt it should conditions warrant. Hellmann," he said to the excited technician, "have them brought to me for interrogation. They may be friends of Bond."

The four hurled Bond savagely into the tent, his head banging the tent pole.

A minute passed. Then he heard the sound of female voices protesting to Holzknicht.

"Kopy! Go-Down!" he cried.

"Iz!"

"Mr. Bond!"

They were dragged kicking and screaming into the tent. Holzknicht, coldly furious, said, "Now, Miss Katz, I am in no mood for trifling. What were you doing in that cave? You were seen blown out to sea. And who is this Japanese woman?"

Bond glommed the two sets of fascinating protuberances and a cylinder in his mind began composing a song, "I'd Love To Be Strayin' Down Mammary Lane," but the other cylinder screamed: *Neck check! neck check!*

His eyes flew back to Kopy's silver AZK chain.

A thrill sped through him.

The plunger was gone.

25
Dem Bones, Dem Bones, Dem Dry Bones

Kopy's all too flimsy yarn of an urge to go spelunking with a friend made Holzknicht even angrier and he slapped her about viciously. Six Nazis had to sit on Bond to restrain him.

At last Holzknicht tired of pummeling the oval face and turned to Hellmann. "Were they carrying any sort of weapons, satchel charges, Calgonite time bombs?"

"*Nein, Herr Doktor*," the man answered. "The guards spotted them almost immediately. Their feet hit one of the trip wires, setting off the alarm. All they had on them was"—he gave the two maidens a long, lascivious look—"all they have on them now."

"BO minus ten and counting, *Herr Doktor*," Von Werner signaled.

"Very well," Holzknicht said. "It appears, Miss Katz, that your foray was unfruitful. Did you expect to upset my plans with those soft powerless hands? Take the *Juden* to the Buddha. I want the lovers to see my rapture when I learn of the detonation."

"And the one he calls Go-Down, *Herr Doktor?*"

"Kill her, Hellmann."

Go-Down Mikimoto spoke in her timid way. "May I kiss him *sayonara*, sir?"

"How poignant," smirked Holzknicht. "Love's last kiss. Be quick about it."

"*Domo arigato, Herr Doktor.* You are generous to your enemies." Go-Down Mikimoto knelt before Bond and kissed the swollen fingers. "Your poor dear hands, hands that have given me such delight. Would that I could free them from these cruel straps!" Then she rose and pressed her lips in longing against his sensual mouth. Her wriggling tongue forced his lips apart and he thought, *Why is she playing the* français *way?* —until he felt the small, sharp object slicing the inside of his cheek.

A *nakawari* shell! An Ama diving girl familiar with the creatures of her environment would, of course, have used such shells in the past to cut ropes, scrape barnacles from her dory, clean fish, etc.

"Good-bye, Mr. Bond." Her eyes flooded as Hellmann grasped her arm and dragged her off.

"Iz," said Kopy, choking on her own tears. "Don't look back."

A Luger roared twice.

Hellmann rejoined them, indifferently wiping blotches of claret from the front of his polo shirt. *"Ach,* so much blood for such a slight girl. I fear this shirt has been ruined permanently." When he saw Bond's jaw bulge, he kicked him in the leg. "Drive all thoughts of revenge from your mind, *Jude.* This is the end."

"BO minus two and counting," said the walkie-talkie in Holzknicht's hand.

Holzknicht held up his hand for the party to halt some three hundred yards from the Great Herrosukka Buddha. Even its impassive face seemed to hold a malicious grin. "Open Buddha."

There was a hissing sound and the Buddha began to divide. As the knees spread apart, there was the bird, slim and white, a swastika painted on its nuclear nose.

"With a phallus like that, no wonder you've been contemplating your navel," said an envious Bond to the deity. Now he felt the utter futility of their risible counterattack. Even if Kopy had put the stuff, whatever it was, into the bird, what possible effect could it have on this one-hundred-foot death-dealer?

"... three, two, one, zero. Ignition!"

Towering steam cumuli roiled out of the earth. The reverberation was deafening. Then the bird lifted off, slowly at first, but it gathered speed and soon was a pencil propelled by a dagger of flame.

Then it was out of sight.

"Auf Wiedersehen, Eretz Israel!" screamed Dr. Ernst Holzknicht, jumping up and down like a schoolboy. "TUSH has avenged *Der Führer!"*

Bond, whose face had been battered by rocks, branches and insects blown about in a dust storm whipped up by the lifting bird, knelt in a prayerful attitude.

Holzknicht laughed. "All the litany from the *Sh'ma Israel* to *Adon Olam* will not help now, *Jude*. The bird is on its way."

Bond *was* praying. But with his tongue tip he was also easing the *nakawari* shell out of the pouch in his right cheek, wincing again and again as the edge scored the sensual inner lining and his lower gum. He got the dull side between his teeth, craned his neck and began to work the sharp one against the saranoflex straps.

It was a long, laborious business. His mouth bled profusely, his head ached and as his jaw bumped his blackish hands, spears of pain ran up his arms.

Now some of the Nazis were coming back from the tent with chairs, a table, a two-way shortwave radio and some refreshments.

"Continue praying, Herr Bond," Holzknicht said. "It is good for the soul. If you like I shall teach you some hymns to Himmler. They would be far more appropriate at the moment."

Bond did not answer and the Nazi laughed again. "Miss Katz, join me in a stein of good Bavarian beer."

"With pleasure, *Herr Doktor*," Kopy said gaily, walking toward the table in a sensual undulation that caused the other nine Nazis to gulp.

"You do not seem distressed at the day's developments," Holzknicht remarked, pouring the beer.

"*Herr Doktor*, I am a scientist also," said Kopy. "Political subdivisions mean nothing to me, nor do shopworn religions. My interest is in science, pure and simple. I have nothing but the greatest admiration for you and your colleagues. To think, you built a missile under Japan's nose!"

That's it, baby. Give me time, time! One strap is severed, but there are four more to go, Bond messaged her.

"Yet you are in love with this God-intoxicated broken vessel of a hero of your own heritage," Holzknicht said keenly.

"Was. And only for his once attractive body, which is not so any more. I admit I tried to save him by stealing in through the caves, but that was before I noticed so many fine German bodies."

A "Hear! hear!" erupted from the assemblage, who began to pound the table.

"Would you prove that, Miss Katz, by yielding to me before this wrecked Hebrew, so that he can see your exquisite pleasure?" Hellmann asked, squeezing his thighs together in his excitation.

"A charming proposal," said Kopy. "Herr Hellmann, you *are* a saucy rascal! Indeed I shall take you on. All of you. But should we not first experience the orgiastic moment of the missile's explosion. In a few minutes or so it will be crisping the sands of Egypt—"

Bond's head bobbed. Three more straps came apart.

"Egypt?" Holzknicht smiled humorlessly. "A joke, Miss Katz, and a poor one."

Kopy Katz stood up tall and proud. *"Herr Doktor..."*

Sit down, darling! Bond telepathed the Xeroxite. *You're overplaying your hand! For God's sake, sit down and button your adorable raspberry-float lips!*

The last strap was half severed. His eyes looked about for a weapon. There—there was something, jagged and bleached, near a *yoni* bush which had been set afire by the heat from the bird. It looked like one of the memorial bones that had been piled near the Buddha's base. It was!

Holzknicht, fiddling with the radio, said, "Go on, Miss Katz."

"You filthy, cold-blooded, murdering kraut!" The mask of levity fell off. "No, your boys didn't find anything on me in Cave Delta. I'd expected a trip-wire warning system, told Go-Down to kick one of them to set up a diversion, and while they were grabbing her I tossed a tiny quantity of a certain liquid into an open hatch on one of your tanks. Shall I give you the scientific formula, *Herr Doktor?*" She rattled off a long string of chemical terms totally incomprehensible to Bond, now crawling toward the burning bush.

Dr. Ernst Holzknicht's golden curls turned ash white. The pasty face began to drip soggy flesh.

"Gott in Himmler!" he screamed. He brought up his Luger, which seemed like a toy in the steam-shovel hand, and shot Kopy Katz in the head at pointblank range.

"Holzknicht, you bastard!"

Israel Bond, his makeshift bludgeon in his hand, sprang onto the table, sending Nazis flying head over heels.

"Die, Holzknicht, die!"

He swung the bleached object down, an incredible electric power surging through his right arm.

The TUSH leader's head exploded in saucer-sized fragments. Claret-soaked curls of golden fleece flew in every direction.

Thwack! Hellmann's hurried Luger shot thumped into Bond's left shoulder, but it was the bite of a mosquito.

Then Hellmann's skull was sundered by a blow from Bond, and Von Werner's, and another Nazi's, and another Nazi's....

One of their shots ripped his thigh, two more smacked into his right shoulder, a fourth creased his sensual scalp, but he steamrollered on and they began to scream in sheer terror, for he seemed to be framed in a golden aura, unafraid, unstoppable, unconquerable, his weapon smashing, crushing, battering, pulverizing....

Then the power was cut off and he fell like a great oak to the earth, the blood pouring out of him like the sea through a breached dike. Next to his ear was the radio, still squawking. "... *Herr Doktor,* something has gone wrong. It is many seconds past detonation time and we have seen nothing. Wait! Something evil comes this way! Something white and swift... something... *eeya-a-a-ah!*"

There was a protracted whine and the Egyptian end of the hookup went dead.

26
Now Heah de Wud of de Lawd

Ten seconds after the *Kyodo Kikaku Kommando* choppers hit the cliff top, buzzing like great cicadas, Baron Cockimamiyama Sanka, a Hanyatti in one hand, a Cal-grenade dangling from his finger, gave a long, low whistle.

"By the belly of Buddha! This is a pocket-size Armageddon! Domo, tell the men to fan out and search. Kill anything that offers opposition."

Nothing did. From the caves came a bevy of Japanese workmen, their hands held high, their eyes fearful as they walked through a landscape of indescribable grue.

One by one the KKK began to stack up the bodies—the Nazis, many of whose heads were shapeless, splintered mounds, and the three dead women.

As Holzknicht's body was dumped on the heap by six sweating Kommandos, Sanka's mouth curled in a sneer and spat a wad of Copenhagen snuff onto the melted face. "Roast in hell!"

"Baron, we have found the Israeli," said Major Domo.

"*Yo-i!* Is he alive?"

"Barely. There is a stertorous rumbling in his chest. He is horribly wounded."

"Tell Dr. Spokko to come at once with plasma."

The pale secret agent lay still in a pool of claret, a strange peace on the cruelly handsome visage.

"That object he continues to clutch so tightly," said Major Domo. "It is blood-red. Apparently he used it as a club against his foes. But I have never before seen any bludgeon like it."

Sanka worked the long, tapering fingers out of the holes they had dug into the weapon. "Dr. Spokko, I suggest an immediate injection of adrenalin straight into the heart. It is the only hope."

"*Hai*," nodded the doctor and prepared it. "Incidentally, my dear Baron and Major, from my considerable knowledge of the higher forms I should say unequivocally that the thing you took from the *gaijin's* hand is the jawbone of an ass."

27
How to Talk to a Jewish Mother

"*Herr Doktor* Ernst Holzknicht played the old shell game with Kopy Katz, and he lost," said Bond, his eyes on the horizon. Soon, he knew, three new ghosts, Kopy, Go-Down and Magma, would be forming out there to haunt him forevermore. Even Sarah Lawrence might decide to re-materialize. He wondered how they'd do it. En masse? In six-hour shifts?

"Explain that, Iz, darling," said Dr. Betty Freudan. "I'm not up on this missile-technology bit."

"In truth, she played the *new* shell game—Super Shell, to be precise. Lavi gave her the formula for Platformate, the ingredient that makes new Super Shell the world's greatest gasoline, and she put it into the hydrocarbon fuel. So powerful was the thrust of just that pinch of Platformate that the inertial-guidance system on the missile couldn't cope with it. The bird overshot Eretz Israel, as Lavi had computed, and nosed into central Egypt. Exeunt one missile base and only heaven knows how many Nazi scientists."

He lit a Raleigh and made a disquieting, though hardly earth-shaking, discovery.

He liked Raleigh cigarettes.

Funny, he ruminated, *maybe I always did. It was only a longing for status that made me snip away at the integrity of Raleigh with all the lousy, snotty jokes. I guess when you reach a certain level of maturity you finally discover what's real and right and true and what's dross. Dammit, I'd smoke Raleighs even if they* didn't *give coupons!*

"And it's worked out so neatly, dearest," trilled the lovely blond psychoanalyst. "Because they need Japanese trade so badly, Red China and Russia have denied they ever monitored the missile flight over their territories. Your pal Goshen of the

CIA has convinced the Tall Texan that the U.S. should stay mum, too. It's the biggest clam-up in history and the Cairo Colonel is being blamed for the detonation. He'll again be an international pariah for a long time and that can't hurt us. Darling, I think you've been out in the sun a flerm of a furge[*] too long. I'd better wheel you back into the kitchen."

He *was* tired. Maybe he was pushing the recovery bit a little too hard. It was only two weeks since he, kept clinically alive by the adrenalin shot and Major Domo's bottle of infection-fighting Excedrins, had been taken in Sanka's Lear jet to the Hadassah Medical Center near Jerusalem, where the real touch-and-go battle had been waged.

Eretz Israel's finest medicos had been rushed from an international convention on fee-splitting in Geneva to toil around the clock. They'd performed six open-heart massages, ten closed ones, and Lord knows how many tracheotomies, given him continual transfusions, even tried a daring innovation—the computer-driven electric *chrysteer*.[**]

It all seemed in vain the night his fever hit 112, but M., dipping into her bag of Hasidic medical lore, had brought it down to 110 by massive infusions of her chicken soup and the rarely used method known as *bankas*.[***] Then she recalled an inspired remedy from her childhood in the Ukrainian village of Baronevkeh, from whence Bond's parents had come also. It was a Guggle Muggle, a mixture of boiling milk, honey, butter and schnapps. But M.'s was no run-of-the-mill Guggle Muggle. The milk came from Schleswig-Holsteins, the sassiest, most pampered cattle on God's green earth; the honey was manufactured under the strict supervision of Kosher queen bees in sterile hives built by the Levitt people; the butter was Breakstone's sweetest and creamiest; the schnapps from the cellar of Dean Martin. Even the glass had been blown from molten jade dust at the command of the grateful Emperor of Japan.

Seconds after he'd drunk it, his temperature fell to 98.6, thus enabling the surgeons to go to work on his body wounds, and the lead they extracted was sufficient for Lavi HaLavi to make Bond an ID bracelet.

---

[*] The solar metric measurement of a pip of a popkin. One achieves it by adding dark matter to the speed of light.
[**] Enema
[***] Cupping

Betty wheeled him into the typical hubbub of the kitchen. "Let's have a little less hub and more bub," Bond said. A weak one-liner, he knew, but the hell with it! Even Jay Burton and Sheldon Keller have their off days.

M. alternated cooking and sending directives to Israeli agents everywhere, who'd be quietly disposing of the remaining TUSH small fry. Op Chief Lazar Beame banged away at his Smith-Corona on an article the *Reader's Digest* had asked him to submit: "Spies Can Be Good Neighbors and Solid Citizens, Too." Z., who'd just cracked a new Syrian code, got so excited he cracked the decoder as well.

And there was Neon Zion, 113, licensed to wound, ashamed to look Bond in the face as he whispered, "And I wanted your Oy Oy Seven number. I'm not fit to polish your bedsocks, Mr. Bond."

"Kid," Bond said tenderly, "you are. Go to it or I'll make a cripple from you, too."

His entrance was the signal for more broad smiles and affectionate words. *One thing I'll say for them,* he thought. *Whenever I come back from a job mutilated they appreciate it.*

"Oy Oy Seven, dear boy!"

It was Lavi HaLavi, dressed in a shepherd's tunic and buskins.

"Lavi!" Bond hugged the little genius to his heart, not caring about the pain. "Lavi, old chum. Your Xerox formula saved my life."

"I'm so happy, Oy Oy Seven. Everything's going splendidly today. My moon probe has just returned after taking samples of the lunar textures. Here, have a taste. It's superfab."

"Lavi, you expect me to eat that awful looking stuff?"

"My dear fellow, a good piece of green cheese never hurt anybody."

The 3-D signal—Danger! Doom! Disaster!—clanged from a large soup tureen on a top shelf.

The hilarity and high jinks stilled. That signal had oft rung before and everyone present knew what it meant.

Z. broke the stillness. "M., look at the two words that just came over the teletype."

The chipper old Number One ripped off the paper, read it, her face gaining ten new wrinkles, and passed it around to the other members of M 33 and 1/3.

It came to Bond last. And as he read the two coded words—TITMOUSE TWEETER—he knew why. Without verbalizing, they were asking him to take the job.

He searched each pair of eyes—Beame's, Z.'s, young Neon's, Betty's and, of course, M.'s—and found the same plea: *Go in there, Oy Oy Seven, and do what must he done.*

He closed his eyes and tried to imagine what TITMOUSE TWEETER would be like. No, a job like that was beyond imagination. He did know what was in store: hot lead would lay open his shoulders, loathsome hirsute things that lurked in the humid Amazon night would sink their fangs into his thighs; his cruelly handsome face would feel the knout, the brass knuckle, the truncheon, the stiffened, calloused fingers of the killer karateist. And my eyes ... and incidentally, are they *gray* or *grey*? Who cares?

Israel Bond rose haltingly from the wheelchair and took a few unsteady steps toward M., the woman to whom he gave his total love and trust.

He ran his long, tapering fingers over her peruke and let them steal down her tabescent cheeks and she smiled her maternal, heart-catching smile.

Quietly and with the heartwarming grin that made him the consummate human being the world had come to adore, he said in a tender tone:

"Fuck it."

He flipped his Double-Oy gold-edged security card to Neon Zion and told the lad, "Go kill and be well." He turned at the door and said in Yiddish:

"*Genig iz shen genig. A mann darft leben.* Enough is enough already ...a man needs to live."

He strode out of the dark kitchen into the sunshine of Jerusalem and in seven seconds was lost in the crowd.

Epis-A-logue

The moving finger, having writ, falls off.
SOL WEINSTEIN
Tokyo and Atami, Japan, 1966.
Levittown, Pa., 1967.
Unemployment and Panic, 1968.

About the Author

We asked Sol Weinstein, author of the Hebrew Secret Agent Israel Bond (Oy Oy Seven) thrillers to describe his fulsome career in three sentences. They are: 1 1/2 – 3 months for kiting checks ... 2 1/2 months for illegally checking kites at a Tokyo kids' fair ... and 1 week for pushing Stepan Novotny, infamous forger, from the top of the Prague National Bank. (The Czech bounced.)

In addition to Oy Oy Seven's capers in *Loxfinger, Matzohball, On the Secret Service of His Majesty the Queen,* and *You Only Live Until You Die,* he wrote a highly sentimental set of music and lyrics to "The Curtain Falls", sung by Kevin Spacey in the biopic *Beyond the Sea* in his role as Bobby Darin.

Sol currently resides in New Zealand, is a member of Temple Sinai in Wellington, and pronounces a favourite ethnic food as "kiegel", not "kugel".

If you enjoyed this book...

...then you are clearly a person of great taste and breeding, the kind of person the world needs more of. Also, you're the sort of person who should visit

Oy-Oy-7.com

to see more about what's going on in the world of M 33 and 1/3.

www.ingramcontent.com/pod-product-compliance
Lightning Source LLC
Chambersburg PA
CBHW032012230426
43671CB00005B/57